INSIDE IRAN

INSIDE IRAN

THE REAL HISTORY AND POLITICS OF THE ISLAMIC REPUBLIC OF IRAN

MEDEA BENJAMIN

O/R

OR Books

New York · London

Library of Congress Cataloging-in-Publication Data: A catalog record for this book is available from the Library of Congress.

British Library Cataloging in Publication Data: A catalog record for this book is available from the British Library.

Typeset by Lapiz Digital, Chennai, India. Printed by BookMobile, USA.

paperback ISBN 978-1-68219-140-8 • ebook ISBN 978-1-68219-142-2

TABLE OF CONTENTS

Map: Joe Perez/Poco Meloso

INTRODUCTION

My first trip to Iran was in 2008. I was traveling with my CODEPINK colleagues Jodie Evans and Ann Wright, and trip organizer Leila Zand. It was just after President Obama's historic election, and we were excited about the possibilities of improving U.S.-Iranian ties, even though Iran was still governed by conservative President Ahmadinejad. We considered ourselves citizen diplomats, modeling the kind of outreach we wanted to see in the new administration.

I must admit that I was apprehensive about traveling to Iran as an American Jew, since for decades the Iranian government has had hostile relations with the United States and Israel. On our very first day, we passed a building with a banner that read "Death to America; Death to Israel." Habib Ahmadzadeh, an Iranian filmmaker who was showing us around, laughed. "Don't take the slogans literally—or personally," he said. "They're meant to show opposition to government policies, not people. You'll find that Iranians love Americans." Indeed, all the Iranians we met expressed admiration for Americans, even though U.S. economic sanctions were making their lives so difficult.

What surprised me even more was their admiration for Jews. "We don't like the policies of the Israeli government, but we love Jews," I was told over and over again. Secular Iranians talked glowingly about Jewish creativity in Hollywood and business. Conservative Muslims said we have the same God, many of the same prophets, and are both are descendants from Abraham. A 2014 poll conducted by the US Anti-Defamation League left the pollsters stunned: It found that the most pro-Jewish people in the Middle East, aside from Israelis, were Iranians.

During this visit we met with all kinds of people, both publicly and privately. We met government officials, as well as people who had been imprisoned by the government. We met religious and secular folks, environmentalists, women's groups, and businesspeople. We had chance meetings with people on the street who invited us into their homes. We were overwhelmed by the world-renowned Iranian hospitality, where a guest is considered a gift from heaven. We were showered with copious amounts of delicious food, endless cups of sweet tea, and more gifts than we could fit in our suitcases.

Iranians, we learned, revere their Persian heritage and culture; they want you to know that they are not Arabs.[1] They speak Farsi, not Arabic, and can recite centuries-old poems by the revered poets Hafez and Rumi. They recall Persian philosophers, artists, and scientists who go back to 500 B.C. They describe in vivid detail how their country has been invaded by Greeks, Arabs, Mongols, British, and Russians, but prevailed with their culture intact. Yes, they are Muslims, and overwhelmingly Shia Muslims, but they celebrate ancient Zoroastrian holidays—to the dismay of conservative clerics. The nation's 2,500-year history shines through in their breathtaking architecture, universally acclaimed literature, and deeply spiritual music.

Since 1979, however, the Islamic revolution has turned the nation into a more sober and isolated society where religious leaders dictate everything from what women must wear in public to who can run for office. It also put U.S.-Iranian government relations on a collision course, starting with a hostage crisis at the U.S. Embassy in Tehran that turned into a 444-day diplomatic standoff.

In more recent times, Iran's nuclear program became a flash point for U.S.-Iranian relations. The U.S., along with Britain,

France, Germany, Russia, and China, spent years negotiating a compromise. An historic breakthrough came in 2015 with the signing of the Iran nuclear deal, known as the Joint Comprehensive Plan of Action (JCPOA). It was the signature foreign policy achievement of the Obama administration, a tribute to reformist Iranian President Rouhani, and an impressive example of what can be achieved when adversaries talk to each other.

Unfortunately, Donald Trump, from the time he was campaigning for president, called it "the worst deal ever" and vowed to tear it up. His first foreign trip as president was to Iran's nemesis, Saudi Arabia, where he crowed about clinching Saudi arms sales worth $110 billion (most of which were deals already signed under Obama) and denounced Iran as a nation that "spreads destruction and chaos across the region." He subsequently looked for ways to quash the nuclear deal, imposed fresh sanctions, and even included Iran on the list of countries whose residents were banned from entering the United States, despite the fact that not a single Iranian has ever taken part in a terrorist attack on U.S. soil.

Trump's effusive embrace of the Saudi rulers and antagonism towards Iran is not really a departure from what has been standard U.S. policy for the past 40 years. The Iranian government is certainly guilty of many abuses, including gross violations of free speech and assembly, restricting the rights of women, imprisoning dissidents, and executing people for nonviolent offenses. But when juxtaposed with Saudi Arabia, the U.S. ally is far more repressive internally. Iran has flawed national elections; Saudi Arabia doesn't have national elections at all. Iran's women are restricted, but Saudi Arabia is a much more gender-segregated society. The West applauded the 2017 Saudi announcement that it would allow movie theatres (albeit segregated), while Iran has had a thriving film, theater, and music industry for decades.

In terms of foreign policy, Iran has plenty of blood on its hands, from its involvement in overseas attacks that have killed civilians to its military support for Bashar al-Assad in Syria. While not excusing Iran's record, it is, nevertheless, fair to hold it up against the track record of Saudi Arabia. For decades, the Saudi regime has been spreading its extremist Wahhabi beliefs, which form the ideological underpinnings of terrorist groups from Al Qaeda to ISIS. In 2011, it crushed the nonviolent democratic uprising in Bahrain, and in 2015 it started bombing neighboring Yemen so mercilessly that millions were left hungry and displaced. I document these abuses in my book *Kingdom of the Unjust: Behind the US Saudi Connections.*

Of course, U.S. foreign policy is even more blood-stained. It is ironic to hear U.S. officials accuse Iran of "meddling in the region," meaning the Middle East, when Iran is part of the region and it is the United States that has been sending its military to "meddle" in the region, including the 1991 Gulf War, the 2003 invasion of Iraq, and the 2011 overthrow of Qaddafi in Libya.

The U.S. also has a sordid track record of meddling in Iran's internal affairs. It helped orchestrate the overthrow of elected Prime Minister Mossadegh in 1953 and re-installed the brutal and unpopular Shah, paving the way for the Islamic Revolution of 1979.

In one of Senator Bernie Sanders's rare foreign policy talks, he used Iran as an example of how U.S. intervention and the use of U.S. military power has produced unintended consequences that have caused incalculable harm. "What would Iran look like today if their democratic government had not been overthrown?" Senator Sanders asked. "What impact did that American-led coup have on the entire region? What consequences are we still living with today?"[2]

While we don't know what Iran would look like today if the United States had not helped engineer the 1953 coup, we can venture a guess that there would not have been an Islamic Revolution, that Iran would be a more secular society, and that it would not be on a collision course with the United States.

We cannot remake the past, but we can help shape the future if we are well-informed about Iran, a nation our government teaches us to hate and our media talks about in such a perverted fashion.

This primer on Iran is meant to give the public a basic understanding of the country, both domestically and internationally. It starts with a brief history of Iran's long and proud past, setting the scene for the 1979 Islamic Revolution. It then looks at how the new regime cracked down on human rights and religious minorities, and circumscribed the role that women could play in society. It covers the economy, including how decades of western sanctions have affected daily life. In terms of foreign policy, it delves into the tumultuous relationship with the United States and its neighbors in the region. Throughout, I strive to highlight the pushback and heroic efforts by Iranians eager to live in a more open, more democratic society free of outside interference.

*****

My second visit to Iran was in 2014, when I was invited to give several talks about my book *Drone Warfare: Killing by Remote Control*. On the second day, I did an interview on one of the major state-run TV stations. I gave examples of grieving families from Pakistan and Yemen whose loved ones had been callously blown away by U.S. pilots sitting in secure control rooms thousands of miles away. That evening a young man stopped by the hotel and waited several hours until I arrived. "I could tell from the interview what hotel you were in, and I hope you don't mind that I stopped by," he said in broken English, as he handed me a beautifully wrapped box of chocolates. "I just wanted to thank you for your compassionate stance on behalf of innocent people who have been hurt by your government's actions."

The next day another man stopped by. He was a medical doctor, and he wanted to run an idea by me. "I have been troubled by all the suffering in the world, and also by the dreadful relations between our countries. I would love to see a group of Iranian and American doctors participate in joint humanitarian missions to help people in poor countries like Haiti or Bangladesh. We could show the world how we, the citizens, can work together to help others—no matter what our governments are doing." I loved the idea and took it to medical groups like Physicians for Social Responsibility and Doctors Without Borders, but couldn't find any group to take it on.

There is a deep longing among the Iranian people for close ties between Iran and the West, for moving beyond the divisions our governments create. In a more rational world, Iran and the United States would have full diplomatic relations. Trade with this nation of 80 million pent-up consumers would be a boon to U.S. businesses. Intelligence-sharing and other forms of cooperation would help ensure the defeat of terrorist groups like ISIS. And greater international interactions would strengthen those inside Iran who are advocating for a more open society, and those of us in the United States who are trying to stop our government from dragging us into another bloody conflict.

I hope that this book, designed to give readers a better understanding of the history and dilemmas facing modern-day Iran, can help ignite more passion and creativity to forge new people-to-people initiatives that model the government relations we want to see—and that can help stop the path toward war.

— Medea Benjamin
Washington, D.C.
January 2018

CHAPTER 1: IRAN BEFORE THE 1979 REVOLUTION

In the United States, it seems we only become interested in the historical background of our adversaries when it is too late. Our interest peaks after we have allowed our political leaders to define other countries as enemies, after we have killed millions of their people and left their cities in ruins. Our most recent wars have all replaced the problems that were the pretexts for using military force in the first place with even more intractable ones, fueling a seemingly endless cycle of global violence.

Many Americans now understand that Vietnam's National Liberation Front (or Viet Cong), created in 1960, was exactly what it claimed to be: a national liberation movement born of French colonialism and Japanese military occupation. It was not, as U.S. leaders claimed at the time, the vanguard of a Communist plot to take over the world and destroy the American way of life. Our failure to understand Vietnam, its people, or its history cost 59,000 American lives and probably more than three million Vietnamese, Cambodian, and Laotian lives, mostly civilians.

The antipathy between the United States and Iran is likewise rooted in our ignorance of that nation's rich history.

How many Americans understand that Iran's militant rejection of foreign interference in its affairs is the culmination of two centuries of foreign intervention by the British and Russians, from the 19th century "Great Game" to their joint invasions of Iran during two world wars? How many understand that the United States lost its credibility as an anti-colonial ally of the Iranian people in 1953, when it plotted with the U.K. to overthrow Iran's popular elected government and re-impose a repressive, autocratic monarchy?

As in Vietnam and other CIA playgrounds in the post-World War II world, U.S. and British planning for the coup in Iran included an elaborate propaganda campaign directed against their own citizens to tar Iranian Prime Minister Mohammad Mossadegh, a life-long champion of democracy and constitutionalism in Iran, as a Communist stooge, and to simplistically define Iran as a Cold War battleground. Mossadegh's real "crime" was his determination to ensure that the Iranian people had the right to develop and benefit from their own oil resources, instead of allowing those resources to be pocketed by the British state-owned company now known as BP.

FROM CYRUS THE GREAT TO THE ARAB INVASION

Unlike most of its neighbors, Iran (traditionally called Persia in English) is not a new country carved out of the ruins of the Ottoman Empire. It is one of the oldest countries in the world, older than any Western power, and it has survived within its present borders or wider ones for 2,500 years.[3]

The empire founded by Cyrus the Great (550-350 B.C.), called the Achaemenid Empire, was the first Persian empire to rule across three continents. It stretched from the Balkans to North Africa and Central Asia, with the seat of power in Persepolis. It was an unprecedented attempt to govern a vast array of ethnic groups based on the principle of equal rights for all, including non-interference in local customs and religions. American historian Will Durant stated, "For the first time in known history, an empire almost as extensive as the United States received an orderly government, a competence of administration, a web of swift communications, a security of movement by men and goods on majestic roads, equaled before our time only by the zenith of Imperial Rome."[4]

Cyrus's successors were less successful, succumbing to various invasions. The next Persian empire was the Sassanid dynasty that ruled Iran and much of the region in the 3rd century. It was the last great Persian empire before the Muslim conquest and the adoption of Islam. Its cultural influence, including architecture, art, writing, and philosophy, extended far beyond the empire's borders to Europe, Africa, China, and India. By the 7th century, it had become exhausted by decades of warfare against the Byzantine Empire and succumbed to attacks from Arab Muslims beginning in 633.

The Arabs, inspired by their new Islamic faith, invaded Iran, and, after several decades, managed to replace the ruling Persians. Over time, a majority of Iranians converted to Islam, although many aspects of Persia's unique evolution remained intact, including its language. A synthesis soon evolved between Iran's new Arab rulers and the rich culture of their new subjects. It is said that while Iran was Islamized, it was not Arabized. Persians remained Persian.

Iranian scholars translated the ancient literature of Iran, Syria, and Greece into Arabic, and the House of Wisdom in Baghdad became the greatest library in the world. The works of Plato, Aristotle, Pythagoras, and Archimedes became the basis for new advances in math, science, and philosophy, centuries before they were rediscovered in Europe during the Renaissance.

INVADED BY MONGOLS AND TIMURIDS, PERSIAN CULTURE REMAINS VIBRANT

In the early 13th century, under the leadership of Genghis Khan, the Mongols from East-Central Asia swept into northeastern Iran. They expanded their vast empire, pillaging and burning cities along the way. The Persian people paid dearly for their resistance to the Mongol invasion, losing millions of lives to war and the famine left it its wake.

After the Mongol invasion, a new scourge fell on Iran in 1380: an invasion led by Timur the Lame. Timur had married a Mongol princess and modeled himself on Genghis Khan, razing cities, massacring the people, and building pillars of human heads to commemorate his conquests, which stretched from Moscow to Delhi. Timur was planning the conquest of China when he died in 1405.

The successive ravages by the Mongols and Timurids left Iran much poorer, with agricultural areas turned back to grassland and many peasants returning to lives of nomadic herding. But Persian culture survived, and even the Timurids fell under its spell.

It is clear that although Iran was repeatedly invaded and militarily defeated, it demonstrated a unique resilience. Many of Iran's former enemies, invaders, and foreign rulers were so influenced by their encounters with Iran that they adopted key elements of Iranian language, literature, architecture, and politics.

PERSIA BECOMES A SHIITE NATION

At the end of the 15th century, the Safavids, a religious-based group of Azerbaijani ancestry from northwestern Iran, gained power among the nomadic people displaced by the Mongol and Timurid invasions. The Safavids followed a form of Sufism that blended beliefs from Shi'ism, Sufism, and other pre-Islamic beliefs, based on the millennial teachings of the Sufi mystic Shaykh Safi (1252–1334).

In 1501, the Safavids conquered the northwestern city of Tabriz. Their leader, Esma'il, declared himself *Shah* (King) of Iran and proclaimed Shiism the new denomination. This was the period when Shi'ism became the official religion, and it is often considered the beginning of modern Persian history.

The peak of the Safavid dynasty was the reign of Abbas the Great (1588–1629). The magnificent capital that Shah Abbas built at Isfahan is widely regarded as the crown jewel of Islamic architecture. He expanded trade with both India and Europe, and in 1616, he granted the British East India Company the right to trade in Iran.

Aided by the British, he took back the Strait of Hormuz from Portugal and reestablished Iran's presence in the Persian Gulf. Shah Abbas defeated the Uzbeks in the east and the Ottomans in the West. He moved provincial governors from province to province to prevent them from establishing independent bases of power, and he moved entire communities from one province to another, like the Christian Armenian community he settled in New Julfa, a suburb of Isfahan, whose descendants still live there today.

The Safavid period saw a new flowering of Iranian culture throughout the Muslim world. While the Safavids in Isfahan still spoke their native Turkic language, Farsi became the language of diplomacy and literature. The stability of the Safavid period also allowed the Shiite clergy to establish a powerful role in Iranian society, and there were occasional bouts of persecution of Sunnis, Sufis, Jews, Christians, Zoroastrians, and other religious minorities.

In 1722, the Safavids were defeated by an Afghan army from Kandahar, but that invasion was short-lived. An Iranian warlord named Nader raised a local army, and by 1729, he managed to drive out the invaders and declare himself Shah. With a thirst for conquest, Nader went on to assemble the largest army in the world at that time, about 375,000 troops, invading and conquering lands from India to Iraq. The demands his wars placed on his own people, however, provoked a revolt in Iran, which he put down with great brutality. He was assassinated in 1747 by his own bodyguards.

Nader's death was followed by a period of anarchy, with his former warlords carving out their own fiefdoms. Plagued by war, disease, and emigration, Iran's population fell from nine million to six million.

RUSSIAN, BRITISH, AND FRENCH RIVALRIES PLAY OUT ON IRANIAN SOIL

At the end of the 18th century, Iran was reunited by Agha Mohammad Khan, the leader of the Qajar tribe. He captured Isfahan in 1785, Tehran in 1786, and Shiraz in 1792. He was crowned Shah of Iran in 1796, and Tehran became the capital of his dynasty.

Although the Qajar dynasty maintained its stronghold until the early 20th century, Agha Mohammad Khan did not live to enjoy power for long, as he was assassinated a year after being crowned. He was succeeded by his nephew, Fath Ali Shah, who reigned for 37 years. After the wars and chaos of the 18th century, this was a period of recovery and peace for the Iranian people.

This period, however, also saw the growth of British, French, and Russian influence, as well as intense rivalry among these foreign powers. The British East India Company sent a 500-strong mission to Iran in 1800, and Fath Ali Shah signed a treaty and an arms deal with the British, granting them commercial privileges to the exclusion of the French.

When Russia aggressively annexed the Iranian province of Georgia, Fath Ali Shah asked the British for help. They refused, as they were now allied with Russia against France. The French exploited these differences and signed a treaty with Iran in 1807, agreeing to replace Britain as Iran's European protector and trading partner. But a month later, France made peace with Russia, and the British sent a new mission to win Iran back.

The U.K. and Iran signed a new treaty in 1809, in which the British promised support against any European power that attacked Iran, including Russia. But in 1812, when the British were called upon to arbitrate a new treaty between Russia and Iran over disputed lands of the Caucasus, the British favored Russia. Iran was forced to hand over Baku, Tbilisi, Darband, and Ganja to Russia, and the Iranian Navy was excluded from entering the Caspian Sea. Iranians began to view the British as duplicitous and self-serving allies, a reputation the British have struggled to overcome in their relations with Iran ever since.

Iranians felt like pawns in what became known as the "Great Game," a term used to describe the 19th century confrontation between the British and Russians over territories in Central and South Asia.

Iran's rulers played into this game, making economic deals with these foreign powers to pay back debts they had accumulated, in part because of their extravagant lifestyles. Beginning in the early 1870s, Iranian leaders granted a series of enormous economic concessions to British interests. The first, in 1872, was known as the Reuters Concession. It handed to Baron Julius de Reuter control over the nation's roads, telegraphs, mills, factories, mineral extraction, forests, and public works. British statesman Lord Curzon called it "the most complete and extraordinary surrender of the entire industrial resources of a kingdom into foreign hands that has probably ever been dreamed of."[5] This deplorable deal was scrapped after only one year due to a combination of local outrage and pressure from Russia.

In 1890, another British businessman, Major G.F. Talbot, was granted full control over the production, sale, and export of tobacco for fifty years.[6] Tobacco was a prized, profitable crop, and the industry employed many local workers. The merchants and *ulama* (Shiite clerics) joined forces to push back against the agreement. The tide turned when leading Shia cleric Mirza Hasan Shirazi issued a *fatwa* (religious ruling) banning the use of tobacco, which was widely consumed at the time. By the next month, the Shah was forced to take the concession back from the British. The cleric Shirazi, for his part, then repealed the *fatwa*. This was the period in which the clerics first realized their ability to sway political decisions.

Another regrettable foreign concession, one with monumental consequences, came in 1901, when Iranian rulers signed over the exclusive rights to drill for oil to British businessman William D'Arcy. This move was the first step in what became the U.K. takeover of Iran's oil resources.

The constant duplicity of the foreign governments, together with the deeply exploitive nature of their companies, established a firm belief in the minds of many Iranians that none of these foreign imperialist powers could be trusted. It also fostered growing public frustration at the failure of Iran's rulers to defend the nation's sovereignty.

THE 1906 CONSTITUTIONAL REVOLUTION

The weakness of Iran's central government and the widespread perception that it was corrupted by foreign interests eventually led to the first of Iran's two 20th century revolutions: the Constitutional Revolution, which began in 1905.

The immediate trigger of the Constitutional Revolution was an economic crisis in 1904–5, caused by the bankruptcy of the government and runaway inflation. The government owed money to foreign powers and tried to collect funds by increasing taxes on bazaar merchants. This led to mass protests by thousands of merchants and students. They presented the Shah with a demand to establish a written constitution and a parliament. On August 5th, a date that is still celebrated as Constitution Day, the Shah signed a proclamation announcing elections for a Constituent Assembly.

A Constituent Assembly was quickly organized, and it oversaw a nationwide election in 1906 for a *Majles* or Parliament (also called the Iranian National Assembly). Although only men could vote (and even they had to be "of higher social status"), this election was nevertheless seen as a breakthrough for a more representative form of government.

The newly elected members of Parliament drafted and approved a constitution based on European models, particularly Belgium's. The Shah remained head of state, but he could only sign laws passed by the Parliament and accept government ministers the Parliament appointed, reducing his role to that of a constitutional monarch, like the heads of royal families in Europe.

The constitution included a bill of rights that gave Iranians the rights of free speech, assembly, and organization; equality before the law; habeas corpus; and protection from arbitrary arrest.

Where this constitution differed from its Western counterparts was in the role of Islam and the Shiite clergy. Shiite Islam was enshrined as Iran's official religion. Only Shiites could hold cabinet positions, and books deemed heretical or anti-religious could be banned. The judiciary was divided between state and *sharia* (religious) courts, and the Parliament could not pass laws deemed to be in conflict with religious law. The Constitution called for the Parliament to elect senior clerics to a Guardian Council to enforce this principle, but this council was never set up until after the 1979 Revolution.

Unfortunately, the first attempt at a representative form of government was short-lived. Several developments strengthened monarchist and reactionary forces, leading to a Civil War that engulfed the nation from 1908 to 1910:

- First, in 1907, the U.K. and Russia signed the Anglo-Russian Convention in which they agreed to divide Iran into British and Russian zones, totally disregarding Iran's national sovereignty. The Parliament was powerless to prevent this, and Iranians learned a hard lesson: the only thing worse than being a pawn in the Great Game between the U.K. and Russia was to confront the two powers working together.

- Second, the parliamentarians soon discovered that tax reform was a hornet's nest of vested interests and traditional privileges that quickly turned many powerful and wealthy Iranians into enemies of the Parliament and the Constitution.

- Third, the liberals stirred up opposition from the clerics by calling for secular reforms on issues like the rights of women and religious minorities. Conservative clerics began to rally huge crowds in opposition.

In June 1908, Mohammad Ali Shah and his supporters, with the encouragement of Russia, staged a military coup against the Parliament, bombarding the building with cannons and killing about 250 people. Six senior members of Parliament were imprisoned; three of them were summarily executed. The coup quickly turned into a civil war when key sectors of Iranian society, from minority groups to Shiite clergy to tribal leaders, took the Constitutional side and opposed the Shah.

When the anti-Shah forces converged in Tehran in 1910, the Shah was forced to abdicate and the Parliament was reconstituted.

More democratic reforms were instituted, including reducing the voting age from 25 to 20 and eliminating status requirements to vote.

The reforms, however, did not resolve an age-old problem: Iran lacked a strong central state capable of collecting revenue. Real power still rested in the hands of the provincial governors and landowners, many of whom had their own private armies and negotiated contracts directly with the British and Russians.

By 1911, the nation was deeply in hock to British and Russian banks. Although the British struck oil in 1908, their first royalty payment to Iran was in 1913—only $15,000, a mere drop in Iran's sea of debt.

When World War I broke out, Iran declared neutrality, but both the British and Russians expanded their occupation of the country. In a brazen display of imperial overreach, the British took advantage of the 1917 Russian revolution to push a scandalous proposal to totally absorb Iran into the British Empire. Britain paid Iran's Prime Minister Vossuq al-Dowleh $600,000 to shepherd this proposal through Parliament, but the entire country rose up against the plan, and the prime minister was forced to resign.

THE RISE OF THE PAHLAVI DYNASTY

In 1921, Reza Khan, a Russian-trained soldier who had risen in the ranks of the Iranian Army, was chosen by the British to lead a brigade to Tehran. Having succeeded in seizing control of the capital, he was initially tasked with heading the army. The ambitious commander, however, wanted more power, and pushed the Parliament to appoint him prime minister. In 1926, the Parliament, dominated by his supporters, crowned him as Shah. Like most Iranians at the time, Reza Khan did not have a surname, and he was informed that he would need a name for his dynasty. This led him to pass a law ordering all Iranians to take a surname; for himself, he chose Pahlavi, the name of the writing system used in ancient Persia.

The Shah succeeded in the task that had stymied every ruler before him: building a strong central state. Using the nation's steadily increasing oil production to provide critical revenues, he created an effective bureaucracy and a large standing army. Although Anglo-Persian Oil paid only a 16 percent royalty on Iran's oil, this nonetheless grew into a tidy sum.

To give Reza Shah his due: he used Iran's oil revenues to build an efficient tax collection and customs system, to build roads across the country, and to invest in new industries. He also built a large, well-equipped military, repressive security services, and new prisons that he filled with thousands of political prisoners. He nearly always wore his military uniform in public, and his government was unapologetically a military regime.

Reza Shah ran a patronage network that made him the richest man in Iran. He reduced the Parliament to a rubber stamp by vetting lists of potential candidates. If the Shah wrote a comment—say, "unpatriotic," "stupid," or "dangerous"—next to a candidate's name, the candidate would be forced to withdraw or end up in prison. Parliamentarians who dared criticize the Shah or his policies fared even worse. Many were killed by death squads or died mysteriously in prison.

The Shah's program of cultural modernization was equally authoritarian. Through military conscription, he forced men to speak Farsi instead of their local dialect and to identify with the state rather than with their own tribe or region. He imposed a national dress code that outlawed tribal and traditional clothes. Men had to wear Western pants, shirts, coats, and the felt-rimmed fedora, or "Pahlavi hat," as it was known. Beards and large mustaches were discouraged.

Women were ordered to remove the *chador* (the traditional dress that covers their bodies and hair, but not their face). The Shah's police would forcibly pull the chadors off women, outraging the Shia clerics and terrorizing women who felt that appearing in public uncovered was tantamount to nakedness.

He called on the international community to change the country's name from Persia to Iran, and to call its citizens Iranians, not Persians.

Reza Shah's government expanded education, but there was little improvement in healthcare, sanitation, or plumbing. Modernization was limited to improvements that would enhance the power of the state and enforce national identity, while things like running water, toilets, and healthcare, which would only improve the lives of its people, were not a priority.

Many of the Shah's measures were consciously designed to break the power of the religious hierarchy. His educational reforms ended the clerics' near monopoly on education, just as the creation of secular courts broke their judicial power. His efforts at Westernization and secularism earned him the enmity of the clerics.

For the most part, the wealthy classes supported or tolerated the Reza Shah regime because they were able to increase their wealth, send their children to universities in Europe, and enjoy the pleasures of modern life. Landowners had the backing of a powerful state to enforce their will on their peasants, and tribal leaders could register formerly common tribal land under their own names, transforming themselves into wealthy, modern landlords.

But Reza Shah was hated by most Iranians, from devout Muslims to exploited working people to educated, middle class Iranians who longed for a democratic state.

In 1934, the Shah signed a new contract with the Anglo-Persian Oil Company, giving it exclusive rights over the nation's oil for the next 60 years in exchange for raising Iran's royalty from 16 percent to 20 percent. This confirmed public suspicion that he was, and had always been, essentially a British puppet.

The Shah was not only negotiating with the British, however. Tired of what he saw as the opportunistic policies of both Britain and the Soviet Union, he sought to counterbalance their influence by encouraging trade with Germany. On the eve of World War II, Germany was Iran's number one trading partner.

Although Reza Shah declared Iran neutral in the war, his ties with Germany backfired when both the Soviets and the British joined forces in 1941 to fight Germany, and decided they needed Iran as a supply route to send war material to the Soviet forces. In August 1941, the British and Soviets both launched a massive air, land, and naval assault against Iran.

The Shah's vaunted army was built to control and oppress his own people, not to resist an invasion. It surrendered after three days. The British gave the stunned Shah a face-saving way out: He could abdicate in favor of his son, Mohammad Reza Pahlavi, if his son would, in turn, allow the British and Soviets to occupy their respective zones in the north and south of the country.

IRAN'S SHORT-LIVED BUT INFLUENTIAL SOCIALIST PARTY: TUDEH

The new Shah, who was only 22 years old, made a show of returning some of his family's ill-gotten land and wealth to the Iranian treasury, ear-marking it to build hospitals, medical colleges, libraries, and a water system. Even as he stressed his Swiss education and Western orientation, he promised the clergy that his government would end his father's Westernization campaign.

The years between 1941 and 1953 marked a brief period of renewed constitutional government, as the Parliament once again became functional. While in the rural areas the majority of seats were controlled by landowners, in the cities a new party began winning over working-class Iranians and young intellectuals: the socialist Tudeh Party. Founded in 1941 by former political prisoners and young graduates of European universities, by 1945 the party held seven seats in the Parliament and three cabinet ministries. Its newspaper *Rahbar* (Leader) had a circulation of 100,000, and about 50,000 people attended its massive rallies in Tehran.

The socialist party made significant gains for workers. When the Tudeh-led Central Council of Federated Trade Unions called a strike against the Anglo-Iranian Oil Company in 1946, the company quickly backed down and granted the strikers' demands for an eight-hour day, overtime pay, higher wages, better housing, and even a paid weekly day off for Friday prayers.

The Tudeh Party went on to push through the first national labor law in the Middle East. It granted all workers most of the same rights the oil workers had won. The law outlawed child labor and established minimum wages based on local conditions, six annual holidays, unemployment compensation, and the right to organize unions.

Sadly, it was the actions of the Soviet Union in 1946 that undermined Iran's socialist party. In opposition to Iran's central government, the Soviets supported popular movements for autonomy in Iranian Kurdistan and Azerbaijan. The Iranian government claimed that Tudeh supported the secessionists, and launched a widespread crackdown. The party's previously powerful united front was split between nationalists who opposed the Soviet-backed secessionist movements and pro-Soviet leftists who felt obliged to support them.

The party was outlawed, and its newspapers were shut down. Many Tudeh leaders were arrested; others fled into exile and were sentenced to death *in absentia*. Even opposition politicians who were not Tudeh members were arrested, and the Shah convened a Constituent Assembly to expand his own powers.

The socialist party was banned and suppressed, but it left a lasting imprint on Iranian politics. It had raised the political consciousness of millions of Iranians and issued the first widespread call for the nationalization of the Anglo-Iranian Oil Company, a call that would only ring louder in the years that followed.

MOSSADEGH COMES TO POWER

Into the political vacuum left by the banning of the Tudeh Party stepped Mohammad Mossadegh, a man in his late 60s, from an aristocratic family. He had been a prominent politician during and after the Constitutional Revolution of 1906, but had been forced out of politics by Reza Shah. He was known as an advocate of two principles: strict adherence to the 1906 Constitution and what he called "negative equilibrium," or strict neutrality in foreign affairs to ensure Iran's sovereignty and independence from foreign domination.

Mossadegh contrasted his concept of "negative equilibrium" with Iran's previous practice of "positive equilibrium," by which Iran gave concessions and privileges to Britain and Russia (as well as to Belgium and France), and then tried desperately to find a balance between them as more and more of its sovereignty was eroded.

He denounced past oil concessions granted to the British and Russians, as well as ongoing negotiations with the Americans for new oil concessions. He took up the call to nationalize Iran's oil industry, insisting that it was Iran's inalienable right to have full control over the production, sale, and export of its own resources.

Due to his conflict with the British over oil nationalization, Mossadegh has been portrayed in the West as anti-British, but he was in fact a great admirer of 19th century British liberal democracy. He was simply opposed to handing Iran's sovereignty or its resources over to any other country, whether it was the U.K., the U.S.S.R., or the U.S.

Iranians regarded Mossadegh as incorruptible because, although he was related by blood and marriage to Iran's most aristocratic and wealthy families, he led a middle-class life and denounced the extravagant lifestyles of his fellow aristocrats. After becoming prime minister in 1951, he insisted on being addressed as "Dr. Mossadegh," not as "Your Excellency."

Mossadegh united different parties and social groups to form a coalition called the National Front. He had the support of Ayatollah Kashani, the most politically active member of the clerical hierarchy. The National Front organized petitions and street demonstrations to mobilize a mass movement for the nationalization of the oil industry. In 1951, he introduced his oil nationalization bill in the Parliament and was elected prime minister with a mandate to carry it out.

Mossadegh and his colleagues created the National Iranian Oil Company (NIOC) and began negotiations with Anglo-Iranian Oil Company (the precursor to BP) to hand over its facilities and operations. When Anglo-Iranian rejected the plan outright, he ordered NIOC to take over its wells, pipelines, refinery, and offices throughout the nation. The British government evacuated most of the company's British personnel from Iran and froze Iranian assets in British banks. Mossadegh closed the British Embassy and broke off diplomatic relations.

In 1952, Mossadegh also tried to reform Iran's election laws to weaken the power of the Shah and the wealthiest landlords. When this failed, he halted the parliamentary elections as soon as he had a quorum of deputies who would support him. Then, he provoked a showdown with the Shah by insisting that, as prime minister, he had the right to appoint the war minister as well as all the other members of his cabinet, a prerogative the Shah had always kept for himself. Mossadegh took to the airwaves and told the nation that he needed control of the military to prevent the Shah and the British from undermining his oil nationalization plan. The public flooded the streets for three days of protests against the Shah, who was forced to back down.

Mossadegh made the most of his victory over the Shah. He transferred lands appropriated by the Shah back to the state; prohibited the Shah from communicating directly with foreign embassies; and exiled the Shah's politically active twin sister, Princess Ashraf.

He also tried to get control over the military. He renamed the War Ministry the Ministry of Defense and promised from then on to buy only defensive weapons. He purged 136 military officers and transferred 15,000 men from the army to the police. He cut the military budget by 15 percent, and appointed a parliamentary commission to investigate the Shah's military procurement practices for corruption.

To counteract the pro-Shah members of Parliament, Mossadegh asked his Parliamentary backers to resign, denying the Parliament the quorum needed to overturn his orders. He then called a referendum to ratify his dissolution of the Parliament. By July 1953, a constitutional committee was debating how to replace Iran's monarchy with a democratic republic.

THE 1953 COUP: STAGED BY THE U.K. AND U.S.

The British had a great deal to lose from the nationalization of the Anglo-Iranian Oil Company. The U.K. government earned $92 million in taxes on its operations and $354 million in foreign exchange from oil sales. The British Royal Navy depended on Iran for 85 percent of its fuel.

But, as the British stressed to their U.S. allies, there were larger issues at stake, relating to control of the global oil industry. If Iran succeeded in nationalizing its oil industry, Indonesia, Venezuela, Iraq, and others would surely follow. The Western cartel that controlled the industry would be broken, with dire consequences for both U.K. and U.S. business and geopolitical interests.

In private negotiations, the British were prepared to increase Iran's share of the profits from its oil production from 20 percent up to as much as 60 percent, and to share Iran's oil with other Western companies, but only with the proviso that ultimate control remained in Western hands.

In public, however, the British blamed the crisis entirely on Mossadegh. Historian Ervand Abrahamian compiled a list of the insulting terms they used to smear him: "fanatical," "crazy," "erratic," "eccentric," "slippery," "unbalanced," "demagogic," "absurd," "childish," "tiresome and single-minded," "inflammatory," "volatile and unstable," "sentimentally mystical," "wild," "wily Oriental," "unwilling to face fact," "dictatorial," "xenophobic," "Robespierre-like," "Frankenstein-like," "unprepared to listen to reason and common sense," and "swayed by martyrdom complex."

There was little disagreement between Washington and London about the result they wanted: to keep Iran's oil under Western control. But for fourteen months in 1951 and 1952, the Americans resisted the British line that Mossadegh had to go. U.S. officials tried to negotiate a compromise that would give the Iranians the illusion of nationalization while keeping real control in Western hands. Only after Mossadegh moved against the Shah in July 1952 did the U.S. Ambassador in Tehran make a report to Washington, saying: "Only a *coup d'etat* could save the situation."

The CIA and the U.K. spy agency MI6 began planning the coup in late 1952. MI6 already had an extensive dossier on all of Iran's senior military officers. The Americans had useful assets as well: 100 U.S. advisors embedded in Iran's military, and good contacts with young Iranian officers who had been sent to the United States for training. Those included tank commanders and a clandestine network of unsavory characters in the Tehran bazaars. In June 1953, Secretary of State John Foster Dulles unveiled the plan to policymakers in Washington, announcing, "This is how we get rid of Mossadegh."[7]

On August 15th, the Shah issued a decree dismissing Mossadegh and appointing a new prime minister, General Zahedi, whom the British had imprisoned during the war as a German collaborator. Mossadegh refused to step down and instead broadcast a message that the Shah, encouraged by "foreign elements," had attempted a coup.

The next day, there were huge demonstrations supporting Mossadegh and the National Front, but CIA provocateurs in the crowd attacked clerics and mosques, forcing Mossadegh to condemn the violence. The U.S. Ambassador met with Mossadegh and threatened to evacuate Americans from Iran because of the chaos in the streets. On August 18th, Mossadegh deployed his police and army to suppress the demonstrations.

On August 19th, CIA-paid gangs and soldiers in civilian clothes staged an aggressive pro-Shah, anti-Mossadegh counter-demonstration that brought the turmoil on the streets of Tehran to a climax. Richard Cottam, who was with the CIA in Tehran at the time, wrote later, "The mob that came into north Tehran and was decisive in the overthrow was a mercenary mob. It had no ideology. That mob was paid for by American dollars."[8]

Amid the mayhem, 32 Sherman tanks rolled into the city and surrounded critical buildings, including Mossadegh's home and the main radio station. Three hours later, the coup leaders captured the radio station and broadcast a proclamation from the Shah naming General Zahedi as Iran's new prime minister. Fighting raged on for another six hours between forces backing the coup and troops loyal to Mossadegh. Outgunned, the loyalists surrendered. The *New York Times* estimated that at least 300 people were killed and 100 wounded.[9]

BITTER AFTERMATH OF THE 1953 COUP

President Eisenhower told the American people that the Iranian people had "saved the day," because of their "revulsion against communism," and "their profound love for their monarchy."

In fact, the coup permanently undermined the legitimacy of the monarchy in Iran. It identified the Shah and his military with the imperialist interests of the British and the Americans, and with Anglo-Iranian and the rest of the Western oil cartel that reaped shares of Iran's oil after the coup. Relations between Iran and the United States were permanently damaged, as the U.S. government was now seen as yet another duplicitous power, in cahoots with the perfidious British who had constrained and thwarted Iran's independence and sovereignty for 150 years. By contrast, Mohammad Mossadegh is remembered by his people as a nationalist leader in the mold of India's Gandhi, Indonesia's Sukarno, and Egypt's Nasser.

The crackdown on the National Front that followed the coup was brutal. There were mass arrests, and many of the leaders were executed. Mossadegh spent three years in prison and the rest of his life under house arrest. When he died in 1967, he was buried in his garden to avoid a public funeral that might have ignited a revolution. (Decades later, on the anniversary of his death, thousands of students still gather outside his house and visit his grave to pay tribute to their hero.)

All the secular parties and organizations that had opposed the Shah were dismantled and banned. The only important institution that maintained some independence and could still speak with moral authority to the concerns of the public was the Shiite clergy, setting the stage for the 1979 Islamic Revolution.

MOHAMMAD REZA SHAH RULES WITH AN IRON FIST

Mohammad Reza Shah was back in charge with even more dictatorial powers, ruling much as his father had done. He continued his father's project of building Iran into a strong, centralized, militarized state. Iran was now receiving a 50 percent share of the annual revenue from its ever-increasing oil output, and the Shah poured much of Iran's oil wealth into his first priority: the military. Iran became the largest weapons purchaser in the world, much like Saudi Arabia today. He built the largest navy in the Persian Gulf, the largest air force in the region, and the fifth largest army in the world. The Shah's arsenal eventually included 1,000 tanks, 100 long-range artillery pieces, 400 helicopters, 2,500 Maverick air-to-ground missiles, and 324 U.S.-built warplanes. In 1978, his last year in power, he ordered $12 billion worth of new weapons, including three destroyers, ten nuclear submarines, and another 449 warplanes.

He also built a terrifying 5,000-man security service called SAVAK, which reportedly recruited one out of every 450 adult Iranian men as an informer. SAVAK enforced draconian censorship, and disappeared, tortured, and killed political dissidents.

Frances FitzGerald, who visited Iran as the niece of the U.S. Ambassador, wrote the following in 1974: "Educated Iranians cannot trust anyone beyond a close circle of friends, and for them the effect is the same as if everyone else belonged (to SAVAK). SAVAK intensifies this fear by giving no account of its activities. People disappear in Iran, and their disappearances go unrecorded."[10]

In 1975, Amnesty International estimated that there were between 25,000 and 100,000 political prisoners in the Shah's prisons. Amnesty noted that Iran had "the highest rate of death penalties in the world, no valid system of civilian courts, and a history of torture that is beyond belief."[11]

THE FAILURE OF THE SHAH'S WHITE REVOLUTION

The highlight of the Shah's development program was his 1963 "White Revolution," framed as a counter to a potential socialist "Red Revolution." It was intended to transform Iran into an economic and industrial power, and included new rights for women. The land reform at the heart of the program, however, still left millions in the countryside with no land, or too little land to support themselves. The population of Tehran mushroomed from 1.5 million to more than 5.5 million as landless peasants flocked to shanty towns around the cities to seek work and some scraps from the relative prosperity of city life.

The central structural problem with the White Revolution was that it was based on what we would now call "trickle-down economics." Iran's oil revenues were funneled to the top 0.1 percent of the economic strata, who were part of the Shah's social circle and patronage system, and most of the wealth simply stayed there. This tiny upper class owned 85 percent of the shares in Iranian corporations, sent their children to university in Europe or the United States, and led extravagant, jet-set lifestyles.

Meanwhile, the Shah tightened his political grip. His rubber-stamp Parliament was run by a two-party system, with a permanent majority for the Shah's Iran-e Novin Party and a permanent minority for the token opposition Mardom Party. In 1975, after the opposition won several by-elections by running local candidates not connected to the Shah's patronage system, its leader was killed in a suspicious car accident, and the Shah dissolved both parties. In their place, he created a one-party totalitarian state under his new Resurgence Party. The Shah now condemned multi-party democracy as a sham and declared that his new party would build a perfect society that would be a model for the East and West alike.

Slipping farther and farther into megalomania, the Shah seemed to genuinely believe in a fantasy vision of himself and his country. He told Italian journalist Oriana Fallaci that he was guided by visions and messages from God and from Imam Ali. "I am accompanied by a force that others can't see, my mythical force. I get messages, religious messages."[12]

Inspired by his delusions, the Shah launched politically suicidal attacks on two powerful interest groups: the bazaar merchants and the Shiite clergy. He blamed the country's economic woes on profiteering by bazaar merchants, and unleashed an army of 10,000 inspectors to harass them. SAVAK security forces set up "Guild Courts" that brought charges against 180,000 merchants, handed down 250,000 fines and 8,000 prison terms, and banished 23,000 merchants from their home towns.

The Shah's call for women's rights—the right to vote, to initiate divorce, to travel without a man's permission—was fiercely opposed by the religious establishment. The Shah also challenged the clergy by proclaiming himself a spiritual as well as a political leader. He replaced the Muslim calendar with a new Imperial Calendar dating from the founding of the Persian Empire in 500 B.C. He sent inspectors to audit religious endowments and took control of Tehran University's Theology College and other religious education institutions. A clerical newspaper accused the Shah of trying to "nationalize" religion.

Living increasingly in his own fantasy world, the Shah seemed convinced to the end that his people really loved him. In reality, he never had support from the Western-educated intelligentsia or the urban working class, who had been politicized by the socialist Tudeh Party in the 1940s, backed Mossadegh's National Front in the 1950s, and saw the Shah as an American and British puppet. The abuses of the Shah and his Resurgence Party severed his last links with the conservative middle class of merchants, landlords, and clerics who had traditionally supported the monarchy.

The Pahlavi dynasty had run its course.

CHAPTER 2: THE ISLAMIC REVOLUTION SHOCKS THE WORLD

To Western observers, it may seem incongruous that a country that supported the socialist Tudeh Party in the 1940s and the anti-imperialist National Front in the early 1950s was consumed in the 1970s by an Islamic revolution that brought to power what Western commentators have labelled a fundamentalist theocracy.

As in all revolutions, the forces driving it were committed to transforming the political regime, but they represented a complex combination of nationalism, populism, and religious radicalism.

THE RISE OF AYATOLLAH KHOMEINI

Key in the religious mix was Sayyid Ruhollah Musavi Khomeini, known in the Western world as Ayatollah Khomeini. Khomeini had been a leading scholar of Shia Islam, teaching political philosophy, Islamic history, and ethics at seminaries in the religious cities of Najaf and Qom. During the 1960s process of Westernization pursued by the Reza Shah Pahlavi, Khomeini became an increasingly vocal opponent, accusing the Shah of submission to the United States and Israel. In 1963, he was arrested for preaching inflammatory sermons calling for the overthrow of the Shah. News of his arrest led to major riots, which resulted in the death of many of his supporters. Khomeini was exiled in 1964, first in Turkey, then Iraq, then France.

From exile, he lectured and wrote extensively about his views on governance. He believed that rule by monarchs or elected parliaments claiming to represent the people was un-Islamic. He insisted that those holding government posts should be well versed in *sharia*, the laws of God, and that the system of clerical rule was necessary to prevent injustice, corruption, and oppression by the powerful over the poor. He believed that clerical rule was the only way to protect the people from anti-Islamic influences and meddling by non-Muslim foreign powers.

Tape recordings of Khomeini's sermons and banned copies of his books circulated underground inside Iran, where he developed a devoted following among the young clergy, students, and merchants.

UNTIMELY DEATH OF INFLUENTIAL CLERIC ALI SHARIATI

A less widely known—but equally important—religious figure was Ali Shariati. Had he lived to see the revolution, it might have taken a very different course.

Shariati was the son of a cleric and teacher in the holy city of Mashad. He taught in a village school before continuing his studies in Arabic and French at Mashad University. There, he translated into Farsi and Arabic the biography of Abu Zarr, one of the Prophet Muhammad's lesser-known companions. The book was titled, *Abu Zarr: The God Worshipping Socialist*. Shariati's father had held up Abu Zarr as a model to his son, and Shariati became known to many Iranians as the "Abu Zarr of Iran."

In the early 1960s, Shariati won a scholarship to study at the Sorbonne in France, where he took part in demonstrations supporting anti-colonial struggles in the Congo and Algeria and studied under French academic experts in Islamic mysticism. He translated into Farsi works by Jean-Paul Sartre, Che Guevara, Franz Fanon and a book about the war in Algeria. He also studied Christian Liberation Theology as he grappled with the role of religion in anti-colonial struggles.

Shariati embraced Shiism's traditional rejection of worldly authority, especially of monarchy, and connected it with the 20th century's anti-colonial and anti-capitalist struggles. He believed that the Prophet Muhammad had come to establish not just a new religion, but a permanent revolution that would lead to a classless society. In Shariati's interpretation, Imam Ali opposed the early Caliphs because they were betraying the true meaning of Islam by compromising with worldly power.

Shariati attacked the Shiite clerical hierarchy and its relationship with the landowning classes, insisting that their financial support was inherently corrupting. "The task at hand is nothing less than the total liberation of Islam from the clergy and the propertied classes," he declared.[13]

When Ali Shariati died in exile in the U.K. in 1977 at the young age of 44, many suspected foul play by SAVAK.

Shariati's death just before the revolution deprived Iran of a powerful voice that might have led it in a different direction and balanced the power of Ayatollah Khomeini and the Shiite hierarchy. While Shariati's ideas appealed more to young, religious intellectuals than to conservative clerics, they were firmly rooted in Shiism's long tradition of opposition to corrupt worldly authority. Many of Khomeini's sayings that became the slogans of the revolution could equally have been written by Shariati: "Islam belongs to the oppressed, not to the oppressors;" "Islam originates from the masses, not from the rich;" and "Islam is not the opiate of the masses."

TRIUMPH OF THE ISLAMIC REVOLUTION

When President Jimmy Carter took office in 1977 and announced that promoting human rights was a new priority of U.S. foreign policy, the Shah actually pulled back from some forms of repression, such as secret trials of dissidents in military courts. More Iranians began to speak out openly against his atrocities and his one-party state, and students in Tehran took to the streets in protest.

When a government-controlled newspaper ran a savage smear of the Ayatollah Khomeini in January 1978, accusing him of immorality and being a British agent, seminary students in the holy city Qom took to the street. The students were demanding the return of Khomeini from exile and the reopening of his Fayzieh seminary. They also demanded the release of political prisoners; an end to Iran's subservient relations with Western powers; freedom of the press; an independent judiciary; and the dissolution of the Shah's Resurgence Party.

They marched to the police station, where they were viciously attacked. The number of students killed is disputed, with estimates ranging wildly from 5 to 100, but their martyrdom became a new rallying cry.

The most senior cleric, Ayatollah Shariatmadari, called a general strike on the 40th day after the killings in Qom, launching a series of escalating protests every 40 days. The February strike provoked a bloody military crackdown on protesters in Tabriz, Shariatmadari's hometown. Angry demonstrators responded by attacking property that symbolized either the repressive state, such as police stations, or Western values, such as luxury hotels and movie theaters. The second strike in March led the Shah to cancel a foreign trip and take personal command of his riot police, who shut down the protests by firing at the crowd, killing over 100. The third strike in May included protest marches in 24 towns and cities. In Qom, police raided Ayatollah Shariatmadari's residence and killed theology students who had taken sanctuary there. The opposition put the death toll in the three strikes at 250, while the government claimed only 22 students had been killed.

On August 19th, 1978, an incident that helped change the course of history occurred at the Rex Cinema in the city of Abadan. While hundreds of people were watching a controversial film about drug addiction and poverty called *Gavaznha* (*The Deer*), a group of men barred the doors of the cinema, doused it with gasoline, and set it on fire. Over 400 people were killed. Incensed, the public blamed the police chief, who was the same person who had ordered the police to fire on the protesting seminary students in Qom in January. They believed the regime had targeted the theater to kill political dissidents who had gathered to watch the film.

To this day, there remains controversy over who really set the theatre on fire. Some believe it was not Shah supporters but Khomeini supporters who wanted to create more anger against the Shah. Others believe it was the Marxist group called MEK, with the same goal of building revolutionary outrage among the public.

In any case, the tragedy did build anti-Shah fervor. After a huge funeral, 10,000 people marched through the city chanting, "Burn the Shah" and "The Shah must go."

According to historian Roy Mottahedeh, "Thousands of Iranians who had felt neutral and had until now thought that the struggle was only between the Shah and supporters of religiously conservative mullahs felt that the government might put their own lives on the block to save itself. Suddenly, for hundreds of thousands, the movement was their own business."[14]

The Shah declared martial law and, on September 8th, his troops opened fire on a demonstration in Tehran's Jaleh Square. The number of deaths varied widely, but 84 people were identified by the Martyrs Foundation that was set up later to compensate the families of the Shah's victims. September 8th, 1978, became known as "Black Friday" and was seen as the critical turning point that sealed the Shah's fate.

In the following weeks, a general strike took hold of the whole country and on December 11th, the climax of the Shiite festival of Ashura, the government called off the military and permitted four huge but orderly marches to meet up in Tehran's Shahyad Square (which after the revolution was renamed Azadi Freedom Square).

An estimated two million people converged, chanting, "The Shah must go." Speakers called for the return of Khomeini, the expulsion of Western powers, and social justice for the "deprived masses." Noting the orderly, peaceful character of the demonstration, the *New York Times* noted, "In a way, the opposition has demonstrated that there already is an alternative government."[15] With the old regime collapsing, on January 16, 1979, the Shah fled the country.

Two weeks later, on February 1st, Ayatollah Khomeini returned to Iran after 15 years in exile. The crowd that greeted Khomeini at the airport was estimated at three million. As the *Washington Post* said at the time, "The religious, the lay, the left, the liberals, the right, everyone who was fed up with the Shah used Khomeini as a convenient symbol of a strong man who for years openly opposed the monarchy."[16]

His first port of call was the Behest-e-Zahra Cemetery, where he paid his respects to the Shah's victims. The revolutionary government later claimed that 60,000 Iranians died resisting the Shah's regime from 1963 until the Revolution, although the Martyrs Foundation was only able to identify about 3,000, mostly killed between 1977 and 1979, and mainly from working-class districts of Tehran.

On February 9th, revolutionary forces broke into armories in Tehran and surrounded the air force headquarters. The chiefs of staff declared the military neutral and confined the troops to their barracks. The French newspaper *Le Monde* compared the scene in the streets of Tehran to the Paris Commune, with thousands of civilians carrying machine guns and other weapons.

On the afternoon of February 11th, Radio Tehran broadcast the historic message: "This is the voice of Iran, the voice of true Iran, the voice of the Islamic Revolution."

KHOMEINI'S VISION PREVAILS OVER CALLS FOR SEPARATION OF CHURCH AND STATE

An Interim Government was set up and charged with drawing up a new constitution. Mehdi Bazargan, an ally of Mohammad Mossadegh and founder of the Iran Liberation Movement in 1961, was named prime minister. Bazargan was a French-educated engineer. He was a devout Shia Muslim, and his Liberation Movement was not as secular as Mossadegh's National Front, but he firmly supported the separation of church and state. Bazargan drafted a new constitution based on the constitution of France's Fifth Republic.

By this point, however, the real power lay with Ayatollah Khomeini and his followers. They had set up a Revolutionary Council and a Central Committee, and they controlled many of the local revolutionary committees that sprang up at mosques around the country.

The sharpest disagreement between Bazargan and Khomeini was over Khomeini's insistence on including the positions of Supreme Leader and Guardian Council, which is a body that was called for in the 1906 Constitution but had never been established. The traditional "guardianship" role of the Shiite clergy was to oversee religious foundations and protect the weakest members of society, especially children, widows, and the mentally ill. Khomeini reinterpreted this guardianship, or *velayat-e faqeh*, to cover society at large. He wanted to ensure that all government laws conformed to the tenets of Islam, extending religious jurisprudence to allow direct clerical rule of society.

The first consequential test of wills between Bazargan and Khomeini was over the April 1979 referendum giving voters the choice of whether or not they wanted to establish an Islamic Republic. Bazargan argued for giving the public a third choice: to vote for a "Democratic Islamic Republic." Khomeini insisted on an up or down vote for an Islamic Republic, arguing that a true Islamic Republic would be perfect and required no qualification based on Western concepts like "democracy." Khomeini won the argument and with a massive 95 percent turnout, an extraordinary 99 percent of the public voted for an Islamic Republic.

Khomeini's supporters likewise dominated the election for a 73-man "Assembly of Experts" to draft the new constitution. The constitution that emerged retained some democratic elements advocated by Bazargan, including direct elections for the president, a 270-member *Majles* (Parliament), and provincial and local councils. But it gave unprecedented authority to Khomeini as the Supreme Leader (and whoever followed him in that role), and tremendous power to the Guardian Council.

The constitution guaranteed civil liberties, from habeas corpus to the presumption of innocence to freedom of religion, speech, assembly, and the press; and freedom from arbitrary arrest, torture, police surveillance, and wiretapping. It met many of the social demands of the working class and the secular opposition to the Shah. It guaranteed old-age pensions, free primary and secondary education, unemployment compensation, disability pay, decent housing, and universal healthcare. It enshrined even loftier goals like eliminating poverty, unemployment, usury, vice, private monopolies, and inequality—even between men and women. It also called for helping the oppressed of the world in their struggles against their oppressors.

The way in which all these rights and promises were to be implemented, however, had to "conform to the principles of Islam," as determined by the Guardian Council.

Prime Minister Bazargan and seven members of the Interim Government signed a petition to Khomeini objecting to the constitution drafted by the Assembly of Experts. They warned that it violated popular sovereignty, lacked public consensus, enshrined the clergy as a "ruling class," and would ultimately backfire by leading the public to blame every future government failure on "Islamic rule." They called the draft constitution "a revolution against the revolution," and threatened to publish their own original draft based on the French constitution.

The Interim Government had important allies for its position, including Ayatollah Shariatmadari, who had never accepted Khomeini's overreaching reinterpretation of clerical guardianship. If the public had been given a choice between the two draft constitutions, it is quite possible that Bazargan and his allies could have won that fight.

We will never know, because, at that critical moment, the United States once again intervened in Iran's affairs by admitting the Shah to the United States for cancer treatment. The public was incensed. Passions previously directed entirely at the Shah were suddenly redirected against the United States, reminding Iranians of the U.S. role in the 1953 coup and raising fears that the CIA station in the U.S. Embassy was once again plotting to impose an autocratic monarchy on Iran. Four hundred university students climbed over the wall of the U.S. Embassy and occupied it for the next 444 days, holding the American staff prisoner in their own embassy.

When Ayatollah Khomeini refused to order the students out of the embassy, Bazargan resigned, and the debate over his and Khomeini's conflicting visions for the constitution and the future of Iran was effectively over. Khomeini had won.

Important secular groups boycotted the national referendum that approved the Islamic Constitution on December 2, 1979, reducing the turnout to 75 percent from the 95 percent who had voted in the earlier referendum on the Islamic Republic. Nevertheless, the constitution was approved by 99 percent of those who voted.

Few observers predicted the success, or even the survival, of the new Islamic Republic, especially when it was immediately faced with a new crisis: war with Iraq.

THE DEVASTATING IRAN-IRAQ WAR 1980–1988

The Iran-Iraq war was started by Iraqi leader Saddam Hussein, who invaded Iran in September 1980 with the aim of seizing the Arvand Rud waterway (known as Shatt al-Arab in Iraq) and Iran's oil-rich southwestern Khuzestan region.

Iran fought back fiercely. The fighters included remnants of the Shah's vaunted military, which totaled 370,000 men under arms. The new government also formed elite regiments of 120,000 Revolutionary Guards, including the super-elite 5,000-man Quds Force. In addition, it raised a volunteer force of 200,000, called Basij-e Mostazefin (Mobilization of the Oppressed), made up mostly of young boys whose homes were under attack. This militia was formed as a support force but its teenage "martyrs" were later used in "human wave" attacks against Iraqi forces.

The Iranians used the Shah's large arsenal of Western-built tanks and warplanes. Israel played a secret but critical role supporting Iran. It became a conduit for spare parts, weapons, and ammunition, keeping many of Iran's weapons operational despite a Western arms embargo.

The war ground on for a total of eight brutal years and was characterized by trench warfare comparable to the horrors of World War I, Iraqi use of chemical and biological weapons, and aerial bombardment of civilians by both sides. The death toll is estimated at somewhere between 400,000 (250,000 Iranians and 150,000 Iraqis) and a staggering one million, with Iranians suffering more of the casualties.

This tragic loss of life and several billion dollars' worth of damages finally came to an end in July 1988, with a UN-brokered ceasefire.

THE ISLAMIZATION OF IRANIAN SOCIETY

Iraq's Saddam Hussein had deliberately started the war at a time when Iran was in a state of upheaval after the 1979 Islamic Revolution. He thought the different groups vying for power would have difficulty creating a unified force to repel his army. He miscalculated, as Iran's revolutionary forces galvanized around this prolonged war with an intense sense of patriotism.

The war also provided the conditions for a massive expansion of the state's role in Iran's economy. All basic goods were rationed, alleviating some of the poverty caused by the war. Up to a quarter of the budget was dedicated to subsidies for bread, rice, sugar, cheese, fuel, cooking oil, electricity, sanitation, and water. The government opened food co-ops, took over factories abandoned by private companies, and nationalized business enterprises that had been part of the Shah's crony-capitalist patronage system. The Iranian state was soon running about 2,000 factories, many of which were losing money, but this prevented mass unemployment.

Many of the confiscated assets of the Shah, his cronies, and foreign partners were placed under the ownership of the Bonyad-e Mostazafan va Janbazan (Foundation for the Oppressed and Disabled). By the late 1980s, its assets amounted to somewhere between $10 and $20 billion, including 140 factories, 470 agribusinesses, 100 construction firms, 64 mines and 250 other companies. These included Zam Zam (the Iranian alternative to Coca-Cola and Pepsi), and the former Hilton and Hyatt hotels.

The government also expanded benefits for the working class. It passed a labor law that guaranteed many of the benefits that had been championed by the socialist Tudeh Party in the 1940s.

At the same time, it formed close ties with the bazaar merchant class, the traditional political allies of the Shiite clergy. Seventy percent of the deputies elected to the revolution's first Parliament were bazaar merchants or other members of the propertied middle class. Ayatollah Khomeini was quick to reassure these allies that the revolution would respect all forms of private property.

THE GOVERNMENT BECOMES INCREASINGLY REPRESSIVE

The war left Iranians ready for strong national leadership, and Ayatollah Khomeini stepped in to take control. The office of Supreme Leader, conceived as a religious authority to be consulted only in certain matters, came to dominate the political system. The reach of Islamic rule was extended throughout society. In the judicial system, all court rulings became subject to appeal all the way to the Guardian Council. Secular and progressive social legislation was repealed. The marriage age was lowered to 13 for girls, and men were allowed to divorce their wives without a court hearing. Women were purged from the judiciary and secular teachers fired. The Baha'i sect was persecuted, with its temples closed down and its leaders imprisoned and executed. An "Islamic code of public appearance" was enforced, favoring the chadour for women (which was later made mandatory) and requiring women to at least wear headscarves and long coats.

The "Islamization" of Iranian society was intended to affect every aspect of life. All publications were subject to censorship, textbooks were rewritten, and secular names of streets and monuments were changed.

The new government also took revenge on its opponents, especially members of the old regime. In the first two years after the revolution, the government executed about 500 of its political opponents, including a former prime minister and six cabinet ministers; 93 SAVAK officers; 205 military officers and soldiers; 35 Baha'is; and a Jewish businessman accused of spying for Israel. Many thousands were imprisoned.

Ayatollah Khomeini also attacked his former allies. Abolhassan Banisadr, for example, had been part of the anti-Shah movement since the 1960s, and returned from exile with Khomeini in 1979. Elected president in 1980, he became openly critical of the Islamic regime. He was impeached by the Parliament in 1981, apparently at the behest of Khomeini, and several of his closest friends were executed. Banisadr fled to Paris and briefly formed an alliance with the opposition group Mojahedin-e-Khalq (MEK), but fell out over the MEK's violent actions.

THE MEK'S VIOLENT RESISTANCE

The MEK, known in English as the People's Mujahideen of Iran, was formed in 1965 by a group of young people who felt the pro-democracy Freedom Movement of Iran was too moderate in its opposition to the Shah. They infused their ideology with a strange mix of Shia Islam and Marxism. When three of the original leaders were killed by the Shah's secret police, Massoud Rajavi took the leadership position.

Espousing an anti-American, anti-Imperialist agenda, while throwing their weight behind Ayatollah Khomeini, the MEK played a significant role in the revolution. From 1975 to 1979, MEK militants were reportedly involved in multiple bombings targeting

military officers, government officials, and American businessmen, including the U.S. information office and the offices of Pepsi,
PanAm, and General Motors.[17] The group routinely joined in calls
for "Death to America" and "Death to Israel."

After the revolution, the MEK was marginalized by Khomeini.
He had viewed them as useful to force the Shah from power, but
later felt they were too leftist and radical to be a part of post-rev-
olutionary Iran. He even described them as *monafeqin* (a religious term meaning hypocrites) and would not allow their leader
Massoud Rajavi to run for president. The MEK boycotted the
national referendum on the Islamic Republic and in 1981 declared
war on the new Iranian government.

Over the course of the next few years, the hybrid Marxist-
Leninist organization attacked, bombed, and assassinated members of the new Iranian leadership. In one attack in 1981, they
exploded a powerful bomb during a leadership meeting of the
Islamic Republic Party in Tehran. The attack killed 73 people,
including Chief Justice Ayatollah Beheshti, four cabinet ministers,
the speaker of the Parliament, 28 deputies, and many other important figures. Soon after that, the MEK bombed the Prime Minister's
office, killing Prime Minister Mohammad Javad Bahonar, President
Mohammad Ali Rajai, and six other government officials. Ali
Khamenei (who later became Supreme Leader) and Akbar Hashemi
Rafsanjani (who later became president) were both wounded in
MEK assassination attempts. The State Department described the
MEK as cutting a "swath of terror" across the country, including
violent attacks on civilians.[18]

Members of the Islamic Republic's security services, essentially
a ragtag group of Khomeini loyalists deputized to restore order,
began cracking down on the MEK. *Hezbollahis* (as these groups
were known) raided meeting places, shut down newsstands, and
arrested suspected members. Much of the leadership was forced

into exile in France and then in Iraq, under the protection of Iran's enemy: Saddam Hussein. In Iraq, the MEK worked with the Iraqi leader to attack Iranian positions during the Iran-Iraq war, a position viewed as treasonous by most Iranians. After the 1988 cease-fire, the MEK, backed by Iraqi warplanes, continued to attack Iran. In retaliation, the Iranian government executed MEK supporters in Iranian prisons.

The government also executed former allies from the Tudeh Party and the National Front. The moderate cleric Ayatollah Shariatmadari was stripped of his title, and he and other opposition leaders were forced to publicly recant their views. In the end, Khomeini executed or imprisoned many more former allies than he did monarchists.

Immediately after the end of the Iran-Iraq War in 1988, and a few months before his death, the Ayatollah authorized another round of mass executions. These killings have been described as a political purge without precedent in modern Iranian history. Amnesty International says that at least 2,000 political prisoners were summarily executed.[19] Iranian dissidents say the numbers were much greater, in the tens of thousands. Most were executed by hanging. Human Rights Watch said that "the deliberate and systematic manner in which these extrajudicial executions took place constitutes a crime against humanity under international law."[20]

Grand Ayatollah Montazeri, previously expected to succeed Khomeini as Supreme Leader, opposed Khomeini's wave of killing and was forced to resign. Historian Ervand Abrahamian interprets this brutal round of mass executions and Khomeini's February 1989 fatwa sentencing writer Salman Rushdie to death, a fatwa that incensed Rushdie's Western supporters, as calculated moves to forestall any accommodation with the secular opposition or the West.

Khomeini died on June 3, 1989. He was replaced by an ayatollah with a similar name, Ali Khamenei.

ATTEMPTS AT REFORM: FROM RAFSANJANI TO KHATAMI

Shortly after Khamenei became the new Supreme Leader, Ali-Akbar Hashemi Rafsanjani was elected president, running as a pragmatist against the Islamic hardliners. He was re-elected in 1993, but by a much smaller margin.

Trying to balance the budget, he launched neoliberal reforms, including abolishing rationing and price controls, opening "free trade" zones, and lowering business taxes. His free market, pro-business policies, along with falling oil prices, led to a substantial increase in foreign debt and massive inflation that intensified class differences.

His government favored renewing ties with the West as part of a strategy to secure more foreign investment and revive the country's war-torn economy. His plans to open Iran to foreign investment featured a $1 billion proposed oil deal with Conoco, a deal that was killed by an executive order from President Bill Clinton. A sanctions bill passed by the U.S. Congress further undercut Rafsanjani's opening to the West. He also alienated Western governments by relaunching Iran's nuclear energy program.

There were some cultural and social openings during his presidency, including a successful family planning program to stabilize Iran's mushrooming population. Young men and women could socialize more openly in public. Literary journals engaged in lively debates, and the film industry flourished. But these openings were attacked by conservative members of the clergy and government, and Rafsanjani's time in office was marked by repressive forces cracking down on writers, filmmakers, academics, and journalists.

The next president, Mohammad Khatami (not to be confused with the Supreme Leaders Khomeini or Khamenei), came to power in 1997 on a reformist ticket. A former minister of culture who had lived in Germany, he had been the director of the National Library and taught courses in Western political thought at Tehran University. He ran on a platform of political pluralism, free expression, and women's rights, and he reinterpreted Iranian history and national identity in more secular terms. "The essence of Iranian history is the struggle for democracy," he declared. Considered a long shot, he was elected in an upset, winning 70 percent of the votes with an 80 percent turnout.

The core of Khatami's support came from the educated middle class, college students, and the urban working class—the same classes that had provided the core support for Tudeh Party and the Mossadegh's National Front. Newspapers published by Khatami's supporters sprung up and soon outsold traditional ones, and they dramatically changed the terms of public debate. Iranian nationalism was reframed in terms that gave attention to Iran's 2,500-year history, its popular struggle against the monarchy, and the nationalization of its oil industry, not just its Islamic traditions.

Khatami and his reform agenda were wildly popular, and the reformers (including some women candidates) won 75 percent of the votes in local elections in 1999, and then 195 of the 290 parliamentary seats in 2000. Khatami was re-elected in 2001 with 80 percent of the vote. The secular leanings of the population were finally finding expression, and the clergy complained that less than two percent of Iranians attended Friday prayers at their local mosques, and less than 30 percent performed their daily prayers.

Khatami reformed some of the repressive practices of the previous era. He disbanded Intelligence Ministry death squads, reformed the prison system, reduced harassment over dress codes and entertainment, raised the marriage age to 15, and improved divorce and child custody laws. The government provided scholarships for women to study abroad, women in government jobs were allowed to wear head-scarves instead of chadours, and schoolgirls began to wear colorful clothes.

But the Guardian Council vehemently pushed back against this reform agenda. It vetoed many of the government's social reforms and disqualified 2,000 candidates, including 87 incumbents, from the next Parliamentary election. The courts shut down at least 60 progressive or secular newspapers.

Despite this pushback at home, and determined to put Iran in good stead with other world powers, Khatami made state visits to foreign capitals from Moscow to Paris to Tokyo. He hosted a conference on "dialogue among civilizations" and a human rights delegation from the European Union, and even expressed regret for the student takeover of the U.S. Embassy during the revolution. The U.K. restored diplomatic relations, President Clinton relaxed U.S. sanctions, and the UN dropped Iran from its list of countries that violate human rights. When the U.S. invaded Afghanistan in 2001, Khatami's government worked closely with the U.S. State Department to help stabilize Afghanistan after the invasion.

This forward movement was reversed, however, in January 2002 when the United States suddenly reinstated and escalated its cold war against Iran. President George W. Bush declared that Iran and North Korea were part of the same "axis of evil" as Iraq, which was already an explicit target of U.S. aggression.

Conservatives in Iran were vindicated in their opposition to improving relations with the West. Secular and progressive Iranians were disillusioned when Khatami's liberal policies were undermined by hardliners. Many progressives gave up on Khatami's brand of reformist politics as an avenue for social progress, and subsequent elections in Iran saw much lower turnout.

AHMADINEJAD AND THE SUPPRESSION OF THE GREEN MOVEMENT

President Mahmoud Ahmadinejad was elected in 2005 on a wave of conservative populism. Ahmadinejad only won six percent of the votes in the first round, but 60 percent in his final runoff with Rafsanjani, then seen by many as a corrupt, cronyist politician. Ahmadinejad ushered in a new phase of conservative policies, including a crackdown on dissent and escalating tensions with the United States.

When running for re-election for a second term in 2009, Ahmadinejad's closest contestant was the reformist and former Prime Minister Mir-Hossein Mousavi. Pundits declared they were running neck and neck. On June 13, however, the government announced Ahmadinejad the winner, insisting he received two-thirds of the votes and Mousavi only 36 percent. Mousavi's supporters cried foul.

Almost two years before the rise of the Arab Spring that rocked the Middle East, hundreds of thousands of Iranians poured into the streets of Tehran and other large cities, shouting "Where is my vote?" These protests marked the beginning of what came to be called the Green Movement. (Green was the color used by Mousavi's campaign, but after the election it became the symbol of the pro-democracy movement.)

Two days after the election, the Supreme Leader Khamenei disappointed the protesters by endorsing the results. Undaunted, the next day Mousavi supporters staged a massive protest of some three million people, the largest protest ever since the 1979 revolution. This protest and subsequent ones were met with riot police and the Basij paramilitary militia armed with bats and chains. The government not only beat and arrested protesters, but raided the homes of prominent reformist politicians and journalists, dragging them off to prison. Mousavi was placed under house arrest.

Citizen journalists began filming the protests and the crackdowns, broadcasting the uprising to the world community. On June 20, the video of a young university student named Neda Agha-Soltan, shot in the chest by a rooftop sniper, went viral. Neda Agha-Soltan became known as one of the many martyrs who died in the pro-democracy movement.

What began as a call for a recount of the votes turned into a call for an end to the Islamic Republic. The protests continued for 20 months, and so did the repression. The government portrayed the Green Movement as a creation of the United States with the goal of destroying the Islamic state, and held show trials where leaders were forced to confess to crimes against the nation. Thousands of dissidents fled, moving mostly to Europe and North America. Newspapers, magazines, and websites were shut down. Iran became the country with the most journalists in prison.

By February 2011, faced with radicalized protesters and massive state repression, including torture in prisons and even executions, the movement's leaders halted calls for more demonstrations. The movement receded from public space into the underground. Its leaders, including Mousavi and former Speaker of Parliament Mehdi Karroubi, were still under house arrest in 2017, due to the intransigence of the Supreme Leader and some of the Revolutionary Guard commanders.

The Green Movement was defeated, but it sowed the seeds that led to the rise of reformist President Hassan Rouhani in 2013, a moderate who encouraged more personal freedom and improved diplomatic relations with the West. Rouhani was re-elected in 2017, but his government also faced pushback from conservatives and a December 2017 uprising among youth and working class people frustrated by economic hardships.

CHANGE THROUGH THE ELECTORAL PROCESS

Despite the profoundly undemocratic pre-election vetting of presidential candidates by Iran's Guardian Council and the power invested in unelected leaders, elections in Iran are serious contests and do matter. Elections are highly contested and unpredictable. Although reformist candidates are often not allowed to run, candidates with varied platforms have made it through the vetting. Iranian elections usually have large turnouts (over 70 percent) because it is one of the few opportunities people have to weigh in on the direction of their country.

Some opposition political parties do exist, such as the reformist Mardom Salari party and the Etemad Melli party, but their members face harassment and their leaders are often arrested.

Most candidates do not belong to political parties but to political factions or alliances. These groups lack the formal structure of political parties but compete just as fiercely. When running for office, some candidates are backed by more than one group, and allegiances often shift. There are factions representing hardline religious interests, pro-reform factions (whose candidates are often disqualified), and pragmatists that fall in the middle of Iran's political spectrum.

The people's desire for reform can be seen in their voting patterns. An analysis of Iran's presidential elections led author/analyst Trita Parsi to conclude that, despite the near limitless powers ascribed to the Supreme Leader, the anti-establishment vote has tended to dominate Iranian elections.[21] In 1997, the Speaker of the Parliament, Ali Akbar Nategh Nouri, was seen as favored by Ayatollah Khamenei, but the Iranian people instead gave their support to a largely unknown reformist candidate, Mohammad Khatami. Eight years later, another unknown candidate, Mahmoud Ahmadinejad, won the anti-establishment vote over the late Ali Akbar Hashemi Rafsanjani, who was perceived as the establishment candidate.

By 2009, the roles had reversed. Ahmadinejad was the establishment candidate running for re-election while Mir Hossein Mousavi, who resurfaced after more than two decades of internal political exile, was considered the anti-establishment candidate. That's why there was such a public outcry when Mousavi was not declared the winner. Again in 2013, the candidate perceived to have the Supreme Leader's support, Saeed Jalili, lost to reform candidate Hassan Rouhani.

Unlike the Supreme Leader, presidents must actually appeal to the electorate directly and are held accountable for policies that affect people's daily lives. The unelected power structures, including the Supreme Leader, the military, judiciary, and intelligence agencies, are often suspicious of the president and try to keep him from gaining too much power.

This power play between Iran's elected and unelected forces will determine Iran's future. The nation's transformation to a truly democratic system will only come with the elimination of the position of Supreme Leader and the clerical bodies under his control. On the other hand, people should not underestimate the political openings that do exist, making Iran one of the more democratic societies in the Middle East.

HOW POWER IS DIVIDED AMONG OFFICIAL GOVERNMENT ENTITIES

An organizational chart of Iran's institutions shows two completely different systems, one democratic and the other theocratic.

While the system is supposed to be a combination of democratic involvement with theocratic oversight, the two often clash, with unelected, unaccountable officials holding the most power.

THE SUPREME LEADER

At the top of Iran's power structure is the Supreme Leader, who is appointed by the Assembly of Experts for this lifetime position. The father of the Iranian Revolution Ayatollah Ruhollah Khomeini and his successor Ayatollah Ali Khamenei, who became Leader upon Khomeini's death in 1989, are the only two men to have held this office since the founding of the Islamic Republic in 1979.

According to Iran's constitution, the Supreme Leader is responsible for setting the direction of Iran's domestic and foreign policies. The Supreme Leader is also commander-in-chief of the armed forces and controls the Islamic Republic's intelligence and security operation. He is the only one who can declare war or peace. Iran is the only state in the world in which the executive branch does not control the armed forces.

The Supreme Leader has the power to appoint and dismiss the leaders of the judiciary, the state radio and television networks, and the Islamic Revolutionary Guard Corps. He also appoints six of the twelve members of the Guardian Council, the powerful body that oversees the activities of Parliament and determines which candidates are qualified to run for public office. The foundations, called *bonyads,* that operate hundreds of companies, are also under the Supreme Leader's control.

The Supreme Leader's sphere of power is extended through his representatives, an estimated 2,000 of whom are sprinkled throughout all sectors of the government and who serve as the Leader's field operatives. His representatives are often more powerful than the president's ministers, since they have the authority to intervene in any matter of state on the Supreme Leader's behalf.

THE PRESIDENT

The president is the second highest ranking official, after the Supreme Leader, and the highest ranking elected official. The president is elected by popular vote for four years and can serve two consecutive terms. Eight vice presidents serve under the president, as well as a cabinet of 22 ministers that must be confirmed by Parliament.

The executive branch is subordinate to the Supreme Leader. Though the president has nominal rule over the Supreme National Security Council and the Ministry of Intelligence and Security, in practice the Supreme Leader is in charge of most foreign and domestic security matters.

Despite these restrictions, over the years the presidency has evolved into a powerful office. One reason is that there used to be a prime minister as well, a position more powerful than the president, but that post was abolished in the 1989 constitutional amendment. Every president that followed has put his stamp on domestic and foreign policies.

THE PARLIAMENT

The Iranian Parliament, called the *Majlis*, is a unicameral legislative body made up of 290 members who are publicly elected every four years. The Parliament drafts legislation, ratifies international treaties, and approves the country's budget. It is also empowered to investigate complaints against the executive branch and the judiciary, approve the president's choice of cabinet ministers, and appoint six members of the 12-person Guardian Council. By a two-thirds majority, it can initiate referenda on proposed amendments to the constitution.

Parliamentary sessions are open to the public; its deliberations are broadcast and its minutes are published.

While reformist candidates tend to win most of the seats and in recent years only a small percentage of the elected deputies have been clerics, the Parliament is still held in check by the Guardian Council, the influential oversight body that examines all laws passed by Parliament to determine their compatibility with sharia law. Over the years, the council has struck down hundreds of laws passed by Parliament.

ASSEMBLY OF EXPERTS

The Assembly of Experts is an obscure governing body that only meets for one week every year. It consists of 86 "virtuous and learned" clerics elected by the public to eight-year terms. Like presidential and parliamentary elections, the Guardian Council determines who can run for a seat in this Assembly of Experts.

Members of the Assembly of Experts in turn elect the Supreme Leader from within their own ranks and periodically reconfirm him. The assembly has never been known to challenge any of the Supreme Leader's decisions or to deny reconfirmation.

GUARDIAN COUNCIL

Twelve jurists comprise the Guardian Council. The Supreme Leader appoints half; the head of the judiciary recommends the remaining six, which are officially appointed by Parliament. All serve for six-year terms.

The Guardian Council has the authority to interpret the constitution and determine if the laws passed by Parliament are in line with Islamic law. This gives the council effective veto power over Parliament. The Council consistently vetoes laws passed by the popularly elected Parliament. If it deems that a law passed by Parliament is incompatible with the constitution or Islamic law, the law is referred back to Parliament for revision. If the Parliament and the Guardian Council cannot decide on a case, it is passed to the Expediency Council for a decision.

The council also has tremendous power over the president and Parliament because it is the body that vets candidates to determine who is "competent" to run and who is not. The Council favors conservative candidates and typically disqualifies most reform candidates. No one who is perceived to be an opponent or critic of the Islamic system is permitted to run for president, and no woman has ever been approved as a presidential candidate. After conservative candidates fared poorly in the 2000 parliamentary elections, the Council disqualified more than 3,600 reformist and independent candidates for the 2004 elections.

In the 2009 election, 476 men and women applied to the Guardian Council to seek the presidency, and only four were approved. Among the arbitrary reasons for disqualifying candidates, without having to furnish any proof, are narcotics addiction or involvement in drug-smuggling, connections to the Shah's pre-revolutionary government, lack of belief in or insufficient practice of Islam, being against the Islamic Republic, or having connections to foreign intelligence services.

EXPEDIENCY COUNCIL

In 1988, when stalemates between Parliament and the Guardian Council proved intractable, Ayatollah Khomeini created the

Expediency Council and charged it with mediating disputes between the two bodies. Now, according to the constitution, the Expediency Council serves as an advisory body to the Supreme Leader.

The council is made up of 34 members who tend to come mostly from the conservative factions. It usually sides with the conservative Guardian Council in its disputes with Parliament, which is why some parliamentary leaders have called for the council to be reformed.

JUDICIARY

The judicial branch of Iran's government is largely controlled by the Supreme Leader, who appoints the head of the judiciary, who in turn appoints the head of the Supreme Court and the chief public prosecutor.

Public courts deal with civil and criminal cases. There are Special Clerical Courts, which function independently of the regular judicial framework, and handle crimes allegedly committed by clerics. There are also "revolutionary courts" that try certain categories of offenses, including crimes against national security, narcotics smuggling, and acts deemed to undermine the Islamic Republic. Decisions rendered in revolutionary courts are final and cannot be appealed.

IRANIAN ARMED FORCES

The Armed Forces consists of the Army, Navy, and the Air Force. There are reportedly about 520,000 Iranians on active service, including 350,000 in the army.

According to Iran's constitution, the regular army is responsible for guarding the independence and territorial integrity of the country and maintaining order. The army falls under the control of the Supreme Leader.

The Islamic Revolutionary Guard Corps, or IRGC, was created in 1979 by Ayatollah Khomeini to protect the revolution and its achievements. It is separate from the regular military, and there has been a rivalry between the two military branches since the founding of the Islamic Republic.

There are about 120,000 members of the IRGC, and it has its own Navy, Air Force, Ground Forces, and Quds Force (special forces). The IRGC also controls the paramilitary volunteer force called *Basij*, which is thought to have about 90,000 active-duty members and 300,000 reservists. The Basij claims is also has a membership of 12 million men and women who are ready to mobilize if/when the need arises, but some outside experts put that figure at 500,000.

The IRGC was put in charge of the military industry. It poured money into the development of its own tanks, radar systems, guided missiles, military vessels, fighter planes, and drones.

Over the years, the IRGC has become among the most autonomous power centers in Iran. In 1982, it sent troops to Lebanon in support of the militant group Hezbollah, and it has since become active in supporting Islamic revolutionary movements in other parts of the Muslim world. It supports Palestinian militant groups in the West Bank, including the Palestinian Islamic Jihad, and Hamas.

MINISTRY OF INTELLIGENCE & SECURITY (MOIS)

The Ministry of Intelligence and Security (MOIS) is a shadowy entity under the control of the Supreme Leader. A special law dictates that the head of the MOIS must be a cleric, which deepens the Supreme Leader's influence.

The ministry is tasked with the "gathering, procurement, analysis, and classification of necessary information inside and outside the country" and disclosing conspiracies that could sabotage the integrity of the Islamic Republic.

The MOIS is infamous for eliminating political dissidents within Iran's borders and plays a key role in organizing and conducting terrorist operations abroad, running operations out of Iranian embassies, consulates, and Islamic centers overseas.

CHAPTER 3: THE STRUGGLE FOR HUMAN RIGHTS IN IRAN

If asked "What first comes to mind when you think about Iran?", many people, especially in the U.S., would list human rights violations. Very few would know that the empire of ancient Persia, now the state of Iran, actually set the precedent of human rights in 539 B.C. when Cyrus the Great conquered Babylon. In a major step forward for humankind, this conqueror set the slaves free and granted them the right to return home, declared that all people had the right to choose their own religion, and established a system of racial equality. Not only did Cyrus the Great take the first stand for establishing these human rights, he actually documented them on a barrel-shaped baked clay tablet inscribed in Babylonian cuneiform writing (now known as the Cyrus Cylinder). This ancient record has been officially recognized as the first human rights charter. The United Nations has translated the text into all six official languages and used it as the basis of the first four articles of the Universal Declaration of Human Rights.[22]

Iran today, unfortunately, is no bastion of freedom. The Islamic Republic has a disastrous track record, ranging from violations of religious freedom and women's rights to the use of torture and capital punishment. On a scale of 100, Freedom House ranks Iran near the bottom, with an abysmal score of 17.[23]

The early years of the revolution were the worst, when moral puritanism swept through the nation. Thousands of prostitutes, drug addicts, and homosexuals were executed. In public places, revolutionaries confronted people who failed to abide by the strict new codes of dress and behavior. Prison sentences and flogging became commonplace for the most minor moral indiscretions, and government offices were purged of the ideologically "unsound." The abuses were amplified when Iraq's army crossed the border into Iran in 1980, leading to a bloody decade of war with Iraq and brutal crackdowns at home.

While the situation has since improved, especially during reform governments, the Iranian government continues to severely restrict civil liberties, including freedoms of assembly, association, speech, religion, and press. There is a lack of due process within the country's legal system, and the government condones the use of torture and capital punishment. The government persecutes human rights defenders, journalists, and trade union leaders. Also facing persecution are religious and ethnic minorities, as well as people of alternative sexualities.

This chapter gives an overview of the human rights situation, highlighting the many violations but also the valiant work of dedicated Iranian activists, at home and abroad, who strive to open more spaces for Iranians to exercise their basic rights.

WHAT RIGHTS DID IRANIANS HAVE UNDER THE SHAH?

Lest one thinks that Iran went from a Western-style form of governance under the Shah to a theocratic dictatorship, it's important to recall the brutality of the Shah's rule. The Shah systematically dismantled the judicial system and violated people's personal liberties. Military courts tried as "terrorists" those brave enough to protest his regime. His infamous intelligence agency SAVAK carried out torture under that friendly guidance of the CIA, which set up SAVAK in 1957 and taught Iranians how to interrogate suspects. The Shah kept tens of thousands of dissidents holed up in prison, where the methods of torture included "whipping and beating, electric shocks, extraction of teeth and nails, boiling water pumped into the rectum, heavy weights hung on the testicles, tying the prisoner to a metal table heated to a white heat, inserting a broken bottle into the anus, and rape."[24]

WHAT HUMAN RIGHTS DOES THE IRANIAN GOVERNMENT RECOGNIZE?

When the revolution came to power, it rewrote the old 1905 constitution. The new constitution, which was amended in 1989, contains a hybrid of theocratic and democratic elements. It recognizes many key human rights, including equal rights for racial and ethnic minorities, gender equality, freedom of association, freedom of expression, and freedom of the press.

At first glance, these guarantees look promising, but there are stipulations and reservations that run counter to these promises. The constitution includes phrases such as "unless the law states otherwise" and "unless they attack the principles of Islam," which leaves the population vulnerable to the whims of interpretation.[25]

Iran was one of the original 51 member states that founded the United Nations in 1951. Since then, it has ratified many of the international declarations relating to human rights, including the Covenant on Economic, Social and Cultural Rights, the International Convention on the Elimination of All Forms of Racial Discrimination, and the International Covenant on Civil and Political Rights. The Convention on the Rights of the Child, a document the United States has never signed, was ratified in 1994. The government also signed additional protocols against child trafficking, child prostitution, child pornography, and the involvement of children in armed conflict. Once again, however, these conventions and covenants were ratified with the catch-all reservation that Iran will adhere to them as long as they are in accordance with Islamic principles.

Iran has not signed the Convention on the Elimination of All Forms of Discrimination Against Women (CEDAW), making it one of only seven countries out of the UN's 194 member states failing to do so (one of the other non-signatories is the United States). The Iranian Parliament discussed signing CEDAW, but the Council of Guardians ruled that the legislation would be "un-Islamic." Iran also refused to sign the Convention Against Torture or adopt the UN protocol abolishing the death penalty.

In December 2016, the government adopted a Charter on Citizens' Rights. It recognizes the right of every citizen to freedom of speech and expression, and the right to freely seek, receive, and publish information using any means of communication. The charter, however, is not legally binding, and the government continues to disrespect these rights.

WHAT ABOUT FREEDOM OF SPEECH, ASSOCIATION, AND ASSEMBLY?

The Iranian constitution claims freedom of expression, but in reality all forms of media, from local magazines to international broadcasts via satellite, are subject to the authorities' discretion. The government has shut down numerous publications, and journalists are regularly subjected to interrogation, surveillance, arrest, and other forms of harassment and intimidation. The government also bans many social media outlets and smartphone applications. Among those regularly blocked are Facebook, Twitter, WhatsApp, Line, Instagram Live, and Tango, although Iranians are very clever at finding ways to counter government interference.[26]

Unfortunately, Iranians have also been blocked from social media by the U.S. side. In 2017, Apple removed a number of popular Iranian apps from its app stores to comply with U.S. sanctions.

Cultural workers also face repression for peacefully exercising their right to free expression. While the Iranian film industry thrives and is acclaimed internationally, films may be censored or banned, and filmmakers arrested. Filmmaker Keyvan Karimi spent five months in prison in 2016 after he was convicted of "propagating against the ruling system" and "insulting religious sanctities" because of a documentary he made about political graffiti.

Music was totally banned at the start of the revolution. Then classical music was allowed on radio and TV stations, with some public concerts held in the late 1980s. In the 1990s, under reformist President Khatami, restrictions were further relaxed. Today, there is a flourishing music scene, but censorship persists. Concerts get canceled, and musicians can be arrested for the content of their music. After a 15-minute trial, music producers Mehdi and Hossein Rajabian were sentenced to six years in prison (reduced to three years on appeal) in 2015 for "insulting the sacred" and "propaganda against the state."[27]

In terms of free association, the constitution says that the formation of political parties, societies, and political or professional associations is permitted, but then adds the usual caveat "provided they do not violate the principles of independence, freedom, national unity, the criteria of Islam or the basis of the Islamic Republic."[28] According to the Interior Ministry, there are over 250 registered political parties or associations. Most are not parties in the Western sense, with membership and detailed party platforms, but more like interest groups and factions. Many appear at election time and then disappear. Parties that oppose the Islamic Revolution are either banned or severely restricted.

NGOs must be registered (as is most countries) and are monitored by the state. The government allows charity and social service organizations, such as those dedicated to helping the poor or sheltering abused women, but routinely cracks down on groups involved in political activities. Severe restrictions on freedom of expression prevent civic groups from openly criticizing state policies. The government is also particularly suspicious of groups with international partners, especially if the international partner is from the United States.

Government-sponsored rallies abound, but permits for non-governmental groups to hold rallies or demonstrations are routinely denied. Protesters, especially students and ethnic minorities demanding human rights, risk government surveillance, harassment, arrest, and imprisonment.

There is a fine line between what is permitted and what is prohibited, and the fate of civic groups is often determined by the government in power and the larger political situation. The reform years of President Khatami from 1997–2005, for example, gave rise to independent civil society organizations of workers, intellectuals, students, and women. After Ahmadinejad was elected in 2005, these public spaces came under attack. Some of the most prominent NGOs were shut down, including the Center for the Defense of Human Rights, led by Nobel Peace Prize winner Shirin Ebadi, and the Organization for the Defense of Prisoners' Rights, led by Emad Baghi. Ebadi ended up leaving Iran, and Baghi was imprisoned on charges of working against national security.

After the Green Movement in 2009, the government crackdown was more severe. Peaceful protests by hundreds of thousands in Tehran were put down brutally. Thousands were detained and more than 100 accused in a televised mass show trial. Prominent opposition leaders were placed under house arrest. These were reformist politician and cleric Mehdi Karroubi;

Mir Hossein Mousavi, former prime minister whose electoral challenge to President Ahmadinejad's re-election sparked the Green Movement; and Mousavi's wife—and women's rights advocate—Zahra Rahnavard. They were punished for publicly disputing the election results and leading peaceful mass demonstrations.

The protests that started in December 2017 and spread throughout the country were also crushed by the policy and Revolutionary Guards, with over 1,000 arrests.

Despite the dangers, there are all sorts of civic groups, many of which come and go depending on the level of government pressure they attract. The Internet has provided new means of collaboration and information sharing, creating conditions for a more diverse range of organizations, but government surveillance of the Internet makes online organizing risky as well.

IMPRISONMENT OF FOREIGNERS AND IRANIANS WITH DUAL NATIONALITY

Particularly volatile have been the arrests of foreigners and dual nationals—people who are citizens of both Iran and another country. Most live overseas and have been arrested, while visiting Iran, on charges related to espionage. Some might well be spies, some are used for prisoner swaps, and others are victims of paranoia against Westerners by Iranian hardliners. The Iranian government does not recognize dual nationality, so when these people are detained they are usually denied access to the services of the embassy where they reside.

A particularly brutal case occurred in 2003, when Iranian-Canadian photojournalist Zahra Kazemi was arrested while taking pictures of grieving mothers outside of Iran's Evin Prison. During her detention, Iranian prison authorities severely tortured her, breaking several bones and allegedly sexually abusing her.

Kazemi was eventually taken to a hospital with internal bleeding and a brain injury. While she was in a coma at the hospital, Iranian officials initially failed to contact Canadian consular officials and refused to allow her family access to her. Kazemi died in the hospital; even then, the Iranian government ignored the wishes of Canadian officials and her family that her remains be returned to Canada for burial.[29]

In 2009, Iranian-American freelance journalist Roxana Saberi was arrested for spying, and held for over 100 days. (Her original sentence was eight years.) Another journalist, Iranian-Canadian Maziar Bahari, was arrested while covering the 2009 Iranian election for *Newsweek* and held for 118 days. That was the same year three American hikers—Joshua Fattal, Sarah Shourd, and Shane Bauer—were arrested on trumped-up charges of espionage after accidentally crossing the Iraq border into Iran, and remained imprisoned until 2011. Their two-year ordeal aggravated relations with the United States, and was seen as part of a tragic power play between the Iranian president, who wanted the Americans released, and the conservative judiciary who wanted to embarrass him.

Several similar cases occurred in 2016, just after the Iran nuclear deal was signed. It was seen as part of a power struggle playing out within the government, pitting reformist President Rouhani against hardliners who wanted to sabotage his openings to the West. An Iranian-American father and son, Baquer and Siamak Namazi, were both sentenced to ten years in prison for "collusion with the enemy state." A young British-Iranian woman, Nazanin Zaghari-Ratcliffe, was arrested in 2016 on her way back to England with her two-year-old daughter. She was sentenced to five years for spreading propaganda following a trial in which her lawyer had only five minutes to argue her defense and she was not allowed to speak.[30] Homa Hoodfar, an Iranian-Canadian academic, was also detained in 2016, then released after a few months.

Perhaps the best known recent case was that of Jason Rezian, an Iranian-American correspondent for the *Washington Post*, who was arrested in 2014 on charges that included spying. He was released in 2016 as part of a prison exchange between the U.S. and Iran.

HOW FAIR IS THE JUDICIAL SYSTEM?

Prior to the Iranian Revolution of 1979, Iran's judicial system was overseen by the Pahlavi Dynasty, and over the course of the 20th century leading up to 1979, the system was largely westernized and secularized, with a constitution that recognized both secular and sharia judiciary authority. Different areas of the law were divided into distinct courts that operated independently, with some cases relegated to the military courts and others to the clerics.

The 1979 revolution led to an overhaul of the legal system to fully incorporate Islamic law. Sharia law is the legal system for Islam that derives from the Quran, Islam's holy text, and the *Sunnah*, or religious traditions based on the sayings of the Prophet Muhammad. It acts as a code of conduct governing many aspects of the personal and public lives of Muslims. The judges are clerics trained in Islamic jurisprudence, and women are banned from being judges.

In addition to problems caused by merging the legal system with religious beliefs, many laws were written in vague terms that then allowed for subjective interpretations and contradictory rulings. Arrests are often made on arbitrary or ambiguous charges, which leads to biased and unfair trials. Trials can move forward without evidence and without conforming to fundamental standards of due process.

Amnesty International has reported that defense lawyers are regularly barred from obtaining case files and meeting directly with their clients before the trial.[31] Within the courts, the testimony of a man is often given twice the weight of that of a woman, and for certain offenses, the testimony of a woman is not even accepted. Detainees are often held in solitary confinement for long periods of time and denied contact with family or a lawyer. Iranian courts accept confessions extracted through torture.

In June 2015, Iran adopted a new, much awaited, criminal procedure code that addressed many flaws in the old code. While the new code stipulates the right to counsel from the moment of arrest through to trial and relative improvements for defense attorneys and the accused, a last minute move by Parliament provided that only selective lawyers may intervene during certain investigations. This provision effectively separated lawyers into two groups—those who are approved by the judiciary and security services, and those who are not.

WHAT ARE THE PRISON CONDITIONS LIKE AND HOW COMMON IS THE USE OF TORTURE?

Iran's prison systems are infamous for their use of torture, especially against detainees during interrogation in order to intimidate them into giving a confession. Common methods of torture include floggings and brutal beatings; more rare are blinding, burnings, and amputations. Other forms of abuse within Iranian prisons— sometimes called "white torture"—is psychological torture that ranges from solitary confinement, sleep deprivation, threats of execution or rape, sexual harassment, virginity tests, and electroshock. Denial of access to proper and necessary medical treatment for detainees is also widely reported. In some cases, depriving a prisoner of medical care is used as a form of punishment.

After the 2009 Green Movement uprising, four detainees died after being tortured in Tehran's Kahrizak Detention Center. Other detainees emerged with stories of rape, torture, and appalling conditions. Ebrahim Sharifi, a 24-year-old student from Tehran, told Amnesty that he was bound, blindfolded and beaten prior to being raped. He also endured severe beatings, and mock executions.[32]

Overcrowding in prisons is also a problem, as it is in prisons around the world. Prisoners may be forced to sleep on floors, in hallways, or in prison yards. In 2016, a member of the National Assembly reported that there were 400,000 prisoners in prisons built for 140,000.

Solitary confinement is a common method used in Iran's prisons to force confessions or to break prisoners. "I haven't experienced death but I think this is how it must feel; in an instant, you are cut off from everything and everyone," said Abbas Hakemzadeh, a student activist who fled Iran after three arrests, including 190 days in solitary.[33]

The three American hikers arrested in 2009 were held in solitary confinement for the first four months of their harrowing ordeal. Upon their release, they made it a point to campaign against solitary confinement in U.S. prisons, once they discovered that U.S. prisons held 80,000 prisoners in solitary in 2005, the last year the federal government released such data. They thought it was important to show that the United States, a country that prides itself on its democratic values, also makes widespread use of a form of punishment that many consider torture.

HOW OFTEN IS THE DEATH PENALTY CARRIED OUT?

The Iranian government has deemed capital punishment a reasonable form of justice not only for violent crimes, but also for nonviolent crimes. After China, Iran executes more people than any other country in the world; when judged on a per capita basis, Iran has the dubious distinction of being number one worldwide. The most common method of execution is hanging, although shooting and stoning have also been used.

Stoning was used in the past as a horrific penalty for adultery. According to this barbaric practice, the convicted offender—woman or man, sometimes both—is partially buried and then bludgeoned to death. Iranian women's groups, along with outside human rights organizations, fought long and hard to end this. World criticism reached a fevered pitch in 2011 when a married woman, Sakieneh Mohammadi Ashtiani, was about to be stoned over "illicit relationships" with two men. The stoning was halted.

A campaign called "Stop Stoning Forever," an initiative of the group Women Living Under Muslim Laws, was successful in getting the Iranian government to prohibit the practice, but lower courts in rural areas still sometimes hand down this dreadful sentence. The last reported case of stoning was in 2009, when a man was stoned to death in the northern city of Rasht.

There are no precise statistics on executions in Iran because the government doesn't publish the figures, but various human rights groups try to cull the information. In the first six months of 2017, the UN said 247 people had been killed, including three women. The number of executions carried out in 2016 is estimated at between 500–600, meaning that at least one person was killed by the state every day. In 2015, the number was even higher—some say over 900, the highest in more than two decades. The vast majority of executions, about 70 percent, are for drug-related offenses, and those executed are mainly poor people from marginalized groups.

Some of the crimes that warrant the death penalty are similar to those in other countries that sanction state killing: premeditated murder, rape, armed robbery, kidnapping, and drug trafficking. Other crimes are more political and religious. Anybody who commits treason, espionage, or a major crime against domestic security or external security may be charged with "corruption on earth, " which can carry the death penalty. Moral crimes that can carry the death penalty include adultery, apostasy, blasphemy against the Prophet, incest, homosexual relations, and publishing pornography.

The UN Special Rapporteur for Human Rights has called on Iran to place a general moratorium on the use of the death penalty, replace the death penalty for drug-related offences with penalties that comply with international standards, and end the practice of public executions.[34]

DOES IRAN EXECUTE JUVENILES?

Although Iran signed the UN Convention on the Rights of the Child, it continues to violate the basic rights of minors. In fact, Iran is the world's top executioner of convicted minors.[35] The penal code was supposedly changed in 2012 to end child execution, but the law still defines puberty, which is age 15 for boys and nine for girls, as the benchmark for when a death sentence can be legally imposed. Minors languish in prison from the time of their conviction until they are 18 when the sentence can be carried out. This was the case for 15-year-old Shaqayeq, who was sentenced to death for the armed robbery of a convenience store.[36] At the end of 2015, at least 160 juveniles were on death row. Human rights groups around the world have called on Iran to immediately end the sentencing of children to death and to commute the death sentences of all children on death row.

HOW ARE ETHNIC MINORITIES TREATED?

Discrimination against ethnic minorities has a long history in Iran. During the time of the Shah, millions of Kurds, Turks, Arabs, Baluchis, and Turkmen were deprived of the right to learn in their mother tongues, and no cultural expression or publication was allowed in their languages. Precisely because of this discriminiation, many ethnic minority activists joined the revolution, but felt bitterly betrayed when the new Islamic government continued the same repressive policies.

Ethnic minority groups are routinely denied the ability to express their cultural heritage, seek adequate housing and employment, or run for political office. In 2016, the government announced that optional Turkish and Kurdish language courses would be offered in schools in two provinces, Kurdistan and West Azerbaijan. That same year, however, three Arab ethnic rights activists were sentenced to a year in prison for organizing Arabic-language classes, and four Azeris were imprisoned on charges of "assembly and collusion against national security" for peacefully advocating the teaching of their mother tongues in local schools.

The limited access to education and employment continues a cycle of economic instability and marginalization for many minorities. If individuals from these minority groups speak out against the violations of their rights, the government often responds with arbitrary arrests, unfair trials, imprisonment, torture, and—in some instances—the death penalty.

One repressed minority are the Baluchis. This group is largely Sunni Muslims, which has contributed to tension with Iran's Shiite government. Baluchis are noticeably underrepresented in government positions. In 2003, a group of Baluchis formed Jundallah, a militant group that organized attacks against government soldiers and seized hostages to dramatize their plight. The government cracked down on Jundallah, as well as on Baluchi journalists and human rights activists.

The Kurds have had the most active separatist movements. Soon after the revolution, they launched a militant movement that was crushed in 1981 by the Iranian army and the Revolutionary Guards. Iranian Kurds have been executed or given long prison sentences for being members or sympathizers of militant groups. The conflict has spilled overseas, where Iranian intelligence agents allegedly killed Kurdish opposition leaders in Vienna in 1989 and Berlin in 1992.

Most Kurdish activists now use nonviolent tactics. When Kurds in Iraq held a non-binding referendum on independence in 2017, Iranian Kurds celebrated in solidarity. Some were arrested for "participation in illegal gatherings and disturbing public order."

Almost all of these minority groups live on the borders, and they often become pawns in larger geopolitical struggles. The United States and Israel have supported separatist groups to destabilize Iran. For the most part, however, Iran's ethnic minorities are less interested in secession or independence—they are more interested in increasing their rights as Iranian citizens.

HOW DOES THE GOVERNMENT TREAT HUMAN RIGHTS ACTIVISTS?

Iranians have a strong history of activism, both pre- and post-revolution. Despite the risks, there are active student groups, journalists advocating the right to free speech, lawyers defending dissidents and promoting the rights of prisoners, women's rights advocates, anti-death penalty activists, and more. Human rights advocates also denounce corruption and impunity within the police forces, and try to stop the police from using violence against protesters.

In Iran today, however, human rights activists are subjected to arrests, interrogations, threats, torture, unfair trials, and other forms of harsh punishment. Of all the prisoners detained in Iran, about 800 are considered by human rights groups to be political prisoners, incarcerated for their activism in pursuit of fundamental human rights.[37]

Iran's government is quick to label opposition groups, political activists, and promoters of human rights as terrorists. In Amnesty International's 2016 country report, the group noted that the authorities had intensified their repression of human rights defenders, subjecting protesters to beatings and arbitrary detention, sentencing them to long prison terms for charges such as "gathering and colluding against national security." The government has also taken action against the families and lawyers of activists and dissidents in order to exert pressure on them.

Organizations are often shut down if the authorities disapprove of their activities. The Association of Iranian Journalists, created in 1997 under the Khatami reform period to protect journalists' rights, was shut down in 2009, but journalists continue to push for its reinstatement. In 2015 they wrote an open letter to President Rouhani calling on him to fulfill his 2013 campaign promise to lift the ban on their organization, but the group remains banned.

Student groups are also active campaigners for student rights. In 2013, 92 student groups rallied together to call for an end of the government's repressive hold on universities.[38]

Among the prominent human rights activists in prison as of 2018 is lawyer Abdolfattah Soltani, who received an 18-year prison sentence in 2012 for his work at the Center for Human Rights Defenders, and for spreading anti-government propaganda, endangering national security, and accepting an illegal prize, the Nuremberg International Human Rights Award. Amnesty International designated him a prisoner of conscience and called him "one of the bravest human rights defenders in Iran."[39] Among well-known women prisoners is Narges Mohammadi, who in 2015 was sentenced to 16 years in prison. The judge found her guilty of "gathering and conspiring with the aim of committing crimes against national security," sentencing her to five years in prison. He added one year for "propaganda against the state" and 10 years for "forming and managing an illegal group." The group, called Legham, was an organization advocating to abolish the death penalty.[40]

Many outside groups support these courageous human rights defenders in Iran, including Amnesty International, Human Rights Watch, United for Iran, the International Campaign for Human Rights in Iran, and the Center for Human Rights in Iran. They help inform the international community, keep track of prisoners, and pressure the government for their release. Without these organizations, it would be even more difficult to know about the plight of human rights activists and how to advocate on their behalf.

CHAPTER 4: "SOCIAL DEVIANTS": GAYS, PROSTITUTES, DRUGS, AND ALCOHOL

In Iran's strict, religious society, people who live outside the "moral norm" set down by the religious authorities live difficult lives. This includes people in the LGBTQ community and people who engage in illicit activities such as prostitution or drug use/dealing. The Iranian government considers these people deviants who have lost the balanced and natural human condition.

HOW DOES THE GOVERNMENT TREAT THE LGBTQ COMMUNITY?

Iran is infamous for repression against people who are not heterosexual. When President Mahmoud Ahmadinejad gave a talk at Columbia University in New York in 2007, he earned widespread condemnation when he replied to a question about gays by saying, "In Iran we don't have homosexuals like in your country. This does not exist in our country." A government spokesperson later insisted that the translation was incorrect. The president didn't mean that there were *no* homosexuals but that there weren't as *many* as in the United States. In any case, the comment was more a reflection of the regime's wishes than the reality. There are certainly many people of various sexual tendencies in Iran, just like in any society.

Before the 1979 revolution, homosexuality was technically illegal but largely tolerated, particularly in large cities. After the revolution, discrimination against non-heterosexual people was based on the notion that such behavior is forbidden by the state's religion. Some of Iran's clerics describe homosexuality as "moral bankruptcy" or "modern Western barbarism."

Being convicted of homosexuality/homosexual acts is punishable by imprisonment, flogging, or even execution. Iran is one of six countries globally where same-sex relationships can carry the death penalty. The other five are Saudi Arabia, Sudan, Yemen, Nigeria, and Somalia.[41]

Hundreds of people have been executed on the basis of their sexual identity, mostly in the early years of the revolution. It still occurs, but usually along with other charges such as male rape and usually in more remote parts of the country. In 2016, a 19-year-old boy, Hassan Afshar, was convicted of raping another teenager and was executed by hanging in Arak Prison in Iran's Markazi Province. He was a 17-year-old high school student when he was arrested. According to Amnesty International, "He had no access to a lawyer and the judiciary rushed through the investigation and prosecution, convicting and sentencing him to death within two months of his arrest."[42]

Until 2012, consensual sexual intercourse between men was a capital offense as well. After a change in the penal code, the "active person" can be punished with up to 100 lashes, while the passive person can still be sentenced to death. Men convicted of *lavat* (sodomy) typically receive more extreme punishment than women convicted of the same "crime." Women can be sentenced to 50 lashes for committing *mosahegheh* (lesbianism) for their first three convictions. If there is a fourth charge, then the punishment can be execution, although there are no confirmed reports of this taking place.

The legal distinctions for non-consensual acts are often vague, meaning that if someone is raped by a person of the same sex, they, too, may be convicted of a crime, although the punishment is less severe. Iran's volunteer paramilitary force, known as the *basij*, are known to entrap and intimidate people who are suspected of being gay, primarily men. Saba, a 32-year-old gay man, told Human Rights Watch that he and a friend were kidnapped by *basij* members, taken to an empty house, and raped before being returned to the street. During the assault, Saba said the man "kept telling me that if I cooperate with them they will not make trouble for us."[43]

Gays and lesbians are not just hounded by the state, but by their own families and society at large. Gay youths have been beaten and sexual assaulted by family members, especially in rural, poor, and less educated households. That's why most gay people in Iran refuse to disclose their sexual identity. Some marry women, but frequent male prostitutes.

In big cities, the situation is different. In Tehran, there is an active gay community and culture. This is especially true among middle- and upper-class Iranians who have the ability to create parallel lives, away from intolerant relatives and the prying eye of the state. There are gay couples who live together, and gay parties in private homes, where the hosts pay off the local morality police so that guests can come and go undisturbed. For the less affluent, there are certain parks known as hook-up spots.

The Internet provides the LGBTQ community a way to communicate. The government monitors and shuts down websites, but new gay dating sites and blogs crop up to replace them.

LGBTQ organizing in Iran is largely underground, but several international human rights groups provide aid, resources, and information to Iranians. One such organization is OutRight Action International, which does research and collects interviews with Iranian members of the community and distributes reports in both English and Farsi.[44] Another, the Iranian Railroad for Queer

Refugees, provides assistance to LGBTQ Iranians who want to leave the country and settle somewhere where they are safe.[45]

Thanks to the hard work of activists inside and outside the country, the government and society are becoming more tolerant. Young Iranians are more accepting, as are Iranians who travel abroad.

DOES THE GOVERNMENT REALLY SUBSIDIZE TRANSGENDER SURGERIES?

One of the remarkable contradictions is that the Iranian government encourages and helps transgender people to undergo sex reassignment surgery. This Islamic republic carries out more sex change operations than any other nation in the world, except for Thailand.

The remarkable transformation of the religious leaders from calling for transsexuals to be executed to helping them change their sex has been credited to the remarkable persistence of Maryam Khatoon Molkara, an Iranian woman who described herself as trapped in a male body.[46] In 1975, several years before the revolution, Molkara began a letter-writing campaign to Ayatollah Khomeini, seeking to convince him that Islam permitted gender reassignment. She had hopes that after the revolution, she would get her wish. Instead, she lost her job, was forcibly injected with male hormones, and institutionalized.

She didn't give up, though. Upon release, she was determined to meet Ayatollah Khomeini, who was then the nation's Supreme Leader. Wearing a man's suit, she approached his heavily guarded compound but was pounced upon by guards. Khomeini's brother, who had witnessed the scene, intervened and ushered her into the house. Granted an audience with Khomeini, Molkara pleaded for religious permission to get sex reassignment surgery. She left with a letter to the head of medical ethics giving her religious authorization to surgically change her gender.

Molkara ultimately got the operation in Thailand, but she returned to Iran to continue her campaign for transgender rights. In 1987, Khomeini issued a fatwa allowing sex reassignment and allowing transsexual women to live as women until they have surgery. The religious justification is that while the Quran bans homosexuality, it doesn't mention transsexuality. This has become the basis for the recognition of transgender people and for Iranian hospitals to carry out the operations. The government even subsidizes the procedures through state health insurance and housing support, and changes the person's identity documents to reflect the gender change.

Although at first glance the Iranian approach to transgender might seem remarkably liberal, it does have a negative side. Some people are pushed into operations they might not want. Many trans people simply wish to be accepted as they are—without surgery.

Also, the difference between being transgender and gay is not well understood in Iran, even within the medical profession, and there have been reports of gay men being pressured into surgery as a way of complying with the law. Some argue that the acceptance of sex-change procedures reinforces the strict gender divide that undermines the rights of the LGBTQ community.

While the government recognizes transgender people, they are still stigmatized in society at large. Families often reject transgender relatives, beating them and expelling them from the home. They may also face attacks from the police and religious fanatics, and discrimination at the workplace.

HOW COMMONPLACE IS PROSTITUTION AND HOW ARE PROSTITUTES TREATED?

Prostitution is illegal in Iran and can yield heavy punishments, including prison sentences, up to 100 lashes, and even execution if the prostitute is a married woman. Despite the potential punishment and societal rejection, prostitution is widespread. The number of prostitutes is unknown, but in certain neighborhoods of Tehran, prostitutes can be seen hanging out on street corners (covered up, of course). One NGO estimates that there are about 10,000 female sex workers in Tehran alone.[47]

While prostitution is illegal, "sigheh," or temporary marriage, is permitted according to Shia law. Temporary marriage allows for short-term sexual relations, lasting from three days to many years. It is a private contract made in a verbal or written format, and it expires automatically without divorce. Sigheh is used in Iran as a legal cover for prostitution.

Most prostitutes are young—high school-age or younger—and have been recruited into the sex trade.[48] Some girls are runaways who fled abuse or were disowned by their conservative families. They connect with other runaways in communities known as *mahfels*, or safe havens, seeking liberation from societal suppression of youth culture and sexuality. Unfortunately, many of these *mahfels* also serve as entry points into sex rings where minors are vulnerable to recruitment by traffickers.

After sex workers age "past their prime" and leave the industry, many have sexually transmitted infections, injuries inflicted by clients, and other trauma that make it difficult for them to re-enter traditional society.

Recognizing the healthcare and psychological issues related to prostitution, the Ministry of Health has established drop-in centers and voluntary counseling/testing centers for female sex workers to get STD checks and medical treatment, as well as counseling.

WHY IS THERE SUCH A MAJOR DRUG PROBLEM IN IRAN?

With drug-related offenses making up the largest category of both prisoners and those executed in prison, there is obviously a big drug problem in Iran—and it's a problem that has been soaring out of control. In this, the U.S. and Iran are similar, both facing a national epidemic that affects young and old, rich and poor, secular and religious. In Iran, the hard drugs include crystal meth, heroin, synthetic hallucinogens, and opium trafficked from neighboring Afghanistan.[49] In 2016, the government estimated that 2.75 percent of the population was addicted (about 2.2 million people); the figure in the United States was 6.8 percent, or 21.6 million Americans. In Iran, those addicted are mostly men, but there are some women and even children who suffer from drug addiction.

One reason for Iran's drug problem is its geographical proximity to Afghanistan. Poppy, the source of opium and heroin, is transported from Afghanistan to Western Europe via Iran. Other socio-economic reasons include high unemployment and social frustration driven by sanctions and restraints imposed by the religious regime. The government has opened thousands of rehabilitation centers using methadone to wean addicts off drugs, and there are private rehab clinics as well.

While the government helps addicts get clean, it has a history of executing the drug dealers—even very small ones. So many Iranians have been hanged for drug offenses that it spurred a movement among elected officials and activists to abolish the death penalty for nonviolent drug-related offences.

In 2016, a year after over 500 people had been executed for drug offenses, human rights advocates succeeded in getting a majority of the nation's 290-seat Parliament to endorse a bill to end capital punishment for drug trafficking. This marked significant progress, as just the year before the same bill had only 70 supporters in Parliament.

In December 2017, President Houhani signed the bill and in January 2018, the law was ratified by the Guardian Council. According to the new law, only those distributing more than 50 kilograms of narcotics like opium, 2 kilograms of heroin or 3 kilograms of crystal meth will be sentenced to death. (Under the previous law, possessing 5kg of opium or 30g of herion was a capital offence.) There is no capital punishment for marijuana possession.

The new law is to be applied retrospectively, meaning that some 5,000 people awaiting execution for drug-related offenses are entitled to have their cases re-examined. This new law is considered a major step forward, but groups will continue pushing for an end to the death penalty for all non-lethal drug-related offenses, as required by international law.

IS ALCOHOL A PROBLEM IN THIS MUSLIM SOCIETY?

Alcohol has been illegal since the 1979 revolution and is taboo for devout Muslims. The Quran mentions the evils of wine but says nothing about drugs, so for a long time alcohol was seen as more dangerous than drugs. People caught drinking can be punished by 80 lashes.

Despite the ban, casual drinking is very commonplace, especially among young people at private parties. Before the revolution, the national drink was aragh sagi, which is distilled from raisins. It is still very popular.

Alcohol is relatively easy to buy. There is a vast, illegal distribution network with alcohol brought in from Iraqi Kurdistan. Dealers will deliver your order to your doorstep. But it is expensive, so many people resort to homemade brew, which is problematic because people can die from alcohol poisoning after consuming low-quality moonshine.

Iranians are said to be the third highest consumers of alcohol in Muslim-majority Middle Eastern countries, just after Lebanon and Turkey (both countries where it is legal to drink). Even official statistics show that at least 10 percent of the population uses alcohol. It is not casual drinking that is a problem, but alcoholism—and there are many alcoholics in Iran.

Previously, the government refused to admit there was an alcohol problem, but for the past several years, Alcoholics Anonymous groups have been allowed to function openly. In 2017, there were over 1,000 AA groups. In 2015, the Health Ministry took a further step in recognizing the problem of alcoholism by ordering drug addiction treatment centers to care for alcoholics. This is in marked contrast to the past. The government is slowly coming to the realization, in the case of drugs and alcohol, that you can't ignore or criminalize addiction out of existence, and that it is best handled by public health institutions and mutual aid groups, not by the criminal justice system.

*****

It is important to recognize that Iran is not a static society. Attitudes towards social issues are slowly evolving. Nowadays, there is more tolerance within society for gay rights, and more of a sense that people who have fallen on hard times, be it through prostitution, drugs, or alcohol, need help. As more activists get involved in these issues, hopefully they will be able to move those in power to embrace people with different sexual preferences and have more compassion for those who have fallen into hard times with drugs, alcohol, and prostitution.

CHAPTER 5: RELIGIOUS FREEDOM, FOR SOME

According to the government, an overwhelming 99.4 percent of Iranians are Muslims. Iranians must disclose their religious affiliation on official documents. Since the government does not recognize non-religious people, such as atheists or agnostics, most people—whether religious or not—formally identify as Muslim.

But there are religious minorities in this Shia-dominated country. There are Sunni Muslims and Muslims who practice Sufism. There are Christians, Zoroastrians, and Jews (groups the government considers "People of the Book"), and there are groups whose religions are not recognized, such as the Baha'is and Yarsan (Ahl-e Haq).

When Iran's President Rouhani addressed the United Nations in September 2017, he proclaimed that Iran, throughout its history, has been a bastion of tolerance for various religions and ethnicities: "We are the same people who rescued the Jews from Babylonian servitude, opened our arms to welcome Armenian Christians in our midst, and created the 'Iranian cultural continent' with a unique mix of diverse religions and ethnicities."

While it is true that Iran is open to some religious minorities, such as Christians, Zoroastrians, and Jews, they crack down on others, particularly the Baha'i. This chapter looks at the ways different religious groups are treated, as well as the fascinating paradox that in this theocratic Muslim state, most Iranians are just not very religious.

HOW DID SHIA ISLAM COME TO DOMINATE?

Before the Islamic conquest of Persia beginning in 637 A.D., Persians were mostly Zoroastrian, with a minority of Christians and Jews. When Islam was introduced by the Arab conquerors, the first to convert were the nobility and city dwellers. Slowly, the peasants also converted so that by the late 11th century, the majority of Persians had become Muslim. But over the centuries, they worked to create and preserve their own distinct version, maintaining their Persian language instead of using Arabic, and infusing their religious rituals with Persian culture.

There are two major strains of Islam, Shia and Sunni. Until the 16th century, most Persians adhered to the Sunni version of Islam. When the ruling Shah Ismail I ascended to power in 1501, he declared Shia Islam the official religion of the state. Those who refused to convert were murdered. The forced conversion continued for the next two centuries, until Iran became predominantly Shia.

Iran today is the largest Shia-dominated country in the world. Government figures show 90 percent of Iranian Muslims are Shia.

Within the Shia sect, there is a particular group called the Twelvers; Iranians are Twelvers, and about 80 percent of all Shia worldwide are Twelvers. Twelvers believe that there were 12 imams. They believe that the last one, Muhammad, is still alive and has been hiding in a cave for more than 1,000 years. They are waiting for him to come out, resume his rule, and establish a reign of peace and justice on earth.

The transformation of Iran into an overtly Shia state after the 1979 Islamic Revolution put Iran at the center of the Shia-Sunni split which dates back to the death of the Prophet Muhammad in 632 A.D. After the Prophet's death, most Muslims believed the new leader should be Abu Bakr, a friend of the Prophet and father of his wife Aisha. This group became known as the Sunnis and today make up about 80 percent of Muslims worldwide.

The minority of Muslims claimed the Prophet had anointed his cousin and son-in-law Ali to be his successor. They became known as Shia, a contraction of "shiaat Ali," or the partisans of Ali. The split deepened when Ali's son Imam Husayn was beheaded in 680 A.D. by Sunni troops. As time went on, the religious beliefs of the two groups became more and more divergent.

Saudi Arabia, home to the holiest Muslim sites of Mecca and Medina, is a Sunni state and considers itself the global center of Islam. Challenged by the Iranian revolution, Saudi rulers began to spread their Sunni version of Islam, Wahhabism, around the world. Both countries revived a centuries-old sectarian rivalry over the true interpretation of Islam. Much of the sectarian violence that has plagued the region can be traced to Saudi-Iranian rivalry.

HOW ARE SUNNI MUSLIMS TREATED?

While Sunni Muslims are the worldwide majority, in Iran they comprise roughly 10 percent of the Muslim population, and are a broad ethnic mix of Kurds, Arabs, Balochs, Persians, Pashtuns, Larestani, and Turkmens.[50] Most of them live in the country's border areas, although some have moved to the cities for more work opportunities. A more recent influx of Sunnis are refugees from Afghanistan.

The Sunnis face considerable persecution and discrimination, in large part because of the country's animosity towards the Sunni-majority Kingdom of Saudi Arabia.

Sunni Muslims do not have the same religious freedom as their Shia counterparts. Although about one million Sunnis live in Tehran, Iranian authorities will not allow them to build a single mosque in the capital city.[51] Officially, the government says that there are no Sunni mosques because Muslims should be united—all mosques are houses of God open to both Shia and Sunni. Some speculate, however, that the real reason is because the government is worried the mosques would be used by radicals to recruit youth who are frustrated with the Islamic Republic's ideology.[52] Authorities do allow small prayer houses for Sunni worship. Unlike mosques, prayers houses are often rental properties tucked away in residential neighborhoods, not prestigious buildings with minarets. The prayer houses usually don't have imams and staff, or religious instruction beyond prayer.

The teaching of Sunni ideology is banned in public schools. In private Sunni schools, the curriculum is regulated and administered by a government council that includes representatives of Iran's Shia Supreme Leader.[53] Sunnis also claim discrimination in employment, citing particular difficulty getting government jobs in the judicial and executive branches.[54]

In 2015, a prayer house in the Pounak neighborhood of western Tehran was raided and closed because, according to the government, the site was illegal and was being used to "recruit foreign citizens."[55]

Religious leaders within the Sunni community have been harassed, detained, arrested, and even executed for practicing their beliefs. At least 120 Sunnis were imprisoned for their faith as of 2016. In August 2016, 22 of them were executed after unfair trials that convicted them of *moharebeh*, which translates to "enmity towards God," and vague charges of involvement with terrorist activities.[56] Iranian authorities have refused to allow an investigation by a UN special rapporteur.

In October 2012, Sunni activists delivered a public letter to Iran's supreme leader, Ali Khamenei, to demand an end to discrimination.[57] The Sunni community welcomed the election of

President Rouhani in 2013 because his campaign included promises to address the discrimination, but very little has changed.

WHAT ABOUT SUFIS?

Sufis can be Shia or Sunni. Sufism is not a branch of Islam, but a practice that developed in the ninth and tenth centuries. Sufism in Iran has grown enormously since 1979. Before the revolution, about 100,000 people declared themselves Sufi Muslims. Today, there are somewhere between two and five million—making Iran the country with the largest Sufi population in the world.

Sufism has an ancient presence in Iran and is often associated with mysticism. It is considered the part of Islamic teaching that deals with the purification of self. Sufis strive to obtain the direct experience of God. Inspired by the mystics of Persian Zoroastrianism, Buddhism, Hinduism, and Christian monks, the early Sufis lived simple, ascetic lives in communal settings.

Sufism produced a flourishing intellectual culture. The most famous is the poet and Sufi master Jalal ad-Din Muhammad Rumi, known in Iran as Molavi. He was born in 1207 in a small village in what is now Afghanistan to Persian-speaking parents. He later traveled to Iran and Syria, ending up in Turkey, where he died in 1273. Rumi was a Sufi mystic who wrote thousands of poems, mostly love poems about the love he had for his mentor Shams of Tabriz, who disappeared three years after they met. Rumi incorporated poetry, music, and dance into religious practice, whirling while he meditated and composed poetry. In his honor, his followers founded the Order of the Whirling Dervishes. Rumi's work is recited, chanted, set to music, and used as inspiration for music, films, poems, and novels—and countless weddings. His peaceful and tolerant message appeals to people worldwide. Books of his writings have sold millions of copies and have been translated from the original Persian into 23 languages. Remarkably, after 800 years, Rumi is still one of the most popular poets, not only in Iran but worldwide.

In 2007, on the 800th anniversary of Rumi's birth, the Iranian government held an international ceremony and conference that was opened by the president. School bells throughout the country rang out on the day of his birth.

Similarly beloved and influential to modern Iranian culture is the 14th century poet Hafez. Like Rumi, Hafez was a Sufi Muslim, and books of his poetry are a fixture in Iranian homes—they are almost as common as the Quran. His home city of Shiraz is known today as Iran's most liberal city, due in part to the lasting influence of the ideas that Hafez expressed in his poetry. He targeted subjects including religious hypocrisy, writing, "Preachers who display their piety in prayer and pulpit behave differently when they're alone. Why do those who demand repentance do so little of it?"[58] Every day, Hafez's tomb in Shiraz is flocked by visitors who recite his poems and celebrate his life and work, keeping his 600-year-old critiques of religious conservatism alive and relevant.

After the revolution, Sufism became especially popular among women and young people. For many, it represents the embodiment of the true, tolerant, liberal Persian culture that is free of restrictions imposed by rigid clerics but also free of Western influence. In a country where playing music in public has been forbidden, music as part of Sufism is tolerated as a form of "alternative religious practice." In thousands of living rooms across the country, especially among the urban middle class, young men and women dance, sing, and recite Sufi-inspired poems.

Even President Rouhani, speaking before the United Nations in 2017, praised Iran's poets as the way Iran has spread its influence—as opposed to military conquest: "Our ambassadors are our poets, our mystics, and our philosophers. We have reached the shores of this side of the Atlantic through Rumi, and spread our influence throughout Asia with Saadi. We have already captured with Hafez."[59]

But the revolution has had a checkered relationship with Sufis. While for the most part, Sufis are tolerated by the government, some traditional clerics see Sufism as a threat. They understand that Sufism became so popular, in part, as a form of opposition to political and state Islam.

Sufi leaders who are critical of the government have been arrested and convicted of vague crimes like "disturbing public order" and "taking action against national security."[60] Sufi centers of worship have been targeted by authorities. In 2006, a Sufi meeting house in Qom was torn down by the political militia known as the Basij, and the approximately 1,200 Sufis who were trying to defend the structure were arrested. In 2007, another Sufi worship space in Borujerd was burned down. When some Sufis expressed their support for the dissident Green Movement in 2009, the government crackdown intensified. Iranian authorities used bulldozers to destroy a Sufi prayer house and the mausoleum of the 19th century Sufi poet Nasir Ali in the city of Isfahan.

In May 2014, approximately 35 Sufis were convicted on charges related to their religious activities and given sentences ranging from three months to four years in prison. Another 10 Sufi activists were either serving prison terms or had cases pending against them.[61]

WHICH NON-MUSLIM GROUPS ARE GRANTED THE RIGHT TO WORSHIP?

As discussed above, Iran is a Shia Muslim state that discriminates against Sunni Muslims and sometimes frowns upon those who practice Sufism. But how are non-Muslims treated?

In sharp contrast to Saudi Arabia, where it is illegal to openly practice a religion other than Islam, the Iranian government recognizes Christians, Zoroastrians, and Jews as "People of the Book." These groups are allowed to openly practice their religion and their freedom to worship is enshrined within the Iranian constitution.[62] They are also granted representation in Parliament, with two seats reserved for Armenian Christians, one for Assyrian and Chaldean Christians, one for Jews, and one for Zoroastrians.[63]

The size of the Christian population is difficult to pin down, with estimates ranging from 270,000–500,000. Most are Armenians and Assyrians.[64] There are about 600 churches in Iran. Christians living in Iran are allowed to drink alcohol and eat pork, even though they are forbidden substances for the majority of Iranians.

Christians are fully integrated into Iranian society. Famous members of Iran's Christian community include the captain of the national football team Andranik Teymourian, well-loved musician Loris Tjeknavorian, and Sombat Hacoupian, who started a men's clothing brand that has become a household name.

Not all Christians, however, are well received by the authorities. Iranians who were not born Christians but converted from Islam face discrimination. Converts may find themselves charged with crimes both secular and religious in nature. Iranian authorities have raided church services and threatened religious leaders who they suspect are involved in proselytizing. Some reports indicate that in 2016, there were about 90 Christians in prison, both converts and people accused of proselytizing. One case is that of Yousef Nadarkhani,[65] a pastor who, in 2009, questioned Islam's monopoly on education. Charged with apostasy (abandoning Islam) and evangelizing Muslims, he was originally sentenced to death. After an international outcry, he was released in 2012.

The second "recognized" minority religion is Zoroastrianism. Zoroastrians have a long history in the region, and they are the oldest surviving religious community in Iran. Founded by the Prophet Zoroaster, it is one of the oldest monotheistic religions. Zoroastrians believe that the god Ahura Mazda, which translates to Wise Lord, created the world and that fire represents the God's wisdom and light. Zoroastrianism not only preceded but is also thought to have influenced the beliefs of the major Abrahamic religions, such as the belief in heaven, hell, and a messianic figure. A 2011 census documented only 25,000 Zoroastrians in Iran, although members of the religious community argue that the number is larger.[66] There is much goodwill among the general population toward Zoroastrianism. Many Muslim Iranians wear a necklace with Faravahar, a Zoroastrian symbol that represents the religion's basic principles: good thoughts, good words, good deeds.

The third officially sanctioned minority religion is Judaism. The Jewish community in Iran is small—about 10,000–20,000. (There are many more Iranian Jews, about 200,000, who live in Israel.) Nevertheless, Jews living in Iran constitute the largest Jewish community in the Middle East outside Israel and the second largest Jewish community in a predominantly Muslim country (Turkey is the first).[67] Prior to the Iranian Revolution, the number of Jews was roughly 80,000, but most fled the country and resettled elsewhere.[68] Many of those who stayed behind claim that while the government is anti-Israel, it is not against Jews. In Tehran alone, there are more than 10 kosher butcher stores, five kosher restaurants, and five Jewish schools.[69] In 2016, the seat in Parliament reserved for a member of the Jewish community was held by a surgeon named Ciamak Morsadegh. Morsadegh claimed that there are about 60 synagogues in Iran and that, unlike some

European countries where synagogues must be guarded from attacks, Jews in Iran felt secure and faced no such threats.[70]

But Iran's standing with the country's Jewish community was badly tarnished under the 2005–2013 presidency of Mahmoud Ahmadinejad, who became infamous internationally for statements denying or downplaying the scale of the Holocaust. His successor Rouhani tried to undo the damage.

On his first visit to the UN General Assembly in New York in 2013, Rouhani was accompanied by Iran's Jewish member of Parliament. Rouhani called the Holocaust a crime against humanity and has been very careful to note that he is a critic of the Israeli government, not the Jewish people. In September 2013, on Rosh Hashanah, the Jewish new year, he made headlines globally by tweeting: "As the sun is about to set here in #Tehran I wish all Jews, especially Iranian Jews, a blessed Rosh Hashanah." The tweet was accompanied by a photo of an Iranian Jew praying at a synagogue in Tehran. Rouhani's government also showed support by donating half a million dollars to Tehran's Jewish hospital.[71]

Anti-Jewish sentiment, however, is still present. Some high-ranking clerics continue to preach anti-Semitic messages and the state has targeted individuals believed to have connections with Israel.[72] But among the public, there is widespread sympathy for Jews. According to a 2014 poll by the U.S.-based Anti-Defamation League, Iranians—who have been accustomed to "Death to Israel" rallies since the time of the revolution—are the most pro-Jewish people in the Middle East (with the exclusion of Israel). In the same poll, when asked if Jews "still talk too much about what happened to them in the Holocaust," only 18 percent of Iranians agreed, compared to 22 percent of Americans.[73]

WHY ARE THE BAHA'I DISCRIMINATED AGAINST?

In contrast to the recognized minority religions are those, such as the Baha'is and Yarsan (Ahl-e Haq), that are not recognized by the state.

The Baha'i are the largest non-Muslim minority in Iran, with a population estimated at 300,000 (and about 6 million worldwide). The Baha'i faith was founded in Iran in the 19th century by its prophet, Baha'u'llah. Iran banned the faith in 1981, soon after the Islamic Revolution.

The Islamic Republic considers the Baha'i faith heretical because it was founded after the death of the Prophet Muhammad, who is perceived in Islam as the final prophet. Former Iranian president Ayatollah Akbar Hashemi Rafsanjani called the Baha'i faith a "deviant sect created by colonialists who we have always and will always oppose." The Iranian regime's typical accusation is that the Baha'i faith is a foreign plot and Baha'is are "agents of Israel and America."[74]

UN officials stated that the Baha'i community is the "most severely persecuted religious minority" in Iran because the multiple forms of discrimination "affect their enjoyment of economic, social and cultural rights."[75] The Iranian Revolutionary Guard and their supporters have demolished or desecrated Baha'i cemeteries and holy places, and confiscated community property.[76] Legally, Baha'is are not even allowed to leave property to their heirs. Hate speech and hate crimes against them are common.

Baha'is are barred from pursuing military careers and face prejudice in many other fields of employment and education. Iranian authorities have seized Baha'i-owned businesses and detained Baha'i students who challenge their lack of access to equal education and employment. In 2014, the government demolished the Baha'i cemetery in Shiraz, where many of the victims are buried.[77]

Leaders of the Baha'i faith are commonly targeted. Scores of Baha'is have been imprisoned for peacefully practicing their religion, with vague charges of threatening national security.

Detained Baha'is have reported torture, such as the alleged torture of 24 Baha'is in Golestan Province in 2016, but the accusations are rarely investigated.[78] Worst of all, Iranian officials have executed more than 200 Baha'i leaders since the revolution in 1979. According to the Center for Human Rights in Iran, more than 80 Baha'is are currently being held in Iranian prisons.[79]

A group known as the "Baha'i 7" were arrested in 2008, charged with "espionage for Israel, insulting religious sanctities and propaganda against the system" and sentenced to 20 years in prison. Amnesty International considered them prisoners of conscience. There is hope that they will be released from their 20-year sentences due to a change in Iran's penal code that allows sentences to be carried out cumulatively instead of consecutively.[80]

Due to this persecution, since 1999 the U.S. government's Commission on International Religious Freedoms has annually labeled Iran as a Country of Particular Concern due to its "systematic, ongoing, and egregious violations of religious freedom, including prolonged detention, torture, and executions based primarily or entirely upon the religion of the accused."[81]

WHAT ABOUT THE OTHER NON-RECOGNIZED RELIGION KNOWN AS YARSAN, OR AHL-E-HAQ?

Yarsan, or Ahl-e-Haq, meaning People of Truth, is a religious minority mostly residing in the Kurdish-dominated province of Kermanshah in the northwest of Iran. The faith also has followers in Iraq and Turkey. Yarsan is a syncretic religion that dates back to the 14th century. Until the 20th century, it was strictly for Kurds who were born into it. Their beliefs include the transmigration of the soul and that human beings go through a cycle of 1001 incarnations, during which they may become more purified based on their actions.

The government of Iran considers this religion a "false cult." Yarsan believers say that the government tries to convert their community to Islam, imprisons their leaders, and violates the social, cultural, and economic rights of its followers.

ARE THERE ATHEISTS IN IRAN?

Certainly there are many atheists in Iran, but there is no way of knowing how many. Iran is one of 13 countries where atheists could be given the death penalty, but this is not enforced. Atheists who don't speak out publicly to advocate their views have no problems. There are even several pro-atheist Facebook groups that poke fun at religious figures, but people participate anonymously.

In an online chat about Iranians and religion, someone wrote, "I am an atheist and an Iranian. I am also anonymous, which speaks volumes." Another Iranian responded differently: "I was raised in Iran in a non-practicing Muslim family and became an atheist when I was around 14. I have never felt any reason to hide it. Some people are surprised if I tell them I don't believe in God, but nobody has ever bothered me and I've never felt intimidated."

CAN MUSLIMS CHANGE THEIR RELIGION?

In Iran, it's a crime for a Muslim to convert to another religion—once born a Muslim, you must remain a Muslim. The act of changing or denouncing your faith, known as apostasy, is a capital offense. It has been decades since anyone was executed for apostasy; the last known case was someone who converted to Christianity in 1990.[82]

Still, anyone converting to another religion tends to do so quietly to avoid government retaliation.

ARE IRANIANS MUSLIMS VERY RELIGIOUS?

One of the fascinating idiosyncrasies of Iran is that while it is a theocratic Muslim state, most Iranians are not particularly religious.

The ruling regime insists that it has created a more religious society since the 1979 revolution, and certainly people are inculcated with a heavy dose of religion in school and through the state-run media. Women must dress according to religious dictates. In the holy month of Ramadan, people cannot eat or drink (even water) in public. When mosques issue their five daily calls to prayer, the call resonates throughout the neighborhoods on loud, outdoor speakers. By law, all public buildings must have prayer rooms.

Yet at office buildings, shopping malls, and bus stations, you see few people praying. In contrast to Saudi Arabia, where workplaces are forced to close for prayer, most Iranian businesses stay open during prayer time.

Polls show that most Iranians say religion is an important part of their daily lives.[83] But with a government that insists on imposing religiosity, many Iranians have rebelled by becoming less and less religious in the traditional sense. Clerics can impose their beliefs on many aspects of Iranian life, but they can't force people to be believers.

CHAPTER 6: THE PARADOXICAL STATUS OF IRANIAN WOMEN

Two key societal restrictions affect the lives of Iranian women: patriarchal values that pre-date the 1979 revolution, and post-1979 institutional structures based on hardline interpretations of Islamic principles. Both influences see women mainly through the lens of wives and mothers, and use this narrow view as a pretext for restricting women's public and private lives. While the restrictions affect all women in some fashion, they are far more pronounced among women who are poor, rural, and/or religious than they are among women who are middle class, educated, urban, and secular.

On the other hand, Westerners who think of Iranian women as passive, hijab-clad individuals relegated to the confines of their homes are quite misinformed. Yes, Iranian women are oppressed— the country ranks 139 out of 145 on the World Economic Forum's 2016 Global Gender Gap report[84]—and the mandatory dress code of the hijab is a visible sign of government interference in their lives. Nevertheless, Iranian women enjoy far greater freedom than women in many other countries in the region, particularly Saudi Arabia, where women live under a much stricter male guardianship system. In Afghanistan, many women remain illiterate and confined to their homes. In striking contrast, Iranian women are well educated, involved in all aspects of society, and are powerful agents of change who continuously fight for their rights, even at great personal risk.

WHAT WERE WOMEN'S RIGHTS UNDER THE SHAH?

While the Pahlavi dynasty (1925–1979) was fraught with repression and corruption, the penchant for Western modernization, coupled with pressure by Iranian women, led to fundamental gains for women. A national referendum in 1963 granted women the right to vote and to run for public office. A woman was promoted to a cabinet position, Minister of Education, in 1968, and in 1969 five female judges were appointed, including future Nobel prize winner Shirin Ebadi.

The Women's Organization of Iran was founded in 1966 to promote women's rights. One of its major victories was the Family Protection Act, enacted in 1967, and updated in 1975. Despite vociferous objections by religious and conservative communities, it gave Iranian women the right to divorce their husbands, object to their husbands' polygamy, and contest their children's custody after divorce. It also raised the minimum age for girls to marry from 13 years to 18 years. In a major breakthrough for women in the region, abortion was legalized.

Immediately after the 1979 Revolution, women lost many of the rights they had achieved. The Family Protection Act was repealed because Supreme Leader Ayatollah Khomeini considered it in violation of Islam and sharia law.

WHAT IS THE NORM TODAY IN TERMS OF MARRIAGE?

Since the beginning of the 20th century, Iran has generally been a monogamous society. Legally, Iranian men can have up to four wives, but polygamy is uncommon and exists mostly among the religious elite.[85]

After the revolution, the marriage age for girls was reduced from 15 years to "puberty," which is nine under Islamic law. In 2002, it was raised to 13, but the girl's father can ask the court for permission to marry off his daughter below this age.[86]

Child marriages can be found among conservative, rural families, as well as poor, women-headed households and families with drug problems. The norm, however, is for Iranians to get married later in life. The average marriage age in 2016 was 24 for women and 27 for men, and even at that age, almost half the young people remain unmarried.[87]

The low marriage rate is attributed to the deterioration of the economy, and the increased opportunities for romantic relationships outside of marriage. Many couples, especially in the big cities, cohabitate without getting married, a practice known as white marriage. Educated, independent women also complain that it is difficult to find open-minded Iranian men who appreciate liberated women.[88]

Arranged marriages do still exist, but mostly in the rural areas. These days, the Internet has become key to matchmaking. Using websites similar to Match.com or e-Harmony, young, urban Iranians find their mates for a lifetime, or for a night. The government tries to crack down on dating sites it considers immoral, but as soon as one site gets blocked, another appears. Finally admitting defeat and following the adage "if you can't beat 'em, join 'em," the government started its own official "spouse-finding" website in 2015, which is mostly used by religious youth. Other, more liberal sites still abound, especially in Tehran, where there is even an app for gay and lesbian singles.[89]

HOW COMMON IS DIVORCE?

A major gain that women had made before the 1979 revolution was the equal right to divorce. One of the revolutionary government's first acts was not only to suspend the Family Protection Act but also to dismantle Family Courts. Men were given the freedom to divorce their wives by simple declaration, and gained exclusive custody of the children. Mothers might be granted custody until the children are seven, but then custody reverts back to the fathers. Even if the father dies, custody does not revert to the mother but to the child's paternal grandfather.

If the husband is unwilling to divorce, the wife must prove that he is abusive, has psychological problems, or is somehow unable to uphold his marital responsibilities.

Divorce is frowned upon by the state and is often considered shameful by the community, particularly in the more conservative parts of the country. It can leave women in a difficult financial and social situation.

Despite the obstacles, the divorce rate in Iran is high. In 2014, about 20 percent of marriages ended in divorce, a statistic decried by the clerics as an affront to the values of the Islamic Republic.[90] Reasons for divorce include adultery, drug addiction, physical abuse, in-law interference, impotence, women's greater financial independence, and greater societal acceptance in more educated, urban households. Conservatives blame it on "growing godlessness" among the youth and the corrupting influences of the West.

IS ABORTION LEGAL?

Among the policies that Iranian women fought for and won during the Shah's time was the 1977 legalization of abortion, which was extremely rare in the Middle East. This changed with the 1979 revolution, however, when the clerics cited the Quran's condemnation of infanticide as the reason to prohibit abortions. Over time, the rules have been slightly loosened to make abortion legal in the case of an abnormal fetus or if the mother's life is in danger.

Otherwise, abortion is forbidden, and those providing or receiving an illegal abortion can be severely punished with a prison term of three to ten years.[91]

But illegal or induced abortions still occur every day, with an estimated 120,000 illegal abortions performed every year.[92] Gynecologists report that illegal, black market abortions have had a terrible impact on women's health.

HOW MANY CHILDREN DO WOMEN HAVE?

At the start of the revolution, Ayatollah Khomeini opposed the Shah's family planning clinics, insisting that birth control was a Western plot to have fewer Muslims in the world. He ordered the destruction of all family planning clinics. The birth rate soared from 2.1 to 4.2, among the highest in the world.

Even the Supreme Leader realized that the growth rate was too much for the country to bear and had to be lowered. The family planning clinics were reopened, and the nation's birth control program of free condoms, vasectomies, pills, and family planning education became a model worldwide—except for the prohibition on abortion.

The push to lower the birthrate was so successful that by 2012, it had plummeted to just 1.7, the lowest in the region. The government now had the opposite concern—that Iran would become a nation of old people. So, at a time when environmentalists are concerned that the global population will surpass eight billion by 2030 (by some calculations, human overpopulation may have occurred at four billion people), Iran switched course once again, setting a goal of doubling the nation's population from 80 million to 150 million by 2050.

To achieve this goal, the government took some steps that were helpful to families, such as increasing maternity leave from six months to a full nine months (compared to three months in the United States) and allowing a two-week leave for fathers. Other measures had a markedly negative impact on women: canceling subsidies for condoms and birth control pills; eliminating free vasectomies; making divorce harder (couples now have to go to counseling first). During President Ahmadinejad's last year in office, the government eliminated the budget for family planning, thus ending one of the most successful programs of its kind in the world.[93]

WHAT IS THE DRESS CODE FOR WOMEN?

For the last 100 years, women's dress in Iran has been an arena of struggle between the government, clergy, men, and women themselves. That's why women's clothing, particularly the veil, is as much a political symbol as a religious one.

During the beginning of the 20th century, most women were isolated in their homes and concealed in public by long chadors, a loose and usually dark-colored cloth that covers the head and body but leaves the face visible. When Reza Shah Pahlavi rose to power in 1925, he pushed a process of modernization and secularization, including encouraging women to adopt Western dress. In 1936, he went even further, issuing a royal decree declaring it illegal for women to wear the traditional chador. Most upper class and educated women happily adopted more Western-styled clothing and shed their chadors, but the decision to ban the veil was vehemently opposed by the clerics and religious women.

Women who chose Islamic dress were harassed by police, and their veils forcibly removed. As a result, rather than appear in public in an "immodest" fashion, religious women often remained at home, either by their choice or at their family's insistence. This meant that fewer religious women were educated or employed outside the home.

Resistance to the ban was so strong that when Mohammed Reza Pahlavi took over from his father in 1941, the ban was lifted. As the Shah's pro-Western government became increasingly repressive, more and more women, including liberal university students, began wearing the headscarf and chador as a symbol of opposition. Many middle and upper class women started wearing the chador to demonstrations as a way so show solidarity with poor women, who were traditionally more religious. Ironically, the veil became a symbol of liberation from the dictatorial state. Little did the women realize that the new government ushered in by the revolution would soon make Islamic dress mandatory.

Once in power, the Supreme Leader called for a return to modesty and Islamic dress, but the government assured women that this was only a recommendation.[94] Then, in 1980, the veil became mandatory in government and public offices, and in 1983 it became mandatory for all women. Women took to the streets in protest on many occasions, but were unsuccessful, leaving them with a profound sense of betrayal.

According to law, women must cover their entire body except for their faces and hands; women who do not wear the chador must wear a long overcoat called a manteau. The manteau is supposed to be loose fitting and thick enough to conceal the clothes underneath. Women are not supposed to wear brightly colored clothes or clothes designed to attract men's attention.

The pendulum had swung to the other side. Now, women who were *not* veiled faced harassment by authorities. *Bad hijab* became a crime and was defined not just by an uncovered head, but also uncovered arms and legs; tight, bright or see-through clothes; clothing with foreign words; makeup; and even nail polish. The punishment in the 1983 Penal Law was 74 lashes, which was changed in 1996 to a prison sentence of up to four months and a monetary fine. Over the years, the rules have been relaxed, with women merely issued a warning.

Some women believe that the dress code liberates them from worrying about their appearance and allows them to focus on more important issues, such as education and employment. Others condemn the practice of forced veiling as repressing their rights of expression and bodily autonomy.

In 2013, the newly elected President Rouhani took a stand, albeit a small one, against the strict adherence to the Islamic dress code favored by his predecessors. Rouhani stated, "If a woman or a man does not comply with our rules for clothing, his or her virtue should not come under question ... In my view, many women in our society who do not respect our hijab laws are virtuous. Our emphasis should be on the virtue."[95] His remarks provoked a critical response from Ayatollah Khamenei and other members of the clergy.

While in pre-revolutionary times women rebelled by wearing the veil, today Iranian women rebel by wearing colorful scarves pushed back to expose as much hair as they can get away with, tight-fitting manteaus, and gobs of makeup. Makeup has become a symbol of defiance, and Iran is the second largest market for cosmetics in the Middle East, right behind Saudi Arabia.[96]

Women who test the boundaries of modesty take a personal risk. As in other Islamic countries, such as Saudi Arabia, Sudan, and Malaysia, Iran has a police force tasked with enforcing the dress code. Iran's morality police, *Gasht-e Ershad*, are constantly on the lookout for "immoral behavior." In 2014, a group of youth released a video of themselves, including women without head scarves, joyfully dancing to Pharrell William's popular song "Happy." The individuals in the video were later arrested and charged with "hurting public chastity." They were sentenced to a year in prison and 91 lashes, but thanks to a fierce international outcry, their sentence was suspended.[97]

While the morality police used to be empowered to impose fines or arrest transgressors, as of 2016 the nation's 7,000-strong force, which includes women, is only supposed to issue warnings to adjust or remove the insulting attire or to report violations to the police, who then decide whether to take action.[98] But that is not always the case, and in some instances the morality police turn violent. In February 2017, a 14-year-old girl was beaten and detained for wearing ripped jeans in public.[99]

Facebook groups such as "My Stealthy Freedom," have popped up with women challenging the dress code by posting photos of themselves unveiled in public places.[100] An initiative started in 2017 by Masih Alinejad, who lives in the United States, used the hashtag #whitewednesdays. It encouraged women to post pictures and videos of themselves wearing white headscarves as symbols of protest, and—if they dared—to take off their headscarves while walking in public.[101] According to Alinejad, in the first two weeks, hundreds of women had already submitted videos, some of which had 500,000 views. One participant said she took the risk because "even if this leads me to jail and sleeping with cockroaches, it would be worth it to help the next generation."

IS IRAN REALLY THE NOSE JOB CAPITAL OF THE WORLD?

One of the most ironic ways that Iranian women snub their noses at the modesty-obsessed clerics is by getting nose jobs. Iran has become the nose job capital of the world, with over 70,000 rhinoplasty operations every year.[102] The women—and increasingly men as well—don't try to hide their surgeries. Going out on the street with a bandaged nose has become a status symbol.

Iranian women also challenge Islamic codes of modesty by obtaining cosmetic surgeries such as liposuction to improve their figures, eyebrow tattoos, botox injections in their cheeks, and collagen in their lips to make them fuller. The public is bombarded with advertisements flaunting photos of clients before and after plastic surgery.

For a group of young women I met on the streets of Tehran, their obsession with their appearance—nose jobs, full lips, lots of makeup, dyed-blonde hair sticking out from the loose-fitting, colorful scarves—definitely represented a form of protest. "The government forces us to cover our heads and our bodies, so we use our faces to display our beauty," smiled a 20-year-old student as she puffed on a cigarette in a Tehran cafe lined with photos of American movie stars. When I asked if she was afraid the morality police would punish her for wearing tight clothes and so much makeup, she laughed. "We just run away from them."

WHAT ACCESS TO EDUCATION DO WOMEN HAVE?

Throughout the first half of the 20th century, there was a slow but steady expansion of women's education. In 1935, the University of Tehran admitted female students to the institution for the first time, and in the ensuing decades, higher education for women became a norm among upper class Iranians.[103]

Education for girls became universal and compulsory in 1944. Primary education, which lasts until ninth grade, is provided free through public schools.[104] High school is not compulsory but is free. Iran boasts that the literacy rate for women and girls between the ages of 15 and 24 is virtually universal, 99 percent.[105]

But the 1979 revolution has had a devastating impact on the quality of girls' education. Coeducation was banned by religious authorities, causing many schools to close their doors to girls. In all-girls schools, the curriculum was often designed by religious leaders to promote gendered career paths, such as running households or working in hospitals.[106] The new regime codified this gendered division of labor by forbidding certain majors. Women were not allowed to study law, and men were not permitted to enroll in studies deemed feminine.[107] Scholarships to study abroad were not available to unmarried women, as the state feared that the women would be negatively affected by foreign influences.[108]

Women pushed for equal educational opportunities, and during the reform period of President Khatami from 1997–2005, many of these restrictions were lifted. In the early 2000s, women's enrollment in university began to surpass the number of male students, and unmarried women were granted the opportunity to pursue scholarships for study abroad, although they still require permission from their fathers.[109]

When Mahmoud Ahmadinejad was elected president in 2005, however, women's gains in education were reversed, as authorities blamed women's education for too much competition in the job market, a rising divorce rate, and the declining fertility rate.[110]

Bans and quotas to cap the number of women were placed on certain majors, and women were only allowed to attend institutions of higher education within their hometowns.[111] Many universities also had gender segregation policies that required separate classes for men and women.

Women hoped to see new education reforms when Hassan Rouhani became president in 2013—during his campaign he directly criticized the university gender quotas that limited the percentage of women.[112] As of 2017, gender-based quotas on admissions and fields of study remain common in Iranian universities, especially since the practice is supported by Supreme Leader Khamenei.[113]

The effects of the backlash on women's education during Ahmadinejad's time and Rouhani's inability to bring about major change led to a decline in the number of Iranian women obtaining higher education. In 2007, 62 percent of students entering university were women. By 2013 that number had plummeted to 48.2 percent, but in ensuing years it once again rose to over 50 percent.[114]

WHAT WORK OPTIONS ARE OPEN FOR WOMEN?

Women are permitted to work in Iran, but there are countless barriers to the type of careers they can pursue, and religious authorities strongly encourage women to stay home to fulfill the traditional roles of wives and mothers. Despite being over 50 percent of university graduates, women only make up 17 percent of the official labor market. Over one-third of university-education women are unemployed.[115]

While many women choose not to enter the job market due to social pressure, unemployment among women willing to work is at least twice as high as the rate for men.[116]

The government formally prohibits discrimination on the basis of gender in the workplace, but the limits placed on women's education and the social/cultural bias towards men in the hiring process combine to result in far fewer professional options for women.[117] In occupations where both men and women compete for the same positions, women in Iran—as in most of the world—are less likely to be hired. Female workers are often paid less than their male counterparts, especially in factories.[118] In the legal arena, women can train as judges, but they can only become assistant judges.

Economic sanctions imposed by the international community have also had a negative impact on women's employment opportunities. The disrupted economy creates more competition between men and women, and in the case of layoffs, women are much more likely to lose their jobs than men.

Women's employment possibilities can also be limited by their families. Although Iran does not have a strict guardianship policy like Saudi Arabia, where men have decision-making power over key aspects of women's lives, some Iranian employers require permission from the father or husband. The husband or father also has the ability to prohibit travel—their permission is needed for a visa application. This can prevent women from being employed in positions where travel is likely. Policies that began in 2014 encouraging women to have more children to reverse the nation's declining fertility rate made it even more difficult for women to find and retain employment, since employers are biased against women who take time off for childcare.

Women had hoped that President Rouhani would address discrimination in the workforce when he came to power in 2013. In July 2016, he temporarily suspended hiring in government agencies that discriminated against women, but the effort produced limited improvements.[119] As in other areas of reform, Rouhani's efforts were slow and halfhearted in the face of opposition from hardliners within the government and religious sector.

Despite all these limitations, many women still thrive in their professions. Iranian women are doctors, lawyers, journalists, engineers, professors, artists, and even truck drivers. Many run their own businesses. The Association of Iranian Business Women lists women-run businesses that range from architectural firms to medical production facilities to family farms.

CAN WOMEN VOTE, RUN FOR OFFICE, AND HOLD POSITIONS OF POWER?

Iranian women secured the right to vote and run for public office in 1963, although these rights were strongly opposed by conservative clerics. That same year, six women were elected to the Iranian Parliament. By 1978, just prior to the Islamic Revolution, there were 22 female members of Parliament.[120]

In the first parliamentary election after the Islamic Revolution, only four women won and many women who had occupied powerful positions, such as judges, were demoted or dismissed. Women's representation in government has remained minimal, with minor ebbs and flows. Some of the greatest gains were under the reform leadership of President Khatami, when record numbers of women were put in senior advisory government positions.

Undeterred by the low odds of winning, women still actively participate in politics and run for office. In 2008, 585 women campaigned for elected office (out of 7,168 total candidates), but only nine were elected.[121]

There has been a raging debate about whether it is legal for women to run for president. Article 115 of the constitution states that the president must be chosen from among the "religious and political *rijal*." The debate revolves around the definition of the word *rijal*. Some insist on the literal Arab translation, which means men. Others, including former President Rafsanjani, argue that in the constitutional context, it simply means "person" and therefore can be a woman.[122]

So far, the male definition has prevailed. In 2009, 42 women attempted to run for president, but all were disqualified by the Guardian Council. In 2013, all 30 women who attempted to get on the presidential ballot were disqualified.[123] In 2017, the highest number of women ever, 137, attempted to run, but all were banned.[124]

In Parliament, however, 17 women were elected to the 290-member body—the highest number since the revolution. This was particularly significant because for the first time, women had more members in Parliament than the clerics, who had only 16 seats.[125]

Still, Iranian women ranked near the bottom in a worldwide comparison of parliaments, placing 178 out of 193 in 2017.[126] Nevertheless, the shift toward electing more women, combined with the declining number of conservative hardliners winning seats in Parliament, is promising. A campaign called "Changing the male face of Parliament" is working toward a goal of 30 percent women by the 2020 election.[127]

CAN IRANIAN WOMEN PLAY SPORTS AND ATTEND SPORTING EVENTS?

Prior to the 1979 revolution, female athletes were encouraged to participate in national and international competitions. Participation declined in the 1980s, but since then there has been a steady increase in women's involvement in both individual and team sports, including soccer, hockey, rugby, volleyball, and even chess. Men are not allowed to attend women's competitions.

Being an athlete offers opportunities for Iranian women to travel abroad, but women do require permission from a male relative, such as a father or husband. Soccer team captain and champion player Niloufar Ardalan couldn't attend the Asian Football Confederation's women's championship in 2015 because her husband wouldn't grant her permission to travel to Malaysia.[128]

Sometimes Iranian athletes face discrimination from international hosts. In 2011, the soccer association FIFA disqualified the Iranian soccer team from the Olympic competition, saying the scarves their government obliged them to wear was a breach of the association's dress code.

Iranian women are also struggling for the right to attend sporting events where males are playing. Iranians share the world's love of volleyball and soccer, but women have been barred from attending. The authorities have justified the ban by insisting that there is a lack of proper infrastructure for women, including bathrooms, and that men used profanities and can become violent.

One famous act of protest was the 1997 "football revolution" when about 5,000 women defied the ban and stormed the gates of the stadium to celebrate the national football team's qualifying for the World Cup.

In 2006, a comical Iranian film called "Offside" portrayed young women sneaking into a World Cup qualifying match. Shot in Iran and inspired by the director's daughter, who did sneak into stadiums, the film received international acclaim but was banned from being shown inside Iran.

The struggle achieved international notoriety in June 2014 when a British-Iranian student, Ghonchech Ghavami, tried to attend a men's volleyball match. She was imprisoned for 100 days, much of the time in solitary confinement.[129] In 2015, the Deputy Minister for Sports announced that women would be permitted to attend some male sporting events. Volleyball, basketball, handball, and tennis matches were opened because they were considered less rowdy, but not soccer or wrestling.

A group of young women started a campaign called Open Stadiums, which identifies itself as "a movement of Iranian women seeking to end discrimination and let women attend stadiums." Prominent male athletes and coaches have called for the ban to be lifted.

In September 2017, the absurdity of the ban was evident at a World Cup qualifying match in Tehran between Iran and Syria. Syrian women were allowed into the stadium to cheer their team while Iranian women left outside, protesting. This led a number of female members of Parliament to condemn the ban.

While Iranians keep pushing from the inside, pressure is also coming from outside the country, including from the international soccer and volleyball federations that threaten to censure Iran if the restrictions on women are not lifted.[130]

HOW SEGREGATED ARE PUBLIC SPACES?

Iran is not as gender segregated as Saudi Arabia, where all the schools, public spaces, and even private businesses like McDonald's are segregated. Public places such as beaches or swimming pools are segregated in Iran, but businesses, parks, and government buildings are not. Perhaps the most segregated space is the mosque, where women are physically partitioned away from men.

Buses are integrated, but there are seats reserved for women, usually in the back. Women can be taxi drivers, but they can only pick up other women. In the Tehran metro, the first and last cars are usually reserved for women. While these cars are marked "Women Only," that doesn't mean women have to ride exclusively in those cars. They can ride in the middle cars with men, but women often choose the segregated cars for safety and security.

HOW COMMON IS VIOLENCE AGAINST WOMEN?

Violence against women is commonplace—domestic violence as well as street harassment and sexual harassment in the workplace. Violence against women is especially prevalent in poor, rural families, where traditional male domination is greater and women have few alternatives. Women in prison are also subjected to sexual violence.

Victims are usually afraid to report the abuses, and government authorities refuse to acknowledge the scale of the problem. In 2014, the country was shocked by a wave of acid attacks in which men on motorcycles threw acid on the faces of women they considered improperly dressed. There were also cases of men throwing acid on women who refused their overtures to date or marry them.

In the case of rape, four male witnesses, or three men and two women, are required to convict someone. If convicted, the penalties can be severe, including the death penalty. But women are generally afraid to report rape for fear that they are the ones who will be punished, not the rapists.

Iran does have shelters for women fleeing abuse, run by both state and private organizations, but there are not enough shelters and they do not provide long-term support—the jobs and housing women need to escape abusive situations.

Another form of violence against women is "honor killing," a murder committed or ordered by a husband, father, or other relatives as punishment for damaging the family's reputation. Honor killings are uncommon in cities and most common among nomads, uneducated people, and conservative ethnic minorities living near Iran's borders. The victims are mostly married women suspected of adultery or young girls suspected of having sexual relations with boys. The deaths are often made to look like suicides by self-immolation, and the perpetrators usually get away with short prison sentences or none at all.

The state is also guilty of violence against women. Premarital sex, while extremely common, is technically a crime that can result in a penalty of up to 100 lashes and between 10 days and two months in prison. These penalties are usually reserved for prostitutes.

WHAT ARE THE PROSPECTS FOR CHANGE?

Despite government repression, Iran has an active women's rights movement. Iranian women activists fall into two categories:

Muslim feminists who want to improve women's status by reinterpreting Islamic law in a more gender-equitable way, and secular feminists who try to challenge the power of religion. While these groups have clashed over the years, they have also been able to come together despite their differences to fight for common goals.

Sometimes, Iran's feminists have support from the country's leadership. This was the case during the time of reformist President Khatami from 1997–2005, but his pro-women policies were constantly challenged by conservative institutions like the Guardian Council, which reviews all laws for their adherence to Islamic principles.

The best-known women's rights movement in recent years was the 2006 One Million Signatures Campaign, which called for equal rights in marriage and inheritance, an end to polygamy, and stricter forms of punishment for honor killings and other forms of violence against women. Over 1,000 people from 20 provinces took part in the campaign's training courses. They reached out to the public by collecting signatures from both men and women on the streets and in public places.

Despite the totally peaceful and mild nature of the campaign, the government cracked down on the organizers. It prevented women from holding meetings. People collecting signatures were attacked and arrested. Campaign leaders were imprisoned for "threatening national security." While the group failed to collect one million signatures due to the repression against the organizers, the women did bring the issues of discrimination into the public sphere and contributed to some legal changes, including limiting a husband's right to prevent his wife from taking a job, creating a new marriage contract that gives women the right to divorce, and changing the inheritance law (traditionally a man was entitled to twice as much inheritance as a woman).

In 2016, the government cracked down on women's organizations that were promoting female candidates for the upcoming elections. Over a dozen activists based in Tehran were interrogated by Revolutionary Guards and threatened with imprisonment on the basis of national security.[131]

Despite the risks, women still organize. In May 2017, 180 prominent female journalists, intellectuals, and activists issued a public statement calling for greater female participation in economic life (doubling women's employment), repeal of discriminatory laws, more female sports, and a quota reserving at least 30 percent of cabinet positions for women.[132]

The struggle of Iranian women for equality and a more free society continues.

CHAPTER 7: THE IRANIAN ECONOMY AFTER DECADES OF SANCTIONS

Iran's economy is dependent on oil, but not to the extent of its oil-rich neighbors. It has a well-developed industrial sector and an agricultural sector that produces much of the food the nation consumes. A visitor to Iran will see fantastic bazaars and stores brimming with products both local and imported, with customers haggling over prices. But beneath the veneer of a bustling economy is a system wracked by decades of international sanctions, corruption, and mismanagement.

Even so, Iran is still the second largest economy in the Middle East, after Saudi Arabia. Its population of almost 80 million makes it the most populous nation the Middle East after Egypt, providing an enormous market. With its wealth of natural resources and educated population, even Goldman Sachs has asserted that Iran has the potential to become one of the world's largest economies.[133]

WHAT WAS THE ECONOMY LIKE UNDER THE YEARS OF THE MONARCHY?

The Pahlavi monarchy that ruled Iran from 1925 to 1979 transformed Iran from an agrarian nation into a booming industrial one that included both manufacturing and oil production. It also brought vast inequalities in wealth, corruption, a stark urban/rural divide, and Western corporate involvement that provoked social unrest.

Modern industrial plants jumped from a mere 20 in 1925 to over 800 by 1940. From the 1950s to the 1970s, increased revenue from oil allowed the regime to further expand industrial sectors and state institutions. But the modernization and focus on industry also led the monarchy to create monopolies and alienate the Iranian labor force that had been previously based in agriculture.

One of the issues that most infuriated the people was the fortunes of the royal family, gained through corruption, bribes, extortion from other businesses, and stealing from the national coffers. During the 53 years of the Pahlavi dynasty, the imperial family amassed billions of dollars. One Iranian economist estimated the assets of the entire royal family—which included 63 princes and princesses—at over $20 billion, a staggering sum in 1979.[134] Most of the wealth came from oil revenues from the National Iranian Oil Company, which the family siphoned off into their own Swiss bank accounts. The Pahlavi Foundation was supposedly a charity, but in reality it was an investment house representing the family's business interests. The foundation owned banks, hotels, casinos, construction firms, and trading companies. Members of the royal family, including the Shah's twin sister Princess Ashraf, were alleged to be deeply involved in the drug trade, exporting opium and hashish and importing heroin and cocaine.[135]

On the eve of the revolution, the economic division was stark. While the royal family traveled the European capitals in the lap of luxury, millions of displaced peasants had streamed into the cities, where they lived in decrepit shantytowns without basic services such as running water, electricity, garbage collection, health care, and education.[136] As these types of encampments increased, the government's solution was to declare them illegal and send bulldozers to destroy people's meager homes. Outside major cities like Tehran, conditions were even worse.

Literacy rose, but with 68 percent of adults illiterate and 60 percent of children not finishing primary school, Iran lagged behind other countries in the region. Iranian healthcare languished even farther behind its neighbors, with some of the highest infant mortality and lowest doctor-patient rates in the Middle East. Instead of addressing the housing shortages, poverty, and the gross socioeconomic inequality, the Pahlavi monarchy spent the majority of the country's budget on themselves, the military, and accommodating Iran's wealthy residents.

WHAT WERE THE ECONOMIC POSITIONS OF THE REVOLUTION?

Equity and social justice were among the proclaimed objectives of the revolution. The lofty goals were part of a quest for an Islamic utopia, where the state would eradicate the elite and establish the rule of the *mostazafan* (oppressed). The state was supposed to be the arbiter and guarantor that would lead to the end of deprivation and poverty.

The revolution was openly antagonistic toward big business and capitalists, especially those affiliated with foreign companies. This led to a major shift in ownership. Banks, insurance companies, and many manufacturing industries were nationalized. Large contracts for nuclear power plants, armaments, and military cooperation were cancelled.

In the early years, takeovers and expropriations of capitalist enterprises were widespread. Revolutionary Islamic Courts confiscated the assets of those found by the Islamic judges to be corrupt. Many businessmen fled the country or shuttered their businesses, and newly formed workers' councils took them over.

Iran's revolutionaries also wanted to disengage from foreign control and from the grip of meddling international institutions, such as the International Monetary Fund (IMF) and the World Bank.

Added to this revolutionary upheaval was the impact of sanctions. In response to the 1979 hostage crisis, the U.S. government froze $12 billion of Iranian government assets in the United States and U.S. banks overseas.

That's not all. A glut in the international oil market from 1985 to 1988 severely depressed prices. The oil boom of the 1970s had been adding over $20 billion a year to Iran's economy; by 1986 oil revenues sunk to less than six billion dollars.

With all these shocks, the economy was in freefall. The gross national product between 1979 and 1981 fell by 64 percent; private investment plummeted by 66 percent.[137]

Plagued by chaotic state-run policies, international sanctions, the enormous financial cost of the war with Iraq, and depressed oil prices, by the end of the Iraq war in 1988 the economic revolutionary project was declared defunct. The search for the Islamic utopia and the claim of establishing rule of the oppressed quietly faded. The Islamic Republic shifted from a populist-revolutionary state to a capitalist one, albeit a capitalist state with a strong state sector.

HOW HAS THE POPULATION FARED?

In the early years, the revolution improved the standard of living and quality of life for many of the nation's poor. Perhaps the greatest achievement was the expansion of educational opportunities, especially for rural families and for women, with increased access to free education from primary school to university. By 1998, the percentage of children in school rose from 60 percent to 90 percent. Another major achievement was improving access to basic services, like electricity, drinking water, and healthcare. One of the best measures of success was the plunge in infant mortality by 1988, dropping from 104 deaths to 25 per 1,000 births.

From the time of the revolution until the end of 2016, life expectancy jumped from 54 years to 75 years; schooling jumped from 9 years to 15 years.[138] But unemployment and inflation took their toll on the public's well-being. General unemployment in 2017 was over 12 percent, but youth unemployment was a staggering 30 percent. Underemployment was also rife.

The 50 percent plunge in the value of the rial in 2012 wiped out the savings of many middle class families. This dramatic devaluation was due mainly to oil and banking sanctions, but some also blamed it on the free-spending policies of President Ahmadinejad. Elected on the slogan "put the oil money on the *sofreh*" (the mat Iranians sit on to eat), President Ahmadinejad took a populist turn, expanding credit, providing cheap housing loans to the poor, and subsidizing gasoline.

These subsidies saddled the economy with an enormous annual bill of $100 billion. In 2010 the government eliminated the energy subsidies, but began a universal cash transfer program of about $40 per person per month to all Iranians, including children, to compensate for the elimination.

The policies fueled inflation just as sanctions began to have an impact.[139] According to one study, the percentage of Iranian families living in poverty increased during Ahmadinejad's term (from 2005 to 2013) from 22 percent to 40 percent.[140]

With the economic devastation caused by 2011 sanctions, workers have seen the value of their wages plummet. The government raised the minimum wage by 25 percent in 2013, but even official criteria deemed this new wage to be just one-third of a living wage for Tehran. A 2016 report by the Iranian parliament said the minimum monthly wage for workers was about $214, while the national poverty line was about $600 a month.

These economic hardships sparked the protests that spread throughout the country at the end of December 2017.

WHO CONTROLS THE NATION'S MAIN RESOURCES?

Iran has a vibrant agricultural sector, employing about 18 percent of workers, while some 34 percent of workers are employed in factories. Many of the rest—nearly one-third of the employed workforce—are self-employed in traditional occupations such as rug makers, carpenters, taxi and truck drivers, street vendors, and shopkeepers.

But most of Iran's economy—by some estimates as much as 60 percent—is in the hands of the state. While it is dominated by oil and gas, the state sector also includes all large-scale industry, foreign trade, major minerals, banking insurance, power generation, radio and television, telephone serves, aviation, shipping, and railroads. There is a significant cooperative sector that operates in accordance with sharia law.

The state sector also manufactures most of its own weapons, from aircraft to artillery to drones—some of which are reverse-engineered from captured U.S. models.

Out of necessity, the role of the private sector has been increasing. A 2003 constitutional amendment allowed 80 percent of state assets to be privatized. Between 2005 and 2010, the government sold half of its $120 billion assets. Many assets, however, were not really privatized since they ended up either in the hands of the Islamic Revolutionary Guard Corps, Iran's security force and the most powerful economic actor in the country, or with its affiliated corporations and religious charities.

The IRGC controls an enormous part of the nation's economy—by some estimates up to one third. Through a tangled web of subsidiaries and trusts, the IRGC has ties to over one hundred companies and an annual revenue of over $12 billion. It gets billions of dollars in no-bid contracts from the Ministry of Petroleum and from government infrastructure projects. It also runs the phone company, makes cars, and builds bridges and roads. Some allege that through its control of the border and ports, the IRGC is also involved in smuggling all types of good, including drugs.

Another unique feature of Iran's economy is the role of large, quasi-state, religious foundations, called *bonyads*. *Bonyads* are a consortium of over 120 tax-exempt organizations that get government subsidies and religious donations. They are under the control of the Supreme Leader. According to some estimates, they control over half the state budget and account for somewhere between 20 to 40 percent of the economy. They operate everything from farms to hotels to shipping lines, and are not subject to audits or the nation's accounting laws.

Established shortly after the revolution, the foundations confiscated billions of dollars in assets from the former royal family, banks, and elites who fled the country. Most of the foundations are exempt from taxes and are involved in activities ranging from trade and commerce to social services and cultural affairs. They have become some of the biggest economic powerhouses in the Middle East. Most of them are the individual fiefs of powerful clerics, and their size crowds out smaller private competitors who might be more efficient.

Seen as unfair competition with the other private businesses, these companies have a reputation of being corrupt, overstaffed, and only viable because of government support.

ARE TRADE UNIONS ALLOWED?

Iran's labor movement has a long history of defending workers' rights. Oil workers played a key role in overthrowing the Shah. After the revolution, a worker-friendly labor law was passed that guaranteed a 40-hour week and made it hard to lay off workers without proof of a serious offense. Employing personnel on consecutive six-month contracts to avoid paying benefits was deemed illegal.

But with the Iran-Iraq war, workers suffered. Conscripted, many young men fought and died on the front lines. Employment also plummeted, since much of the nation's infrastructure was destroyed, especially in the southwestern part of the country. The economic chaos of the early years also led to a crackdown on workers. Independent unions were destroyed, and labor disputes began to be settled by state-sponsored Islamic Labor Councils, which must be approved by employers and usually rule in favor of the employers.[141]

In 1997, temporary contracts were made legal, leading to the massive erosion of permanent positions. In 2002, businesses with under ten employees were deemed exempt from the labor law, further eroding workers' conditions. Employers try to keep their employees under ten so they can hire workers without contracts.

Iran is a member of the International Labor Organization (ILO), which calls for independent trade unions, but the unions that do exist are closely monitored by the state, including the official state union called the Workers' House. Strikes and work stoppages, mostly by transport, education, and factory workers, are common but illegal and often suppressed, including through the imprisonment of labor leaders.

During the reform era of President Khatami, there was a new wave of trade unionism, including by petrochemical workers, construction workers, sugarcane workers, teachers, and bus drivers, but even these were suppressed. In 2004, construction workers at a copper plant operated by a Chinese contractor held a strike calling on the company to fulfill its hiring promises. Security forces attacked the strikers, leaving four workers killed, 300 wounded, and many arrested.[142]

In 2005, workers at the Tehran Bus Company formed an independent union called the Vahed Bus Workers Union. A strike in 2005 led to the imprisonment of hundreds of bus drivers and their supporters. Soon after, a national teachers association (ITTA) was created, organizing strikes against low wages, and many other sectors began independent unions. But when President Ahmadinejad came to power in 2005, most of these union leaders were arrested. ITTA leader Esmail Abdi was sentenced to six years in prison for "distributing propaganda against the establishment" and "disrupting public order and security."

With the signing of the Iran nuclear deal and lifting of some sanctions, labor leaders perceived a new opportunity to organize. "Iran is very eager to attract European companies and do business with them, and this could be a chance for Iranian activists, since all EU companies are committed to guaranteeing responsible business behavior," said Hadi Ghaemi, executive director of the New York-based Center for Human Rights in Iran.[143]

WHAT IS THE ROLE OF OIL AND GAS?

Iran has about 10 percent of the world's proven oil reserves and 15 percent of its gas reserves. According to the U.S. Energy Information Administration, Iran has the world's second-largest natural gas reserves and the fourth-largest oil reserves. Oil exports contribute about 80 percent of the nation's public revenue.

The history of oil in Iran dates back to 1901, when British speculator William D'Arcy received a concession from the Iranian government giving him exclusive rights to prospect for oil. After searching for years without success in finding sellable amounts of oil, D'Arcy and team were about to go bankrupt when in 1908, a fifty-foot gusher of petroleum shot up the drilling rig, revealing such large quantities of oil that a new corporate structure was created to work the concession.[144] This led to the formation of the Anglo-Persian Oil Company and direct British control over Iranian oil fields.

In 1950, Iran attempted to nationalize the industry and created the National Iranian Oil Company, but three years later, U.S. and British intelligence agencies overthrew the Iranian prime minister committed to nationalization and reasserted their claim to half of the profits.[145]

The 1979 revolution brought a reversal of fortunes. Iran cut the international deals, and the state-owned NIOC took full control of the country's oil. Driven by the need for revenue during the exhausting Iran-Iraq war, Iran adopted a more aggressive approach to oil to maximize exports, investing billions to expand oil fields and export to Africa, Asia, and Europe.[146]

Despite efforts to diversify, Iran's economy remains dependent on oil and gas. When some international sanctions were lifted in January 2016, Iran was producing 1.5 million barrels of oil per day. Within five months, it had bumped up production to 2.6 million barrels per day, with plans to increase production to 5 million barrels per day by 2021.[147]

While this allowed foreign currency to flow in, it did little to create jobs because the oil sector is not labor-intensive.

WHAT HAVE BEEN THE EFFECTS OF SANCTIONS?

It's a wonder that the Iranian economy functions as well as it does, given the crippling restrictions it is been subjected to since the time of the 1979 revolution. Sanctions started with the U.S. Embassy hostage crisis, when the Carter administration banned Iranian oil imports, froze $12 billion in Iranian government assets in the United States, and imposed an embargo on travel to Iran. Some of these restrictions were lifted when the hostages were released, but the Reagan administration, after the 1983 bombing of a U.S. Marine compound in Lebanon, blocked World Bank loans to Iran and later banned all US imports from Iran.

Starting in 1995, the Clinton administration used sanctions to punish Iran for links to groups it defined as terrorists—Hezbollah, Hamas, and Palestinian Islamic Jihad. The administration placed a total trade and investment embargo on Iran. Congress went even further with a 1996 sanctions bill pressuring foreign companies to refrain from investing in Iran's oil and gas industry. In 2005, the Bush administration froze the assets of individuals and firms, including Russian and Chinese companies, that it deemed involved in Iran's "support for terrorism" and its nuclear and missile programs. It also prosecuted individuals and companies changed with selling weapons to Iran.

The Obama administration continued and intensified these sanctions. Congressional measures passed in 2010 targeted insurance companies that insured Iranian shipping, and squeezed the oil and gas sector further. Sanctions had already cobbled Iran's refineries, forcing this oil-rich nation to import 30 percent of its refined gasoline. New bans targeted non-U.S. firms supplying Iran with refined petroleum products.

Through the U.S. Treasury Department's Office of Foreign Assets Control, billions of dollars in penalties have been inflicted on U.S. branches of foreign-owned banks for sanctions violations. As a result, many banks adopted a "de-risking" strategy, refusing to conduct even permissible business with Iran for fear of coming under regulatory scrutiny. U.S. measures also greatly restricted the access of Iranian banks to the global financial system, as well as its Central Bank's access to its own $150 billion of foreign exchange money that the U.S. froze—funds that were only released after the nuclear deal was signed.

By 2010, other major European countries joined U.S. sanctions in a concerted effort to force Iran to cease its nuclear program. These crippling measures included a ban on dealings with Iran's Central Bank, a ban on imports of Iranian oil, and a ban on trade in gold, diamonds, and precious metals. In 2012, the European Union joined the U.S. effort to close off Iran's oil trade. The pressure further increased when Iranian banks were shut out of the SWIFT global electronic payments system.

A look at the website of the Treasury Department's Office of Foreign Assets Control shows the vast concoction of bureaucratic punishments the U.S. government cooked up over the years to squeeze Iran economically. They include 27 Executive Orders, 11 Statutes, 23 Interpretive Guidance documents.[148] They are meant to scare U.S. companies from even contemplating deals with Iran, but they are also meant to influence foreign companies around the globe.

Many Iranians interpreted these draconian measures not as a way to force a nuclear deal but as an insidious international plan to weaken Iran to the benefit of pro-Western governments in the region, like Israel and Saudi Arabia. President Ahmadinejad called them "the heaviest economic onslaught on a nation in history. Every day, all our banking and trade activities and our agreements are being blocked."[149]

An Iranian women's rights activist reflected, "The sanctions started 32 years ago. I don't know of any people who have suffered these kinds of sanctions over such a long period, except Palestinians and Cubans. They toppled our democratically elected government in 1953. After the revolution, they helped prolong the war with Iraq, and as such helped push the Iranian government to the right. I don't know what the West has gained from all this. I only ask: Why do they hate us so much?"[150]

One of the most difficult issues for businesses has been access to financing, especially for smaller businesses. Thousands of businesses were forced to close, leaving workers stranded. With a constrained economy and lack of investment, many educated Iranians left to seek employment abroad, leading to a brain drain among some of the nation's brightest young people.

Economic sanctions are blunt policy instruments that often harm the civilian population far more than the state. In the case of Iran, sanctions destroyed the purchasing power of ordinary citizens. Prices for food, rent, fuel, and other basic necessities rose steeply— by 100 percent in some instances. Despite subsidies intended to help the poor, in 2012 prices for staples such as milk, bread, yogurt, and vegetables doubled, prompting food riots. Middle class families began living on rice and beans. Many medicines for serious illnesses became scarce or prohibitively expensive. Theft, something rare in Iran, shot up. Imported goods became unaffordable, and the government was forced to embark on an emergency campaign to substitute imports with domestic production.

Sanctions have also led to greater corruption. In 2016, Transparency International ranked Iran among the world's more corrupt countries, with a rating of 131 out of 176 nations.[151] Often the only way to get basic goods is through the black market, so government entities and businesses that control the black market reap windfall profits. Paying bribes to get access to scarce goods or to reduce taxes, fees, and custom duties became routine. And the hardline Islamic Revolutionary Guards Corps, with its unfair advantages over private businesses, gained control over vast sectors of the country's economy. This also means that, while one of the goals of sanctions is to weaken the government, sanctions actually strengthen the government's hand vis-a-vis the public. People become more dependent on the government for their economic survival.

Sanctions and corruption have also led to a yawning wealth gap between the rich and the poor that mirrors the pre-revolutionary society of haves and have-nots. When Mahmoud Ahmadinejad was president, he complained that 60 percent of the nation's wealth was controlled by just 300 people. Luxury apartments and fancy cars line the streets in the wealthy neighborhoods in North Tehran while families cram together in small, rented rooms in the poorer South Tehran. In the rural areas, especially areas depleted from drought, the poverty is even worse,

Another insidious, little-known effect of sanctions has been the environmental impact. Not only was Iran barred from selling its crude oil, but it was also barred from importing refined gasoline. This forced the country to quickly come up with a way to refine its own oil. The result was poor-quality oil, leading to tremendous air pollution in the cities and skyrocketing deaths from respiratory diseases. In Tehran, the days of "healthy air" dropped from 300 days in 2009 to 150 days in 2011.[152] Air quality got so bad that there were days the capital city had to be shut down for people's safety and health. As one reporter quipped, "No longer are Iranians merely suffering from the economic effects of wide-ranging international sanctions; they are literally choking to death from them."[153]

There is one silver lining from these decades of economic strangulation: a focus on self-reliance. Cut off from the outside, the government's call for a "resistance economy" has promoted decades of local development and diversification. Iranian researchers and entrepreneurs have stepped in to fill the thousands of voids, showing the remarkable creativity and skill of the Iranian people. It has also helped preserve Iranian culture. Without a Starbucks on every corner, local tea shops thrive; without U.S. fast food chains, Iranians continue to appreciate their delicious Persian cuisine. There are pseudo-American chains like Pizza Hat and Kabooki Fried Chicken, but the restaurants are locally owned and operated.

DID SANCTIONS BRING IRAN TO THE NEGOTIATING TABLE?

The short answer is "not really."

The common assumption in the U.S. is that the pressure of sanctions forced a crippled Iran to cry uncle and make a deal. President Obama offered up this narrative, as did his staff—and even detractors of the diplomatic initiatives.[154] The reality, however, is more complex.

What most of the argument ignores is that the Iranians played their own pressure track as well. In what could be described as a game of diplomatic chicken, the Iranians met pressure with pressure by accelerating their nuclear program.[155] From 2009, when Obama's first attempt at a negotiated settlement failed, to 2013, when talks finally bore fruit, the number of Iranian centrifuges and the amount of enriched uranium increased dramatically. The nation's technological know-how became so advanced that they were less than three months away from having enough fissile material for a bomb.[156]

So the fact that the Iranians had accelerated their program in response to the sanctions would suggest that the sanctions achieved the opposite of their intended objective.

Several other points also bear noting. First, implying that sanctions brought Iran to the table ignores the fact that Iran was already at the table. Negotiations had been ongoing since 2009, albeit in fits and starts and with little to no progress. Nonetheless, Iran had already committed to talks. The team around President Rouhani, particularly Foreign Minister Javad Zarif, had displayed a willingness to engage diplomatically. Zarif was already engaged with the United States in another diplomatic initiative, helping to bring together the various factions within Afghanistan for the signing of the Bonn Agreement.

The problem was not Iran's willingness to negotiate, but the terms of the negotiations. It was only after Obama recognized Iran's right to enrich that progress was made. After years of frustrations and talking over each other with regurgitated demands, Obama finally relented. But so did the Iranians. They allowed for a robust and invasive inspections regime led by the International Atomic Energy Agency, and they agreed to limits on enrichment. Thus, compromise was the final push needed to get an agreement.

In the end, no single element made the deal a success. This isn't to deny that sanctions hurt the Iranians, they did. But they weren't the decisive factor bringing the Iran to the table or creating the conditions for the agreement signed on July 14, 2015 between the six countries involved in the talks.

WHAT HAPPENED AFTER THE SIGNING OF THE NUCLEAR DEAL?

Some $100 billion in frozen assets were released after the completion of the nuclear deal, which went mostly to pay outstanding debts and modernize the oil industry and the air fleet. Other sanctions, however, remained. Those were sanctions imposed in response to Iran's missile program and sanctions in opposition to Iran's ties with groups like Hamas and Hezbollah. So while Iran did reap some benefit from the lifting of nuclear-related sanctions, it was not as much as expected. Many Iranians felt cheated by the deal, as their lives failed to improve. In a January 2017 poll, 73 percent of Iranians said the nuclear deal had not improved their living conditions.[157]

At the end of December 2017, the economic dissatisfaction erupted in protests that roiled the country for several weeks. The demonstrators voiced their discontent over cuts in government subsidies, economic mismanagement, corruption, and wealth inequality. While the government managed to crush the uprising, it felt the heat and new economic reforms may well be in the offing.

The government is hoping that economic relief might come with the inking of several major deals with foreign companies anxious to get a foothold in such a potentially enormous market. One such deal is with the American company Boeing and its European competitor Airbus, a deal to sell up to 140 commercial planes. The Iranian government is desperate to upgrade its aging civilian fleet. The wear and tear from operating the same planes for decades, and the inability to buy spare parts, has led to plane crashes and the deaths of hundreds of passengers. But President Trump might scuttle the deal, a deal that Boeing says would support up to 118,000 American jobs.

Another major investment involves the French energy giant Total. In July 2017, Total announced its plan to invest $1 billion in Iran to develop the giant South Pars gas field, the largest natural gas field in the world. This was the biggest deal by a Western energy company in Iran in more than a decade. Royal Dutch Shell also signed several memorandums of understanding for projects in Iran.

The French carmaker PSA had been heavily invested in Iran since the 1960s. At that time it claimed almost 30 percent of Iran's car market. Under the weight of international sanctions, it was forced to pull out in 2011. With the easing of restrictions in 2016, it re-entered the market, committing $320 million to manufacture Citroen cars in Iran. In the meantime, however, Chinese rivals had grabbed up a good chunk of the car market.[158]

India has been one of Iran's most reliable trading partners. In 2017, a consortium of Indian businesses announced it would offer up to $11 billion to develop another of Iran's natural gas fields. Iran is the second-largest supplier of crude oil to India, and India is one of the largest foreign investors in Iran's oil and gas industry. However, international restrictions have impacted these investments as well. With U.S. banking restrictions still in place in 2018, India could not trade with Iran in dollars and had to revert to payments in rupees or euros.

WHAT ABOUT IRAN'S ECONOMIC RELATIONSHIP WITH CHINA?

During a decade of international restrictions, Western companies dealing in everything from oil to communications to cars had been replaced by Chinese ones. China became Iran's number one investor and trade partner. Iranian streets soon overflowed with Chinese consumer products.

For Iranian leaders, China represents an important outlet for international trade and finance. For China, Iran is a vital transport and logistics hub. China is providing $1.8 billion to establish a high-speed rail connection linking key Iranian cities of Tehran, Qom, and Isfahan, and another $1.5 billion to electrify the rail line from Tehran to the city of Mashad. In exchange, Iran is slashing transit tariffs for Chinese goods. The Iranian route from Tehran to the east will be part of China's 3,200 kilometer New Silk Road rail link that starts in China's western Xinjiang province and ends in the Iranian capital, connecting Kazakhstan, Kyrgyzstan, Uzbekistan, and Turkmenistan along the way.

China also became a key source of weapons and nuclear technology. But the Chinese, too, have been subjected to U.S. pressure, and Iranians have complained of Chinese failures to deliver on promised deals. Iranian producers also complained that cheap Chinese imports undercut local manufacturing. Iranian leaders have also been wary of relying too much on China and have been trying to work with a greater spectrum of foreign companies.

*****

Despite these major deals, foreign investment has fallen short of anticipated levels. The uncertainly about sanctions and the nuclear deal made international banks reluctant to finance projects and companies jittery abut the risks posed by investing in Iran.

The Trump administration and the U.S. Congress continue to destabilize Iran's economy. Instead of lifting restrictions, they impose new ones. The Trump administration argues that strengthening the Iranian economy by lifting sanctions just shores up the regime and its support for groups such as Hezbollah and Hamas. But European nations and human rights advocates argue that supporting Iran's economy is the best way to boost political moderates. They also argue that integrating Iran into the global economy creates incentives for the country to abide by the nuclear agreement and to reduce tensions in the region.

A similar debate has been occurring inside Iran. Political and religious hardliners have opposed opening up the nation's economy to foreign capital, especially to Western businesses. These conservatives have reaped the benefits of controlling the nation's key industries and have much to lose from a more open economy.

On the other side is President Rouhani and his supporters, who want more international investment, especially from the West. Most Iranians support the opening as well, but not if the benefits remain in the pockets of the elites.

In any case, the government is under intense internal pressure to improve the economy and spread the gains. The very future of the regime rests on its ability to deliver more economic benefits to the working class and the urban middle class, and to create more job oppportunities for the nation's restless youth.

CHAPTER 8: IRAN'S RELATIONS WITH THE US AND THE WEST

Iran has a long history of interacting with the rest of the world—initially as the various empires discussed in earlier chapters, and now as the Islamic Republic. The resentment and suspicion of foreign interference found in the Iranian political culture are a direct result of historic deals with foreigners that took power away from the local elites, including *bazaaris* and the *clerics*.

Through the 1800s to the early half of the 1900s, Russia and Britain were the main foreign interventionist forces and therefore became the focus of the public's vitriol. As the 20th century evolved, the United States began playing a larger role in Iran, due primarily to Cold War dynamics. As American policy in Iran came to resemble the earlier Russian and British imperial policies, anger towards the United States grew. That resentment boiled over and was a key factor in the 1979 revolution.

HOW AND WHEN DID THE U.S. BECOME THE FOCAL POINT FOR IRAN'S INTERACTIONS WITH THE WEST?

Starting in the 1830s, American missionaries began arriving in Iran, but it would take another 20 years before there would be any official diplomatic recognition between the two nations. That came in 1856 with the signing of a Treaty of Commerce and Navigation. Even then, the U.S. role remained minimal.

Iran really became important to the United States after World War II, in the context of the burgeoning Cold War with the Soviets. During World War II, the Allies had agreed to leave Iran six months after the war ended. Yet after victory was finally sealed in September 1945, U.S. and British forces left Iran within the agreed timeframe, but Soviet forces remained, expanding their areas of control and supporting local Kurdish and Azeri separatists.

The Shah secured U.S. support to push the Soviets out by painting the crisis in Cold War colors. U.S. diplomatic pressure and Iranian negotiations were successful in demanding a Soviet withdrawal. In 1947, Iran was included in the Truman Doctrine, the policy established by President Truman that said the United States would use its economic, political, and military power to contain Soviet threats anywhere in the world. As Iran became increasingly critical to blocking Soviet expansion, American support for Iran's monarchy increased.

The U.S. alliance with Iran came crashing down in 1953, however, when the recently inaugurated American President Dwight D. Eisenhower approved CIA plans to overthrow the government of elected Prime Minister Mohammad Mossadegh, who had incurred the wrath of both British and American oil companies and governments by nationalized oil fields. Once Mossadegh was deposed, the U.S. became the main ally of the new Shah and helped to develop the Iranian military and infamous secret police.

For many Iranians, this was the moment that the U.S. went from friend to foe. Originally thought to be a supporter of Iran's movement towards democracy, the U.S. had instead orchestrated a coup. This resentment would be one of the major driving forces, 25 years later, when a popular protest movement ultimately overthrew the U.S.-backed Shah. It also lies at the very foundation of the current government's anti-Americanism.

As the CIA's first successful covert operation to overthrow a government that refused to bend to U.S. economic and political interests, the overthrow of Mossadegh also became a model for similar operations around the globe, such as the overthrow of Guatemalan President Arbenz in 1954, Congolese Prime Minister Patrice Lumuba in 1960, and the failed intervention in Cuba in 1961.

HOW DID THE REVOLUTION AFFECT THE U.S. RELATIONSHIP?

America's role in ousting Mossadegh vaulted it to the top of Iran's most-hated list, a position once held by the Russians and the British. The United States became the focus for the anti-imperialists within Iran.

Tensions ran high in 1963 when the U.S. and Iran signed a Status of Forces Agreement (SOFA) that gave Americans immunity from punishment under the law. This meant that all American personnel accused of wrongdoing in Iran, including the large number of U.S. military personnel who were training the Shah's military forces, would be free from prosecution by Iranian authorities.

A relatively minor cleric at the time, Ayatollah Ruhollah Khomeini, used this agreement to speak out against the Shah and the United States. He gave a famous speech decrying that in the eyes of the Shah and his American allies, Iranians were worth less than American dogs.[159] The Shah responded by forcing Khomeini into exile in 1964.

Over the years, anti-Shah and anti-U.S. tensions continued to mount. Both the U.S. State Department and intelligence services missed the writing on the wall, underestimating the breadth and depth of the opposition. In one evaluation, six months prior to the 1979 revolution, the CIA reported that "Iran is not in a revolutionary or even pre-revolutionary situation."[160]

U.S. President Jimmy Carter seemed oblivious to the changing landscape. After pressuring the Shah to improve his human rights record, President Carter visited Iran in late December 1977. During a New Year's toast, Carter described Iran as "an island of stability in one of the most troublesome regions in the world."[161] In the same speech, he talked about how popular the Shah was among Iranians. In a little over a year, the Shah was ousted from power.

Shortly after the Shah fled, Ayatollah Khomeini, who had been the main face of the growing opposition movement, returned from exile in France. Despite Khomeini's anti-American rhetoric, some U.S. officials felt it was necessary to meet with the new revolutionary government. As 1979 progressed, however, anti-American sentiment grew, especially when President Carter allowed the Shah to enter the U.S. as a "private citizen" to receive cancer treatment. The Shah's presence in the United States was seen by many Iranians as a disgrace and an insult that ignored the enormous pain and suffering they had endured under his rule, with the approval of the U.S. government.

For Iran's revolutionaries, many of whom blamed the US for the 1953 coup, Carter's decision was a clear signal that the Shah was planning a counter-revolution with America's help.[162] They wanted the Shah extradited, tried, and executed for his crimes against the Iranian population. The revolutionaries did not get their wish, but they did find a new target—the U.S. Embassy.

HOW AND WHY DID THE TAKEOVER OF THE U.S. EMBASSY HAPPEN?

Originally planned as a sit in, on November 4, 1979, students climbed the fences and stormed the U.S. Embassy compound. Ransacking offices and detaining embassy personnel, their radical actions surprised both the U.S. government and Iran's provisional government. Khomeini originally backed a plan to forcibly remove the protesters from the embassy, but then endorsed their actions once he realized he could use the seizure to solidify power. The revolution had risked spiraling out of control as the various factions were openly clashing in the streets. The embassy seizure was a symbolic way to synergize around a cause while also showing that Iran could stand up for itself. The provisional government resigned due to its disapproval of the takeover.

Fifty-two American diplomats were held hostage for 444 days. This act marked a breaking point in relations between Iran and the United States. Diplomatic relations were severed and have officially been frozen ever since. Americans saw the takeover as a breach of the one inviolable law governing relations between countries—the sanctity of embassies. The revolutionaries viewed it as a way to prevent a counter-coup and to hit back at decades of foreign interference in Iran's internal affairs.

Attempts at negotiating for the release of the hostages were stymied by Ayatollah Khomeini's prohibition on speaking to American officials and a lack of overall stability within Iran. With Khomeini's goals of crushing other factions and solidifying power, settling with the U.S. was not in the cards. If he had negotiated, he would have gone against his own narrative. Meanwhile, the U.S. could not adopt a policy of patience, since Carter was in the middle of a re-election campaign. And what country is patient when their diplomats are being held hostage?

As the domestic pressure on President Carter mounted, in April 1980 he approved an ill-fated rescue attempt called Operation Eagle Claw. It failed in large part because a severe desert sandstorm caused several helicopters to collide as they were taking off for Tehran. Eight American servicemen were killed, and the operation was aborted.

Just a few months later, the Shah, Mohammad Reza Pahlavi, died of cancer. Khomeini responded by tasking his subordinates with finding a solution to the hostage crisis.

In the middle of negotiations to release the hostages, Iraq invaded Iran, delaying talks until November 1980. By the time an agreement was signed, Carter had already lost the presidential election to Ronald Reagan. In a slap in the face to President Carter, Khomeini delayed the release of the hostages until the day Ronald Reagan was sworn into office.

For many older Americans, the lens through which they view Iran is still tinted by the hostage crisis. Each night, from the very beginning of the crisis, the U.S. press updated the public on the status of the hostages and efforts to get them released. Every night for 444 days, Ted Koppel's ABC News special *America Held Hostage: The Iran Crisis* (which later became *Nightline*) reminded Americans that Iranians had kidnapped their diplomats. But for many Iranians, the U.S. history of violating their sovereignty outweighs their responsibility for the hostage crisis.

WHAT POSITION DID THE U.S. TAKE DURING THE 1980–88 IRAN-IRAQ WAR?

Officially, the United States remained neutral during the war that broke out in 1980 after Iraq invaded Iran, but, in reality, it was arming both sides. Shortly after taking office in 1981, the Reagan administration secretly worked with Israel to ship several billion dollars of American weapons to Iran, despite the U.S. embargo against such sales. Then in 1982, when the CIA warned Reagan that Iraq was on the verge of being beaten on the battlefield by Iran, the U.S. government secretly provided Iraq with highly classified intelligence, including on Iranian troop movements, and covertly shipped American weapons to Iraq.[163] Basically, the United States was arming both sides so that neither side would dominate this key oil region. By 1983, however, the U.S. began to favor Iraq, turning a blind eye while U.S. arms dealers sold sophisticated Soviet arms to Iraqi strongman Saddam Hussein.

Even worse, the Reagan administration sold Iraq biological agents, including anthrax, and vital ingredients for chemical weapons—all the while knowing that the Iraqi leader Saddam Hussein was regularly using these horrific weapons against the Iranian people and against his own Iraqi citizens. The 1983 photo of Middle East envoy Donald Rumsfeld shaking hands with Saddam Hussein is chilling. Years later, in 2003, the U.S. government used the very biological weapons it sold Hussein as a pretext to invade Iraq. A morbid joke at that time had George W. Bush saying, "We know Saddam Hussein has chemical weapons—we have the receipts."

WHY DID THE U.S. SHOOT DOWN AN IRANIAN AIRBUS IN 1988?

During the brutal eight years of the Iran-Iraq war, Iraq and then Iran used air attacks to target foreign tankers transporting each other's oil exports through the Persian Gulf. This led the U.S. and other nations to deploy warships to protect their tankers in international waters.

On July 3, 1988, a terrible tragedy occurred: U.S. personnel on the warship *USS Vincennes* shot down a commercial passenger airline, Iran Air Flight 655, which was flying along its official route from Tehran to Dubai. All 290 people on board—274 passengers and 16 crew—were killed.

According to the U.S. government, this was a regrettable accident. The crew incorrectly identified the Iranian Airbus A300 as an attacking F-14 Tomcat fighter.

Most Iranians, however, believed it was a deliberate war crime. This belief was reinforced when the U.S. government tried to mislead the world about the details of the incident. It made a series of false claims that the plane was not on a normal flight path but was diving toward the ship rather than climbing after taking off from Bandar Abbas airport in southern Iran; that its identification transponder was not working or had been altered; and that the *Vincennes* was either rushing to the aid of a merchant ship or pursuing hostile Iranian patrol boats.

Months before the plane was shot down, air traffic controllers and the crews of other warships in the Persian Gulf had been warning that poorly trained U.S. crews, especially the gung-ho captain and crew of the *Vincennes* (or "Robocruiser," as other crews had nicknamed it), were constantly misidentifying civilian aircrafts over the Persian Gulf, making this horrific massacre entirely predictable.

Adding insult to injury when, two years later, the U.S. Navy awarded combat medals to the warship's captain and crew. The town of Vincennes, Indiana, for which the ship was named, even launched a fundraising campaign for a monument. The monument was not to remember the tragedy or the Iranians killed, but to honor the ship and its crew.

In 1996, in response to an Iranian lawsuit at the International Court of Justice, the U.S. agreed to a settlement, granting $213,000 per passenger to the victim's families. But the U.S. government still refused to formally apologize or acknowledge wrongdoing.

While most Americans have no memory of this incident, in Iran the date of the deaths of 290 Iranian citizens at the hands of the U.S. military is marked every year just as the 9/11 attack is remembered every year in the United States. To some Iranians, it is just one more example of the callousness of U.S. policy.

WAS IRAN INVOLVED IN 1983 MARINE BOMBING?

Another incident that has impacted U.S.-Iranian relations was the bombing in 1983 of the U.S. Marine barracks in Beirut, Lebanon that killed 241 U.S. service personnel. The explosion came from a truck bomb at the compound. There were 1,800 Marines stationed in Beirut at the time as part of a multinational peacekeeping force. The bombing was traced to the Iranian-affiliated militia group, Hezbollah, and the U.S. accused Iran of being behind the attack. In April 2016, the U.S. Supreme Court ruled that frozen Iranian bank assets could be used to pay $1.75 billion to the survivors and family members of those killed. As of early 2018, however, those funds have still not been disbursed to the families.

WHAT WAS THE IRAN-CONTRA AFFAIR? HOW DID THAT AFFECT THE RELATIONSHIP?

Even though the U.S. and Iran did not have official relations after 1979, there were still points of engagement. In most cases, these have been one-off affairs and limited in scope.

One of the earliest such cases was the issue known as the Iran-Contra Affair. Starting in 1985, only a few years after the U.S. Embassy hostages were released and ties officially severed, Iran, the U.S., and Israel found themselves entangled in an illegal, secret web of confusion, misaligned interests, and shady middlemen.

Enmeshed in a brutal war with Iraq, Iran was in dire need of spare parts for its military, but there was a U.S. embargo on selling arms to Iran. At the same time, the Reagan administration was anxious to bring home seven Americans being held hostage in Lebanon by Hezbollah, a paramilitary group with ties to Iran. Despite the American position that it would never negotiate with hostage takers, the Reagan administration decided to sell weapons to Iran in exchange for Iran's help in freeing the U.S. hostages.

Given the illegality of selling weapons to Iran, however, the Israelis were brought in as go-betweens. Their job was to ship weapons to Iran, and then the U.S. would resupply Israel.

This scheme became even more complicated when U.S. Marine Lt. Colonel Oliver North of the National Security Council became involved in late 1985. He modified the plan so that a portion of the proceeds from the weapon sales to Iran would be diverted to fund the "Contras," an armed rebel group in Nicaragua that was trying to overthrow the leftist Sandinistas. There was a congressional prohibition on arming the Contras, so this was an attempt to subvert the prohibition.

This sordid affair now involved violating one congressional order against arms sales to Iran, then using the proceeds from that illegal operation to fund a project violating another congressional order banning the provision of arms to the Contras. Both acts breached the constitution.

The scheme was doomed from the start. When the first weapons shipment arrived in Iran, only one of the seven American hostages in Lebanon was released. The Iranians realized that it was in their best interest to slow walk their obligations so they could maintain the flow of weapons and spare parts. With two subsequent shipments, two more hostages were released, but two more hostages were taken. The U.S., for its part, sent old weapons and never agreed to send enough to alter the outcome of the Iran-Iraq war. Both sides were playing each other and had arrived at an impasse.

U.S. officials covertly traveled to Iran to work out a new deal but were blindsided when reports of the meeting were leaked to the media and made worldwide headlines.[164] "Arms for Hostages" did not make good PR for either side, and all negotiations ceased.

America's PR nightmare became even worse when it was revealed that proceeds from the weapons sales were used to purchase arms for the Nicaraguan Contras in flagrant violation of U.S. law.[165] Fourteen of Reagan's aides were indicted, including the Secretary of Defense and two national security advisors, and 11 were convicted. Reagan's presidency was tarnished by the sordid affair, and it was a further setback for U.S.-Iranian relations. None of the 14 went to jail, and President George H.W. Bush, who was vice president under Reagan, pardoned all of them in his final days in office.

WHAT SHIFTS TOOK PLACE IN THE 1990S?

In the waning days of the 1980s, Iran and Iraq agreed to a ceasefire, and Ayatollah Khomeini passed away. There was hope that the subsequent increase in trade between Iran and the U.S., coupled with the new Supreme Leader Ayatollah Ali Khamenei, would lead to improved relations. U.S. hostages were still being held in Lebanon, but Iran seemed more amenable to working for their release. Additionally, Saddam Hussein's decision to invade Kuwait in 1990 lent more credibility to Iran's assertion that he was the aggressor during their eight-year war.

When President Reagan's vice president, George H.W. Bush, was elected to succeed him, Bush seemed like a candidate who could help lead the détente. In his inaugural address, he promised to "reciprocate goodwill with goodwill." Iranian President Akbar Hashemi Rafsanjani saw this as a positive sign that the Americans were willing to take concrete steps to improve their relationship. To test their resolve, Rafsanjani pulled the necessary strings to have the Americans held hostage in Lebanon released. But the Bush administration reneged on its offer to meet goodwill with goodwill, damaging the potential for rapprochement.

Cooperation with Iran did occur during the 1991 Gulf War, when the U.S.-led Operation Desert Storm pushed Iraq out of Kuwait. While not directly joining the fight against Iraq, the Iranians allowed coalition airplanes overflight rights. After the war, Iran tried to build a Gulf-based security coalition that could provide regional stability.

The Bush administration, however, had its own plans. It organized a conference to discuss the future of the region, but did not invite Iran. Naturally, the Iranians saw this as yet another example of U.S. double dealing.

The decision to leave Iran out of the conference was largely due to Israeli pressure. The Israelis had been worried about rapprochement between Iran and the United States. Israel considered Iran a threat not because it was militarily dangerous, but because economically it provided a bigger potential market for U.S. goods and businesses than Israel. The Israelis worried that U.S.-Iran détente would mean Israel would lose its special relationship with the U.S.

Leaving the Iranians out of the regional security apparatus also meant that Iran was free to be the spoiler. Tehran did just that, embarking on a policy to make the U.S. decision to isolate Iran as costly as possible. Many of the problems in the region today stem from the Bush White House's decision to isolate Iran.

After Bush lost his re-election bid and Bill Clinton moved into the Oval Office, not much changed in the adversarial relationship between the two nations. The Israeli government continued to play a large role in preventing the U.S. from reaching out to Iran, convincing the Clinton administration of the need to contain both Iraq's Saddam Hussein and Iran's Islamic government. This policy, known as dual containment, was a shift from previous strategies that sought to balance one with the other.

The Clinton administration had also become preoccupied with the peace process between Israel and Palestine. In an effort to move that forward, the Clinton White House caved to Israeli pressure aimed at targeting Iran. Initially this was in language only, utilizing the now commonplace phrases of "state sponsor of terrorism" and "ardent opponent of the peace process" to describe the Iranian government. But more importantly, Israel pushed for tougher sanctions on Iran.

The Iranians had offered Conoco, an American oil company, a lucrative oil field concession in 1995. It was a significant move, heavy with symbolism. The Clinton administration was aware of the ongoing negotiations between Conoco and the Iranian government. Within a month of the deal being announced, however, the pro-Israel lobby was out in full force in Washington working to squash it. Pressured by this powerful lobby and its allies in Congress, Clinton once again caved to Israeli demands. By issuing two executive orders prohibiting trade with Iran, he essentially snuffed out Conoco's hard-earned deal. Congress, not to be outdone in their anti-Iran efforts, went one step further and codified those executive orders by passing the Iran-Libya Sanctions Act in 1996. The sanctions effectively blocked any effort to improve relations with Iran.

The Iranians were incensed and responded by attacking the Israeli peace process. Tehran began building relationships with Palestinian militant organizations. Since the revolution, Iran had only verbally attacked Israel, never actually following through with their threats. But as Israel spearheaded efforts to isolate Iran, Iranian rhetoric turned to action, further jeopardizing U.S.-Iranian détente.

The 1990s saw hopes of rapprochement dashed by both the Bush and Clinton administrations. Under heavy pro-Israel lobbying and still nursing old wounds from the hostage crisis, both

Democrats and Republicans joined the anti-Iran bandwagon. But it was also in the 1990s that the U.S. and European stances toward Iran began to diverge, with the Europeans favoring détente and economic cooperation. After Congress passed the 1996 Sanctions Act, countries in the European Union protested and continued to do business with Iran.

HOW DID 9/11 AFFECT IRAN'S RELATIONS WITH THE WEST?

The George W. Bush administration had been in office less than eight months in 2001 when the 9/11 terror attacks occurred, attacks that fundamentally changed the region and its relationship with the United States. One might think that 9/11 would have shifted the U.S. alliance from Saudi Arabia to Iran, given that 15 of the 19 hijackers were Saudis and that the attacks were perpetrated by Al Qaeda, a Sunni-based extremist group whose fundamentalist ideology is based on the Saudi's Wahhabist version of Islam. Iran, on the other hand, is a Shia country that had no ties to Al Qaeda.

Moreover, the 9/11 attacks were planned in Afghanistan, where Al Qaeda leadership lived under the protection of the Taliban. Since the mid-1990s, the Iranians had been fighting the Taliban, primarily by assisting their adversaries, the Northern Alliance.

Iranians, both the government and the public, were also very sympathetic towards the United States after the attack. Unlike the celebrations in some Arab nations, where people saw the attacks on the U.S. as a well-deserved blow to Israel's main supporter, Iranians poured into the streets to hold candlelight vigils.[166] Iran's political leaders expressed their condolences and thought the attack might result in a warming of U.S.-Iranians relations. When the Bush administration declared war on the Sunni fundamentalist Taliban regime in Afghanistan that had not only harbored Al Qaeda but had murdered Iranian diplomats, the Iranian government offered assistance. As before, however, the U.S. was reluctant to accept Iran's help, in large part due to continued Israeli pressure.

The U.S. forces invaded Afghanistan, toppled the Taliban from power and pushed Al Qaeda's networks into Pakistan. President Bush then needed a plan to rebuild Afghanistan, and it was here that the Iranians offered assistance. Iran's extensive knowledge of Afghanistan and the connections it had made by backing the anti-Taliban alliance was of enormous help in getting all sides together in Bonn, Germany to try to work out an agreement for an interim government.

James Dobbins, the U.S. special envoy to Afghanistan at the time, described the tense gathering in Bonn, where the disparate factions had reached an impasse. Everything was about to fall apart until the intervention by the Iranian representative Javad Zarif, the same person who 14 years later negotiated the Iran nuclear deal. Zarif talked privately to the Northern Alliance delegate, who then compromised and saved the day. "It was indicative that Iran was collaborating quite constructively with the United States and with the rest of the international community to assure a positive outcome of the conference," Dobbins said.[167]

At the international donors' conference to help rebuild Afghanistan, Iran also played a positive role, pledging a staggering $500 million in assistance—the same amount as the United States. Iran was so eager to continue helping that it even offered to pay to rebuild the Afghan Army, an offer the U.S. refused.[168] Iranian officials were also helpful in extraditing Al Qaeda fighters who had fled Afghanistan and were living in Iran.

Inside the George W. Bush White House, debates were raging about whether to continue collaborating with Iran. The discussions came to a crashing halt when President Bush, in his fateful January 29, 2002 State of the Union address, called Iran part of the "axis of evil."

Bush's speech undercut any movement for positive relations with Iran. Iranian reformists who had lobbied to engage the United States felt betrayed and were throttled by both Bush's rebuke and condemnation from hardliners inside Iran. The opportunity to improve U.S.-Iranian relations in the wake of the 9/11 attacks had been torpedoed by conservative, pro-Israel U.S. politicians.

HOW DID THE 2003 U.S. INVASION OF IRAQ AFFECT RELATIONS?

Then came the U.S.-led invasion of Iraq in March 2003. The Iranian government was delighted to see Saddam Hussein's regime attacked; after all, the Iraqi leader had invaded Iran in 1980 and was responsible for the deaths of hundreds of thousands of Iranians. Iraq was also a majority Shia country where the Shia had been brutally persecuted under Saddam Hussein, and Iran had a long history of supporting its Shia brethren. But the speed with which the U.S. military overthrew Saddam Hussein, doing in three weeks what Iran could not do in eight years of war with Iraq, worried Iran's political leadership. They wanted to make sure that any new Iraqi government would not be a threat to Iran's security.

Initially, Iran held off from sowing seeds of discord. In fact, via Swiss intermediaries, the Iranians sent a proposal to the U.S. State Department laying out the terms of a "grand bargain." It was, in essence, a bold peace treaty that put everything on the table. It offered to negotiate nearly every issue the U.S. had been concerned with—Iran's nuclear program, support for Palestinian militant groups, policy in Iraq, and accepting Israel's right to exist. In return, the U.S. would have to give up hostile behavior towards Iran, end economic sanctions, allow access to peaceful nuclear technology, clampdown on the terrorist group MEK, and acknowledge Iran's security interests.

The Bush administration, elated by its quick victory in defeating Saddam Hussein and believing that regime change in Iran could come next, saw no need to negotiate, and even rebuked the Swiss for playing the role of intermediary. Iran's offer never even received a reply.

The hubris of the Bush officials made them believe their quick success in toppling Saddam Hussein signaled the long-term viability of their agenda to create a new, pro-Western, stable government in Iraq. Instead, their refusal to negotiate with Iran hurt U.S. chances of controlling events on the ground in Iraq. It also sent a message to the hardliners in Iran that the only way to force the United States to treat Iran as a sovereign nation was to be a thorn in its side. That's when Iran began funding, training, and equipping Shia militias inside Iraq.

The first Iraqi election, which took place one year after the U.S. government's pro-consul Paul Bremer had been running the country, put Prime Minister Nouri Maliki in office. Maliki had spent much time in Iran during Saddam Hussein's dictatorship, and his first trip as prime minister was to Tehran. From 2005 onward, successive Iraqi governments have had expensive ties with Iran, much to the consternation of U.S. officials.

HOW DID THE EUROPEANS AFFECT U.S.-IRANIAN NEGOTIATIONS?

In June 2003, just months after the U.S. invasion of Iraq, the U.K., Germany, and France launched a diplomatic effort to address their growing concern about Iran's nuclear policy. The U.S. refused to join the talks. A few months later, the parties reached an agreement known as the Tehran Declaration, where Iran agreed to fully cooperate with the International Atomic Energy Agency (IAEA) and to suspend all uranium enrichment. For the Iranians, they felt the negotiations with the Europeans were a prelude to deeper talks that would include the U.S., but the U.S. was not interested. The buzz phrase in the Bush White House was "we don't talk to evil."[169]

By 2005, the situation had changed. Iraq was a mess, and the Bush administration finally decided that engaging Iran was worth a shot. Rather than recognize that Iran had already suspended uranian enrichment, however, the White House demanded that Iran give up fuel production altogether as a precondition for talks. The Iranians refused.

In the meantime, presidential elections in Iran were looming. Western governments were hopeful that former President Hashemi Rafsanjani, a reformist, would win. They did not bank on the conservative former Tehran mayor Mahmoud Ahmadinejad edging out Rafsanjani. Reformists had stuck their necks out on multiple occasions to build a more positive relationship with the United States. In return, the U.S. had shut the door or ignored their overtures. With Ahmadinejad in office, whatever political capital the reformists still had soon evaporated. Now the hardliners had the green light.

Almost immediately after Ahmadinejad took office, Iran restarted its suspended nuclear program. By mid-2006, after a failed attempt at restarting negotiations, the Germans stepped in and persuaded the Bush administration to try again. The Germans realized there would not be any long-term solution without U.S. involvement, but Bush's team once again insisted that the suspension of uranium enrichment was a precondition. For the Iranians, this was a non-starter. They had already suspended their program once and received nothing in return.

The Bush administration was surprised Iran said "no," but it should not have been. In the waning days of the second Bush White House, Iran's nuclear program was gaining ground, and it was clear Iran would also gain from the chaos in Iraq. Bush had, through his own hubris, neutered America's ability to build a consensus around Iran. It took the election of a new U.S. president for that to be rebuilt.

WHAT DID OBAMA'S 'UNCLENCHED FIST' DIPLOMATIC INITIATIVE DO TO IMPROVE RELATIONS?

In November 2008, the United States elected Barack Obama, who had promised to improve America's relations with the rest of the world, especially the Middle East. His approach extended to Iran as well. After 12 years of American failure to recognize openings, Obama's election was a breath of fresh air and a time of hope.

Almost immediately after taking office in late January 2009, President Obama sent clear signals that he sought to engage the Iranians, both private citizens and the government. Just a few weeks after taking office, President Obama sent a video message to the Iranian people for the Persian New Year, Nowruz.[170] It was intended to show the Iranians that Obama appreciated their culture and understood the importance of hospitality and respect. The Iranians were appreciative of his message.

Progress on any diplomatic initiative was muted, though, because of the pending Iranian presidential elections in June 2009, in which conservative President Ahmadinejad was vying for another term. The Obama administration had hoped that someone more amenable to diplomatic efforts would be elected. They almost got their wish with challenger Mir-Hossein Mousavi. On election day, the two were neck and neck, but the official results gave Ahmadinejad a landslide victory. The public cried foul.

In the ensuing days and weeks, protests raged across the country. The movement for a recount and for more transparency became known as the Green Movement. International media outlets endlessly covered the unfolding events, but as time progressed the Iranian government was determined to move forward with Ahmadinejad as president. Instead of letting the protests die out, they decided to violently crack down on citizens who had taken to the streets.

The Obama administration had hoped to jumpstart diplomatic efforts after the election was over. Now they were scrambling to figure out how to respond to the protests. Obama wanted to support the Green Movement but did not want to eliminate the possibility of future engagement with the government. Conservatives in the U.S. Congress called for more sanctions and more public support for the Green Movement. Ironically, the movement did not want open support from the U.S. government, as such support would jeopardize the legitimacy of the opposition.[171]

Several months later, however, Obama sought to engage the Iranian government regarding their nuclear program. Over a series of meetings, diplomats from the five permanent members of the UN Security Council (the U.S., UK, France, Russia, and China) plus Germany (P5+1) met with Iranian officials to deal with Iran's low enriched uranium stockpile. If Iran could enrich it further, the stockpile would be enough to reach the highly enriched uranium necessary for a nuclear weapon. A complex proposal involving shipments between Russia, France, and Iran had traction, but a deal was never reached.

Frustrated, the Obama administration set a different course. Rather than trying to engage Iran, the White House doggedly pursued building a consensus among the P5+1 to impose even tougher sanctions. The Chinese and Russians were initially reluctant, but after months of negotiations and Iran's intransigence, they agreed to support new UN Security Council sanctions.

Just as the UN Security Council was debating new sanctions, two upstart countries, Turkey and Brazil, tried to give diplomacy another chance. After getting tepid approval from the Obama administration, Turkish and Brazilian diplomats went to Iran to re-engage on the nuclear issue. [172] To everyone's surprise, they were successful in getting an agreement that essentially mirrored what had been discussed six months earlier. Iran would exchange a portion of its low enriched uranium for fuel pads. Only this time, the deal was too little too late. The Obama administration scuttled the new deal, because Iran's enriched uranium stockpile had nearly doubled, and international consensus had already been built around a new set of sanctions. That little glimmer of hope created by Turkey and Brazil was snuffed out by the United States.

Sanctions on Iran passed the UN Security Council, and for the next two years, as the U.S. turned up the pressure on Iran, the two countries were locked in a stalemate over the nuclear issue. Iran accelerated its program, increasing stockpiles of enriched uranium and increasing the number of centrifuges. Both countries engaged in tit-for-tat cyberattacks on each other's infrastructure. And in early 2012, the U.S. Congress passed sanctions on Iran's Central Bank, which essentially cut Iran off from participating in global commerce.

Around the same time as the banking sanctions, new rounds of talks were starting with a secret back channel via the government of Oman.[173] Over the course of the next year, the secret talks would continue building trust, but no agreement.

When Hassan Rouhani became Iran's new president in June 2013, new life was breathed into the back channel. President

Obama had been forced to reconsider his position on zero enrichment. There was pressure from the Omanis and Europeans, as well as recognition that the sanctions were having a diminishing impact. All the while, Iran's nuclear program was advancing.

As the back channel continued to hammer out a framework for enrichment, inspections, and removal of sanctions, the P5+1 renewed its meetings as well. In November 2013 they reached an interim agreement and tried to hash out the final sticking points, including the future of a heavy water reactor at Natanz, the release of Iranian frozen assets held in U.S. banks, and limitations on enrichment and research bans.

The global public watched with bated breath, as deadlines kept getting extended. At several moments it seemed that the entire deal would collapse, as each side threatened to walk away. Finally, after a 12-year-standoff, 20 months of on-and-off talks, and a final 17-day marathon round of uninterrupted negotiations, an historic deal was reached on July 14, 2015.

Then came the next step: a Herculean effort by both the Obama administration and the grassroots organizations to get the necessary congressional approval. Despite heavy lobbying by the pro-Israel organization AIPAC (American Israeli Public Affairs Committee) and other lobby groups created specifically to quash the deal, Congress failed to block the agreement, giving victory to a hard-fought diplomatic battle.

Negotiations were also taking place regarding a different issue: a prisoner swap. Several Iranian-American dual nationals were being held in Iranian prisons, most notably *Washington Post* journalist Jason Rezaian. In exchange for their release, the U.S. agreed to release several Iranians held in American jails. Adding to the complexity was the fact that several U.S. sailors, after a series of mistakes and navigation equipment malfunctions, had drifted into Iranian waters and were detained by the Iranian

Revolutionary Guard's Navy. Leaning on the already good rapport between Secretary of State John Kerry and Iranian Foreign Minister Javad Zarif, the sailors were released after 16 hours.

The U.S. and Iran had figured out a diplomatic solution to the nuclear impasse and the trust they had built allowed them to hammer out other agreements. But the two countries remained at odds over many issues, including Iran's role in the unrest in Iraq and Syria. Another concern was Iran's continued testing of missiles, even though this was not directly prohibited under the nuclear accords.

As the Obama administration prepared to leave office, hopes were high that the next president would build on his efforts. Both countries had gone a long way to establish trust and institutionalize their interactions. What they did not anticipate, however, was Donald Trump becoming the next president.

WILL TRUMP'S "MAKE AMERICA GREAT AGAIN" LEAD US TO A FAMILIAR PATH?

Riding a wave of right-wing populism, Donald Trump was elected to replace Barack Obama. He promised to bring jobs back, renegotiate trade deals that hurt Americans, and—notably—tear up the Iran nuclear deal that he called the "worst deal ever negotiated."[174]

Despite Iran's compliance with the terms of the agreement, President Trump insisted on the contrary. On October 13, 2017, Trump dealt a blow to the pact by refusing to certify that Iran was in compliance with the accord, despite all evidence by U.S. and international specialists that Iran had compiled. If the U.S. abandons the nuclear accord, the other P5+1 countries have said they would remain committed to it. What Trump is risking, however, is that Iran will say the deal has been violated and restart its enrichment program.[175] We could be in for a long road of increased instability and conflict in an already tumultuous region.

WHY HAVE U.S. POLICYMAKERS BEEN SO SUPPORTIVE OF THE MEK?

In 1997, the MEK (People's Mujahedeen of Iran) was listed by the United States as a terrorist group. Indeed, it has a sordid history of violent attacks, first against the Shah and U.S. businessmen in Iran, and later against the Islamic Republic once it fell out of favor with Ayatollah Khomeini. MEK members were early examples of suicide bombers, strapping themselves with explosives and blowing up civilians in Iran. Israel used the MEK to penetrate Iran and assassinate nuclear scientists. The MEK also took their attacks overseas, targeting Iranian diplomatic missions in 13 countries.

The MEK is a cult-like organization run by Massoud Rajavi and his wife Maryam. A 1994 State Department report documented how Massoud Rajavi "fostered a cult of personality around himself that had alienated most Iranian expatriates, who assert they do not want to replace one objectionable regime for another." A 2009 Rand study described the group as having "cultic practices," including mandatory divorce and celibacy, because "love for the Rajavis was to replace love for spouses and family." In 2013, a George Mason University study found that only five percent of Iranians showed any support for the MEK.[176]

In the United States, however, the group launched a hard-core lobbying campaign to get itself off the terrorist list and rehabilitate itself as a legitimate opposition to the Iranian regime. It has large sums of money for the campaign, reportedly coming from Israel, Saudi Arabia, and a handful of wealthy Iranian-Americans.

Their campaign became a classic case in how to buy influence in Washington DC. The MEK used its funds to secure the backing of an astounding array of U.S. politicians across the political spectrum—from liberal Democrat Howard Dean to conservative Republican Newt Gingrich. It gathered support from pro-Israel figures, including Holocaust survivor Elie Wiesel and Harvard law professor Alan Dershowitz.[177]

Many of its high-profile advocates—including members of Congress, Washington lobby groups, and influential former officials— received large contributions for their support.[178] The funds were disbursed as speaker and lobby fees, campaign contributions, and expensive travel reimbursements. The MEK paid up to $100,000 for people to make public appearances at their events.

As the *New York Times* noted, "Rarely in the annals of lobbying in the capital has so obscure a cause attracted so stellar a group of supporters: former directors of the CIA and the FBI, retired generals and famous politicians of both parties."[179]

Their campaign worked. In 2012, Secretary of State Hillary Clinton announced that the MEK had been removed from the State Department's list of terrorist organizations.

While the MEK continues to have many supporters within Congress and a large pool of big name advocates, a group that fought alongside Saddam Hussein in the Iran-Iraq war, has ties to the CIA and Israel's Mossad, and functions in a cult-like manner is hard pressed to be a viable alternative to Iran's present government. The group might have been able to buy support in the U.S. capital, but it has virtually zero support inside Iran.

CHAPTER 9: IRAN IN THE MIDDLE EAST AND BEYOND

With the Middle East on fire, Iran is certainly involved in many of the region's conflicts. As a Shia nation in a predominantly Sunni region, and a Persian country in an Arab world, Iran has felt surrounded by threats. Iran is the Muslim country in the Middle East that has been most adamantly opposed to radical Sunni terrorist groups, from the Taliban to Al Qaeda to ISIS. Iran has been fighting all of those groups in other countries in the region, somehow managing—for the most part—to keep the fighting away from its own homeland.

That's why Iranians were so shocked by an unprecedented terrorist attack in June 2017 in the heart of Tehran, hitting the Parliament and the mausoleum of Ayatollah Khomeini. Seventeen people were killed and dozens injured. ISIS took credit for the attack, which seems to have been carried out by disaffected Iranian Kurds.[180] Iran sees all of these fanatical Sunni groups as being nurtured, in one way or another, by the Wahhabists in Saudi Arabia. It is one more reason why Iran's relations with the rest of the world have to be filtered through the lens of its intense hostility with Saudi Arabia, and to a lesser extent with the United States and Israel.

WHAT'S BEHIND THE SAUDI/IRAN RIVALRY?

Saudi leaders see Iran's post-1979 policies as part of an expansionist, sectarian agenda aimed at empowering Shia Muslims in the region at the expense of Sunnis. Iranian leaders attribute similar motives to their Saudi counterparts.

It wasn't always this way. The religious division between Sunni and Shia dates back to the religion's founding in the seventh century, but Sunni and Shia have coexisted without significant conflict for much of the history of the Middle East.

With the 1979 Islamic Revolution, the initial message of the Iranian leader, Ayatollah Khomeini, was not only anti-imperialist but anti-monarchy. He claimed that Islam was incompatible with hereditary monarchies. Khomeini tried to position himself as the leader of all Muslims, regardless of their denomination. In doing so, he challenged the legitimacy of the Saudi royal family and called into question its status as guardian of Islam's two holy sites, Mecca and Medina. The Saudi rulers' response was to denounce Iran's revolution as a power play by heretical Shiites.

In essence, the Saudi–Iran rivalry is not religious, but political. When Shah Pahlavi ruled Iran from 1941 to 1979, the two nations had a decent relationship. Both were original members of the oil cartel OPEC. The problem between the two countries arose when revolutionary religious leaders in Iran posed an ideological threat to the Saudi regime.

During the Iran–Iraq war in the 1980s, Saudi Arabia took the side of Saddam Hussein's Iraq as a way to weaken Iran. This caused tremendous anger among Iranians.

Relations were further strained in 1987, when 275 Iranians died at the hands of Saudi police during a pilgrimage to Mecca. While in Mecca, the Iranians had organized, as they did every year, a demonstration against the United States and Israel. This time, however, they were brutally attacked by Saudi riot police. In response, protesters in Iran occupied the Saudi Embassy and a Saudi diplomat died when he fell out of an embassy window.

Saudi Arabia severed relations with Iran in 1988; they were later restored in 1991.

Relations improved in the late 1990s, when Saudi Crown Prince Abdullah visited Iran in 1997, followed by an official visit to Saudi Arabia by Iranian reformist President Mohammad Khatami the following year. The 2003 U.S. invasion of Iraq, however, led to more turmoil. The power vacuum created by the overthrow of Saddam Hussein and disastrous U.S. policies, such as firing hundreds of thousands of Sunnis in the ruling Baath Party, unleashed fierce infighting between Iraq's Sunni and Shia communities. Iran supported Iraqi Shia; Saudi Arabia supported Iraqi Sunnis.

The enmity between Saudi Arabia and Iran became even fiercer eight years later, in 2011, with the Arab Spring. As some regimes were toppled and others desperately clung to power, the Saudis and Iranians competed for influence and dominance. By 2016, the Saudis accused Iran of waging proxy wars in Iraq, Syria, Yemen, Bahrain, Kuwait, and even inside the kingdom itself; Iran viewed Saudi Arabia as destabilizing the entire Middle East. While many of the claims were false or exaggerated, both countries had a hand in the regional conflicts.

Another area of tension was Iran's nuclear program. The Saudis seemed to be less concerned about Iran's nuclear ambitions than the possibility that a deal would bring Iran back into the international fold and threaten the cozy U.S.–Saudi alliance. The Saudis eventually gave a nod of approval for the deal when President Obama pledged more weapons sales to Saudi Arabia and beefed up military support to defend itself against potential missile strikes, maritime threats, and cyberattacks from Iran.

In September 2015, hundreds of Iranians were killed in a stampede during the annual Hajj pilgrimage in Mecca, Saudi Arabia. Iran accused the Saudis of gross negligence and mismanagement, and Saudi officials accused Iran of playing politics in the aftermath of a tragedy.

Another bone of contention has been Iran's connection with dissident Shia groups in eastern Saudi Arabia and Bahrain (where Shia are the majority). The Shia populations in both countries have been oppressed, and Iran has occasionally entered the fray to offer support.

Relations between the two nations came to a breaking point in 2016, when Saudi Arabia executed anti-government activist and Shiite cleric Nimr al-Nimr on trumped-up charges of terrorism. The killing of the nonviolent sheikh, beloved by the Shia community at home and abroad, predictably outraged many Shia in Iran. They staged violent protests at the Saudi Embassy in Tehran, including setting it on fire. Saudi Arabia cut off all diplomatic and economic ties with Iran.

Saudi Arabia and Iran were also on opposite sides in the conflicts in Syria and then in Yemen. They came close to direct confrontation after Saudi Arabia held Iran responsible for a ballistic missile fired from Yemen on November 4, 2017 that landed near the airport in Saudi's capital city Riyadh.

When Donald Trump became president in 2017, he exacerbated tensions by publicly cozying up to the Saudis, continuing to sell them weapons, and expanding U.S. support for the Yemen war. Emboldened by U.S. support—and with power in the hands of the rash, young Crown Prince Mohammad bin Salman—Saudi Arabia stepped up its actions to isolate Iran.

HOW DOES IRAN RELATE TO THE OTHER GULF COUNTRIES?

In 1981, against the backdrop of the Iranian revolution and the Iran-Iraq war, the Gulf States banded together to form the Gulf

Cooperation Council (GCC). It was composed of the six Arab monarchies in the Persian Gulf: Saudi Arabia, Bahrain, Kuwait, Oman, Qatar, and the United Arab Emirates (UAE). De facto leadership of the GCC was in the hands of Saudi Arabia.

While the GCC countries have many common interests, ranging from trade to ensuring that their monarchies remain intact to promoting Sunni dominance in the region, the GCC is not a monolith. Tensions can be high within that organization as well, as happened in 2017 when Saudi Arabia and a few other nations broke off diplomatic relations with GCC member Qatar. Kuwait and Oman refused to go along with Saudi demands.

One of the reasons for the Saudi decision to isolate Qatar was that Qatar, despite opposing Iran in the conflicts in Syria and Yemen, openly advocated for better relations with Iran. Qatar and Iran share control over the vast South Pars/North Dome oil and natural gas field. The field sits offshore and northeast of Qatar and just south of Iran. The Iranians have been slow to exploit the enormous offshore resources, but the shared resource is a major incentive for Qatar to maintain positive relations with Iran.

Qatar, a tiny nation with enormous wealth thanks to natural gas, refused to comply with the Saudi demand that it cut ties with Iran. The Saudis responded with a blockade. This move, however, only pushed Qatar and Iran closer together since Iran stepped in to supply whatever imports Qatar needed and allowed Qatar Airlines to fly over Iranian territory so the airlines could continue its routes to Europe and Asia.

Other GCC states have business ties to Iran as well. This includes Kuwait, with its large Iranian expat population. Iran's largest GCC economic partner is Dubai, one of the United Arab Emirates. During the Iran-Iraq War, while most of the GCC countries sided with Iraq, Dubai allowed Iran to use its territory for resupplying its military. Prior to the imposition of hard-hitting sanctions in 2012, trade between Dubai and Iran accounted for nearly 25 percent of Iran's international trade. After a 2009 financial crisis and bailout from another UAE emirate, Abu Dhabi, Dubai caved to external pressure and began rolling back trade with Iran. But as Iran's economy picked back up after the 2015 signing of the nuclear deal, Dubai became the main beneficiary in the Gulf.

Iran has maintained close ties with the Gulf state of Oman. Before the Iranian revolution, Iran helped the Sultan of Oman fight off a rebellion, and after the revolution, they continued to have positive relations. At times, Oman serves as the interlocutor for countries dealing with Iran. This was the case when U.S. and Iranian officials held secret talks starting in 2011 regarding Iran's nuclear program.

There are also some ongoing territorial disputes with Iran that strain regional relations. The UAE has laid claim to three islands Iran has occupied prior to the revolution. Iran does not acknowledge the UAE's claim.

HOW CAN THE RELATIONSHIP WITH ISRAEL BE DEFINED?

It's hard to imagine two more bitter enemies than Iran and Israel, with Iranian leaders calling for Israel's demise and Israeli leaders calling Iran an existential threat to Israel. Yet this animosity is relatively new. Before Iran's 1979 revolution, the two nations were allies. Iranian diplomats in Europe saved thousands of Jews from the Holocaust. Although the Shah voted against 1947 Partition Plan for Palestine at the end of the British Mandate, rightly asserting that it would lead to violence, Iran was still the second Muslim-majority country to formally recognize Israel.

Iran and Israel saw each other as natural regional allies, in large part due to their non-Arab backgrounds and their common Sunni

Arab enemies. The two nations shared intelligence and weapons. Their ties were further cemented through various joint ventures and robust trade. Both were closely allied with the United States.

Iran remained neutral in all three Arab-Israeli wars. Even during the Arab oil boycott of the 1970s, Iran continued to supply Israel with oil. Iran's population of some 100,000 Jews was another factor tying the nations together.

After the 1979 revolution, the relationship did an about-face. Iran's new rulers viewed Israel as an American lackey and denounced Israel's suppression of Palestinian rights. But even though the rhetoric was heated, Israel continued to supply arms to Iran during the Iran/Iraq war and Israel served as a middleman during the Reagan administration's arms-for-hostages deal.

As the Iran-Iraq war ended, Iran stepped up its support for Hezbollah in Lebanon and formed new alliances with Palestinian militias. Through funding and training of Palestinian militants, Iran played a role in several bombing attacks inside Israel, as well as the bombing of the Israeli Embassy and a Jewish Center in Argentina.

The staunchest ally of the Palestinians in the region, however, was Iraq's Saddam Hussein. Iraq had declared war on the Jewish state in 1948, sent armies to fight Israel in 1948, 1968, and 1973, and subsidized families of Palestinian martyrs (including suicide bombers). When the 1991 Gulf War severely weakened Saddam Hussein, the Israelis swtiched to identifying Iran as their major threat in the region. Israel used its close relationship with the U.S. to lobby for isolating Iran. Israel pushed for increased sanctions and in 1995 was responsible for scuttling a major oil deal between Iran and the U.S. oil company Conoco.

After the U.S. invaded and occupied Iraq, the Iranians offered up a grand bargain in which they indicated they would be open to recognizing Israel's right to exist, but their offer never received a response.

In the 2000s, Iran's nuclear program became an even bigger focus for the Israelis, despite the fact that Israel had illegally developed its own nuclear weapons and refused to sign onto the Nuclear Non-Proliferation Treaty.

Israel seized on every new Iranian effort to develop and protect its nuclear industry, such as the discovery of its Natanz underground uranium enrichment site in 2002, as evidence that Iran would have a nuclear bomb within a few years.

As Trita Parsi documented in his book, *A Single Roll of the Dice: Obama's Diplomacy with Iran*, President Obama's "dual-track" approach to Iran's nuclear program during his first term was a political compromise between hawks and doves in Washington. The hawks, who were allied with Netanyahu and the Israel lobby, were determined to destroy Iran's nuclear program by crippling sanctions or even by war. The doves wanted to avoid war with Iran and resolve the nuclear scare through diplomacy.

The Obama administration was also dogged by the fear that Israel would follow through on its threats to take matters into its own hands by launching a unilateral strike on Iran's nuclear program. The fact that Israel had done this twice before, in Iraq and Syria, gave the threats more credence. Iran's allies, including Hezbollah and Hamas, would surely have responded by striking deep inside Israeli territory. It was clear any attack by Israel would likely pull the U.S. into yet another regional conflict.[181]

Israel vigorously opposed the Iran nuclear deal, directly lobbying the White House and Congress, including getting the Republican congressional leadership to give Israeli Prime Minister Netanyahu an unprecedented invitation to speak about Israel's opposition to the nuclear agreement to a 2015 joint session of Congress without even informing the White House of the invitation.

Israel was also implicated in a more brutal tactic to oppose the nuclear deal: the assassination of nuclear scientists inside Iran.

Between 2010 and 2012, at least five scientists associated with Iran's nuclear program were killed. Darioush Rezaeinejad, an electrical engineer, was killed by gunmen on motorcycles in July 2011. Mostafa Ahmadi Rosham, deputy head of Iran's nuclear enrichment program, was killed in January 2012 by a bomb attached to his car door—also by men on motorcycles.[182] While these assassinations were not directly attributed to Israel, strong evidence points in that direction. NBC reported that U.S. officials, speaking off-record, claimed Israel's Mossad had trained Iranian exiles from the MEK for the assassination campaign.[183] Israeli Defense Minister Moshe Ya'alon did not explicitly deny Israeli responsibility, instead ominously claiming he bore no responsibility "for the life expectancy of Iranian scientists," and that Israel would "act in any way" to prevent a nuclear-armed Iran.[184]

When the nuclear deal was finally negotiated in 2015 and was received with near unanimous international consensus, Israel was the outlier with its condemnation of the agreement.

Iran's involvement in Syria has also caused concern for Israel. The successful effort by Russia, Iran, and Hezbollah to prop up the Assad regime meant stronger, better equipped, Iranian-backed militias on Israel's borders with both Lebanon and Syria. Israel saw the spread of Iranian-backed militias to Syria as a serious shift in the military balance on its borders, which is why it launched several airstrikes in Syria against them and quietly supported the Al Qaeda-linked forces the Iranians were fighting.

In its efforts to push back against Iran, Israel found an odd bedfellow: Saudi Arabia. With the old adage that "the enemy of my enemy is my friend," the Israelis made common cause with Saudi Arabia, the only country in the Middle East where it would be illegal to build a synagogue.

WHAT DEFINES IRAN'S RELATIONSHIP WITH OTHER NEIGHBORS ON ITS BORDERS?

Not only does Iran have to navigate turbulent relations with GCC countries that sit along its 1,500 mile coastline on the Persian Gulf, but it must also traverse an equally stormy set of relationships with seven other neighbors with whom it shares 3,300 miles of borders: Afghanistan, Armenia, Azerbaijan, Iraq, Pakistan, Turkey and Turkmenistan.

These countries, at some point in their histories, have been part of one of the various Persian empires. Travelers will often find cultural, social, and linguistic commonalities in these countries based on centuries-old contact. But today's relations are forged through a complex blend of wars, sanctions, religious identities, ideology, shifting alliances, and economic interests. Each relationship is unique, and fluctuates according to the breathtaking pace and scope of changes that have been taking place in the region.

IRAQ

Iran's longest border is the one with Iraq—over 900 miles long. Historically, that border has been porous, due in large part to extensive cross-border trade and tourism. Every year, hundreds of thousands of Iranians make pilgrimages to Shia religious shrines in Najaf and Karbala in southern Iraq. This geographic closeness, along with the fact that both Iran and Iraq are majority Shia, means that the two nations are, for better or worse, inextricably linked.

Relations were tense before the Iranian revolution, with the Shah trying to organize a coup against Saddam Hussein in 1971 and Saddam Hussein supporting insurgencies against the Shah. But the real catastrophe came in 1980, when Iraq invaded Iran, sparking an eight-year war that left over a million dead and wounded.

After the ceasefire with Iraq, Iran continued to play host to several Iraqi Shia dissident groups. These groups would end up forming the core of Iran's influence in Iraq for decades to come.

When the U.S. decided to invade Iraq in 2003, Iran was hesitant to get involved. The ensuing chaos brought on by the U.S. occupation and Baathist insurgency forced Iran's hand. Using its extensive network of Shia dissident groups, the Iranians fought both the U.S. occupying forces and the Iraqi army.

Despite the massive American presence, it was the Iranians who played kingmaker in Iraq. Iraq's Shia militias and political leaders coalesced around the new Iranian-backed leadership. All three Iraqi prime ministers since 2006 owed their positions to Iranian influence, and ironically, Iran owed its influence to the U.S. overthrow of Saddam Hussein.

After the U.S. withdrew its troops in 2011 and ISIS (formed primarily by men who had been imprisoned in Iraq by U.S. forces) grabbed control over swaths of western and northern Iraq, Iran re-mobilized the Shia militias it had controlled during the U.S. occupation. Iranian-backed militias fought alongside the Iraqi Army and Kurdish Peshmerga to push ISIS out of Iraq.

Once ISIS was defeated by the end of 2017, however, Shia militias joined the Iraqi Army to confront their former allies, the Peshmerga, and push the Kurds out of the northern, oil-rich city of Kirkuk.

While U.S. officials deny it, the fight against ISIS in Iraq involved a tacit U.S. alliance with Iran. A coalition of mainly Shia Iraqi militias, known as the Popular Mobilization Units (PMUs), were officially formed in 2014 and were key to defeating ISIS. U.S. officials fear that these Shia militias, even though they are technically part of the Iraqi Armed Forces, will eventually become much like Hezbollah or even the Iranian Revolutionary Guard—armed Shia groups independent of the official military, ready to do Iran's bidding.

But there are limits to Iran's influence. The U.S. has been pressing the Iraqi leaders to send Iranian fighters home and minimize Iran's power. There is also tremendous resentment among the sizable Sunni population in Iraq, some of whom have been terrorized by Shia militia for years.

The Iraqi leaders know they are walking a tightrope, trying to please both their American patrons and their Iranian allies. To keep control, defeat Sunni extremist groups, and prevent the total breakaway of Iraqi Kurdistan, Iraqi leaders are aware they need both the Iranians and the Americans. So far, they have been brilliantly playing the two off each other.

There is no doubt, however, that the U.S. overthrow of Iran's archrival in Iraq, Saddam Hussein, turned out not only to be a catastrophe for Iraqis, but for the Sunni-Shia sectarian violence it unleashed that opened the door for Iran to play a major role in the future of Iraq.

AFGHANISTAN

Iran's eastern neighbor, Afghanistan, has experienced 40 years of coups and wars, including the longest war ever waged by the United States. Iran's influence has mainly been along the border in the western, mostly Tajik, Farsi-speaking city and province of Herat, which is sometimes referred to as "Little Iran." Most Afghan Tajiks are Sunni Muslims, but both Hazaras and a Tajik minority called the Farsiwan are Shia, giving them another link with Iran. During the Soviet invasion in the 1980s, two million Afghans fled and took refuge in Iran.

With the emergence of the Taliban government in 1996 and its harsh treatment of Afghan minorities, Iran refused to recognize the Taliban and instead provided military support to the

Tajik-majority Northern Alliance opposition. Relations further deteriorated in 1998, when the Taliban attacked the Iranian consulate in Afghanistan, killing ten diplomats and a journalist.

Iran's support for the Northern Alliance helped the United States topple the Taliban in 2001. When the various anti-Taliban forces came together to negotiate the post-Taliban peace, Iran's links with the Northern Alliance were the key to getting all sides to come to an agreement. Iran was also set to play a larger role in the post-Taliban reconstruction of Afghanistan until President George W. Bush decided to take a hostile stance against Iran.

Iran says its goal in Afghanistan is to have a stable country on its border, which means eliminating the Taliban and Al Qaeda. It wants a greater focus on drug trafficking. Afghanistan is the world's largest source of opium, and Iran is the main conduit for international traffickers to get the drugs out to Europe. The trafficking through Iran has created a chronic drug problem in Iran, and hundreds of Iranian security agents have been killed in clashes with drug traffickers.

Over the years, Iran has spent hundreds of millions of dollars in reconstruction investments in Afghanistan, including the building of a railroad to the western city of Herat. It has spearheaded an ambitious, politically charged project to connect Afghanistan to the Iranian port of Chabahar, creating a route that would significantly shorten the distance between Afghanistan and the Persian Gulf and compete with the traditional roadway through Pakistan.

A major Iranian goal in Afghanistan, however, is to see that U.S. troops leave; Iran does not want American soldiers on its border. With the Trump administration upping troop numbers and military involvement in Afghanistan, Iran has been trying to undermine the U.S. presence.

Some reports allege that Iran's strategy includes support for the Taliban in their attacks on US forces, which the Iranian government denies. Major support for the Afghan Taliban still comes from Pakistan. Iran insists that its contacts with the Taliban have only been to encourage them to pursue peace talks rather than continue their military activities.[185]

Both the United States and Iran are worried about a new development in Afghanistan: the presence of ISIS groups. A mini-caliphate was established in 2017 in the province of Jawzjan, started by disaffected Taliban elements and fighters streaming out from Iraq and Syria.[186] Given the ISIS attacks that took place in the heart of Iran in June 2017, Iran's leaders are determined to make sure that Afghanistan does not become a haven for ISIS fighters.

Moreover, while the war in Afghanistan is the longest in U.S. history, the Iranians are convinced that, at some point, the U.S. military will get tired and go home. Iran, Afghanistan's next door neighbor, will remain and will continue to use its influence with successive Afghan governments.

TURKEY

Turkey and Iran are descendants of historic empires that share geographic, ethnic, and linguistic ties. Their relationship in modern times has been mainly peaceful, but often tense and suspicious.

After the 1979 Iranian revolution, relations remained cool even though Turkey supplied Iran with much-needed goods during the Iran-Iraq war. The main flash point early on was the religious-secular divide, with Turkey being a constitutionally secular state before the ascent of Recep Tayyip Erdogan's Islamist party in 2002. There were also concerns over support for separatist groups, particularly Kurds, within each country. Turkey's membership in NATO brought U.S. troops to Iran's borders, which made Iran nervous.[187]

The rise of Erdogan's Justice and Development Party (AKP) in 2002 and his "zero problems with neighbors" policy saw relations start to warm. At the behest of the Turkish government, Iran even reduced its contacts with the Kurdish groups it had previously supported. And in 2010, Erdogan—along with Brazilian President Lula da Silva—spearheaded an effort to find an international solution to the nuclear impasse with Iran.

Just a year later, tensions flared as Iran and Turkey found themselves on opposite sides during the Arab Spring. The worst flashpoint was Syria. Turkey was determined to see Bashar al-Assad toppled; Iran was determined to see his government survive. Iran accused Turkey of being the supply source for ISIS in the region, and Turkey said Iran's role in supporting Assad was irresponsible.[188]

The two countries found themselves with mutual interests, however, when the Saudis boycotted Qatar in 2017. Both Iran and Turkey came to Qatar's aid, and trade among the three countries increased.[189]

Bilateral trade between Iran and Turkey is focused on the energy sector. Iran has significant oil and gas reserves, but due to sanctions has trouble exploiting them. Turkey has money and access to technology. In the future, ties on that front will likely improve if Turkish companies can find ways to avoid becoming embroiled in U.S. sanctions on Iranian industries.

PAKISTAN

While Iran's relationship with Turkey has improved, its relationship with Pakistan has soured. Pakistan is a Sunni-majority country with a large Shia population. Prior to the revolution, the two countries were close—Iran was quick to reach out to Pakistan when Pakistan became a nation in 1947.

Multiple fissures emerged after the 1979 Iranian revolution. First, Pakistan became home to Sunni extremists. General Zia-ul-Haq, who had seized power in Pakistan in 1977 and imposed sharia law, was a staunch follower of Sunni Islam and strengthened ties with the Saudis. He gave the Saudis free rein to create Islamic schools across the country to fill the gap of a collapsed education system. Flush with cash from soaring oil prices, the Saudis funded schools and mosques to teach their Wahhabi extremist version of Sunni Islam, an ideology that paints Shia as infidels. This exacerbated the Sunni-Shia sectarian divide, both in Pakistan and beyond its borders, hurting relations with Iran.

Second, Pakistan and Iran conflict over trade. Both countries are anxious to connect Central Asia to international markets. Pakistan already provides Afghanistan with overland access, but Iran is planning an alternative to bypass the Pakistani route. Iran's plans to link Kandahar, Afghanistan, with Iran's new port at Chabahar could put Pakistan's trade route out of business, primarily because the road is shorter and safer than the one in Pakistan.

To make matters worse, Pakistan's adversary, India, is helping Iran develop the Chabahar port. Pakistan views this and other Indian investments in Iran as part of an Indian plot to encircle and isolate Pakistan. At the same time, Pakistan's strong economic ties with Saudi Arabia are threatening to Iran.

Third, border issues have led to finger pointing on both sides. Iran blames Pakistan for the rise of Sunni militancy along Iran's southeast border. Iran's southeast is also restless due to a Baluchi insurgency, which is funded by illicit trading and drug smuggling. Iran has called for greater cooperation with Pakistan to counter smuggling, trafficking, and Baluchi separatist groups.[190]

AZERBAIJAN, ARMENIA, AND TURKMENISTAN

The Azeri, Armenian, and Turkmen peoples were all part of Iran or the Iranian Empire for many centuries, but large parts of their historic territories were conquered by Russia during the expansion of the Russian Empire in the 18th and 19th centuries.

When the Soviet Union broke up at the end of the Cold War, the Soviet parts of these territories became independent countries, while other parts remained within the borders of Iran and other countries in the region. Roughly 55 percent of the world's Azeri population, 22 percent of Turkmen, and two percent of Armenians still live in Iran.

Ties with Azerbaijan should, on the surface, be strong. Both countries are Shia and have a shared history, as well as cultural and linguistic ties. Most of the world's Azeris live in Iran, not in Azerbaijan. But after a brief, positive relationship after the fall of the Soviet Union in the early 1990s, the two countries have spent the intervening years viewing each other with intense suspicion.[191]

Azerbaijan, a secular state anxious to disentangle itself from Russia, sought cooperation with the West, making Iran wary of a pro-Western country on its border. When the Azeris in Azerbaijan decided to advocate for reunification with the Azeri portion of Iran, Tehran began supporting Azerbaijan's bitter rival, Armenia, during their clash over the disputed territory of Nagorno-Karabakh.

Azerbaijan has been gaining influence internationally, mostly due to increased revenues from oil and gas. A deeper treasury has brought them new trading partners. In 2012, to the consternation of Iran, they signed a $1.6 billion military agreement with Israel. Around the same time, the Azerbaijani government claimed it broke up an Iranian cell that had planned to attack the Israeli Embassy in Azerbaijan.

More recently, however, the two sides have moved closer. Energy and transport links have increased, and in October 2017, Iran, Russia, and Azerbaijan met to discuss a framework to strengthen trilateral ties.

Iran's relations with Azerbaijan's neighbor, Armenia, have remained cordial. Iran's large Christian Armenian population is influential, despite different religious preferences. Iran has viewed Armenia as a gateway to Western markets.[192]

With respect to Turkmenistan, Iran was the first country to recognize it as an independent state in 1991. Although the authoritarian government of Turkmenistan represses that nation's small Shia community, Iran still feels compelled to work closely with it to prevent a spillover of destabilizing Islamic extremists from Afghanistan.. Turkmenistan, like Iran, has also taken a hardline stance against Sunni extremists.[193]

The two nations work together to stem the flow of illegal drugs from Afghanistan. In 2013, Turkmen police oversaw the largest ever seizure of Afghan opium on their border, an operation that was part of a larger anti-drug campaign to crack down on both the drug trade and domestic drug abuse. The two countries have also focused on large-scale oil and gas projects.

WHAT HAS BEEN IRAN'S ROLE IN SYRIA?

Since the Iranian revolution, Syria and Iran have been strategic allies, despite the conflict between Assad's secular Arab nationalism and Iran's revolutionary Islamic ideology. The nations' ties have been political, not religious. (The Assad family belongs to the Alawite branch of Shi'a Islam—Iran's Supreme Leader Ayatollah Khomeini did not even consider Assad to be a true Muslim.) Syria was the first Arab state to recognize the Islamic Republic in 1979.

Both nations shared an antipathy towards Saddam Hussein, as well as towards Israel and the United States. With a few exceptions, the Syrian government was the odd man out in the Arab world in supporting Iran in the Iran-Iraq war.

Both Iran and Syria supported Hezbollah in its struggles against Israel. The U.S. invasion of Iraq, along with the 2006 failed Israeli invasion into Lebanon, brought the countries closer together. Iran supplied Syria with military equipment and heavily invested in the Syrian economy.

Since the 2011 Syrian internal strife, Iran and its Revolutionary Guards weighed in on the side of Assad, sending advisors, special forces, and frontline troops. While it was Russia's military intervention to prop up Assad that was the turning point in the war with ISIS and Western-supported militias, Iran also gained a multi-layered presence in Syria that included local Shiite militants. Iran's Revolutionary Guard was anxious to institutionalize the pro-Iranian militias it had built up in Syria. The Guard wanted to turn the Syrian militias into semi-state actors akin to how Hezbollah operates in Lebanon. This put Iran's Revolutionary Guard at odds with Russia, which wanted to reinforce Syrian state institutions. Iran's President Rouhani, anxious to improve relations with the West, was amenable to disbanding the militias.

It is still unclear how peace will come to war-torn Syria, and what role Iran will play in that process. As of early 2018, however, Syria's future was being decided by Russia, Turkey, and Iran.

WHAT IS IRAN'S RELATIONSHIP WITH THE VARIOUS NON-STATE MILITANTS GROUPS IN THE MIDDLE EAST?

Since the 1979 revolution and its eight-year war with Iraq in the 1980s, Iran has been looking for ways to both protect itself and spread its influence. Using the special forces arm of the Revolutionary Guard—the Quds Force—Iran has sought alliances with non-state actors to pursue its foreign policy objectives. The United States designates some of these non-state actors, such as Hezbollah in Lebanon, as terrorist organizations.

The U.S. cites Iran's links to these groups as the main reason for putting Iran on its list of state sponsors of terrorism. According to the 2016 State Department *Country Reports on Terrorism*, Iran is the foremost state sponsor of terrorism in the world. The report accused Iran of backing anti-Israeli groups, as well as supporting proxies that have destabilized Iraq, Syria, and Yemen. It also accused Iran of supplying weapons, money, and training to militant Shia groups in Bahrain, maintaining cyber terrorism programs, and refusing to prosecute senior members of Al Qaeda that it had detained.[194]

But, as the saying goes, one person's terrorist is another person's freedom fighter. It all depends on where you sit. For many people in the Middle East, Israel is a nation that illegally occupies Palestine and brutally represses the Palestinian people. They see Hezbollah in Lebanon and Hamas in Gaza as legitimate resistance fighters against enemies who are infinitely better armed and have more sophisticated means of killing.

HEZBOLLAH

Iran's most successful non-state relationship is with Hezbollah, whose name is Arabic for Party of God. Starting in the late 1970s, Lebanon's Shia community was ripe with resentment. Despite being the largest sect within Lebanon, the Shia had been left out of much of the decision making in the religious-based political system put in place by the French at a time when Sunnis and Christians made up a larger percentage of the population. Shia strongholds in the south and in parts of Beirut also became home to thousands of Palestinian refugees. Cross border skirmishes with Israel became common.

In 1982, Israel invaded south Lebanon to attack Palestinian militants. Shia leaders, looking for a way to resist the Israeli occupation, challenged the mainstream Shia Amal movement and formed an armed movement that would later become Hezbollah. Early on, they sought support from Iran, and their targets were the Israelis and their American backers.

The United States blamed Hezbollah and Iran for the bombings of the U.S. Embassy and U.S. Marine barracks in Lebanon in 1983. The Marine barracks attack left 258 Americans servicemen dead; at the embassy, the death toll was 63, including 17 Americans. Another bombing at the US Embassy in 1984 left 24 dead.

Hezbollah, which was officially formed in 1985 after years of mobilization, denied any involvement, and a previously unknown group called "Islamic Jihad" took credit for the bombings. Caspar Weinberger, the U.S. Defense Secretary at the time, insisted that U.S. officials never discovered who was responsible.

Hezbollah continued its guerrilla war against Israeli forces in South Lebanon, but also began to play an active role in Lebanese politics. While the U.S. press portrays Hezbollah as an Iranian agent, for Lebanese it is one of the most popular political parties in the country, where it routinely wins among the highest number of votes in the parliament, and where it is widely viewed as a legitimate political party, with an armed wing that succeeded in liberating and defending the country from Israel twice: in 1982 and in 2006.

Iran has used its ties to Hezbollah not just to keep Israel out of Lebanon but also to expand Iran's reach in the region. For Iran, a Shia, Farsi-speaking country in a Sunni-dominated, Arabic-speaking region, Hezbollah not only added military strength but also provided Arabic-speaking cadre who could maneuver more easily in the Arab world. After the U.S. invasion of Iraq in 2003, Iran called on Hezbollah to help train Shiite militias in Iraq to fight U.S. forces. These militias also became involved in sectarian violence, both on their own and in support of the U.S.-installed Shia-dominated government's repression against Sunnis.

In Syria, as the uprising against Bashar al-Assad threatened to topple his regime, Iran intervened to support Assad. When Syrian rebels led by the Nusra Front took control of territory along the Syrian-Lebanese border, Hezbollah joined the fight. Along with the Lebanese Army, they fought a three-year battle to uproot the rebels, including ISIS forces, and succeeded in dislodging ISIS from the border area in August 2017.

Both Hezbollah and Iran emerged as winners in the battle to save Assad and defeat ISIS. But Hezbollah's growing strength contributed to a rise in regional tension, alarming Israel, the United States, and Saudi Arabia. The Saudis were also angry about Hezbollah's condemnation of the U.S.-Saudi bombing of Yemen.

That's why in November 2017, the Saudi Crown Prince concocted a bizarre plan to get at Iran and Hezbollah. He brought the Lebanese Prime Minister Saad Hariri, long backed by Saudi Arabia, to the Saudi capital and pressured him to resign—ostensibly because of the presence of Hezbollah in the Lebanese government. The plan backfired. Returning home, Hariri rescinded his resignation, and the Saudi misadventure only brought more support for Hezbollah, indirectly benefitting Iran.

HAMAS

Iran has also built alliances with Palestinian militia, most notably Hamas, the Palestinian Islamic Jihad, and the Popular Front for the Liberation of Palestine—General Command. The longest relationship is with Islamic Jihad, but the deepest ties have tended to be with Hamas. After the Islamic Revolution, Iran supported the Palestinian cause rhetorically but was not very active. After the Oslo Peace Accords in 1993, which Iran opposed, the Iranians began supporting Hamas and other Palestinian groups that also opposed the U.S.-backed peace process.[195]

With Iran's support of Assad, however, tensions between these Palestinian militias and Iran increased, as some Palestinians— including Hamas—became concerned about the treatment of Palestinian refugees in Syria and spoke out against Assad. In 2012, Hamas broke with Iran. Hamas had never been completely dependent on or a proxy for Iran, but the break meant that Hamas had to forgo much of the funding they had been receiving from Iran, and instead turned to Qatar and Turkey. Since the summer of 2017, there has been somewhat of a reconciliation with Iran.[196]

HOUTHIS IN YEMEN

There is a common misconception that the Houthi rebellion in Yemen is part of a larger Iranian proxy war against Saudi Arabia. The Houthi rebellion grew out of internal political dynamics in Yemen, not Iranian agitation.[197] The Houthis, officially called Ansar Allah, are a homegrown movement that originated in northern Yemen in the 1990s and fought against Yemen's government from 2004 to 2010.

In 2014, charging that the government had failed to provide for the needs of the people in northern Yemen, the Houthis rose up against the central government. Some reports insist that Iran was providing weapons, money, and training to the Houthis before they even entered the capital Sana'a in 2014. Others claim that the

Iranians were not involved early on and that they had actually advised the Houthis not to take over the capital.

After the Saudi-led bombing campaign started in March 2015, however, Iran helped the Houthis with training, mostly through Hezbollah (although the Houthis were already experienced fighters from their past wars with the Yemeni central government). Weapons shipments to the Houthis have been reduced by the Saudi's sea blockade, but Iran has reportedly shipped weapons via Somalia, then transferred them to small fishing boats, which are hard to spot because they are so common. Most of the weapons used by the Houthis, however, had been taken from government armories—mostly, weapons the United States had sold to Yemen.

While there are no ideological or strategic imperatives tying Iran and the Houthis, support for the Houthis helps Iran keep the Saudis bogged down in a costly, protracted quagmire that has brought them international condemnation because of the bombing of civilians and civilian infrastructure that has devastated Yemen.

WHAT IS IRAN'S RELATIONSHIP WITH RUSSIA?

Iran and Russia have a long history. Dating back to the Safavid period in Iran, historians can point to various interactions between Persians and Russians. The relationship has often been filled with suspicion and tension due to Russia's historical interference in Iran's internal affairs.

More recently, Russia and Iran have come together due to shared interests. First, Syria has strategic importance for the two nations, and both were anxious to make sure Assad was not overthrown. Additionally, both wanted to push back against Sunni extremism globally. Since the time of the Soviet-Afghan war in the 1980s, Tehran and Moscow have had a shared animosity towards

Sunni Islamist groups and have been wary of the links some Western powers had forged with these groups.

A second factor for closer ties has been the isolation both countries have faced from the West. Iran has been isolated due to its nuclear program and its links with groups like Hezbollah. Russia's actions in Ukraine and Crimea have left it facing sanctions from the West.

Russia played a key role in negotiating the Iran nuclear deal, and after the accord was signed, its relationship with Iran became stronger. Iran had already relied heavily on Russian weapons to supply its military, but those ties deepened as Russia removed its own restrictions on selling more sophisticated weapons to Iran.

Additionally, the countries have extensive trade links. In 2017 alone, they signed energy agreements worth $30 billion. These range from the development of Iran's oil and gas fields to collaboration on research. They have moved beyond trade in fossil fuels into telecoms and agriculture, and they plan to expand multilateral cooperation in Central Asia and the Caucasus.

On the negative side, Russia has developed a military connection with Israel that concerns Iran, and Russia has increased its ties to some of Iran's Arab adversaries, including Saudi Arabia.[198]

Friction has also developed around Syria. While Russia and Iran worked together in their military campaigns to support Assad, in negotiating Syria's future, Iran felt that Russia had negotiated with the United States and others behind its back.

WHAT RELATIONSHIP DOES IRAN HAVE WITH THE ASIAN POWERS? CHINA? INDIA? JAPAN? SOUTH KOREA? AUSTRALIA?

When it comes to regional powers in the east, many of Iran's relationships are centered around oil. China, India, Japan, Korea, and even Australia require oil and its derivatives to fuel their economic growth—and Iran has the oil.

China's interest, however, goes even further. China is seeking to check American power in the Middle East, just as they are in every other region. They see Iran as a lynchpin for their objectives. China is seeking Iranian partnership in implementing its Silk Road Economic Belt initiative, and is trying to build a transportation network that connects China to Europe, bypassing the Red Sea and Mediterranean.[199]

For Iran, China provides a market for its energy resources, and receives critical investment and help modernizing its oil and natural gas sector. Ironically, the Chinese foothold in Iran came about because Western sanctions on Iran kept Western firms out of Iranian markets.[200]

Additionally, Iran and China have slowly built a solid military relationship, including weapons sales, training, and joint naval exercises in the Persian Gulf.[201] This relationship could prove far more advantageous to Iran than its military relationship with Russia, mainly because the Chinese do not have military ties to Iran's adversaries in the Middle East.

Japan and South Korea's alliance with the U.S. makes their relationships with Iran much more problematic. Like China, these countries need access to oil, but they also rely on the U.S. security umbrella. Deeper ties beyond the energy sector would cause tension with the United States.[202] Additionally, Iran's closeness with China makes both Japan and South Korea nervous. With the removal of some sanctions after the signing of the nuclear deal, however, both nations have upped their investments in Iran.[203]

Australia's relations have taken a different path. While access to energy is important, Australia has made its relationship with the U.S. paramount. Trade with Iran has been minimal, especially after Australia imposed its own set of sanctions in 2008. Australia does see some common interests, viewing Iran as a partner in fighting ISIS and creating a stable Iraq. But on balance, the relationship remains limited at best.[204]

India, like China, is a significant importer of Iranian crude oil. Sanctions have slowed trade between both countries, but recently the Indians have stepped up investment inside Iran, including funding for the new port of Chabahar. India wants to develop the north-south corridor that connects Central Asia to the Persian Gulf. Closer ties between India and Iran have caused tension with Pakistan.[205]

WHAT RELATIONSHIP DOES IRAN HAVE WITH LATIN AMERICA AND AFRICA?

Latin America and Africa often get overlooked when discussing Iran's relations across the globe. While not nearly as influential or extensive as the U.S. or China, Iran nonetheless has established a foothold on both continents. Iran's aims are centered around three main factors: easing its Western-imposed isolation due to sanctions, countering U.S.-Israeli-Saudi influence, and creating strategic depth in case Iran is attacked.

In Africa, Iran has engaged Shia communities in various African countries to challenge Saudi Arabia's Sunni influence. It has set up schools and brings thousands of students from across Africa to study in Iran's religious center, Qom. It has also helped fund Shia social welfare centers, with soup kitchens and homeless shelters. Saudi diplomatic cables released in 2015 by WikiLeaks reveal Saudi concern about Iran's Shiite expansion in Mali, Mauritania, Burkina Faso, and Nigeria in West Africa.[206] The funds and the outreach, however, pale in comparison to the billions of dollars and the thousands of schools and mosques set up by the Saudis.

In terms of allies at the national level in Africa, Sudan was once a solid Iranian ally. The Sudanese relationship was built on a mutual distrust of the Western-dominated international system. Despite representing different sects of Islam, the two countries developed a robust military relationship. Iran had even used Sudan as a land route to smuggle weapons to Hamas. But in 2016, the Sudanese severed ties with Iran due to pressure from Saudi Arabia, which financed Sudan after its loss of revenue when oil-rich South Sudan gained independence in 2011.[207]

Sudan's neighbor, Eritrea, is another of Iran's curious alliances, given that it is a country of Christians and Sunni Muslims. As the Eritreans emerged from a long conflict to gain independence from Ethiopia in 1991, many Eritreans hoped their nation would come into the Western orbit. But continued U.S. support for Ethiopia forced Eritrea to look elsewhere. Iran saw Eritrea's disgruntlement as an opportunity to gain a foothold in the Red Sea. It wanted to use Eritrea as a waystation for funneling weapons to the Houthis in Yemen, as well as to Hamas in Gaza. Iran's operations in Eritrea are part of its larger goal of controlling the Bab el Mandeb strait and the water route to the Suez Canal. Also, the United States and France have large bases in neighboring Djibouti, so a presence in Eritrea could help Iran with intelligence gathering.

Oddly enough, Israel also operates in Eritrea, maintaining a listening facility to monitor Iranian activities in the Red Sea.[208] Cooperating with Israel was a way for the Eritrean government to balance its controversial relationship with Iran. Even odder was the revelation in a 2016 report by the UN Monitoring Group on Somalia and Eritrea that Eritrea had sent 400 soldiers to fight alongside the Saudis in Yemen against the Houthis, who are supported by Iran; Eritrea denied the report.[209]

Iran's relations with other African countries may cause some anxiety in the West and with the Saudis, but their activities have been minimal, and their African hosts seem to easily switch sides when a better deal is offered.[210]

LATIN AMERICA

Heading west to Latin America, we see similar trends. Iran has formed ties with leaders searching for ways to buck the U.S.-led international order. Iran's most important partner in Latin America has been Venezuela. Since 1999, when the revolutionary leader Hugo Chavez came to power, the relationship experienced a rapid expansion. Both countries saw themselves as the vanguard against U.S. interference in the region, and both have been the victims of US sanctions. Their relationship has mainly focused on oil, manufacturing, and trade partnerships.

Iran built close relations with Bolivia when Evo Morales became president in 2006. As in Venezuela, the relationship was built on opposition to the U.S.-led global order. Cuba, Ecuador, and Nicaragua also developed closer links along the same lines.

Another partner in the region has been Brazil, due to trade in the energy sector. In 2010, the Brazilians, along with Turkey, attempted to find a solution to the nuclear impasse with Iran. While they were able to get an agreement from Iran, the United States and other international players refused to honor their attempts.

Iran has been seeking relationships in Africa and Latin America in hopes of curtailing its sanctions-imposed isolation. After signing the nuclear deal, Iran's need for immediate and sizable investment meant it would lean more heavily on Russia and China, leaving out smaller and poorer countries in Africa and Latin America. Also, increased trade and cooperation with the U.S. by some potential partners has meant Iran faces a dwindling number of choices. Most countries are unwilling to give up lucrative trade with the powerful United States in exchange for comparatively paltry deals with Iran.

*****

While Iran is a mid-level power battered by decades of sanctions, it is still remarkable to see how the government of Iran has leveraged its meager resources and ideological fervor to have a major influence abroad. Many Iranians, however, would much prefer that their government focus on improving the lives of its citizens and building beneficial trade relations instead of spreading its theology and military zeal beyond its borders.

CHAPTER 10: THE WAY FORWARD

As I conclude this book in early 2018, Iran has just emerged from a period of internal turmoil. A series of protests that began on December 28, 2017 and lasted for several weeks shook the nation. The protests, which began over economic hardships suffered by the young and working class, quickly spread to more than 80 cities and towns, making them the largest public manifestation of discontent in Iran since the disputed 2009 presidential election.

The protests reflected the unfulfilled expectations of Iran's working class and young people. President Rouhani had won re-election in 2017 by promising more jobs for Iran's youth through more foreign investment, as well as more social justice, individual freedom, and political tolerance. The economic promises rested on the notion that Rouhani would be able to deliver a nuclear deal that would lift sanctions and revive the economy. Rouhani delivered on the nuclear deal, but the infusion of funds that came with the partial lifting of sanctions did not improve the lives of ordinary Iranians.

To make matters worse, in December 2017, the government undertook a number of economic austerity measures that led to a hike in fuel prices and other basic goods. An epidemic of avian influenza killed 15 million chickens, further inflating the price for eggs and chicken, the most popular and affordable foods for Iranians.

That same month, Iranian President Hassan Rouhani had proposed a new budget and made it open for the public to see. Many were angry when they discovered that it called for slashing subsidies for the poor while allocating enormous funds for Iran's wealthy religious foundations, some of which were linked to corrupt credit institutions that had depleted the savings of many Iranians. Some people were also upset to see such a large chuck of the budget going to the powerful military and paramilitary forces, including $8 billion for the Revolutionary Guards.

The protests that broke out in December 2017 initially focused on high prices and corruption. But they soon took on a rare political dimension, rejecting the entire system and denouncing Supreme Leader Ayatollah Khamenei, President Rouhani, and the Revolutionary Guards. Some of the protesters also condemned Iran's overseas interventions, calling for the nation's resources to be spent at home.

Many speculated that conservative opponents of moderate President Rouhani had started the demonstrations as a way to capitalize on public frustration but that they quickly lost control of both the message and the actions.

While most protesters were peaceful, some became violent, attacking shops, cars, government buildings, and even police stations. The government called in the police and Revolutionary Guards to quash the demonstrations. Twenty-two people were killed in clashes and more than 1,000 were arrested. The government also countered the protests by organizing large pro-government rallies.

The Revolutionary Guard blamed the unrest on the United States, Israel, and Saudi Arabia, as well as the exiled opposition group MEK (the People's Mujahadeen of Iran) and supporters of the monarchy that had been overthrown in the 1979 revolution.

President Rouhani was more sympathetic. He said that despite the exploitation of the protests by outsiders, the demonstrators had legitimate economic, political, and social grievances. He also pointed out the generational element to the unrest, saying, "We cannot pick a lifestyle and tell two generations after us to live like that. It is impossible... The views of the young generation about life and the world is different than ours." Over 90 percent of the people arrested during the protests were under age 25.

To the dismay of the Trump administration and other anti-regime forces, the protests fizzled out after a few weeks. Their demise was due to the government crackdown, but also because they had no central leadership, did not put forth coherent demands, failed to get widespread support, and posed no realistic alternative to the regime. But they did strike a chord, revealing a level of anger and frustration that will remain until the government takes concrete steps to address their economic grievances.

It will be difficult to significantly improve the economy, however, as long as the fate of nuclear deal and sanctions hang in the balance. When the nuclear agreement was signed in 2015, many Iranians rejoiced over the chance to "rejoin the world" because the deal was not just about nukes. It was also about the future direction of Iran. Just as American conservatives tried to scuttle the deal, so did conservatives in Iran. They wanted Iran to stand up to the West, not negotiate. They were afraid that Western influence would pollute the revolution—and diminish their power. They feared that President Rouhani would end up like President Mikhail Gorbachev, whose reforms and detente with the West led to the unraveling of the Soviet Union.

The nuclear deal marked a triumph over the hardliners in both countries. A milestone for diplomacy, it was a tectonic shift from the past, when officials from Iran and the United States were not even authorized to speak to one another. In the course of the intense negotiations, American and Iranian diplomats became acquainted—some would even say they became friends. Republicans in Washington chided Secretary of State John Kerry for what they considered his "chummy relationship" with Iran's American-educated Foreign Minister Mohammad Javad Zarif.

The triumphant negotiations led many to believe that the nuclear deal would pave the way for talks on a wide range of other issues, from Iran's development of ballistic missiles to the conflicts in Afghanistan, Iran, Syria, and Yemen. Coordination on these critical areas could have helped to bring an end to those long, agonizing conflicts.

Storming into this fragile space like a bull in a China shop came Donald Trump, excoriating the nuclear deal and blaming Iran for all the troubles in the Middle East. He ran over to Saudi Arabia to sell more weapons—and participate in a traditional war dance with the Saudi king. Not only did Trump and King Salman bond, but a "bromance" developed between the next generation: Salman's young, aggressive son and heir to the throne, Mohammed bin Salman, and Trump's son-in-law Jared Kushner.

President Trump managed to infuriate Iranians of all political stripes when he added Iran to the list of countries whose citizens would be banned from entering the United States, hurting countless Iranian families who had nothing to do with the hostilities.

Another example of Trump's ability to offend all Iranians was when he accused Iran of harassing American ships "in the Arabian Gulf." The Arabian Gulf? Really? Iranians went wild. All Iranians call this body of water that separates them from their Arab neighbors "the Persian Gulf." So do cartographers. President Rouhani ridiculed Trump for his ignorance of geography. "Trump should ask his military what is written as the name of this gulf," he jested. Nearly three million Iranians bombarded Trump's Instagram account with nasty comments.

When protests broke out at the end of Demember 2017, Trump gave his full support, saying "The people of Iran are finally acting against the brutal and corrupt Iranian regime," and ridiculously tried to take the issue to the UN Security Council. The Iranian government condemned what it called "grotesque interference" in the country's domestic affairs, and used this interference to rally internal support for the government. Whether Iranians were pro- or anti-government, the idea that Donald Trump cared about their well-being seemed like a cruel joke.

*****

The American demonization of Iran did not start with Trump. Since 1979, it has run deep and wide in mainstream US politics, among both Democrats and Republicans. Officials in both parties have repeatedly declared themselves ready and eager to "strike" and "obliterate" Iran. Republican Senator John McCain sang, "Bomb, bomb, bomb Iran," to the tune of an old Beach Boys song and embraced the murderous MEK that is so hated by most Iranians.[211] Democratic Congressman Brad Sherman said U.S. sanctions should be strong enough to "hurt the Iranian people."[212] Billionaire political funder Sheldon Adelson called for an unprovoked nuclear attack on Iran.

The U.S. military has been threatening Iran as well. General Joseph Votel, head of the U.S. Central Command, told Congress that the U.S. must be prepared to use military means to confront and defeat the "greatest destabilizing force in the Middle East."[213] Admiral James Lyons Jr., former commander of the U.S. Pacific Fleet, said the U.S. military was prepared to "drill them back to the fourth century."[214]

President Trump took the dregs of this belligerence and turned it into his foreign policy. He brought the most diehard Iran-haters into his cabinet. He surrounded himself with people itching to, in the words of Senator John McCain, "Bomb, bomb, bomb Iran."

*****

To single out Iran as the source of global terrorism is absurd. According to the Global Terrorism Database of King's College

London, more than 94 percent of the deaths caused by Islamic terrorism from 2001 to 2016 were perpetrated by ISIS, Al Qaeda, and other Sunni jihadists. Iran is fighting those groups, not fueling them. Iran is a Shia nation combatting Sunni jihadists who consider Shia, and Westerners, infidels. Not one Iranian has ever been linked to a terrorist attack in the United States.

If Americans want to assign blame for Middle Eastern instability and terrorism, how about starting with the United States? The greatest single action in modern history to destabilize the region was the 2003 U.S. invasion of Iraq. American interventions in the Middle East have ignited civil wars, religious fanaticism, and vicious sectarianism.

Another appropriate place to point the finger is Saudi Arabia. Saudi money and ideology have fueled Sunni jihadists from the time of the mujahedeen in Afghanistan. The Saudis only stopped funding Al Qaeda and ISIS after those groups started biting the hand that fed them. In the West, almost every terrorist attack has had some connection to Saudi Arabia. Why, then, did the Trump administration put Iranians, not Saudis, on the list of people banned from entry to the United States?

"The United States cast off the most populous, cohesive country in the region, Iran, in favor of a bunch of corrupt, venal, terrorist-supporting dudes in Saudi Arabia. It is unconscionable," said Colonel Larry Wilkerson, former chief of staff for Colin Powell, who was Secretary of State under the Bush administration.[215]

Sadly, even tragically, that's not how most Americans see it. Following the narrative propagated by politicians and the mainstream media, Americans rank Iran alongside North Korea as one of their "greatest enemies."[216]

This doesn't make any sense. Iran is not a credible threat to the United States. Its military may be good at confronting ISIS, but it is no match for the U.S. military. Iran spends somewhere between

$15 billon and $30 billion a year on its military while the United States spends $700 billion.[217] U.S. ally Saudi Arabia, with one-third of Iran's population, has far superior weaponry, thanks to U.S. weapons sales. In terms of military spending, Saudi Arabia ranks third in the world, after the behemoths U.S. and China, while Iran ranks number 19.[218] Even Turkey and Egypt, two other major powers in the region, are militarily superior to Iran.

What about Iran's nuclear threat? The inspections regime Iran agreed to under the nuclear deal is the most rigorous inspections regime ever negotiated. And while the world would be a safer place if Iran did not have nuclear weapons, the same can be said of *all* nations. We agonize over Iran's potential to acquire a nuclear bomb while our ally, Israel, has somewhere between 80 and 200 nuclear warheads and, in stark contrast to Iran, has flatly refused to sign the non-proliferation treaty (NPT). The volatile and repressive government of Pakistan, on Iran's border, also has nuclear weapons. And, what about the United States itself? The U.S. is a signatory to the NPT but has defied its treaty obligations by spending outrageous sums of money to upgrade its nuclear arsenal and by failing to make real progress in nuclear disarmament.

Iran is a powerful nation, but it will never be a superpower. Iran tries to increase its influence by spreading Shi'ism, but this brand of Islam represents only about 10–15 percent of Muslims worldwide. The overwhelming majority of Muslims are Sunni. So even in a religious war, Iran could never win.

While the U.S. accuses Iran of pursuing regional hegemony, ironically, Iran's regional strength has come mainly from the American overthrow of the Taliban in Afghanistan and Saddam Hussein in Iraq. Contrary to U.S. propaganda, Iran's aim is not to take over in the Middle East but to preserve itself. Given the lingering trauma of the war with Iraq, the Saudi-Sunni rivalry, and the hostility of the U.S. superpower, Tehran's primary objective is defense and survival. It wants friendly and stable governments on its borders. Unlike more distant powers, Iran has permanent interests in neighboring Iraq, Syria, and Afghanistan and is affected when there is conflict in neighboring countries. Iran wants to ensure that it will not be attacked by unfriendly nations, whether Israel, the United States, Saudi Arabia, or an aggressive neighbor (such as the attack by Iraq in 1980). It also wants to protect itself from terrorist activities at home.

The U.S. military concurs. According to the U.S. Defense Department, "Iran's military doctrine is defense. It is designed to deter an attack, survive an initial strike, retaliate against an aggressor, and force a diplomatic solution to hostilities while avoiding any concessions that challenge its core interests."[219]

*****

If Iran is no threat to the United States, then why is the U.S. government so hostile towards Iran? The answer is that U.S. policy in the Middle East has been hijacked by a variety of actors who are out for their own interests.

For starters, there is the long-standing U.S. relationship with the Saudi monarchy, which is obsessed with its rival Iran. The United States should not be taking sides in this regional feud. In an April 2016 interview in *The Atlantic*, President Obama expressed his frustration with the destabilizing Saudi-Iranian rivalry. "The competition between the Saudis and the Iranians—which has helped to feed proxy wars and chaos in Syria and Iraq and Yemen—requires us to say to our friends [the Saudis] as well as to the Iranians that they need to find an effective way to share the neighborhood and institute some sort of cold peace," Obama said.[220] Instead of encouraging the Saudis, the U.S. should be pushing them to "share the neighborhood."

U.S. policy has also been hijacked by the Israeli government, especially under Prime Minister Benjamin Netanyahu. For

Netanyahu, Iran acts as a foil to divert attention from his own oppressive policies toward Palestinians in the West Bank, Gaza, and East Jerusalem. Obama was willing to defy Netanyahu's opposition to the Iran deal, but Trump swallowed the Netanyahu position—hook, line, and sinker. When Trump decertified the Iran deal, Netanyahu was elated, calling it "a very brave decision that is right for the world."

The leaders of Israel and Saudi Arabia have been so eager to shape a more aggressive U.S. policy toward Iran that they downplayed their animosity towards each other and began collaborating. Former Secretary of State John Kerry said that leaders of both nations pressured Obama to bomb Iran instead of signing a deal. "Each of them said to me, you have to bomb Iran, it's the only thing they are going to understand," Kerry said.[221] Tragically, what this really suggests is that threats and bombing are the only things that the present leaders of Israel and Saudi Arabia understand.

U.S. policy towards Iran has also been hijacked by weapons makers and Pentagon contractors whose very lucrative livelihoods (and shareholder benefits) are tied to peddling fear and justifying a constant state of war. For these "merchants of death," as Pope Francis calls them, Iran is a gold mine. They rake in enormous profits from U.S. military assistance and weapons sales to anti-Iran countries such as Israel, Saudi Arabia, the Emirates and Bahrain. They also make a fortune from what American taxpayers spend to keep about 30,000 U.S. troops, ships, and aircraft in the Gulf (somewhere between $50 billion and $90 billion a year).

Finally, others who influence U.S. policy towards Iran are the bottom feeders who suck up the crumbs—the American politicians who receive donations from pro-Israel groups, the lobbyists in the pay of the weapons industries and foreign governments, the pundits whose "think tanks" are bankrolled by Lockheed Martin or some Saudi prince, and national-security bureaucrats whose careers and bank accounts are enhanced by the constant threat of war.

WHERE WILL CHANGE COME FROM?

Iranians needs to get out from under the yoke of both internal hardliners and international pressure so that they can transform the nation into a more open and democratic society.

Some say the only way this transformation will happen is by overthrowing the present regime. They point to the election of three presidents claiming to be reformists—Akbar Hashemi Rafsanjani, Mohammad Khatami, and Hassan Rouhani. All three were unable to implement most of their promised reforms. They also point to the crushing of the nonviolent, reformist Green Movement and the more recent quashing of the January 2018 wave of protests.

But is violent revolution an option? Who could overthrow the regime? The National Council of Resistance in Iran, which is really the same as the People's Mujahedeen of Iran (MEK), puts itself forward as a group with cadre inside Iran, ready to take over. But this group has almost zero support inside Iran.

What about separatist minority groups rising up to overthrow the regime? Together, these minority groups make up quite a large portion of the population—about 40 percent. For many years, the United States covertly supported separatist groups inside Iran to destabilize the country. Of the minorities, the Kurds have historically been the group pressing the hardest for greater autonomy or separation. The militant Kurdish separatists were defeated in the 1980s, although the CIA, together with Israel's Mossad, continued to provide covert support during the Bush years and, according to the Iranian government, the Obama years as well. There are also separatists among the Baluchis in southeastern Iran, Arabs in the southwest, and some Azeri Turks in the northwest. But these minorities have been part of Iran for ages, and most are well integrated. The Azeris, Iran's largest minority, are the most fully integrated. The Supreme Leader Ayatollah Ali Khamenei is Azeri. Efforts over the years to encourage uprisings by these various ethnic groups have come to naught. Meanwhile, the regime's coercive apparatus has only become more heavily armed, more organized, and more battle-hardened.

How about more sanctions? Could even tighter sanctions cause the regime to crumble? This strategy hasn't worked since 1979—and has even less chance of working now. Since the signing of the nuclear deal, the rest of the world is moving ahead with all kinds of business ventures. The White House would face a major international backlash if it unilaterally reinstated nuclear-related sanctions, including secondary sanctions on foreign firms doing business with Iran.

Looking at the recent history of the Middle East, a more important question to ask is: Even if the regime could be overthrown, what would follow? Another failed state like Iraq, Afghanistan, Libya, and Syria? The track record for regime change in the region is dismal.

CHANGE FROM WITHIN

A nonviolent process of transformation from within is really the only option. Fortunately, demographics are on the side of change.

The sector holding back change is primarily the older, religious generation, and that generation is, literally, dying out. Supreme Leader Ali Khamenei is elderly and in poor health; so are many of the clerics and politicians from the days of the revolution.

MEDEA BENJAMIN

Most Iranians were born after 1979; two-thirds of the population is under 25. The nation's restless youth, particularly those living in urban areas, want more economic options and social freedom.

The government tries to control the population in ways that range from operations by the secret police to vetting candidates for election to pervasive propaganda, but Iranians are well educated and generally well informed. While the state controls television broadcasting, and satellite dishes are technically illegal, some 70 percent of Iranians own satellite receivers and have access to programs from all over the world. The government blocks some websites like Facebook and Reddit, but Iranians easily find ways around the blocks or use encrypted messaging apps like Telegram. There are about 75,000 bloggers; the Internet is abuzz with critiques and ideas. Out of 80 million people, 48 million Iranians have smartphones and 40 million use Telegram messenger.

Iranians are also not physically isolated. Many travel to Europe or the United States on vacation or to study. There are about 50,000 Iranians studying around the world, some 9,000 of them in the United States.

About five million Iranians live abroad, mostly in North America, Europe, Australia, and the greater Middle East. This number keeps growing every year, as some 160,000 Iranians emigrate in search of better economic opportunities. Many of them maintain regular contact with their family and friends in Iran. With constant travel in and out of the country, Iranians understand the pros and cons of other societies, and this information informs and elevates their push for change back home.

*****

Looking at the history of Iran in the last century alone, we see that Iranians have a remarkable record of political activism. In more recent history, since the 1979 upheaval, Iranians have been putting their lives at risk to organize human rights groups, women's organizations, unions, legal collectives, and other forms of social activism. They have come out on the streets to protest. Iranian prisoners of conscience have gone on prolonged hunger strikes to call attention to their plight. Activists have staged hunger strikes outside prisons to protest the mistreatment of prisoners and the lack of due process. Women regularly defy the government-imposed dress code. Student groups protest the rising costs of higher education, the privatization of student services, gender and religious discrimination, and the presence of security forces on campuses.

Many activists end up in prison. Others escape and seek refuge abroad. Most, however, remain in Iran and continue their courageous work. They have had success in opening up opportunities for women, invigorating the electoral system, loosening the dress code, creating more government transparency, fighting corruption, making the judicial system more accountable, decreasing the use of the death penalty, and pushing for economic subsidies for the poor. For many, however, the reforms have been painfully slow and as the December 2017 protests showed, there is little articulaton between the organized activst groups and the unorganized, pent-up frustration of Iranian youth.

The best way that we, as outsiders, can help speed up the process of reform is to stop our governments from threatening Iran, imposing more sanctions, destroying the nuclear deal, or actually waging war. When international tensions ease, Iranians have more breathing room. Our job is to get our governments out of the way so that the Iranian people can, as they have done so brilliantly in their past, transform their own nation.

*****

On the last day of my visit to Iran in 2014, I spent some time shopping for gifts to take home. In one of the lovely craft stores, I fell into a conversation with the owner. He was delighted that I was from the United States, and had lots of questions: What did I think of Barack Obama? Did I like Iranian food? Did I know his cousin in Los Angeles? We chatted for a while, and then I left without buying anything.

The storekeeper ran after me, holding a beautiful painting in his hand. "I want to give you this," he said. "It was painted by a friend of mine." He handed me a painting of a large, traditional family sitting on the floor in front of a low table brimming with food—kebabs, rice, beef kofte, flatbread, pomegranates. "When you go home, I want you to think of the people of our two nations sitting around a table together, eating good food, enjoying good conversation, meeting each other's families. That is how it should be."

I tearfully accepted the glorious gift. Once home, I put it in a gold frame and hung it on the wall in the entryway to our house. I look at it as I go in and out of the house every day. It serves as a reminder of the generosity of the Iranian people and the way things might one day evolve between our nations.

Prime Minister Mossadegh and President Truman, 1951. Mossadegh
was overthrown in a CIA coup in 1953.
Photo credit: Abbie Rowe.

Man in US with sign during Iran hostage crisis, 1979.
Photo credit: Marion S. Trikosko.

Coronation of Reza Shah, 1926.

Morality police (woman in chador) chastising a young Iranian for wearing an "improper" hijab.

Young Iranian man and woman socializing at a cafe in Tehran, 2015.
Photo credit: Medea Benjamin.

Author (third from right) visits woman-owned medical supplies business, 2015.
Photo credit: Medea Benjamin.

Protesting voter fraud during the Green Movement in 2011.
Getty Images.

Secretary of State John Kerry and Foreign Minister Javad Zarif during
Iran Nuclear Deal talks.
Photo credit: Dominick Reuter/AFP/Getty Images.

Iranian President Hassan Rouhani, elected in 2013 and re-elected in
2017.

Isfahan Mosque highlights Iran's beautiful 5,000 year old culture.

Women elected to the Iranian National Assembly in 2017.
Photo credit: Shahrvand.

Statue of Shah being torn down during 1979 Revolution.

Zoroastrian temple in Yazd.
Photo credit: Zenith210.

Vank Cathedral, Armenian Quarter, Isfahan, Iran.
Photo credit: Mike Gadd.

Young Iranian Kurds.
Photo credit: Abdul Hamid Zibari.

ACKNOWLEDGEMENTS

Hats off to Sandy Davies for his invaluable work on the history of Iran that became the basis for chapters one and two, and to David Shams for his rigorous help on the very complicated chapters about Iran's relations with the U.S., the Middle East, and beyond. David's personal understanding of Iran helped me navigate some treacherous political waters.

A big thanks to Brienne Kordis for being such a terrific assistant and great researcher and editor. I give my deepest appreciation to Leila Zand for her deep insights into her beautiful culture and country, from taking us there to giving critical feedback on the book. Crystal Zevon gave me marvelous editing help, as did the very knowledgeable Ann Wright. Thanks to Marin Kirk for your research and Elliot Swain for being a critical reader, and helping to gather the photos. I so appreciate Phyllis Bennis and Vijay Prashad for helping me sort out some of the thorny political points concerning Iran's regional allies.

My ever encouraging and upbeat publisher John Oakes and the entire OR team are a delight to work with.

My life partner, Tighe Barry, has been sweetly tolerant of my late night writing and constantly supportive—from hot tea to shoulder rubs. Thanks to my daughters, Maya and Arlen, and their families, for their shared concerns and efforts to make the world a more peaceful place.

I am ever indebted to CODEPINK cofounder Jodie Evans, with whom I have had the great honor and privilege of working with for the past 16 years, sharing our grief at the violence that surrounds us and optimism that citizen activism can lead the way to a more loving planet. I so appreciate the CODEPINK family that I get to work so closely with, including Farida Sharalam, Ariel Gold, Taylor Morley, Nancy Mancias, Mark Folkman, Mariana Mendoza, and Haley Pedersen. Paki Wieland, our "house mom" in D.C., makes the CODEPINK house glow with warmth even on the coldest days.

I am indebted to the work of the National Iranian American Council (NIAC), especially Trita Parsi. I so appreciate Trita's analysis and dedication to stop the U.S. and Iran from going to war. I also thank Marjan Shallal for helping me understand and fall in love with Iranian culture.

Finally, I send my thanks to the many people I have met on trips to Iran who fill me with hope and inspire me to bring our nations closer together.

FURTHER RESOURCES

A History of Iran: Empire of the Mind
Michael Axworthy
Renowned Arab and Islamic Studies professor Michael Axworthy writes eloquently and authoritatively about Iran's fascinating and complex history, taking us through each era from the early Zoroastrians to the challenges of modern-day Iran.

A History of Modern Iran
Ervand Abrahamian
As Abrahamian trances Iran's traumatic journey through the twentieth century, he adroitly negotiates the twists and turns of the country's regional and international politics--always keeping the people of Iran at the center of the narrative.

Losing an Enemy: Obama, Iran, and the Triumph of Diplomacy
Trita Parsi
This book focuses on President Obama's strategy toward Iran's nuclear program and reveals how the historic agreement of 2015 broke the persistent stalemate in negotiations that had blocked earlier efforts.

Bitter Friends, Bosom Enemies: Iran, the U.S., and the Twisted Path to Confrontation
Barbara Slavin

Slavin reveals that relations between Washington and Tehran have been riddled with contradictions for decades and details missed opportunities for reconciliation.

Iran Without Borders
Hamid Dabashi
Acclaimed cultural critic and scholar of Iranian history traces the evolution of this worldly culture from the eighteenth century to the present day.

Close Up
Hamid Dabashi
Dabashi dissects the idea of the oriental in western perceptions of Iranian cinema and details the way that film festivals and distribution in the west have shaped domestic output in Iran.

Operation Ajax
Mike de Seve
This is the story of the CIA coup that removed the democratically elected Mossadegh and reinstated the monarchy.

In the Rose Garden of the Martyrs
Christopher de Bellaigue
An insider's account of Iran and its people, it glides easily between memoir and history of the Islamic revolution and the terrible legacy of the Iran-Iraq war.

All the Shah's Men: An American Coup and the Roots of Middle East Terror
Stephen Kinzer
Kinzer's account of the CIA-orchestrated coup in 1953 makes vital reading for anyone interested in the roots of the revolution.

The Ayatollah Begs to Differ: the Paradox of Modern Iran
Hooman Majd
The grandson of an ayatollah and the son of an Iranian diplomat, Hooman Majd offers a unique perspective on Iran's complex culture.

The Last Great Revolution: Turmoil and Transformation in Iran
Robin B. Wright
A rich history of the events of the 1979 Islamic revolution and its aftermath, including wide-ranging interviews with a variety of Iranians.

Lipstick Jihad
Azadeh Moaveni
A young reporter who grew up in California returns to her parents' homeland in this insightful memoir with illuminating anecdotes.

The Essential Rumi
Jalal al-Din Rumi
Rumi, the 13th century Persian poet, is widely acknowledged as being the greatest Sufi mystic of his age. He was the founder of the brotherhood of the Whirling Dervishes. This is a collection of his exquisite poetry.

Poems from the Divan of Hafiz
Gertrude Bell, translator
Khwaja Shemsundin Mahommad Hifiz-e Sirazi, or simply Hafiz, was a14th century mystical poet of Shiraz. His collected works (The Divan) represent a masterpiece of Persian poetry and are to be found in the homes of many Iranians, who learn his poems by heart and still use them as proverbs and sayings.

Modern Iran: Roots and Results of Revolution
Nikki R Keddie
Updated version of the classic work includes a probing and perceptive guide to more than two decades of tumultuous developmentments, including Iran's nuclear policy and US relations.

Iran Awakening: A Memoir of Revolution and Hope
Shirin Ibadi
Shirin Ebadi won the 2003 Nobel Peace Prize for her work advocating for oppressed peoples. *Iran Awakening* is Ebadi's memoir in which she describes her upbringing in pre-Revolutionary Iran, as well as the ways in which the Revolution changed her marriage, her faith, and her career. It is a powerful condemnation of the Islamic regime.

Days of God: The Revolution in Iran and its Consequences
James Buchan
Persian scholar and a former foreign correspondent writes an in-depth account of the revolutionary birth of theocracy in Iran, using declassified diplomatic papers and Persian-language news report and interviews.

Shah of Shahs
Ryszard Kapuscinski
Travel writer and war correspondent Kapuscinski describes the final years of the Shah with a compelling history of conspiracy, repression, fanatacism, and revolution.

The Mantle of the Prophet: Religion and Politics in Iran
Roy Mottahedeh
A great read for anyone interested in an in-depth look at Ayatollah Khomeini, the roots of the revolution, and the origins of the Islamic Republic.

Persia through Writers' Eyes
David Blow
A wonderful series of selections from 3,000 years of descriptive writing, including everyone from Herodotus to John Simpson.

The Blindfold Horse: Memories of a Persian Childhood
Shusha Guppy
An enchanting account of growing up in Persia before the revolution in a society balanced between traditional Islamic life and the transforming forces of westernization.

Persepolis, the Story of a Childhood and Persepolis 2, the Story of a Return
Marjan Satrapi
Satrapi uses the form of the graphic novel to describe life in Iran before and after the revolution through her eyes as a child. Magnificent, moving, and highly original.

Children of Paradise: The Struggle for the Soul of Iran
Laura Secor
This deep look inside Iranian society shows that beneath the country's monolithic exterior, there are dreamers and doers who are shaping Iran's future.

My Uncle Napoleon: A Novel
Iraj Pezeshkzad
A hilarious tale of family life in early 1940s Tehran. This satirical novel features an aristocratic Iranian family led by "Dear Uncle Napoleon" who oversees the group with an iron fist. The story is told from the perspective of Dear Uncle's least favorite nephew and reflects the end of the pre-Revolutionary era.

Jasmine and Stars, Reading More Than Lolita in Tehran
Fatemeh Keshavarz
Blending first-hand recollections of her own life in 1960s Shiraz, Keshavarz shows the intellectual complexity of Iran.

My Father's Notebook
Kader Abdolah
Abdolah's autobiographical novel sees Iran's recent history through the eyes of a father and son, unraveling an intricate tale of moving from the silent world of a village carpet-mender to the increasingly hostile environment of modern Iran.

GUIDEBOOKS
Iran, Bradt Travel Guide
Hilary Smith
A great guide to Iran, combining practical information and detailed historical and cultural background, with lots of practical travel information and detailed maps.

Iran, Lonely Planet Planet Guide
Constantly updated advice on what to see, what to eat, where to stay, as well as key cultural insights and advice.

MEDEA BENJAMIN

Culture Smart! Iran
Stuart Williams, 2016
A concise, well-illustrated and practical guide to local customs, etiquette, and culture.

ENDNOTES

INTRODUCTION

1 "Persia" was the official name of Iran in the Western world prior to 1935. Iranian and Persian are often used interchangeably but Persian relates to a particular ethnicity, while Iranian is a nationality. Modern Iran is comprised of a large number of different ethnic and tribal groups. People who identify as Persian account for the majority, but there are also Azeri, Galati, and Kurdish people. While all are citizens of Iran are Iranians, only some can identify their lineage as Persian.

2 https://www.vox.com/world/2017/9/21/16345600/bernie-sanders-full-text-transcript-foreign-policy-speech-westminster

CHAPTER 1

3 The main sources for the historical material in this chapter, supplemented as noted, are Michael Axworthy's *A History of Iran: Empire of the Mind*, New York, NY: Basic Books, 2008 and Ervand Abrahamian's *A History of Modern Iran*, New York, NY: Cambridge UP, 2008.

4 Durant, Will. "Persia in the History of Civilization," *Addressing 'Iran-America Society*. Mazda Publishers, Inc. July 23, 2011.

5 George Curzon, *Persia and the Persian Question*, p.136.

6 https://nvdatabase.swarthmore.edu/content/iranian-resistance-tobacco-concession-1891-1892

7 Kermit Roosevelt. *Countercoup: the Struggle for the Control of Iran*. New York, NY: McGraw-Hill, 1979. p. 6.

8 Brian Lapping. *End of Empire*. New York, NY: St. Martin's Press, 1985. pp. 204–223

9 https://partners.nytimes.com/library/world/mideast/082053iran-army.html

10 Frances FitzGerald, "Giving the Shah everything he wants." *Harper's*. November 1974.

11 Reza Baraheni, "Terror in Iran." *The New York Review of Books*. October 28 1976. http://www.nybooks.com/articles/1976/10/28/terror-in-iran/#fn-1

12 Ervand Abrahamian, *A History of Modern Iran*. New York, NY: Cambridge UP, 2008, p. 53.

CHAPTER 2

13 Ervand Abrahamian, *The Iranian Mojahedin*, Yale University Press, p121.

14 Roy Mottahedeh, *The Mantle of the Prophet: Religion and Politics in Iran*, 2004, p375.

15 Adam Roberts and Timothy Garton Ash, *Civil Resistance and Power Politics: The Experience of Non-violent Action*, Oxford University Press, 2009, p.51.

16 https://www.washingtonpost.com/archive/politics/1979/01/21/khomeini-from-oblivion-to-the-brink-of-powerlong-exile-from-iran-is-khomeinis-badge-and-handicap/02b4fc68-c0ae-4c71-b3ae-94ef68fefaae/?utm_term=.1013f5afb588

17 https://www.theguardian.com/politics/2012/sep/21/qanda-mek-us-terrorist-organisation

18 https://www.theguardian.com/world/2016/sep/09/iranian-opposition-groups-camp-ashraf-closes

19 https://www.amnesty.org/en/documents/MDE13/021/1990/en/

20 https://www.hrw.org/legacy/backgrounder/mena/iran1205/2.htm

21 https://www.niacouncil.org/kingmaker-irans-presidential-election/

CHAPTER 3

22 http://www.humanrights.com/what-are-human-rights/brief-history/

23 https://freedomhouse.org/report/freedom-world/2017/iran

24 http://www.thecrimson.com/article/1979/12/6/life-under-the-shah-pit-was/

25 https://freedomhouse.org/report/freedom-world/2017/iran
26 Ibid.
27 Situation of Human Rights in the Islamic Republic of Iran, UN Special Rapporteur on Human Rights, August 4, 2017.
28 https://berkleycenter.georgetown.edu/quotes/constitution-of-iran-article-26-freedom-of-association
29 https://www.ccij.ca/cases/kazemi/
30 Situation of Human Rights in the Islamic Republic of Iran, UN Special Rapporteur on Human Rights, August 4, 2017, p10.
31 http://www.li.com/docs/default-source/future-of-iran/2012-future-of-iran-by-karim-lahidji-the-history-of-the-judiciary-in-iran.pdf?sfvrsn=2
32 http://www.telegraph.co.uk/news/worldnews/middleeast/iran/8102358/Rape-in-Irans-prisons-the-cruellest-torture.html
33 https://www.amnesty.org/en/countries/middle-east-and-north-africa/iran/report-iran
34 Situation of Human Rights in the Islamic Republic of Iran, UN Special Rapporteur on Human Rights, August 4, 2017, p10.
35 http://www.ihrr.org/ihrr_article/violence-en_islamic-republic-of-iran-promoting-violence-against-children/
36 https://www.theguardian.com/artanddesign/gallery/2016/jan/08/inside-iran-jail-where-children-face-execution-in-pictures
37 http://www.iranhrdc.org/english/publications/human-rights-data/chart-of-prisoners/1000000595-chart-of-prisones.html
38 https://www.amnesty.org/en/countries/middle-east-and-north-africa/iran/report-iran
39 https://www.amnesty.org/en/latest/news/2012/03/iran-overturn-jail-sentence-human-rights-lawyer/
40 https://www.nytimes.com/2016/09/29/world/asia/narges-mohammadi-iran-sentencing.html?_r=0

CHAPTER 4

41 http://www.telegraph.co.uk/news/2017/10/04/us-votes-against-un-resolution-condemning-death-penalty-gay/
42 http://www.jpost.com/Middle-East/Iran-News/Iran-executes-gay-teenager-in-violation-of-international-law-463234

43 https://www.hrw.org/sites/default/files/reports/
iran1210webwcover_0.pdf

44 https://www.outrightinternational.org/region/islamic-republic-
iran

45 http://irqr.ca/2016/

46 https://www.theguardian.com/world/2005/jul/27/gayrights.iran

47 http://www.economist.com/node/2137652

48 https://www.theguardian.com/world/iran-blog/2014/oct/10/
iran-prostitution-sex-work-runaways

49 http://www.latimes.com/world/la-fg-iran-drug-addiction-2016-
story.html

CHAPTER 5

50 https://www.cia.gov/library/publications/the-world-factbook/
geos/ir.html (via Wikipedia)

51 https://www.theatlantic.com/international/archive/2016/01/
iran-sunnis-saudi/422877/

52 https://www.theatlantic.com/international/archive/2016/01/
iran-sunnis-saudi/422877/

53 http://www.mei.edu/content/article/iran%E2%80%99s-uneasy-
relationship-its-sunni-minorities

54 http://journal.georgetown.edu/iran-vs-its-people-abuses-against-
religious-minorities-by-katrina-lantos-swett/

55 https://www.al-monitor.com/pulse/originals/2017/09/iran-
tehran-sunni-mosque-prayer-space-pounak.html

56 https://freedomhouse.org/report/freedom-world/2017/iran

57 http://www.aljazeera.com/indepth/features/2014/03/iranian-
sunnis-complain-discrimination-2014397125688907.html

58 http://www.bbc.com/news/magazine-29648166

59 http://www.haaretz.com/middle-east-news/iran/1.813519

60 http://www.al-monitor.com/pulse/originals/2013/12/sufi-
practices-questioned-by-iranian-clerics.html

61 http://www.uscirf.gov/sites/default/files/USCIRF%202016%20
Annual%20Report.pdf

62 https://web.archive.org/web/20080422184053/http://www.fidh.
org/asie/rapport/2003/ir0108a.pdf

63 http://iranprimer.usip.org/blog/2016/jan/11/trends-parliamentary-elections
64 https://www.nytimes.com/2014/03/15/opinion/irans-oppressed-christians.html
65 http://www.uscirf.gov/youcef-nadarkhani
66 http://www.thenational.ae/news/world/middle-east/iran-is-young-urbanised-and-educated-census
67 https://www.jewishvirtuallibrary.org/jewish-population-of-the-world
68 Wright, *The Last Great Revolution*, (2000), p.207 (via Wikipedia)
69 https://www.timesofisrael.com/jewish-iranian-mp-lauds-countrys-religious-freedom/
70 http://www.independent.co.uk/news/world/middle-east/irans-jews-on-life-inside-israels-enemy-state-we-feel-secure-and-happy-a6934931.html
71 https://www.theguardian.com/world/2015/jun/01/first-christian-football-captain-in-iran-as-rouhani-puts-focus-on-minorities
72 http://www.uscirf.gov/sites/default/files/Iran.2017.pdf
73 http://www.bbc.com/news/world-middle-east-27438044
74 https://www.criticalthreats.org/briefs/iran-news-round-up/iran-news-round-up-may-16-2016-1
75 http://www.uscirf.gov/sites/default/files/Iran.2017.pdf
76 http://www.uscirf.gov/news-room/op-eds/the-wall-street-journal-whoever-wins-irans-election-its-religious-minorities-lose
77 http://www.uscirf.gov/news-room/op-eds/the-wall-street-journal-whoever-wins-irans-election-its-religious-minorities-lose
78 https://www.amnesty.org/en/countries/middle-east-and-north-africa/iran/report-iran/
79 https://www.iranhumanrights.org/2016/02/24-bahais-in-golestan-long-prison-sentences/
80 http://www.uscirf.gov/news-room/op-eds/the-wall-street-journal-whoever-wins-irans-election-its-religious-minorities-lose
81 http://www.uscirf.gov/sites/default/files/Iran.2017.pdf
82 http://www.loc.gov/law/help/apostasy/#iran
83 http://www.gallup.com/poll/114211/alabamians-iranians-common.aspx

CHAPTER 6

84 http://reports.weforum.org/global-gender-gap-report-2016/
economies/#economy=IRN

85 https://www.amnesty.org/en/latest/news/2011/11/iranian-women-fight-controversial-polygamy-bill/

86 http://iranprimer.usip.org/resource/womens-movement

87 http://reports.weforum.org/global-gender-gap-report-2016/
economies/#economy=IRN

88 http://www.latimes.com/world/la-fg-iran-unmarried-snap-story.html

89 http://www.atlanticcouncil.org/blogs/iraninsight/love-and-marriage-iranian-style

90 http://www.reuters.com/article/us-iran-divorce-idUSKCN0IB0GQ20141022

91 http://www.iranchamber.com/society/articles/abortion_iranian_law.php

92 DeJong, Jocelyn; Iman Mortagy; Bonnie Shepard (2005). "The Sexual and Reproductive Health of Young People in the Arab Countries and Iran." *Reproductive Health Matters*. **13** (25): 49–59.

93 http://iranprimer.usip.org/resource/womens-movement

94 https://euphrates.org/unveiling-and-reveiling-in-iran/

95 https://www.theguardian.com/world/2013/jul/02/iran-president-hassan-rouhani-progressive-views

96 http://www.nydailynews.com/life-style/makeup-speaks-volumes-iran-38-million-women-article-1.1841672

97 http://www.mei.edu/content/article/irans-headscarf-politics

98 http://www.bbc.com/news/world-middle-east-36101150

99 http://www.independent.co.uk/news/world/middle-east/iran-morality-police-14-year-old-girl-teenage-ripped-jeans-sharia-guidance-patrols-womens-right-a7582206.html

100 http://www.mei.edu/content/article/irans-headscarf-politics

101 http://www.bbc.com/news/world-middle-east-40218711

102 http://www.independent.co.uk/news/world/middle-east/lipstick-revolution-irans-women-are-taking-on-the-mullahs-1632257.html

103 Shavarini, Mitra K. (2005-01-01). "The Feminisation of Iranian Higher Education". International Review of Education /

Internationale Zeitschrift für Erziehungswissenschaft / Revue Internationale de l'Education. 51 (4): 329–347, 331, 333, 334, 335. JSTOR 25054545. (via Wikipedia)

104 http://wenr.wes.org/2017/02/education-in-iran

105 http://www.un.org/en/ga/search/view_doc. asp?symbol=A/70/352

106 Mehran, Golnar (2003-08-01). "The Paradox of Tradition and Modernity in Female Education in the Islamic Republic of Iran". Comparative Education Review. 47 (3): 269–286. ISSN 0010-4086. doi:10.1086/378248. (via Wikipedia)

107 Shavarini, Mitra K. (2005-01-01). "The Feminisation of Iranian Higher Education"

108 Mehran, Golnar (2003-08-01). "The Paradox of Tradition and Modernity in Female Education in the Islamic Republic of Iran".

109 Shavarini, Mitra K. (2005-01-01). "The Feminisation of Iranian Higher Education."

110 https://www.iranhumanrights.org/2015/02/womenreport-womens-education/

111 Povey, Tara; Rostami-Povey, Elaheh (2012). *Women, Power and Politics in 21st Century Iran*. Ashgate Publishing, Ltd. p. 42. ISBN 1409402053.

112 https://www.iranhumanrights.org/2015/02/womenreport-womens-education/

113 https://www.iranhumanrights.org/2015/02/womenreport-womens-education/

114 http://www.un.org/en/ga/search/view_doc. asp?symbol=A/70/352

115 https://www.hrw.org/report/2017/05/24/its-mens-club/discrimination-against-women-irans-job-market

116 https://www.hrw.org/report/2017/05/24/its-mens-club/discrimination-against-women-irans-job-market

117 https://www.iranhumanrights.org/2015/02/womenreport-womens-education/

118 https://www.usnews.com/news/best-countries/articles/2017-05-24/in-iran-women-want-rights-jobs-and-a-seat-at-the-table

119 https://www.hrw.org/report/2017/05/24/its-mens-club/
    discrimination-against-women-irans-job-market
120 Ibid
121 Ibid
122 http://www.al-monitor.com/pulse/originals/2016/12/iran-
    cabinet-reshuffle-women-vp-ministers-shojaei-ahmadipour.html
123 Ibid
124 http://indianexpress.com/article/world/iran-presidential-
    elections-women-who-were-never-candidates-4661542/
125 http://www.bbc.com/news/world-middle-east-36182796
126 http://www.ipu.org/wmn-e/classif.htm
127 http://www.al-monitor.com/pulse/originals/2016/02/iran-
    rouhani-women-vote-parliament-elections.html
128 https://www.rferl.org/a/iran-female-soccer-star-protests-
    husband-travel-ban/27248135.html
129 https://www.nytimes.com/2016/07/03/sports/iranian-women-
    push-for-more-open-stadiums.html?_r=0
130 https://www.nytimes.com/2016/07/03/sports/iranian-women-
    push-for-more-open-stadiums.html?_r=0
131 https://www.amnesty.org/en/latest/news/2016/08/iran-
    womens-rights-activists-treated-as-enemies-of-the-state-in-
    renewed-crackdown/
132 https://www.usnews.com/news/best-countries/
    articles/2017-05-24/in-iran-women-want-rights-jobs-and-a-seat-
    at-the-table

CHAPTER 7

133 https://www.bloomberg.com/news/articles/2012-08-07/
    goldman-sachs-s-mist-topping-brics-as-smaller-markets-
    outperform
134 https://www.washingtonpost.com/archive/politics/1979/01/17/
    pahlavi-fortune-a-staggering-sum/ef54b268-15c5-4ee5-b0a1-
    194f90d87bba/?utm_term=.5f4b40f4560c
135 https://www.washingtonpost.com/archive/politics/1979/01/17/
    pahlavi-fortune-a-staggering-sum/ef54b268-15c5-4ee5-b0a1-
    194f90d87bba/?utm_term=.5f4b40f4560c

136 http://www.truth-out.org/news/item/22118-fruits-of-irans-revol ution?tmpl=component&print=1

137 Farhad Mumani and Sohrab Behdad. *Class and Labor in Iran: Did the Revolution Matter?*, Syracuse University Press, 2006, p 39.

138 http://www.ir.undp.org/content/iran/en/home/countryinfo. html

139 http://journal.georgetown.edu/the-ahmadinejad-presidency-and-the-future-of-irans-economy/

140 http://www.ft.com/content/4d017b7a-3cc2-11e3-86ef-00144feab7de?mhq5j=e1

141 http://www.ilo.org/dyn/natlex/docs/WEBTEXT/21843/64830/ E90IRN01.htm

142 http://www.pbs.org/wgbh/pages/frontline/ tehranbureau/2011/04/labors-struggle-for-independent-unions. html

143 https://www.equaltimes.org/iranian-workers-continue-to#. WawlvoqQw0o

144 Daniel Yergin, *The Prize: The Epic Quest for Oil, Money and Power.* Free Press, 2008, p.119.

145 https://en.wikipedia.org/wiki/Petroleum_industry_in_Iran#cite_ note-15 (possibly sourced from *Kinzer, All the Shah's Men: An American Coup and the Roots of Middle East Terror* (John Wiley & Sons, 2003), p.166)

146 https://en.wikipedia.org/wiki/Petroleum_industry_in_Iran#cite_ note-15 (Curtis, Glenn; Eric Hooglund. Iran, a country study (PDF). Washington D.C.: Library of Congress. pp. 160–163. ISBN 978-0-8444-1187-3)

147 http://oilprice.com/Energy/Crude-Oil/Iran-Plans-To-Raise-Crude-Oil-Production-Capacity-By-3-Million-Bpd.html

148 https://www.treasury.gov/resource-center/faqs/Sanctions/Pages/ faq_iran.aspx

149 http://www.cnn.com/2012/01/23/world/meast/iran-sanctions-effects/index.html

150 Killing them Softly: The Start Impact of Sanctions on the Lives of Ordinary Iranians, International Civil Society Action Network, July 2012.

151 https://www.transparency.org/country/IRN

152 https://ajammc.com/2013/10/03/15-ways-sanctions-hurt-ordinary-iranians/
153 https://ajammc.com/2013/01/24/seeing-through-the-haze-the-politics-of-reporting-sanctions-and-smog-in-tehran/
154 http://www.newsmax.com/Newsfront/Iran-nuclear-deal-sanctions/2015/04/08/id/637354/
155 Parsi. *Losing an Enemy*. Pg 141
156 http://foreignpolicy.com/2014/05/14/no-sanctions-didnt-force-iran-to-make-a-deal/
157 https://www.bloomberg.com/news/articles/2017-04-06/leading-iranian-cleric-enters-election-in-threat-to-rouhani
158 http://www.reuters.com/article/us-peugeot-iran-idUSKCN10127V

CHAPTER 8

159 Slavin, Barbara. Bitter Friends, Bosom Enemies. Pg. 145–146
160 https://www.theguardian.com/world/iran-blog/2015/feb/11/us-general-huysers-secret-iran-mission-declassified
161 http://www.presidency.ucsb.edu/ws/?pid=7080
162 lombert. Negotiating. Pgs 99–101
163 http://www.nytimes.com/1992/01/26/world/us-secretly-gave-aid-to-iraq-early-in-its-war-against-iran.html?pagewanted=all
164 Slavin. *Bitter Friends*. Pg. 178
165 https://en.wikipedia.org/wiki/Iran%E2%80%93Contra_affair
166 http://www.nytimes.com/2001/09/21/world/a-nation-challenged-tehran-iran-softens-tone-against-the-united-states.html
167 http://www.pbs.org/wgbh/pages/frontline/showdown/themes/slapface.html
168 Parsi, Trita. Losing an Enemy. Pg. 43
169 Parsi. *Losing an Enemy*. Pg. 50
170 http://www.washingtonpost.com/wp-dyn/content/article/2009/03/20/AR2009032000398.html
171 Parsi. *Losing an Enemy*. Pg 85
172 Parsi, Trita. *A Single Roll of the Dice*. Pg. 183–84
173 Ibid. Pg. 161–73
174 http://thehill.com/homenews/administration/351323-trump-iran-nuclear-deal-an-embarrassment

175 http://foreignpolicy.com/2017/09/26/the-myth-of-a-better-iran-deal/

176 http://www.al-monitor.com/pulse/originals/2013/04/iranian-americans-human-rights-military.html

177 https://www.theguardian.com/commentisfree/2012/sep/23/iran-usa

178 https://www.theguardian.com/world/2012/sep/21/iran-mek-group-removed-us-terrorism-list

179 http://www.nytimes.com/2012/09/22/world/middleeast/iranian-opposition-group-mek-wins-removal-from-us-terrorist-list

CHAPTER 9

180 http://www.newsweek.com/surely-some-mistake-why-did-isis-attack-iran-625253

181 http://iranprimer.usip.org/resource/iran-and-israel

182 https://www.theguardian.com/world/2012/jan/11/secret-war-iran-timeline-attacks?intcmp=239

183 https://www.theglobeandmail.com/news/world/the-undeclared-war-on-irans-nuclear-program/article4210032/

184 http://www.jpost.com/Middle-East/Iran/Israel-behind-assassinations-of-Iran-nuclear-scientists-Yaalon-hints-411473#/

185 https://www.nytimes.com/2017/08/05/world/asia/iran-afghanistan-taliban.html

186 https://www.reuters.com/article/us-afghanistan-islamic-state/islamic-state-seizes-new-afghan-foothold-after-luring-taliban-defectors-idUSKBN1DV3G5

187 http://iranprimer.usip.org/resource/iran-and-turkey

188 https://www.al-monitor.com/pulse/originals/2015/09/iran-turkey-relations.html

189 https://www.huffingtonpost.com/entry/consequences-of-qatar-rapprochement-with-iran-and-turkey_us_59bab51ce4b02c642e4a1494

190 https://thediplomat.com/2017/07/iran-pakistan-at-the-crossroads/

191 https://www.foreignaffairs.com/articles/united-states/2013-01-15/tangle-caucasus

192 https://www.al-monitor.com/pulse/fr/originals/2015/11/iran-armenia-cooperation.html

193 https://thediplomat.com/2016/05/has-iran-finally-found-a-security-partner-in-central-asia/

194 https://www.pbs.org/newshour/world/iran-still-top-state-sponsor-terrorism-u-s-report-says

195 http://iranprimer.usip.org/resource/iran-and-israel

196 https://www.theatlantic.com/international/archive/2017/06/qatar-crisis-saudi-arabia-hamas-iran-syria-gcc-gaza/530229/

197 https://www.washingtonpost.com/news/monkey-cage/wp/2016/05/16/contrary-to-popular-belief-houthis-arent-iranian-proxies/?utm_term=.344ef5ce2449

198 https://www.theguardian.com/world/iran-blog/2016/apr/25/iran-russia-israel-tehranbureau

199 https://thediplomat.com/2016/01/chinas-relations-with-iran-a-threat-to-the-west/

200 http://iranprimer.usip.org/resource/iran-and-china

201 http://www.atlanticcouncil.org/blogs/iraninsight/the-u-s-is-pushing-iran-toward-china-2

202 http://www.mei.edu/content/map/japan-s-return-iran-risky-business

203 http://iranprimer.usip.org/blog/2016/may/23/south-korea-iran-boost-ties

204 https://newmatilda.com/2016/03/30/a-guide-to-australias-relationship-with-iran/

205 https://thediplomat.com/2016/07/the-reality-of-india-iran-ties/

206 https://www.bloomberg.com/news/features/2017-03-08/as-trump-makes-threats-iran-makes-friends

207 https://warisboring.com/irans-other-shadow-war-is-in-africa/

208 http://www.mepc.org/iran-horn-africa-outflanking-us-allies

209 https://reliefweb.int/report/eritrea/report-monitoring-group-somalia-and-eritrea-pursuant-security-council-resolution-2244

210 http://nationalinterest.org/feature/irans-awkward-diplomacy-africa-15571?page=2

CHAPTER 10

211 https://www.youtube.com/watch?v=o-zoPgv_nYg
212 https://www.huffingtonpost.com/ryan-costello/rep-sherman-favors-more-c_b_4352122.html
213 https://www.cnbc.com/2017/03/29/general-calls-iran-destabilizing-force-suggests-us-disrupt-regime-by-military-means.html
214 https://www.huffingtonpost.com/barry-lando/a-secret-war-against-iran_b_42218.html
215 Private conversation with Col. Wilkerson, October 22, 2017, Washington DC.
216 http://news.gallup.com/poll/116236/iran.aspx
217 http://www.politifact.com/truth-o-meter/statements/2015/apr/09/barack-obama/obama-iran-spends-30-billion-defense-us-about-600-/
218 https://en.wikipedia.org/wiki/List_of_countries_by_military_expenditures#List
219 http://www.politifact.com/truth-o-meter/statements/2015/apr/09/barack-obama/obama-iran-spends-30-billion-defense-us-about-600-/
220 https://www.theatlantic.com/magazine/archive/2016/04/the-obama-doctrine/471525/
221 http://www.newsweek.com/israel-and-egypt-pressured-obama-bomb-iran-nuclear-deal-725577

INDEX

the worst came to the worst, it would be impossible to beat them out of *Norway* and *Greenland*, provided the Northern Crowns hold together, and the Czar of *Muscovy* stand Neuter.

He further told us for our Comfort, That there were vast Tracts of Land about the Pole, inhabited neither by Protestants nor Papists, and of greater Extent than all the *Roman* Catholick Dominions in *Europe*.

When we had fully discussed this Point, my Friend the Upholsterer began to exert himself upon the present Negotiations of Peace, in which he deposed Princes, settled the Bounds of Kingdoms, and ballanced the Power of *Europe*, with great Justice and Impartiality.

I at length took my Leave of the Company, and was going away; but had not been gone Thirty Yards, before the Upholsterer hemm'd again after me. Upon his advancing towards me, with a Whisper, I expected to hear some secret Piece of News, which he had not thought fit to communicate to the Bench; but instead of that, he desired me in my Ear to lend him Half a Crown. In Compassion to so needy a Statesman, and to dissipate the Confusion I found he was in, I told him, if he pleased, I would give him Five Shillings, to receive Five Pounds of him when the Great Turk was driven out of *Constantinople*; which he very readily accepted, but not before he had laid down to me the Impossibility of such an Event, as the Affairs of *Europe* now stand.

This Paper I design for the particular Benefit of those worthy Citizens who live more in a Coffee-house than in their Shops, and whose Thoughts are so taken up with the Affairs of the Allies, that they forget their Customers.

No. 164
Thursday, April 27, 1710
[Steele on the Reception of the Paper]

Qui sibi promittit Cives, Urbem, sibi Curae
Imperium fore, & Italiam, & Delubra Deorum,
Quo Patre sit natus, num ignotâ Matre inhonestus,
Omnes Mortales curare & quaerere cogit.[1]
— Hor.

From my own Apartment, April 26.

I have lately been looking over the many Pacquets of Letters which I have receiv'd from all Quarters of *Great Britain*, as well as from Foreign Countries, since my entring upon the Office of *Censor*, and indeed am very much surprized to see so great a Number of them, and pleased to think that I have so far encreased the Revenue of the *Post-Office*. As this Collection will grow daily, I have digested it into several Bundles, and made proper Endorsements on each particular Letter, it being my Design, when I lay down the Work that I am now engaged in, to erect a Paper-Office, and give it to the Publick.

I could not but make several Observations upon reading over the Letters of my Correspondents: As first of all, on the different Tasts that reign in the different Parts of this City. I find, by the Approbations which are given me, That I am seldom famous on the same Days on both Sides of *Temple-Bar*;[2] and that when I am in the greatest Repute within the Liberties,[3] I dwindle at the Court End of the Town. Sometimes I sink in both these Places at the same Time; but for my Comfort, my Name hath then been up in the Districts of *Wapping* and *Rotherhithe*. Some of my Correspondents desire me to be always serious, and others to be always merry. Some of them entreat me to go to Bed and fall into a Dream, and like me better when I am

---

[1] *Qui sibi . . . cogit:* From Horace, *Satires* 1.6.34–37 (altered):

> Thus when one thrusts himself upon the State,
> And cries, Come, I'll sustain the nation's weight,
> The empire and religion be my care,
> I'll manage all: This makes the people stare,
> This makes them ask, what is he, whence came he?
> What was his mother, what his family?
> Or is he base, his sire of mean degree? [Bond]

[2] *Temple-Bar:* Temple-Bar is a gate that historically marked the western part of London. There was an ideological and social divide between the eastern districts, where many tradespeople lived, and the more fashionable and elite districts to the west.

[3] *the Liberties:* The area around Fleet prison where prisoners were allowed to live.

asleep than when I am awake: Others advise me to sit all Night upon the Stars, and be more frequent in my Astrological Observations; for that a Vision is not properly a Lucubration. Some of my Readers thank me for filling my Paper with the Flowers of Antiquity, others desire News from *Flanders*. Some approve my Criticisms on the Dead, and others my Censures on the Living. For this Reason, I once resolved in the new Edition of my Works, to range my several Papers under distinct Heads, according as their principal Design was to benefit and instruct the different Capacities of my Readers, and to follow the Example of some very great Authors, by writing at the Head of each Discourse, *Ad Aulam, Ad Academiam, Ad Populum, Ad Clerum.*[4]

There is no Particular in which my Correspondents of all Ages, Conditions, Sexes, and Complexions, universally agree, except only in their Thirst after Scandal. It is impossible to conceive how many have recommended their Neighbours to me upon this Account, or how unmercifully I have been abused by several unknown Hands, for not publishing the secret Histories of Cuckoldom that I have received from almost every Street in Town.

It would indeed be very dangerous for me to read over the many Praises and Eulogiums which come Post to me from all the Corners of the Nation, were they not mixed with many Checks, Reprimands, Scurrilities, and Reproaches, which several of my good-natured Countrymen cannot forbear sending me, though it often costs them Two-pence or a Groat, before they can convey them to my Hands: So that sometimes when I am put into the best Humour in the World, after having read a Panegyrick upon my Performance, and looked upon my self as a Benefactor to the *British* Nation, the next Letter perhaps I open, begins with, *You old Doting Scoundrel — Are not you a sad Dog — Sirrah, you deserve to have your Nose slit.* And the like ingenious Conceits. These little Mortifications are necessary to suppress that Pride and Vanity which naturally arise in the Mind of a received Author, and enable me to bear the Reputation which my courteous Readers bestow upon me, without becoming a Coxcomb by it. It was for the same Reason, that when a *Roman* General entered the City in the Pomp of a Triumph, the Commonwealth allowed of several little Drawbacks to his Reputation, by conniving at such of the Rabble as repeated Libels and Lampoons upon him

---

[4] *Ad Aulam ... Ad Clerum:* To the court, the academy, the general population, the clergy.

within his Hearing, and by that Means engaged his Thoughts upon his Weakness and Imperfections, as well as on the Merits that advanced him to so great Honours. The Conqueror however was not the less esteemed for being a Man in some Particulars, because he appeared as a God in others.

There is another Circumstance in which my Countrymen have dealt very perversely with me; and that is, in Searching not only into my own Life, but also into the Lives of my Ancestors. If there has been a Blot in my Family for these Ten Generations, it hath been discovered by some or other of my Correspondents. In short, I find the ancient Family of the *Bickerstaffs* has suffered very much through the Malice and Prejudice of my Enemies. Some of them twit me in the Teeth with the Conduct of my Aunt *Margery*: Nay, there are some who have been so disingenuous, as to throw *Maud* the Milk-Maid into my Dish, notwithstanding I my self was the first who discovered that Alliance. I reap however many Benefits from the Malice of these my Enemies, as they let me see my own Faults, and give me a View of my self in the worst Light; as they hinder me from being blown up by Flattery and Self-Conceit; as they make me keep a watchful Eye over my own Actions, and at the same Time make me cautious how I talk of others, and particularly of my Friends and Relations, or value my self upon the Antiquity of my Family.

But the most formidable Part of my Correspondents are those whose Letters are filled with Threats and Menaces. I have been treated so often after this Manner, that not thinking it sufficient to fence well, in which I am now arrived at the utmost Perfection, and carry Pistols about me, which I have always tuck'd within my Girdle; I several Months since made my Will, settled my Estate, and took Leave of my Friends, looking upon my self as no better than a dead Man. Nay I went so far as to write a long Letter to the most intimate Acquaintance I have in the World, under the Character of a departed Person, giving him an Account of what brought me to that untimely End, and of the Fortitude with which I met it. This Letter being too long for the present Paper, I intend to print it by it self very suddenly; and at the same Time I must confess, I took my Hint of it from the Behaviour of an old Soldier in the Civil Wars, who was Corporal of a Company in a Regiment of Foot, about the same Time that I my self was a Cadet in the King's Army.

This Gentleman was taken by the Enemy; and the Two Parties were upon such Terms at that Time, that we did not treat each other as Prisoners of War, but as Traitors and Rebels. The poor Corporal being condemned to die, wrote a Letter to his Wife when under Sentence of Execution. He writ on the *Thursday*, and was to be executed on the *Friday*: But considering that the Letter would not come to his Wife's Hands till *Saturday*, the Day after Execution, and being at that Time more scrupulous than ordinary in speaking exact Truth, he formed his Letter rather according to the Posture of his Affairs when she should read it, than as they stood when he sent it: Though it must be confessed, there is a certain Perplexity in the Style of it, which the Reader will easily pardon, considering his Circumstances.

Dear Wife,
   'Hoping you are in good Health, as I am at this present Writing, This is to let you know, that Yesterday, between the Hours of Eleven and Twelve, I was hanged, drawn and quartered. I died very penitently, and every Body thought my Case very hard. Remember me kindly to my poor Fatherless Children.

Yours till Death,
W. B.'

It so happened, that this honest Fellow was relieved by a Party of his Friends, and had the Satisfaction to see all the Rebels hanged who had been his Enemies. I must not omit a Circumstance which exposed him to Raillery his whole Life after. Before the Arrival of the next Post, that would have set all Things clear, his Wife was married to a Second Husband, who lived in the peaceable Possession of her; and the Corporal, who was a Man of plain Understanding, did not care to stir in the Matter, as knowing that she had the News of his Death under his own Hand, which she might have produced upon Occasion.

No. 178
Tuesday, May 30, 1710
[Steele on The Tatler *as Antidote*
for News-Addiction]

Sheer Lane, May 29.

When we look into the delightful History of the most ingenious *Don Quixot* of the *Mancha*,[1] and consider the Exercises and Manner of Life of that renowned Gentleman, we cannot but admire the exquisite Genius and discerning Spirit of *Michael Cervantes*, who has not only painted his Adventurer with great Mastery in the

---

[1] *Don Quixot of the Mancha:* The protagonist of the satirical romance by Miguel de Cervantes Saavedra (1547–1616), *Don Quixote* (1605 and 1615).

conspicuous Parts of his Story, which relate to Love and Honour, but also intimated in his ordinary Life, Oeconomy and Furniture, the infallible Symptoms he gave of his growing Phrenzy, before he declared himself a Knight-Errant. His Hall was furnished with old Launces, Halbards, and Morrions; his Food, Lentils; his Dress, amorous. He slept moderately, rose early, and spent his Time in Hunting. When by Watchfulness and Exercise he was thus qualified for the Hardships of his intended Peregrinations, he had nothing more to do but to fall hard to study; and before he should apply himself to the Practical Part, get into the Methods of making Love and War by reading Books of Knighthood. As for raising tender Passion in him, *Cervantes* reports, That he was wonderfully delighted with a smooth intricate Sentence; and when they listened at his Study-Door, they could frequently hear him read aloud. *The Reason of the Unreasonableness, which against my Reason is wrought, doth so weaken my Reason, as with all Reason I do justly complain on your Beauty.* Again, he would pause till he came to another charming Sentence, and with the most pleasing Accent imaginable be loud at a new Paragraph: *The high Heavens, which, with your Divinity, do fortify you divinely with the Stars, make you Deserveress of the Deserts that your Greatness deserves.* With these, and other such Passages, (*says my Author*) the poor Gentleman grew distracted, and was breaking his Brains Day and Night to understand and unravel their Sense.

As much as the Case of this distempered Knight is received by all the Readers of his History as the most incurable and ridiculous of all Phrensies, it is very certain we have Crowds among us far gone in as visible a Madness as his, tho' they are not observed to be in that Condition. As great and useful Discoveries are sometimes made by accidental and small Beginnings, I came to the Knowledge of the most Epidemick Ill of this Sort, by falling into a Coffee-house where I saw my Friend the Upholsterer, whose Crack towards Politicks I have heretofore mention'd. This Touch in the Brain of the *British* Subject, is as certainly owing to the reading News-Papers, as that of the *Spanish* Worthy above-mention'd to the reading Works of Chivalry. My Contemporaries the Novelists[2] have, for the better spinning out Paragraphs, and working down to the End of their Columns, a most happy Art in saying and unsaying, giving Hints of Intelligence, and Interpretations of indifferent Actions, to the great Disturbance of the Brains of ordinary Readers. This Way of going on in the Words, and

[2] *the Novelists:* Newspaper journalists.

making no Progress in the Sense, is more particularly the Excellence of my most ingenious and renowned Fellow-Labourer the *Post-Man*; and it is to this Talent in him that I impute the Loss of my Upholsterer's Intellects. That unfortunate Tradesman has for Years past been the chief Orator in ragged Assemblies, and the Reader in Alley-Coffee-houses. He was Yesterday surrounded by an Audience of that Sort, among whom I sat unobserved through the Favour of a Cloud of Tobacco, and saw him with the *Post-Man* in his Hand, and all the other Papers safe under his Left Elbow. He was intermixing Remarks, and reading the *Paris* Article of *May* 30, which says, *That it is given out that an Express arrived this Day, with Advice, that the Armies were so near in the Plain of* Lens, *that they cannonaded each other.* (Ay, ay, here we shall have Sport.) *And that it was highly probable the next Express would bring us an Account of an Engagement.* (They are welcome as soon as they please.) *Tho' some others say, That the same will be put off till the 2d or 3d of* June, *because the Mareschal* Villars *expects some further Reinforcements from* Germany, *and other Parts, before that Time.* What-a-Pox does he put it off for? Does he think our Horse is not marching up at the same Time? But let us see what he says further. *They hope, that Monsieur* Albergotti *being encouraged by the Presence of so great an Army, will make an extraordinary Defence.* Why then I find, *Albergotti* is one of those that love to have a great many on their Side — Nay, I'll say that for this Paper, he makes the most natural Inferences of any of them all. *The Elector of* Bavaria[3] *being uneasy to be without any Command, has desired Leave to come to Court to communicate a certain Project to his Majesty — Whatever it be, it is said, that Prince is suddenly expected, and then we shall have a more certain Account of his Project, if this Report has any Foundation.* Nay, this Paper never imposes upon us, he goes upon sure Grounds; for he won't be positive the Elector has a Project, or that he will come, or if he does come at all; for he doubts, you see, whether the Report has any Foundation.

What makes this the more lamentable, is, that this Way of Writing falls in with the Imagination of the cooler and duller Part of Her Majesty's Subjects. The being kept up with one Line contradicting another, and the whole, after many Sentences of Conjecture, vanishing in a Doubt whether there is any Thing at all in what the Person

---

[3] *The Elector of Bavaria:* The Elector Max Emmanuel (1662–1726) was an ally of Louis XIV throughout the War of the Spanish Succession (1701–14).

has been reading, puts an ordinary Head into a Vertigo, which his natural Dulness would have secured him from. Next to the Labours of the *Post-Man*, the Upholsterer took from under his Elbow honest *Icabod Dawks's*[4] Letter, and there, among other Speculations, the Historian takes upon him to say, *That it is discoursed that there will be a Battel in* Flanders *before the Armies separate, and many will have it to be to Morrow, the great Battel of* Ramellies *being fought on a* Whit-Sunday.[5] A Gentleman who was a Wag in this Company laughed at the Expression, and said, By Mr. *Dawks's* Favour, I warrant ye, if we meet them on *Whit-Saturday*, or *Monday*, we shall not stand upon the Day with them, whether it be before or after the Holydays. An Admirer of this Gentleman stood up and told a Neighbour at a distant Table the Conceit, at which indeed we were all very merry. These Reflections in the Writers of the Transactions of the Times, seize the Noddles of such as were not born to have Thoughts of their own, and consequently lay a Weight upon every Thing which they read in Print. But Mr. *Dawks* concluded his Paper with a courteous Sentence, which was very well taken and applauded by the whole Company. *We wish,* says he, *all our Customers a merry* Whitsuntide, *and many of them.* Honest *Icabod* is as extraordinary a Man as any of our Fraternity, and as particular. His Style is a Dialect between the Familiarity of Talking and Writing, and his Letter such as you cannot distinguish whether Print or Manuscript,[6] which gives us a Refreshment of the Idea from what has been told us from the Press by others. This wishing a good Tide had its Effect upon us, and he was commended for his Salutation, as showing as well the Capacity of a Bellman as an Historian. My distempered old Acquaintance read in the next Place the Account of the Affairs abroad in the *Courant*;[7] but the Matter was told so distinctly, that these Wanderers thought there was no News in it; this Paper differing from the rest as an History from a Romance. The Tautology, the Contradictions, the Doubts, and Wants of Confirmations, are what keep up imaginary Entertainments

---

[4] *Icabod Dawks:* Ichabod Dawks is mentioned with John Dyer as an "Epistolary Historian" in *Spectator* No. 457. Bond notes that Dawks printed his newsletter in a script type that gave the appearance of handwritten letters.

[5] *Battel of Ramellies . . . Whit-Sunday:* This battle, in the Netherlands, was a turning point in the War of the Spanish Succession. It was won in May 1706 for the English and their allies against French forces by John Churchill, Duke of Marlborough. Whitsunday is the seventh Sunday after Easter and marks the Christian festival of Pentecost, celebrating the descent of the Holy Spirit.

[6] *whether Print or Manuscript:* Whether set in type or written out by hand, as by Ichabod Dawks.

[7] *the Courant:* Printed by Samuel Buckley, the *Daily Courant* was the first daily paper published in England.

in empty Heads, and produce Neglect of their own Affairs, Poverty, and Bankruptcy, in many of the Shop-Statesmen; but turn the Imaginations of those of a little higher Orb into Deliriums of Dissatisfaction, which is seen in a continual Fret upon all that touches their Brains, but more particularly upon any Advantage obtained by their Country, where they are considered as Lunaticks, and therefore tolerated in their Ravings.

What I am now warning the People of is, That the News-Papers of this Island are as pernicious to weak Heads in *England* as ever Books of Chivalry to *Spain*; and therefore shall do all that in me lies with the utmost Care and Vigilance imaginable to prevent these growing Evils. A flaming Instance of this Malady appeared in my old Acquaintance at this Time, who, after he had done reading all his Papers, ended with a Thoughtful Air, *If we should have a Peace, we should then know for certain whether it was the King of* Sweden *that lately came to* Dunkirk. I whispered him, and desired him to step aside a little with me. When I had Opportunity, I decoyed him into a Coach, in order for his more easy Conveyance to *Moorfields*. The Man went very quietly with me; and by that Time he had brought the *Swede* from the Defeat by the Czar to the *Boristhenes*, we were passing by *Will*'s Coffee-house, where the Man of the House beckoned to us. We made a full Stop, and could hear from above a very loud Voice swearing, with some Expressions towards Treason, That the Subject in *France* was as free as in *England*. His Distemper would not let him reflect, that his own Discourse was an Argument of the contrary. They told him, One would speak with him below. He came immediately to our Coach-Side. I whispered him, That I had an Order to carry him to the *Bastile*. He immediately obeyed with great Resignation: For to this Sort of Lunatick, whose Brain is touched for the *French*, the Name of a Gaol in that Kingdom has a more agreeable Sound than that of a Paternal Seat in this their own Country. It happen'd a little unluckily bringing these Lunaticks together, for they immediately fell into a Debate concerning the Greatness of their respective Monarchs; one for the King of *Sweden*, the other for the Grand Monarch of *France*. This Gentleman from *Will*'s is now next Door to the Upholsterer, safe in his Apartment in my *Bedlam*,[8] with proper Medicaments, and the *Mercure Gallant*[9] to sooth his Imagination that he is actually in *France*. If therefore he should escape to

---

[8] *Bedlam:* "Bedlam," a colloquial corruption of "Bethlehem," refers to St. Mary of Bethlehem, a hospital for the insane.

[9] *Mercure Gallant:* A popular French miscellany paper.

Covent-Garden[10] again, all Persons are desired to lay hold of him, and deliver him to Mr. *Morphew*,[11] my Overseer. At the same Time, I desire all true Subjects to forbear Discourse with him, any otherwise than when he begins to fight a Battle for *France*, to say, *Sir, I hope to see you in* England.

No. 224
Thursday, September 14, 1710
[Addison on Advertisements]

Materiam superabat Opus.[1]
— Ovid.

From my own Apartment, September 13.

It is my Custom, in a Dearth of News, to entertain my self with those Collections of Advertisements that appear at the End of all our publick Prints. These I consider as Accounts of News from the little World, in the same Manner that the foregoing Parts of the Paper are from the great. If in one we hear that a Sovereign Prince is fled from his Capital City, in the other we hear of a Tradesman who hath shut up his Shop, and run away. If in one we find the Victory of a General, in the other we see the Desertion of a private Soldier. I must confess, I have a certain Weakness in my Temper, that is often very much affected by these little Domestick Occurrences, and have frequently been caught with Tears in my Eyes over a melancholy Advertisement.

But to consider this Subject in its most ridiculous Lights, Advertisements are of great Use to the Vulgar: First of all, as they are Instruments of Ambition. A Man that is by no Means big enough for the *Gazette*,[2] may easily creep into the Advertisements; by which Means we often see an Apothecary in the same Paper of News with a Plenipotentiary, or a Running-Footman with an Ambassador. An Advertisement from *Pickadilly* goes down to Posterity, with an Article from *Madrid*; and *John Bartlett* of *Goodman*'s *Fields* is celebrated in

---

[10] *Covent-Garden:* Established in 1670, Covent Garden was the chief flower, fruit, and vegetable market in London. It was located in the midst of the theater district and acquired a reputation as a center of dissipated pleasures.

[11] *Mr. Morphew:* John Morphew.

[1] *Materiam superabat Opus:* From Ovid, *Metamorphoses* 2.5: "The workmanship surpasses the material" [Bond].

[2] *the Gazette:* England's official newspaper, edited by Steele at this time, the *Gazette*'s advertisements consisted mostly of bankruptcy notices.

the same Paper with the Emperor of *Germany*. Thus the Fable tells us, That the Wren mounted as high as the Eagle, by getting upon his Back.

A Second Use which this Sort of Writings have been turned to of late Years, has been the Management of Controversy, insomuch that above half the Advertisements one meets with now-a-Days are purely Polemical. The Inventors of *Strops for Razors* have written against one another this Way for several Years, and that with great Bitterness; as the whole Argument *pro* and *con* in the Case of the *Morning-Gowns* is still carried on after the same Manner. I need not mention the several Proprietors of Dr. *Anderson*'s Pills; nor take Notice of the many Satyrical Works of this Nature so frequently published by Dr. *Clark*, who has had the Confidence to advertize upon that learned Knight, my very worthy Friend, Sir *William Read:*[3] But I shall not interpose in their Quarrel; Sir *William* can give him his own in Advertisements, that, in the Judgment of the Impartial, are as well penned as the Doctor's.

The Third and last Use of these Writings is, to inform the World where they may be furnished with almost every Thing that is necessary for Life. If a Man has Pains in his Head, Cholicks in his Bowels, or Spots in his Clothes, he may here meet with proper Cures and Remedies. If a Man would recover a Wife or a Horse that is stolen or strayed; if he wants new Sermons, Electuaries,[4] Asses Milk, or any Thing else, either for his Body or his Mind, this is the Place to look for them in.

The great Art in writing Advertisements, is the finding out a proper Method to catch the Reader's Eye; without which, a good Thing may pass over unobserved, or be lost among Commissions of Bankrupt. Asterisks and Hands were formerly of great Use for this Purpose. Of late Years, the *N.B.* has been much in Fashion; as also little Cuts and Figures, the Invention of which we must ascribe to the Author of Spring-Trusses. I must not here omit the blind *Italian* Character, which being scarce legible, always fixes and detains the Eye, and gives the curious Reader something like the Satisfaction of prying into a Secret.

But the great Skill in an Advertizer, is chiefly seen in the Style which he makes use of. He is to mention *the universal Esteem, or general Reputation*, of Things that were never heard of. If he is a

---

[3] *Sir William Read:* Sir William Read (d. 1715) served as oculist to Queen Anne and was knighted in 1705 for curing soldiers and sailors of blindness.

[4] *Electuaries:* Medicinal pastes made up of a powder mixed with honey, syrup, or preserves.

Physician or Astrologer, he must change his Lodgings frequently, and (though he never saw any Body in them besides his own Family) give publick Notice of it, *For the Information of the Nobility and Gentry.* Since I am thus usefully employed in writing Criticisms on the Works of these diminutive Authors, I must not pass over in Silence an Advertisement which has lately made its Appearance, and is written altogether in a *Ciceronian* Manner.[5] It was sent to me, with Five Shillings, to be inserted among my Advertisements; but as it is a Pattern of good Writing in this Way, I shall give it a Place in the Body of my Paper.

The highest compounded Spirit of Lavender, the most glorious (if the Expression may be used) enlivening Scent and Flavour that can possibly be, which so raptures the Spirits, delights the Gust, and gives such Airs to the Countenance, as are not to be imagined but by those that have tried it. The meanest Sort of the Thing is admired by most Gentlemen and Ladies; but this far more, as by far it exceeds it, to the gaining among all a more than common Esteem. It is sold (in neat Flint Bottles fit for the Pocket) only at the Golden-Key in Warton's-Court near Holborn-Bars, for 3s. 6d. with Directions.

At the same Time that I recommend the several Flowers in which this Spirit of Lavender is wrapped up, (if the Expression may be used) I cannot excuse my Fellow-Labourers for admitting into their Papers several uncleanly Advertisements, not at all proper to appear in the Works of polite Writers. Among these I must reckon the *Carminitive Wind-expelling* Pills. If the Doctor had called them only his Carminitive Pills, he had been as cleanly as one could have wished; but the Second Word entirely destroys the Decency of the First. There are other Absurdities of this Nature so very gross, that I dare not mention them; and shall therefore dismiss this Subject, with a publick Admonition to *Michael Parrot*, That he do not presume any more to mention a certain Worm he knows of, which, by the Way, has grown Seven Foot in my Memory; for, if I am not much mistaken, it is the same that was but Nine Foot long about Six Months ago.

By the Remarks I have here made, it plainly appears, that a Collection of Advertisements is a kind of Miscellany; the Writers of which, contrary to all Authors, except Men of Quality, give Money to the

---

[5] *Ciceronian Manner:* The complex periodic prose style of the Roman orator, philosopher, and statesman Marcus Tullius Cicero (106–43 B.C.) is a high-flown vehicle for an advertisement for lavender water.

Booksellers who publish their Copies. The Genius of the Bookseller is chiefly shown in his Method of ranging and digesting these little Tracts. The last Paper I took up in my Hands, places them in the following Order:

The True Spanish Blacking for Shoes, *&c.*
The Beautifying Cream for the Face, *&c.*
Pease and Plaisters, *&c.*
Nectar and Ambrosia, *&c.*
Four Freehold Tenements of 15. *l.* per Annum, *&c.*
***The Present State of England, *&c.*
†‡†Annotations upon the Tatler, *&c.*
A Commission of Bankrupt being awarded against *B.L.* Bookseller, *&c.*

No. 229
Tuesday, September 26, 1710
[Addison on The Tatler's *Imitators*]

Quaesitam Meritis sume Superbiam.[1]
— Hor.

From my own Apartment, September 25.

The whole Creation preys upon it self: Every living Creature is inhabited. A Flea has a Thousand invisible Insects that teaze him as he jumps from Place to Place, and revenge our Quarrels upon him. A very ordinary microscope[2] shows us, that a Louse is it self a very lousy Creature. A Whale, besides those Seas and Oceans in the several Vessels of his Body, which are filled with innumerable Shoals of little Animals, carries about it a whole World of Inhabitants; insomuch that, if we believe the Calculations some have made, there are more living Creatures which are too small for the naked Eye to behold about the Leviathan, than there are of visible Creatures upon the Face of the whole Earth. Thus every nobler Creature is as it were the Basis and Support of Multitudes that are his Inferiors.

---

[1] *Quaesitam Meritis sume Superbiam:* From Horace, *Odes* 3.30.14–15 (altered): "Proudly claim the just renown / Thy merits and immortal lays have won" [Bond].
[2] *microscope:* A simple, single-lens microscope was in use by the mid–fifteenth century. By 1674, the Dutch naturalist Antonie van Leeuwenhoek (1632–1723) had developed a lens powerful enough to observe bacteria.

This Consideration very much comforts me, when I think on those numberless Vermin that feed upon this Paper, and find their Sustenance out of it: I mean, the small Wits and Scribblers that every Day turn a Penny by nibbling at my Lucubrations. This has been so advantageous to this little Species of Writers, that, if they do me Justice, I may expect to have my Statue erected in *Grub-street*,[3] as being a common Benefactor to that Quarter.

They say, when a Fox is very much troubled with Fleas, he goes into the next Pool with a little Lock of Wool in his Mouth, and keeps his Body under Water till the Vermin get into it; after which he quits the Wool, and diving, leaves his Tormentors to shift for themselves, and get their Livelihood where they can. I would have these Gentlemen take Care that I do not serve them after the same Manner; for though I have hitherto kept my Temper pretty well, it is not impossible but I may some Time or other disappear; and what will then become of them? Should I lay down my Paper, What a Famine would there be among the Hawkers, Printers, Booksellers, and Authors? It would be like Dr. *B——s's*[4] dropping his Cloak with the whole Congregation hanging upon the Skirts of it. To enumerate some of these my doughty Antagonists, I was threatened to be answered Weekly *Tit for Tat*: I was undermined by the *Whisperer*, haunted by *Tom Brown's Ghost*, scolded at by a *Female Tatler*, and slandered by another of the same Character, under the Title of *Atalantis*.[5] I have been *annotated*, *retattled*, *examined*, and *condoled*: But it being my standing Maxim never to speak ill of the Dead, I shall let these Authors rest in Peace, and take great Pleasure in thinking that I have sometimes been the Means of their getting a Belly-full. When I see my self thus surrounded by such formidable Enemies, I often think of the Knight of the *Red-Cross* in *Spencer's Den of Error*, who after he has cut off the Dragon's Head, and left it wallowing in a Flood of Ink, sees a Thousand monstrous Reptiles making their Attempts upon

---

[3] *Grub-street:* An actual street inhabited by professional freelance writers near Moorfields in London, Grub Street also refers to the whole symbolic realm of "low" literary culture produced by "hack" writers purely for financial gain.

[4] *Dr. B——s's:* Dr. Daniel Burgess (1645–1713) was a Presbyterian minister. In March 1710 a mob rioted in support of the fanatic High Church Anglican Tory Henry Sacheverell (1674?–1724), who had been convicted of sedition; the rioters gutted Burgess's meetinghouse in Lincoln's Inn Fields.

[5] *Tit for Tat . . . Whisperer . . . Tom Brown's Ghost . . . Female Tatler . . . Atalantis:* All actual publications, the first four periodical papers like *The Tatler*, the last a scandalous roman à clef, *The New Atalantis*, written by Mary de la Rivière Manley, who also wrote much of *The Female Tatler*.

him, one with many Heads, another with none, and all of them without Eyes.

> *The same so sore annoyed has the Knight,*
>   *That well nigh choaked with the deadly Stink,*
>   *His Forces fail, he can no longer fight;*
>   *Whose Courage when the Fiend perceived to shrink,*
>   *She poured forth out of her Hellish Sink*
>   *Her fruitful cursed Spawn of Serpents small,*
>   *Deformed Monsters, foul, and black as Ink;*
>   *Which swarming all about his Legs did crawl,*
> *And him encombred sore, but could not hurt at all.*

> *As gentle Shepherd in sweet Even-tide,*
>   *When ruddy* Phoebus *gins to welk in West,*
>   *High on an Hill, his Flock to viewen wide,*
>   *Marks which do bite their hasty Supper best;*
>   *A Cloud of combrous Gnats do him molest,*
>   *All striving to infix their feeble Stings,*
>   *That from their Noyance he no where can rest;*
>   *But with his clownish Hands their tender Wings*
> *He brusheth oft, and oft doth mar their Murmurings.*[6]

If ever I should want such a Fry of little Authors to attend me, I
shall think my Paper in a very decaying Condition. They are like Ivy
about an Oak, which adorns the Tree at the same Time that it eats
into it; or like a great Man's Equipage, that do Honour to the Person
on whom they feed. For my Part, when I see my self thus attacked, I
do not consider my Antagonists as malicious, but hungry, and therefore am resolved never to take any Notice of them.

As for those who detract from my Labours without being
prompted to it by an empty Stomach, in Return to their Censures I
shall take Pains to excel, and never fail to perswade my self, that their
Enmity is nothing but their Envy or Ignorance.

Give me Leave to conclude, like an old Man and Moralist, with a
Fable:

The Owls, Bats, and several other Birds of Night, were one Day
got together in a thick Shade, where they abused their Neighbours in
a very sociable Manner. Their Stayr at last fell upon the Sun, whom
they all agreed to be very troublesome, impertinent, and inquisitive.
Upon which the Sun, who overheard them, spoke to them after this

---

[6] This passage is from Book 1 of Edmund Spenser's (1552–1599) long allegorical
poem, *The Faerie Queene*, which appeared in a series of volumes in the later years of
the sixteenth century.

Manner: Gentlemen, I wonder how you dare abuse one that you know could in an Instant scorch you up, and burn every Mother's Son of you: But the only Answer I shall give you, or the Revenge I shall take of you, is, to *shine on.*

No. 271
Tuesday, January 2, 1711
[The Last Tatler: Steele's Apology]

The Printer having informed me, that there are as many of these Papers printed as will make Four Volumes, I am now come to the End of my Ambition in this Matter, and have nothing further to say to the World, under the Character of *Isaac Bickerstaff.* This Work has indeed for some Time been disagreeable to me, and the Purpose of it wholly lost by my being so long understood as the Author. I never designed in it to give any Man any secret Wound by my Concealment, but spoke in the Character of an old Man, a Philosopher, an Humorist, an Astrologer, and a Censor, to allure my Reader with the Variety of my Subjects, and insinuate, if I could, the Weight of Reason with the Agreeableness of Wit. The general Purpose of the whole has been to recommend Truth, Innocence, Honour, and Virtue, as the chief Ornaments of Life; but I considered, that Severity of Manners was absolutely necessary to him who would censure others, and for that Reason, and that only, chose to talk in a Mask. I shall not carry my Humility so far as to call my self a vicious Man; but at the same Time must confess, my Life is at best but pardonable. And with no greater Character than this, a Man would make but an indifferent Progress in attacking prevailing and fashionable Vices, which Mr. *Bickerstaff* has done with a Freedom of Spirit that would have lost both its Beauty and Efficacy, had it been pretended to by Mr. *Steele.*

As to the Work it self, the Acceptance it has met with is the best Proof of its Value; but I should err against that Candour which an honest Man should always carry about him, if I did not own, that the most approved Pieces in it were written by others, and those which have been most excepted against by my self. The Hand that has assisted me in those noble Discourses upon the Immortality of the Soul, the glorious Prospects of another Life, and the most sublime Idea's of Religion and Virtue, is a Person who is too fondly my Friend ever to own them;[1] but I should little deserve to be his, if I usurped the Glory of them. I must acknowledge at the same Time, that I think the finest Strokes of Wit and Humour in all Mr. *Bickerstaff*'s Lucubrations are those for which he is also beholden to him.

As for the Satyrical Parts of these Writings, those against the Gentlemen who profess Gaming are the most licentious; but the main of them I take to come from losing Gamesters, as Invectives against the Fortunate; for in very many of them, I was very little else but the Transcriber. If any have been more particularly marked at, such Persons may impute it to their own Behaviour, (before they were touched upon) in publickly speaking their Resentment against the Author, and professing they would support any Man who should insult him. When I mention this Subject, I hope Major-General *Davenport*, Brigadier *Bisset*, and my Lord *Forbes*, will accept of my Thanks for their frequent good Offices, in professing their Readiness to partake any Danger that should befal me in so just an Undertaking, as the Endeavour to banish Fraud and Couzenage from the Presence and Conversation of Gentlemen.

But what I find is the least excusable Part of all this Work is, That I have, in some Places in it, touched upon Matters which concern both the Church and State. All I shall say for this is, That the Points I alluded to are such as concerned every Christian and Freeholder[2] in *England*; and I could not be cold enough to conceal my Opinion on Subjects which related to either of those Characters. But Politicks apart, I must confess, it has been a most exquisite Pleasure to me to frame Characters of Domestick Life, and put those Parts of it which are least observed into an agrecable View; to enquire into the Seeds of Vanity and Affectation, to lay before my Readers the Emptiness of Ambition; and in a Word, to trace Human Life through all its Mazes and Recesses, and show much shorter Methods than Men ordinarily practise, to be happy, agreeable, and great.

But to enquire into Men's Faults and Weaknesses has something in it so unwelcome, that I have often seen People in Pain to act before me, whose Modesty only make them think themselves liable to Censure. This, and a Thousand other nameless Things, have made it an

---

[1] *my Friend . . . them:* Joseph Addison, whose involvement in *The Tatler* had increased through the course of its production.

[2] *Freeholder:* A person who owns a freeholder estate, or an estate held in fee-simple (in absolute possession), fee-tail (entailed or limited to some particular class of heirs), or for the term of life. The freeholder was distinguished from those who held property as copyholders or tenants. Most simply, it designated a class of property owners.

irksome Task to me to personate Mr. *Bickerstaff* any longer; and I believe it does not often happen, that the Reader is delighted where the Author is displeased.

All I can now do for the further Gratification of the Town, is to give them a faithful Index and Explication of Passages and Allusions, and sometimes of Persons intended in the several scattered Parts of the Work. At the same Time, the succeeding Volumes shall discover which of the whole have been written by me, and which by others, and by whom, as far as I am able, or permitted.[3]

Thus I have voluntarily done what I think all Authors should be able to do when call'd upon. I have published my Name to my Writings, and given my self up to the Mercy of the Town, (as *Shakespear* expresses it) with all my Imperfections on my Head. The indulgent Readers

Most Obliged,
Most Obedient
Humble Servant,
RICHARD STEELE.

---

[3] ... *or permitted:* This promise was, unhappily, never carried out. Steele provided Tickell, editor of Addison's *Works* in 1721, with an incomplete list of Addison's contributions [Bond].

The Spectator

No. 1
Thursday, March 1, 1711
[Addison Introduces the Character of Mr. Spectator]

Non fumum ex fulgore, sed ex fumo dare lucem
Cogitat, ut speciosa debinc miracula promat.[1]
— Hor.

I have observed, that a Reader seldom peruses a Book with Pleasure 'till he knows whether the Writer of it be a black or a fair Man, of a mild or cholerick Disposition, Married or a Batchelor, with other Particulars of the like nature, that conduce very much to the right Understanding of an Author. To gratify this Curiosity, which is so natural to a Reader, I design this Paper, and my next, as Prefatory Discourses to my following Writings, and shall give some Account in them of the several Persons that are engaged in this Work. As the chief Trouble of Compiling, Digesting and Correcting will fall to my Share, I must do my self the Justice to open the Work with my own History.

I was born to a small Hereditary Estate, which, according to the Tradition of the Village where it lies, was bounded by the same Hedges and Ditches in *William* the Conqueror's Time[2] that it is at present, and has been delivered down from Father to Son whole and entire, without the Loss or Acquisition of a single Field or Meadow, during the Space of six hundred Years. There runs a Story in the Family, that when my Mother was gone with Child of me about three Months, she dreamt that she was brought to Bed of a Judge: Whether this might proceed from a Law-Suit which was then depending in the Family, or my Father's being a Justice of the Peace, I cannot determine; for I am not so vain as to think it presaged any Dignity that I should arrive at in my future Life, though that was the Interpretation which the Neighbourhood put upon it. The Gravity of my Behaviour

---

[1] *Non fumum . . . promat:* From Horace, *Ars Poetica* 143–44: "Not smoke after flame does he plan to give, but after smoke the light, that then he may set forth striking and wondrous tales" [Bond].

[2] *William the Conqueror's Time:* The time of the Norman invasion led by William, Duke of Normandy (1028–1087), who conquered Anglo-Saxon England in 1066.

at my very first Appearance in the World, and all the Time that I sucked, seemed to favour my Mother's Dream: For, as she has often told me, I threw away my Rattle before I was two Months old, and would not make use of my Coral 'til they had taken away the Bells from it.

As for the rest of my Infancy, there being nothing in it remarkable, I shall pass it over in Silence. I find, that, during my Nonage, I had the Reputation of a very sullen Youth, but was always a Favourite of my School-Master, who used to say, *that my Parts were solid and would wear well.* I had not been long at the University, before I distinguished my self by a most profound Silence: For, during the Space of eight Years, excepting in the publick Exercises of the College, I scarce uttered the Quantity of an hundred Words; and indeed do not remember that I ever spoke three Sentences together in my whole Life. Whilst I was in this Learned Body I applied my self with so much Diligence to my Studies, that there are very few celebrated Books, either in the Learned or the Modern Tongues, which I am not acquainted with.

Upon the Death of my Father I was resolved to travel into Foreign Countries, and therefore left the University, with the Character of an odd unaccountable Fellow, that had a great deal of Learning, if I would but show it. An insatiable Thirst after Knowledge carried me into all the Countries of *Europe*, in which there was any thing new or strange to be seen; nay, to such a Degree was my Curiosity raised, that having read the Controversies of some great Men concerning the Antiquities of *Egypt*, I made a Voyage to *Grand Cairo*, on purpose to take the Measure of a Pyramid; and as soon as I had set my self right in that Particular, returned to my native Country with great Satisfaction.

I have passed my latter years in this City, where I am frequently seen in most publick Places, tho' there are not above half a dozen of my select Friends that know me; of whom my next Paper shall give a more particular Account. There is no Place of general Resort, wherein I do not often make my Appearance; sometimes I am seen thrusting my Head into a Round of Politicians at *Will*'s, and listning with great Attention to the Narratives that are made in those little Circular Audiences. Sometimes I smoak a Pipe at *Child*'s;[3] and whilst

---

[3] *Will's ... Child's*: These were popular coffeehouses, Will's a resort associated with its literary clientele, and Child's a meeting place for authors, booksellers, physicians, and clergy. See *Tatler* No. 1, p. 49.

I seem attentive to nothing but the *Post-Man*, overhear the Conversation of every Table in the Room. I appear on *Sunday* Nights at *St. James*'s Coffee-House,[4] and sometimes join the little Committee of Politicks in the Inner-Room, as one who comes there to hear and improve. My Face is likewise very well known at the *Grecian*, the *Cocoa-Tree*,[5] and in the Theaters both of *Drury-Lane*, and the *Hay-Market*. I have been taken for a Merchant upon the *Exchange* for above these ten Years, and sometimes pass for a Jew in the Assembly of Stock-Jobbers at *Jonathan*'s.[6] In short, where-ever I see a Cluster of People I always mix with them, tho' I never open my Lips but in my own Club.

Thus I live in the World, rather as a Spectator of Mankind, than as one of the Species; by which means I have made my self a Speculative Statesman, Soldier, Merchant and Artizan, without ever medling with any Practical Part in Life. I am very well versed in the Theory of an Husband, or a Father, and can discern the Errors in the Oeconomy, Business, and Diversion of others, better than those who are engaged in them; as Standers-by discover Blots,[7] which are apt to escape those who are in the Game. I never espoused any Party with Violence, and am resolved to observe an exact Neutrality between the Whigs and Tories, unless I shall be forc'd to declare my self by the Hostilities of either side. In short, I have acted in all the parts of my Life as a Looker-on, which is the Character I intend to preserve in this Paper.

I have given the Reader just so much of my History and Character, as to let him see I am not altogether unqualified for the Business I have undertaken. As for other Particulars in my Life and Adventures, I shall insert them in following Papers, as I shall see occasion. In the mean time, when I consider how much I have seen, read and heard, I begin to blame my own Taciturnity; and since I have neither Time nor Inclination to communicate the Fulness of my Heart in Speech, I

[4] *St. James's Coffee-House:* Popular with Whigs and men of fashion.

[5] *the Grecian, the Cocoa-Tree:* The Grecian was one of the oldest coffeehouses; its clientele consisted of lawyers, Greek scholars, and fellows of the Royal Society. The Cocoa-Tree was a chocolate house patronized by Tory extremists.

[6] *Exchange . . . Jonathan's:* The Royal Exchange, in London's central financial district on Threadneedle Street, provided a meeting place for businessmen and housed nearly two hundred shops. The first Royal Exchange, established by Sir Thomas Gresham (1518–1579) in 1566–68, was destroyed in the Great Fire of London (1666) and rebuilt in 1669 from designs by Edward Jarman. See also *Spectator* No. 69, p. 203. Jonathan's was a coffeehouse near the Royal Exchange in Exchange Alley, frequented by stockbrokers.

[7] *Blots:* In the board game backgammon, a blot is an exposed playing piece liable to be taken by one's opponent.

am resolved to do it in Writing; and to Print my self out, if possible, before I Die. I have been often told by my Friends, that it is Pity so many useful Discoveries which I have made, should be in the Possession of a Silent Man. For this Reason therefore, I shall publish a Sheet-full of Thoughts every Morning, for the Benefit of my Contemporaries; and if I can any way contribute to the Diversion or Improvement of the Country in which I live, I shall leave it, when I am summoned out of it, with the secret Satisfaction of thinking that I have not Lived in vain.

There are three very material Points which I have not spoken to in this Paper, and which, for several important Reasons, I must keep to my self, at least for some Time: I mean, an Account of my Name, my Age, and my Lodgings. I must confess I would gratify my Reader in any thing that is reasonable; but as for these three Particulars, though I am sensible they might tend very much to the Embellishment of my Paper, I cannot yet come to a Resolution of communicating them to the Publick. They would indeed draw me out of that Obscurity which I have enjoy'd for many Years, and expose me in publick Places to several Salutes and Civilities, which have been always very disagreeable to me; for the greatest Pain I can suffer, is the being talked to, and being stared at. It is for this Reason likewise, that I keep my Complexion and Dress, as very great Secrets; tho' it is not impossible, but I may make Discoveries of both in the Progress of the Work I have undertaken.

After having been thus particular upon my self, I shall in to-Morrow's Paper give an Account of those Gentlemen who are concerned with me in this Work. For, as I have before intimated, a Plan of it is laid and concerted (as all other Matters of Importance are) in a Club. However, as my Friends have engaged me to stand in the Front, those who have a mind to correspond with me, may direct their Letters *To the Spectator*, at Mr. *Buckley*'s in *Little Britain*.[8] For I must further acquaint the Reader, that tho' our Club meets only on *Tuesdays* and *Thursdays*, we have appointed a Committee to sit every Night, for the Inspection of all such Papers as may contribute to the Advancement of the Publick Weal.

---

[8] *Mr. Buckley's in Little Britain*: Samuel Buckley was already a successful printer and bookseller, best known perhaps for the *Daily Courant*, thc first daily newspaper to be published in England, which since 1702 had been issued from Buckley's shop (he continued to print it until September 24, 1714) [Bond].

No. 2
Friday, March 2, 1711
[Steele Introduces the Club]

... Ast Alii sex
Et plures uno conclamant ore.[1]
— Juv.

The first of our Society[2] is a Gentleman of *Worcestershire*, of antient Descent, a Baronet, his Name Sir ROGER DE COVERLY. His great Grandfather was Inventor of that famous Country-Dance which is call'd after him. All who know that Shire, are very well acquainted with the Parts and Merits of Sir ROGER. He is a Gentleman that is very singular in his Behaviour, but his Singularities proceed from his good Sense, and are Contradictions to the Manners of the World, only as he thinks the World is in the wrong. However, this Humour creates him no Enemies, for he does nothing with Sowrness or Obstinacy; and his being unconfined to Modes and Forms, makes him but the readier and more capable to please and oblige all who know him. When he is in Town he lives in *Soho-Square*: It is said he keeps himself a Batchelour by reason he was crossed in Love, by a perverse beautiful Widow of the next County to him. Before this Disappointment, Sir ROGER was what you call a fine Gentleman, had often supped with my Lord *Rochester* and Sir *George Etherege*, fought a Duel upon his first coming to Town, and kick'd Bully *Dawson*[3] in a publick Coffee-house for calling him Youngster. But being ill used by

---

[1] ... *Ast Alii ... ore:* From Juvenal, *Satires* 7.167–68: "Six and more cry with one voice" [Bond].

[2] *our Society:* Here Mr. Spectator introduces the members of the famed "Spectator Club." The characters represent a range of social types: the old-fashioned Tory country gentleman (Sir Roger); the young law student; the Whig businessman (Sir Andrew Freeport); the military man (Captain Sentry); the rakish, if aging, representative of Restoration high life (Will Honeycomb); and the clergyman. According to *Spectator* No. 1, the club was to meet twice a week and appoint a committee "to sit every Night" for the inspection of all the papers. The characters presented here reappear in later issues, especially Sir Roger, Sir Andrew, and Will Honeycomb.

[3] *Lord Rochester ... Sir George Etherege ... Bully Dawson:* John Wilmot, Earl of Rochester (1647–1680), a lyric poet and satirist, was a leading member of the group of court wits surrounding Charles II. Sir George Etherege (1635?–1691), a successful playwright and also a member of the group of Restoration wits, wrote satirical comedies of manners, including his best-known play, *The Man of Mode, or, Sir Fopling Flutter* (1676). Bully Dawson was a noted cardsharper and dissolute man-about-town. These references place the young Sir Roger in the most fashionable and most debauched society in Restoration London.

the abovementioned Widow, he was very serious for a Year and a half; and tho' his Temper being naturally jovial, he at last got over it, he grew careless of himself and never dressed afterwards; he continues to wear a Coat and Doublet of the same Cut that were in Fashion at the Time of his Repulse, which, in his merry Humours, he tells us, has been in and out twelve Times since he first wore it. 'Tis said Sir ROGER grew humble in his Desires after he had forgot this cruel Beauty, insomuch that it is reported he has frequently offended in Point of Chastity with Beggars and Gypsies: But this is look'd upon by his Friends rather as Matter of Raillery than Truth. He is now in his Fifty sixth Year, cheerful, gay, and hearty, keeps a good House both in Town and Country; a great Lover of Mankind; but there is such a mirthful Cast in his Behaviour, that he is rather beloved than esteemed: His Tenants grow rich, his Servants look satisfied, all the young Women profess Love to him, and the young Men are glad of his Company: When he comes into a House he calls the Servants by their Names, and talks all the way up Stairs to a Visit. I must not omit that Sir ROGER is a Justice of the *Quorum*;[4] that he fills the Chair at a Quarter-Session with great Abilities, and three Months ago gain'd universal Applause by explaining a Passage in the Game-Act.

The Gentleman next in Esteem and Authority among us, is another Batchelour, who is a Member of *the Inner-Temple*;[5] a Man of great Probity, Wit, and Understanding; but he has chosen his Place of Residence rather to obey the Direction of an old humoursome Father than in Pursuit of his own Inclinations. He was plac'd there to study the Laws of the Land, and is the most learned of any of the House in those of the Stage. *Aristotle* and *Longinus* are much better understood by him than *Littleton* or *Cooke*.[6] The Father sends up every Post Questions relating to Marriage-Articles, Leases, and Tenures, in the Neighbourhood; all which Questions he agrees with an Attorney

---

[4] *Justice of the Quorum:* Justice of the Peace.

[5] *Inner-Temple:* One section of the Temple-Bar, one of the four Inns of Court housed along Fleet Street in London. Originally owned by the Knights Templar, a medieval religious and military order, this series of buildings, known collectively as the Temple, was presented by James I to lawyers for their professional use. It housed both residential and professional legal apartments.

[6] *Aristotle and Longinus . . . Littleton or Cooke:* That is, the law student's tastes are more literary than legal. He would rather read Aristotle's (384–322 B.C.) *Poetics* and Dionysus Cassius Longinus's (210?–274) rhetorical criticism in his *On the Sublime* than Sir Edward Coke's (1552–1634) *First Part of the Institutes of the Lawes of England: or Commentarie upon Littleton* (1628). Sir Thomas Littleton's (1442–1481) *Littleton upon Tenures* was the first important legal document to be written in English rather than Latin and to be little influenced by Roman civil law.

to answer and take care of in the Lump: He is studying the Passions themselves, when he should be inquiring into the Debates among Men which arise from them. He knows the Argument of each of the Orations of *Demothenes* and *Tully*, but not one Case in the Reports of our own Courts. No one ever took him for a Fool, but none, except his intimate Friends, know he has a great deal of Wit. This Turn makes him at once both disinterested and agreeable: As few of his Thoughts are drawn from Business, they are most of them fit for Conversation. His Taste of Books is a little too just for the Age he lives in; he has read all, but approves of very few. His Familiarity with the Customs, Manners, Actions, and Writings of the Antients, makes him a very delicate Observer of what occurs to him in the present World. He is an excellent Critick, and the Time of the Play, is his Hour of Business; exactly at five he passes through *New-Inn*,[7] crosses through *Russel-Court*, and takes a Turn at *Will's* till the Play begins;[8] he has his Shooes rubb'd and his Perriwig powder'd at the Barber's as you go into the *Rose*. It is for the Good of the Audience when he is at a Play, for the Actors have an Ambition to please him.

The Person of next Consideration is Sir ANDREW FREEPORT, a Merchant of great Eminence in the City of *London*: A Person of indefatigable Industry, strong Reason, and great Experience. His Notions of Trade are noble and generous, and (as every rich Man has usually some sly Way of Jesting, which would make no great Figure were he not a rich Man) he calls the Sea the *British Common*. He is acquainted with Commerce in all its Parts, and will tell you that it is a stupid and barbarous Way to extend Dominion by Arms; for true Power is to be got by Arts and Industry. He will often argue, that if this Part of our Trade were well cultivated, we should gain from one Nation; and if another, from another. I have heard him prove, that Diligence makes more lasting Acquisitions than Valour, and that Sloth has ruin'd more Nations than the Sword. He abounds in several frugal Maxims, among which the greatest Favourite is, 'A Penny saved is a Penny got.' A General Trader of good Sense, is pleasanter Company than a general Scholar; and Sir ANDREW having a natural unaffected Eloquence, the Perspicuity of his Discourse gives the same Pleasure that Wit would in another Man. He has made his Fortunes himself; and says that *England* may be richer than other Kingdoms, by as plain Methods as he himself is richer than other Men; tho' at

---

[7] *New-Inn:* An Inn of Chancery Court.
[8] *Will's till the Play begins:* Will's was a coffeehouse frequented by the literary set. Plays began around six in the evening.

the same Time I can say this of him, that there is not a Point in the Compass but blows home a Ship in which he is an Owner.

Next to Sir ANDREW in the Club-room sits Captain SENTRY, a Gentleman of great Courage, good Understanding, but invincible Modesty. He is one of those that deserve very well, but are very awkard at putting their Talents within the Observation of such as should take notice of them. He was some Years a Captain, and behaved himself with great Gallantry in several Engagements and at several Sieges; but having a small Estate of his own, and being next Heir to Sir ROGER, he has quitted a Way of Life in which no Man can rise suitably to his Merit, who is not something of a Courtier as well as a Souldier. I have heard him often lament, that in a Profession where Merit is placed in so conspicuous a View, Impudence should get the Better of Modesty. When he has talked to this Purpose I never heard him make a sower Expression, but frankly confess that he left the World because he was not fit for it. A strict Honesty and an even regular Behaviour, are in themselves Obstacles to him that must press through Crowds who endeavour at the same End with himself, the Favour of a Commander. He will however in this Way of Talk excuse Generals for not disposing according to Mens Desert, or enquiring into it: For, says he, that great Man who has a Mind to help me, has as many to break through to come at me, as I have to come at him: Therefore he will conclude, that the Man who would make a Figure, especially in a military Way, must get over all false Modesty, and assist his Patron against the Importunity of other Pretenders by a proper Assurance in his own Vindication. He says it is a civil Cowardice to be backward in asserting what you ought to expect, as it is a military Fear to be slow in attacking when it is your Duty. With this Candour does the Gentleman speak of himself and others. The same Frankness runs through all his Conversation. The military Part of his Life has furnish'd him with many Adventures, in the Relation of which he is very agreeable to the Company; for he is never overbearing, tho' accustomed to command Men in the utmost Degree below him; nor ever too obsequious, from an Habit of obeying Men highly above him.

But that our Society may not appear a Set of Humourists unacquainted with the Gallantries and Pleasures of the Age, we have among us the gallant WILL. HONEYCOMB, a Gentleman who according to his Years should be in the Decline of his Life, but having ever been very careful of his Person, and always had a very easy Fortune, Time has made but very little Impression, either by Wrinkles on his

Forehead, or Traces in his Brain. His Person is well turn'd, of a good Height. He is very ready at that Sort of Discourse with which men usually entertain Women. He has all his Life dressed very well, and remembers Habits as others do Men. He can smile when one speaks to him, and laughs easily. He knows the History of every Mode, and can inform you from which of the *French* King's[9] Wenches our Wives and Daughters had this Manner of curling their Hair, that Way of placing their Hoods; whose Frailty was covered by such a Sort of Petticoat, and whose Vanity to shew her Foot made that Part of the Dress so short in such a Year. In a Word, all his Conversation and Knowledge has been in the female World: As other Men of his Age will take Notice to you what such a Minister said upon such and such an Occasion, he will tell you when the Duke of *Monmouth*[10] danced at Court such a Woman was then smitten, another was taken with him at the Head of his Troop in the *Park*.[11] In all these important Relations, he has ever about the same Time received a kind Glance or a Blow of a Fan from some celebrated Beauty, Mother of the present Lord such-a-one. If you speak of a young Commoner that said a lively thing in the House, he starts up, 'He has good Blood in his Veins, *Tom Mirabell* begot him, the Rogue cheated me in that Affair; that young Fellow's Mother used me more like a Dog than any Woman I ever made Advances to.' This Way of Talking of his very much enlivens the Conversation among us of a more sedate Turn; and I find there is not one of the Company but my self, who rarely speak at all, but speaks of him as of that Sort of Man who is usually called a well-bred fine Gentleman. To conclude his Character, where Women are not concerned, he is an honest worthy Man.

I cannot tell whether I am to account him whom I am next to speak of, as one of our Company; for he visits us but seldom, but when he does it adds to every Man else a new Enjoyment of himself. He is a Clergyman, a very philosophick Man, of general Learning, great Sanctity of Life, and the most exact good Breeding. He has the

---

[9] *the French King:* Louis XIV (1638–1715), who ruled from 1643 to 1715.

[10] *the Duke of Monmouth:* James Scott, Duke of Monmouth (1649–1685), illegitimate son of Charles II and a Welshwoman named Lucy Waters. Backed by powerful Whigs led by Anthony Ashley Cooper, Earl of Shaftesbury, Monmouth was involved in a conspiracy against Charles II known as the Rye House Plot (1682–83) and then in an armed rebellion against the recently crowned James II in 1685. The rebellion failed and Monmouth was beheaded in 1685. Before he began asserting his claim to the throne, Monmouth was a great favorite at Charles's court and a powerful military leader.

[11] *the Park:* St. James's Park, the oldest of London's royal parks and a resort of the sovereigns and their courts through the Restoration.

Misfortune to be of a very weak Constitution, and consequently cannot accept of such Cares and Business as Preferments in his Function would oblige him to: He is therefore among Divines what a Chamber-Councellor is among Lawyers. The Probity of his Mind, and the Integrity of his Life, create him Followers, as being eloquent or loud advances others. He seldom introduces the Subject he speaks upon; but we are so far gone in Years, that he observes, when he is among us, an Earnestness to have him fall on some divine Topick, which he always treats with much Authority, as one who has no Interests in this World, as one who is hastening to the Object of all his Wishes, and conceives Hope from his Decays and Infirmities. These are my ordinary Companions.

No. 10
Monday, March 12, 1711
[Addison on the Popularity of the Papers]

Non aliter quam qui adverso vix flumine lembum
Remigiis subigit: si brachia forte remisit,
Atque illum in præceps prono rapit alveus amni.[1]
— Virg.

It is with much Satisfaction that I hear this great City inquiring Day by Day after these my Papers, and receiving my Morning Lectures with a becoming Seriousness and Attention. My Publisher tells me, that there are already Three Thousand of them distributed every Day: So that if I allow Twenty Readers to every Paper, which I look upon as a modest Computation, I may reckon about Three-score thousand Disciples in *London* and *Westminster*, who I hope will take care to distinguish themselves from the thoughtless Herd of their ignorant and unattentive Brethren. Since I have raised to my self so great an Audience, I shall spare no Pains to make their Instruction agreeable, and their Diversion useful. For which Reasons I shall endeavour to enliven Morality with Wit, and to temper Wit with Morality, that my Readers may, if possible, both Ways find their Account in the Speculation of the Day. And to the End that their Virtue

---

[1] *Non aliter . . . amni:* From Virgil, *Georgics* 1.201–03: "As if one, whose oars can scarce force his skiff against the stream, should by chance slacken his arms, and lo! headlong down the current the channel sweeps it away" [Bond].

and Discretion may not be short transient intermitting Starts of Thought, I have resolved to refresh their Memories from Day to Day, till I have recovered them out of that desperate State of Vice and Folly into which the Age is fallen. The Mind that lies fallow but a single Day, sprouts up in Follies that are only to be killed by a constant and assiduous Culture. It was said of *Socrates*,[2] that he brought Philosophy down from Heaven, to inhabit among Men; and I shall be ambitious to have it said of me, that I have brought philosophy out of Closets and Libraries, Schools and Colleges, to dwell in Clubs and Assemblies, at Tea-Tables, and in Coffee-Houses.

I would therefore in a very particular Manner recommend these my Speculations to all well regulated Families, that set apart an Hour in every Morning for Tea and Bread and Butter; and would earnestly advise them for their Good to order this Paper to be punctually served up, and to be looked upon as a Part of the Tea Equipage.

Sir *Francis Bacon*[3] observes, that a well-written Book compared with its Rivals and Antagonists, is like *Moses*'s Serpent, that immediately swallow'd up and devoured those of the *Ægyptians.* I shall not be so vain as to think, that where the SPECTATOR appears, the other publick Prints will vanish; but shall leave it to my Readers Consideration, whether, Is it not much better to be let into the Knowledge of ones-self, than to hear what passes in *Muscovy* or *Poland*; and to amuse our selves with such Writings as tend to the wearing out of Ignorance, Passion, and Prejudice, than such as naturally conduce to inflame Hatreds and make Enmities irreconcileable?

In the next Place, I would recommend this Paper to the daily Perusal of those Gentlemen whom I cannot but consider as my good Brothers and Allies, I mean the Fraternity of Spectators who live in the World without having any thing to do in it; and either by the Affluence of their Fortunes, or Laziness of their Dispositions, have no other Business with the rest of Mankind but to look upon them. Under this Class of Men are comprehended all contemplative Tradesmen, titular Physitians, Fellows of the Royal Society,[4] Templers[5] that

---

[2] *Socrates:* Cicero (106–43 B.C.), *Tusculan Disputations* 5.4.10 [Bond].

[3] *Sir Francis Bacon:* Bacon (1561–1626) was an early empirical philosopher and essayist whose *Great Instauration* probed the workings of nature and the mysteries of science. This allusion is to a passage in the first part of that work, *The Advancement of Learning* (1605), Book 2 [Bond].

[4] *Royal Society:* A scientific society based on the empirical philosophy of Francis Bacon, the Royal Society for the Improving of Natural Knowledge was instituted by Royal Charter in 1662.

[5] *Templers:* Men in the legal professions housed in the Temple.

are not given to be contentious, and Statesmen that are out of Business. In short, every one that considers the World as a Theatre, and desires to form a right Judgment of those who are the Actors on it.

There is another Set of Men that I must likewise lay a Claim to, whom I have lately called the Blanks of Society, as being altogether unfurnish'd with Ideas, till the Business and Conversation of the Day has supplied them. I have often considered these poor Souls with an Eye of great Commiseration, when I have heard them asking the first Man they have met with, whether there was any News stirring? and by that Means gathering together Materials for thinking. These needy Persons do not know what to talk of, till about twelve a Clock in the Morning; for by that Time they are pretty good Judges of the Weather, know which Way the Wind sits, and whether the *Dutch* Mail be come in. As they lie at the Mercy of the first Man they meet, and are grave or impertinent all the Day long, according to the Notions which they have imbibed in the Morning, I would earnestly entreat them not to stir out of their Chambers till they have read this Paper, and do promise them that I will daily instil into them such sound and wholesome Sentiments, as shall have a good Effect on their Conversation for the ensuing twelve Hours.

But there are none to whom this Paper will be more useful, than to the female World. I have often thought there has not been sufficient Pains taken in finding out proper Employments and Diversions for the Fair ones. Their Amusements seem contrived for them rather as they are Women, than as they are reasonable Creatures; and are more adapted to the Sex, than to the Species. The Toilet is their great Scene of Business, and the right adjusting of their Hair the principal Employment of their Lives. The sorting of a Suit of Ribbons, is reckon'd a very good Morning's Work; and if they make an Excursion to a Mercer's or a Toy-shop,[6] so great a Fatigue makes them unfit for any thing else all the Day after. Their more serious Occupations are Sowing and Embroidery, and their greatest Drudgery the Preparation of Jellies and Sweetmeats. This, I say, is the State of ordinary Women; tho' I know there are Multitudes of those of a more elevated Life and Conversation, that move in an exalted Sphere of Knowledge and Virtue, that join all the Beauties of the Mind to the Ornaments of Dress, and inspire a kind of Awe and Respect, as well as Love, into their Male-Beholders. I hope to encrease the Number of these by pub-

---

[6] *Toy-shop:* Not a shop selling toys for children, but one selling fashionable trinkets, knick-knacks, and ornamental adornments for adults.

lishing this daily Paper, which I shall always endeavour to make an innocent if not an improving Entertainment, and by that Means at least divert the Minds of my female Readers from greater Trifles. At the same Time, as I would fain give some finishing Touches to those which are already the most beautiful Pieces in humane Nature, I shall endeavour to point out all those Imperfections that are the Blemishes, as well as those Virtues which are the Embellishments, of the Sex. In the mean while I hope these my gentle Readers, who have so much Time on their Hands, will not grudge throwing away a Quarter of an Hour in a Day on this Paper, since they may do it without any Hindrance to Business.

I know several of my Friends and Well-wishers are in great Pain for me, lest I should not be able to keep up the Spirit of a Paper which I oblige my self to furnish every Day: But to make them easy in this Particular, I will promise them faithfully to give it over as soon as I grow dull. This I know will be Matter of great Raillery to the small Wits; who will frequently put me in mind of my Promise, desire me to keep my Word, assure me that it is high Time to give over, with many other little Pleasantries of the like Nature, which Men of a little smart Genius cannot forbear throwing out against their best Friends, when they have such a Handle given them of being witty. But let them remember, that I do hereby enter my Caveat against this Piece of Raillery.

No. 49
Thursday, April 26, 1711
[Steele on Coffeehouse Society]

. . . Hominem pagina nostra sapit.[1]
— Mart.

It is very natural for a Man who is not turned for Mirthful Meetings of Men, or Assemblies of the fair Sex, to delight in that sort of Conversation which we find in Coffee-houses. Here a Man, of my Temper, is in his Element; for, if he cannot talk, he can still be more agreeable to his Company, as well as pleased in himself, in being only

---

[1] *. . . Hominem pagina nostra sapit:* From Martial, *Epigrams* 10.4.10: "Our book savours of the man" [Bond].

an Hearer. It is a Secret known but to few, yet of no small use in the Conduct of Life, that when you fall into a Man's Conversation, the first thing you should consider is, whether he has a greater Inclination to hear you, or that you should hear him. The latter is the more general Desire, and I know very able Flatterers that never speak a word in Praise of the Persons from whom they obtain daily Favours, but still practise a skilful Attention to whatever is uttered by those with whom they converse. We are very Curious to observe the Behaviour of Great Men and their Clients; but the same Passions and Interests move Men in lower Spheres; and I (that have nothing else to do, but make Observations) see in every Parish, Street, Lane, and Alley of this Populous City, a little Potentate that has his Court, and his Flatterers who lay Snares for his Affection and Favour, by the same Arts that are practised upon Men in higher Stations.

In the Place I most usually frequent, Men differ rather in the time of Day in which they make a Figure, than in any real Greatness above one another. I, who am at the Coffee-house at Six in a Morning, know that my friend *Beaver* the Haberdasher has a Levy of more undissembled Friends and Admirers, than most of the Courtiers or Generals of *Great Britain.* Every man about him has, perhaps, a News Paper in his Hand, but none can pretend to guess what Step will be taken in any one Court of *Europe,* 'till Mr. *Beaver* has thrown down his Pipe, and declares what Measures the Allies must enter into upon this new Posture of Affairs. Our Coffee-house is near one of the Inns of Court, and *Beaver* has the Audience and Admiration of his Neighbours from Six 'till within a Quarter of Eight, at which time he is interrupted by the Students of the House; some of whom are ready Dress'd for *Westminster,* at Eight in a Morning, with Faces as busie as if they were retain'd in every Cause there; and others come in their Night-Gowns to Saunter away their Time, as if they never designed to go thither. I do not know that I meet, in any of my Walks, Objects which move both my Spleen and Laughter so effectually, as those Young Fellows at the *Grecian, Squire*'s, *Searle*'s,[2] and all other Coffee-houses adjacent to the Law, who rise early for no other purpose but to publish their Laziness. One would think these young *Virtuoso*'s[3] take a gay Cap and Slippers, with a Scarf and Party-

---

[2] *Grecian, Squire's, Searle's:* Three coffeehouses near the Inns of Court ("adjacent to the Law"). See *Spectator* No. 2, note 5 (p. 84).

[3] *Virtuoso's:* Virtuoso, used ironically here, refers to a person with an interest in natural curiosities or the fine arts. Virtuosos were often collectors and engaged in their hobbies of collecting and connoisseurship with great fervor.

colour'd Gown, to be Ensigns of Dignity; for the vain Things approach each other with an Air, which shows they regard one another for their Vestments. I have observed, that the Superiority among these proceeds from an Opinion of Gallantry and Fashion: The Gentleman in the Strawberry Sash, who presides so much over the rest, has, it seems, subscribed to every Opera this last Winter, and is supposed to receive Favours from one of the Actresses.

When the Day grows too busie for these Gentlemen to enjoy any longer the Pleasures of their *Deshabilé*,[4] with any manner of Confidence, they give Place to Men who have Business or good Sense in their Faces, and come to the Coffee-house either to transact Affairs or enjoy Conversation. The Persons to whose Behaviour and Discourse I have most regard, are such as are between these two sorts of Men; Such as have not Spirits too Active to be happy and well pleased in a private Condition, nor Complexions too warm to make them neglect the Duties and Relations of Life. Of these sort of Men consist the worthier Part of Mankind; of these are all good Fathers, generous Brothers, sincere Friends, and faithful Subjects. Their Entertainments are derived rather from Reason than Imagination: Which is the Cause that there is no Impatience or Instability in their Speech or Action. You see in their Countenances they are at home, and in quiet Possession of the present Instant, as it passes, without desiring to Quicken it by gratifying any Passion, or prosecuting any new Design. These are the Men formed for Society, and those little Communities which we express by the Word *Neighbourhoods*.

The Coffee-house is the Place of Rendezvous to all that live near it, who are thus turned to relish calm and ordinary Life. *Eubulus* presides over the middle Hours of the Day, when this Assembly of Men meet together. He enjoys a great Fortune handsomely, without launching into Expence, and exerts many noble and useful Qualities, without appearing in any publick Employment. His Wisdom and Knowledge are serviceable to all that think fit to make use of them; and he does the Office of a Council, a Judge, an Executor, and a Friend to all his Acquaintance, not only without the Profits which attend such Offices, but also without the Deference and Homage which are usually paid to them. The giving of Thanks is displeasing to him. The greatest Gratitude you can show him, is to let him see you are the better Man for his Services; and that you are as ready to oblige others, as he is to oblige you.

---

[4] *Deshabilé*: Casual dress.

In the private Exigencies of his Friends he lends, at legal Value, considerable Sums, which he might highly increase by rolling in the Publick Stocks. He does not consider in whose Hands his Mony will improve most, but where it will do most Good.

Eubulus has so great an Authority in his little Diurnal Audience, that when he shakes his Head at any Piece of publick News, they all of them appear dejected; and, on the contrary, go home to their Dinners with a good Stomach and chearful Aspect, when *Eubulus* seems to intimate that Things go well. Nay, their Veneration towards him is so great, that when they are in other Company they speak and act after him; are Wise in his Sentences, and are no sooner sat down at their own Tables, but they hope or fear, rejoice or despond as they saw him do at the Coffee-house. In a word, every Man is *Eubulus* as soon as his Back is turn'd.

Having here given an Account of the several Reigns that succeed each other from Day-break 'till Dinner-time, I shall mention the Monarchs of the Afternoon on another occasion, and shut up the whole Series of them with the History of *Tom* the Tyrant; who, as first Minister of the Coffee-house, takes the Government upon him between the Hours of Eleven and Twelve at Night, and gives his Orders in the most Arbitrary manner to the Servants below him, as to the Disposition of Liquors, Coal and Cinders.

No. 124
Monday, July 23, 1711
[Addison on the Essay Form]

Μέγα βιβλίον, μέγα κακόν.[1]

A man who publishes his Works in a Volume, has an infinite Advantage over one who communicates his Writings to the World in loose Tracts and single Pieces. We do not expect to meet with any thing in a bulky Volume, till after some heavy Preamble, and several Words of Course, to prepare the Reader for what follows: Nay Authors have established it as a Kind of Rule, That a Man ought to be dull sometimes; as the most severe Reader makes Allowances for many Rests and Nodding-places in a voluminous Writer. This gave

---

[1] Adapted from Callimachus, *Fragments* 359: "A great book is a great evil" [Bond].

Occasion to the famous *Greek* Proverb which I have chosen for my Motto, *That a great Book is a great Evil.*

On the contrary, those who publish their Thoughts in distinct Sheets, and as it were by Piece-meal, have none of these Advantages. We must immediately fall into our Subject and treat every Part of it in a lively Manner, or our Papers are thrown by as dull and insipid: Our Matter must lie close together, and either be wholly new in itself, or in the Turn it receives from our Expressions. Were the Books of our best Authors thus to be retailed to the Publick, and every Page submitted to the Taste of forty or fifty thousand Readers, I am afraid we should complain of many flat Expressions, trivial Observations, beaten Topicks, and common Thoughts, which go off very well in the Lump. At the same Time, notwithstanding some Papers may be made up of broken Hints and irregular Sketches, it is often expected that every Sheet should be a kind of Treatise, and make out in Thought what it wants in Bulk: That a Point of Humour should be worked up in all its Parts; and a Subject touched upon in its most essential Articles, without the Repetitions, Tautologies, and Enlargements that are indulg'd to longer Labours. The ordinary Writers of Morality prescribe to their Readers after the Galenick Way; their Medicines are made up in large Quantities. An Essay Writer must practise in the Chymical Method, and give the Virtue of a full Draught in a few Drops. Were all Books reduced thus to their Quintessence, many a bulky Author would make his Appearance in a Penny Paper: There would be scarce such a thing in Nature as a Folio.[2] The Works of an Age would be contained on a few Shelves; not to mention Millions of Volumes that would be utterly annihilated.

I cannot think that the Difficulty of furnishing out separate Papers of this Nature has hindered Authors from communicating their Thoughts to the World after such a Manner: Though I must confess I am amazed that the Press should be only made use of in this Way by News-Writers, and the Zealots of Parties; as if it were not more advantageous to Mankind to be instructed in Wisdom and Virtue, than in Politicks; and to be made good Fathers, Husbands, and Sons, than Counsellours and Statesmen. Had the Philosophers and great Men of Antiquity, who took so much Pains in order to instruct Mankind, and leave the World wiser and better than they found it; had they, I say, been possessed of the Art of Printing, there is no Question but they would have made such an Advantage of it, in dealing out their

---

[2] *Folio:* The largest common book size, usually about fifteen inches high.

Lectures to the Publick. Our common Prints would be of great Use were they thus calculated to diffuse good Sense through the Bulk of a People, to clear up their Understandings, animate their Minds with Virtue, dissipate the Sorrows of a heavy Heart, or unbend the Mind from its more severe Employments with innocent Amusements. When Knowledge, instead of being bound up in Books, and kept in Libraries and Retirements, is thus obtruded upon the Publick; when it is canvassed in every Assembly, and exposed upon every Table; I cannot forbear reflecting upon that Passage in the *Proverbs*, *Wisdom cryeth without, she uttereth her Voice in the Streets: She cryeth in the chief Place of Concourse, in the Openings of the Gates. In the City she uttereth her Words, saying, How long, ye simple ones, will ye love Simplicity? and the Scorners delight in their Scorning? and Fools hate Knowledge?*

The many Letters which come to me from Persons of the best Sense in both Sexes, (for I may pronounce their Characters from their Way of Writing) do not a little encourage me in the Prosecution of this my Undertaking: Besides that, my Bookseller tells me, the Demand for these my Papers increases daily. It is at his Instance that I shall continue my *rural Speculations* to the End of this Month; several having made up separate Sets of them, as they have done before of those relating to Wit, to Operas, to Points of Morality, or Subjects of Humour.

I am not at all mortified, when sometimes I see my Works thrown aside by Men of no Taste nor Learning. There is a kind of Heaviness and Ignorance that hangs upon the Minds of ordinary Men, which is too thick for Knowledge to break through: Their Souls are not to be enlightned.

> . . . *Nox atra cavâ circumvolat umbra.*[3]

To these I must apply the Fable of the Mole, That after having consulted many Oculists for the bettering of his Sight, was at last provided with a good Pair of Spectacles; but upon his endeavouring to make use of them, his Mother told him very prudently, 'That Spectacles, though they might help the Eye of a Man, could be of no use to a Mole.' It is not therefore for the Benefit of Moles that I publish these my daily Essays.

---

[3] . . . *umbra:* From the Roman poet Virgil's (70–19 B.C.) epic *Aeneid* 2.360: "Black night surrounded [us] with its enfolding shadows."

But besides such as are Moles through Ignorance, there are others who are Moles through Envy. As it is said in the *Latin* Proverb, 'That one Man is a Woolf to another;' so, generally speaking, one Author is a Mole to another Author. It is impossible for them to discover Beauties in one another's Works; they have Eyes only for Spots and Blemishes: They can indeed see the Light, as it is said of the Animals which are their Namesakes, but the Idea of it is painful to them; they immediately shut their Eyes upon it, and withdraw themselves into a wilful Obscurity. I have already caught two or three of these dark undermining Vermin, and intend to make a String of them, in order to hang them up in one of my Papers as an Example to all such voluntary Moles.

No. 262
Monday, December 31, 1711
[Addison Declares The Spectator Is Not a Newspaper]

Nulla venenato Littera mista Joco est.[1]
— Ov.

I think my self highly obliged to the Publick for their kind Acceptance of a Paper which visits them every Morning, and has in it none of those *Seasonings* that recommend so many of the Writings which are in vogue among us.

As, on the one Side, my Paper has not in it a single Word of News, a Reflection in Politicks, nor a Stroke of Party; so, on the other, there are no fashionable Touches of Infidelity, no obscene Ideas, no Satyrs upon Priesthood, Marriage, and the like popular Topicks of Ridicule; no private Scandal, nor any thing that may tend to the Defamation of particular Persons, Families, or Societies.

There is not one of these abovementioned Subjects that would not sell a very indifferent Paper, could I think of gratifying the Publick by such mean and base Methods: but notwithstanding I have rejected every thing that savours of Party, every thing that is loose and immoral, and every thing that might create Uneasiness in the Minds of particular Persons, I find that the Demand for my Papers has

---

[1] *Nulla . . . est:* From Ovid, *Tristia* 2.866: "'Mongst what I write no venom doth appear" [Bond].

encreased every Month since their first Appearance in the World. This does not perhaps reflect so much Honour upon my self, as on my Readers, who give a much greater Attention to Discourses of Virtue and Morality, than ever I expected, or indeed could hope.

When I broke loose from that great Body of Writers who have employed their Wit and Parts in propagating Vice and Irreligion, I did not question but I should be treated as an odd kind of Fellow that had a Mind to appear singular in my Way of Writing: But the general Reception I have found, convinces me that the World is not so corrupt as we are apt to imagine; and that if those Men of Parts who have been employed in viciating the Age had endeavoured to rectify and amend it, they needed not have sacrificed their good Sense and Virtue to their Fame and Reputation. No Man is so sunk in Vice and Ignorance, but there are still some hidden Seeds of Goodness and Knowledge in him; which give him a Relish of such Reflections and Speculations as have an Aptness to improve the Mind and to make the Heart better.

I have shewn in a former Paper, with how much Care I have avoided all such Thoughts as are loose, obscene, or immoral; and I believe my Reader would still think the better of me, if he knew the Pains I am at in qualifying what I write after such a Manner, that nothing may be interpreted as aimed at private Persons. For this Reason when I draw any faulty Character, I consider all those Persons to whom the Malice of the World may possibly apply it, and take care to dash it with such particular Circumstances as may prevent all such ill-natured Applications. If I write any thing on a black Man,[2] I run over in my Mind all the eminent Persons in the Nation who are of that Complection: When I place an imaginary Name at the Head of a Character, I examine every Syllable and Letter of it, that it may not bear any Resemblance to one that is real. I know very well the Value which every Man sets upon his Reputation, and how painful it is to be exposed to the Mirth and Derision of the Publick, and should therefore scorn to divert my Reader at the Expence of any private Man.

As I have been thus tender of every particular Person's Reputation, so I have taken more than ordinary Care not to give Offence to those who appear in the higher Figures of Life. I would not make my self merry even with a Piece of Pasteboard that is invested with a publick

---

[2] *black Man:* Not a person of African descent but rather a European with a dark complexion.

Character; for which Reason I have never glanced upon the late designed Procession of his Holiness[3] and his Attendants, notwithstanding it might have afforded Matter to many ludicrous Speculations. Among those Advantages which the Publick may reap from this Paper, it is not the least, that it draws Mens Minds off from the Bitterness of Party, and furnishes them with Subjects of Discourse that may be treated without Warmth or Passion. This is said to have been the First Design of those Gentlemen who set on Foot the Royal Society; and had then a very good Effect, as it turned many of the greatest Genius's of that Age to the Disquisitions of natural Knowledge, who, if they had engaged in Politicks with the same Parts and Application, might have set their Country in a Flame. The Air-Pump, the Barometer, the Quadrant, and the like Inventions, were thrown out to those busy Spirits, as Tubs and Barrels are to a Whale, that he may let the Ship sail on without Disturbance, while he diverts himself with those innocent Amusements.

I have been so very scrupulous in this Particular of not hurting any Man's Reputation, that I have forborn mentioning even such Authors as I could not name with Honour. This I must confess to have been a Piece of very great Self-denial: For as the Publick relishes nothing better than the Ridicule which turns upon a Writer of any Eminence, so there is nothing which a Man that has but a very ordinary Talent in Ridicule may execute with greater Ease. One might raise Laughter for a Quarter of a Year together upon the Works of a Person who has published but a very few Volumes. For which Reasons I am astonished, that those who have appeared against this Paper have made so very little of it. The Criticisms which I have hitherto published, have been made with an Intention rather to discover Beauties and Excellencies in the Writers of my own Time, than to publish any of their Faults and Imperfections. In the mean while I should take it for a very great Favour from some of my underhand Detractors, if they would break all Measures with me so far, as to give me a Pretence for examining their Performances with an impartial Eye: Nor shall I look upon it as any Breach of Charity to criticise the Author, so long as I keep clear of the Person.

In the mean while, till I am provoked to such Hostilities, I shall from Time to Time endeavour to do Justice to those who have

---

[3] *Procession of his Holiness:* Taking place on November 17, 1711, this was a mock procession, strongly Protestant and Whig, anti-Papist and anti-Tory, of wax effigies of the Pope, the Pretender, and the Devil, four cardinals, four Jesuits, and four friars [Bond].

distinguished themselves in the politer Parts of Learning, and to point out such Beauties in their Works as may have escaped the Observation of others. . . .

No. 367
Thursday, May 1, 1712
[Addison on the Benefits of the Paper]

. . . *perituræ parcite chartæ.*[1]
— Juv.

I have often pleas'd my self with considering the two kinds of Benefits which accrue to the Publick from these my Speculations, and which, were I to speak after the manner of Logicians, I would distinguish into the *Material* and the *Formal.* By the latter I understand those Advantages which my Readers receive, as their Minds are either improved or delighted by these my daily Labours; but having already several times descanted on my Endeavours in this Light, I shall at present wholly confine my self to the Consideration of the former. By the Word *Material* I mean those Benefits which arise to the Publick from these my Speculations, as they consume a considerable quantity of our Paper Manufacture, employ our Artisans in Printing, and find Business for great Numbers of Indigent Persons.

Our Paper Manufacture takes into it several mean Materials which could be put to no other use, and affords Work for several Hands in the collecting of them, which are incapable of any other Employment. Those poor Retailers, whom we see so busie in every Street, deliver in their respective Gleanings to the Merchant. The Merchant carries them in Loads to the Paper-Mill, where they pass thro' a fresh Sett of Hands, and give Life to another Trade. Those who have mills on their Estates by this means considerably raise their Rents, and the whole Nation is in a great measure supplied with a Manufacture, for which formerly she was obliged to her Neighbours.

The Materials are no sooner wrought into Paper, but they are distributed among the Presses, where they again set innumerable Artists at Work, and furnish Business to another Mystery. From hence, ac-

---

[1] . . . *perituræ parcite chartæ*: From Juvenal, *Satires* 1.18: "Spare a few sheets already doom'd to dye" [Bond].

cordingly as they are stained with News or Politicks, they fly thro' the Town in *Post-Men, Post-boys, Daily-Courants, Reviews, Medleys* and *Examiners*.[2] Men, Women and Children contend who shall be the first Bearers of them, and get their daily Sustenance by spreading them. In short, when I trace in my Mind a bundle of Rags to a Quire[3] of *Spectators*, I find so many Hands employ'd in every Step they take thro' their whole Progress, that while I am writing a *Spectator*, I fancy my self providing Bread for a Multitude.

If I do not take care to obviate[4] some of my witty Readers, they will be apt to tell me, that my Paper, after it is thus Printed and Published, is still beneficial to the Publick on several Occasions. I must confess, I have lighted my Pipe with my own Works for this Twelve-month past: My Landlady often sends up her little Daughter to desire some of my old *Spectators*, and has frequently told me, that the Paper they are printed on is the best in the World to wrap Spice in. They likewise make a good Foundation for a Mutton-pye, as I have more than once experienced, and were very much sought for, last *Christmas*, by the whole Neighbourhood.

It is pleasant enough to consider the Changes that a Linnen-fragment undergoes, by passing through the several Hands above-mentioned. The finest Pieces of Holland,[5] when worn to tatters, assume a new Whiteness more beautiful than their first, and often return in the shape of Letters to their Native Country. A Lady's Shift may be metamorphosed into Billets doux, and come into her Possession a second time. A Beau may peruse his Cravat after it is worn out, with greater Pleasure and Advantage than ever he did in a Glass. In a word, a piece of Cloath, after having officiated for some Years as a Towel or a Napkin, may by this means be raised from a Dung-hill, and become the most valuable piece of Furniture in a Prince's Cabinet.

The politest Nations of *Europe* have endeavoured to vie with one another for the Reputation of the finest Printing; Absolute Governments, as well as Republicks, have encouraged an Art which seems to be the noblest and most beneficial that was ever invented among the Sons of Men. The Present King of *France*, in his Pursuits after Glory, has particularly distinguished himself by the promoting of this useful Art, insomuch that several Books have been printed in the *Louvre* at

[2] *Post-Men . . . Examiners:* A list of popular contemporary newspapers.
[3] *Quire:* A set of twenty-four or twenty-five sheets of paper.
[4] *obviate:* To forestall, anticipate.
[5] *Holland:* A glazed cotton or linen fabric.

his own Expence, upon which he sets so great a value, that he considers them as the noblest Presents he can make to Foreign Princes and Ambassadors. If we look into the Commonwealths of *Holland* and *Venice*, we shall find that in this Particular they have made themselves the Envy of the greatest Monarchies. *Elzevir* and *Aldus*[6] are more frequently mentioned than any Pentioner of the one, or Doge[7] of the other.

The several Presses which are now in *England*, and the great Encouragement which has been given to Learning for some Years last past, has made our own Nation as glorious upon this Account, as for its late Triumphs and Conquests. The new Edition which is given us of *Cæsar*'s Commentaries[8] has already been taken notice of in Foreign *Gazettes*, and is a Work that does Honour to the *English* Press. It is no wonder that an Edition should be very correct, which has passed through the Hands of one of the most Accurate, Learned and Judicious Writers this Age has produced. The Beauty of the Paper, of the Character, and of the several Cuts with which this noble Work is Illustrated, makes it the finest Book that I have ever seen; and is a true Instance of the *English* Genius, which, though it does not come the first into any Art, generally carries it to greater heights than any other Country in the World. I am particularly glad that this Author comes from a *British* Printing-house in so great a Magnificence, as he is the first who has given us any tolerable Account of our Country.

My Illiterate Readers, if any such there are, will be surprised to hear me talk of Learning as the Glory of a Nation, and of Printing as an Art that gains a Reputation to a People among whom it flourishes. When Mens Thoughts are taken up with Avarice and Ambition, they cannot look upon any thing as great or valuable, which does not bring with it an extraordinary Power or Interest to the Person who is concerned in it. But as I shall never sink this Paper so far as to engage with *Goths* and *Vandals*,[9] I shall only regard such kind of Reasoners with that Pity which is due to so deplorable a degree of Stupidity and Ignorance.

[6] *Elzevir and Aldus:* The Elzevir family were printers in Holland in the seventeenth century. "Aldus" refers to the Venetian printing house established by Aldus Manutius in the late fifteenth century [Bond].

[7] *Doge:* An elected magistrate in the former republics of Venice and Genoa.

[8] *Caesar's Commentaries: Commentarii de Bello Gallico*, Julius Caesar's (c. 100?–46 B.C.) account of his conquest of Gaul. The "new Edition" referred to is by Dr. Samuel Clarke [Bond].

[9] *Goths and Vandals:* Germanic tribes that conducted campaigns of conquest against the ancient Roman empire. They invaded and occupied Gallic, Latin, and African provinces throughout the fifth century A.D. They were the original "barbarians at the gate" of civilization.

No. 435
Saturday, July 19, 1712
[Addison on the Distinction between "Occasional" and "Immutable" Papers]

Nec duo sunt at forma duplex, nec fœmina dici
Nec puer ut possint, neutrumque & utrumque videntur.[1]
— Ovid.

Most of the Papers I give the Publick are written on Subjects that never vary, but are for ever fixt and immutable. Of this kind are all my more Serious Essays and Discourses; but there is another sort of Speculations, which I consider as Occasional Papers, that take their Rise from the Folly, Extravagance, and Caprice of the present Age. For I look upon my self as one set to watch the Manners and Behaviour of my Countrymen and Contemporaries, and to mark down every absurd Fashion, ridiculous Custom, or affected Form of Speech that makes its Appearance in the World, during the Course of these my Speculations. The Petticoat no sooner begun to swell, but I observed its Motions. The Party-patches had not time to muster themselves before I detected them. I had Intelligence of the Coloured Hood the very first time it appeared in a Publick Assembly. I might here mention several other the like Contingent Subjects, upon which I have bestowed distinct Papers. By this Means I have so effectually quashed those Irregularities which gave Occasion to 'em, that I am afraid Posterity will scarce have a sufficient Idea of them to Relish those Discourses which were in no little Vogue at the time when they were written. They will be apt to think that the Fashions and Customs I attacked, were some Fantastick Conceits of my own, and that their Great-Grandmothers cou'd not be so whimsical as I have represented them. For this Reason, when I think on the Figure my several Volumes of Speculations will make about a Hundred Years hence, I consider them as so many Pieces of old Plate, where the Weight will be regarded, but the Fashion lost.

---

[1] *Nec duo . . . videntur:* From Ovid, *Metamorphoses* 4.378–79: "Both bodies in a single body mix, / A single body with a double sex"[Bond].

No. 452
Friday, August 8, 1712
[Addison and Pope on the Popular Taste for News]

Est natura Hominum Novitatis avida.[1]
— Plin. apud Lill.

There is no Humour in my Countrymen, which I am more en-
clined to wonder at, than their general Thirst after News. There are
about half a Dozen Ingenious Men, who live very plentifully upon
this Curiosity of their Fellow-Subjects. They all of them receive the
same Advices from abroad, and very often in the same Words; but
their way of Cooking it is so different, that there is no Citizen, who
has an Eye to the Publick Good, that can leave the Coffee-house with
Peace of Mind, before he has given every one of them a Reading.
These several Dishes of News are so very agreeable to the Palate of
my Countrymen, that they are not only pleased with them when they
are served up hot, but when they are again set cold before them, by
those penetrating Politicians who oblige the Publick with their Reflections and Observations upon every Piece of Intelligence that is sent us
from abroad. The Text is given us by one Sett of Writers, and the
Comment by another.

But notwithstanding we have the same Tale told us in so many different Papers, and if Occasion requires in so many Articles of the
same Paper; Notwithstanding in a scarcity of Foreign Posts we hear
the same Story repeated, by different Advices from *Paris, Brussels,*
the *Hague,* and from every great Town in *Europe;* Notwithstanding the Multitude of Annotations, Explanations, Reflections, and various Readings which it passes through, our Time lies heavy on our
Hands till the Arrival of a fresh Mail: We long to receive further Particulars, to hear what will be the next Step, or what will be the Consequences of that which has been already taken. A Westerly Wind
keeps the whole Town in Suspence, and puts a stop to Conversation.

This general Curiosity has been raised and inflamed by our late
Wars, and, if rightly directed, might be of good use to a Person who
has such a Thirst awakened in him. Why should not a Man, who
takes Delight in reading every thing that is new, apply himself to History, Travels, and other Writings of the same kind, where he will find

---

[1] *Est natura ... avida:* From Pliny the Elder, *Natural History* 12.5 (as cited in
Lilly's Latin Grammar): "Human nature is greedy for novelty"[Bond].

perpetual Fuel for his Curiosity, and meet with much more Pleasure and Improvement, than in these Papers of the Week? An honest Tradesman, who languishes a whole Summer in expectation of a Battel, and perhaps is balked at last, may here meet with half a dozen in a Day. He may read the News of a whole Campain, in less time than he now bestows upon the Products of any single Post. Fights, Conquests and Revolutions lie thick together. The Reader's Curiosity is raised and satisfied every Moment, and his Passions disappointed or gratified, without being detained in a State of Uncertainty from Day to Day, or lying at the Mercy of Sea and Wind. In short, the Mind is not here kept in a perpetual Gape after Knowledge, nor punished with that Eternal Thirst, which is the Portion of all our Modern News-mongers and Coffee-house Politicians.

All Matters of Fact, which a Man did not know before, are News to him; and I do not see how any Haberdasher in *Cheapside* is more concerned in the present Quarrel of the Cantons, than he was in that of the League.[2] At least, I believe every one will allow me, it is of more Importance to an *Englishman* to know the History of his Ancestors, than that of his Contemporaries, who live upon the Banks of the *Danube* or the *Borysthenes*. As for those who are of another Mind, I shall recommend to them the following Letter, from a Projector, who is willing to turn a Penny by this remarkable Curiosity of his Countrymen.

Mr. SPECTATOR,

'You must have observed, the Men who frequent Coffee-houses, and delight in News, are pleased with every thing that is Matter of Fact, so it be what they have not heard before. A Victory, or a Defeat, are equally agreeable to them. The shutting of a Cardinal's Mouth pleases them one Post, and the opening of it another. They are glad to hear the *French* Court is removed to *Marli*, and are afterwards as much delighted with its Return to *Versailles*. They read the Advertisements with the same Curiosity as the Articles of Publick News; and are as pleased to hear of a Pye-bald Horse that is stray'd out of a field near *Islington*, as a whole Troop that has been engaged in any Foreign Adventure. In short, they have a Relish for every thing that is News, let the matter of it be what it will; or to speak more

---

[2] *Quarrel of the Cantons . . . the League:* Cantons are Swiss states. At this time the Protestant states Zug and Bern were quarreling with five Roman Catholic cantons. The Holy League, or Catholic League, was established in 1576 to oppose the rule of the Protestant Bourbon king, Henry IV of Navarre (1553–1610).

properly, they are Men of a Voracious Appetite, but no Taste. Now, Sir, since the great Fountain of News, I mean the War, is very near being dried up; and since these Gentlemen have contracted such an inextinguishable Thirst after it; I have taken their Case and my own into Consideration, and have thought of a Project which may turn to the Advantage of us both. I have Thoughts of Publishing a daily Paper, which shall comprehend in it all the most remarkable Occurences in every little Town, Village and Hamlet, that lie within ten Miles of *London*, or in other Words, within the Verge of the Penny-Post. I have pitched upon this Scene of Intelligence for two Reasons; first, because the Carriage of Letters will be very cheap; and secondly, because I may receive them every Day. By this means my Readers will have their News fresh and fresh, and many worthy Citizens, who cannot Sleep with any Satisfaction at present, for want of being informed how the World goes, may go to Bed contentedly, it being my Design to put out my paper every Night at nine a Clock precisely. I have already established Correspondencies in these several Places, and received very good Intelligence.

'By my last Advices from *Knights-bridge* I hear that a Horse was clapped into the Pound on the third Instant, and that he was not released when the Letters came away.

'We are inform'd from *Pankridge*, that a dozen Weddings were lately celebrated in the Mother Church of that Place, but are referred to their next Letters for the Names of the Parties concerned.

'Letters from *Brompton* advise, That the Widow *Blight* had received several Visits from *John Milldew*, which affords great matter of Speculation in those Parts.

'By a Fisherman which lately touched at *Hammersmith*, there is Advice from *Putney*, that a certain Person well known in that Place, is like to lose his Election for Church-warden; but this being Boat News, we cannot give entire Credit to it.

'Letters from *Paddington* bring little more, than that *William Squeak*, the Sow-gelder, passed through that Place the 5th Instant.

'They advise from *Fulham*, that things remained there in the same State they were. They had Intelligence, just as the Letters came away, of a Tub of excellent Ale just set abroach at *Parsons Green*; but this wanted confirmation.

'I have here, Sir, given you a Specimen of the News with which I intend to entertain the Town, and which, when drawn up regularly in the form of a News Paper, will, I doubt not, be very acceptable to many of those Publick-Spirited Readers, who take more delight in acquainting themselves with other Peoples Business than their own. I hope a Paper of this kind, which lets us know what is done near home, may be more useful to us, than those which are filled with Advices from *Zug* and *Bender*, and make some Amends for that Dearth of Intelligence, which we may justly apprehend from times of Peace. If I find that you receive this Project favourably, I will shortly trouble you with one or two more; and in the mean time am, most worthy Sir, with all due Respect,

Your most obedient,
and most humble Servant.'

No. 542
Friday, November 21, 1712
[Addison on Letters to The Spectator]

Et sibi præferri se gaudet . . .[1]
— Ov.

When I have been present in Assemblies where my Paper has been talked of, I have been very well pleased to hear those who would detract from the Author of it observe, that the Letters which are sent to the *Spectator* are as good, if not better, than any of his Works. Upon this Occasion many Letters of Mirth are usually mentioned, which some think the *Spectator* writ to himself, and which others Commend because they fancy he received them from his Correspondents: Such are those from the *Valetudinarian*; the Inspector of the Sign-posts; the Master of the Fan Exercise: with that of the Hooped Petticoat; that of *Nicholas Hart* the annual Sleeper; that from Sir *John Envill*; that upon the *London* Cries; with Multitudes of the same Nature. As I love nothing more than to mortifie the Ill-natured, that I may do it effectually, I must acquaint them, they have very often praised me when they did not design it, and that they have approved my Writings when they thought they had derogated from them. I have heard several of these unhappy Gentlemen proving, by undeniable Arguments, that I was not able to pen a Letter which I had written the Day before. Nay, I have heard some of them throwing out ambiguous

---

[1] *Et sibi præferri se gaudet . . . :* From Ovid, *Metamorphoses* 2.430: "He heard, / Well pleased, himself before himself preferred" — ADDISON [Bond].

Expressions, and giving the Company Reason to suspect that they themselves did me the Honour to send me such or such a particular Epistle, which happened to be talked of with the Esteem or Approbation of those who were present. These rigid Criticks are so afraid of allowing me any thing which does not belong to me, that they will not be positive whether the Lion, the wild Boar, and the Flower-pots in the Play-house did not actually write those Letters which came to me in their Names. I must therefore inform these Gentlemen, that I often chuse this way of casting my Thoughts into a Letter, for the following Reasons; First, out of the Policy of those who try their Jest upon another, before they own it themselves. Secondly, because I would extort a little Praise from such who will never applaud any thing whose Author is known and certain. Thirdly, because it gave me an Opportunity of introducing a great variety of Characters into my Work, which could not have been done, had I always written in the person of the *Spectator.* Fourthly, because the Dignity Spectatorial would have suffered, had I published as from my self those several ludicrous Compositions which I have ascribed to fictitious Names and Characters. And lastly, because they often serve to bring in, more naturally, such additional Reflections as have been placed at the End of them.

There are others who have likewise done me a very particular Honour, though undesignedly. These are such who will needs have it, that I have translated or borrowed many of my Thoughts out of Books which are written in other Languages. I have heard of a Person, who is more famous for his Library than his Learning, that has asserted this more than once in his private Conversation. Were it true, I am sure he could not speak it from his own Knowledge; but had he read the Books which he has collected, he would find this Accusation to be wholly groundless. Those who are truly learned will acquit me in this Point, in which I have been so far from offending, that I have been scrupulous perhaps to a Fault in quoting the Authors of several Passages which I might have made my own. But as this Assertion is in reality an Encomium on what I have published, I ought rather to glory in it, than endeavour to confute it.

Some are so very willing to alienate from me that small Reputation which might accrue to me from any of these my Speculations, that they attribute some of the best of them to those imaginary Manuscripts with which I have introduced them. There are others, I must confess, whose Objections have given me a greater Concern, as they seem to reflect, under this Head, rather on my Morality than on my

Invention. These are they who say an Author is guilty of Falsehood, when he talks to the Publick of Manuscripts which he never saw, or describes Scenes of Action or Discourse in which he was never engaged. But these Gentlemen would do well to consider, there is not a Fable or Parable which ever was made use of, that is not liable to this Exception; since nothing, according to this Notion, can be related innocently which was not once Matter of Fact. Besides, I think the most ordinary Reader may be able to discover, by my way of writing, what I deliver in these Occurences as Truth, and what as Fiction.

Since I am unawares engaged in answering the several objections which have been made against these my Works, I must take Notice that there are some who affirm a Paper of this Nature should always turn upon diverting Subjects, and others who find Fault with every one of them that hath not an immediate Tendency to the advancement of Religion or Learning. I shall leave these Gentlemen to dispute it out among themselves, since I see one half of my Conduct patronized by each side. Were I serious on an improper Subject, or trifling in a serious one, I should deservedly draw upon me the Censure of my Readers; or were I conscious of any thing in my Writings that is not innocent at least, or that the greatest part of them were not sincerely designed to discountenance Vice and Ignorance, and support the interest of true Wisdom and Virtue, I should be more severe upon my self than the Publick is disposed to be. In the mean while I desire my Reader to consider every particular Paper or Discourse as a distinct Tract by it self, and independant of every thing that goes before or after it.

I shall end this Paper with the following Letter, which was really sent me, as some others have been which I have published, and for which I must own my self indebted to their respective Writers.

SIR,

'I was this Morning in a Company of your Well-wishers, when we read over, with great Satisfaction, *Tully*'s Observations on Action adapted to the *British* Theatre: Though, by the way, we were very sorry to find that you have disposed of another Member of your Club. Poor Sir *Roger* is dead, and the worthy Clergyman dying. Captain *Sentry* has taken Possession of a fair Estate, *Will. Honeycomb* has married a Farmer's Daughter, and the *Templar* withdraws himself into the Business of his own Profession. What will all this end in! We are afraid it portends no Good to the Publick. Unless you very speedily fix a Day for the Election of new Members, we are under

Apprehensions of losing the *British Spectator*. I hear of a Party of
Ladies who intend to address you on this Subject, and question not, if
you do not give us the Slip very suddenly, that you will receive Addresses from all Parts of the Kingdom to continue so useful a Work.
Pray deliver us out of this Perplexity, and among the Multitude of
your Readers you will particularly oblige

Your most Sincere Friend and Servant,

Philo-Spec.'

No. 568
Friday, July 16, 1714
[Addison on the Political Misreading of The Spectator*]*

. . . Dum recitas, incipit esse Tuus.[1]
— Mart.

I was Yesterday in a Coffee-House not far from the *Royal Exchange*,[2] where I observed three Persons in close Conference over a
Pipe of Tobacco; upon which, having filled one for my own use, I
lighted it at the little Wax Candle that stood before them; and after
having thrown in two or three Whiffs amongst them, sat down, and
made of the Company. I need not tell my Reader, that lighting a
Man's Pipe at the same Candle, is looked upon among Brother-
smokers as an Overture to Conversation and Friendship. As we here
lay our Heads together in a very amicable Manner, being intrenched
under a Cloud of our own raising, I took up the last SPECTATOR, and
casting my Eye over it, *The* SPECTATOR, says I, *is very witty to Day*;
upon which a lusty lethargick old Gentleman who sat at the Upper-
end of the Table, having gradually blown out of his Mouth a great
deal of Smoke, which he had been collecting for some Time before,
Ay, says he, *more witty than wise I am afraid*. His Neighbour who
sat at his right Hand immediately coloured, and being an angry
Politician, laid down his Pipe with so much Wrath that he broke it in
the Middle, and by that Means furnished me with a Tobacco-stopper.
I took it up very sedately, and looking him full in the Face, made use

[1] *. . . Dum recitas, incipit esse Tuus*: From Martial, *Epigrams* 1.38.2 (altered):
"When you rehearse my verse, it is not mine but thine" [Bond].
[2] *Royal Exchange*: A meeting place for businessmen that housed nearly two hundred shops.

of it from Time to Time all the while he was speaking: *This Fellow,* says he, *can't for his Life keep out of Politicks. Do you see how he abuses* four *great Men here?* I fix'd my Eye very attentively on the Paper, and asked him if he meant those who were represented by Asterisks. *Asterisks,* says he, *do you call them? They are all of them Stars. He might as well have put Garters to 'em. Then pray do but mind the two or three next Lines! Ch–rch and P–dd–ng in the same Sentence! Our Clergy are very much beholden to him.* Upon this the third Gentleman, who was of a mild Disposition, and, as I found, a Whig in his Heart, desired him not to be too severe upon the SPECTATOR neither; *For,* says he, *you find he is very cautious of giving Offence, and has therefore put two Dashes into his Pudding. A Fig for his Dash,* says the angry Politician. *In his next Sentence he gives a plain Innuendo, that our Posterity will be in a sweet P–ckle. What does the Fool mean by his Pickle? Why does not he write it at length if he means honestly?* I have read over the whole Sentence, says I; *but I look upon the Parenthesis in the Belly of it to be the most dangerous Part, and as full of Insinuations as it can hold. But who,* says I, *is my Lady* Q–p–t–s? *Ay, Answer that if you can, Sir,* says the furious Statesman to the poor Whig that sat over against him. But without giving him Time to reply, *I do assure you,* says he, *were I my Lady* Q–p–t–s, *I would sue him for* Scandalum Magnatum. *What is the World come to? Must every Body be allowed to —— ?* He had by this time filled a new Pipe, and applying it to his Lips, when we expected the last Word of his Sentence, put us off with a Whiff of Tobacco; which he redoubled with so much Rage and Trepidation that he almost stifled the whole Company. After a short Pause, I owned that I thought the SPECTATOR had gone too far in writing so many Letters of my lady Q–p–t–s's Name; *but however,* says I, *he has made a little Amends for it in his next Sentence, where he leaves a blank Space without so much as a Consonant to direct us;* I mean, says I, *after those Words,* The Fleet, that used to be the Terrour of the Ocean, should be Wind-bound for the Sake of a —— ; *after which ensues a Chasm, that, in my Opinion, looks modest enough. Sir,* says my Antagonist, *you may easily know his Meaning by his Gaping; I suppose he designs his Chasm, as you call it, for an Hole to creep out at, but I believe it will hardly serve his Turn. Who can endure to see the Great Officers of State, the* B—y's *and* T—t's, *treated after so scurrilous a Manner?* I can't for my Life, says I, *imagine who they are the* SPECTATOR *means?* No! says he, —— *Your humble Servant Sir!* Upon which he flung himself back in his chair after a contemptuous Manner, and smiled upon the old lethargick Gentleman on his Left Hand, who I found was his great Admirer. The Whig however had begun to conceive a Good-will towards me, and seeing my Pipe out, very generously offered me the use of his Box; but I declined it with great Civility, being obliged to meet a Friend about that Time in another Quarter of the City.

At my leaving the Coffee-house, I could not forbear reflecting with my self upon that gross Tribe of Fools who may be termed the *Overwise*, and upon the Difficulty of writing any thing in this censorious Age, which a weak Head may not construe into private Satyr and personal Reflection.

A Man who has a good Nose at an Innuendo, smells Treason and Sedition in the most innocent Words that can be put together, and never sees a Vice or Folly stigmatized, but finds out one or other of his Acquaintance pointed at by the Writer. I remember an empty pragmatical Fellow in the Country, who upon reading over *the whole Duty of Man*, had written the Names of several Persons in the Village at the Side of every Sin which is mention'd by that excellent Author; so that he had converted one of the best Books in the World into a Libel against the 'Squire, Church-wardens, Overseers of the Poor, and all other most considerable Persons in the Parish. This Book with these extraordinary marginal Notes fell accidentally into the Hands of one who had never seen it before; upon which there arose a current Report that Some-body had written a Book against the 'Squire and the whole Parish. The Minister of the Place having at that Time a Controversy with some of his Congregation upon the Account of his Tythes, was under some Suspicion of being the Author, till the good Man set his People right by shewing them that the satyrical Passages might be applied to several others of two or three neighbouring Villages, and that the Book was writ against all the Sinners in *England*.

No. 625
Friday, November 26, 1714
[Tickell on Thomas Quid-nunc]

. . . amores
A tenero meditatur Ungui.[1]
— Hor.

The *Love-Casuist* hath referred to me the following Letter of Queries, with his Answers to each Question, for my Approbation. I have accordingly considered the several Matters therein contained, and hereby confirm and ratifie his Answers, and require the gentle Querist to conform her self thereunto.

SIR,

'I was Thirteen the Ninth of *November* last, and must now begin to think of settling my self in the World, and so I would humbly beg your Advice, what I must do with Mr. *Fondle*, who makes his Addresses to me. He is a very pretty Man, and hath the blackest Eyes and whitest Teeth you ever saw. Though he is but a younger Brother, he dresses like a Man of Quality, and no Body comes into a Room like him. I know he hath refused great Offers, and if he cannot Marry me, he will never have any Body else. But my Father hath forbid him the House, because he sent me a Copy of Verses; for he is one of the greatest Wits in Town. My elder Sister, who, with her good Will, would call me *Miss* as long as I live, must be married before me, they say. She tells them, that Mr. *Fondle* makes a Fool of me, and will spoil the Child, as she calls me, like a confident Thing as she is. In short, I am resolved to marry Mr. *Fondle*, if it be but to spite her. But because I would do nothing that is imprudent, I beg of you to give me your Answers to some Questions I will write down, and desire you to get them printed in the SPECTATOR, and I do not doubt but you will give such Advice as, I am sure, I shall follow.

'When Mr. *Fondle* looks upon me for half an Hour together, and calls me *Angel*, is he not in Love?'

Answer, *No.*

'May not I be certain he will be a kind Husband, that has promised me half my Portion in Pin-mony, and to keep me a Coach and Six in the Bargain?'

---

[1] *. . . amores . . . Ungui:* From Horace, *Odes* 3.6.23–24 (altered): "Plans amours from childhood" [Bond].

No.

'Whether I, who have been acquainted with him this whole Year almost, am not a better Judge of his Merit, than my Father and Mother, who never heard him talk, but at Table?'

No.

'Whether I am not old enough to chuse for my self?'

No.

'Whether it would not have been rude in me to refuse a Lock of his Hair?'

No.

'Should not I be a very barbarous Creature, if I did not pity a Man that is always sighing for my Sake?'

No.

'Whether you would not advise me to run away with the poor Man?'

No.

'Whether you do not think, that if I won't have him, he won't drown himself?'

No.

'What shall I say to him the next time he asks me if I will marry him?'

No.

The following Letter requires neither Introduction, nor Answer.

Mr. SPECTATOR,

'I wonder that, in the present Situation of Affairs, you can take Pleasure in writing any thing but News; for, in a Word, who minds any thing else? The Pleasure of increasing in Knowledge, and learning something new every Hour of Life, is the noblest Entertainment of a Rational Creature. I have a very good Ear for a Secret, and am naturally of a communicative Temper; by which Means I am capable of doing you great Services in this way. In order to make my self useful, I am early in the Antichamber, where I thrust my Head into the thick of the Press, and catch the News, at the opening of the Door, while it is warm. Sometimes I stand by the Beef-Eaters,[2] and take the Buz as it passes by me. At other times I lay my Ear close to the Wall, and suck in many a valuable Whisper, as it runs in a streight Line from Corner to Corner. When I am weary with standing, I repair to one of the neighbouring Coffee-houses, where I sit sometimes for a whole Day,

---

[2] *Beef-Eaters:* Yeomen of the Royal Guard and Warders of the Tower of London.

and have the News, as it comes from Court, fresh and fresh. In short Sir, I spare no pains to know how the World goes. A Piece of News loses its Flavour when it hath been an Hour in the Air. I love, if I may so speak, to have it fresh from the Tree; and to convey it to my Friends before it is faded. Accordingly my Expences in Coach-hire make no small Article; which you may believe, when I assure you, that I post away from Coffee-house to Coffee-house, and forestall the *Evening-Post*[3] by two Hours. There is a certain Gentleman, who hath given me the slip twice or thrice, and hath been before-hand with me at *Child*'s. But I have played him a Trick. I have purchased a Pair of the best Coach-horses I could buy for Money, and now let him out-strip me if he can. Once more, Mr. SPECTATOR, let me advise you to deal in News. You may depend upon my Assistance. But I must break off abruptly, for I have twenty Letters to write.

> *Yours, in haste,*
> Tho. Quid-nunc.'[4]

Cultural Contexts

JOSIAH WOODWARD

From An Account of the Societies for Reformation of Manners in England and Ireland

First published in 1699, this text chronicles the institution and the successes of these reforming societies. Comprising Low Church Anglicans and Dissenters (radical Protestant sects outside the official Anglican church), these societies were active in London and in provincial towns between 1690 and 1738. They campaigned for stricter enforcement of moral legislation by magistrates, pursuing prosecutions for drunkenness, swearing, prostitution, and other criminal vices. The Society lacked broad-based support and was rendered inoperative by 1740.

---

[3] *Evening-Post:* There was a newspaper with this title published in 1706, but the allusion here is more likely to the evening mail [Bond].

[4] *Quid-nunc:* A person who is always asking "what now?," a gossip. *Quid nunc* means "what now?" in Latin.

It may be hoped, That this plain Discourse will meet no other Enemies than such as are likewise Enemies to *Religion* and *Virtue,* and are lost to the Sense of *Good* and *Evil,* since the only *Design* of it is evidently to promote the true Interest of *Religion*; and it does not oppose any one Man's honest Advantage, or encounter any common Opinion, that I know of, among us: The Observation having been long since made, That how many Disputes soever there have been rais'd among the too various Denominations of Christians, concerning *the Power of the Magistrate in Matters of Religion,* with respect either to *Faith* or *Worship,* it hath never been a Dispute, Whether *the Magistrate hath Power to Punish Immoralities:* The *Prosecution* of Men for their *Vices* hath never been reckoned *Persecution.* It being as plainly the Duty of the *Magistrate,* from the Word of GOD, which obliges him to *Execute Wrath upon those that do Evil,*[1] as it is evident, from the dismal Effects of *Vice* and *Wickedness* in all Ages, that Laws against **Prophaneness** and **Debauchery** are necessary for the Preservation of *Communities,* as that *Piety* and *Virtue* are requisite to their Well-being; and that unrestrained *Vice* and *Prophaneness* are as fatal to *Publick Societies*, as they are destructive to *Private Persons.*

But though LAWS are necessary to the very Being of *Communities,* and *Good Laws* to their Happiness; yet they cannot be supposed, by any Rational Man, to be any more sufficient of themselves, to procure the Welfare of the *Body Politick*, without *Execution*, than the best *Medicines* can procure the *Health* of the *Natural Body,* without the Use and Application of them.

If therefore the *Execution of Good Laws* be necessary, as is proved, to the Welfare of *Communities;* and those that concern *Matters of Religion,* as do those for the Punishment of *Prophaneness* and *Debauchery,* are allow'd, in a Christian Country, to deserve the greatest regard; the Interest of *Religion,* and the Welfare of the *Community* being so deeply concerned therein, it cannot be a matter of Dispute, whether it becomes Men that call themselves *Christians,* to promote the *Execution* of such *Laws.* Nay, it cannot be well imagined, how Men can have a *Zeal* for the Service of the Great GOD of Heaven and Earth, or can have a *due Love* to Mankind, who have no regard to the *Honour* of God, or *Welfare* of their *Country;* as shall hereafter more fully appear.

Now, what becomes all Men, in their several Capacities, to do, in the Promoting of the *Execution* of our *Laws* against **Prophaneness**

---

[1] *. . . those that do Evil:* Romans 13.4.

and **Debauchery,** my Business, in the first place, is to shew is Practicable, and that it may be done by us of this Nation; and that not only from what was done some Years ago, in the Times of *Usurpation,* but what hath been done within Eight Years past, in and about this City, and other Parts of the Kingdom.

It is very well known, that in the late times **Prophane Swearing** and **Cursing, Drunkenness, Open-Lewdness,** and **Prophanation** of the **Lord's-Day,** were generally discouraged, and suppressed. And it is as well known, to our Shame, that those Sins have not only since revived among us, by reason of the Impunity of Offenders, the Countenance and Preferment they have met with, and the Contagion of great and ill Examples, but have been committed with great Impudence, and without Controul; without either Shame, or the Fear of the Laws; so that they were seen and heard at *Noon-Day,* and in our *Open Streets;* and as if we were resolved to out-do the Impieties of the very *Heathens, Prophaneness,* and even *Blasphemy,* was too often the Wit and Entertainment of our *Scandalous Play-Houses,* and *Sincere Religion* became the Jest and Scorn of our *Courts* in the late Reigns.

And thus *Debauchery* diffused it self throughout the whole Body of the Nation, till, at last, our *Morals* were so corrupted, that *Virtue* and *Vice* had with too many changed their Names; it was reckoned *Breeding* to *Swear, Gallantry to be Lewd, good Humour to be Drunk,* and *Wit* to despise *Sacred things;* and it was enough to have rendred one suspected of *Phanaticism,* or an abjectness of Spirit, and a matter of Reproach, not to suffer ones self to be carried away with this *Torrent of Wickedness,* and not to glory in those *fashionable Vices.* Nay, it was thought an unpardonable Rudeness, even for a *Clergy-Man* or *Magistrate,* to reprove or punish one that was Guilty of them, notwithstanding the Solemn Obligations of their *Oaths* and *Vows* to do it. And even after the Accession of His present Majesty to the Crown, tho' *Popery* immediately vanished, *Immorality* and *Prophaneness* still kept their ground, as if they expected an *Establishment* with our *Liberties,* after so long and *Peaceable a Possession.*

Reformation was indeed talkt of by some Persons as an Excellent thing, and as a proper way of Expressing our Thankfulness to Almighty God for his Mercies to this Nation, and to procure a Continuance of them to us, and to our Posterity: But *Vice* was lookt upon as too formidable an Enemy to be provok'd, and *Publick Reformation* was thought so difficult an Undertaking, that those that gave it very good Words, judged it not safe to set about it in the time of War, whilst there were so many in Arms on the other side; and therefore they seemed to decline the Thoughts of it till we should see the End of the uncertain War we were ingag'd in; tho' they were, I conceive, otherwise instructed by *God's* express Command to the *Jews*. *When the Host goeth forth against thine Enemy, then keep thy self from every evil thing.*[2] When things were in this dismal and almost desperate State, it came into the Hearts, it seems, of *Five* or *Six* private *Gentlemen* of the *Church of England,* to engage in this difficult and hazardous Enterprize; who considering that the higher the Tide of Wickedness was, the more need there was of Opposing it; that our crying Sins were our greatest Enemies, and most threatned our Ruin; that we have Laws in Force against them; and that they should have the Laws of *God,* with the Prayers of *good Men* on their side, resolved, whatever Difficulties they met with, to make their Efforts for Promoting the *Execution* of our Laws against *Prophaneness* and *Debauchery,* and the Suppressing of them by advisable Methods.

This was such an Undertaking as we might well believe would soon alarm the Enemy, but which the *Patrons* of *Vice* would make no doubt to defeat, before any Progress could be made; and which the Prudent and Wise Men of the World, who rely on second Causes, with too little regard to the first, the Almighty Creator and Governor of the World, *with whom,* as King Asa expresses it in his Prayer, *it is nothing to help, whether with many, or with those that have no power,*[3] would look on with Pity, if not with Derision; and so it proved, that the Champions and Advocates of *Debauchery* put themselves in Array to defend their wretched and infamous Liberties; they set themselves to Ridicule, to Defame, and to Oppose this Design, and to Overthrow the Hopes and Expectations of the Undertakers: And some others, whom in Charity we would not look on as Enemies of Religion and Virtue, tho' we cannot easily esteem them our Friends, whose Conduct has so greatly obstructed the Progress of this Design, consulting Human Prudence, or rather Worldly Policy, too much, and perhaps their own Obligations too little, were very forward to censure these Attempts as the Effect of an imprudent and an unseasonable Zeal; But notwithstanding a furious Opposition from Adversaries, the ill Offices of those from whom better things might have been expected, and the unkind Neutrality of Friends, these *Gentlemen,* who in a little time began to add some others to their Number, not only kept their Ground, but made farther Advances; for

---

[2] *When . . . from every evil thing:* Deuteronomy 23.9.

[3] *. . . those that have no power:* 2 Chronicles 14.10. One of the kings of Judah, Asa worked toward religious reform by abolishing idol worship.

our late Excellent QUEEN of Glorious Memory, having this Affair laid before Her, in the Absence of the King, by a Prelate of great Learning and Fame, (the late Lord Bishop of *Worcester*).[4] She had just Sentiments of it, and therefore thought it became Her to give it Countenance; She Graciously condescended to Thank those who were concerned in it, and readily promised them Her Assistance; and afterwards, upon this Application made to Her Majesty, She was pleased to send Her *Letter* to the *Justices of Middlesex,* commanding them to *put the Laws against Prophaneness and Vice in Execution with all Fidelity and Impartiality; and to this end, that they should be careful and diligent in encouraging all Persons to do their part in giving Informations against Offenders, as they were obliged by their Oath, as Magistrates, to do;* and when there was further Occasion, She shew'd She was in earnest to promote this Design, by taking other more effectual Methods for that purpose. But as it may well be supposed, That the Queen's patronizing of these Endeavours could not but give Credit and Strength to them; so the Affair, by Her Death (it may as easily be imagined) must lose a great Advantage: But yet the Loss (tho' it appeared exceedingly great) did not discourage those that were ingaged in this Enterprize. For as they first set about it with little or no Expectation of such a Patroness, because they thought it would be an acceptable Service to the King of Kings, and that it would promote the true Interests of *Religion,* and the Welfare of their *Country:* So the same Considerations obliged them to pursue their Design with equal Vigour and Zeal, tho' they were deprived of so great a Friend and Protector. And Divine Providence had by this time seemed to favour their Endeavours, by the great and remarkable Success that had attended them; for Multitudes of Offenders had been by their means brought to Punishment. The *Publick Opposition* that was at first made to their *Undertaking* was broke through, (which the Lord Bishop of *Gloucester,* who hath been a great Encourager of this Undertaking, gave an Account of in his *Vindication* of it, which, it may be wished, there may never be any further Occasion to remember) and the Honesty of it had recommended it to the Virtuous and Unprejudiced part of the Nation, whom the Account of these Matters had reached; the Enemy, after a severe Examination, having not been able to discover, that any *illegal Methods* had been used, or that any *secular Interest* was pursued by those, who bestow'd their *Time* and

---

[4] *QUEEN . . . Lord Bishop of Worcester:* Queen Mary II (1662–1694), daughter of James II. Her husband, William III (William of Orange, 1650–1702), was invited to assume the English throne in 1688 by Protestant opponents of James II.

their *Pains* in carrying on so ungrateful and hazardous a Work, as that of *Reformation* will be always found, since it is the Opposing of ill Men, in their sinful Indulgencies, which are often more desirable to them than their very Lives. With these Encouragements they prosecuted their Business, increasing their Number by the Addition of Persons of considerable Note, and of the best Character; some of whom, tho' they were of different Opinions from those of the *Establish'd Church*, as to some Points concerning *Religion*, were willing to unite their Strength in the common Cause of Christianity, and engage in so Noble a Design, that had done so much Good: By whose *joint Endeavours*, great Advances have been made towards a *Reformation of Manners*, which is every Day getting ground, Persons of *various Ranks*, of *considerable Fortunes*, and of the *clearest Character*, offering Assistance to it, not only in and about the City of *London*, but from several Parts of the Kingdom.

. . . The forming therefore of *Good Men* into such *pious Combinations*, for the overbalancing those of *Vice*, the countermining the contrary *Attempts* of all *wicked Men*, and recovering the *Power*, as well as *Form* of *Religion*, is most earnestly recommended to all the Friends of *Piety* and *Virtue*. And methinks it may be expected from all, that have any sincere regard to *God's Honour*, their *own* and their *Country's Happiness*, that they should exert themselves in their several Capacities, with a noble *Zeal* and *Emulation* for the *Perfecting* of this great *Undertaking*. And now especially the *Times of Peace* are returned, which we have been told, are the Times of *Reformation*, surely none that carry the Face of Christians can with Confidence offer new Excuses any longer to postpone it; we may now hope for the Assistance of some, at least, of the *Cautious* and *prudent Men* amongst us, who have hitherto, with great *Gravity*, stood *Neuters* in this Affair, and that they will at last answer the Expectation of Good Men from them, and suffer the Generations to come to call them Blessed. 'Tis at least to be hoped, that if they are too *Great* and *Wise* to *ingage* in the *Work* themselves, they will not, however, *obstruct* it more than the *open Enemies* of it can do, by their calling it an *Impracticable Undertaking*, whispering groundless *Jealousies* of the Design, or uncharitable and disadvantageous *Characters* of the *Persons* concerned in the Promoting it; but rather, that they will let the World see that their *Zeal* is ingaged in the Carrying on of *wiser Methods*, for the Effecting of a *National Reformation*. And one would think, that the Employing our *Labour* or *Authority* in this *Noble Design*, of being *Instrumental* in doing Good to Multitudes of Souls, by Suppressing of *National Sins,* and, by consequence, the Reviving the Power and Reputation of *Religion,* and thereby Preventing *National Judgments,* should be more worth the *Concern* and *Application* of Christians, and should afford a more true and solid Satisfaction than the pursuit of our Worldly Interest or Pleasures. All indeed are not *Capable* of being *Serviceable* in the same way; but whether it be by *Executing the Laws,* or by *Preaching, Discoursing, Writing, Informing, Setting up of Societies,* or otherwise contributing towards it, which way soever it be that we can further this *Glorious Work,* it will, I think, be hard to find a good Excuse for any that shall decline their Concurrence, according to their Advantages and Opportunities, in an Undertaking which it would become the greatest Man upon Earth to promote, which is now so far facilitated by the *Schemes* that are laid, and the *Methods* it is put into.

We have seen some *few Persons,* ingaging in this *Enterprize,* before they had any *Methods* to direct them, or many *Examples* to incourage them, encountring *Opposition* in the first *forming* their Design, from *open Enemies,* and perhaps *false Friends,* suffering cruel *Mockings,* unkind *Censures,* and unjust *Reproaches,* and yet not *giving way.* We have seen them surmounting their *greatest Difficulties,* so that the main brunt seems now near over, and going on with that *Resolution* and *Success,* that the *Deluge* of *publick Wickedness* is visibly abated. We are told, that many *Thousands* have been brought to Punishment for *Swearing* and *Cursing,* by their means; *Seventy* or *Eighty Warrants* a Week having been executed on these Offenders, in and about this City only, since the late *Act of Parliament* against **Swearing** and **Cursing** was made, which hath given so great and remarkable a Check to those *Scandalous Sins,* that our *Constables* sometimes of late have found it difficult to take up a *Swearer* in divers of our *Streets* and *Markets,* where, within a few years past, *horrid Oaths, Curses,* and *Imprecations,* were heard Day and Night; that a multitude of *Drunkards,* and *Prophaners* of the *Lord's-Day,* some of whom kept, as it were, *open Markets* within a few Years past, have been made *Examples* by their means; that *Hundreds* of *Disorderly Houses,* which were little better than Stews, and Nests for *Thieves, Clippers* and *Coiners,*[5] &c. have been rooted out and suppressed; and that some *Thousands* of *Lewd Persons* have been

---

[5] *Clippers and Coiners:* Clippers are people who clipped the edges of coins for their silver; coiners are counterfeiters.

Imprisoned, Fined, and *Whipt;* so that the *Tower-End* of the Town, and many of our *Streets,* have been much purg'd of that *pestilent Generation* of **Night-Walkers,**[6] that used to *infest* them, which were a *Reproach* to this *Noble City,* and a *Scandal* to *Christianity; Forty* or *Fifty* of them having been sent in a Week to *Bridewell,*[7] where they have of late received such *Discipline,* that a considerable Number of them hath chose rather to be Transported to our *Plantations,*[8] to work there for an honest Subsistence, than to expose themselves, by their lewd way of Living, to *Shame* and *Punishment,* to *Poverty* and *Disease,* to all sorts of wicked Practices, and the Danger of the *Gallows,* to which, in the Conclusion, they are often, if not generally brought.

DANIEL DEFOE

Mercure Scandale: or, Advice from the Scandalous Club (*From* Review Vol. 1, Nos. 2, 63, 53, and 57)

Written for Daniel Defoe's (1661?–1731) *Review of the State of the English Nation,* these selections from "Advice from the Scandalous Club" anticipate the journalistic fiction of Addison and Steele's Spectator Club. Although perhaps best known today for his novels — *Robinson Crusoe, Moll Flanders, Roxana* — Defoe was a prolific journalist. He produced the *Review* single-handedly from 1704 to 1713. This paper, which focused on military, political, and financial news, appeared first once, then twice, and finally three times a week. Originally a part of the *Review,* the "Advice from the Scandalous Club" was for a short time printed seperately as *The Little Review.* Defoe's *Review* was a groundbreaking success in the history of the English periodical. In the selections reprinted here, Defoe takes on the reformation of news writers. In the following excerpts, the club lays out its aims; considers whether or not it

[6] *Night-Walkers:* Prostitutes.
[7] *Bridewell:* Originally a royal palace built between 1515 and 1520 for Henry VIII, Bridewell was named after a holy well dedicated to St. Bride. In 1553, Edward VI gave the palace to the city of London to house vagrants and homeless children and to serve as a correctional institution for petty offenders and wayward women. In 1556 the city took possession and with the confirmation of Queen Mary turned the palace into a prison, hospital, and workhouse.
[8] *Transported to our Plantations:* A common punishment for criminals was to be transported to English colonies in the Americas.

is good manners to expose crimes in a public paper; and responds to letters from a young man and a young woman who have, respectively, slept with an unmarried partner.

Vol. 1, No. 2
Saturday, February 26, 1704

Translated out of *French*.[1]

This Society is a Corporation long since established in *Paris*, and we cannot compleat our Advices from *France*, without entertaining the World with every thing we meet with from that Country.

And, tho' Corresponding with the Queen's Enemies[2] is prohibited; yet since the Matter will be so honest, as only to tell the World of what every body will own to be scandalous, we reckon we shall be welcome.

This Corporation has been set up some Months, and open'd their first Sessions about last *Bartholomew* Fair[3] but having not yet obtain'd a Patent, they have never, till now, made their Resolves publick.

The Business of this Society is to censure the Actions of Men, not of Parties, and in particular, those Actions which are made publick so by the Authors, as to be, in their own Nature, an Appeal to the general Approbation.

They do not Design to expose Persons but Things; and of them, none but such as more than ordinarily deserve it; they who would not be censur'd by this Assembly, are desired to act with caution enough, not to fall under their Hands; for they resolve to treat Vice, and Villanous Actions, with the utmost Severity.

The First considerable Matter that came before this Society, was about *Bartholomew* Fair; but the Debates being long, they were at last adjourned to the next Fair, when we suppose it will be decided;

---

[1] *Translated out of French:* In semi-ironic parody of French journals like *Le Mercure Courant*, Defoe represents these sections as translations of those papers. The French were stereotyped as addicted to scandal.

[2] *the Queen's Enemies:* The English were engaged with the French in the War of the Spanish Succession (1701–14).

[3] *Bartholomew Fair:* Founded at Smithfield in 1102 by Henry I's jester, Bartholomew Fair was the greatest cloth fair in the country until the seventeenth century, when it became a center of popular entertainment featuring strolling minstrels, wrestlers, fire-eaters, and dwarfs. The fair was seen by its critics as a place of public licentiousness and excess.

so being not willing to trouble the World with any thing twice over, we refer that to next *August*.

On the 10th of *September* last, there was a long Hearing, before the Club, of a Fellow that said he had kill'd the Duke of *Bavaria*. Now, as *David* punish'd the Man that said he had kill'd King *Saul*,[4] whether it was so or no, 'twas thought this Fellow ought to be delivered up to Justice, tho' the Duke of *Bavaria* was alive.

Upon the whole, 'twas voted a scandalous Thing, That News-Writers shou'd kill Kings and Princes, and bring them to life again at pleasure; and to make an Example of this Fellow, he was dismiss'd, upon Condition he should go to the Queen's bench once a Day, and bear *Fuller*, his Brother of the Faculty, Company two Hours for fourteen Days together; which cruel Punishment was executed with the utmost Severity.

The Club has had a great deal of trouble about the News-Writers, who have been continually brought before them for their ridiculous Stories, and imposing upon Mankind; and tho' the Proceedings have been pretty tedious, we must give you the trouble of a few of them in our next.

Vol. 1, No. 63
October 10, 1704
[Restatement of Purpose]

The following Letter the Society have thought fit to Publish here, because it seeming to strike at the Justice of their Undertaking; which tho' they have often defended, yet they think themselves bound to protect by Arguments, or submit and lay it down.

Gentlemen,

I Desire your Answer to these following Queries: First, Whether the Method taken, to expose Men in Publick Papers, is not in its Consequence pernicious, and perfectly contrary to good Manners? Secondly, Whether you may not be impos'd upon either by the Malice of some, the Ignorance of others, or the Multiplicity of Business upon your Hands, which hinders you from making an exact Scrutiny in the several Cases before you: So that the wisest and best of Men, may be render'd the Scorn of the Publick, and their Reputation expos'd to

---

[4] *David . . . Saul:* 2 Samuel 1.15.

*Scandal and Ridicule? Lastly, Whether it be not a very great Hard-
ship upon any Gentleman, to be exposed to the Publick, for a single
Miscarriage; since the utmost Care to mend the Defect, and to be
very correct for the future, can come to the Knowledge but of a few.
Be pleased to answer this, in your Paper the first Opportunity, and
you'll oblige.*

Gentlemen,
Your humble Servant,
B. T.

To the first of these Queries, the Society Oppose the Declaration
made by them in the Introduction to their Work, in the very first
Paper they began to Act in; wherein they told the World, they should
always choose to Treat of Things, not of Persons,[5] and have as Carefully kept to their profess'd Principle in that Clause, as possible, with
this only Exception, Where the Criminal has taken Care, first to
make himself so Publick, as that the Crime cannot go without the
Person; or where it has been Committed in defyance of Law, Shame,
and Publication, and in those Cafes they humbly Answer in the Negative, it is neither of *Pernicious Consequence,* nor *Contrary to good
Manners.*

To the Second they Answer, They may be Impos'd upon, for they
are not infallible; but to this they Reply, That as no Man is Answerable for more than is in his possible Power, they have always used the
utmost Caution, and they appeal to those many Gentlemen, whose
Letters and Relations have been unanswered by them, who may conclude 'tis for want of Satisfaction in the Particulars, and they have the
good Fortune to find they Trespass very little that way.

To the last, they Answer No; supposing he here means of Printing,
since the first Cautions of this Society were very Publick, and Authors
had thereby Notice to look out: and Secondly, because they always
give any Author time to Revise and Correct; and Lastly, frankly own
the Ingenuity of such as do.

If these are not sufficient Answers to the Design of the Letter, the
Writer is desired to Reply, and farther satisfaction shall be endeavoured for him.

---

[5] *Treat of Things, not of Persons:* Defoe protests, as do Addison and Steele, that
his reform addresses the abuse, not the person. Personal attack or scandal risked both
a libel suit and, as here, a charge of incivility.

Vol. 1, No. 53
September 5, 1704
[Letter from a Troubled Young Man]

This Letter they Order'd to be Translated as well as such sort of *Latin* will bear it; that the Ladyes,[6] for whose Instruction they Write this, may not be at the trouble to enquire the Meaning.

> I am a young Man, and lately courted *a young Woman*, and we had promis'd one another; but being not able to obtain her Friends consent to Marry, I us'd my best endeavours to get to Bed to her without it; which I easily effected. I had no sooner done this, but I began to talk of it, *(keeping a secret being none of my Talent,)* and now her Father Threatens to go to Law with me: Therefore I pray your Assistance in this Affair.

Tho' the Society thought the Publication of this a sufficient Caution *to the Sex, in General,* how they venture upon the Honour of the Men, yet they could not but add some necessary Remarks here. *As,*

1. A Woman that will take a Man's word in this *Cafe*, really ought to expect such Usage.
2. He that Lyes with a Woman on a promise of Matrimony, is a Knave if he does not perform his promise, and a Fool if he does.
3. A Woman ought in Policy, *tho' no such thing as Conscience was concern'd in it,* never to admit a Man on the most Sacred promise in the World, for the following Reasons;

1. Because she is under his Lash for ever, and Subject to the Insults of his Tongue.
2. He will always plead his Merit, and think her obliged to him.
3. He can never believe she will be Honest, because, *Once a Whore and always so.*
4. She Forfeits the Dignity of her Office, *as Wife,* and makes her Consent of Marriage, which should be esteemed a Favour obtain'd by her Husband, be a Bounty bestow'd upon her.

But as to *the young Rake[7] that sent us the Letter,* the Society Ordered him to be told,

---

[6] *the Ladyes:* Literate women typically lacked the classical education in Greek and Latin that men of their class obtained. Here Defoe undertakes the instruction of women in issues of personal morality.

[7] *Rake:* A libertine; a high-living, dissolute man-about-town.

1. That his *Latin* is *as bald* as his Action is *Villainous,* and so he might as well have wrote *English*, if he had known how.

2. He ought to be Punish'd for deluding the young Woman, but he ought to be hang'd for telling of it afterward.

3. He has Committed two Crimes against Man, *for we suppose he don't trouble himself about that against his Maker.*

1. A Crime against *the Family,* in Debauching a Person they thought too good for him to Marry.

2. A Crime against *the Sex,* for betraying the highest Confidence could be plac'd in him; and therefore of all Villanies in the World, this must be allow'd to be *the most Ungenerous.*

At last this Gentleman desires the Assistance of the Society, by which they understand, he means their Advice, which they are free to give him as follows,

1. That he immediately apply himself to the Father, and offer to Marry the young Woman, *if she be Fool enough to have him.*

2. That he agree to tell all the World *his Name,* that no other weak Sister may venture upon him.

3. That since he has declar'd himself such a Villain, as not to be fit for Human Society, he would please to dispose of himself into her Majesty's Service, where he may Expiate his Crime by the Service of his Country, and perhaps stop a Bullet from killing an honester Man.

4. There is another Method to rid his Native Country of such a Betrayer of Secrets, and that is, to *hang himself out of the way;* but they Advise him to let that be the last Remedy he takes, when all other means fail.

Vol. 1, No. 57
September 19, 1704
[Reply from a Young Lady]

Tho' the Society have a great many Letters upon their Hands Unanswer'd, yet they could not but give the Lady's the Diversion of the following Epistle; They are not Inquisitive, whether it be a History or a Fable; whether the Writer be really a Woman, or pretends only; but since 'tis Written as from a Woman, and seems to be a Woman's Hand, they shall take it for Granted.

Gentlemen!

In the Second Remark after the Villain's Letter,[8] *who so Grosly abused the Poor Lady, Review 53. Being a Party in a Case of the like Nature, I cannot without some Concern, take Notice of your severe Sentence.*

My Case is thus.

Being too Young to have too much Wit; under too strict a Discipline to be long bore with; Over Head and Ears in Love to Boot;

Reason forsook Me, and I became Subject to the tempting Youth, who upon Devout Promises of M————, made a Conquest over all my Prerogatives.

I cannot tax him of a Breach of Promise, for he is always ready, on demand, to perform the Ceremony.

Since I read Your said Review, *I am at a stand, to know what Character my Gentleman lies under, for what he has done; and if he be already a Knave, whether I had better have a Knave, for a spark, or a Fool for a Husband; Your Answer in this, will Engage me upon all Occasions to acknowledge my Self,*

Your most Obliged Servant,
ARABELLA

For Answer, Madam, to this *Question,* and in order to come at the Gentleman's *Character;* 'tis absolutely necessary to examine your Own.

1. A Young Lady, *very young,* and *very forward too, Madam* it seems, since you were willing to have a Man, before you could be expected to have much Wit.

2. *Strictly Educated,* but very Ungovernable, it seems, by our own Consession; a pretty Jest upon your Self; your *Sober Parents* seeing your Vicious Inclination, and willing to keep you from being Debauch'd, kept a severe hand over you, and this you call a *thing not to be born.*

3. *In Love,* but with what? with the *Vice,* it seems, not with the *Man;* for, you say, he is willing to Marry you at Demand, and if it is not done 'tis you stick out; and it must be your Fault.

Since then, Madam, under these Circumstances, you Demand the Societies Opinion, they give you for Answer,

---

[8] *the Villain's Letter:* Printed in *Review* Vol. 1, No. 53 (see p. 126).

That they advise you to Marry him by all means, that both of you may be made Examples to the World; in the worst Punishment Matrimony is Capable of, *viz.*

That you, Madam, may have a Fool to your Husband, and he may have a W——e to his Wife; and if you are not both undone, the Author begs your Pardon for being Mistaken.

A Lady That Knows Everything
(From The Female Tatler *Nos. 1 and 98)*

One of the earliest and most successful imitators of *The Tatler* was *The Female Tatler*, which first appeared on July 8, 1709, and continued until March 31, 1710. It came out three times a week on those days that Steele and Addison's paper did not run, at first under the guise of the satirical persona Mrs. Crackenthorpe, and then of a "Society of Ladies." The authorship of *The Female Tatler* has been attributed to the playwright Thomas Baker (fl. 1700–09) and to the Tory journalist (*The Examiner*) and author of *The New Atalantis*, Mary de la Rivière Manley (1663–1724). While it is likely that *The Female Tatler* was a joint production of both Baker and Manley, there were a number of other contributors, including the physician and satirist Bernard Mandeville and perhaps also the playwright Susannah Centlivre. The fictional narrator, a Mrs. Phoebe Crackenthorpe, is shown at the head of each issue with the epithet: "a Lady that knows ever'y thing." The paper concerns itself with those scenes of life that were accessible to women: the drawing room, the shopping street, the opera, the park. There is no coverage of news or politics. It shares the focus of *The Tatler* and *The Spectator*, the reform of manners and morals, and like them, undertakes this reformation through social satire. In its personal focus and single-essay format, *The Female Tatler* anticipates the transition from *The Tatler*, with its varied content, to the more unified and ethically oriented *Spectator*. Although most certainly written at least in part by women and addressed expressly to women, *The Female Tatler* is not a feminist paper in any sense that we would recognize today. Although it asserts the wit and intelligence of Mrs. Crackenthorpe and some of her allies, it adheres to and indeed promotes the prevailing gender ideology of the time.

Excerpted here are Nos. 1 and 98 from *The Female Tatler*, ed. Fidelis Morgan (Rutland, VT: Charles Tuttle/Everyman's, 1992), 1–3 and 186–88.

Female  Tatler.

By Mrs. Crackenthorpe, *a Lady that knows every thing.*

From **Monday** August 22, to **Wednesday** August 24, 1709.

MR. *Christopher Coppy-wise,* Sollicitor in Chancery, is certainly the most accomplish'd of Cavaliers, he is so equally divided between Beau and Business, that neither of 'em gains the Superiority, having the same Genius, and giving the like Thought, Concern, and strenuous Application to both. You meet him plentifully dirty, loaded with Bills, Answers, Pleas, Demurrers and Exceptions; he's a perfect Squirrel in the Law, skips from *Westminster* to the *Temple,* to the Rolls, to the Register, is in the violent'st flutter about one Pauper Cause, and makes a blustering in the Court, as if the Council were assembl'd, and the well Fee'd Sir *Thomas* had comb'd out his most Ingenious Perriwig, open'd his Cherry Colour Bag, and study'd his quaint Phrases and Rhetorical Ambiguities,—*May it please you, my Lord, tho' I cou'd not be Attorney-General, I am Council for the Plaintiff in this Case,*—Upon matters of no greater Importance, than to get an Alms-Woman TwentyPounds: He's at threescore Coffee-houses three times ev'ry day, enquiring for Letters and Messages, and seems to have as much Employment as if he were Sollicitor to all the litigious Widows in the Kingdom; meet him in the Street, he can't possibly speak to you, having a Reference before a Master, Affidavits to File, Orders to draw up, and a Subpœna to take out returnable immediate, and is as industrious about nothing, as a Beau that calls at Chocolate Houses for Letters he wrote to himself, or a decay'd Serjeant that hurries to *Guild-Hall* when he has no other Business in the City than to sponge a Dinner at my Lord Mayor's. When the hurry of the day is over, as Men cannot toil incessantly, Mr. *Coppy-wise* becomes the Reverse of himself, the Taylor, the Hosier, the Semptress, the Barber, are in an Uproar to equip him; you see him in Lac'd Linnen, Pearl Colour Silk Stockings, Silver long Pockets, and a *French* Night-Cap; he is invited to a Dancing Bout, going to *Spring Garden,* or ingag'd at Cards with some fine Ladies; ask him to go to the Tavern, he has appointed Ladies, Ladies are impatient for him, and all that you can get out of him, is, *Ladies;* his Chambers at *Lincolns Inn,* are a perfect Lady's Apartment, he has his Toilet, his Peer Glasses, his Tea-Tables, his *French* Prints, and a fine set o' Window-Curtains of his own Stiching; Ladies admire his Niceties, he makes elegant Entertainments for 'em, and his Collations are all in China The *Chancery* Office are alarm'd at his Proceedings, he has no Estate, his traversing the Town is but Business in Appearance, yet they envy his Happiness in the Fair Sex, and fancy some great Lady, who has an uncommon Regard for him, is the Fund of his Extravagancies: But as this prying World has an increasing itch to find out one anothers Intrigues, when Mr. *Coppy-wise* had publish'd to all *Chancery-Lane,* that several Ladies of the first Quality were to Sup with him; *Ned Buisy,* the Impertinent of the Office, bolts into his Chambers, was charm'd at the Number of Wax Lights, and began to doubt the strength of his Brain, to behold in reality all the Beauties of *Hampton Court.* His Curiosity, indeed, was prettily satisfy'd, and his Senses more confounded than he imagin'd; when the *Agreeables,* the *Adorables,* the *Invincibles,* and the reported Quality he expected to find there, were Mrs. *Sage-Tea,* the Coffee Woman, Mrs. *Instep* the Shoe-makers Lady, Madam *Neckloit* at the Blue Perriwig, Mrs. *Single mug* at the Carpenter's Arms, Madam *Stay-tape* the Taylor's Wife, with her two well-bred Daughters, and the Quality Vintner's Lady at the *Devil. Coppy-wise* was struck dumb at the Discovery, the Ladies rose, and desired *Buisy* to make one with 'em at *Cribbage* or *All-Fours;* but he retir'd, between Wonder and Ridicule, with the greatest Precipitation imaginable; the News spread, the Examiners Office took it to pieces, 'twas enter'd with the Register, and inroll'd in Chancery; *Coppy-wise,* it seems, has run himself deeply in Debt, and frequently entertains these Creatures, that they may perswade their Husbands to give him further Credit; and at present, he's so much upon the Totter, that if some Charitable Attorney don't give him one Cause more, he'll be forc'd to visit *Carolina* with the *Palatines:* Such a Composition of Extreams we shall rarely meet with; 'tis true, this Person seems to have a design, tho' with little prospect of Success; a pretence to Business gains a Man no ill Character; 'tis good to be in the way, but an old Attorney wou'd no more trust a Cause of Consequence, to a Fellow that has a Notion of Foppery and Impertinence, than a cautious Lady wou'd an Intrigue to a Gossiping Visiter, that shall tell it the whole Town for a Secret: These Women too, who aim at Ceremonies, nice Treats, and things above their Sphere, may for a while by prejudicing their Husbands, bear out his false Pride; but such Matters are soon blown up, a Consumptive Person is, in some Measure supported by Art, but Nature still wasting, the Party languishes unil expires; but to leave the Man of Business, and speak a little more to the Fop, what shall we say of a set of People, Men of real Estates, whose Natures are so groveling, Souls so uninform'd, and are so very destitute of Ambition, that they have no Notion of Society above Tradesmen and Trollops, who ask the Taylor to drink Tea with 'em, the spruce Barber is invited to Dinner, and make Dancing Bouts for the second hand Fry; Sempstresses and Ladies Women, and sometimes

First page of *The Female Tatler* No. 21 (Monday, August 22, to Wednesday, August 24, 1709).

No. 1
Friday, July 8, 1709

I hope Isaac Bickerstaff, Esq.[1] will not think I invade his property, by undertaking a paper of this kind, since tatling was ever adjudg'd peculiar to our sex; my design is not to rival his performance, or in the least prejudice the reputation he has deservedly gain'd: but as more ridiculous things are done every day than ten such papers can relate, I desire leave to prate a little to the town, and try what diversion my intelligence can give 'em. My acquaintance, which is a very great part of the town (for I am intimate with everybody at first sight) have encourag'd me to this attempt, by saying I have the character of knowing everybody's actions, and have sometimes pretended to declare people's intentions. 'Tis true I have twice a week a very great assembly of both sexes, from his Grace my Lord Duke to Mr Sagathie the spruce Mercer in the City; and from her Grace my Lady Duchess, to Mrs Top Sail, the sea captain's wife at Wapping.[2] Not that my drawing room ever had the least ill character, tho' a foolish baronet once call'd it the scandal office. But as I am courteous to all persons, and strangers have the same respect paid 'em as my former acquaintance, half the nation visits me, where I have a true history of the world; and to oblige those who are absent from me, by turns, shall endeavour to give it 'em again. I shall date all my advices from my own apartment, which comprehends, White's, Will's, the Grecian, Garraway's, in Exchange-Alley,[3] and all the India houses[4] within the Bills of Mortality.[5] Since grave statesmen, airy beaus, lawyers, cits,[6] poets and parsons, and ladies of all degrees assemble there, each person delivers himself according to his talent, which gives me a superficial smattering for all of 'em.

The variety of our conversation affords general satisfaction; books are canvas'd, removals at court suggested, law cases disputed, the price of stocks told, the beaus and ladies inform us of new fashions, and the first long pocket that was seen in town receiv'd its reputation

---

[1] *Isaac Bickerstaff, Esq.:* The fictional persona of *The Tatler.*

[2] *Wapping:* A docking and shipping area east of the Tower on the banks of the Thames River.

[3] *White's . . . in Exchange-Alley:* A group of fashionable coffeehouses in a busy street off Lombard Street near the Royal Exchange.

[4] *India houses:* Shops that sell tea and other imported goods.

[5] *Bills of Mortality:* Those areas of the City of London entered into the official returns of the London death rate.

[6] *beaus . . . cits:* Beaus were men of fashion; cits were men from the commercial classes of the City of London.

from being approved of at Mrs Crackenthorpe's drawing room. But when we get into general tittle-tattle, 'tis every little story that happens to get air, those of quality are as liable to reflection as their inferiors, and seldom any person obliges the company with a new piece of scandal, but 'tis repaid him with above twenty more. And tho' to support my visiting days, I am forc'd to act the good Lady Praise-all myself, yet the moment any visitor retires to give place to a fresh comer-in, some one of the company breaks out into (if a gentleman), 'Really, Mrs Crackenthorpe, Sir Charles is mighty good company wou'd he not rail at people so behind their backs.' 'Pray what estate has he?' says another, 'I hear but small and they say damnably dipp'd.'[7] (If a Lady) 'Cousin Crackenthorpe, D'you think that lady handsome? She's horrid silly however, and not a bit genteel; but what a load of jewels she had on!' 'Ay,' says another, 'they say she lies in 'em; I don't believe her earrings were right.'

As to particular stories, I shall begin my second paper with them; but in that, and every following piece, as I find encouragement to proceed, shall be very careful, unjustly or ungenteely not to reflect upon any person whatsoever, but gently to correct the vices and vanities which some of distinction, as well as others, wilfully commit. Shou'd we be so bless'd as to procure an honourable and lasting peace,[8] things of this kind will be a very good amusement for the public, when our news papers are laid aside; peace will produce plenty, plenty makes every body grow mercurial; and when a happiness so long wish'd for, and with such difficulty obtain'd shall, instead of promoting religion, virtue, and sobriety, so far intoxicate men's minds as to draw 'em into pride, luxury, and all manner of ridiculous excursions, an ingenious tatler will conduce more to the reformation of mankind than an hypocritical society,[9] who have made a trade of it. Would people of rank proceed with honour, justice, and a nobleness of spirit, and let their actions, not their equipage, support the dignity of their station, we might hope for a true Golden Age; but when we daily hear of unaccountable whims and extravagant frolics committed by the better sort, we must expect those of inferior classes will imitate them in their habits of mind, as well as body, and the only way to correct great men's foibles, is handsomely to ridicule

[7] *dipp'd:* Mortgaged.
[8] *peace:* England at this time was in the eighth year of the War of the Spanish Succession (1701–14).
[9] *hypocritical society:* The Society for the Reformation of Manners and Morals.

'em; a seasonable banter has often had a reclaiming effect, when serious advice from a grave divine has been thought impudence.

I wou'd intreat those who are not particularly acquainted with me, that they wou'd not imagine I write this paper merely for the profit that may accrue to me by it; for all that I have the honour to be intimate with, know that I have an estate of £300 *per annum* and always kept two maids and a footman; but if I should happen to succeed beyond my expectation, it might so far advance my fortune that I may be able to keep a coach as well as my sister Micklethwaite. I shall follow Mr Bickerstaff's method to get a footing into the world, and deliver the first paper *gratis*, afterwards those that will receive them at the price of 1d[10] will in some measure repay the charge and trouble of such an undertaking; and to prevent mistakes, which may happen by peoples' enquiring for either of the tatlers, I shall publish mine the contrary days, *viz*. Mondays, Wednesdays and Fridays.

Phoebe Crackenthorpe

No. 98
Friday, February 24, to Monday, February 27
Emilia's Day

I had no sooner concluded my letter, but in came my sister Rosella with a city lady, an admirer of fashionable wit, one that could no more smile at a sentence than like a handkerchief that was not of the newest invention; one that drinks Mr Bull's coffee and Mr Shepherd's tea, but because they are well spoken of. She had no sooner seated herself in the elbow chair, but she begun. 'Pray, Mrs Emilia,' says she. 'What news do you hear? Will these French headclothes take? Is the lottery[11] full? Does the trial come on next Monday? Is there any certainty of a peace?'[12] To all this answered as brief and as satisfactory as possible, and then questioned in my turn, 'Pray, Madam, how do you like *The Female Tatler*?' 'Like?' said she. 'I should like it well enough if the authors would not be so much upon the reserve. There was once scandal sufficient to have pleased our end of the town, but why should I confine myself to that. The Court dotes on scandal, and, should they not, we should quickly hold it in disgrace.

---

[10] *gratis . . . 1d:* For free and then for one penny (in Latin, *denarius*).

[11] *lottery:* The government started a state lottery in 1709 to help meet the expenses of the war. See *Tatler* No. 124, notes 3 and 10 (p. 177); and *Tatler* No. 203 (p. 181).

[12] *peace:* To the War of the Spanish Succession. See note 8.

'But of late the authors of *The Female Tatler* set up for morality and are as insipid as anything in print. Well! This morality is a wicked mistake in writers. 'Tis monstrous and abominable to pretend we want their monitions. Mrs Emilia, we want diversion, instruction apart for our children. Pray who would give a half a penny to read what they know already, or what they are certain they can never be the better for. Yet, if they are severe, 'tis on some general vice. They give one very rarely to know who they aim at, and that is what we hate. I love to find an acquaintance exposed or a neighbor ridiculed. It is not a farthing matter whether they deserve it or not. There is my intimate Mrs Friendly and her two daughters. They are as good people as ever lived, but so awkward that they would make admirable figures in *The Female Tatler* and oblige the town for two days. Mrs Emilia, if you know any of the Tatlers, I'll give you their descriptions. They are creatures would oblige everybody in a clumsy manner. They are brimful of good nature, without one regard to ceremony and they'll entertain you a whole afternoon with housewifery and family stories. If you offer them any snuff they hold out the back of their hands, and then make you deaf with sneezing. Coffee and tea they count slop tawdries, but as soon as you appear they call for a tankard of ale, and before you go it is ten to one that they bring you a glass of surfeit water.[13] They know just as much of the fashion as if they lived in Greenland, but very inquisitive concerning taxes.' 'Sure,' said my sister Rosella, 'this family contributes greatly to your mirth.' 'O,' says she, 'since my father will still live at this odious end of the town. Cheapside had been the death of me, but for the pleasure I take in laughing at these dear creatures.'

'By your description,' said I, 'I know the originals. I visit there sometimes and have ever remarked them for sober, hospitable, worthy friends, ignorant of the vices, and guiltless of the follies of the town, and should they read this paper, might take an honest pride in seeing their pictures, even as they are drawn by yourself. But thus it is we all laugh at one another and believe everything a folly or a fault that differs from our own opinions or manners. The gayest wit, though never so bright, among a company of prudes would pass but for a ridiculous scene, and it was the advice of an admirable pen, "Not to value ourselves upon our judgments, nor flatter ourselves with reason, a brisk buffoonery will run it down, and the false glittering of a youthful fancy will turn to ridicule our most delicate conver-

---

[13] *surfeit water:* A medicinal drink to relieve indigestion.

sations." The ingenious Mr Rose-hast mistook his way into a coffee-room dedicate to stock-jobbing, and there said things would have been set down in every commonplace book[14] at Whites. But for an unlucky error as to time and company, he has by all those solemn and misunderstanding politicians been despised for a shallow half-witted person, and made the subject of their heavy mirth and harmless railing of the rest of the week. What pity was he had not prevented their scoffs by taking his own infallible rule not to pass for a fool in one company, who is sure to be regarded as a philosopher in another.

'It is easy to secure ourselves by sorting with equal capacities and agreeing opinions, but public papers must share the common fate of the reverse. You, Madam, want scandal. Another cries out for the liberty of the press that dares encourage anything of that kind. One says they are the improvement and diversion of the town, others that they are a tax upon public houses and invented to ruin them. A lady assured me yesterday that *The Female Tatler* was the best paper extant, and, not knowing I writ any of them, advised me to take them in, and this evening another seemed to hint that there was nothing at all in them, who shall I believe or which should I oblige, 'tis the old story of Aesop's travelling family, and I think to follow my own measures, to do as little mischief and as much good as possible, and endeavour to entertain all that are foes to vice, and friends to virtue, to lash guilty follies and criticise on the failings of all who imagine themselves perfect.' Here the lady rose and took her leave, and because I think her own picture would be more diverting than what she drew for her friends, I intend to give it another opportunity.

RICHARD FLECKNOE

Character of a Common Newsmonger
(*From* Seventy Eight Characters)

In this character sketch of a common newsmonger we see an earlier example of the conventional satiric type that appears in *Spectator* No. 625 as Thomas Quid-nunc. This portrait is one of a collection of "characters" written by the poet, dramatist, and traveler Richard Flecknoe

---

[14] *commonplace book:* A notebook for recording witticisms and epigrams.

(1600–1678), perhaps best known as the butt of John Dryden's *Mac-Flecknoe* (1682). Based on the generalized, imaginary portraits of the Greek rhetorician Theophrastus (fl. 372 B.C.), character writing thrived in England and France from the sixteenth through the early eighteenth centuries. A satiric genre, character writing works from a single, undesirable, defining trait (pride, greed, sloth) and then fills out the portrait with descriptions of the speech, attitudes, and manners through which this trait manifests itself. In the seventeenth and eighteenth centuries especially, writers began to add contemporary social types to their collections of moral characters. *The Tatler* and *The Spectator* are full of portraits in the tradition of Theophrastan character writing.

His word is, *What news! What news!* And he may well be added to the Cryes of *London*,[1] with that word in his Mouth; he is an excellent *Embrotherer of Lies,* for any ground serves him to work on; and for a need he can do it, without any ground at all. He deals more with *Conjectures* than *Almanack Makers,* and will venture the repute of a *Lier* twenty times, for that of a *Prophet* once. He wishes more for ill news, than *ingrossers* of *Corn*,[2] do for dear years, and is sorry with *Caligula*,[3] when none happens in his time. He runs faster away with a Rumor, than a Pack of Hounds do with a full Scent, and warrants it for true, though it be never so great a lye for his publick news; the *Gazette*[4] with some Comments of his own, are his *Pourlieus;*[5] and the *Coffee-House,* the place where he vents it afterwards: But for his *Avisi secreti,* or secret Advice, he has some other *Authors* who deserve to be whipt for their pains, and he too for divulging it, it being commonly the defaming some Noble Persons, taxing of the State, or Rumors tending to Sedition.

---

[1] *Cryes of London:* Street-vendors who called out to advertise their wares as they traveled through the city.

[2] *ingrossers of Corn:* Those who speculated in the future market in grain.

[3] *Caligula:* An eccentric and despotic Roman emperor who ruled from A.D. 37 to 41.

[4] *Gazette:* The official newspaper of the English government.

[5] *Pourlieus:* The places where he is apt to be found.

ANONYMOUS

The Character of a Coffee-House, with the Symptomes of a Town-Wit

Character sketches or "characters" were written of coffeehouses as well as of the town wits that frequented them (see "A Common Newsmonger," p. 135). This anonymous Restoration satire describes a typical coffeehouse and its denizens. Like Edward Ward's descriptions in *The London Spy*, here the coffeehouse — smoky, dirty, and full of knaves and fools — contrasts sharply with the picture that historical social theorists like Jürgen Habermas draw of the coffeehouse as a place of rational and genteel discourse. It differs as well from the sometimes satiric, but never grotesque, accounts of coffeehouse life found in *The Tatler* and *The Spectator*. Yet in its excessively vivid way, this early description gives a good sense of the range of functions served by coffeehouses in Restoration and early-eighteenth-century England.

A Coffee-House is a *Lay-Conventicle*, Good-fellowship turn'd *Puritan*, Ill-husbandry in *Masquerade*, whither people come, after *Toping*[1] all day, to purchase, at the expence of their last peny, the repute of *sober Companions*; a *Rota-Room*[2] that (like *Noahs* Ark) receives Animals of every sort, from the precise *diminutive Band*, to the *Hectoring Cravat* and Cuffs in *Folio*; a *Nursery* for training up the smaller Fry of *Virtuosi*[3] in confident Tattling, or a Cabal of *Kittling*[4] *Criticks* that have only learn't to *Spit* and *Mew*; a Mint of *Intelligence*, that to make each man his *peny-worth*,[5] draws out into petty parcels, what the Merchant receives in Builion: He that comes often saves *two pence* a week in *Gazets*,[6] and has his News and his Coffee for the same charge, as at a *three peny Ordinary*[7] they give in Broth to your Chop of Mutton; 'tis an *Exchange* where Haberdashers of

[1] *Toping:* Getting drunk.

[2] *Rota-Room:* A political club; so called after the political club founded in 1659 by the political philosopher James Harrington (1611–1677).

[3] *Virtuosi:* Men with scientific pretensions. See *Spectator* No. 49, note 3 (p. 92).

[4] *Kittling:* To puzzle with questions or riddles; here also with the sense of infantile, like kittens who "have only learn't to *Spit* and *Mew*."

[5] *peny-worth:* The cover, or entrance cost, of the coffeehouse.

[6] *Gazets:* The official English government newspaper was the *Gazette*.

[7] *three peny Ordinary:* A restaurant where a meal cost three pence.

Political small wares meet, and mutually abuse each other, and the Publique, with bottomless stories, and headless notions; the Rendezvous of *idle Pamphlets*, and persons more idly imployd to read them; a *High Court of Justice,* where every little Fellow in a *Chamlet-Cloak*[8] takes upon him to transpose Affairs both in Church and State, to shew reasons against *Acts* of Parliament, and condemn the Decrees of *General Councels.* . . .

The Room stinks of *Tobacco* worse than Hell of *Brimstone,* and is as full of *smoak* as their Heads that frequent it, whose humours are as various as those of *Bedlam*[9] and their discourse oft-times as *Heathenish* and *dull* as their Liquor; that Liquor, which by its looks and taste, you may reasonably guess to be *Pluto's Diet-drink;*[10] that Witches tipple out of *dead mens Skulls,* when they ratifie to *Belzebub*[11] their Sacramental Vows.

This *Stygian-Puddle-seller*[12] was formerly notorious for his ill-favour'd *Cap,* that Ap'd a *Turbant,* and in Conjunction with his *Antichristian face,* made him appear perfect *Turk:*[13] But of late his *Wife* being grown acquainted with Gallants, and the provocative virtue of *Chocolet,* he finds a *Broad-brim'd Hat* more necessary: When he comes to fill you a Dish, you may take him for *Guy Faux* with a *dark Lanthern* in's hand, for no sooner can you taste it, but it scalds your throat, as if you had swallowed the *Gunpowder-Treason:*[14] though he seem never so demure, you cannot properly call him *Pharisee,*[15] for he never *washes* either out or inside of his *pots* or *dishes,* till they be as black as an Usurers Conscience; and then only scraping off the contracted Soot, makes use of it, in the way of his Trade, instead of

---

[8] *Chamlet-Cloak:* An angora cloak.

[9] *Bedlam:* Bethlehem Hospital for the insane.

[10] *Pluto's Diet-drink:* Coffee. Pluto is the Roman god of the underworld.

[11] *Belzebub:* Beelzebub is one of the seven archdemons; he is identified with the sin of gluttony.

[12] *Stygian-Puddle-seller:* The proprietor of the coffeehouse. "Stygian-Puddle" refers to coffee, here vilified as water from the river Styx, one of the five rivers in the ancient classical underworld.

[13] *Turk:* At this time, most coffee came from the Levant. The coffeehouse proprietor is denounced as a foreigner and an infidel.

[14] *Gunpowder-Treason:* A reference to the Gunpowder Plot led in 1605 by Guy Fawkes and other Catholics who conspired to blow up James I and Parliament during the state opening on November 5. The plot was discovered and Fawkes was executed.

[15] *Pharisee:* A member of the ancient Jewish sect active in Palestine during the Second Temple period (515 B.C.–A.D. 70). The Pharisees emphasized adherence to both the written law (as contained in the Torah) and the unwritten set of laws that grew up through the interpretation and application of the Torah. Here the reference is to the dietary practices of the Pharisees, what we would call "keeping kosher." Because of their portrayal in the New Testament, in colloquial usage *pharisee* can mean a hypocrite.

Coffee-powder; their taste and virtue being so near of Kin, he dares defie the veriest *Coffee-Critick* to distinguish them: Though he be no great *Traveller,* yet he is in continual *motion,* but 'tis only from the fire side to the Table, and his *tongue* goes infinitely faster than his *feet,* his grand study being readily to eccho an answer to that thredbare question, *What News have you Master?* Then with a grave whisper (yet such as all the Room may hear it) he discovers some mysterious *Intrigue* of State told him last night by *one* that is *Barber to the Taylor of a mighty great Courtiers man,* relating this with no less formality than a young *Preacher* delivers his *first Sermon,* a sudden *Hickup* surprizes him, and he is forced twenty times to break the thred of his Tale with such necessary Parenthesis's, *Wife, Sweep up those loose Corns of Tobacco, and see the Liquor boil not over:* He holds it as part of his Creed, that the *Great Turk* is a very good Christian, and of the Reformed Church, because he drinks Coffee, and swears that *Pointings* for celebrating its virtues in *doggerel* deserves to be *Poet Laureat:* yet is it not only this hot *Hell-broth* that he sells, for never was Mountebank furnisht with more variety of poysonous *drugs,* then he of *liquors, Tea* and *Aromatique* for the sweet-tooth'd Gentleman, *Betony* and *Rosade*[16] for the *addle-headed Customer,* Back recruiting *Chocolet* for the Consumptive Gallant, *Herefordshire Redstreak*[17] made of rotten apples at the *three Cranes,* true *Brunswick-Mum*[18] brew'd at S. *Katherines,* and *Ale* in peny *Mugs,* not so big as a Taylors Thimble.

As you have a hodge-podge of Drinks, such too is your Company, for each man seems a Leveller,[19] and ranks and files himself as he lifts, without regard to degrees or order; so that oft you may see a silly *Fop,* and a worshipful *Justice,* a griping *Rook,*[20] and a grave *Citizen,* a worthy *Lawyer,* and an errant *Pickpocket,* a Reverend *Nonconformist,*[21] and a Canting *Mountebank;* all blended together; to compose an *Oglio*[22] of Impertinence.

[16] *Betony and Rosade:* Types of wine.

[17] *Herefordshire Redstreak:* A variety of cider.

[18] *Brunswick-Mum:* A kind of strong beer originally brewed at Brunswick, Germany.

[19] *Leveller:* A member of the radical republican and democratic faction formed in England in 1645–46 and active during the Civil Wars and Commonwealth. Advocates of property reform, they were called "levelers" by their opponents because they were understood to want to "level" men's estates.

[20] *Rook:* A con artist or extortionist.

[21] *Nonconformist:* A member of one of the Protestant sects outside the Anglican Church.

[22] *Oglio:* A mishmash.

. . . The *Arch-Devil,* wherewith this *Smoke-hole* is haunted, is the *Town-wit,* one that playes *Rex*[23] where ever he comes, and makes as much hurry as *Robin Goodfellow* of old amongst our *Granams Milkbouls;*[24] He is a kind of a *Squib*[25] on a Rope, a *meteor* compos'd of Self-conceit and noise, that by *blazing and crackling* engages the wonder of the ignorant, till on a sudden he vanishes and leaves a *stench,* if not *infection* behind him; he is too often the *stain* of a good Family, and by his debaucht life blots the noble *Coat*[26] of his Ancestors, A *wilde unbuck'd Colt,* whose *brains* are not half *codled,* indebted for his *cloaths* to his Tailor, and for his wit (such as it is) to his Company: The School had no sooner *'dued*[27] him with a few superficial besprinklings, but his *Mothers indulgence* posted him to Town for *Genteeler breeding,* where three or four wilde *Companions,* half a dozen bottles of *Burgundy,* two leaves of *Leviathan,*[28] a brisk encounter with his *Landlords Glasswindowes,* the charmes of a little *Miss,*[29] and the sight of a new *Play* dub'd him at once both a *Wit* and a *Hero,* ever since he values himself mainly for *understanding the Town,* and indeed *knows* most things in it that are not *worth knowing:* The two *Poles* whereon all his discourses turn are *Atheism* and *Bawdry;* Bar him from being prophane or obscene, and you *cramp* his Ingenuity, which forthwith *Flags* and becomes *useless,* as a meer *Common Lawyer* when he has cross'd the *Channel.*

He is so refractory to *Divinity* that Morality it self cannot hold him, he affirms humane Nature knows no such things as principles of Good and evil, and will swear *all women* are *whores,* though his *Mother* and *Sister* both stand by: Whatever is sacred or serious he seeks to render Ridiculous, and thinks Government and Religion fit objects for his *idle* and fantastick *Buffoonry,* his *humor* is proud and assuming, as if he would palliate his ignorance by *Scoffing* at what he understands not, and therefore with a *pert* and *pragmatique* scorn de-

[23] *Rex:* King, in Latin.

[24] *Robin Goodfellow . . . Granams Milk-bouls:* In English folk legend, a sprite that curdled milk.

[25] *Squib:* A firecracker. Also commonly used of a noisy, bantering would-be wit.

[26] *Coat:* Coat of arms, a family's heraldic emblem of its ancestry and distinctions.

[27] *'dued:* Endued, or provided.

[28] *Leviathan:* The chief work of the English mathematician, political theorist, and philosopher Thomas Hobbes (1588–1679). *The Leviathan* (1651) sets out Hobbes's theories of social contract and natural rights. Materialist, secular, and radically skeptical, *The Leviathan* became popularly associated with freethinking and libertinism.

[29] *Landlords Glasswindowes . . . little Miss:* Pursuing the conventional pastimes of the town rake, the town wit breaks windows and seduces the daughters of respectable citizens.

preciates all things of nobler moment, but most passionately affects *pretty a la mode*[30] words, And is as covetous of a *New Song* or Ayre, as an Antiquary of *Cato's*[31] *Statue* with ne'r an arm, and but half a nose, These keep him alwaies imployd, and fill up the *Grotesco's*[32] of his conversation, whilst with a stately Gallantry once in every half hour he *Combes out his Wig, Carreens*[33] his breeches, and new marshalls his *Garniture,* to the Tune of *Methinks the poor Town has been troubled too long.*

His mind used to *whistle* up and down in the levities of Fancy, and effeminated by the childish *Toyings* of a rampant imagination finds it self indisposed for all solid imployment, especially the serious exercises of *Piety* and *Virtue,* which begets an aversion to those *Lovely Beauties,* and that prompts him on all occasions to expose them as ridiculous and vain: Hence by degrees he comes to abuse *Sacred Scripture,* makes a mock of eternal Flames, Joque on the venerable Mysteries of Religion, and in fine, scoffe at that *All Glorious* and *Tremendous Majesty* before whom his brother *Wits below* tremble;[34] Tis true he will not confess himself *Atheist,* yet in his heart the Fool hath said it, and boasts aloud that he holds his *Gospel* from the *Apostle of Malmsbury,*[35] though it is more than probable he ne'r read, at least understood *ten* leaves of that *unlucky Author;* Talk of *Witches* and you Tickle him, speak of *Spirits* and he tels you he knowes none better than those of Wine, name but *Immaterial Essence,* and he shall shout at you as a dull Fop incapable of sense, and unfit for Conversation; Nor is he ever better pleas'd than when he can here hedge in some young *raw Divine* to *Bulbait* with scurrility and all kind of profaneness.

By means of some small *Scraps of learning* matcht with a far greater stock of Confidence, a voluble Tongue, and bold delivery, he has the ill-luck to be celebrated by the vulgar; for a man of *Parts,*[36]

---

[30] *a la mode:* Trendy. French phrases were especially fashionable at this time.

[31] *Cato's:* Cato Marcus Porcius (234–149 B.C.), a Roman statesman famous for his uncompromising morality and patriotism.

[32] *Grotesco's:* The bizarrely fanciful ornaments of his conversation (grotesque).

[33] *Carreens:* Nautical term. He repairs (careens) his pants as one repairs, cleans, and caulks a ship.

[34] *Majesty . . . tremble:* He scoffs at God whose majesty awes even the fallen angels ("his brother *Wits below*").

[35] *Apostle of Malmsbury:* William of Malmesbury (d. 1143?), the librarian of Malmesbury Abbey and historian of England. His *Gesta Regum Anglorum* (*Exploits of the English Kings*) and its companion *Historia Novella* (*Recent History*) trace the history of England from 449 into the twelfth century.

[36] *a man of Parts:* A talented and accomplished man.

which opinion gains credit to his Insolences, and sets him on further extravigances to maintain his Title of a *Wit* by continuing his practice of *Fooling*, whereas all his mighty parts are sum'd up in this Inventory.

Imprimis, A *pedling way* of Fancy, a *Lucky bit of Quibbling*, now and then an *odd metaphor*, a conceited *Irony*, a ridiculous *Simile*, a *wilde fetch*, an unexpected *Inference*, a *Minick Gesture*, a pleasing *knack* in humouring a Tale, and lastly an irresistable Resolution to speak *last*, and never be *dasht* out of Countenance:

By these *Arts* dexterously manag'd he engrosses a vaste *Repute*, The grave Citizen calls him shrewd man, and notable *Headpiece*, The *Ladies* (we mean the things so called of his acquaintance) vote him a most *accomplisht Gentleman* and the Blades swear he is a *Walking Comedy*, the only *Merry Andrew* of the Age, that scatters *Wit* wherever he comes, as *Beggars* do *Lice*, or Muskcats perfumes, and that *nothing in Nature and all* that can compare with him.

You would think he had got the *Lullian Art*,[37] for he speaks *Extempore* on all subjects, and ventures his words without the Relief of *Sense* to second them, his thoughts start from his *imagination*, and he never troubles himself to Examine their decency, or solidity by Judgement. To discourse him seriously is to read the *Ethicks to a Monkey*, or make an Oration to *Caligula's Horse*,[38] whence you can only expect a *weehee* or *Jadishspurn*,[39] after the most convincing Arguments, if he can but muster up one plausible *joque* you are routed, For he that understood not your *Logick*, apprehends his droll, and though *Syllogismes* may be answered, yet Jests and loud *laughter* can never be confuted, but have more sway to degrade things with the *unthinking crowd*, than *demonstrations;* There being a Root of envy in too many Men, that invites them to applaud that which Exposes and villifies what they cannot comprehend, He pretends great skill in curing the *Tetters*[40] and *Ring-worms* of State, but blowes in the sores till they Rankle with his poisonous breath, he shoots *libels* with his forked tongue at his Superiors and abusest his dearest *Friends*, chus-

---

[37] *Lullian Art:* A reference to the philosophy of the Spanish mystic Lullius (Raymond Lull, 1234–1315), who tried to identify the common elements in Judaism, Christianity, and Islam.

[38] *Caligula's Horse:* The Roman emperor Caligula (12–41) was (falsely) reputed to have made his horse consul.

[39] *weehee or Jadishspurn:* A *weehee* is a whinny or neigh. The meaning of *Jadishspurn* is not known to me.

[40] *Tetters:* Skin diseases like eczema, psoriasis, and herpes.

ing to forfeit his neck to the *Gibbet,* or his shoulders to the *Batoon* rather than lose the driest of his idle *Quibbles;* In brief he is the *Jack-pudding of Society,* a *fleering Buffoon,* a better kind of *Ape* in the judgement of all *Wisemen,* but an incomparable *Wit* in his *own.*

Thus have we led you from *Board to Board,* like the fellow in the Tower, to shew you *strange Beasts* wherewith this place is sometimes frequented. To take now a *farewel view* of the House will be difficult, since tis always shifting Scenes and like *O Brazile* (the Inchanted Island) seldome appears twice in a posture; The *wax Candles* burning, and low devout whispers sometimes strike a kind of Religious Awe, whilst the modish Gallant swears so oft by Iesu[41] an Ignorant Catholick would take it for a Chappel, and think he were saying our Ladies Psalter; In some places the *Organs* speak it a Musick Room, at others a pair of *Tables and draught board,* a smal gaming house; on a sudden it turns *Exchange,* or a Warehouse for all sorts of *Commodities,* where fools are drawn in by inch of Candles as we betray and catch *Larks* with a Glass; The Bully-*Rook* makes it his *Bubbling* pond,[42] where he angles for *Fops,* singles out his man, insinuates an *acquaintance,* offers the wine, and at next Tavern sets upon him with *high Fullums,*[43] and *plucks* him: The *Ingenius* use it for an after *Rehearsal,* where they bring *Plays* to Repetition, sift each *Scene* examine every *uncorrected Line,* and *damn* beyond the fury of the *Rota,* whilst the *incognito Poet* out of an overweening affection to his *Infant Wit,* steals in *muffled* up in his Cloake, and sliely *Evesdrops* like a *mendicant Mother* to praise the *prettyness* of the *Babe* she has newly pawm'd on the Parish.[44]

But 'tis time to be *gone,* who knows what *Magick* may be a working, For, behold! the *Coffee-Powder* settles at the bottome of our dish in form of a most terrible *Saracens Head.* For a parting blow then give us leave to *unbend* a little, and say,

A *Coffee-House* is a *Phanatique Theatre,* a *Hot-House* to flux in for a *clapt understanding*[45] a *Sympathetical* Cure for the *Gonorrhea* of the Tongue, or a *refin'd Baudy-House,* where *Illegitimate Reports* are got in close *Adultery* between *Lying lips* and *Itching Ears.*

---

[41] *by Iesu:* By Jesus.
[42] *Bubbling pond:* The source of people he can "bubble" or trick out of their money.
[43] *high Fullums:* Presumably meaning "with brash, overriding arrogance."
[44] *pawm'd on the Parish:* Abandoned to be raised by public charity.
[45] *Hot-House . . . understanding:* An infirmary in which diseased (with gonorrhea) minds sweat out their toxins.

EDWARD WARD

A Visit to a Coffee-House
(From The London Spy)

A tavern keeper and prolific satirist, Edward "Ned" Ward (1667–1731) published his *London Spy* in eighteen monthly installments from November 1698 to May 1700. Presented as a series of rambles a country man takes through the city, in its self-consciously vulgar idiom *The London Spy* documents the seedier sides of metropolitan life. A great observer of characters, the Spy trains his gaze on the carnivalesque life of the London streets, shops, coffeehouses, taverns, brothels, and baths. By adopting the stance of an outsider and a reformer, Ward's Spy seems to anticipate Bickerstaff and Mr. Spectator, but a huge difference in sensibility separates the Spy from these personae of Addison and Steele. The pictures Ward draws of London life are marked by hyperbole, an aggressively "low" style, and an almost obsessive occupation with the sensory world. Where Bickerstaff and the Spectator seem all eyes, Ward's Spy engages in the full repertoire of the senses — sight and hearing certainly, but also the more directly palpable perceptions of taste, touch, and smell. We see in Ward's description of this London coffee-house many of the same types (the virtuoso, the spark) that we meet in *The Tatler* and *The Spectator,* but the whole mood of the experience is different. The feeling of immersion in the smoke and soot, the sheer strength of the sensations recorded by Ward resonate more fully with the earlier "Character of the Coffee-House" than with Addison and Steele's more distanced, mediated, and controlled portraits.

The text included here has been taken from *The London Spy,* ed. Paul Hyland (East Lansing, MI: Colleagues Press, 1993), 18–20.

'Come,' says my friend, 'let us step into this coffee-house here. As you are a stranger to the Town it will afford you some diversion.' Accordingly, in we went, where a parcel of muddling muckworms were as busy as so many rats in an old cheese-loft; some going, some coming, some scribbling, some talking, some drinking, others jangling, and the whole room stinking of tobacco like a Dutch scoot, or a boatswain's cabin. The walls were hung with gilt frames, as a farrier's shop with horseshoes, which contained abundance of rarities, viz., Nectar and Ambrosia, May Dew, Golden Elixirs, Popular Pills,

Liquid Snuff, Beautifying Waters, Dentifrices, Drops, Lozenges, all as infallible as the Pope. 'Where everyone' (as the famous Saffold[1] has it) 'above the rest, Deservedly has gained the name of best.' Good in all cases, curing all distempers; and every medicine, being so catholic, pretends to nothing less than universality. Indeed, had not my friend told me 'twas a coffee-house I should have took it for Quacks' Hall, or the parlour of some eminent mountebank.

When we had each of us stuck in our mouths a pipe of sotweed,[2] we began to look about us. 'Do you mind,' says my friend, 'yonder old sophister[3] with an Indian pipe between his meagre jaws, who sits staring at the candle with as much steadfastness as a country passenger at Bow Steeple, or a child at a raree-show?[4] That's a strange, whimsy-headed humorist. Observe his posture; he looks like the picture of Aesculapius[5] behind an apothecary's counter! And he has as many maggots in his noddle as there are mice in an old barn, or nits in a mumper's[6] doublet. He has a wonderful projecting head, and has lately contrived one of the prettiest pocket-engines for the speedy blanching of hazel-nuts and filbert kernels that ever was invented; he'll crack and skin two for a squirrel's one, and in a few years, by a little alteration, will improve it to the use of walnuts. I'll assure you he's a member of the Royal Society[7] and had as great a hand, for many years together, in bringing the weather-glass to perfection, as any of them. He puts great faith in the philosophers' stone[8] and believes he shall one time or other be as rich as Croesus,[9] though he has almost beggared himself in the search on't, and has as large a pair of bellows in his laboratory as ever an alchemist in Town.

'He tried a notable experiment the other day, in setting fire to a large haystack he had in the country, and ordered the ashes to be brought to Town, from whence he proposed to prepare a medicine, called *Sal-Graminis*,[10] which should infallibly cure all distempers in

[1] *Saffold:* Thomas Saffold (d. 1691) was an astrologer and a quack doctor.

[2] *sotweed:* Tobacco.

[3] *sophister:* Teacher.

[4] *raree-show:* A show carried about the streets in a box, a peep show.

[5] *Aesculapius:* Greek god of healing.

[6] *mumper's:* Beggar's.

[7] *Royal Society:* The Royal Society of London for the Improving of Natural Knowledge was established in 1660 and incorporated by Charles II's royal charter in 1662.

[8] *philosophers' stone:* The stone sought by medieval alchemists as the catalyst that would turn base metals into gold.

[9] *Croesus:* The last king of ancient Libya (c. 560–546 B.C.), proverbially the richest man in the world.

[10] *Sal-Graminis:* Latin for "salt of the pasture."

horses, and be the rarest medicine for cows, sheep, or oxen, and all sorts of creatures that feed upon grass, that any grazier or farrier can use in any distemper. But sending it up in an ill season, the ashes got wet in their carriage and quite lost their virtue, so that he was forced to sell them to a West Country bargeman in order to dung land. But, it's thought by the wise, he might have sold it in the hay to ten times the advantage.

'He has abundance of whims in him, very remarkable. He lives over against the church, so that when he dies he might not have far to travel upon four men's shoulders. As soon as the clock begins nine, if he gets not his shoes off before it has done striking, in order for bed, he is immediately seized with such a violent fit of the gout that he roars like a Tower lion[11] at a woman pregnant with a male child. If he is not up just as the clock strikes five in the morning, he thinks himself bedridden. If his victuals be not brought to the table whilst the clock goes twelve, he eats nothing all that day; his stomach is always at the meridian height the same time as the sun is, and if he finds by his observation it's declined, he is as much out of humour for letting slip the critical minute as a married lady (without children to employ her thoughts) is for losing of her lap-dog.

'He's a wonderful antiquary, and has a closet of curiosities that outdoes Gresham College.[12] He tells ye that he has a toothpick of Epicurus,[13] which he always uses after eating. It is made of the claws of an American humming-bird, and is to be used like a rake, and will pick four teeth at once. He has Diogenes'[14] lantern, which he carried about Athens at noonday to seek for an honest man. He says he has some of Heraclitus's[15] tears, which dropped from him in a hard winter and are frozen into crystal. They are set in a locket, and everytime

---

[11] *Tower lion:* Lions were kept in the Tower of London and were one of the obligatory sights of the city.

[12] *Gresham College:* Designed by Sir Thomas Gresham and established in 1597 as a venue for public lectures on divinity, law, rhetoric, music, astronomy, and other learned topics. The college first met at Gresham's house in Broad Street, and from the weekly meetings of this learned society, the Royal Society developed.

[13] *Epicurus:* An ancient Greek philosopher, Epicurus (341–271 B.C.) taught that life should be based on the evidence of the senses, without reliance on superstition and belief in the supernatural. Epicureanism identifies pleasure with the good, but holds that pleasure actually lies in limiting and controlling one's desires. A popular distortion of Epicurean philosophy associates it with hedonistic abandon.

[14] *Diogenes:* Diogenes (c. 440–323 B.C.) was an ancient Athenian Cynic philosopher.

[15] *Heraclitus:* The "weeping philosopher," Heraclitus (c. 540–480 B.C.) believed that all things were in a state of constant flux.

anybody looks upon it they cannot forbear weeping. Also a tenpenny nail drawn out of the Ark, and though it's iron, toss it into a tub of water and 'twill swim like a feather. He pretends to have one of Judas's thirty pence, and everytime he looks upon't he is ready to hang himself. A mighty collection of these sort of trinkets he tells the world he's master of, and some give credit to his ridiculous romances.

'Mind that spark who has just come in. Four years since, his reputation was but slender, and in so little a time he has had three wives, all good fortunes to him, and now is looked upon to be worth ten thousand pounds.' ''Tis observed,' said I, 'that money is thrown into the very mouths of Fortune's minions, and some men must grow rich if all the lucky accidents that Chance can give will make them so.' My friend, in pursuance of this particular, expressed himself to this purpose: that he believed there was some foul play practised, because, says he, it is a thing so common in this city for a man to grow rich by plurality of wives, and send them one after another so methodically to the grave, as if he had a flight of translating them into another world a little before their time. 'For, I must confess,' says he, 'I know an apothecary who, if a man will trust him with the care of his family, once in a twelvemonth's time will certainly take an opportunity to do him such a piece of service if he gives him but the least item of his slender affections towards his helpmate. And I have often heard him say that women are always the best patients, especially if they die under his hands, for then, says he, let me make never so unreasonable a bill, it's never disputed but generously satisfied, with as good a will as a married man pays the tax for the birth of the first child, or an extravagant heir the charges of his father's funeral.

'Mind the little blade in the cloak that's talking with a parson. He's a bookseller in this city, and has got an estate by starving authors. I'll warrant you, the priest has been conjuring his brains together and has raised some wonderful work to the Church's glory and his own fame. He has been providing "A Scourge for the Pope's Jacket; or a Cudgel for Antichrist," or else a mess of good Protestant porridge to scald the mouth of an unbeliever, or some such business. But as to the wit-monger, I'll tell you, he's as honest a man as ever betrayed his trust, or built his own welfare upon another's ruin. He was appointed trustee for a young gentlewoman, and had the charge of an estate of between two or three hundred pounds per annum, which he very carefully secured to himself by marrying her to his apprentice and obliging him, upon that consideration, to buy his stock, whereby he became well paid for a great deal of waste paper. So he is crept into the estate, and they are got into his books for it. There is abundance of such sort of plain dealing practised amongst our worthy citizens, for you must know they do not always tell the truth in their shops, or get their estates by their honesty.'

Being half-choked with the steam that arose from their soot-coloured ninny-broth, their stinking breaths and the suffocating fumes of their nasty puffing-engines, my friend and I paid for our Muhammadan gruel[16] and away we came.

JOHN GAY

The Present State of Wit

"The Present State of Wit," by the English poet and dramatist John Gay (1685–1732), is an epistolary essay. Here Gay uses the conventional device of a "letter to a friend in the country" to frame his report to an eager recipient of the latest intelligence from London. This is news about the news. The letter demonstrates the necessity of keeping up with the times in order not to be "at a loss in Conversation among the *Beau Monde*." News and fashionable life intermingle in a society where polite conversation is supplied in good part by the periodical press. Published as a pamphlet on May 29, 1711, this "letter" was actually written to evaluate the state of the periodical market in London between 1709 and 1711 and was meant to be read by Londoners.

The text is taken from *John Gay: Poetry and Prose*, ed. Vinton A. Dearing, Vol. 1 (Oxford: Clarendon Press, 1974), 449–56. Dearing's notes are credited [Dearing].

SIR,

You Acquaint me in your last, that you are still so busie Building at ——— , that your Friends must not hope to see you in Town this Year: At the same time you desire me that you may not be quite at a loss in Conversation among the *Beau Monde*[1] next Winter, to send

---

[16] *soot-coloured ninny-broth ... Muhammadan gruel:* Coffee, which at this time came from the Moslem countries of the Levant.
[1] *Beau Monde:* Fashionable society.

you an account of the present State of Wit in Town; which, without further Preface, I shall therefore endeavour to perform, and give you the Histories and Characters of all our *Periodical Papers*, whether Monthly, Weekly, or Diurnal, with the same freedom I used to send you our other Town News.

I shall only premise, that as you know I never cared one Farthing either for *Whig* or *Tory*, So I shall consider our Writers purely as they are such, without any respect to which Party they may belong.[2]

Dr. King[3] has for some time lain down his *Monthly Philosophical Transactions*, which the Title Page informed us at first, were only to be continued as they Sold; and tho' that Gentleman has a World of Wit, yet as it lies in one particular way of Raillery, the Town soon grew weary of his Writings; tho' I cannot but think, that their Author deserves a much better Fate, than to Languish out the small remainder of his Life in the *Fleet* Prison.[4]

About the same time that the Doctor left off Writing, one Mr. *Ozell* put out his *Monthly Amusement*,[5] (which is still continued) and as it is generally some *French* Novel or Play indifferently Translated, is more or less taken Notice of, as the Original Piece is more or less Agreeable.

As to our Weekly Papers, the Poor *Review*[6] is quite exhausted, and grown so very Contemptible, that tho' he has provoked all his Brothers of the Quill round, none of them will enter into a Controversy with him. This Fellow, who had excellent Natural Parts, but wanted a small Foundation of Learning, is a lively instance of those Wits, who, as an Ingenious Author says, will endure but one Skimming.

The Observator[7] was almost in the same Condition, but since our Party-Struggles have run so high, he is much mended for the better; which is imputed to the Charitable Assistance of some out-lying Friends.

These Two Authors might, however, have flourish'd some time

---

[2] *. . . to which Party they may belong:* The conventional pose of the politically disinterested observer. Gay was a Whig but shortly after writing his tract joined the Tories.

[3] *Dr. King:* William King (1662–1712) was a doctor of canon law; he published his *Useful Transactions in Philosophy* in three numbers in 1709. Swift got King appointed gazetteer in place of Steele in 1711.

[4] *Fleet Prison:* A debtors' prison near Ludgate Circus.

[5] *Monthly Amusement:* John Ozell's periodical ran from April to September 1709.

[6] *Poor Review:* Daniel Defoe's *Review* ran from 1704 to 1713 and came out three times a week during its last seven years.

[7] *The Observator:* A Whig semiweekly that ran from 1702 to 1712.

longer, had not the Controversie been taken up by much abler Hands.

The Examiner[8] is a Paper, which all Men, who speak without Prejudice, allow to be well Writ. Tho' his Subject will admit of no great Variety, he is continually placing it in so many different Lights, and endeavouring to inculcate the same thing by so many Beautiful Changes of Expressions, that Men, who are concern'd in no Party, may Read him with Pleasure. His way of assuming the Question in Debate, is extremely Artful; and his Letter to Crassus,[9] is, I think, a Master-piece. As these Papers are suppos'd to have been Writ by several Hands, the Criticks will tell you, That they can discern a difference in their Stiles and Beauties, and pretend to observe, that the first Examiners abound chiefly in Wit, the last in Humour.

Soon after their first appearance, came out a Paper from the other Side, called the Whig Examiner,[10] writ with so much Fire, and in so excellent a Stile, as put the Tories in no small pain for their favourite Hero, every one cry'd Bickerstaff[11] must be the Author, and People were the more confirm'd in this opinion, upon its being so soon lay'd down; which seem'd to shew, that it was only writ to bind the Examiners to their good Behaviour, and was never design'd to be a Weekly Paper. The Examiners therefore have no one to Combat with at present, but their Friend the Medley;[12] The Author of which Paper, tho' he seems to be a Man of good Sense, and expresses it luckily enough now and then, is, I think, for the most part, perfectly a Stranger to fine Writing.

I presume I need not tell you that the Examiner carries much the more Sail, as 'tis supposed to be writ by the Direction, and under the Eye of some Great Persons who sit at the helm of Affairs, and is consequently look'd on as a sort of publick Notice which way they are steering us.

The reputed Author is Dr. S——t, with the assistance, sometimes, of Dr. Att——y, and Mr. P——r.[13]

---

[8] *The Examiner:* The Tory weekly that ran from 1710 to 1714. It was started by the prominent Tory, Henry St. John, later Viscount Bolingbroke.

[9] *Letter to Crassus:* Written by the satirist, journalist, and Anglican divine Jonathan Swift (1667–1745), this appeared on February 8, 1710, in No. 27. "Crassus" is Marlborough [Dearing].

[10] *Whig Examiner:* Addison wrote this Whig weekly for a run of five numbers in September and October 1710.

[11] *Bickerstaff:* The persona of *The Tatler.*

[12] *the Medley:* A Whig weekly that appeared 1710–12.

[13] *Dr. S——t . . . Dr. Att——y and Mr. P——r:* Jonathan Swift; Francis Atterbury, future bishop of Rochester; and the poet Matthew Prior (1664–1721).

The Medley, is said to be Writ by Mr. *Old——n*, and supervised by Mr. *Mayn——g*,[14] who perhaps might intirely write those few Papers which are so much better than the rest.

Before I proceed further in the account of our Weekly Papers, it will be necessary to inform you, that at the beginning of the Winter, to the infinite surprize of all Men, Mr. *Steele* flung up his *Tatler*,[15] and instead of *Isaac Bickerstaff* Esq; Subscrib'd himself *Richard Steele* to the last of those Papers, after an handsome Compliment to the Town for their kind acceptance of his Endeavours to divert them. The Chief Reason he thought fit to give for his leaving off writing, was, that having been so long look'd on in all publick Places and Companies as the Author of those Papers, he found that his most intimate Friends and Acquaintance were in Pain to Act or Speak before him. The Town was very far from being satisfied with this Reason; and most People judg'd the true cause to be, either that he was quite spent, and wanted matter to continue his undertaking any longer, or that he lay'd it down as a sort of Submission to, and Composition with the Government for some past Offences;[16] Or lastly, that he had a Mind to vary his Shape, and appear again in some new Light.

However that were, his disappearing seem'd to be bewailed as some general Calamity, every one wanted so agreeable an Amusement, and the Coffee-houses began to be sensible that the Esquires Lucubrations alone, had brought them more Customers than all their other News Papers put together.

It must indeed be confess'd, that never Man threw up his Pen under Stronger Temptations to have imployed it longer: His Reputation was at a greater height than, I believe, ever any living Author's was before him. 'Tis reasonable to suppose that his Gains were proportionably considerable; Every one Read him with Pleasure and Good Will, and the *Tories*, in respect to his other Good Qualities, had almost forgiven his unaccountable Imprudence in declaring against them.

Lastly, It was highly improbable that if he threw off a Character, the Ideas of which were so strongly impress'd in every one's mind, however finely he might write in any new form, that he should meet with the same reception.

---

[14] *Mr. Old——n . . . Mr. Mayn——g:* John Oldmixon (1673–1742), the historian and pamphleteer, and Arthur Maynwaring (1688–1712), the Whig politician.

[15] *Tatler:* The *Tatler* ran three times a week from April 1709 until January 1711.

[16] *for some past Offences:* It is probable that Steele gave up *The Tatler* in a political deal that allowed him to keep his lucrative post as commissioner for stamp duties (see Introduction, p. 1).

To give you my own thoughts of this Gentleman's Writings, I shall in the first place observe, that there is this noble difference between him and all the rest of our Polite and Gallant Authors: The latter have endeavour'd to please the Age by falling in with them, and incouraging them in their fashionable Vices, and false notions of things. It would have been a jest, sometime since, for a Man to have asserted, that any thing Witty could be said in praise of a Marry'd State, or that Devotion and Virtue were any way necessary to the Character of a fine Gentleman. *Bickerstaff* ventur'd to tell the Town, that they were a parcel of Fops, Fools, and vain Cocquets; but in such a manner, as even pleased them, and made them more than half enclin'd to believe that he spoke Truth.

Instead of complying with the false Sentiments or Vicious tasts of the Age, either in Morality, Criticism, or Good Breeding, he has boldly assur'd them, that they were altogether in the wrong, and commanded them with an Authority, which perfectly well became him, to surrender themselves to his Arguments, for Vertue and Good Sense.

'Tis incredible to conceive the effect his Writings have had on the Town; How many Thousand follies they have either quite banish'd, or given a very great check to; how much Countenance they have added to Vertue and Religion; how many People they have render'd happy, by shewing them it was their own fault if they were not so; and lastly, how intirely they have convinc'd our Fops, and Young Fellows, of the value and advantages of Learning.

He has indeed rescued it out of the hands of Pedants and Fools, and discover'd the true method of making it amiable and lovely to all mankind: In the dress he gives it, 'tis a most welcome guest at Tea-tables and Assemblies, and is relish'd and caressed by the Merchants on the Change; accordingly, there is not a Lady at Court, nor a Banker in *Lumbard-Street*,[17] who is not verily perswaded, that *Captain Steele*[18] is the greatest Scholar, and best Casuist, of any Man in *England*.

Lastly, His Writings have set all our Wits and Men of Letters upon a new way of Thinking, of which they had little or no Notion before; and tho' we cannot yet say that any of them have come up to the Beauties of the Original, I think we may venture to affirm, that every

[17] *Lumbard-Street:* Lombard Street was a central corridor in the heart of the city's financial district.

[18] *Captain Steele:* Richard Steele had served as a captain in the Coldstream Guards.

one of them Writes and Thinks much more justly than they did some time since.

The vast variety of Subjects which he has treated of in so different manners, and yet All so perfectly well, made the World believe that 'twas impossible they should all come from the same hand. This set every one upon guessing who was the Esquires Friend, and most people at first fancied it must be Dr. *Swift;* but it is now no longer a Secret, that his only great and constant assistant was Mr. *Addison.*

This is that excellent Friend to whom Mr. *Steele* ow's so much, and who refuses to have his Name set before those Pieces, which the greatest Pens in *England* would be Proud to own. Indeed, they could hardly add to this Gentleman's Reputation, whose Works in *Latin* and *English* Poetry, long since convinc'd the World, that he was the greatest Master in *Europe* of those Two Languages.

I am assur'd from good hands, That all the *Visions,*[19] and other Tracts in that way of Writing, with a very great number of the most exquisite Pieces of Wit and Raillery throughout the Lucubrations, are intirely of this Gentleman's Composing; which may in some Measure account for that different Genius, which appears in the Winter Papers from those of the Summer; at which time, as the *Examiner* often hinted, this Friend of Mr. *Steele*'s was in *Ireland.*[20]

Mr. *Steele* confesses in his last Volume of the *Tatlers,* that he is oblig'd to Dr. *Swift* for his *Town Shower,* and the *Description of the Morn,*[21] with some other hints received from him in Private Conversation.

I have also heard, that several of those Letters, which came as from Unknown Hands, were writ by Mr. *Henly;*[22] which is an Answer to your Query, Who those Friends are, whom Mr. *Steele* speaks of in his last *Tatler?*

But to proceed with my account of our other Papers: The Expiration of *Bickerstaff's Lucubrations,* was attended with much the same Consequences as the Death of *Melibæus*'s Ox in *Virgil;*[23] as the latter

[19] *Visions:* The conceit of the dream vision, a common rhetorical device in both *The Tatler* and *The Spectator.* See, for example, Addison's vision of Lady Credit in *Spectator* No. 3 (p. 188).

[20] *Ireland:* As secretary to the Lord-Lieutenant, Addison was in Ireland during the summers of 1709 and 1710 but sent essays to Steele in London.

[21] *Town Shower ... Description of the Morn:* Swift's poems "A Description of a City Shower" and "A Description of the Morning" appeared, respectively, in *Tatler* Nos. 238 and 239.

[22] *Mr. Henly:* Anthony Henly was a Whig M.P.

[23] *Melibæus's Ox in Virgil: Georgics* 4.315–558 [Dearing].

engendred Swarms of Bees, the former immediately produc'd whole Swarms of little Satyrical Scriblers.[24]

One of these Authors, call'd himself *The Growler*,[25] and assur'd us, that to make amends for Mr. *Steele*'s Silence, he was resolv'd to *Growl* at us Weekly, as long as we should think fit to give him any Encouragement. Another Gentleman, with more Modesty, call'd his Paper *The Whisperer*;[26] and a Third, to Please the Ladies, Christen'd his, *The Tell-Tale*.[27]

At the same time came out several *Tatlers*;[28] each of which, with equal Truth and Wit, assur'd us, That he was the Genuine *Isaac Bickerstaff*.

It may be observ'd, That when the Esquire laid down his Pen, tho' he could not but foresee that several Scriblers would soon snatch it up, which he might, one would think, easily have prevented, he Scorn'd to take any further Care about it, but left the Field fairly open to any Worthy Successor. Immediately some of our Wits were for forming themselves into a Club, headed by one Mr. *Harrison*,[29] and trying how they could shoot in this Bow of *Ulysses*;[30] but soon found that this sort of Writing, requires so fine and particular a manner of Thinking, with so exact a Knowledge of the World, as must make them utterly Despair of Success.

They seem'd indeed at first to think, that what was only the *Garnish* of the former *Tatlers*, was that which recommended them, and not those *Substantial Entertainments* which they every where abound in.

Accordingly they were continually talking of their *Maid*, *Night-Cap*, *Spectacles*, and *Charles Lillie*.[31] However there were now and then some faint endeavours at Humour and *Sparks* of Wit, which the Town, for want of better Entertainment, was content to hunt after, through an heap of Impertinencies; but even those are at present, become wholly invisible, and quite swallow'd up in the *Blaze of the Spectator*.[32]

---

[24] *Swarms of little Satyrical Scriblers:* In *Tatler* No. 229 Bickerstaff remarks on "those numberless Vermin that feed upon this Paper" (see p. 74).

[25] *The Growler:* Ran for six issues, from January to February 1711.

[26] *The Whisperer:* Appeared only once, in October 1709 [Dearing].

[27] *The Tell-Tale:* Possibly *The Female Tatler* (see p. 129).

[28] *several Tatlers:* John Baker and John Morphew each published continuations of *The Tatler*.

[29] *Mr. Harrison:* William Harrison was an associate of Swift's [Dearing].

[30] *Bow of Ulysses:* Suggests that these men are taking on a task (writing *Tatler* papers) beyond their strength. In Book 21 of Homer's *Odyssey*, Odysseus returns home in disguise and easily strings the bow he had left, a feat no other could perform.

[31] *Charles Lillie:* A perfumer who published *The Tatler* with John Morphew.

[32] *Spectator:* The first number of *The Spectator* appeared on March 1, 1711.

You may remember I told you before, that one Cause assign'd for the laying down the *Tatler* was, want of Matter; and indeed this was the prevailing Opinion in Town, when we were Surpriz'd all at once by a Paper called *The Spectator*, which was promised to be continued every day, and was writ in so excellent a Stile, with so nice a Judgment, and such a noble profusion of Wit and Humour, that it was not difficult to determine it could come from no other hands but those which had penn'd the *Lucubrations*.

This immediately alarm'd these Gentlemen, who (as 'tis said Mr. *Steele* phrases it) had *The Censorship in Commission*.[33] They found the new *Spectator* come on like a Torrent and swept away all before him; they despaired ever to equal him in Wit, Humour, or Learning; (which had been their true and certain way of opposing him) and therefore, rather chose to fall on the Author, and to call out for help to all Good Christians, by assuring them again and again, that they were the First, Original, True, and Undisputed *Isaac Bickerstaff*.

Mean while *The Spectator*, whom we regard as our shelter from that Flood of False Wit and Impertinence which was breaking in upon us, is in every ones Hand, and a constant Topick for our Morning Conversation at Tea-Tables, and Coffee-Houses. We had at first indeed no manner of Notion, how a *Diurnal Paper* could be continu'd in the Spirit and Stile of our present *Spectators*; but to our no small Surprize, we find them still rising upon us, and can only wonder from whence so Prodigious a Run of Wit and Learning can proceed; since some of our best Judges seem to think that they have hitherto, in general, out-shone even the Esquires first *Tatlers*.

Most People Fancy, from their frequency, that they must be compos'd by a Society; I, with all, Assign the first Places to Mr. *Steele* and *His Friend*.

I have often thought that the Conjunction of those two Great Genius's (who seem to stand in a Class by themselves, so high above all our other Wits) resembled that of two famous States-men in a late Reign, whose Characters are very well expressed in their two Mottoes (*viz.*) *Prodesse quam conspici*, and *Otium cum Dignitate*.[34] Accordingly the first was continually at work behind the Curtain, drew up and prepared all those Schemes and Designs, which the latter Still

---

[33] *The Censorship in Commission:* In *Tatler* No. 144, Bickerstaff styles himself "Censor of Great Britain" (see p. 55).

[34] *two famous States-men . . . Otium cum Dignitate:* The two men are John Lord Somers and Charles Montagu [Dearing]. The "late Reign" is that of William III (1650–1702), who ruled from 1688 to 1702. The Latin mottoes mean, respectively, "to benefit as much as to be admired" and "leisure with dignity."

drove on, and stood out exposed to the World to receive its Praises or Censures.

Mean time, all our unbyassed wellwishers to Learning, are in hopes, that the known Temper and Prudence of one of these Gentlemen, will hinder the other from ever lashing out into Party, and rend'ring that wit which is at present a Common Good, Odious and Ungrateful to the better part of the Nation.

If this piece of imprudence do's not spoil so excellent a Paper, I propose to my self, the highest Satisfaction, in Reading it with you over a Dish of Tea, every Morning next Winter.

As we have yet had nothing new since the *Spectator*, it only remains for me to assure you, that I am

Yours, *&c.*

Westminster, May 3, 1711.   J.G.

RICHARD STEELE

Guarding the Public
(From The Guardian Nos. 1, 98, and 114)

The Guardian, which was conceived as a continuation of *The Spectator*, was written by Richard Steele and Joseph Addison with the help of a number of other contributors, including the young Alexander Pope; George Berkeley, the Anglo-Irish empiricist philosopher; Eustace Budgell, who was Addison's cousin and a contributor to *The Spectator*; and Thomas Tickell, Addison's friend and protégé. *The Guardian* also featured the device of a fictional persona: here, it is Nestor Ironside, an elderly bachelor, who presides. While suggesting a greater moral gravity than *The Tatler* and a more personal interest in the world than *The Spectator*, *The Guardian* (see No. 98) claims a direct lineage with these predecessors. Isaac Bickerstaff is "a Man nearly related to the Family of the Ironsides," and Mr. Spectator "a Gentleman of the same Family."

The Guardian first appeared on March 12, 1713, and for the first six weeks was edited and largely written by Steele, since Addison was at the time preoccupied with the production of his tragedy *Cato* at the Drury Lane Theatre. Addison's first contribution appeared as No. 67 on May 28. In July, while Steele was occupied with political business, Addison took on the sole editorship. Concerned with morals and manners, *The*

Guardian also solicited and printed letters from correspondents. Indeed, according to Nos. 98 and 114, Nestor Ironside had a special lion's head constructed outside Button's Coffee-house so that readers could deposit their letters in the lion's mouth.

Like *The Tatler* and *The Spectator, The Guardian* addressed itself to the ladies as well as the gentlemen of the town. Indeed, the fictional Lizard family, managed by Lady Jane Lizard and her widowed daughter-in-law, Lady Aspasia Lizard, seems specifically designed to engage the domestic and familiar interests of its female readers, unlike the exclusively male Spectator Club. Like the Spectator Club, however, the Lizard family soon moved to the background as the essays addressed broader, more diffuse topics. *The Guardian* never enjoyed the vast success of *The Tatler* and *The Spectator.* And perhaps because of low sales and pressure on Steele to produce a more explicitly political paper, it ceased publication in October 1713, and Steele immediately began writing the Whig *Englishman.*

The text included here comes from *The Guardian*, ed. John Calhoun Stephens (Lexington: UP of Kentucky, 1982), 41–43, 348–50, 387–89. Stephens's notes are credited [Stephens].

No. 1
Thursday, March 12, 1713

—— *Ille quem requiris.*[1]
— Mart.

There is no Passion so universal, however diversified or disguised under different Forms and Appearances, as the Vanity of being known to the rest of Mankind, and communicating a Man's Parts, Virtues or Qualifications to the World; this is so strong upon Men of great Genius, that they have a restless Fondness for satisfying the World in the Mistakes they might possibly be under, with relation even to their Physiognomy. Mr. *Airs*,[2] that excellent Penman, has taken care to affix his own Image opposite to the Title Page of his

---

[1] —— *Ille quem requiris:* From Martial, *Epigrams* 1.2.1: "Him whom you seek" [Stephens].

[2] *Mr. Airs:* John Ayres (fl. 1680–1704) was the preeminent writing-master of his day. Steele is probably referring to his best-known work, *The Tutor to Penmanship* (1698?), which includes a portrait of the author engraved by John Sturt (1658–1730) [Stephens].

Learned Treatise, wherein he instructs the Youth of this Nation to arrive at a flourishing Hand. The Author of *the Key to Interest, both Simple and Compound, containing Practical Rules plainly expressed in Words at length for all Rates of Interest, and Times of Payment, for what time soever,* makes up to us the Misfortune of his living at *Chester,* by following the Example of the abovemention'd *Airs,* and coming up to Town, over-against his Title Page in a very becoming Periwig, and a flowing Robe or Mantle, inclosed in a Circle of Foliages; below his Portraiture, for our farther Satisfaction, as to the Age of that useful Writer, is subscribed *Johannes Ward*[3] *de Civitat. Cestriæ, Ætat. suæ 58. An. Dom.* 1706. The serene Aspect of these Writers, join'd with the great Encouragement I observe is given to another, or, what is indeed to be suspected, in which he indulges himself, confirmed me in the Notion I have of the prevalence of Ambition this way. The Author whom I hint at shall be nameless,[4] but his Countenance is communicated to the Publick in several Views and Aspects drawn by the most eminent Painters, and forwarded by Engravers, Artists by way of Metsotinto, Etchers, and the like. There was, I remember, some Years ago one *John Gale,*[5] a Fellow that play'd upon a Pipe, and diverted the Multitude of Dancing in a Ring they made about him, whose Face became generally known, and the Artists employ'd their Skill in delineating his Features, because every Man was judge of the Similitude of them. There is little else than what this *John Gale* arriv'd at in the Advantages Men enjoy from common Fame, yet do I fear it has always a Part in moving us to exert our selves in such things, as ought to derive their beginnings from nobler Considerations: But I think it is no great matter to the Publick what is the Incentive which makes Men bestow time in their Service, provided there be any thing useful in what they produce; I shall proceed therefore to give an Account of my intended Labours, not without some hope of having my Vanity, at the end of them, indulged in the sort above-mention'd.

---

[3] *Johannes Ward:* The portrait of John Ward (c. 1648–post-1723), which appears as the frontispiece to his *Clavis Usurae: Or, A Key to Interest . . .* (1710), was engraved by Michael Van der Gucht (1660–1725) [Stephens]. The Latin inscription reads, "John Ward of the city of Chester, age 58, in the year of our Lord 1706."

[4] *nameless:* This refers to Dr. Henry Sacheverell (1674–1724), a fanatic Tory Anglican [Stephens]. In *Spectator* No. 57, Addison describes a lady who has a snuffbox, handkerchief, and fan inscribed with Sacheverell's portrait.

[5] *John Gale:* John Gale (c. 1633–post-1702), a deaf mute, was well known for accompanying condemned criminals to Tyburn, where they were hanged [Stephens].

I should not have assumed the Title of *Guardian*, had I not maturely considered, that the Qualities necessary for doing the Duties of that Character, proceed from the Integrity of the Mind more than the Excellence of the Understanding: The former of these Qualifications it is in the Power of every Man to arrive at; and the more he endeavours that Way, the less will he want the Advantages of the latter; to be Faithful, to be Honest, to be Just, is what you will demand in the Choice of your Guardian; or if you find added to this, that he is Pleasant, Ingenious, and Agreeable, there will overflow Satisfactions which make for the Ornament, if not so immediately to the Use, of your Life. As to the Diverting Part of this Paper, by what Assistance I shall be capacitated for that, as well as what Proofs I have given of my Behaviour as to Integrity in former Life, will appear from my History to be delivered in ensuing Discourses. The main Purpose of the Work shall be to protect the Modest, the Industrious, to celebrate the Wise, the Valiant, to encourage the Good, the Pious, to confront the Impudent, the Idle, to contemn the Vain, the Cowardly, and to disappoint the Wicked and Prophane. This Work cannot be carried on but by preserving a strict Regard, not only to the Duties but Civilities of Life, with the utmost Impartiality towards Things and Persons. The unjust Application of the Advantages of Breeding and Fortune is the Source of all Calamity both Publick and Private; the Correction therefore, or rather Admonition, of a Guardian, in all the Occurrences of a various Being, if given with a benevolent Spirit, would certainly be of General Service.

In order to contribute as far as I am able to it, I shall publish in respective Papers whatever I think may conduce to the Advancement of the Conversation of Gentlemen, the Improvement of Ladies, the Wealth of Traders, and the Encouragement of Artificers. The Circumstance relating to those who excel in Mechanicks, shall be consider'd with particular Application. It is not to be immediately conceived by such as have not turned themselves to Reflections of that Kind, that Providence, to enforce and endear the Necessity of Social Life, has given one Man Hands to another Man's Head, and the Carpenter, the Smith, the Joiner are as immediately necessary to the Mathematician, as my Amanuensis will be to me, to Write much fairer than I can my self. I am so well convinced of this Truth, that I shall have a particular regard to Mechanicks, and to show my Honour for them, I shall place at their head the Painter. This Gentleman is as to the Execution of his Work a Mechanick, but as to his Conception, his Spirit and Design, he is hardly below even the Poet, in Liberal Art. It will be from these Considerations useful to make the World see the Affinity between all Works which are beneficial to Mankind is much nearer, than the illiberal Arrogance of Scholars will, at all times allow. But I am from Experience convinced of the Importance of Mechanick Heads, and shall therefore take them all into my Care, from *Rowley*,[6] who is improving the Globes of the Earth and Heavens in *Fleetstreet*, to *Bat Pidgeon* the Hair Cutter in the *Strand*.

But it will be objected upon what Pretensions I take upon me to put in for the *prochain amy*, or nearest Friend of all the World. How my Head is accomplished for this Employment towards the Publick, from the long Exercise of it in a private Capacity, will appear by reading me the two or three next Days with Diligence and Attention. There is no other Paper in Being which tends to this Purpose. They are most of them Histories of Advices of Publick Transactions; but as those Representations affect the Passions of my Readers, I shall some-times take Care, the Day after a Foreign Mail, to give them an Account of what it has brought. The Parties among us are too violent to make it possible to pass them by without Observation. As to these Matters, I shall be impartial, tho' I cannot be Neuter. I am, with Relation to the Government of the Church, a Tory, with Regard to the State, a Whig.

The Charge of Intelligence, the Pain in compiling and digesting my Thoughts in proper Stile, and the like, oblige me to value my Paper an Half-penny above all other Half-Sheets. And all Persons, who have any thing to communicate to me, are desired to direct their Letters (Postage paid) to *Nestor Ironside*, Esq; at Mr. *Tonson*'s in the *Strand*.[7] I declare before hand, that I will at no Time be conversed with any other ways than by Letter; for as I am an Antient Man, I shall find enough to do to give Orders proper for their Service, to whom I am by Will of their Parents Guardian, tho' I take that to be too narrow a Scene for me to pass my whole Life in. But I have got my Wards so well off my Hands, and they are so able to act for themselves, that I have little to do but give an Hint, and all that I desire to be amended is altered accordingly.

My Design upon the whole is no less, than to make the Pulpit, the Bar, and the Stage, all act in Concert in the Care of Piety, Justice and

[6] *Rowley:* John Rowley (d. 1728), Master of Mechanics to George I and Engine Keeper under the Board of Works, was the foremost mathematical instrument maker of his day. His shop was in Fleet Street [Stephens].

[7] *Mr. Tonson's in the Strand:* Jacob Tonson (1682–1735) had also been the publisher of *The Spectator* from October 1712.

Virtue. For I am past all the Regards of this Life, and have nothing to manage with any Person or Party, but to deliver my self as becomes an Old Man with one Foot in the Grave, and one who thinks he is passing to Eternity. All Sorrows which can arrive at me are comprehended in the Sense of Guilt and Pain; If I can keep clear of these two Evils, I shall not be apprehensive of any other. Ambition, Lust, Envy, and Revenge, are Excrescencies of the Mind which I have cut off long ago: But as they are Excrescencies which do not only deform, but also torment those on whom they grow, I shall do all I can to persuade all others to take the same Measures for their Cure which I have.

No. 98
Friday, July 3, 1713

In sese redit ——— [8]
— Virg.

The first who undertook to instruct the World in single Papers, was *Isaac Bickerstaff* [9] of famous Memory; a Man nearly related to the Family of the IRONSIDES. We have often smoked a Pipe together, for I was so much in his Books, that at his Decease he left me a Silver Standish, a pair of Spectacles, and the Lamp by which he used to write his Lucubrations.

The venerable *Isaac* was succeeded by a Gentleman of the same Family, [10] very memorable for the Shortness of his Face and of his Speeches. This Ingenious Author published his Thoughts, and held his Tongue, with great Applause, for two Years together.

I NESTOR IRONSIDE have now for some Time undertaken to fill the Place of these my two renowned Kinsmen and Predecessors. For it is observed of every Branch of our Family, that we have all of us a wonderful Inclination to give good Advice, though it is remarked of some of us, that we are apt on this occasion rather to give than take.

However it be, I cannot but observe with some secret Pride, that this way of Writing diurnal Papers has not succeeded for any space of Time in the Hands of any Persons who are not of our Line. I believe I speak within compass, when I affirm that above a hundred different Authors have endeavoured after our Family-way of Writing. Some of

---

[8] *In sese redit:* From Virgil, *Georgics* 4.444: "To himself returns" [Stephens].

[9] *Isaac Bickerstaff:* The fictional narrator of *The Tatler.*

[10] *Gentleman of the same Family:* Mr. Spectator, who refers to his squat face in, for example, *Spectator* No. 17.

which have been Writers in other kinds of the greatest Eminence in the Kingdom; but I do not know how it has happened, they have none of them hit upon the Art. Their Projects have always dropt after a few unsuccessful Essays. It puts me in mind of a Story which was lately told me by a pleasant Friend of mine, who has a very fine Hand on the Violin. His Maid Servant seeing his Instrument lying upon the Table, and being sensible there was Musick in it, if she knew how to fetch it out, drew the Bow over every part of the Strings, and at last told her Master she had tried the Fiddle all over, but could not for her Heart find whereabout the Tune lay.

But though the whole Burden of such a Paper is only fit to rest on the Shoulders of a *Bickerstaff* or an *Ironside*; there are several who can acquit themselves of a single Day's Labour in it with suitable Abilities. These are Gentlemen whom I have often invited to this Tryal of Wit, and who have several of them acquitted themselves to my private Emolument, as well as to their own Reputation. My Paper among the Republick of Letters is the *Ulysses* his Bow,[11] in which every Man of Wit or Learning may try his Strength. One who does not care to write a Book without being sure of his Abilities, may see by this means if his Parts and Talents are to the Publick Taste.

This I take to be of great Advantage to Men of the best Sense, who are always diffident of their private judgment, till it receives a Sanction from the publick. *Provoco ad Populum*, I appeal to the People, was the usual Saying of a very excellent Dramatick Poet,[12] when he had any Disputes with particular Persons about the Justness and Regularity of his Productions. It is but a melancholy Comfort for an Author to be satisfied that he has written up to the Rules of Art, when he finds he has no Admirers in the World besides himself. Common Modesty should, on this Occasion, make a Man suspect his own Judgment, and that he misapplies the Rules of his Art, when he finds himself singular in the Applause which he bestows upon his own Writings.

The Publick is always Even with an Author who has not a just Deference for them. The Contempt is reciprocal. I laugh at every one, said an old Cynick,[13] who laughs at me. Do you so? replied the Philosopher; then let me tell you, you live the merriest Life of any Man in *Athens*.

---

[11] *Ulysses his Bow:* See "The Present State of Wit," where Gay uses the same figure (note 30, p. 154).

[12] *Dramatick Poet:* Possibly John Dryden. Steele translates the Latin in the phrase that follows.

[13] *old Cynick:* Not identified.

It is not therefore the least Use of this my Paper, that it gives a timorous Writer, and such is every good one, an Opportunity of putting his Abilities to the Proof, and of sounding the Publick before he launches into it. For this Reason I look upon my Paper as a kind of Nursery for Authors, and question not but some, who have made a good Figure here, will hereafter flourish under their own Names in more long and elaborate Works.

After having thus far inlarged upon this Particular, I have one Favour to beg of the Candid and Courteous Reader, that when he meets with any thing in this Paper which may appear a little dull or heavy, (tho' I hope this will not be often) he will believe it is the Work of some other Person, and not of NESTOR IRONSIDE.

I have, I know not how, been drawn in to tattle of my self, *more Majorum*,[14] almost the length of a whole *Guardian*. I shall therefore fill up the remaining Part of it with what still relates to my own Person, and my Correspondents. Now I would have them all know that on the twentieth Instant it is my Intention to erect a Lion's Head in Imitation of those I have described in *Venice*,[15] through which all the private Intelligence of that Commonwealth is said to pass. This Head is to open a most wide and voracious Mouth, which shall take in such Letters and Papers as are conveyed to me by my Correspondents, it being my Resolution to have a particular Regard to all such Matters as come to my Hands through the Mouth of the Lion. There will be under it a Box, of which the Key will be in my own Custody, to receive such Papers as are dropped into it. Whatever the Lion swallows I shall digest for the Use of the Publick. This Head requires some Time to finish, the Workman being resolved to give it several Masterly Touches, and to represent it as Ravenous as possible. It will be set up in *Button*'s Coffee-house in *Covent-Garden*, who is directed to shew the Way to the Lion's Head, and to instruct any young Author how to convey his Works into the Mouth of it with Safety and Secrecy.

---

[14] *more Majorum:* According to the way of my ancestors.

[15] *in Venice:* In *Guardian* No. 71, Ironside discusses how the "Name of a Lion" came to be used "to any one that is a great Man's Spy." He relates an anecdote about how in Venice, those who would convey secret intelligence to the State would slip a piece of paper into the mouth of one of the huge stone lions that stood outside the Doge's palace. In *Guardian* No. 114, he discusses the lion's head "now erected at *Button's* Coffee-house in *Russel street*, *Covent-Garden*" (see p. 164). Addison and Steele were prominent among the club of Whigs that frequented Button's Coffee-house.

No. 114
Wednesday, July 22, 1713

Alveos accipite, et ceris opus infundite,
Fuci recusant, apibus conditio placet.[16]
— Phædr.

I think my self obliged to acquaint the Publick, that the Lion's Head, of which I advertised them about a Fortnight ago, is now erected at *Button*'s Coffee-house[17] in *Russel street, Covent-Garden,* where it opens its Mouth at all Hours for the Reception of such Intelligence as shall be thrown into it. It is reckoned an excellent Piece of Workmanship, and was designed by a great Hand in Imitation of the Antique *Ægyptian* Lion, the Face of it being Compounded out of that of a Lion and a Wizzard. The Features are strong and well furrow'd. The Whiskers are admired by all that have seen them. It is planted on the Western Side of the Coffee house, holding its Paws under the Chin upon a Box, which contains every thing that he swallows. He is indeed a proper Emblem of *Knowledge* and *Action*, being all Head and Paws.

I need not acquaint my Readers, that my Lion, like a Moth or Book Worm, feeds upon nothing but Paper, and shall only beg of them to Diet him with wholsom and substantial Food. I must therefore desire that they will not gorge him either with Nonsense or Obscenity; and must likewise insist, that his Mouth be not defiled with Scandal, for I would not make use of him to revile the Human Species, and Satyrise those who are his Betters. I shall not suffer him to worry any Man's Reputation, nor indeed fall on any Person whatsoever, such only excepted as disgrace the Name of this generous Animal, and under the Title of Lions contrive the Ruin of their Fellow-Subjects.[18] I must desire likewise, that Intrieguers will not make a Pimp of my Lion, and by his means convey their Thoughts to one another. Those who are read in the History of the Popes observe, that the *Leo's* have been the best, and the *Innocents* the worst of that Species, and I hope that I shall not be thought to derogate from my Lion's Character, by representing him as such a peaceable good-natured well-designing Beast.

---

[16] *Alveos accipite . . . placet:* From Phædrus, *Aesopic Fables* 3.13.9 and 12 [Stephens]: "Take the beehive and pour in the work of wax, / The drones refuse, the bees are pleased with the proposal" [my translation].

[17] *Button's Coffee-house:* See *Guardian* No. 98, note 15 (p. 163).

[18] *Fellow-Subjects:* See *Guardian* No. 98, note 15 (p. 163).

I intend to publish once every Week *the roarings of the Lion*, and hope to make him roar so loud as to be heard over all the *British* Nation.

If my Correspondents will do their Parts in prompting him, and supplying him with suitable Provision, I question not but the Lion's Head will be reckoned the best Head in *England*.

There is a Notion generally received in the World, that a Lion is a dangerous Creature to all Women who are not Virgins, which may have given occasion to a foolish Report, that my Lion's Jaws are so contrived, as to snap the Hands of any of the Female Sex, who are not thus qualified to approach it with Safety.[19] I shall not spend much time in exposing the falsity of this Report, which I believe will not weigh any thing with Women of Sense, I shall only say, that there is not one of the Sex in all the Neighborhood of *Covent Garden*,[20] who may not put her Hand in the Mouth with the same Security as if she were a Vestal. However that the Ladies may not be deterred from corresponding with me by this Method, I must acquaint them, that the Coffee-Man has a little Daughter of about four Years old who has been virtuously educated, and will lend her Hand, upon this Occasion, to any Lady that shall desire it of her.

In the mean time I must further acquaint my fair Readers, that I have Thoughts of making a Provision for them at my Ingenious Friend Mr. *Motteux*'s, or at *Corticelli*'s,[21] or some other Place frequented by the Wits and Beauties of the Sex. As I have here a Lion's Head for the Men, I shall there erect an Unicorn's Head for the Ladies, and will so contrive it that they may put in their Intelligence at the top of the Horn, which shall convey it into a little Receptacle at the bottom prepared for that purpose. Out of these two Magazines I shall supply the Town from time to time with what may tend to their Edification, and at the same Time carry on an epistolary Correspondence between the two Heads, not a little Beneficial both to the Publick and to my self. As both these Monsters will be very insatiable, and devour great Quantities of Paper, there will no small Use redound from them to that Manufacture in particular.

The following Letter having been left with the Keeper of the Lion, with a Request from the Writer that it may be the first Morsel which

---

[19] *Safety:* In *Spectator* No. 13 Addison relates "the received Opinion that a Lion will not hurt a Virgin."

[20] *Covent Garden:* The neighborhood was a notorious haunt of prostitutes.

[21] *Mr. Motteux's . . . Corticelli's:* Both these men ran fashionable shops. Motteux sold China and Japan ware, teas, and muslins. Corticelli specialized in Italian goods.

is put into his Mouth, I shall communicate it to the Publick as it came to my Hand, without examining whether it be proper Nourishment, as I intend to do for the future.

Mr. GUARDIAN,

'Your Predecessor, the *Spectator*, endeavour'd, but in vain, to improve the Charms of the fair Sex, by exposing their Dress whenever it launched into Extremities. Among the rest the great Petticoat came under his Consideration,[22] but in Contradiction to whatever he has said they still resolutely persist in this Fashion. The Form of their Bottom is not, I confess, altogether the same; for whereas before it was of an orbicular Make, they now look as if they were press'd, so that they seem to deny Access to any Part but the Middle. Many are the Inconveniencies that accrue to Her Majesty's loving Subjects from the said Petticoats, as hurting Mens Shins, sweeping down the Ware of industrious Females in the Street, *&c.* I saw a young Lady fall down, the other Day, and, believe me Sir, she very much resembled an overturned Bell without a Clapper. Many other Disasters I could tell you of that befall themselves as well as others, by means of this unwieldy Garment. I wish, Mr. GUARDIAN, you would join with me in showing your Dislike of such a monstrous Fashion, and I hope when the Ladies see 'tis the Opinion of two of the wisest Men in *England*, they will be convinced of their Folly.'

I am SIR, Your daily Reader and Admirer,

Tom. Plain.

---

[22] *Consideration:* Mr. Spectator discusses the hoop-petticoat in Nos. 127, 145, and 294. See also Bickerstaff's trial of the hoop-skirt in *Tatler* No. 116 (p. 482).

"A Perspective View of the Bank of England" from William Maitland, *The History and Survey of London from Its Foundation to the Present Time*, 3rd ed. (London: T. Osborne, 1760), vol. 2, facing page 846.

2

Getting and Spending: Commerce, Finance, and Consumption

Life in eighteenth-century England was becoming increasingly saturated by commerce and its quantitative values, its standards of profit and loss, and the premium it put on novelty and impermanence. Modern historians often refer to a "financial revolution," a "commercial revolution," and a "consumer revolution" that took place from the 1690s on (Dickson; Hill; McKendrick). The late seventeenth and eighteenth centuries witnessed an intensified commercialization of land, an increase in the extent of wage labor, and the establishment of the National Debt and the Bank of England, which funded that debt. The Treaty of Utrecht not only ended the War of the Spanish Succession in 1714 but further secured England's power in the Americas with the signing of the Asiento, which granted England exclusive rights to supply slaves to Spanish America. In the early eighteenth century, as England's imperial entanglements escalated, great wealth flowed into the country, especially from the slave and sugar enterprises in Barbados and Jamaica in the British West Indies. This brought as well an ever-greater dependence on these colonies, both as suppliers of valuable commodities, such as sugar, rum, and tobacco, and as export markets. Overcoming its Dutch rivals, England established a presence in the East Indies as well. Laying the foundation for England's future imperial control, the East India Company extended its reach over India.

This widening network of trade brought an influx of foreign goods and stimulated innovation and intensification in domestic manufactures. Contemporary accounts of English life reveal a world focused very closely on buying and selling. Discussions of not only financial and commercial transactions, but also social relations and cultural production are often embedded, if only to react against it, in an economically inflected discourse of exchange whose rhetoric and values seem to seep into all facets of life.

The commercialization of life is an ongoing theme in *The Tatler* and *The Spectator*. This section includes papers and contextual materials that most directly address the major commercial and financial institutions of the day: the Bank of England and the credit economy, the Royal Exchange, the lotteries used by the government to finance the War of the Spanish Succession, commercial imperialism and its domestic effects, trade and its status as a profession in early-modern England, money and its proper role in human life, shopping. These papers illustrate some of the ways in which *The Tatler* and *The Spectator,* and their contemporaries, address the challenges that commerce and finance present to social relations, psychological stability, and ethical norms. In accommodating credit capitalism and commercial imperialism to a morally sustainable vision of personal and social life, these papers show as well one of the ideological foundations of England's emerging colonial, commercial, and industrial power.

But we must not mistake accommodation for indiscriminate, whole-hearted endorsement of every aspect and effect of the new commercial and financial economies. The texts collected here level sharp criticism at the financial and commercial markets they take as their subjects. The incorporation of modern capitalist institutions did not go unchallenged in late-seventeenth- and early-eighteenth-century England. While Mr. Spectator may celebrate the "harmonizing," "one world" rationale for commercial imperialism in *Spectator* No. 69, he is deeply critical of the greed, luxury, and ruinous personal debt that commerce often fostered (see *Spectator* Nos. 11, 55, 82, and 114).

The accommodation of capitalism and its sociocultural effects takes place through an ongoing critical debate over the effects of a commercialized world on virtue and social cohesion. In *The Fable of the Bees,* Bernard Mandeville relentlessly drives home the sharp divergence between conventional moral ideals and the forces that fuel the economy. Private vices like greed, luxury, and selfishness are,

Mandeville insists, public benefits, for they yield the markets that support commerce and industry. We find somewhat the same thinking in Nicholas Barbon's *Discourse of Trade,* which notes that "Prodigality is a Vice that is prejudicial to the Man, but not to *Trade*" (see p. 238). The "scandal" of Mandeville's satire is to some extent his refusal to ethically normalize or rationalize capitalism and its social effects. Mandeville presents a critical picture of commerce, trade, and consumption, but his is a polarized and perverse world where one must choose either virtue and starvation or vice and prosperity. Certainly, such a choice cancels out any positive accommodation of capitalism and its institutions.

The treatment of commerce and consumption in *The Tatler* and *The Spectator* is itself hardly free of the very contradictions Mandeville wants to call hypocrisies. Yet their view is more supportive of both morality and the market than Mandeville's, and consequently more useful to society and the individual. While there is no "right choice" to be made in Mandeville's moral universe, in *The Tatler* and *The Spectator* there are clearly right and wrong uses of wealth, good and bad patterns of consumption, honest and dishonest modes of transacting business. Faced with the divide between moral and market values, the emerging bourgeoisie did not thrive by making the doomed choice offered by Mandeville, but by thinking of ways to be both virtuous and prosperous, to consume without falling into overindulgent luxury, to pursue profit without incurring the guilt of avarice, to concentrate on business affairs without degenerating into one-dimensional materialism. In their papers, Addison and Steele figure out how to achieve these goals and thus how to integrate the commercial, the financial, and the material with the ethically and socially beneficial. It is a matter not of choosing between polarities but of drawing distinctions between the use and abuse of wealth, between honest business and ruthless greed, between tasteful consumption and vulgar ostentation, between participating in the world's marketplaces and becoming their creature. Capitalism does not thrive on the Mandevillean plan of brazen amorality but through the more moderate, explicitly moral program of the bourgeois ideology we see at work in *The Tatler* and *The Spectator.* One point we can note is that the rationalized allowance of exactly the sort of contradictions exposed by Mandeville is necessary for the integration of capitalist institutions into the social and ethical worlds of the eighteenth century.

Even those texts that may at first seem to celebrate commercial expansion, on closer inspection reveal ambiguities and equivocations.

Spectator No. 69, one of the best-known panegyrics to commercial imperialism, stands in a well-established literary and ideological tradition established by John Denham's *Coopers Hill* and continued in Alexander Pope's *Windsor-Forest*. These texts figure English commerce as a harmonizing force; all must disavow the exploitation, violence, and destruction that actually attends English commercial imperialism. Through commercial exchange and the military-political domination that secured it, England is inundated with exotic commodities and to a lesser degree with exotic peoples, those "Feather'd People" that crowd the banks of the Thames at the close of *Windsor-Forest* (see p. 265). These features — the growth of the luxury market and the encounter with foreign "primitive" peoples — are two major sticking points in the liberal adaptation of imperialism to enlightened sensibilities. Various rationalizing strategies allow men like Pope, Addison, and Steele, to embrace the benefits of imperialism while disowning its ethically and socially dubious effects.

So while Pope, no less than Addison, supports England's commercial conquests, he is critically ambivalent about the ways in which these foster domestic consumption, as is clear from his satire on Belinda's toilet in *The Rape of the Lock*. As Laura Brown argues, in this scene as in Addison's proto-Britannia figure in *Spectator* No. 69 and his depiction of the ideally outfitted woman in *Tatler* No. 116, woman becomes both the reified product of and the alibi for England's commercial imperialism (*Ends of Empire* 116; *Alexander Pope* 44–45). Women are the consumers; it is for women's pleasure, for women's adornment, that England goes to the ends of the earth searching for new markets, new goods, and new scenes of production. At the same time, women are relegated more and more to an exclusively consumerist role in the economy. According to the genteel, bourgeois standards emerging at this period, a woman's respectable social standing depends, in good part, on her absence from public scenes of commercial production and distribution. Women selling things, as we see in *Spectator* No. 155 and in Ward's description of the shopgirls at the New Exchange, are often misunderstood as women for sale.

Domestic consumption, then, is one problematic effect of commercial expansion and one that is gendered in ways that depend upon, and further, negative stereotypes of women. In order to examine the second problem of commercial imperialism — the exploitation of primitive peoples — we can return to *Windsor-Forest* and then look at the tale of Inkle and Yarico in *Spectator* No. 11. In *Windsor-Forest* we find Pope, apparently against all reason, figuring England's colonizing project as the end of conquest and slavery and the advent of global peace. Pope celebrates English imperialism by contrasting it with the ruthless empire-building of Spain. This defense was already well-established, indeed was almost obligatory, in the rhetoric that rationalized England's presence in the Caribbean. England's influence, so Pope's imperial, impossible vision at the end of *Windsor-Forest* asserts, will displace military conquest and restore peace, right rule, liberty, and prosperity. England's dominion is achieved, so the myth maintains, through purely peaceful commercial exchange, not through the brutal coercion of military might:

> Oh stretch thy Reign, fair *Peace!* from Shore to Shore
> Till Conquest cease, and Slav'ry be no more:
> Till the freed *Indians* in their native Groves
> Reap their own Fruits, and woo their Sable Loves,
> *Peru* once more a race of Kings behold,
> And other *Mexico's* be roof'd with Gold. (ll. 407–12; see p. 265)

Of course we know, and we no better than Pope, that it was precisely through conquest and slavery that England and other European nations thrived in the Americas. But Pope's thinking can be understood to follow imperialism to a certain kind of logical conclusion: once England has conquered every nation and made all peoples its subjects, then there need be no more conquest, and once all mankind understands the benefits of willingly working on English sugar plantations, there need no longer be slavery. What is obnoxious to Pope's sensibility, as to Addison's and to Steele's, are the naked facts of coercion, greed, and brutality necessary to imperial conquest. Coercion is at odds with rational, liberal ideals of social governance; greed is an affront to a moral schema that transcends naked self-interest and materialism; and brutality violates ideals of human sympathy.

The problem of slavery in the Americas emerges in *The Spectator* with the story of Inkle and Yarico. Clearly, Mr. Spectator condemns the betrayal of the Amerindian Yarico by her European lover, Inkle. His outpouring of compassionate tears affirms the moral superiority of women over men that Arietta, the narrator, asserts in her story. On one level, this tale relates a moral competition between the sexes and enlists the reader's sympathy for the virtuous and victimized woman. Figuring the heroine's virtue chiefly through her brutal victimization, the story of Inkle and Yarico bears all the hallmarks of sentimental discourse.

But the story of Inkle and Yarico speaks not only of woman's age-old betrayal by man, but also of contemporary colonization and enslavement. Although considerably embellished by Steele, the tale comes from Richard Ligon's *True and Exact History of the Island of Barbados* (1657). Within the discourse of imperialism, what this tale does is to sentimentalize slavery and disown the brutality and greed of merchants like Inkle. *Spectator* No. 11 submits Inkle's bottom-line mentality to sentimental critique. The product of the vulgar City culture Addison and Steele seek to reform, Inkle's ethical depravity is part and parcel of his heartless commercial sensibility. His father "had taken particular Care to instill into his Mind an early Love of Gain, by making him a perfect Master of Numbers, and consequently giving him a quick View of Loss and Advantage, and preventing the natural Impulses of his Passions, by Prepossession towards his Interests." It is only "with a Mind thus turned" that Inkle can dally with and then betray the innocent Yarico (see p. 194). Inkle, then, embodies the threats that commercialism poses to the human heart. Steele's exposure of these dangers does not lay a blanket condemnation on commerce per se, as much as it selectively acknowledges and disowns this instance of exploitation and betrayal as an egregious abuse of commercial imperial power. By joining with Mr. Spectator and Arietta in their sentimental censure of Inkle and empathy for Yarico, readers are reassured that a humane, ethical standard is still in place. The paper suggests not that commercial imperialism be abandoned but that a kinder, gentler approach be adopted, one that resolves the tension between ethics and commerce and thus accommodates capitalism to the imperatives of the human heart.

The Tatler and *The Spectator* seem simultaneously to celebrate and condemn commercial imperialism. Yet it is important to understand how the moral criticism levied against Inkle supports the celebration of imperialism sustained in a paper like *Spectator* No. 69: if one fully condemns the evils of commerce, one may with an easier conscience embrace all the goods of commerce.

The Tatler

From No. 25
Tuesday, June 7, 1709
[Steele on the Worthy Businessman
versus the Mere "Cit"]

. . . I had too much Bowels to be insincere to a Man who came yesterday to know of me, with which of two eminent Men in the City he should place his Son: Their Names are *Paulo* and *Avaro*.[1] This gave me much Debate with my self, because not only the Fortune of the Youth, but his Virtue also, depended upon this Choice. The Men are equally wealthy; but they differ in the Use and Application of their Riches, which you immediately see upon entring their Doors.

The Habitation of *Paulo* has at once the Air of a Nobleman and a Merchant. You see the Servants act with Affection to their Master, and Satisfaction in themselves: The Master meets you with an open Countenance, full of Benevolence and Integrity: Your Business is dispatch'd with that Confidence and Welcome which always accompanies honest Minds: His Table is the Image of Plenty and Generosity, supported by Justice and Frugality. After we had din'd here, our Affair was to visit *Avaro*: Out comes an aukward Fellow with a careful Countenance; Sir, would you speak with my Master? May I crave you Name? After the first Preambles, he leads us into a noble Solitude, a great House that seem'd uninhabited; but from the End of the spacious Hall moves towards us *Avaro*, with a suspicious Aspect, as if he believ'd us Thieves; and as for my Part, I approach'd him as if I knew him a Cut-purse. We fell into Discourse of his noble Dwelling, and the great Estate all the World knew he had to enjoy in it: And I, to plague him, fell a commending *Paulo*'s Way of living. *Paulo*, answer'd *Avaro*, is a very good Man; but we who have smaller Estates, must cut our Coat according to our Cloth. Nay, says I, Every Man knows his own Circumstance best; you are in the Right, if you han't wherewithal. He look'd very sowr; for it is, you must know, the

---

[1] *Paulo and Avaro:* The *Gentleman's Magazine* (lx. 679) [reports] that these referred to Sir James Bateman and Sir Gilbert Heathcote, directors of the Bank of England and subscribers to both *The Tatler* and *The Spectator* [Bond]. Paulo and Avaro also serve as more generalized stereotypes of men who use wealth in, respectively, the right and the wrong way.

utmost Vanity of a mean spirited rich Man to be contradicted, when he calls himself poor. But I was resolv'd to vex him by consenting to all he said; the main Design of which was, that he would have us find out, he was one of the wealthiest Men in *London*, and liv'd like a Beggar. We left him, and took a Turn on the Change. My Friend was ravish'd with *Avaro*: This (said he) is certainly a sure Man. I contradicted him with much Warmth, and summ'd up their different Characters as well as I could. This *Paulo* (said I) grows wealthy by being a common Good; *Avaro*, by being a general Evil: *Paulo* has the Art, *Avaro* the Craft of Trade. When *Paulo* gains, all Men he deals with are the better: Whenever *Avaro* profits, another certainly loses. In a Word, Paulo is a Citizen, and *Avaro* a Cit.[2] I convinc'd my Friend, and carried the young Gentleman the next day to *Paulo*, where he will learn the Way both to gain, and enjoy a good Fortune. And tho' I cannot say, I have, by keeping him from *Avaro*, sav'd him from the Gallows, I have prevented his deserving it every Day he lives: For with *Paulo* he will be an honest Man, without being so for Fear of the Law; as with Avaro, he would have been a Villain within the Protection of it.

[2] *a Cit:* A usually derogatory term applied to a member of the commercial classes living in the City of London. The term was used to distinguish the shopkeeper ("Cit") from the gentleman. Here Steele uses it to distinguish the Cit from the more worthy businessman.

From No. 124
Tuesday, January 24, 1710
[Steele on the Lottery]

—— *Ex humili summa ad Fastigia Rerum*
Extollit, quoties voluit Fortuna jocari.[1]
— Juv.

From my own Apartment, January 23.

I went on *Saturday* last to make a Visit in the City;[2] and as I passed through *Cheapside*, I saw Crowds of People turning down towards the *Bank*,[3] and struggling who should first get their Money into the new-erected Lottery.[4] It gave me a great Notion of the Credit of our present Government and Administration, to find People press as eagerly to pay Money, as they would to receive it; and at the same Time a due Respect for that Body of Men who have found out so pleasing an Expedient for carrying on the Common Cause, that they have turned a Tax into a Diversion. The Chearfulness of Spirit, and the Hopes of Success, which this Project has occasioned in this great City, lightens the Burden of the War,[5] and puts me in Mind of some Games which they say were invented by wise Men who were Lovers of their Country, to make their Fellow-Citizens undergo the Tediousness and Fatigues of a long Siege. I think there is a Kind of Homage due to Fortune, (if I may call it so) and that I should be wanting to my self if I did not lay in my Pretences to her Favour, and pay my Compliments to her by Recommending a Ticket to her Disposal. For this Reason, upon my Return to my Lodgings, I sold off a Couple of Globes and a Telescope, which, with the Cash I had by me, raised the Sum that was requisite for the Purpose. I find by my Calculations,

---

[1] *Ex humili . . . jocari:* From Juvenal, *Satires* 3.39–40 (altered): "[Fortune,] for her pleasure, can her Fools advance; / And toss 'em topmost on the Wheel of Chance" — DRYDEN [Bond].

[2] *the City:* The financial and commercial districts on the eastern side of Greater London.

[3] *the Bank:* Founded in 1694 in order to float the debt for the French-Dutch War with Sir John Houblon as the first Governor. The Bank began operations in Mercers' Hall and then moved to Grocers' Hall in Poultry Street, where it was housed at this time.

[4] *Lottery:* The government ran a series of lotteries in order to raise money, mostly for the war effort. This lottery was to raise £1,500,000 by issuing 150,000 tickets in March at £10 each. The lottery winner would be drawn around the end of September [Bond].

[5] *the War:* The War of the Spanish Succession (1701–14).

that it is but an Hundred and Fifty Thousand to One against my being worth a Thousand Pounds *per Annum* for Thirty two Years; and if any Plumb[6] in the City will lay me an Hundred and Fifty Thousand Pounds to Twenty Shillings (which is an even Bett) that I am not this fortunate Man, I will take the Wager, and shall look upon him as a Man of singular Courage and Fair-dealing, having given Orders to Mr *Morphew*[7] to subscribe such a Policy in my Behalf, if any Person accepts of the Offer. I must confess, I have had such private Intimations from the Twinkling of a certain Star in some of my Astronomical Observations, that I should be unwilling to take Fifty Pounds a Year for my Chance, unless it were to oblige a particular Friend. My chief Business at present is, to prepare my Mind for this Change of Fortune; For as *Seneca*, who was a greater Moralist, and a much richer Man than I shall be with this Addition to my present Income, says, *Munera ista Fortunae putatis? Insidiae sunt.*[8] *What we look upon as Gifts and Presents of Fortune, are Traps and Snares which she lays for the Unwary.* I am arming my self against her Favours with all my Philosophy; and that I may not lose my self in such a Redundance of unnecessary and superfluous Wealth, I have determined to settle an Annual Pension out of it upon a Family of *Palatines*, and by that means give these unhappy Strangers a Tast of *British* Property.[9] At the same Time, as I have an excellent Servant Maid, whose Diligence in attending me has increased in Proportion to my Infirmities, I shall settle upon her the Revenue arising out of the Ten Pounds, and amounting to Fourteen Shillings *per Annum*, with which she may retire into *Wales*, where she was born a Gentlewoman, and pass the remaining Part of her Days in a Condition suitable to her Birth and Quality. It was impossible for me to make an Inspection into my own Fortune on this Occasion, without seeing at the same Time the Fate of others who are embarked in the same Adventure. And indeed it was a great Pleasure to me to observe, That

---

[6] *Plumb:* The sum of £100,000.

[7] *Morphew:* The printer of *The Tatler*.

[8] *Seneca . . . Insidiae sunt:* From Seneca, *Epistulae Morales (Moral Epistles)* 8.3 [Bond]. Seneca (c. A.D. 4–65) was a Roman Stoic philosopher and rhetorician. His letters and prose were popular in England during the seventeenth and eighteenth centuries.

[9] *Palatines . . . British Property:* Palatines were Italian immigrants from the Roman Palatine Hills. According to a contemporary pamphlet, *The State of the Palatines for Fifty Years Past to this Present Time* (1710), "There are now some Thousands of them Lodg'd in Tents at *Black heath* and *Camberwell*, where they spend their Time very Religiously and Industriously, hearing Prayers Morning and Evening . . . " (15) [Bond].

the War, which generally impoverishes those who furnish out the Expence of it, will by this means give Estates to some, without making others the poorer for it. I have lately seen several in Liveries, who will give as good of their own very suddenly; and took a particular Satisfaction in the Sight of a young Country Wench, whom I this Morning passed by as she was whirling her Mop, with her Petticoats tucked up very agreeably, who, if there is any Truth in my Art, is within Ten Months of being the handsomest great Fortune in Town. I must confess, I was so struck with the Foresight of what she is to be, that I treated her accordingly, and said to her, Pray, young Lady, permit me to pass by. I would for this Reason advise all Masters and Mistresses to carry it with great Moderation and Condescension towards their Servants till next Michaelmas,[10] lest the Superiority at that Time should be inverted. I must likewise admonish all my Brethren and Fellow-Adventurers, to fill their minds with proper Arguments for their Support and Consolation in case of ill Success. It so happens in this Particular, that tho' the Gainers will have Reason to rejoice, the Losers will have no Reason to complain. I remember, the Day after the Thousand Pound Prize was drawn in the Penny Lottery,[11] I went to visit a splenatick Acquaintance of mine, who was under much Dejection, and seemed to me to have suffered some great Disappointment. Upon Enquiry, I found he had put Two-pence for himself and his Son into the Lottery, and that neither of them had drawn the Thousand Pound. Hereupon this unlucky Person took Occasion to enumerate the Misfortunes of his Life, and concluded with telling me, That he never was successful in any of his Undertakings. I was forced to comfort him with the common Reflection upon such Occasions, That Men of the greatest Merit are not always Men of the greatest Success, and that Persons of his Character must not expect to be as happy as Fools. I shall proceed in the like Manner with my Rivals and Competitors for the Thousand Pounds a Year which we are now in Pursuit of; and that I may give general Content to the whole Body of Candidates, I shall allow all that draw Prizes to be fortunate, and all that miss them to be wise.

[10] Michaelmas: The feast of St. Michael on September 29, one of the quarter-days in the English business year, on which accounts were settled between debtors and creditors, rents paid, and so on.

[11] Penny Lottery: This was one of the private lotteries in 1698, before they were forbidden by law the following year [Bond]. In 1709/10 the government reestablished state lotteries.

I must not here omit to acknowledge, that I have received several Letters upon this Subject, but find one common Error running through them all, which is, That the Writers of them believe their Fate in these Cases depends upon the Astrologer, and not upon the Stars, as in the following Letter from one, who, I fear, flatters himself with Hopes of Success, which are altogether groundless, since he does not seem to me so great a Fool as he takes himself to be.

SIR,

'Coming to Town, and finding my Friend Mr. *Partridge* dead and buried, and you the only Conjurer in Repute, I am under a Necessity of applying my self to you for a Favour, which nevertheless I confess it would better become a Friend to ask, than one who is, as I am altogether, a Stranger to you; but Poverty, you know, is impudent; and as that gives me the Occasion, so that alone could give me the Confidence to be thus importunate.

'I am, Sir, very poor, and very desirous to be otherwise; I have got Ten Pounds, which I design to venture in the Lottery now on foot. What I desire of you is, that by your Art, you will choose such a Ticket for me as shall arise a Benefit sufficient to maintain me. I must beg Leave to inform you, That I am good for nothing, and must therefore insist upon a larger Lot[12] than would satisfie those who are capable by their own Abilities of adding something to what you should assign 'em; whereas I must expect an absolute, independant Maintenance, because, as I said, I can do nothing. 'Tis possible, after this free Confession of mine, you may think I don't deserve to be rich; but I hope you'll likewise observe, I can ill afford to be poor. My own Opinion is, I am well qualified for an Estate, and have a good Title to Luck in a Lottery; but I resign my self wholly to your Mercy, not without Hopes that you will consider, the less I deserve, the greater the Generosity in you. If you reject me, I have agreed with an Acquaintance of mine to bury me for my Ten Pounds. I once more recommend my self to your Favour, and bid you *Adieu*.'

---

[12] *larger Lot:* The "great" or "chief" lot, terms for the highest prize in the lottery.

Ut tu Fortunam, sic nos te, Celse, feremus.[1]
— Hor.

From my own Apartment, July 26.

It is natural for the Imaginations of Men, who lead their Lives in too solitary a Manner, to prey upon themselves, and form from their own Conceptions Beings and Things which have no Place in Nature. This often makes an Adept as much at a Loss when he comes into the World as a meer Savage. To avoid therefore that Ineptitude for Society, which is frequently the Fault of us Scholars, and has to Men of Understanding and Breeding something much more shocking and untractable than Rusticity it self, I take Care to visit all publick Solemnities, and go into Assemblies as often as my Studies will permit. This being therefore the first Day of the Drawing of the Lottery,[2] I did not neglect spending a considerable Time in the Crowd: But as much a Philosopher as I pretend to be, I could not but look with a Sort of Veneration upon the Two Boys which received the Tickets from the Wheels, as the impartial and equal Dispensers of the Fortunes which were to be distributed among the Crowd, who all stood expecting the same Chance. It seems at first Thought very wonderful, that one Passion should so universally have the Preeminence of another in the Possession of Men's Minds as that in this Case; all in general have a secret Hope of the great Ticket:[3] And yet Fear in another Instance, as in going into a Battle, shall have so little Influence, as that tho' each Man believes there will be many Thousands slain, each is confident he himself shall escape. This Certainty proceeds from our Vanity; for every Man sees abundance in himself that deserves Reward, and nothing which should meet with Mortification. But of all the Adventurers that filled the Hall, there was one who stood by me, who I could not but fancy expected the Thousand Pounds *per Annum*, as a meer Justice to his Parts and Industry. He had his Pencil and Table-Book, and was at the drawing of each Lot, counting how much a

---

[1] *Ut tu . . . feremus:* From Horace, *Epistles* 1.8.17: "We will bear you, Celsus, as you your fortune bear" [Bond].

[2] *Lottery:* The government ran a series of lotteries in order to raise money, mostly for the war effort.

[3] *great Ticket:* The highest prize in the lottery.

Man with Seven Tickets was now nearer the great Prize, by the striking out another, and another Competitor. This Man was of the most particular Constitution I had ever observed; his Passions were so active, that he worked in the utmost Stretch of Hope and Fear. When one Rival fell before him, you might see a short Gleam of Triumph in his Countenance, which immediately vanished at the Approach of another. What added to the Particularity of this Man, was, that he every Moment cast a Look either upon the Commissioners, the Wheels, or the Boys. I gently whispered him, and asked, When he thought the Thousand Pounds would come up? Pugh! says he, Who knows that? And then looks upon a little List of his own Tickets, which were pretty high in their Numbers, and said it would not come this Ten Days. This Fellow will have a good Chance, tho' not that which he has put his Heart on. The Man is mechanically turned, and made for getting. The Simplicity and Eagerness which he is in, argues an Attention to his Point; tho' what he is labouring at does not in the least contribute to it. Were it not for such honest Fellows as these, the Men who govern the rest of their Species would have no Tools to work with: For the outward Show of the World is carried on by such as cannot find out that they are doing nothing. I left my Man with great Reluctance, seeing the Care he took to observe the whole Conduct of the Persons concerned, and compute the Inequality of the Chances with his own Hands and Eyes. Dear Sir, said I, they must rise early that cheat you. As, said he, there's nothing like a Man's minding his Business himself. 'Tis very true, said I, The Master's Eye makes the Horse fat.

As it is much the greater Number who are to go without Prizes, it is but very Expedient to turn our Lecture to the forming just Sentiments on the Subject of Fortune. One said this Morning, That the Chief Lot[4] he was confident would fall upon some Puppy; but this Gentleman is one of those wrong Tempers who approve only the Unhappy, and have a natural Prejudice to the Fortunate. But as it is certain that there is a great Meanness in being attached to a Man purely for his Fortune, there is no less a Meanness in disliking him for his Happiness. It is the same Perverseness under different Colours, and both these Resentments arise from meer Pride.

The true Greatness of Mind consists in valuing Men apart from their Circumstances, or according to their Behaviour in them. Wealth is a Distinction only in Traffick; but it must not be allowed as a Recommendation in any other Particular, but only just as it is applied. It

---

[4] *Chief Lot:* Another term for the highest prize in the lottery.

was very prettily said, That we may learn the little Value of Fortune by the Persons on whom Heaven is pleased to bestow it. However, there is not an harder Part in human Life, than becoming Wealth and Greatness. He must be very well stock'd with Merit, who is not willing to draw some Superiority over his Friends from his Fortune: For it is not every Man that can entertain with the Air of a Guest, and do good Offices with the Mien of one that receives them.

I must confess, I cannot conceive how a Man can place himself in a Figure wherein he can so much enjoy his own Soul, and that greatest of Pleasures, the just Approbation of his own Actions, than as an Adventurer on this Occasion, to sit and see the Lots go off without Hope or Fear, perfectly unconcerned as to himself, but taking Part in the good Fortune of others.

I will believe there are happy Tempers in being, to whom all the good that arrives to any of their Fellow-Creatures gives a Pleasure. These live in a Course of substantial and lasting Happiness, and have the Satisfaction to see all Men endeavour to gratify them. This State of Mind not only lets a Man into certain Enjoyments, but relieves him from as certain Anxieties. If you will not rejoice with happy Men, you must repine at them. *Dick Reptile* alluded to this when he said, He would hate no Man out of pure Idleness. As for my own Part, I look at Fortune quite in another View than the rest of the World; and, by my Knowledge in Futurity, tremble at the approaching Prize.

No. 249
Saturday, November 11, 1710
[Addison on the History of a Shilling]

Per varios Casus, per tot Discrimina Rerum,
Tendimus.[1]

— Virg.

From my own Apartment, November 10.

I was last Night visited by a Friend of mine who has an inexhaustible Fund of Discourse, and never fails to entertain his Company with a Variety of Thoughts and Hints that are altogether new and uncommon. Whether it were in Complaisance to my Way of

[1] *Per varios . . . Tendimus:* From Virgil, *Aeneid* 1.204–05: "Through various Hazards, and Events we move" — DRYDEN [Bond].

Living, or his real Opinion, he advanced the following Paradox, That it required much greater Talents to fill up and become a retired Life, than a Life of Business. Upon this Occasion he rallied very agreeably the busie Men of the Age, who only valued themselves for being in Motion, and passing through a Series of trifling and insignificant Actions. In the Heat of his Discourse, seeing a Piece of Money lying on my Table, I defie, says he, any of these active Persons to produce half the Adventures that this Twelvepenny-Piece has been engaged in, were it possible for him to give us an Account of his Life.

My Friend's Talk made so odd an Impression upon my Mind, that soon after I was a-Bed I fell insensibly into a most unaccountable *Resverie*, that had neither Moral nor Design in it, and cannot be so properly called a Dream as a Delirium.

Methoughts the Shilling that lay upon the Table reared it self upon its Edge, and turning the Face towards me, opened its Mouth, and in a soft Silver Sound gave me the following Account of his Life and Adventures.

I was born, says he, on the Side of a Mountain, near a little Village of *Peru*,[2] and made a Voyage to *England* in an Ingot, under the Convoy of Sir *Francis Drake*.[3] I was, soon after my Arrival, taken out of my *Indian* Habit, refined, naturalized, and put into the *British* Mode, with the Face of Queen *Elizabeth* on one Side, and the Arms of the Country on the other.[4] Being thus equipped, I found in me a wonderful Inclination to ramble, and visit all the Parts of the new World into which I was brought. The People very much favoured my natural Disposition, and shifted me so fast from Hand to Hand, that before I was Five Years old, I had travelled into almost every Corner of the Nation. But in the Beginning of my Sixth Year, to my unspeakable Grief, I fell into the Hands of a miserable old Fellow, who clapped me into an Iron Chest, where I found Five Hundred more of my own Quality who lay under the same Confinement. The only Relief we had, was to be taken out and counted over in the fresh Air every

---

[2] *Peru:* Silver shillings had been coined in England since 1503 [Bond]. Silver was largely obtained from South America.

[3] *Sir Francis Drake:* Drake (1540?–1596) was a circumnavigator and admiral. He made three voyages to the West Indies in 1570–72. Between 1577 and 1578 he sailed around the Cape of Good Hope and so circumnavigated the world. On his return in 1581 he was knighted by Queen Elizabeth.

[4] *Indian Habit . . . the other:* That is, the ingot of silver (its "*Indian*" Habit) was melted down and made into a shilling stamped with the image of the queen and the arms of the country. Queen Elizabeth (1533–1603), daughter of Henry VIII, reigned from 1558 to 1603.

Morning and Evening. After an Imprisonment of several Years, we heard some Body knocking at our Chest, and breaking it open with an Hammer. This we found was the old Man's Heir, who, as his Father lay a dying, was so good as to come to our Release: He separated us that very Day. What was the Fate of my Companions, I know not: As for my self, I was sent to the Apothecary's Shop for a Pint of Sack.[5] The Apothecary gave me to an Herb-Woman, the Herb-Woman to a Butcher, the Butcher to a Brewer, and the Brewer to his Wife, who made a Present of me to a Nonconformist Preacher.[6] After this Manner I made my Way merrily through the World; for, as I told you before, we Shillings love nothing so much as travelling. I sometimes fetched in a Shoulder of Mutton, sometimes a Play-Book, and often had the Satisfaction to treat a Templer at a Twelvepenny Ordinary,[7] or carry him with Three Friends to *Westminster-Hall*.[8]

In the Midst of this pleasant Progress which I made from Place to Place, I was arrested by a superstitious old Woman, who shut me up in a greazy Purse, in Pursuance of a foolish Saying, That while she kept a Queen *Elizabeth*'s Shilling about her, she should never be without Money. I continued here a close Prisoner for many Months, till at last I was exchanged for Eight and Forty Farthings.

I thus rambled from Pocket to Pocket till the Beginning of the Civil Wars,[9] when, to my Shame be it spoken, I was employed in raising Soldiers against the King:[10] For being of a very tempting Breadth, a Serjeant made Use of me to inveigle Country Fellows, and list them in the Service of the Parliament.

---

[5] *Sack:* A type of strong, dry wine from Spain and the Canary Islands, imported to England during the sixteenth and seventeenth centuries.

[6] *Nonconformist Preacher:* One that did not "conform" to the tenets of the Anglican Church; a member of one of the many dissenting sects.

[7] *Templer at a Twelvepenny Ordinary:* A law student at a cheap restaurant where dinner cost twelve pennies.

[8] *Westminster-Hall:* The surviving remnant of the original Palace of Westminster, built as an extension of Edward the Confessor's palace in 1097, Westminster Hall served as the center of administrative life outside the city walls (Westminster is west of the city). From the thirteenth century until 1882, the building contained the courts of law. During the seventeenth and eighteenth centuries, the hall also served as an emporium for books, gewgaws, and clothes.

[9] *Civil Wars:* The period of civil strife in England between 1642 and 1651. Conflicts between Charles I and Parliament were traceable to a breakdown in relations between the crown and the political nation during the reigns of James I and Charles I. This strife was simultaneously religious and political. Puritans generally supported the claims of Parliament, while Anglicans and Catholics lined up on the side of the king.

[10] *King:* King Charles I (1600–1649), son of James I, ruled England from 1625 to 1649; he was executed by Parliamentary forces for treason.

As soon as he had made one Man sure, his Way was to oblige him to take a Shilling of a more homely Figure, and then practise the same Trick upon another. Thus I continued doing great Mischief to the Crown, till my Officer chancing one Morning to walk abroad earlier than ordinary, sacrificed me to his Pleasures, and made Use of me to seduce a Milk-Maid. This Wench bent me, and gave me to her Sweetheart, applying more properly than she intended the usual Form of, *To my Love and from my Love.* This ungenerous Gallant marrying her within few Days after, pawned me for a Dram of Brandy, and drinking me out next Day, I was beaten flat with an Hammer, and again set a running.

After many Adventures, which it would be tedious to relate, I was sent to a young Spendthrift, in Company with the Will of his deceased Father. The young Fellow, who I found was very extravagant, gave great Demonstrations of Joy at the receiving the Will; but opening it, he found himself disinherited and cut off from the Possession of a fair Estate, by Vertue of my being made a Present to him. This put him into such a Passion, that after having taken me in his Hand, and cursed me, he squirred[11] me away from him as far as he could fling me. I chanced to light in an unfrequented Place under a dead Wall, where I lay undiscovered and useless during the Usurpation of *Oliver Cromwell.* [12]

About a Year after the King's Return,[13] a poor Cavalier that was walking there about Dinner-time fortunately cast his Eye upon me, and, to the great Joy of us both, carried me to a Cook's-Shop, where he dined upon me, and drank the King's Health. When I came again into the World, I found that I had been happier in my Retirement than I thought, having probably by that Means escaped wearing a monstrous Pair of Breeches.

Being now of great Credit and Antiquity, I was rather looked upon as a Medal than an ordinary Coin; for which Reason a Gamester laid hold of me, and converted me to a Counter, having got together some

---

[11] *squirred:* To throw with a rapid, skimming motion.

[12] *Oliver Cromwell:* Cromwell (1599–1658) was a soldier, a politician, and the Lord Protector during the Interregnum period (1653–58). As head of the army, Cromwell led the most successful opposition to the crown during the Civil Wars and founded his Republic on military strength, dissolving the Parliament by force. In 1657, Cromwell turned down the offer of the crown. He was briefly succeeded by his ineffectual son, Richard, before the restoration of the Stuart monarchy.

[13] *the King's Return:* The restoration of the Stuart monarchy with Charles II (1630–1685) in 1660.

Dozens of us for that Use. We led a melancholy Life in his Possession, being busy at those Hours wherein Current Coin is at Rest, and partaking the Fate of our Master, being in a few Moments valued at a Crown, a Pound, or a Sixpence, according to the Situation in which the Fortune of the Cards placed us. I had at length the good Luck to see my Master break, by which Means I was again sent abroad under my primitive Denomination of a Shilling.

I shall pass over many other Accidents of less Moment, and hasten to that fatal Catastrophe when I fell into the Hands of an Artist who conveyed me under Ground, and with an unmerciful Pair of Sheers cut off my Titles, clipped my Brims, retrenched my Shape, rubbed me to my inmost Ring, and, in short, so spoiled and pillaged me, that he did not leave me worth a Groat. You may think what a Confusion I was in to see my self thus curtailed and disfigured. I should have been ashamed to have shown my Head, had not all my old Acquaintance been reduced to the same shameful Figure, excepting some few that were punched through the Belly. In the midst of this general Calamity, when every Body thought our Misfortune irretrievable, and our Case desperate, we were thrown into the Furnace together, and (as it often happens with Cities rising out of a Fire) appeared with greater Beauty and Lustre than we could ever boast of before. What has happened to me since this Change of Sex which you now see, I shall take some other Opportunity to relate. In the mean time I shall only repeat Two Adventures, as being very extraordinary, and neither of them having ever happened to me above once in my Life. The First was, my being in a Poet's Pocket, who was so taken with the Brightness and Novelty of my Appearance, that it gave Occasion to the finest Burlesque Poem in the *British* Language, Entitled from me, *The Splendid Shilling*.[14] The Second Adventure, which I must not omit, happened to me in the Year 1703, when I was given away in Charity to a blind Man; but indeed this was by a Mistake, the Person who gave me having heedlessly thrown me into the Hat among a Pennyworth of Farthings.

---

[14] *The Splendid Shilling:* By John Philips (1705).

The Spectator

No. 3
Saturday, March 3, 1711
[Addison on the Bank of England
and the Allegory of Lady Credit]

Quoi quisque ferè studio devinctus adhæret:
Aut quibus in rebus multùm sumus antè morati:
Atque in quâ ratione fuit contenta magis mens;
In somnis eadem plerumque videmur obire.[1]
— Lucr. l. 4.

In one of my late Rambles, or rather Speculations, I looked into the great Hall where the Bank is kept,[2] and was not a little pleased to see the Directors, Secretaries, and Clerks, with all the other Members of that wealthy Corporation, ranged in their several Stations, according to the Parts they act in that just and regular Oeconomy. This revived in my Memory the many Discourses which I had both read and heard concerning the Decay of Publick Credit,[3] with the Methods of restoring it, and which, in my Opinion, have always been defective, because they have always been made with an Eye to separate Interests, and Party Principles.

The Thoughts of the Day gave my Mind Employment for the whole Night, so that I fell insensibly into a kind of Methodical Dream, which dispos'd all my Contemplations into a Vision or Allegory, or what else the Reader shall please to call it.

Methoughts I returned to the Great Hall, where I had been the Morning before, but, to my Surprize, instead of the Company that I left there, I saw towards the Upper-end of the Hall, a beautiful Virgin, seated on a Throne of Gold. Her Name (as they told me) was *Publick Credit*. The Walls, instead of being adorned with Pictures and Maps, were hung with many Acts of Parliament written in

---

[1] *Quoi quisque . . . obire:* From Lucretius 4.962–65: " . . . What studies please, what most delight, / And fill men's thoughts, they dream them o'er at night" — CREECH [Bond].

[2] *the great Hall where the Bank is kept:* Grocers' Hall at the upper end of Grocers' Alley.

[3] *many Discourses . . . Publick Credit:* Addison has in mind such things as Defoe's *Essay upon Publick Credit*, published during the preceding summer, on August 23 [Bond].

Golden Letters. At the Upper-end of the Hall was the *Magna Charta*,[4] with the Act of Uniformity on the right Hand, and the Act of Toleration on the left. At the Lower-end of the Hall was the Act of Settlement,[5] which was placed full in the Eye of the Virgin that sat upon the Throne. Both the Sides of the Hall were covered with such Acts of Parliament as had been made for the Establishment of publick Funds. The Lady seemed to set an unspeakable Value upon these several Pieces of Furniture, insomuch that she often refreshed her Eye with them, and often smiled with a Secret Pleasure, as she looked upon them; but, at the same time, showed a very particular Uneasiness, if she saw any thing approaching that might hurt them. She appeared indeed infinitely timorous in all her Behaviour: And, whether it was from the Delicacy of her Constitution, or that she was troubled with Vapours,[6] as I was afterwards told by one who I found was none of her Well-wishers, she changed Colour, and startled at every thing she heard. She was likewise (as I afterwards found) a greater Valetudinarian than any I had ever met with, even in her own Sex, and subject to such Momentary Consumptions, that in the twinkling of an Eye, she would fall away from the most florid Complexion, and the most healthful State of Body, and wither into a Skeleton. Her Recoveries were often as sudden as her Decays, insomuch that she would revive in a Moment out of a wasting Distemper, into a Habit of the highest Health and Vigour.

I had very soon an Opportunity of observing these quick Turns and Changes in her Constitution. There sat at her Feet a Couple of

[4] *Magna Charta:* The Great Charter of English personal and political liberty was signed by King John under pressure from the barons in 1215. The Charter served as the basis in disputes between the sovereign and his subjects.

[5] *Act of Uniformity . . . Act of Toleration . . . Act of Settlement:* The Act of Uniformity and the Act of Settlement were two differing responses to the problem of religious coherence in post-Restoration England. The Act of Uniformity was passed in 1662 by the Cavalier (pro-Stuart) Parliament and proposed a series of regulations to insure greater conformity to the tenets of the episcopal Anglican church. It required the reordination of many pastors and instituted punishments for any adult attending religious meetings not in accordance with its stipulations. A 1665 revision prohibited any nonconforming citizen from living within five miles of London. Passed in 1689 after the ascension of William of Orange, the Act of Toleration maintained the episcopal structure of the established church but allowed dissenting groups to meet in licensed chapels. The Act of Settlement, passed in 1701, offered the royal succession to the descendants of Sophia of Hanover in the event that William III and Queen Anne died without heirs. It guaranteed the Protestant succession, disregarding other claims to the throne, based on descent, made by the Stuart Pretenders, who were Catholic.

[6] *Vapours:* A fashionable nervous disorder marked by anxiety, depression, and fainting fits.

Secretaries, who received every Hour Letters from all Parts of the World, which the one or the other of them was perpetually reading to her; and, according to the News she heard, to which she was exceedingly attentive, she changed Colour, and discovered many Symptoms of Health or Sickness.

Behind the Throne was a prodigious Heap of Bags of Mony, which were piled upon one another so high that they touched the Ceiling. The Floor, on her right Hand, and on her left, was covered with vast Sums of Gold that rose up in Pyramids on either side of her: But this I did not so much wonder at, when I heard, upon Enquiry, that she had the same Virtue in her Touch, which the Poets tell us a *Lydian King*[7] was formerly possess'd of; and that she could convert whatever she pleas'd into that precious Metal.

After a little Dizziness, and confused Hurry of Thought, which a Man often meets with in a Dream, methoughts the Hall was alarm'd, the Doors flew open, and there entered half a dozen of the most hideous Phantoms that I had ever seen (even in a Dream) before that Time. They came in two by two, though match'd in the most dissociable Manner, and mingled together in a kind of Dance. It would be tedious to describe their Habits and Persons, for which Reason I shall only inform my Reader that the first Couple were Tyranny and Anarchy, the second were Bigotry and Atheism, the third the Genius of a Common-Wealth, and a young Man[8] of about twenty two Years of Age, whose Name I could not learn. He had a Sword in his right Hand, which in the Dance he often brandished at the Act of Settlement; and a Citizen, who stood by me, whisper'd in my Ear, that he saw a Spunge in his left Hand. The Dance of so many jarring Natures put me in Mind of the Sun, Moon and Earth, in the *Rehearsal*,[9] that danced together for no other end but to eclipse one another.

The Reader will easily suppose, by what has been before said, that the Lady on the Throne would have been almost frighted to Distrac-

---

[7] *Lydian King:* King Midas, the legendary king of ancient Phrygia, who had the power to turn everything he touched into gold.

[8] *a young Man:* The Old Pretender, James Francis Edward Stuart (1688–1766), the son of the deposed James II. Supported by the pro-Stuart Jacobites as James III of England and James VIII of Scotland, and proclaimed King of England by the French monarch Louis XIV, he made several attempts to regain the throne. His son Charles, the Young Pretender, "Bonnie Prince Charlie," led one last Jacobite rebellion in Britain in 1745.

[9] *the Rehearsal:* A play by George Buckingham (1628–1687) that parodies Restoration heroic tragedies. In the final act, the protagonist, a tragic playwright named Bayes, has his actors, as the moon, the earth, and the sun, dance together.

tion, had she seen but any one of these Spectres; what then must have been her Condition when she saw them all in a Body? She fainted and dyed away at the Sight.

> *Et neque jam color est misto candore rubori;*
> *Nec Vigor, & Vires & quæ modo visa placebant;*
> *Nec Corpus remanet . . .*[10]
> — Ov. *Met.*, Lib. 3.

There was as great a Change in the Hall of Mony Bags, and the Heaps of Mony, the former shrinking, and falling into so many empty Bags, that I now found not above a tenth Part of them had been filled with Mony. The rest that took up the same Space, and made the same Figure as the Bags that were really filled with Mony, had been blown up with Air, and called into my Memory the Bags full of Wind, which *Homer* tells us his Hero receiv'd as a Present from *Æolus*.[11] The great Heaps of Gold, on either side the Throne, now appeared to be only Heaps of Paper, or little Piles of notched Sticks, bound up together in Bundles, like *Bath*-Faggots.[12]

Whilst I was lamenting this sudden Desolation that had been made before me, the whole Scene vanished: In the Room of the frightful Spectres, there now entered a second Dance of Apparitions very agreeably matched together, and made up of very amiable Phantoms. The first Pair was Liberty, with Monarchy at her right Hand: The second was Moderation leading in Religion; and the third a Person whom I had never seen,[13] with the Genius of *Great Britain*. At their first Entrance the Lady reviv'd, the Bags swell'd to their former Bulk, the Piles of Faggots and Heaps of Paper changed into Pyramids of Guineas: And for my own Part I was so transported with Joy, that I awaked, tho' I must confess I would fain have fallen asleep again to have closed my Vision, if I could have done it.

[10] *Et neque . . . remanet:* From Ovid [43 B.C.–A.D. 17?], *Metamorphoses* 3.491–93: "No longer has [she] that ruddy color mixing with the white, no longer that vigor and strength, and all that lately was so pleasing to behold; hardly does [her] body remain . . . " [Bond].

[11] *Æolus:* Homer (fl. eighth century B.C.) composed the ancient Greek epics, the *Iliad* and the *Odyssey*. Æolus is the Greek god of the winds. Here Addison refers to the *Odyssey*, Book 10.

[12] *Piles of notched Sticks . . . like Bath-Faggots:* This refers to the tallies notched to keep track of payments received or owed. Addison compares them to a pile of firewood gathered to heat water for a bath.

[13] *a Person whom I had never seen:* This refers to Prince George (1660–1727), son of the Electress of Hanover and thus heir to the throne. The Whigs complained that he had never been invited to visit Britain [Bond].

No. 11
Tuesday, March 13, 1711
[Steele on Inkle and Yarico]

Dat veniam corvis, vexat censura columbas.[1]
— Juv.

Arietta is visited by all Persons of both Sexes, who have any Pretence to Wit and Gallantry. She is in that time of Life which is neither affected with the Follies of Youth, or Infirmities of Age; and her Conversation is so mixed with Gaiety and Prudence, that she is agreeable both to the Young and the Old. Her Behaviour is very frank, without being in the least blameable; and as she is out of the Tract of any amorous or ambitious Pursuits of her own, her Visitants entertain her with Accounts of themselves very freely, whether they concern their Passions or their Interests. I made her a Visit this Afternoon, having been formerly introduced to the Honour of her Acquaintance, by my Friend *Will. Honeycomb*, who has prevailed upon her to admit me sometimes into her Assembly, as a civil, inoffensive Man. I found her accompanied with one Person only, a Common-Place Talker, who, upon my Entrance, rose, and after a very slight Civility sat down again; then turning to *Arietta*, pursued his Discourse, which I found was upon the old Topick, of Constancy in Love. He went on with great Facility in repeating what he talks every Day of his Life; and, with the Ornaments of insignificant Laughs and Gestures, enforced his Arguments by Quotations out of Plays and Songs, which allude to the Perjuries of the Fair, and the general Levity of Women. Methought he strove to shine more than ordinarily in his Talkative Way, that he might insult my Silence, and distinguish himself before a Woman of *Arietta*'s Taste and Understanding. She had often an Inclination to interrupt him, but could find no Opportunity, 'till the Larum ceased of its self; which it did not 'till he had repeated and murdered the celebrated Story of the *Ephesian* Matron.[2]

[1] *Dat veniam . . . columbas:* From Juvenal, *Satires* 2.63: "He shows indulgence toward the crows and censures the doves" [Bond].
[2] *Ephesian Matron:* This story is told by the first century A.D. Roman satirist Petronius in his *Satyricon*. In it, a grief-stricken Ephesian widow, renowned for her fidelity, is seduced at her dead husband's tomb by a soldier placed to guard the bodies of several crucified corpses. When it is discovered that one of the crucified bodies is missing, the widow offers the body of her husband to replace the stolen body and so saves her soldier lover from punishment for neglecting duty. The story is told as evidence of the fickleness of female affection.

Arietta seemed to regard this Piece of Raillery as an Outrage done to her Sex, as indeed I have always observed that Women, whether out of a nicer Regard to their Honour, or what other Reason I cannot tell, are more sensibly touched with those general Aspersions, which are cast upon their Sex, than Men are by what is said of theirs.

When she had a little recovered her self from the serious Anger she was in, she replied in the following manner.

Sir, When I consider, how perfectly new all you have said on this Subject is, and that the Story you have given us is not quite two thousand Years Old, I cannot but think it a Piece of Presumption to dispute with you: But your Quotations put me in Mind of the Fable of the Lion and the Man.[3] The Man walking with that noble Animal, showed him, in the Ostentation of Human Superiority, a Sign of a Man killing a Lion. Upon which the Lion said very justly, *We Lions are none of us Painters, else we could show a hundred Men killed by Lions, for one Lion killed by a Man.* You Men are Writers, and can represent us Women as Unbecoming as you please in your Works, while we are unable to return the Injury. You have twice or thrice observed in your Discourse, that Hipocrisy is the very Foundation of our Education; and that an Ability to dissemble our Affections, is a professed Part of our Breeding. These, and such other Reflections, are sprinkled up and down the Writings of all Ages, by Authors, who leave behind them Memorials of their Resentment against the Scorn of particular Women, in Invectives against the whole Sex. Such a Writer, I doubt not, was the celebrated *Petronius*, who invented the pleasant Aggravations of the Frailty of the *Ephesian* Lady; but when we consider this Question between the Sexes, which has been either a Point of Dispute or Raillery ever since there were Men and Women, let us take Facts from plain People, and from such as have not either Ambition or Capacity to embellish their Narrations with any Beauties of Imagination. I was the other Day amusing my self with *Ligon*'s Account of *Barbadoes*; and, in Answer to your well-wrought Tale, I will give you (as it dwells upon my Memory) out of that honest Traveller, in his fifty fifth Page, the History of *Inkle* and *Yarico*.[4]

---

[3] *Fable of the Lion and the Man:* Aesop, Fable 219 [Bond].

[4] *Ligon's . . . Inkle and Yarico:* In his *True and Exact History of the Island of Barbados* (1657), Richard Ligon tells the story of "an *Indian* Woman" who worked as a servant in his household who was pregnant with the child of a European servant. She had been sold into slavery by her English lover whom she had saved from attack by her countrymen (54–55). This story became quite popular in England, appearing in plays, novels, and poems. Steele's account embellishes and personalizes Ligon's, naming the characters and highlighting the sentimental pathos of Yarico's plight.

Mr. *Thomas Inkle* of *London*, aged 20 Years, embarked in the *Downs* on the good Ship called the *Achilles*, bound for the *West-Indies*, on the 16th of *June* 1647, in order to improve his Fortune by Trade and Merchandize. Our Adventurer was the third Son of an eminent Citizen, who had taken particular Care to instill into his Mind an early Love of Gain, by making him a perfect Master of Numbers, and consequently giving him a quick View of Loss and Advantage, and preventing the natural Impulses of his Passions, by Prepossession towards his Interests. With a Mind thus turned, young *Inkle* had a Person every way agreeable, a ruddy Vigour in his Countenance, Strength in his Limbs, with Ringlets of fair Hair loosely flowing on his Shoulders. It happened, in the Course of the Voyage, that the *Achilles*, in some Distress, put into a Creek on the Main of *America*, in Search of Provisions: The Youth, who is the Hero of my Story, among others, went ashore on this Occasion. From their first Landing they were observed by a Party of *Indians*, who hid themselves in the Woods for that Purpose. The *English* unadvisedly marched a great distance from the Shore into the Country, and were intercepted by the Natives, who slew the greatest Number of them. Our Adventurer escaped among others, by flying into a Forest. Upon his coming into a remote and pathless Part of the Wood, he threw himself, tired and breathless, on a little Hillock, when an *Indian* Maid rushed from a Thicket behind him: After the first Surprize, they appeared mutually agreeable to each other. If the *European* was highly Charmed with the Limbs, Features, and wild Graces of the Naked *American*; the *American* was no less taken with the Dress, Complexion, and Shape of an *European*, covered from Head to Foot. The *Indian* grew immediately enamoured of him, and consequently sollicitous for his Preservation: She therefore conveyed him to a Cave, where she gave him a Delicious Repast of Fruits, and led him to a Stream to slake his Thirst. In the midst of these good Offices, she would sometimes play with his Hair, and delight in the Opposition of its Colour, to that of her Fingers: Then open his Bosome, then laugh at him for covering it. She was, it seems, a Person of Distinction, for she every day came to him in a different Dress, of the most beautiful Shells, Bugles and Bredes.[5] She likewise brought him a great many Spoils, which her other Lovers had presented to her; so that his Cave was richly adorned with all the spotted Skins of Beasts, and most Party-coloured Feathers of Fowls, which that World afforded. To make his Confine-

[5] *Bugles and Bredes:* Glass ornaments and braiding.

ment more tolerable, she would carry him in the Dusk of the Evening, or by the favour of Moon-light, to unfrequented Groves and Solitudes, and show him where to lye down in Safety, and sleep amidst the Falls of Waters, and Melody of Nightingales. Her Part was to watch and hold him in her Arms, for fear of her Country-men, and wake him on Occasions to consult his Safety. In this manner did the Lovers pass away their Time, till they had learn'd a Language of their own, in which the Voyager communicated to his Mistress, how happy he should be to have her in his Country, where she should be Cloathed in such Silks as his Wastecoat was made of, and be carried in Houses drawn by Horses, without being exposed to Wind or Weather. All this he promised her the Enjoyment of, without such Fears and Alarms as they were there Tormented with. In this tender Correspondence these Lovers lived for several Months, when *Yarico*, instructed by her Lover, discovered a Vessel on the Coast, to which she made Signals, and in the Night, with the utmost Joy and Satisfaction accompanied him to a Ships-Crew of his Country-Men, bound for *Barbadoes*. When a Vessel from the Main arrives in that Island, it seems the Planters come down to the Shoar, where there is an immediate Market of the *Indians* and other Slaves, as with us of Horses and Oxen.

To be short, Mr. *Thomas Inkle*, now coming into *English* Territories, began seriously to reflect upon his loss of Time, and to weigh with himself how many Days Interest of his Mony he had lost during his Stay with *Yarico*. This Thought made the Young Man very pensive, and careful what Account he should be able to give his Friends of his Voyage. Upon which Considerations, the prudent and frugal young Man sold *Yarico* to a *Barbadian* Merchant; notwithstanding that the poor Girl, to incline him to commiserate her Condition, told him that she was with Child by him: But he only made use of that Information, to rise in his Demands upon the Purchaser.

I was so touch'd with this Story, (which I think should be always a Counterpart to the *Ephesian* Matron) that I left the Room with Tears in my Eyes; which a Woman of *Arietta*'s good Sense, did, I am sure, take for greater Applause, than any Compliments I could make her.

No. 21
Saturday, March 24, 1711
[Addison on the Social Status of Trade]

. . . Locus est & pluribus Umbris.[1]
— Hor.

I am sometimes very much troubled, when I reflect upon the three great Professions of Divinity, Law and Physick; how they are each of them over-burdened with Practitioners, and filled with Multitudes of Ingenious Gentlemen that starve one another.

We may divide the Clergy into Generals, Field-Officers, and Subalterns. Among the first we may reckon Bishops, Deans and Arch-Deacons. Among the second are Doctors of Divinity, Pre-bendaries, and all that wear Scarfs.[2] The rest are comprehended under the Subalterns. As for the first Class, our Constitution preserves it from any Redundancy of Incumbents, notwithstanding Competitors are numberless. Upon a strict Calculation, it is found that there has been a great Exceeding of late Years in the second Division, several Brevets having been granted for the converting of Subalterns into Scarf-Officers; insomuch that within my Memory the price of Lutestring[3] is raised above two Pence in a Yard. As for the Subalterns, they are not to be numbred. Should our Clergy once enter into the corrupt Practice of the Laity, by the splitting of their Freeholds, they would be able to carry most of the Elections in *England*.

The Body of the Law is no less encumbered with superfluous Members, that are like *Virgil*'s Army,[4] which he tells us was so crouded many of them had not Room to use their Weapons. This prodigious Society of Men may be divided into the Litigious and Peaceable. Under the first are comprehended all those who are carried down in Coach-fulls to *Westminster-Hall*,[5] every Morning in Term-time. *Martial*'s Description of this Species of Lawyers is full of Humour:

---

[1] *. . . Locus est & pluribus Umbris:* From Horace, *Epistles* 1.5.28: "There's room too for several uninvited guests" [Bond].

[2] *Scarfs:* Ecclesiastical scarves. At this time it denoted specifically the scarf worn by a nobleman's chaplain [Bond].

[3] *Lutestring:* A glossy silk fabric.

[4] *Virgil's Army: Aeneid* 10. 432–34 [Bond].

[5] *Westminster-Hall:* Center of administrative life outside of London; contained courts of law until 1882.

Iras & Verba locant.[6]

Men that hire out their Words and Anger; that are more or less passionate according as they are paid for it, and allow their Client a quantity of Wrath proportionable to the Fee which they receive from him. I must however observe to the Reader, that above three Parts of those whom I reckon among the Litigious, are such as are only quarrelsome in their Hearts, and have no Opportunity of showing their Passion at the Bar. Nevertheless, as they do not know what Strifes may arise, they appear at the Hall every Day, that they may show themselves in a Readiness to enter the Lists, whenever there shall be Occasion for them.

The Peaceable Lawyers are, in the first place, many of the Benchers of the several Inns of Court, who seem to be the Dignitaries of the Law, and are endowed with those Qualifications of Mind that accomplish a Man rather for a Ruler, than a Pleader. These Men live peaceably in their Habitations, Eating once a Day, and Dancing once a Year, for the Honour of their respective Societies.

Another numberless Branch of Peaceable Lawyers, are those young Men who being placed at the Inns of Court in order to study the Laws of their Country, frequent the Play-House more than *Westminster-Hall,* and are seen in all publick Assemblies, except in a Court of Justice. I shall say nothing of those Silent and Busie Multitudes that are employed within Doors, in the drawing up of Writings and Conveyances; nor of those greater Numbers that palliate their want of Business with a Pretence to such Chamber-practice.

If, in the third place, we look into the Profession of Physick, we shall find a most formidable Body of Men: The Sight of them is enough to make a Man serious, for we may lay it down as a Maxim, that When a Nation abounds in Physicians it grows thin of People. *Sir William Temple*[7] is very much puzzled to find out a Reason why the Northern Hive, as he calls it, does not send out such prodigious Swarms, and over-run the World with *Goths* and *Vandals,*[8] as it did

---

[6] *Iras & Verba locant:* The line is not from the Roman epigrammatist Martial (c. A.D. 40–c. 103) but from the Roman philosopher and dramatist Seneca (4 B.C.?–A.D. 65) (*Hercules Furens* 173–74) [Bond].

[7] *Sir William Temple:* Sir William Temple (1628–1699) was an English statesman and diplomat. His essays were collected and published posthumously by Jonathan Swift, who served as Temple's secretary from 1689 to 1699. Bond notes that Addison is referring to Temple's Miscellanea, part ii (*Works*, 1720, i. 212).

[8] *Goths and Vandals:* Germanic tribes that conducted campaigns of conquest against the Roman empire. They invaded and occupied Gallic, Latin, and North

formerly; but had that Excellent Author observed that there were no Students in Physick among the Subjects of *Thor* and *Woden*,[9] and that this Science very much flourishes in the North at present, he might have found a better Solution for this Difficulty, than any of those he has made use of. This Body of Men, in our own Country, may be described like the *British* Army in *Caesar*'s time: Some of them slay in Chariots, and some on Foot.[10] If the Infantry do less Execution than the Charioteers, it is because they cannot be carried so soon into all Quarters of the Town, and dispatch so much Business in so short a Time. Besides this Body of Regular Troops, there are Stragglers, who without being duly listed and enrolled, do infinite Mischief to those who are so unlucky as to fall into their Hands.

There are, besides the abovementioned, innumerable Retainers to Physick, who, for want of other Patients, amuse themselves with the stifling of Cats in an Air Pump, cutting up Dogs alive, or impaling of Insects upon the point of a Needle for Microscopical Observations; besides those that are employed in the gathering of Weeds, and the Chase of Butterflies: Not to mention the Cockleshell-Merchants and Spider-catchers.[11]

When I consider how each of these Professions are crouded with Multitudes that seek their Livelihood in them, and how many Men of Merit there are in each of them, who may be rather said to be of the Science, than the Profession; I very much wonder at the Humour of Parents, who will not rather chuse to place their Sons in a way of Life where an honest Industry cannot but thrive, than in Stations where the greatest Probity, Learning and Good Sense may miscarry. How many Men are Country-Curates, that might have made themselves Aldermen of *London*, by a right Improvement of a smaller Sum of Mony than what is usually laid out upon a learned Education? A sober, frugal Person, of slender Parts and a slow Apprehension, might have thrived in Trade, tho' he starves upon Physick; as a Man would be well enough pleased to buy Silks of one, whom he would not ven-

---

African provinces throughout the fifth century A.D. They were the original "barbarians at the gate" of civilization.

[9] *Thor and Woden:* Thor is the Norse god of thunder. The Anglo-Saxon Woden (or Odin) is the supreme deity and creator of the cosmos, a god of wisdom and culture.

[10] *Caesar's time . . . on Foot:* Caesar, *Commentaries* 4.33 [Bond]; Julius Caesar's (c. 100?–46 B.C.) account of his conquest of Gaul.

[11] *. . . Spider-catchers:* Here Addison mocks the scientific *virtuosi*. *Virtuosi* were persons interested in natural curiosities or the fine arts; they often engaged in collecting and connoisseurship with great fervor.

ture to feel his Pulse. *Vagellius* is careful, studious and obliging, but withal a little thick-skull'd; he has not a single Client, but might have had abundance of Customers. The Misfortune is, that Parents take a Liking to a particular Profession, and therefore desire their Sons may be of it. Whereas, in so great an Affair of Life, they should consider the Genius and Abilities of their Children, more than their own Inclinations.

It is the great Advantage of a trading Nation, that there are very few in it so dull and heavy, who may not be placed in Stations of Life which may give them an Opportunity of making their Fortunes. A well-regulated Commerce is not, like Law, Physick or Divinity, to be overstocked with Hands; but, on the contrary, flourishes by Multitudes, and gives Employment to all its Professors. Fleets of Merchantmen are so many Squadrons of floating Shops, that vend our Wares and Manufacturers in all the Markets of the World, and find out Chapmen under both the Tropicks.

No. 55
Thursday, May 3, 1711
[Addison's Allegory of Luxury and Avarice]

... *Intus, & in jecore ægro*
Nascuntur Domini ...[1]
— Pers.

Most of the Trades, Professions, and Ways of Living among Mankind, take their Original either from the Love of Pleasure or the Fear of Want. The former, when it becomes too violent, degenerates into *Luxury*, and the latter into *Avarice*. As these two Principles of Action draw different Ways, *Persius* has given us a very humorous Account of a young Fellow who was rouzed out of his Bed, in order to be sent upon a long Voyage by *Avarice*, and afterwards overpersuaded and kept at Home by *Luxury*. I shall set down at length the Pleadings of these two imaginary Persons, as they are in the Original, with Mr. *Dryden*'s Translation of them. ...

[1] ... *Intus ... Domini* ... : From Persius, *Satires* 5.129–30: "But if thy passions lord it in thy breast, / Art thou not still a slave, and still oppress'd?" — DRYDEN [Bond].

Whether alone, or in thy Harlot's Lap,
When thou would'st take a lazy Morning's Nap;
Up, Up, says *AVARICE*; thou snor'st again,
Stretchest thy Limbs, and yawn'st, but all in vain.
The rugged Tyrant no Denial takes;
At his Command th'unwilling Sluggard wakes.
What must I do? he cries; What? says his Lord:
Why rise, make ready, and go streight Aboard:
With Fish, from *Euxine* Seas, thy Vessel freight;
Flax, Castor, *Coan* Wines, the precious Weight
Of Pepper, and *Sabean* Incense, take
With thy own Hands, from the tir'd Camel's Back,
And with Post-haste thy running Markets make.
Be sure to turn the Penny; Lye and Swear,
'Tis wholesome Sin: But *Jove*, thou say'st, will hear.
Swear, Fool, or Starve; for the *Dilemma*'s even:
A Tradesman thou! and hope to go to Heav'n?

Resolv'd for Sea, the Slaves thy Baggage Pack,
Each saddled with his Burden on his Back:
Nothing retards thy Voyage, now; but He,
That soft voluptuous Prince, call'd *LUXURY*;
And he may ask this civil Question; Friend,
What dost thou make a Shipboard? To what end?
Art thou of *Bethlem*'s noble College[2] free?
Stark, staring mad, that thou wou'dst tempt the Sea?
Cubb'd[3] in a Cabbin, on a Mattress laid,
On a brown *George*, with lowsie Swobbers fed,
Dead Wine that stinks of the *Borachio*, sup
From a foul Jack,[4] or greasie Maple Cup?
Say, wou'dst thou bear all this, to raise thy Store,
From Six i'th'Hundred, to Six Hundred more?
Indulge, and to thy Genius freely give:
For, not to live at Ease, is not to live:
Death stalks behind thee, and each flying Hour
Does some loose Remnant of thy Life devour.
Live, while thou liv'st; for Death will make us all,
A Name, a nothing but an Old Wife's Tale.

[2] *Bethlem's noble College:* Bethlehem, or "Bedlam," Hospital for the insane.
[3] *Cubb'd:* Confined.
[4] *brown George . . . Borachio . . . foul Jack:* A loaf of a coarse kind of brown bread; a leather bottle or bag used in Spain for wine; a leather jug or tankard [Bond].

> Speak, wilt thou *Avarice*, or *Pleasure* chuse
> To be thy Lord? Take one, and one refuse.[5]

When a Government flourishes in Conquests, and is secure from foreign Attacks, it naturally falls into all the Pleasures of Luxury; and as these Pleasures are very expensive, they put those who are addicted to them upon raising fresh Supplies of Mony, by all the Methods of Rapaciousness and Corruption; so that Avarice and Luxury very often become one complicated Principle of Action, in those whose Hearts are wholly set upon Ease, Magnificence, and Pleasure. The most Elegant and Correct of all the *Latin* Historians[6] observes, that in his time, when the most formidable States of the World were subdued by the *Romans*, the Republick sunk into those two Vices of a quite different Nature, Luxury and Avarice: And accordingly describes *Catiline*[7] as one who coveted the Wealth of other Men, at the same time that he squandred away his own. This Observation on the Commonwealth, when it was in its height of Power and Riches, holds good of all Governments that are settled in a State of Ease and Prosperity. At such times Men naturally endeavour to outshine one another in Pomp and Splendor, and having no Fears to alarm them from abroad, indulge themselves in the Enjoyment of all the Pleasures they can get into their Possession; which naturally produces Avarice, and an immoderate Pursuit after Wealth and Riches.

As I was humouring my self in the Speculation of these two great Principles of Action, I could not forbear throwing my Thoughts into a little kind of Allegory or Fable, with which I shall here present my Reader.

There were two very powerful Tyrants engaged in a perpetual War against each other: The Name of the first was LUXURY, and of the second AVARICE. The Aim of each of them was no less than Universal Monarchy over the Hearts of Mankind. *Luxury* had many Generals under him, who did him great Service, as *Pleasure, Mirth, Pomp,* and *Fashion. Avarice* was likewise very strong in his Officers, being

[5] *... refuse:* John Dryden's (1631–1700) translation of Persius's fifth Satire (ll. 132–55). Persius (A.D. 34–62) was a Stoic poet and, with Horace and Juvenal, one of the three greatest Latin satirists. In the 1690s, toward the end of his life, the English poet John Dryden translated the satires of Persius and Juvenal.

[6] *Latin Historians:* Sallust (86–35 B.C.), *Bellum Catilinae* 5.4 [Bond].

[7] *Catiline:* Lucius Sergius Catilina (100–62 B.C.) was a Roman patrician of the late period of the Republic. In 63 he ran for the consulship held by Cicero, the incumbent. Defeated, Catiline attempted to overthrow the Republic; he was killed in 62. The Roman historian Sallust (86–35 B.C.) documented these events in *The Conspiracy of Catiline.*

faithfully served by *Hunger, Industry, Care* and *Watchfulness*: He had likewise a Privy-Counsellor who was always at his Elbow, and whispering something or other in his Ear: the Name of this Privy-Counsellor was *Poverty*. As *Avarice* conducted himself by the Counsels of *Poverty*, his Antagonist was entirely guided by the Dictates and Advice of *Plenty*, who was his first Counsellor and Minister of State, that concerted all his Measures for him, and never departed out of his sight. While these two great Rivals were thus contending for Empire, their Conquests were very various. *Luxury* got Possession of one Heart, and *Avarice* of another. The Father of a Family would often range himself under the Banners of *Avarice*, and the Son under those of *Luxury*. The Wife and Husband would often declare themselves on the two different Parties; nay, the same Person would very often side with one in his Youth, and revolt to the other in his old Age. Indeed the Wise Men of the World stood *Neuter*; but alas! their Numbers were not considerable. At length, when these two Potentates had wearied themselves with waging War upon one another, they agreed upon an Interview, at which neither of their Counsellors were to be present. It is said that *Luxury* began the Parly, and after having represented the endless State of War in which they were engaged, told his Enemy, with a Frankness of Heart which is natural to him, that he believed they two should be very good Friends, were it not for the Instigations of *Poverty*, that pernicious Counsellor, who made an ill use of his Ear, and filled him with groundless Apprehensions and Prejudices. To this *Avarice* replied, that he looked upon *Plenty*, (the first Minister of his Antagonist) to be a much more destructive Counsellor than *Poverty*, for that he was perpetually suggesting Pleasures, banishing all the necessary Cautions against Want, and consequently undermining those Principles on which the Government of *Avarice* was founded. At last, in order to an Accommodation, they agreed upon this Preliminary; That each of them should immediately dismiss his Privy-Counsellor. When things were thus far adjusted towards a Peace, all other Differences were soon accommodated, insomuch that for the future they resolved to live as good Friends and Confederates, and to share between them whatever Conquests were made on either side. For this Reason, we now find *Luxury* and *Avarice* taking Possession of the same Heart, and dividing the same Person between them. To which I shall only add, that since the discarding of the Counsellors above mentioned, *Avarice* supplies *Luxury* in the room of *Plenty*, as *Luxury* Prompts *Avarice* in the place of *Poverty*.

No. 69
Saturday, May 19, 1711
[Addison on the Royal Exchange]

Hic segetes, illic veniunt felicius uvæ:
Arborei fœtus alibi, atque injussa virescunt
Gramina. Nonne vides, croceos ut Tmolus odores,
India mittit ebur, molles sua thura Sabæi?
At Chalybes nudi ferrum, virosaque Pontus
Castorea, Eliadum palmas Epirus equarum?
Continuo has leges æternaque fœdera certis
Imposuit Natura locis . . .[1]

— Vir.

There is no Place in the Town which I so much love to frequent as the *Royal-Exchange*.[2] It gives me a secret Satisfaction, and, in some measure, gratifies my Vanity, as I am an *Englishman*, to see so rich an Assembly of Country-men and Foreigners consulting together upon the private Business of Mankind, and making this Metropolis a kind of *Emporium* for the whole Earth. I must confess I look upon High-Change[3] to be a great Council, in which all considerable Nations have their Representatives. Factors in the Trading World are what Ambassadors are in the Politick World; they negotiate Affairs, conclude Treaties, and maintain a good Correspondence between those wealthy Societies of Men that are divided from one another by Seas

[1] *Hic segetes, . . . Natura locis . . .*: From Virgil, *Georgics* 1.54–61:

> This Ground with *Bacchus*, that with *Ceres* suits:
> That other loads the Trees with happy Fruits.
> A fourth with Grass, unbidden, decks the Ground:
> Thus *Timolus* is with yellow Saffron crown'd:
> *India*, black Ebon and white Ivory bears:
> And soft *Idume* weeps her od'rous Tears.
> Thus *Pontus* sends her Beaver Stones from far;
> and naked *Spanyards* temper Steel for War.
> *Epirus* for th' *Elean* Chariot breeds,
> (In hopes of Palms,) a Race of running Steeds.
> This is the Orig'nal Contract; these the Laws
> Impos'd by Nature, and by Nature's Cause,
> On sundry Places. — DRYDEN [Bond]

[2] *Royal-Exchange*: The Royal Exchange, in London's central financial district on Threadneedle Street, provided a meeting place for businessmen and housed nearly two hundred shops. The first Royal Exchange was established by Sir Thomas Gresham (1518–1579) in 1566–68. This building was destroyed in the Great Fire of London (1666), and the Exchange was rebuilt in 1669 from designs by Edward Jarman.

[3] *High-Change*: The busiest period of the day on the Exchange.

and Oceans, or live on the different Extremities of a Continent. I have often been pleased to hear Disputes adjusted between an Inhabitant of *Japan* and an Alderman of *London*, or to see a Subject of the *Great Mogul* entering into a League with one of the *Czar* of *Muscovy*. I am infinitely delighted in mixing with these several Ministers of Commerce, as they are distinguished by their different Walks and different Languages: Sometimes I am justled among a Body of *Armenians*: Sometimes I am lost in a Crowd of *Jews*, and sometimes make one in a Groupe of *Dutch-men*. I am a *Dane, Swede,* or *French-Man* at different times, or rather fancy my self like the old Philosopher, who upon being asked what Country-man he was, replied, That he was a Citizen of the World.[4]

Though I very frequently visit this busie Multitude of People, I am known to no Body there but my Friend, Sir ANDREW, who often smiles upon me as he sees me bustling in the Croud, but at the same time connives at my Presence without taking any further notice of me. There is indeed a Merchant of *Egypt*, who just knows me by sight, having formerly remitted me some Mony to *Grand Cairo*; but as I am not versed in the Modern *Coptick*, our Conferences go no further than a Bow and a Grimace.[5]

This grand Scene of Business gives me an infinite Variety of solid and substantial Entertainments. As I am a great Lover of Mankind, my Heart naturally overflows with Pleasure at the sight of a prosperous and happy Multitude, insomuch that at many publick Solemnities I cannot forbear expressing my Joy with Tears that have stolen down my Cheeks. For this reason I am wonderfully delighted to see such a Body of Men thriving in their own private Fortunes, and at the same time promoting the Publick Stock; or in other Words, raising Estates for their own Families, by bringing into their Country whatever is wanting, and carrying out of it whatever is superfluous.

Nature seems to have taken a particular Care to disseminate her Blessings among the different Regions of the World, with an Eye to this mutual Intercourse and Traffick among Mankind, that the Natives of the several Parts of the Globe might have a kind of Dependance upon one another, and be united together by their common Interest. Almost every *Degree* produces something peculiar to it.

---

[4] *Citizen of the World:* The old philosopher who gave this answer was Diogenes the Cynic, according to Diogenes Laertius (6.63) [Bond]. Diogenes (c. 440–323 B.C.) was a Greek philosopher who championed the natural life and rejected conventional standards of human happiness, including personal property and personal relationships.

[5] *Grimace:* Here, a facial expression acknowledging acquaintance.

The Food often grows in one Country, and the Sauce in another. The Fruits of *Portugal* are corrected by the Products of *Barbadoes*: The Infusion of a *China* Plant sweetned with the Pith of an *Indian* Cane: The *Philippick* Islands[6] give a Flavour to our *European* Bowls. The single Dress of a Woman of Quality is often the Product of an hundred Climates. The Muff and the Fan come together from the different Ends of the Earth. The Scarf is sent from the Torrid Zone, and the Tippet from beneath the Pole. The Brocade Petticoat rises out of the Mines of *Peru*,[7] and the Diamond Necklace out of the Bowels of *Indostan.*

If we consider our own Country in its natural Prospect, without any of the Benefits and Advantages of Commerce, what a barren uncomfortable Spot of Earth falls to our Share! Natural Historians tell us, that no Fruit grows originally among us, besides Hips and Haws, Acorns and Pig-Nutts, with other Delicacies of the like Nature; That our Climate of it self, and without the Assistances of Art, can make no further Advances towards a Plumb than to a Sloe, and carries an Apple to no greater a Perfection than a Crab: That our Melons, our Peaches, our Figs, our Apricots, and Cherries, are Strangers among us, imported in different Ages, and naturalized in our *English* Gardens; and that they would all degenerate and fall away into the Trash of our own Country, if they were wholly neglected by the Planter, and left to the Mercy of our Sun and Soil. Nor has Traffick more enriched our Vegetable World, than it has improved the whole Face of Nature among us. Our Ships are laden with the Harvest of every Climate: Our Tables are stored with Spices, and Oils, and Wines: Our Rooms are filled with Pyramids of *China*, and adorned with the Workmanship of *Japan*: Our Morning's-Draught comes to us from the remotest Corners of the Earth: We repair our Bodies by the Drugs of *America*, and repose our selves under *Indian* Canopies. My Friend Sir ANDREW calls the Vineyards of *France* our Gardens; the Spice-Islands our Hot-Beds; the *Persians* our Silk-Weavers, and the *Chinese* our Potters. Nature indeed furnishes us with the bare Necessaries of Life, but Traffick gives us a great Variety of what is Useful, and at the same time supplies us with every thing that is Convenient and Ornamental. Nor is it the least part of this our Happiness, that whilst we enjoy the remotest Products of the North and South, we are free from those Extremities of Weather which give them Birth; That our Eyes

---

[6] *Philippick Islands:* The Philippines.
[7] *Mines of Peru:* The garment is embroidered with thread made of silver from Peru.

are refreshed with the green Fields of *Britain*, at the same time that our Palates are feasted with Fruits that rise between the Tropicks.

For these Reasons there are not more useful Members in a Commonwealth than Merchants. They knit Mankind together in a mutual Intercourse of good Offices, distribute the Gifts of Nature, find Work for the Poor, add Wealth to the Rich, and Magnificence to the Great. Our *English* Merchant converts the Tin of his own Country into Gold, and exchanges his Wooll for Rubies. The *Mahometans* are cloathed in our *British* Manufacture, and the Inhabitants of the Frozen Zone warmed with the Fleeces of our Sheep.

When I have been upon the '*Change*, I have often fancied one of our old Kings standing in Person, where he is represented in Effigy, and looking down upon the wealthy Concourse of People with which that Place is every Day filled. In this Case, how would he be surprized to hear all the Languages of *Europe* spoken in this little Spot of his former Dominions, and to see so many private Men, who in his Time would have been the Vassals of some powerful Baron, Negotiating like Princes for greater Sums of Mony than were formerly to be met with in the Royal Treasury! Trade, without enlarging the *British* Territories, has given us a kind of additional Empire: It has multiplied the Number of the Rich, made our Landed Estates infinitely more Valuable than they were formerly, and added to them an Accession of other Estates as Valuable as the Lands themselves.

No. 82
Monday, June 4, 1711
[Steele on Being in Debt]

... *Caput domina venale sub hasta.*[1]
— Juv.

Passing under *Ludgate*[2] the other Day I heard a Voice bawling for Charity, which I thought I had somewhere heard before. Coming near to the Grate the Prisoner called me by my Name, and desired I would throw something into the Box: I was out of Countenance for

[1] ... *Caput domina venale sub hasta:* From Juvenal, *Satires* 3.33: "Or put up slaves for sale under the authority of the spear" [Bond].

[2] *Ludgate:* A debtors' prison in the City, situated on the east side of Ludgate Street. At this time, creditors could have their debtors imprisoned until the debt was paid.

him, and did as he bid me, by putting in half a Crown. I went away reflecting upon the strange Constitution of some Men, and how meanly then behave themselves in all Sorts of Conditions. The Person who begged of me is now, as I take it, Fifty: I was well acquainted with him till about the Age of Twenty five; at which Time a good Estate fell to him, by the Death of a Relation. Upon coming to this unexpected good Fortune, he ran into all the Extravagancies imaginable; was frequently in drunken Disputes, broke Drawers[3] Heads, talked and swore loud; was unmannerly to those above him, and insolent to those below him. I could not but remark that it was the same Baseness of Spirit which worked in his Behaviour in both Fortunes: The same little Mind was insolent in Riches, and shameless in Poverty. This Accident made me muse upon the Circumstance of being in Debt in general, and solve in my Mind what Tempers were most apt to fall into this Errour of Life, as well as the Misfortune it must needs be to languish under such Pressures. As for my self, my natural Aversion to that Sort of Conversation which makes a Figure with the Generality of Mankind, exempts me from any Temptations to Expence; and all my Business lies within a very narrow Compass, which is, only to give an honest Man who takes care of my Estate proper Vouchers for his quarterly Payments to me, and observe what Linnen my Laundress brings and takes away with her once a Week: My Steward brings his Receipt ready for my signing, and I have a pretty Implement with the respective Names of Shirts, Cravats, Handkerchiefs and Stockings, with proper Numbers to know how to reckon with my Laundress. This being almost all the Business I have in the World for the Care of my own Affairs, I am at full Leisure to observe upon what others do, with Relation to their Equipage and Oeconomy.

When I walk the Street, and observe the Hurry about me in this Town,

> *Where with like Haste, tho' different Ways, they run,*
> *Some to undo, and some to be undone.*[4]

I say, when I behold this vast Variety of Persons and Humours, with the Pains they both take for the Accomplishment of the Ends mentioned in the above Verses of *Denham*, I cannot much wonder at the Endeavor after Gain; but am extremely astonished that Men can be

---

[3] *Drawers:* Men who drew drinks at taverns; waiters and bartenders.
[4] *Where . . . to be undone:* From John Denham's (1615–1669) *Coopers Hill* (see Cultural Contexts, p. 243).

so insensible of the Danger of running into Debt. One would think it impossible a Man who is given to contract Debts should know, that his Creditor has from that Moment in which he transgresses Payment, so much as that Demand comes to in his Debtor's Honour, Liberty and Fortune. One would think he did not know that his Creditor can say the worst thing imaginable of him, to wit, *That he is unjust*, without Defamation, and can sieze his Person without being guilty of an Assault. Yet such is the loose and abandoned Turn of some Mens Minds, that they can live under these constant Apprehensions, and still go on to encrease the Cause of them. Can there be a more low and servile Condition, than to be ashamed, or afraid, to see any one Man breathing? yet he that is much in debt, is in that Condition with relation to twenty different People. There are indeed Circumstances wherein Men of honest Natures may become liable to Debts, by some unadvised Behaviour in any great Point of their Life, or mortgaging a Man's Honesty as a Security for that of another, and the like; but these Instances are so particular and circumstantiated, that they cannot come within general Considerations: For one such Case as one of these, there are, where a Man, to keep up a Farce of Retinue and Grandeur within his own House, shall shrink at the Expectation of surly Demands at his Doors. The Debtor is the Creditor's Criminal, and all the Officers of Power and State whom we behold make so great a Figure, are no other than so many Persons in Authority to make good his Charge against him. Humane Society depends upon his having the Vengeance Law allots him; and the Debtor owes his Liberty to his Neighbour, as much as the Murderer does his Life to his Prince.

Our Gentry are, generally speaking, in debt; and many Families have put it into a kind of Method of being so from Generation to Generation. The Father mortgages when his Son is very young, and the Boy is to marry as soon as he is at Age, to redeem it, and find Portions for his Sisters. This, forsooth, is no great Inconvenience to him, for he may wench, keep a publick Table, or feed Dogs like a worthy *English* Gentleman, till he has outrun half his Estate, and leave the same Incumbrance upon his First-born, and so on, till one Man of more Vigour than ordinary goes quite thorough the Estate, or some Man of Sense comes into it, and scorns to have an Estate in Partnership, that is to say, liable to the Demand or Insult of any Man living. There is my Friend Sir ANDREW, tho' for many Years a great and general Trader, was never the Defendant in a Law Suit, in all the Perplexity of Business, and the Iniquity of Mankind at present: No one had any Colour for the least Complaint against his Dealings with him. This is certainly as uncommon, and in its Proportion as laudable in a Citizen, as it is in a General never to have suffered a Disadvantage in Fight. How different from this Gentleman is *Jack Truepenny*, who has been an old Acquaintance of Sir ANDREW and my self from Boys, but could never learn our Caution. *Jack* has a whorish unresisting good Nature, which makes him incapable of having a Property in any thing. His Fortune, his Reputation, his Time, and his Capacity, are at any Man's Service that comes first. When he was at School he was whipp'd thrice a Week for Faults he took upon him to excuse others; since he came into the Business of the World, he has been arrested twice or thrice a Year for Debts he had nothing to do with but as Surety for others; and I remember when a Friend of his had suffered in the Vice of the Town, all the Physick his Friend took was conveyed to him by *Jack*, and inscribed, 'A Bolus or an Electuary for Mr. *Truepenny*.' *Jack* had a good Estate left him, which came to nothing; because he believed all who pretended to Demands upon it. This Easiness and Credulity destroy all the other Merit he has; and he has all his Life been a Sacrifice to others, without ever receiving Thanks or doing one good Action.

I will end this Discourse with a Speech which I heard *Jack* make to one of his Creditors (of whom he deserved gentler Usage) after lying a whole Night in Custody at his Suit.

SIR,

'Your Ingratitude for the many Kindnesses I have done you, shall not make me unthankful for the Good you have done me, in letting me see there is such a Man as you in the World. I am obliged to you for the Difference I shall have all the rest of my Life: *I shall hereafter trust no Man so far as to be in his Debt.*'

No. 114
Wednesday, July 11, 1711
[Steele on Extravagance]

. . . Paupertatis pudor & fuga . . .[1]
— Hor.

Oeconomy in our Affairs, has the same Effect upon our Fortunes which good Breeding has upon our Conversations. There is a pretending Behaviour in both Cases, which instead of making Men esteemed, renders them both miserable and comtemptible. We had Yesterday at Sir ROGER's a Set of Country Gentlemen who dined with him; and after Dinner the Glass was taken, by those who pleased, pretty plentifully. Among others I observed a Person of a tolerable good Aspect, who seemed to be more greedy of Liquor than any of the Company, and yet, methought, he did not taste it with Delight. As he grew warm, he was suspicious of every thing that was said; and as he advanced towards being fudled, his Humour grew worse. At the same Time his Bitterness seemed to be rather an inward Dissatisfaction in his own Mind, than any Dislike he had taken at the Company. Upon hearing his Name, I knew him to be a Gentleman of a considerable Fortune in this Country, but greatly in Debt. What gives the unhappy Man this Peevishness of Spirit, is, that his Estate is dipp'd,[2] and is eating out with Usury; and yet he has not the Heart to sell any Part of it. His proud Stomach, at the Cost of restless Nights, constant Inquietudes, Danger of Affronts, and a thousand nameless Inconveniences, preserves this Canker in his Fortune, rather than it shall be said he is a Man of fewer Hundreds a Year than he has been commonly reputed. Thus he endures the Torment of Poverty, to avoid the Name of being less rich. If you go to his House you see great Plenty; but served in a Manner that shews it is all unnatural, and that the Master's Mind is not at home. There is a certain Waste and Carelesness in the Air of every thing, and the whole appears but a covered Indigence, a magnificent Poverty. That Neatness and Chearfulness which attends the Table of him who lives within Compass, is wanting, and exchanged for a libertine Way of Service in all about him.

This Gentleman's Conduct, tho' a very common way of Management, is as ridiculous as that Officer's would be, who had but few

---

[1] *. . . Paupertatis pudor & fuga . . .*: From Horace, *Epistles* 1.18.24: "The shame and dread of being poor" [Bond].

[2] *dipp'd:* Mortgaged.

Men under his Command, and should take the Charge of an Extent of Country rather than a small Pass. To pay for, personate, and keep in a Man's Hands, a greater Estate than he really has, is of all others the most unpardonable Vanity, and must in the End reduce the Man who is guilty of it to Dishonour. Yet if we look round us in any County of *Great-Britain*, we shall see many in this fatal Errour, if that may be call'd by so soft a Name, which proceeds from a false Shame of appearing what they really are, when the contrary Behaviour would in a short Time advance them to the Condition which they pretend to.

Laertes has fifteen hundred Pounds a Year, which is mortgaged for six thousand Pounds; but it is impossible to convince him, that if he sold as much as would pay off that Debt he would save four Shillings in the Pound, which he gives for the Vanity of being the reputed Master of it. But if *Laertes* did this, he would, perhaps, be easier in his own Fortune, but then *Irus*, a Fellow of Yesterday, who has but twelve hundred a Year, would be his Equal. Rather than this shall be, *Laertes* goes on to bring well-born Beggars into the World, and every Twelve-month charges his Estate with at least one Year's Rent more by the Birth of a Child.

Laertes and *Irus* are neighbours, whose Way of living are an Abomination to each other. *Irus* is moved by the Fear of Poverty, and *Laertes* by the Shame of it. Though the Motive of Action is of so near Affinity in both, and may be resolved into this, 'That to each of them Poverty is the greatest of all Evils, yet are their Manners very widely different.' Shame of Poverty makes *Laertes* launch into unnecessary Equipage, vain Expence, and lavish Entertainments; Fear of Poverty makes *Irus* allow himself only plain Necessaries, appear without a Servant, sell his own Corn, attend his Labourers, and be himself a Labourer. Shame of Poverty makes *Laertes* go every Day a Step nearer to it; and Fear of Poverty stirs up *Irus* to make every Day some further Progress from it.

These different Motives produce the Excesses which Men are guilty of in the Negligence of and Provision for themselves. Usury, Stock-Jobbing, Extortion and Oppression, have their Seed in the Dread of Want; and Vanity, Riot and Prodigality from the Shame of it: But both these Excesses are infinitely below the Pursuit of a reasonable Creature. After we have taken Care to command so much as is necessary for maintaining our selves in the Order of Men suitable to our Character, the Care of Superfluities is a Vice no less extravagant, than the Neglect of Necessaries would have been before.

Certain it is that they are both out of Nature when she is followed with Reason and good Sense. It is from this Reflection that I always read Mr. *Cowley*[3] with the greatest Pleasure: His Magnanimity is as much above that of other considerable Men as his Understanding; and it is a true distinguishing Spirit in the elegant Author[4] who published his Works, to dwell so much upon the Temper of his Mind and the Moderation of his Desires: By this Means he has render'd his Friend as amiable as famous. That State of Life which bears the Face of Poverty with Mr. *Cowley*'s *great Vulgar*,[5] is admirably described; and it is no small Satisfaction to those of the same Turn of Desire, that he produces the Authority of the wisest Men of the best Age of that World, to strengthen his Opinion of the ordinary Pursuits of Mankind.

It would methinks be no ill Maxim of Life, if, according to that Ancestor of Sir ROGER whom I lately mentioned, every Man would point to himself what Sum he would resolve not to exceed. He might by this Means cheat himself into a Tranquility on this Side of that Expectation, or convert what he should get above it to nobler Uses than his own Pleasures or Necessities. This Temper of Mind would exempt a Man from an ignorant Envy of restless Men above him, and a more inexcusable Contempt of happy Men below him. This would be sailing by some Compass, living with some Design; but to be eternally bewildered in Prospects of future Gain, and putting on unnecessary Armour against improbable Blows of Fortune, is a Mechanick Being which has not good Sense for its Direction, but is carried on by a Sort of acquired Instinct towards things below our Consideration and unworthy our Esteem. It is possible that the Tranquility I now enjoy at Sir ROGER's may have created in me this Way of Thinking, which is so abstracted from the common Relish of the World: But as I am now in a pleasing Arbour surrounded with a beautiful Landskip, I find no Inclination so strong as to continue in these Mansions, so remote from the ostentatious Scenes of Life; and am at this present Writing Philosopher enough to conclude with Mr. *Cowley*;

---

[3] *Mr. Cowley:* Abraham Cowley (1618–1667), seventeenth-century English metaphysical poet.

[4] *the elegant Author:* Thomas Sprat, who prefixed "An Account of the Life and Writings of Mr. Abraham Cowley" to Cowley's *Works* (1668) [Bond].

[5] *Mr. Cowley's great Vulgar:* From the opening paragraph of Cowley's essay "Of Greatness" [Bond].

If e'er Ambition did my Fancy cheat,
With any Wish so mean as to be Great;
Continue, Heav'n, still from me to remove,
The humble Blessings of that Life I love.[6]

From No. 155
Tuesday, August 28, 1711
[Steele on Women Proprietors of Coffeehouses and Shops]

> ... *Hæ nugæ seria ducunt*
> *In mala ...*[1]
> — Hor.

I have more than once taken Notice of an indecent License taken in Discourse, wherein the Conversation on one Part is involuntary, and the Effect of some necessary Circumstance. This happens in travelling together in the same hired Coach, sitting near each other in any publick Assembly, or the like. I have upon making Observations of this sort received innumerable Messages, from that Part of the fair Sex, whose Lot in Life it is to be of any Trade or publick Way of Life. They are all to a Woman urgent with me to lay before the World the unhappy Circumstances they are under, from the unreasonable Liberty which is taken in their Presence, to talk on what Subject it is thought fit by every Coxcomb who wants Understanding or Breeding. One or two of these Complaints I shall set down.

Mr. SPECTATOR,

'I keep a Coffee-house, and am one of those whom you have thought fit to mention as an Idol[2] some Time ago: I suffered a good deal of Raillery upon that Occasion; but shall heartily forgive you, who were the Cause of it, if you will do me Justice in another Point. What I ask of you, is to acquaint my Customers (who are otherwise

---

[6] ... *Life I love:* Also from Cowley's "Of Greatness" [Bond].

[1] ... *Hæ nugæ seria ducunt / In mala ...:* From Horace, *Ars Poetica* 451 (altered; used also as motto for Tatlers Nos. 103 and 269): "These things which now seem frivolous and slight, / Will prove of serious consequence" — ROSCOMMON [Bond].

[2] *Idol:* Mentioned in *Spectator* Nos. 73 and 87, an Idol is a female type "wholly taken up in the Adorning of her Person" in order to seduce men (see *Spectator* No. 73, p. 506).

very good ones) that I am unavoidably hasped in my Bar, and cannot help hearing the improper Discourses they are pleased to entertain me with. They strive who shall say the most immodest things in my Hearing: At the same time half a dozen of them loll at the Bar staring just in my Face, ready to interpret my Looks and Gestures, according to their own Imaginations. In this passive Condition I know not where to cast my Eyes, place my Hands, or what to employ my self in: But this Confusion is to be a Jest, and I hear them say in the End, with an insipid Air of Mirth and Subtlety, Let her alone, she knows as well as we for all she looks so. Good Mr. SPECTATOR, perswade Gentlemen that this is out of all Decency. Say it is possible a Woman may be modest, and yet keep a publick House. Be pleas'd to argue, that in Truth the Affront is the more unpardonable because I am obliged to suffer it, and cannot fly from it. I do assure you, Sir, the Chearfulness of Life which would arise from the honest Gain I have, is utterly lost to me from the endless, flat, impertinent Pleasantries which I hear from Morning to Night. In a Word, it is too much for me to bear, and I desire you to acquaint them, that I will keep Pen and Ink at the Bar and write down all they say to me, and send it to you for the Press. It is possible when they see how empty they speak, without the Advantage of an impudent Countenance and Gesture, will appear, they may come to some Sense of themselves, and the Insults they are guilty of towards me. I am,

Sir,

Your most humble Servant,

The Idol.'

This Representation is so just, that it is hard to speak of it without an Indignation which perhaps would appear too elevated to such as can be guilty of this inhumane Treatment, where they see they affront a modest, plain, and ingenuous Behaviour. This Correspondent is not the only Sufferer in this Kind, for I have long Letters both from the *Royal* and *New Exchange*[3] on the same Subject. They tell me that a young Fop cannot buy a Pair of Gloves, but he is at the same Time

---

[3] *Royal and New Exchange:* The Royal Exchange, in London's central financial district on Threadneedle Street, provided a meeting place for businessmen and housed nearly two hundred shops. The first Royal Exchange was established by Sir Thomas Gresham (1518–1579) in 1566–68. This building was destroyed in the Great Fire of London (1666). The Exchange was rebuilt in 1669 from designs by Edward Jarman. The New Exchange was an emporium of stalls in the Strand where fashionable goods were sold. It was built in 1608–09, and gained in popularity after the Restoration (1660), especially after the Great Fire, when it took over much of the business of the Royal Exchange. The New Exchange was demolished in 1737.

straining for some ingenious Ribaldry to say to the young Woman who helps them on. It is no small Addition to the Calamity, that the Rogues buy as hard[4] as the plainest and modestest Customers they have; besides which they loll upon their Counters half an Hour longer than they need, to drive away other Customers, who are to share their Impertinencies with the Milliner, or go to another Shop. Letters from '*Change Alley*[5] are full of the same Evil, and the Girls tell me except I can chace some eminent Merchants from their Shops they shall in a short Time fail. It is very unaccountable, that Men can have so little Deference to all Mankind who pass by them, as to bear being seen toying by two's and three's at a Time, with no other Purpose but to appear gay enough to keep up a light Conversation of commonplace Jests, to the Injury of her whose Credit is certainly hurt by it, tho' their own may be strong enough to bear it. When we come to have exact Accounts of these Conversations, it is not to be doubted but that their Discourses will raise the usual Stile of buying and selling: Instead of the plain down-right lying, and asking and bidding so unequally to what they will really give and take, we may hope to have from these fine Folks an Exchange of Complements. There must certainly be a great deal of pleasant Difference between the Commerce of Lovers, and that of all other Dealers, who are, in a Kind, Adversaries. A sealed Bond or a Bank Note, would be a pretty Gallantry to convey unseen into the Hands of one whom a Director is charmed with; otherwise the City Loiterers are still more unreasonable than those at the other End of the Town: At the *New Exchange* they are eloquent for want of Cash, but in the City they ought with Cash to supply their want of Eloquence.

If one might be serious on this prevailing Folly, one might observe, that it is a melancholy thing, when the World is mercenary even to the buying and selling our very Persons, that young Women, tho' they have never so great Attractions from Nature, are never the nearer being happily disposed of in Marriage; I say it is very hard under this Necessity, it shall not be possible for them to go into a Way of Trade for their Maintenance, but their very Excellences and personal Perfections shall be a Disadvantage to them, and subject them to be treated as if they stood there to sell their Persons to Prostitution. There cannot be a more melancholy Circumstance to one who has made any Observation in the World, than one of these erring

---

[4] *buy as hard:* Drive a hard bargain in order to pay as little as possible.

[5] '*Change Alley:* A small but busy mercantile street running between Cornhill and Lombard Streets in the City, in front of the Royal Exchange on Threadneedle Street.

Creatures exposed to Bankrupcy. When that happens, none of these toying Fools will do any more than any other Man they meet to preserve her from Infamy, Insult, and Distemper. A Woman is naturally more helpless than the other Sex; and a Man of Honour and Sense should have this in his View in all Manner of Commerce with her. Were this well weighed, Inconsideration, Ribaldry, and Nonsence would not be more natural to entertain Women with than Men; and it would be as much Impertinence to go into a Shop of one of these young Women without buying, as into that of any other Trader.

No. 174
Wednesday, September 19, 1711
[Steele on the Debate between Sir Roger de Coverly and Sir Andrew Freeport]

Hæc memini & victum frustra contendere Thyrsin.[1]
— Virg.

There is scarce any thing more common than Animosities between Parties that cannot subsist but by their Agreement: This was well represented in the Sedition of the Members of the human Body in the old *Roman* Fable.[2] It is often the Case of lesser confederate States against a superiour Power, which are hardly held together though their Unanimity is necessary for their common Safety: And this is always the Case of the landed and trading Interest of *Great Britain*; the Trader is fed by the Product of the Land, and the landed Man cannot be cloathed but by the Skill of the Trader; and yet those Interests are ever jarring.

We had last Winter an Instance of this at our Club, in Sir ROGER DE COVERLY and Sir ANDREW FREEPORT, between whom there is generally a constant, though friendly, Opposition of Opinions. It happened that one of the Company, in an historical Discourse, was observing, that *Carthaginian* Faith[3] was a proverbial Phrase to intimate Breach of Leagues. Sir ROGER said it could hardly be otherwise:

[1] *Hæc . . . Thyrsin:* From Virgil, *Eclogues* 7.69: "These rhymes I did to memory commend, / When vanquish'd Thyrsis did in vain contend" — DRYDEN [Bond].

[2] *Roman Fable:* The fable of the interdependence of the parts of the body (Livy, *History* 2.32, and elsewhere). . . . In L'Estrange's *Fables of Aesop* (1692) it is Fable No. 50 [Bond].

[3] *Carthaginian Faith:* The North African (modern Tunisia) Carthaginians were a great commercial nation in the ancient Mediterranean world. Founded by the Phoenicians in the ninth century B.C., Carthage was a military rival of Rome.

That the *Carthaginians* were the greatest Traders in the World; and as Gain is the chief End of such a People; they never pursue any other: The Means to it are never regarded; they will, if it comes easily, get Money honestly; but if not, they will not scruple to attain it by Fraud or Cosenage: And indeed what is the whole Business of the Trader's Accompt, but to over-reach him who trusts to his Memory? But were that not so, what can there great and noble be expected from him whose Attention is for ever fixed upon ballancing his Books, and watching over his Expences? And at best, let Frugality and Parsimony be the Virtues of the Merchant, how much is his punctual Dealing below a Gentleman's Charity to the Poor, or Hospitality among his Neighbours?

Captain SENTRY observed Sir ANDREW very diligent in hearing Sir ROGER, and had a Mind to turn the Discourse, by taking Notice in general from the highest to the lowest Parts of human Society, there was a secret, tho' unjust Way among Men, of indulging the Seeds of ill Nature and Envy, by comparing their own State of Life to that of another, and grudging the Approach of their Neighbour to their own Happiness; and on the other Side, he who is the less at his Ease repines as the other who, he thinks, has unjustly the Advantage over him. Thus the civil and military List look upon each other with much ill Nature; the Soldier repines at the Courtier's Power, and the Courtier rallies the Soldier's Honour; or to come to lower Instances, the private Men in the Horse and Foot of an Army, the Carmen and Coachmen in the City-streets, mutually look upon each other with ill Will, when they are in Competition for Quarters or the Way in their respective Motions.

It is very well, good Captain, interrupted Sir ANDREW: You may attempt to turn the Discourse, if you think fit, but I must however have a Word or two with Sir ROGER; who, I see, thinks he has paid me off, and been very severe upon the Merchant. I shall not, continued he, at this Time remind Sir ROGER of the great and noble Monuments of Charity and publick Spirit which have been erected by Merchants since the Reformation,[4] but at present content my self with what he allows us, Parsimony and Frugality. If it were consistent with

---

[4] *Reformation:* A sixteenth-century religious movement aimed at reforming the Roman Catholic Church in Western Europe that resulted in the establishment of Protestant religions. Its three great leaders were Martin Luther (1483–1546) in Germany, John Calvin (1509–1564) in Geneva, and John Knox (c. 1514–1572) in Scotland. Protestants stressed the authority of scriptures over that of priests and justification by faith rather than by works, and they rejected the doctrine of transubstantiation, the cult of the Virgin Mary, and the authority of the pope.

the Quality of so antient a Baronet as Sir ROGER, to keep an Accompt or measure things by the most infallible Way, that of Numbers, he would prefer our Parsimony to his Hospitality. If to drink so many Hogsheads is to be hospitable, we do not contend for the Fame of that Virtue; but it would be worth while to consider, whether so many Artificers at work ten Days together by my Appointment, or so many Peasants made merry on Sir ROGER's Charge, are the Men more obliged: I believe the Families of the Artificers will thank me, more than the Housholds of the Peasants shall Sir ROGER. Sir ROGER gives to his Men, but I place mine above the Necessity or Obligation of my Bounty. I am in very little Pain for the *Roman* Proverb upon the *Carthaginian* Traders; the *Romans* were their professed Enemies: I am only sorry no *Carthaginian* Histories have come to our Hands; we might have been taught perhaps by them some Proverbs against the *Roman* Generosity, in fighting for and bestowing other People's Goods. But since Sir ROGER has taken Occasion from an old Proverb to be out of Humour with Merchants, it should be no Offence to offer one not quite so old in their Defence. When a Man happens to break[5] in *Holland*, they say of him that *he has not kept true Accompts.* This Phrase, perhaps, among us would appear a soft or humorous way of speaking, but with that exact Nation it bears the highest Reproach; for a Man to be mistaken in the Calculation of his Expence, in his Ability to answer future Demands, or to be impertinently sanguine in putting his Credit to too great Adventure, are all Instances of as much Infamy, as with gayer Nations to be failing in Courage or common Honesty.

Numbers are so much the Measure of every thing that is valuable, that it is not possible to demonstrate the Success of any Action or the Prudence of any Undertaking without them. I say this in Answer to what Sir ROGER is pleased to say, That little that is truly noble can be expected from one who is ever poring on his Cash-book or ballancing his Accompts. When I have my Returns from abroad, I can tell to a Shilling by the Help of Numbers the Profit or Loss by my Adventure; but I ought also to be able to shew that I had Reason for making it, either from my own Experience or that of other People, or from a reasonable Presumption that my Returns will be sufficient to answer my Expence and Hazard; and this is never to be done without the Skill of Numbers. For Instance, if I am to trade to *Turkey*, I ought before-hand to know the Demand of our Manufactures there as well

---

[5] *to break:* To go bankrupt.

as of their Silks in *England*, and the customary Prices that are given for both in each Country. I ought to have a clear Knowledge of these Matters before-hand, that I may presume upon sufficient Returns to answer the Charge of the Cargo I have fitted out, the Freight and Assurance out and home, the Customs to the Queen, and the Interest of my own Money, and besides all these Expences a reasonable Profit for my self. Now what is there of Scandal in this Skill? What has the Merchant done that he should be so little in the good Graces of Sir Roger? he throws down no Man's Enclosures,[6] and tramples upon no Man's Corn; he takes nothing from the industrious Labourer; he pays the poor Man for his Work; he communicates his Profit with Mankind; by the Preparation of his Cargo and the Manufacture of his Returns, he furnishes Employment and Subsistance to greater Numbers than the richest Nobleman; and even the Nobleman is oblig'd to him for finding out foreign Markets for the Produce of his Estate, and for making a great Addition to his Rents; and yet 'tis certain that none of all these things could be done by him without the Exercise of his Skill in Numbers.

This is the Oeconomy of the Merchant, and the Conduct of the Gentleman must be the same, unless by scorning to be the Steward, he resolves the Steward shall be the Gentleman. The Gentleman no more than the Merchant is able without the Help of Numbers to account for the Success of any Action or the Prudence of any Adventure. If, for Instance, the Chace is his whole Adventure, his only Returns must be the Stag's Horns in the great Hall, and the Fox's Nose upon the Stable Door. Without Doubt Sir Roger knows the full Value of these Returns; and if before-hand he had computed the Charges of the Chace, a Gentleman of his Discretion would certainly have hang'd up all his Dogs, he would never have brought back so many fine Horses to the Kennel, he would never have gone so often like a Blast over Fields of Corn. If such too had been the Conduct of all his Ancestors, he might truly have boasted at this Day that the Antiquity of his Family had never been sullied by a Trade; a Merchant had never been permitted with his whole Estate to purchase a Room for his Picture in the Gallery of the Coverlys, or to claim his Descent from the Maid of Honour. But 'tis very happy for Sir Roger that the Merchant paid so dear for his Ambition. 'Tis the Misfortune of many other Gentlemen to turn out of the Seats of their Ancestors, to make Way for such new Masters as have been more exact in their

---

[6] *Enclosures:* Private fields that are fenced or hedged in.

Accompts than themselves; and certainly he deserves the Estate a great deal better who has got it by his Industry, than he who has lost it by his Negligence.

No. 218
Friday, November 9, 1711
[Steele on Reputation and Credit]

> *Quid de quoque viro & cui dicas sæpe caveto.*[1]
> — Hor.

I happened the other Day, as my Way is, to strole into a little Coffee-house beyond *Aldgate*;[2] and as I sat there, two or three very plain sensible Men were talking of the SPECTATOR. One said, he had that Morning drawn the great Benefit Ticket; another wished he had; but a third shaked his Head and said, it was pity that the Writer of that Paper was such a sort of Man, that it was no great Matter whether he had it or no. He is, it seems, said the good Man, the most extravagant Creature in the World; has run through vast Sums, and yet been in continual Want; a Man, for all he talks so well of Oeconomy, unfit for any of the Offices of Life, by reason of his Profuseness. It would be an unhappy thing to be his Wife, his Child, or his Friend; and yet he talks as well of those Duties of Life as any one. Much Reflection has brought me to so easy a Contempt for every thing which is false, that this heavy Accusation gave me no Manner of Uneasiness; but at the same Time it threw me into deep Thought upon the Subject of Fame in general; and I could not but pity such as were so weak, as to value what the common People say out of their own talkative Temper, to the Advantage or Diminution of those whom they mention, without being moved either by Malice or Good-will. It would be too long to expatiate upon the Sense all Mankind have of Fame, and the inexpressible Pleasure which there is in the Approbation of worthy Men, to all who are capable of worthy Actions; but methinks one may divide the general Word Fame into three different Species, as it regards the different Orders of Mankind who have any thing to do with it. Fame therefore may be divided into Glory, which respects the

---

[1] *Quid . . . caveto:* From Horace, *Epistles* 1.18.68: "Take heed of whom you speak, and what it is, / Take heed to whom. . . ." — CREECH [Bond].

[2] *Aldgate:* A section in the eastern part of the City, north of the Tower of London.

Hero; Reputation, which is preserved by every Gentleman; and Credit, which much be supported by every Tradesman. These Possessions in Fame are dearer than Life to those Characters of Men, or rather are the Life of these Characters. Glory, while the Hero pursues great and noble Enterprizes, is impregnable; and all the Assailants of his Renown do but shew their Pain and Impatience of its Brightness, without throwing the least Shade upon it. If the Foundation of an high Name be Virtue and Service, all that is offered against it is but Rumour, which is too short-lived to stand up in Competition with Glory, which is everlasting.

Reputation, which is the Portion of every Man who would live with the elegant and knowing Part of Mankind, is as stable as Glory if it be as well founded; and the common Cause of humane Society is thought concerned when we hear a Man of good Behaviour calumniated: Besides which, according to a prevailing Custom amongst us, every Man has his Defence in his own Arm; and Reproach is soon checked, put out of Countenance, and overtaken by Disgrace.

The most unhappy of all Men, and the most exposed to the Malignity of Wantonness of the common Voice, is the Trader. Credit is undone in Whispers: The Tradesman's Wound is received from one who is more private and more cruel than the Ruffian with the Lanthorn and Dagger. The Manner of repeating a Man's Name, As *Mr. Cash, Oh! do you leave your Money at his Shop? Why do you know Mr. Searoom? He is indeed a general Merchant.* I say, I have seen, from the Iteration of a Man's Name, hiding one Thought of him, and explaining what you hide by saying something to his Advantage when you speak, a Merchant hurt in his Credit; and him who every Day he lived litterally added to the Value of his native Country, undone by one who was only a Burthen and a Blemish to it. Since every Body who knows the World is sensible of this great Evil, how careful ought a Man to be in his Language of a Merchant. It may possibly be in the Power of a very shallow Creature to lay the Ruine of the best Family in the most opulent City; and the more so, the more highly he deserves of his Country; that is to say, the farther he places his Wealth out of his Hands, to draw home that of another Climate.

In this Case an ill Word may change Plenty into Want, and by a rash Sentence a free and generous Fortune may in a few Days be reduced to Beggary. How little does a giddy Prater imagine, that an idle Phrase to the Disfavour of a Merchant may be as pernicious in the Consequence, as the Forgery of a Deed to bar an Inheritance would be to a Gentleman? Land stands where it did before a Gentleman was calumniated, and the State of a great Action is just as it was before

Calumny was offered to diminish it, and there is Time, Place, and Occasion expected to unravel all that is contrived against those Characters; but the Trader who is ready only for probable Demands upon him, can have no Armour against the Inquisitive, the Malicious, and the Envious, who are prepared to fill the Cry to his Dishonour. Fire and Sword are slow Engines of Destruction, in Comparison of the Babbler in the Case of the Merchant.

For this Reason I thought it an imitable Piece of Humanity of a Gentleman of my Acquaintance, who had great Variety of Affairs, and used to talk with Warmth enough against Gentlemen by whom he thought himself ill dealt with; that he would never let any thing be urged against a Merchant (with whom he had any Difference) except in a Court of Justice. He used to say, that to speak ill of a Merchant was to begin his Suit with Judgment and Execution. One cannot, I think, say more on this Occasion, than to repeat, That the Merit of the Merchant is above that of all other Subjects; for while he is untouched in his Credit, his Hand-writing is a more portable Coin for the Service of his Fellow-Citizens, and his Word the Gold of *Ophir*[3] in the Country wherein he resides.

No. 336
Wednesday, March 26, 1712
[Steele on a Shopkeeper's Complaint]

Mr. SPECTATOR,

'I have formerly read with great Satisfaction, your Papers about Idols, and the Behaviour of Gentlemen in those Coffee-houses where Women officiate,[1] and impatiently waited to see you take India and China Shops into Consideration: But since you have pass'd us over in Silence, either that you have not as yet thought us worth your Notice, or that the Grievances we lie under have escap'd your discerning Eye, I must make my Complaints to you, and am encourag'd to do it because you seem a little at leisure at ths present Writing. I am, dear Sir, one of the top China-Women[2] about Town; and though I say it, keep

---

[3] *Ophir:* A place frequently mentioned in the Old Testament for its fine gold. Its location is uncertain [Bond].

[1] ... *where Women officiate:* See *Spectator* No. 155 on women proprietors of coffeehouses (p. 213).

[2] *China-Women:* Women who run shops selling equipment for the tea table.

as good things, and receive as fine Company as any o' this end of the Town, let the other be who she will: In short, I am in a fair way to be easy, were it not for a Club of Female Rakes,[3] who, under Pretence of taking their innocent Rambles forsooth, and diverting the Spleen,[4] seldom fail to plague me twice or thrice a Day, to cheapen[5] Tea or buy a Screen, *what else should they mean?* as they often repeat it. These Rakes are your idle Ladies of Fashion, who have nothing to do, employ themselves in tumbling over my Ware. One of these No-Customers (for by the way they seldom or never buy any thing) calls for a Set of Tea Dishes, another for a Bason, a third for my best Green Tea, and even to the Punch-Bowl there's scarce a Piece in my Shop but must be displac'd, and the whole agreeable Architecture disorder'd, so that I can compare 'em to nothing but to the Night-Goblins that take a Pleasure to over-turn the Disposition of Plates and Dishes in the Kitchens of your housewifely Maids. Well, after all this Racket and Clutter, this is too dear, that is their Aversion, another thing is charming but not wanted: The Ladies are cur'd of the Spleen, but I am not a Shilling the better for it: Lord! what signifies one poor Pot of Tea, considering the Trouble they put me to? Vapours,[6] Mr. SPECTATOR, are terrible things; for tho' I am not possess'd by 'em my self, I suffer more from 'em than if I were. Now I must beg you to admonish all such Day-Goblins, to make fewer Visits, or to be less troublesome when they come to one's Shop; and to convince 'em, that we honest Shop-keepers have something better to do, than to cure Folks of the Vapours *gratis*. A young Son of mine, a School-Boy, is my Secretary; so I hope you'll make Allowances. I am Sir,

Your constant Reader
and very humble Servant,
Rebecca *the distress'd.*'

March the 22d.

---

[3] *Rakes:* The term is commonly applied to dissolute, high-living, hooliganish, wellborn men; the female rakes here are a breed of fashionable ladies. Rather than beat up guards of the watch and break windows like their male counterparts, these ladies wreak havoc in the shops they visit.

[4] *Spleen:* According to humoral theories of physiognomy, the spleen is the site of melancholy feelings. In the eighteenth century it referred, like the term *vapors*, to a fashionable mood disorder characterized by depression, anxiety, and irritability.

[5] *cheapen:* Bargain down for a better price.

[6] *Vapours:* Understood as exhalations from corporeal organs, vapors were thought to exert a morbid effect on the health. As the name for the psychosomatic disorder that resulted, vapors, like spleen, refers to a nervous condition.

No. 442
Monday, July 28, 1712
[Steele's Call for Papers on the Theme of "Money" and One Reply]

Scribimus Indocti Doctique . . .[1]
— Hor.

I do not know whether I enough explained my self to the World, when I invited[2] all Men to be assistant to me in this my Work of Speculation; for I have not yet acquainted my Readers, that besides the Letters and valuable Hints I have from Time to Time received from my Correspondents, I have by me several curious and extraordinary Papers sent with a Design (as no one will doubt when they are publish'd) that they might be printed entire, and without any Alteration, by way of *Spectator*. I must acknowledge also, that I my self being the first Projector of the Paper, thought I had a Right to make them my own, by dressing them in my own Stile, by leaving out what wou'd not appear like mine, and by adding whatever might be proper to adapt them to the Character and Genius of my paper, with which it was almost impossible these cou'd exactly correspond, it being certain that hardly two Men think alike, and therefore so many Men so many *Spectators*. Besides, I must own my Weakness for Glory is such, that if I consulted that only, I might be so far sway'd by it, as almost to wish that no one could write a *Spectator* besides my self; nor can I deny, but upon the first Perusal of those Papers, I felt some secret Inclinations of ill Will towards the Persons who wrote them. This was the Impression I had upon the first reading them; but upon a late Review (more for the Sake of Entertainment than Use) regarding them with another Eye than I had done at first, (for by converting them as well as I cou'd to my own Use, I thought I had utterly disabled them from ever offending me again as *Spectators*) I found my self mov'd by a Passion very different from that of Envy; sensibly touch'd with Pity, the softest and most generous of all Passions, when I reflected what a cruel Disappointment the Neglect of those Papers must needs have been to the Writers, who impatiently long'd to see them appear in Print, and who, no Doubt, triumph'd to themselves in

---

[1] *Scribimus Indocti Doctique . . .* : From Horace, *Epistles* 2.1.117: "And skilful, or unskilful, all must write" — CREECH [Bond].

[2] *I invited*: In *Spectator* No. 428. For a response to letters on the theme of money proposed here, see *Spectator* No. 450 (p. 226).

the Hopes of having a Share with me in the Applause of the Publick;
a Pleasure so great, that none but those who have experienc'd it can
have a Sense of it. In this Manner of viewing those Papers, I really
found I had not done them Justice, there being something so extremely natural and peculiarly good in some of them, that I will appeal to the World whether it was possible to alter a Word in them
without doing them a manifest Hurt and Violence; and whether they
can ever appear rightly, and as they ought, but in their own native
Dress and Colours: And therefore I think I shou'd not only wrong
them, but deprive the World of a considerable Satisfaction, shou'd I
any longer delay the making them publick.

After I have publish'd a few of these *Spectators*, I doubt not but I
shall find the Success of them to equal, if not surpass, that of the best
of my own. An Author should take all Methods to humble himself in
the Opinion he has of his own Performances. When these Papers appear to the World, I doubt not but they will be followed by many
others; and I shall not repine, tho' I my self shall have left me but
very few Days to appear in Publick: But preferring the general Weal
and Advantage to any Considerations of my self, I am resolv'd for the
Future to publish any *Spectator* that deserves it, entire, and without
any Alteration; assuring the World (if there can be Need of it) that it
is none of mine; and if the Authors think fit to subscribe their Names,
I will add them.

I think the best way of promoting this generous and useful Design,
will be by giving our Subjects or Themes of all Kinds whatsoever, on
which (with a Preamble of the extraordinary Benefit and Advantage
that may accrue thereby to the Publick) I will invite all manner of
Persons, whether Scholars, Citizens, Courtiers, Gentlemen of the
Town or Country, and all Beaux, Rakes, Smarts, Prudes, Coquets,
Housewives, and all Sorts of Wits, whether Male or Female, and
however distinguish'd, whether they be True-Wits, Whole, or Half-
Wits, or whether Arch, Dry, Natural, Acquir'd, Genuine, or Deprav'd
Wits; and Persons of all Sorts of Tempers and Complexions, whether
the Severe, the Delightful, the Impertinent, the Agreeable, the
Thoughtful, Busy, or Careless; the Serene or Cloudy, Jovial or Melan-
choly, Untowardly or Easy; the Cold, Temperate, or Sanguine; and of
what Manners or Dispositions soever, whether the Ambitious or
Humble-minded, the Proud or Pitiful, Ingenuous or Base-minded,
Good or Ill-natur'd, Publick-spirited or Selfish; and under what For-
tune or Circumstance soever, whether the Contented or Miserable,
Happy or Unfortunate, High or Low, Rich or Poor (whether so thro'

Want of Money, or Desire of more), Healthy or Sickly, Marry'd or
Single; nay, whether Tall or Short, Fat or Lean; and of what Trade,
Occupation, Profession, Station, Country, Faction, Party, Perswa-
sion, Quality, Age or Condition soever, who have ever made Thinking a Part of their Business or Diversion, and have any thing worthy
to impart on these Subjects to the World, according to their several
and respective Talents or Genius's, and as the Subject given out hits
their Tempers, Humours, or Circumstances, or may be made profitable to the Publick by their particular Knowledge or Experience in
the Matter propos'd, to do their utmost on them by such a Time; to
the End they may receive the inexpressible and irresistible Pleasure of
seeing their Essays allow'd of and relish'd by the rest of Mankind.

I will not prepossess the Reader with too great Expectation of the
extraordinary Advantages which must redound to the Publick by
these Essays, when the different Thoughts and Observations of all
Sorts of Persons, according to their Quality, Age, Sex, Education,
Professions, Humours, Manners and Conditions, &c. shall be set out
by themselves in the clearest and most genuine Light, and as they
themselves wou'd wish to have them appear to the World.

The Thesis *propos'd for the present Exercise of the Adventurers to
write* Spectators, *is* MONEY, *on which Subject all Persons are desired
to send in their Thoughts within Ten Days after the Date hereof.*

No. 450
Wednesday, August 6, 1712
[Steele on the Moral Value of Money]

*. . . Quærenda pecunia primum
Virtus post nummos.*[1]

Mr. SPECTATOR,[2]

'All Men, through different Paths, make at the same common
thing, *Money*; and it is to her we owe the Politician, the Merchant,
and the Lawyer; nay, to be free with you, I believe to that also we are
beholden for our *Spectator*. I am apt to think, that could we look into

---

[1] *. . . Quærenda . . . nummos:* From Horace, *Epistles* 1.1.53–54 (altered): "Gold
must first be sought, / Then Virtue" — CREECH [Bond].

[2] *Mr.* SPECTATOR: This letter is a response to Steele's ruminations on the theme of
money in *Spectator* No. 442. It is uncertain whether this is an actual letter received
from a reader or one written by Steele himself.

our own Hearts, we should see Money ingraved in them in more lively and moving Characters than Self-Preservation; for who can reflect upon the Merchant hoisting Sail in a doubtful Pursuit of her, and all Mankind sacrificing their Quiet to her, but must perceive that the Characters of Self-Preservation (which were doubtless originally the brightest) are sullied, if not wholly defaced; and that those of Money (which at first was only valuable as a Mean to Security) are of late so brightened, that the Characters of Self-Preservation, like a less Light set by a greater, are become almost imperceptible? Thus has Money got the upper Hand of what all Mankind formerly thought most dear, *viz.* Security; and I wish I could say she had here put a Stop to her Victories; but, alass! common Honesty fell a Sacrifice to her. This is the Way Scholastick Men talk of the greatest Good in the World; but I, a Tradesman, shall give you another Account of this Matter in the plain Narrative of my own Life. I think it proper, in the first Place, to acquaint my Readers, that since my setting out in the World, which was in the Year 1660, I never wanted Money; having begun with an indifferent good Stock in the Tobacco Trade, to which I was bred; and by the continual Successes it has pleased Providence to bless my Endeavours with, am at last arrived at what they call a *Plumb.*[3] To uphold my Discourse in the Manner of your Wits or Philosophers, by speaking fine things, or drawing Inferences, as they pretend, from the Nature of the Subject, I account it vain; having never found any thing in the Writings of such Men, that did not savour more of the Invention of the Brain, or what is stiled Speculation, than of sound Judgment or profitable Observation. I will readily grant indeed, that there is what the Wits call Natural in their Talk; which is the utmost those curious Authors can assume to themselves, and is indeed all they endeavour at, for they are but lamentable Teachers. And what, I pray, is Natural? That which is Pleasing and Easy: And what are Pleasing and Easy? Forsooth, a new Thought or Conceit dressed up in smooth quaint Language, to make you smile and wag your Head, as being what you never imagined before, and yet wonder why you had not; meer frothy Amusements! fit only for Boys or silly Women to be caught with.

'It is not my present Intention to instruct my Readers in the Methods of acquiring Riches, that may be the Work of another Essay; but to exhibit the real and solid Advantages I have found by them in my long and manifold Experience: nor yet all the Advantages of so worthy and valuable a Blessing, (for who does not know or imagine the

---

[3] *Plumb: Plum* is a slang term used to denote £100,000.

Comforts of being warm or living at Ease? and that Power and Pre-heminence are their inseparable Attendants?) but only to instance the great Supports they afford us under the severest Calamities and Mis-fortunes; to shew that the Love of them is a special Antidote against Immorality and Vice, and that the same does likewise naturally dis-pose Men to Actions of Piety and Devotion: All which I can make out by my own Experience, who think my self no ways particular from the rest of Mankind, nor better nor worse by Nature than generally other Men are.

'In the year 1665, when the Sickness was,[4] I lost by it my Wife and two Children, which were all my Stock. Probably I might have had more, considering I was married between 4 and 5 Years; but finding her to be a teeming Woman, I was careful, as having then little above a Brace of thousand Pounds to carry on my Trade and maintain a Family with. I loved them as usually Men do their Wives and Chil-dren, and therefore could not resist the first Impulses of Nature on so wounding a Loss; but I quickly rouzed my self, and found Means to alleviate, and at last conquer my Affliction, by reflecting how that she and her Children having been no great Expence to me, the best Part of her Fortune was still left; that my Charge being reduced to my self, a Journeyman, and a Maid, I might live far cheaper than before; and that being now a childless Widower, I might perhaps marry a no less deserving Woman, and with a much better Fortune than she brought, which was but 800 *l.* And to convince my Readers that such Consid-erations as there were proper and apt to produce such an Effect, I re-member it was the constant Observation at that deplorable Time, when so many Hundreds were swept away daily, that the Rich ever bore the Loss of their Families and Relations far better than the Poor; the latter having little or nothing before-hand, and living from Hand to Mouth, placed the whole Comfort and Satisfaction of their Lives in their Wives and Children, and were therefore inconsolable.

'The following Year happened the Fire;[5] at which Time, by good Providence, it was my Fortune to have converted the greatest Part of my Effects into ready Money, on the Prospect of an extraordinary Advantage which I was preparing to lay Hold on. This Calamity was very terrible and astonishing, the Fury of the Flames being such, that whole Streets, at several distant Places, were destroyed at one and the

---

[4] *1665, when the Sickness was:* The Great Plague, which swept through London in that year.
[5] *the Fire:* The Great Fire of London of 1666, which destroyed much of the city.

same Time, so that (as it is well known) almost all our Citizens were burnt out of what they had. But what did I then do? I did not stand gazing on the Ruins of our noble Metropolis; I did not shake my Head, wring my Hands, sigh, and shed Tears; I considered with my self what cou'd this avail; I fell a plodding what Advantages might be made of the ready Cash I had, and immediately bethought my self that wonderful Pennyworths might be bought of the Goods that were saved out of the Fire. In short, with about 2000 *l.* and a little Credit, I bought as much Tobacco as raised my Estate to the Value of 10000 *l.* I then *looked on the Ashes of our City, and the Misery of its late Inhabitants, as an Effect of the just Wrath, and Indignation of Heaven towards a sinful and perverse People.*

'After this I married again, and that Wife dying, I took another; but both proved to be idle Baggages; the first gave me a great deal of Plague and Vexation by her Extravagancies, and I became one of the By-words of the City. I knew it would be to no manner of Purpose to go about to curb the Fancies and Inclinations of Women, which fly out the more for being restrain'd; but what I cou'd I did. I watch'd her narrowly, and by good Luck found her in the Embraces (for which I had two Witnesses with me) of a wealthy Spark[6] of the Court-end of the Town; of whom I recover'd 15000 Pounds, which made me Amends for what she had idly squander'd, and put a Silence to all my Neighbours, taking off my Reproach by the Gain they saw I had by it. The last died about two Years after I marry'd her, in Labour of three Children. I conjecture they were begotten by a Country Kinsman of hers, whom, at her Recommendation, I took into my Family, and gave Wages to as a Journey-man. What this Creature expended in Delicacies and high Diet with her Kinsman (as well as I could compute by the Poulterers, Fishmongers, and Grocers Bills) amounted in the said two Years to One hundred eighty six Pounds, four Shillings, and five Pence Half-penny. The fine Apparel, Bracelets, Lockets, and Treats, *&c.* of the other, according to the best Calculation, came in three Years and about three Quarters to Seven hundred forty four Pounds, seven Shillings and nine Pence. After this I resolved never to marry more, and found I had been a Gainer by my Marriages, and the Damages granted me for the Abuses of my Bed, (all Charges deducted) Eight thousand three hundred Pounds within a Trifle.

[6] *Spark:* A fancy, fashionable man-about-town.

'I come now to shew the good Effects of the Love of Money on the Lives of Men towards rendring them honest, sober, and religious. When I was a young Man, I had a Mind to make the best of my Wits, and over-reach'd a Country Chap[7] in a Parcel of unsound Goods; to whom, upon his upbraiding, and threatning to expose me for it, I return'd the Equivalent of his Loss; and upon his good Advice, wherein he clearly demonstrated the Folly of such Artifices, which can never end but in Shame, and the Ruin of All Correspondence, I never after transgress'd. Can your Courtiers, who take Bribes, or your Lawyers or Physicians in their Practice, or even the Divines who intermeddle in worldly Affairs, boast of making but one Slip in their Lives, and of such a thorough and lasting Reformation? Since my coming into the World I do not remember I was ever overtaken in Drink, save nine times, one at the Christening of my first child, thrice at our City Feasts, and five times at driving of Bargains. My Reformation I can attribute to nothing so much as the Love and Esteem of Money; for I found my self to be extravagant in my Drink, and apt to turn Projector, and make rash Bargains. As for Women, I never knew any, except my Wives: For my Reader must know, and it is what he may confide in as an excellent Recipe, That the Love of Business and Money is the greatest Mortifier of inordinate Desires imaginable, as employing the Mind continually in the careful Oversight of what one has, in the eager Quest after more, in looking after the Negligences and Deceits of Servants, in the due Entring and Stating of Accounts, in hunting after Chaps, and in the exact Knowledge of the State of Markets; which Things whoever thoroughly attends, will find enough and enough to employ his Thoughts on every Moment of the Day: So that I cannot call to Mind, that in all the Time I was a Husband, which, off and on, was about twelve years, I ever once thought of my Wives but in Bed. And, lastly, for Religion, I have ever been a constant Church-man, both Forenoons and Afternoons on *Sundays*, never forgetting to be thankful for any Gain or Advantage I had had that Day; and on *Saturday* Nights, upon casting up my Accounts, I always was grateful for the Sum of my Week's Profits, and at *Christmas* for that of the whole Year. It is true perhaps, that my Devotion has not been the most fervent; which, I think, ought to be imputed to the Evenness and Sedateness of my Temper, which never would admit of any Impetuosities of any Sort: And I can remember, that in

---

[7] *Chap*: A chapman, or customer.

my Youth and Prime of Manhood, when my Blood ran brisker, I took greater Pleasure in Religious Exercises than at present, or many Years past, and that my Devotion sensibly declined as Age, which is dull and unweildy, came upon me.

'I have, I hope, here proved, that the Love of Money prevents all Immorality and Vice; which if you will not allow, you must, that the Pursuit of it obliges Men to the same Kind of Life as they would follow if they were really virtuous: Which is all I have to say at present, only recommending to you, that you would think of it, and turn ready Wit into ready Money as fast as you can. I conclude,

Your Servant,

Ephraim Weed.'

Cultural Contexts

NICHOLAS BARBON

From A Discourse of Trade

Nicholas Barbon (1640–1698) was an economist and is credited as the founder of fire insurance. He is the author of two economic tracts, *A Discourse of Trade* and *A Discourse Concerning Coining the New Money Lighter* . . . (1696), both of which participate in the central economic debates of their day. One crucial debate, over how to correct the debilitating shortage of coin in England, revolved around the fundamental issue of value and how to secure it. Should England, as John Locke and others thought, be kept to a silver standard and so not coin more money than it could back in bullion? Does silver even have an intrinsic value and can it serve as a stable standard for currency? Or, as Barbon and his party maintained, are silver and gold themselves simply commodities in a financial market where values shift in response to supply and demand? If silver cannot serve as a standard, how then can the value of money be determined? According to Barbon, this can be achieved only by "law," and the difference in value can be known not by the metal of the coin but only "by the stamp."

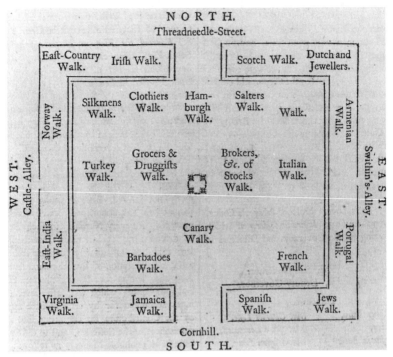

Floor plan of the Royal Exchange.

These questions about the standard of value shift easily from the monetary to the ethical, as we can see in Barbon's discussion of credit: "There are Two Sorts of Credit; the one, is Grounded upon the Ability of the Buyer; the other, upon the Honesty" (see p. 235). Ethical questions also move to the foreground in debates over the relative benefits and drawbacks of domestic consumption. In his discussion "Of the Chief Causes that Promote Trade," Barbon draws a careful distinction between liberality, which promotes trade through an abundance of consumption and does no ethical damage, and both prodigality and covetousness. Prodigality, while it may promote trade, "is prejudicial to the Man"; and covetousness is "prejudicial both to Man & Trade" (p. 238). The discourse of political economy and of ethics shade in and out of one another, for both involve, at the most basic level, questions of value. Discussions of the value of currency and of commercial well-being touch, often to the quick, the fundamental issues of human desire and behavior, but they also question the very possibility of stable standards of value in a society increasingly conscious of the impact of commerce on its institutions.

Of Mony, Credit and Interest.

Mony is a Value made by a Law; And the Difference of its Value is known by the Stamp, and Size of the Piece.

One Use of M O N Y is, It is the Measure of Value, By which the Value of all other things are reckoned; as when the Value of any thing is expressed, its said, It's worth so many shillings, or so many Pounds: Another Use of Mony is; It is a Change or Pawn for the Value of all other Things: For this Reason, the Value of Mony must be made certain by Law, or else it could not be made a certain Measure, nor an Exchange for the Value of all things.

It is not absolutely necessary, Mony should be made of Gold or Silver; for having its sole Value from the Law, it is not Material upon what Metal the Stamp be set. Mony hath the same Value, and performs the same Uses, if it be made of Brass, Copper, Tin, or any thing else. The Brass Mony of *Spain*, the Copper Mony of *Sweeden*, and Tin Farthings of *England*, have the same Value in Exchange, according to the Rate they are set at, and perform the same Uses, to Cast up the Value of things, as the Gold and Silver Mony does; Six Pence in Farthings will buy the same thing as Six Pence in Silver; and the Value of a thing is well understood by saying, It is worth Eight Farthings, as that it is worth Two Pence: Gold and Silver, as well as Brass, Copper and Tin Mony, change their Value in those Countries, where the Law has no Force, and yield no more than the Price of the Metal that bears the S T A M P: Therefore, all Foreign Coins go by Weight, and are of no certain Value, but rise and fall with the Price of the Metal. Pieces of Eight, yield sometimes 4 *sh*. 6 *d.*, 4 *sh*. 7 *d.* and 4 *sh*. 8 *d.*[1] as the Value of Silver is higher or lower: And so doth Dollars, and all Foreign Coin, change their Value; and were it not for the Law that fixeth the Value, an *English* Crown Piece would now yield Five Shillings and Two Pence, for so much is the Value of it, if it were melted, or in a Foreign Country. But the chief Advantage of making Mony of Silver and Gold, is to prevent Counterfeiting; for Silver and Gold, being Metals of great Value, those who design Profit by Counterfeiting the Coin, must Counterfeit the Metals, as well as the Stamp, which is more difficult than the Stamp. There's another Benefit to the Merchant, by such Mony; for Gold and Silver being Commodities for other Uses, than to make Mony; to make Plate, Gold &

---

[1] . . . *4 sh. 8 d.*: Four shillings, eight *denarii* (pence or cents). English usage maintained the Latin abbreviation for *denarii* (a Roman silver coin) when referring to their own pence.

Silver Lace, Silks, &c. And Coins of little Bulk, in respect of their Value, the Merchant transmits such Mony from Place to Place, in *Specie*, according as he finds his Advantage, by the Rise of Bulloin; though this may be a Conveniency to the Merchant, it often proves a Prejudice to the State, by making Mony scarce: Therefore, there are Laws in most Countries, that Prohibit the Transportation of Mony, yet it cannot be prevented; for in *Spain*, though it be Capital, yet in Two Months after the Gallions are come home, there is scarce any Silver Mony to be seen in the Country.

Some Men have so great an Esteem for Gold and Silver, that they believe they have an intrinsick Value in themselves, and cast up the Value of every thing by them: The Reason of the Mistake, is, Because Mony being made of Gold and Silver, they do not distinguish betwixt Mony, and Gold and Silver. Mony hath a certain Value, because of the Law; but the Value of Gold and Silver are uncertain, & varies their Price, as much as Copper, Lead, or other Metals: And in the Places where they are dug, considering the smalness of their Veins, with the Charges of getting them, they do not yield much more Profit than other Minerals, nor pay the Miners better Wages for digging them.

And were it not for the Waste, made of Gold and Silver, by Plate, Lace, Silks, and Guilding, and the Custom of the *Eastern* Princes, to lay them up and bury them, that Half which is dug in the *West*, is buryed in the *East*. The great Quantities dug out of the Earth, since the Discovery of the *West-Indies*, would have so much lessened the Value, that by this time, they would not have much exceeded the Value of Tin, or Copper: Therefore, How greatly would those Gentlemen be disappointed, that are searching after the *Philosopher's Stone*,[2] if they should at last happen to find it? For, if they should make but so great a Quantity of Gold and Silver, as they, and their Predecessors have spent in search after it, it would so alter, and bring down the Price of those Metals, that it might be a Question, whether they would get so much *Over-plus* by it, as would pay for the Metal they change into Gold and Silver. It is only the Scarcity that keeps up the Value, and not any Intrinsick Vertue or Quality in the Metals; For if the Vertue were to be considered, the *Affrican* that gives Gold for Knives, and Things made of Iron, would have the Odds in the Exchange; Iron being a much more Useful Metal, than either Gold or

---

[2] *Philosopher's Stone:* The substance thought by alchemists to have properties that would change base metals into gold.

Silver. To Conclude this Objection, Nothing in it self hath a certain Value; One thing is as much worth as another: And it is time, and place, that give a difference to the Value of all things.

Credit is a Value raised by Opinion, it buys Goods as Mony doe's; and in all Trading Citys, there's more Wares sold upon Credit, then for present Mony.

There are Two Sorts of Credit; the one, is Grounded upon the Ability of the Buyer; the other, upon the Honesty: The first is called a Good Man, which implys an Able Man; he generally buys upon short Time; to pay in a Month, which is accounted as ready Mony, and the Price is made accordingly. The other is accounted an Honest Man; He may be poor; he Generally buys for three and Six Months or longer, so as to pay the Merchant by the Return of his own Goods; and therefore, the Seller relys more upon the Honesty of the Buyer, than his Ability: Most of the Retail Traders buy upon this Sort of Credit, and are usually Trusted for more than double they are worth.

In Citys of great Trade, there are publick Banks of Credit, as at *Amsterdam* and *Venice:* They are of greater Advantage to Trade, for they make Payments easie, by preventing the Continual Trouble of telling over Mony, and cause a great Dispatch in Business: Publick Banks are of so great a Concern in Trade, that the Merchants of *London*, for want of such a Bank,[3] have been forced to Carry their Cash to Gold-Smiths, and have thereby Raised such a Credit upon Gold-Smiths Notes, that they pass in Payments from one to another like Notes upon the Bank; And although by this way of Credit, there hath been very Vast Sums of Mony lost, not less then too Millions within five and Twenty Years, yet the Dispatch and Ease in Trade is so great by such Notes, that the Credit is still in some Measure kept up.

Therefore, it is much to be wondered at, that since the City of *London* is the Largest, Richest, and Chiefest City in the World, for Trade; Since there is so much Ease, Dispatch, and Safety in a Publick Bank; and since such vast Losses has Happened for want of it; That the Merchant and Traders of *London* have not long before this time Addressed themselves, to the Government, for the Establishing of a Publick Bank.

The Common Objection, that a Publick Bank cannot be safe in a Monarchy, is not worth the Answering; As if Princes were not Governed by the same Rules of Policy, as States are, To do all things for the Well-fair of the Subjects, wherein their own Interest is concerned.

---

[3] *Bank:* The Bank of England was not instituted until 1694.

It is True, in a Government wholly Dispotical, whose Support is altogether in it's Millitary Forces; where Trade hath no Concern in the Affaires of the State; Brings no Revenue, There might be a Jealousy, That such a Bank might tempt a Prince to Seize it; when by doing it, he doth not Prejudice the Affairs of his Government: But in *England*, where the Government is not Dispotical; But the People Free; and have as great a Share in the Soveraign Legislative Power, as the Subjects of any States have, or ever had; where the Customs makes great Figures, in the Kings Exchequer; where Ships are the Bullworks of the Kingdom; and where the Flourish of Trade is as much the Interest of the King as of the People, There can be no such Cause of Fear: For, What Objections can any Man make, that his Mony in the Bank, may not be as well secured by a Law, as his Property is? Or; Why he should be more afraid of Losing his Mony, than his Land or Goods?

Interest is the Rent of Stock, and is the same as the Rent of Land: The First, is the Rent of the Wrought or Artificial Stock; the Latter, of the Unwrought, or Natural Stock.

Interest is commonly reckoned for Mony; because the Mony Borrowed at Interest, is to be repayed in Mony; but this is a mistake: For the Interest is paid for Stock: for the Mony borrowed, is laid out to buy Goods, or pay for them before bought: No Man takes up Mony at Interest, to lay it by him, and lose the Interest of it.

One use of Interest: It is the Rule by which the Trader makes up the Account of Profit and Loss; The Merchant expects by Dealing, to get more then Interest by his Goods; because of bad Debts, and other Hazards which he runs; and therefore, reckons all he gets above Interest, is Gain; all under, Loss; but if no more than Interest, neither Profit, nor Loss.

Another use of Interest, is, It is the measure of the Value of the Rent of Land; it sets the Price in Buying and Selling of Land: For, by adding three Years Interest more than is in the Principle, Makes the usual Value of the Land of the Country; The difference of three Year is allowed; Because Land is more certain than Mony or Stock. Thus in *Holland*, where Mony is at three *per. Cent.* by reckoning how many times three is in a Hundred Pounds, which is Thirty Three; and Adding three Years more; makes Thirty Six Years Purchase; the Value of the Land in *Holland*: And by the same Rule, interest being at six *per Cent.* in *England*, Land is worth but Twenty Years Purchase; and in *Ireland*, but Thirteen; Interest being there at Ten *per*

Cent: so that, according to the Rate of Interest, is that Value of the Land in the Country.

Therefore, Interest in all Countrys is setled by a Law, to make it certain; or else it could not be a Rule for the Merchant to make up his Account, nor the Gentleman, to Sell his Land By.

Of the Use and Benefit of Trade.

The Use of *Trade* is to make, and provide things Necessary: Or useful for the Support, Defence, Ease, Pleasure, and Pomp of Life: Thus the Brewers, Bakers, Butchers, Poulterers, and Cooks, with the Apothecaries, Surgeons, and their Dependencies provide Food, and Medicine for the support of Life: The Cutlers, Gun-smiths, Powder-makers, with their Company of *Traders*, make things for Defence; The Shoomakers, Sadlers, Couch, and Chair-makers, with abundance more for the Ease of Life: The Perfumers, Fidlers, Painters, and Book-sellers, and all those Trades that make things to gratifie the Sense, or delight the Mind, promote Pleasure: But those Trades that are imploy'd to express the Pomp of Life, are Infinite; for, besides those that adorn Mans Body, as the Glover, Hosier, Hatter, Semstriss, Taylor, and many more, with those that make the Materials to Deck it; as Clothier, Silk-Weaver, Lace-Maker, Ribbon-Weaver, with their Assistance of Drapers, Mercers,[4] and Milliners, and a Thousand more: Those Trades that make the Equipage[5] for Servants, Trappings for Horses; and those that Build, Furnish, and Adorn Houses, are innumerable. . . .

Of the Chief Causes that Promote Trade.

The Chief Causes that Promote *Trade*, (not to mention Good Government, Peace, and Scituation, with other Advantages) are Industry in the Poor, and Liberality in the Rich: Liberality, is the free Usage of all those things that are made by the Industry of the Poor, for the Use of the Body and Mind; It Relates chiefly to Man's self, but doth not hinder him from being Liberal to others.

---

[4] *Drapers, Mercers:* Both drapers and mercers were retail dealers in textiles. Mercers dealt in fine fabrics such as silk.

[5] *Equipage:* Here, simply, outfits, or livery. Servants that waited on their masters on public ceremonial occasions wore uniforms that signaled their affiliation to the household that employed them.

The Two Extreams to this Vertue, are Prodigality and Covetousness: Prodigality is a Vice that is prejudicial to the Man, but not to
Trade; It is living a pace, and spending that in a Year, that should last
all his Life: Covetousness is a Vice, prejudicial both to Man *& Trade*;
It starves the Man, and breaks the Trader; and by the same way the
Covetous Man thinks he grows rich, he grows poor; for by not consuming the Goods that are provided for Man's Use, there ariseth a
dead Stock, called Plenty, and the Value of those Goods fall, and the
Covetous Man's Estates, whether in Land, or Mony, becomes less
worth: And a Conspiracy of the Rich Men to be Covetous, and not
spend, would be as dangerous to a Trading State, as a Forreign War;
for though they themselves get nothing by their Covetousness, nor
grow the Richer, yet they would make the Nation poor, and the Government great Losers in the Customs and Excises that ariseth from
Expence.

Liberality ought Chiefly to be Exercised in an equal Division of the
Expence amongst those things that relate to Food, Cloaths, and
Lodging; according to the Portion, or Station, that is allotted to every
Man, with some allowance for the more refined Pleasures of the
Mind; with such Distributions, as may please both sect of Philoso-
phers, *Platonist* and *Epicureans*:[6] The Belly must not be starved to
cloath the Back-Part.

Those Expences that most Promote *Trade*, are in Cloaths and
Lodging: In Adorning the Body and the House, There are a Thousand
Traders Imploy'd in Cloathing and Decking the Body, and Building,
and Furnishing of Houses, for one that is Imploy'd in providing
Food. Belonging to Cloaths, is Fashion; which is the Shape or Form
of Apparel.

In some places, it is fixt and certain; as all over *Asia*, and in *Spain*;
but in *France*, *England*, and other places, the Dress alters; Fashion or
the alteration of Dress, is a great Promoter of *Trade*, because it occasions the Expence of Cloaths, before the Old ones are worn out: It is
the Spirit and Life of *Trade*; It makes a Circulation, and gives a Value
by Turns, to all sorts of Commodities; keeps the great Body of *Trade*
in Motion; it is an Invention to Dress a Man, as if he Lived in a perpetual Spring; he never sees the Autum of his Cloaths: The following
of the Fashion, Is a Respect paid to the Prince and his Court, by ap-

---

[6] *Platonist and Epicureans:* The Platonist would be pleased with those things that
promoted "the more refined Pleasures of the Mind," the Epicureans with more material pleasures.

proving his Choice in the shape of the Dress. It lyes under an ill Name amongst many Grave and Sober People, but without any Just Cause; for those that Exclaim against the Vanity of the New Fashion, and at the same time, commend the Decency of the Old one, forget that every Old Fashion was once New, and then the same Argument might have been used against it. And if an *Indian*, or Stranger, that never saw any person Cloathed before, were to be Judge of the Controversy, and were to Determin upon seeing at the same time a well Drest Courtier in the New Fashion, and another in the Old, which is accounted Decent; and a third in the Robes of an Officer, which by common Esteem, had a Reverence: It will be Two to One, against any One of the Grave Fashions; for it's only Use and Custom by which Habits become Grave and Decent, and not any particular Conveniency in the shape; for if Conveniency were the Rule of Commendation, there would arise a Question not Easily to be Determined, Whether the *Spanish* Garb made strait to the Body, or the loose Habit of the *Turks*, were to be Chosen? And therefore since all Habits are equally handsome, and hard to know which is most Convenient: The Promoting of New Fashions, ought to be Encouraged, because it provides a Livelihood for a great Part of Mankind.

The next Expence that chiefly promotes *Trade*, is Building, which is natural to Mankind, being the making of a Nest or Place for his Birth, it is the most proper and visible Distinction of Riches, and Greatness, because the Expences are too Great for Mean Persons to follow. It is a Pleasure fit to entertain Princes; for a Magnificent Structure doth best represent the Majesty of the Person that lives in it, and is the most lasting and truest History of the Greatness of his Person.

Building is the chiefest Promoter of *Trade*; it Imploys a greater Number of Trades and People, than Feeding or Cloathing: The Artificers that belong to Building, such as *Bricklayers, Carpenters, Plaisterers*, &c. imploy many Hands; Those that make the Materials for Building, such as *Bricks, Lyme, Tyle*, &c. imploy more; and with those that Furnish the Houses, such as *Upholsterers, Pewterers*, &c. they are almost Innumerable.

In *Holland*, where *Trade* hath made the Inhabitants very Rich, It is the Care of the Government, to Incourage the Builder, and at the Charge of the *State*, the Grafts and Streets are made. And at *Amsterdam*, they have three Times, at great Expence, Thrown down the Walls of their City, and Dreined the Boggs, to make Room for the Builder: For Houses are the Places where the Artificers make their

Goods, and Merchants Sell them; and without New Houses, the Trades and Inhabitants could not Increase.

Beside, There is another great Advantage to *Trade*, by Enlarging of Cities; the Two Beneficial Expences of Cloathing and Lodging, are Increased; Man being Naturally Ambitious, the Living together, occasion Emulation, which is seen by Out-Vying one another in Apparel, Equipage, and Furniture of the House; whereas, if a Man lived Solitary alone, his chiefest Expence, would be Food. It is from this very Custom; If the Gentry of *France* Living in Cities, with the Invention of Fashion; That *France*, tho' a Country no way fitted for *Trade*, has so great a share of it: It is from Fashion in Cloaths, and Living in Cities, That the King of *France*'s Revenues is so great, by which he is become troublesome to his Neighbours, and will always be so, while he can preserve Peace within his own Country; by which, those Fountains of Riches, may run Interrupted into his *Exchequer*.

Of the Chief Causes of the Decay of Trade *in England, and Fall of the* Rents *of* Land.

The Two Chief Causes of the Decay of *Trade*, are the many Prohibitions and high Interest.

The Prohibition of *Trade*,[7] is the Cause of its Decay; for all Forreign Wares are brought in by the Exchange of the Native: So that the Prohibiting of any Foreign Commodity, doth hinder the Making and Exportation of so much of the Native, as used to be Made and Exchanged for it. The Artificers and Merchants, that Dealt in such Goods, lose their Trades; and the Profit that was gained by such Trades, and laid out amongst other Traders, is Lost. The Native Stock for want of such Exportation, Falls in Value, and the Rent of the Land must Fall with the Value of the Stock.

The common Argument for the Prohibiting Foreign Commodities, is, That the Bringing in, and Consuming such Foreign Wares, hinders the Making and Consuming the like sort of Goods of our own Native Make and Growth; therefore *Flanders*-Lace, *French* Hats, Gloves,

---

[7] *Prohibition of Trade:* Barbon refers to restrictions and embargoes placed on trade. Some of these prohibitions respond to military-political pressures, such as embargoes during wartime, and others to commercial-political pressures, such as protectionist restrictions on certain imports in order to promote the consumption of domestically produced goods. The textile manufacturers had an especially strong pull in England and lobbied for a ban on certain imported fabrics, like East Indian muslins. Barbon writes as a laissez-faire economist at a time when the protectionist policies of mercantilism were in force.

Silks, *Westphalia*-Bacon, *&c.* are Prohibited, because it is supposed, they hinder the Consumption of *English*-Lace, Gloves, Hats, Silk, Bacon, *&c.* But this is a mistaken Reason, and ariseth by not considering what it is that Occasions *Trade.* It is not Necessity that causeth the Consumption, Nature may be Satisfied with little; but it is the wants of the Mind, Fashion, and desire of Novelties, and Things scarce, that causeth *Trade.* A Person may have *English*-Lace, Gloves, or Silk, as much as he wants, and will Buy no more such; and yet, lay out his Mony on a Point of *Venice, Jessimine*-Gloves,[8] or *French*-Silks; he may desire to Eat *Westphalia*-Bacon, when he will not *English*; so that, the Prohibition of Forreign Wares, does not necessarily cause a greater Consumption of the like sort of *English*.

Besides, There is the same wants of the Mind in Foreigners, as in the *English*; they desire Novelties; they Value *English*-Cloth, Hats, and Gloves, and Foreign Goods, more than their Native make; so that, tho' the Wearing or Consuming of Forreign Things, might lessen the Consuming of the same sort in *England*; yet there may not be a lesser Quantity made; and if the same Quantity be made, it will be a greater Advantage to the Nation, if they are Consumed in Foreign Countries, than at Home; because the Charge, and Imploy of the Freight, is Gained by it, which in bulky Goods, may be a Fourth Part of the whole Value.

The particular *Trades* that expect an Advantage by such Prohibition, are often mistaken; For if the Use of most Commodities depending upon Fashion, which often alters; The Use of those Goods cease. As to Instance, Suppose a Law to Prohibit Cane-Chairs; It would not necessarily follow, That those that make *Turkey*-Work Chairs,[9] would have a better *Trade.* For the Fashion may Introduce, Wooden, Leather, or Silk Chairs, (which are already in Use amongst the Gentry, The Cane-Chairs being grown too Cheap and Common) or else, they may lay aside the Use of all Chairs, Introducing the Custom of Lying upon Carpets; the Ancient *Roman* Fashion; still in Use amongst the *Turks, Persians,* and all the *Eastern* Princes.

Lastly, If the Suppressing or Prohibiting of some sorts of Goods, should prove an Advantage to the *Trader,* and Increase the Consumption of the same sort of our Native Commodity: Yet it may prove a Loss to the Nation. For the Advantage to the Nation from

[8] *Jessimine-Gloves:* Jasmine gloves, that is, gloves scented with oil of jasmine.
[9] *Turkey-Work Chairs:* Chairs upholstered with Turkish tapestry (like Turkish rugs).

Trade, is, from the Customs, and from those Goods that Imploys most Hands. So that, tho' the Prohibition may Increase, as the Consumption of the like sort of the Native; yet if it should Obstruct the Transporting of other Goods which were Exchanged for them, that Paid more Custom, Freight, or Imployed more Hands in making; The Nation will be a loser by the Prohibition: As to Instance, If Tobacco or Woollen-Cloth were used to Exchange for *Westphaly*-Bacon, The Nation loseth by the Prohibition, tho' it should Increase the Consumption of *English*-Bacon; because the First, Pays more Freight, and Custom; and the Latter, Imploys more Hands. By this Rule it appears, That the Prohibition of all unwrought Goods, such as raw Silk, Cotton, Flax, *&c.* and all Bulky Goods; such as Wines, Oyls, Fruits, *&c.* would be a Loss to the Nation; because nothing can be sent in Exchange that Imploys fewer Hands than the First, or Pays greater Freight than the Latter.

It doth not alter the Case, If the Ballance of the Account, or all the Foreign Goods, were bought by Silver or Gold; For Silver and Gold, are Foreign Commodities; Pay but little Freight, and Imploy but few Hands in the Working; And are at First brought into *England*, by the Exchange of some Native Goods, and having Paid for their coming hither, must Pay for the Carriage out. It is true, That if our Serge, Stuffs, or Cloth, are Exchanged for Unmanufactured Goods, it would be a greater Advantage to the Nation, because of the difference in Number of Hands in the making of the First, and the Later.

But all Trading Countries Study their Advantage by *Trade*, and Know the difference of the Profit by the Exchange of wrought Goods, for unwrought: And therefore, for any Nation to make a Law to Prohibit all Foreign Goods, but such only as are most Advantageous; Is to put other Nations upon making the same Laws; and the Consequence will be to Ruine all Foreign *Trade*. For the Foundation of all Foreign *Trade*, is, from the Exchange of the Native Commodities of each Country, for one another.

To Conclude, If the bringing in of Foreign Goods, should hinder the making and consuming of the Native, which will very seldom happen; this disadvantage is not to be Remedied by a Prohibition of those Goods; but by Laying so great Duties upon them, that they may be always Dearer than those of our Country make: The Dearness will hinder the common Consumption of them, and preserve them for the Use of the Gentry, who may Esteem them, because they are Dear; and perhaps, might not Consume more of the *English* Growth, were the other not Imported. By such Duties, the Revenue of the Crown, will be Increased; And no Exceptions can be taken by any Foreign Prince, or Government; Since it is in the Liberty of every Government, To Lay what Duty or Imposition they please. *Trade* will continue Open, and Free; and the *Traders*, Enjoy the Profit of their *Trade:* The Dead Stock of the Nation, that is more than can be Used, will be Carried off, which will keep up the *Price* of the Native Stock, and the *Rent* of the *Land.*

JOHN DENHAM

From Coopers Hill

John Denham (1615–1669), a Royalist poet, is best known for his historical-political poem *Coopers Hill* (1642/1655) and for the blank-verse historical tragedy *Sophy* (performed in 1641). During the Interregnum, Denham worked for the Stuart cause in England and on the Continent, where he had fled in 1648. In 1660, with the restoration of Charles II, Denham was appointed Surveyor General. He was later knighted and made a member of the Royal Society.

Along with Edmund Waller, John Denham is credited with the development of the closed heroic couplet, a form that in the work of John Dryden and Alexander Pope came to characterize early-eighteenth-century poetry. In this selection from Denham's poem *Coopers Hill*, the poet surveys the Thames River from this promontory in the northwest corner of Surrey. The view includes Windsor Forest, the site of Alexander Pope's later poem, which is modeled on *Coopers Hill* (p. 259). *Coopers Hill*, like *Windsor-Forest*, is largely concerned with questions of authority and the productive, rather than destructive, exercise of power. Denham conducts his parallel survey of the English landscape and English history as a political meditation. In the Thames passage, the river is figured as the embodiment of balanced power and becomes an emblem not only of just authority, but also of a harmonious poetics: "O could I flow like thee, and make thy stream / My great example, as it is my theme! / Though deep, yet clear, though gentle, yet not dull, / Strong without rage, without ore-flowing full" (ll. 189–92, see p. 245). In *Coopers Hill*, balanced power and peace are established through the logic of *concordia discors,* a harmonious fusion of opposites. As embodied and emblematized by the Thames, this peaceful, harmonious confluence is linked to the fruitful effects of England's commercial expansion. The

Thames ". . . makes both *Indies* ours; / Finds wealth where 'tis, bestows it where it wants." This notion of commerce as a corrective to imbalances of wealth and of power was widely held and is central to the apologies for trade advanced by, for example, Defoe, Addison, and Pope.

The text excerpted here is taken from *Expans'd Hieroglyphicks: A Critical Edition of Sir John Denham's Coopers Hill,* ed. Brendan Hehir (Berkeley: U of California P, 1969), 148–53.

My eye descending from the Hill,° surveys
Where *Thames* amongst the wanton vallies strays.   160
Thames, the most lov'd of all the Oceans sons,
By his old Sire to his embraces runs,
Hasting to pay his tribute to the Sea,
Like mortal life to meet Eternity.
Though with those streams he no resemblance hold,   165
Whose foam is Amber, and their Gravel Gold;
His genuine, and less guilty wealth t'explore,
Search not his bottom, but survey his shore;
Ore which he kindly spreads his spacious wing,
And hatches plenty for th'ensuing Spring.   170
Nor then destroys it with too fond a stay,
Like Mothers which their Infants overlay.
Nor with a sudden and impetuous wave,
Like profuse Kings, resumes the wealth he gave.
No unexpected inundations spoyl   175
The mowers hopes, nor mock the plowmans toyl:
But God-like his unwearied Bounty flows;
First loves to do, then loves the Good he does.
Nor are his Blessings to his banks confin'd,
But free, and common, as the Sea or Wind;   180
When he to boast, or to disperse his stores
Full of the tributes of his grateful shores,
Visits the world, and in his flying towers
Brings home to us, and makes both *Indies*° ours;

159. *the Hill:* Coopers Hill, in the northern part of Egham district, in the county of Surrey. The hill rises above the Thames Valley.

184. *both Indies:* The East Indies (India and Southeast Asia) and the West Indies (the Caribbean islands).

Finds wealth where 'tis, bestows it where it wants   185
Cities in deserts, woods in Cities plants.
So that to us no thing, no place is strange,
While his fair bosom is the worlds exchange.
[Rome only conquerd halfe the world, but trade
One commonwealth of that and her hath made
And though the sunn his beame extends to all
Yet to his neighbour sheds most liberall
Least God and Nature partiall should appeare
Commerse makes everything grow everywhere]°
O could I flow like thee, and make thy stream
My great example, as it is my theme!   190
Though deep, yet clear, though gentle, yet not dull,
Strong without rage, without ore-flowing full.
Heaven her *Eridanus*° no more shall boast,
Whose fame in thine, like lesser Currents lost,
Thy Nobler streams shall visit Jove's aboads,°   195
To shine amongst the Stars, and bath the Gods.
Here Nature, whether more intent to please
Us or her self, with strange varieties,
(For things of wonder give no less delight
To the wise Maker's, than beholders sight.   200
Though these delights from several causes move
For so our children, thus our friends we love)
Wisely she knew, the harmony of things,
As well as that of sounds, from discords springs.
Such was the discord, which did first disperse   205
Form, order, beauty through the Universe;
While driness moysture, coldness heat resists
All that we have, and that we are, subsists.
While the steep horrid roughness of the Wood
Strives with the gentle calmness of the flood.   210
Such huge extreams when Nature doth unite,

[Rome . . . everywhere]: These six lines were added in holograph by Denham to his
own copy of 1668. . . . In the second line "that" presumably is "the world," and "her"
presumably "Rome" [Hehir].
   193. *Eridanus:* The Milky Way; also a name for the Po River in Italy.
   195. *Jove's aboads:* The heavens, home of the gods. Jove is the chief god in the
Roman pantheon, as Zeus is in the Greek.

Wonder from thence results, from thence delight
The stream is so transparent, pure, and clear,
That had the self-enamour'd youth gaz'd here,
So fatally deceiv'd he had not been,   215
While he the bottom, not his face had seen.
But his proud head the aery Mountain hides
Among the Clouds; his shoulders, and his sides
A shady mantle cloaths; his curled brows
Frown on the gentle stream, which calmly flows,   220
While winds and storms his lofty forehead beat:
The common fate of all that's high or great.
Low at his foot a spacious plain is plac't,
Between the mountain and the stream embrac't:
Which shade and shelter from the Hill derives,   225
While the kind river wealth and beauty gives;
And in the mixture of all these appears
Variety, which all the rest indears.

EDWARD WARD

The Royal Exchange (From The London Spy*)*

In the selections collected here, Ward's *London Spy* takes a skeptical
and damning look at some central commercial and financial institutions
of late-seventeenth-century London: the Royal Exchange; the lottery;
Jonathan's Coffee-house; and the New Exchange. As with his descriptions of coffeehouses collected in Chapter 1 of this edition, Ward's perspective on the Royal Exchange may be fruitfully contrasted with that
much more attractive and celebratory view given by Addison in *Spectator* 69. For more information about *The London Spy,* see Chapter 1,
Cultural Contexts, p. 144.

The account of a visit to the Royal Exchange is from Part 3; the description of lotteries from Part 14; the description of Jonathan's Coffee-
house from Part 16; and the description of shopgirls at the New Exchange from Part 9. All excerpts are from Paul Hyland's edition of
Edward Ward's *The London Spy* (4th ed. 1709) (East Lansing, MI: Colleagues Press, 1993), 58–62, 257–61, 297–98, and 162–64.

[A Visit to the Royal Exchange]

We then proceeded and went on to the 'Change,[1] turned to the right, and jostled in amongst a parcel of swarthy buggerantoes[2] (preternatural fornicators, as my friend called them) who would ogle a handsome young man with as much lust as a true-bred English whore-master would gaze upon a beautiful virgin. Advertisements hung as thick round the pillars of each walk as bells about the legs of a morris dancer,[3] and an incessant buzz, like the murmurs of the distant ocean, stood as a diapason[4] to our talk, like a drone to a bagpipe. The wainscot was adorned with quacks' bills, instead of pictures; never an empiric[5] in the town but had his name in a lacquered frame, containing a fair invitation for a fool and his money to be soon parted. Thus he that wants physic for a clap,[6] or a wet-nurse for a child, may be furnished here at a minute's warning.

After we had squeezed ourselves through a crowd of bum-firking[7] Italians, we fell into a throng of strait-laced monsters in fur and thrum-caps,[8] with huge logger heads, effeminate waists, and buttocks like a Flanders mare, with slovenly mien and swinish looks, whose upper lips were gracefully adorned with turd-coloured whiskers. These, with their gloves under their arms, and their hands in their pockets, were grunting to each other like hogs at their peas. These, my friend told me, were the water-rats of Europe,[9] who love nobody but themselves, and fatten upon the spoils, and build their own welfare upon the ruin of their neighbours.

We had no sooner jostled through this cluster of Commonwealth's-men,[10] but we were got amongst a parcel of lank-haired

---

[1] *'Change:* The Royal Exchange, in London's central financial district on Threadneedle Street, provided a meeting place for businessmen and housed nearly two hundred shops. The first Royal Exchange was established by Sir Thomas Gresham (1518–1579) in 1566–68. This building was destroyed in the Great Fire of London (1666), and the Exchange was rebuilt in 1669 from designs by Edward Jarman.

[2] *buggerantoes:* "Buggers" or sodomites, here Italians.

[3] *morris dancer:* Morris (from "moorish") dancers are English folk dancers who perform seasonal dance narratives in colorful costumes.

[4] *diapason:* (Ironic) a full outpouring of harmonious sound.

[5] *empiric:* A disreputable, or "quack," doctor.

[6] *a clap:* A case of gonorrhea.

[7] *bum-firking:* Bum-fucking; sodomitical.

[8] *thrum-caps:* A cap made of coarse wool or hemp.

[9] *the water-rats of Europe:* The Dutch, so called because of the canals for which Amsterdam is famous.

[10] *Commonwealth's-men:* Republicans.

formalists, in flat crowned hats and short cloaks, walking with as much state and gravity as a snail o'er the leaf of a cabbage, with a box of tobacco-dust[11] in one hand, and the other employed in charging their nostrils from whence it drops into their moustaches, which are always as full of snuff as a beau's wig is full of powder. Every sentence they spoke was graced with a shrug of the shoulders, and every step they took was performed with as much leisure as a cock strides. These, my friend told me, were Spaniards. Says he, 'you may know them by their smell, for they stink as strong of garlic as a Bologna sausage.'

These were confusedly jumbled among people of sundry nations such as our neighbouring antics the French, who talk more with their heads and hands than with their tongues. They commonly speak first and think afterwards, step a minuet as they walk, and sit as gracefully on an Exchange bench as if in a great saddle. Their bodies always dance to their tongues, and they are so great lovers of action that they were ready to wound every pillar with their canes as they passed by, either in tierce, carte, or seconde.[12]

There, likewise, were the Lord's vagabonds, the Jews, who were so accursed for their infidelity that they are generally the richest people in all nations where they dwell. Like the wicked Spaniards, they were such great consumers of the wicked weed in snuff that their upper lips looked as if they excreted through their nostrils and had forgot to use bumfodder. 'These,' says my friend, 'are the hawks of mankind, the spies of the universe, the only trade-politicians, subtle knaves, and great merchants.'

Here were also a few amber-necklace sellers, as my friend called them; men with fur caps, long gowns and grave countenances, seeming wise in their carriage, retaining something of the old Grecian grandeur in their comely deportment. Among them there was one very handsome young fellow, which my companion bid me take particular notice of, 'for,' says he, 'that spark in the red gown was very familiar with some of our sweet-lipped ladies of the City. He was very much admired and courted by several topping benefactresses at this end of the town, to receive their favours, till the fool, proud of his happiness, must needs boast of their kindnesses to the disreputation of his humble servants; so they all discarded him with such ha-

---

[11] *tobacco-dust:* Snuff.

[12] *tierce, carte, or seconde:* Fencing terms for the positions from which a parry or thrust can be made.

tred and contempt that he is now become the scorn and ridicule of every woman in the City.'

'Pray,' said I, 'what tall, sober-looked gentleman is that, in so grave a dress, in the long black wig and formal hat that stands as level in the brim as a pot-lid? He seems to be wonderfully reverenced by a great many much finer than himself.' 'That man,' says my friend, 'is the greatest merchant we have in England, and those fellows that keep astern, and now and then come upon his quarter with their topsails lowered, are commanders of ships who are soliciting for employment. He that plies him so close, they call Honour and Glory, who lately bore command in the Service. He was originally a poor fisherman, but did a very notable exploit (by the help of his man Jack) that recommended him to a commission. But either for want of discretion or honesty, he is turned out, and I suppose rather than return to his nets, he is willing to enter into the merchant service.'

In the next walk we went into were a parcel of swordsmen in twisted wigs and laced hats, with broad faces and flattish noses, saluting one another commonly by the title of Captain. But they looked as if they had been a long while out of commission, for most of them were out of repair, some like gentlemen without estates, and others like footmen out of places, many of them picking their teeth, often plucking out large tobacco-boxes to cram a wad in their mouths, as if most of their food was minced meat.

The other sort were a kind of lean, carrionly creatures with reddish hair and freckly faces, being very much given to scratching and shrugging, as if they held lousiness no shame and the itch no scandal; stooping a little in the shoulders as if their backs had been used to a pedlar's pack. Amongst them was a poor parson who came to the wrong place to look for a benefice. These, I found, were a compound of Scotch and Irish, who looked as if they rather came to seek for business than dispatch any.

We now came to the back gate of the 'Change, on the east side of which sat a parcel of women, some looking like jilts who wanted cullies,[13] and others like servants who wanted places.

We passed by them, and squeezed amongst coasters[14] and English traders, who were as busy in outwitting one another as if plain dealing was a crime and cozenage a virtue.

---

[13] *like jilts who wanted cullies:* Like prostitutes who need customers.
[14] *coasters:* Sailors in the coastal trade.

'Take notice,' says my companion, 'of that camel-backed spark. He is dignified with the title of My Lord and has as many maggots in his head as there are holes in a colander. Though the rickets have crushed him into that lump of deformity, he has the happiness, or curse, I know not which, to have a very handsome woman for a wife, whose prevailing glances have tempted such custom to her shop that he can afford to spend three or four hundred pounds a year in a tavern without doing himself a prejudice. This she very generously allows him to do out of her gettings, as some censorious people are apt to imagine as a gratuity for his toleration for her liberty of conscience. She is never without a shopful of admirers, whom she poisons with her eyes; and bubbles as she pleases. Give her her due, she's as beautiful as an angel, but as subtle as the Devil; as courteous as a courtesan, but sharp as a needle; very free, but very jiltish; very inviting, yet some say very virtuous.'

'Now,' says my friend, 'we are got amongst the Plantation traders. This may be called Kidnappers' Walk,[15] for a great many of these Jamaicans and Barbadians, with their kitchen-stuff countenances, are looking as sharp for servants as a gang of pickpockets for booty. But we have given these their characters already in the *Trip to Jamaica*,[16] therefore we shall speak but little of them here. I'll warrant you, if they knew the author was among them, they'd hustle him about, as the Whigs would a Jacobite[17] at the election of a Lord Mayor, or the Quakers would a drunken Ranter that should disturb 'em at their Meeting.'

'Pray,' said I, 'what is the meaning of this inscription in golden capitals over the passage, "My Lord Mayor's Court"?' My friend replied that it was the nest of City cormorants who, by scraping a little out of many men's estates, raise great ones to themselves, by which they teach fools wit, and bring litigious knaves to repentance.

Within that entry is an office of intelligence, pretending to help servants to places, and masters to servants. They have a knack of bubbling silly wenches out of their money, who loiter hereabouts, upon this expectancy, till they are picked up by the Plantation kidnappers and spirited away into a state of misery and whoredom.

---

[15] *Kidnappers' Walk*: So called because of the notorious practice of kidnapping people into servitude to work on West Indian plantations.

[16] *Trip to Jamaica*: A satirical account of Jamaica by Ward (1698). The "characters" he gives of Jamaicans are those of rogues and whores.

[17] *Jacobite*: Supporter of James II after his deposition in the Glorious Revolution of 1688. For the Whig and Tory parties, see Introduction (p. 1).

'Now,' says my friend, 'let us walk on the middle of the 'Change and view the statue. This,' says he, 'is the figure of King Charles II,[18] and those are stockjobbers[19] who are hovering about him, and are, by report, a pack of as great knaves as ever he had in his dominions. The rest are a mixed multitude of all nations, and not worth describing. Now I'll conduct you upstairs, where we'll first take a view of the fair ladies, and so adjourn to the tavern and refresh ourselves with a bottle.'

Accordingly we went up, where women sat in their pinfolds[20] begging of custom with such amorous looks, and after so affable a manner, that I could not but fancy they had as much mind to dispose of themselves as the commodities they dealt in. My ears on both sides were so baited with 'Fine linen, sir!' 'Gloves and ribbons, sir!' that I had a milliner's and a sempstress' shop in my head for a week together. 'Well,' says my friend, 'what do you think of all these pretty ladies?' I answered, I thought of them as I did of the rest of their sex; I supposed they were all ready to obey the laws of nature and answer the end of their creation. Says he, 'You have guessed right, for this place is the merchants' seraglio, a nursery of young wagtails for the private consolation of incontinent citizens; for most that you see here come under Chaucer's character of a sempstress, and so we'll leave them.'

'She keeps shop for countenance
And swyves for mountenance.'[21]

[The Lotteries]

We now turned back again to our buzzing metropolis, the City, where modesty and plain dealing were laid aside to pursue the wonderful expectancies so many thousands had from a mixture of projectors'[22] knavery and their own folly. The *Gazette* and *Post* papers[23]

[18] *King Charles II:* The Stuart king exiled during the Commonwealth (1649–60) and restored to the throne in 1660. He ruled until his death in 1685.

[19] *stockjobbers:* Stockbrokers.

[20] *pinfolds:* Pens for cattle; here, stalls for shopkeepers.

[21] *. . . And swyves for mountenance:* "She keeps a shop for the sake of appearances / and copulates for maintenance." This is an inexact quotation of the last lines from "The Cook's Tale" in Geoffrey Chaucer's (1340?–1400) *Canterbury Tales:* "And hadde a wyf that heeld for countenance / A shoppe, and swyved for hir sustenance."

[22] *projectors':* A projector is a deviser of schemes for financial or social improvement.

[23] *Gazette and Post papers:* The *Gazette* was the government's official biweekly newspaper; the *Post* is probably *The Post-Boy,* a thrice-weekly Tory paper.

lay by, neglected, and nothing was pored over in the coffee-houses but the Ticket catalogues.[24] No talking of the Jubilee,[25] the want of current trade with France, or the Scotch settlement at Darien;[26] nothing buzzed about by the purblind trumpeters of State news, but Blank and Benefit.[27] 'My son had five pounds in such a lottery but got nothing' 'My daughter,' says another, 'had but five shillings, and got the twenty-pound prize.' People were running up and down the streets in crowds and numbers, as if one end of the town was on fire, and the other were running to help 'em off with their goods. One stream of coachmen, footmen, apprentice boys and servant wenches flowing one way, with wonderful hopes of getting an estate for threepence; knights, esquires, gentlemen and traders, married ladies, virgin madams, jilts, concubines and strumpets, moving on foot, in sedans, chariots and coaches, another way, with a pleasing expectance of getting six hundred a year for a crown.

Thus were all the fools in Town so busily employed in running up and down from one lottery to another, that it was as much as London could do to conjure together such numbers of knaves as might cheat 'em fast enough of their money. The unfortunate cried out, 'A cheat, a cheat, a confounded cheat; nothing of fairness in't.' The fortunate, in opposition to the other, crying, ''Tis all fair, all fair; the fairest adventure that ever was drawn.' And thus everybody, according to their success, expressed variously their sentiments, though the losers, who may be said to be in the wrong of it to venture their money, were most right in their conjectures of the project; and the gainers, who were in the right of it to hazard their money, because they won, were most wrong in their opinion of the matter. For I have much ado to forbear believing that luck in a bag is almost as honest as fortune in a wheel, or any other of the like projects.

'Truly,' says my friend, 'I confess I cannot conceive any extraordinary opinion of the fairness of any lottery, for I am apt to believe that whenever such a number of fools fall into a knave's hand he will make the most of 'em, and I think the Parliament could not have given the nation greater assurances of their especial regard to the welfare of the public than by suppressing all lotteries, which only serve to buoy up the mistaken multitude with dreams of golden showers to

[24] *Ticket catalogues:* For the lotteries.

[25] *the Jubilee:* The Papal Jubilee (fiftieth anniversary) of 1700.

[26] *Scotch settlement at Darien:* The proposal to settle a Scotch colony at Darien, on the Isthmus of Panama. The project was abandoned in 1698.

[27] *Blank and Benefit:* a losing and a winning lottery ticket, respectively.

the expense of that little money which with hard labour they have earned, and often to the neglect of their business, which doubles the inconvenience. The gentry, indeed, might make it their diversion, but the common people make it a great part of their care and business, hoping thereby to relieve a necessitous life, instead of which they plunge themselves further into an ocean of difficulties. What if one man in ten thousand gets five hundred pounds? What benefit is that to the rest, who have struggled hard for fools' pence to make up that sum, which perhaps falls to one who stood not in need of Fortune's favours?

'Prithee,' says my friend, 'let's go to Mercers' Chapel and see how the crowd behave themselves there. Ten to one, we shall see something or other that may be diverting to ourselves, and worth rendering to the public.' Accordingly we directed ourselves thither, to which rendezvous of adventurers, as well as ourselves, abundance of fools from all parts of the town were flocking, none showing a despairing countenance, but all expressing as much hopes in their looks as if every one had an assurance from a Moorfields conjurer of having the great prize. Some were thoughtful how to improve it, should it so happen; some how happily they'd enjoy it; women, what fine clothes they'd wear; maids, what handsome husbands they'd have; beaus, what fine wigs they'd wear; and sots, what rare wine they'd drink; the religious, what charitable works they'd do; and young libertines, what fine whores they'd keep.

In the porch, or entry of the hall, was a bookseller's shop, where the printed benefits were sold, for which the people were so impatient that there could not be more clawing amongst mumpers[28] at a nobleman's gate (when he goes out of town) at the distribution of his charity. With much ado we crowded into the hall, where young and old, rich and poor, gentle and simple, were mixed higgledy-piggledy, all gaping for a benefit, like so many Fortune's minions waiting for a windfall from her blind lady's Golden Pippin tree, whilst the projector and the honourable trustees sat, laughing in their sleeves, to see fair play dealt out to the attentive assembly, whose avaricious hearts went pit-a-pat at the drawing of every ticket.

Every now and then, when a benefit arose, some impatient novice or other crying out, 'That's mine,' bustled up to the trustees, producing his ticket to prevent that fraud which, though he had ventured his money, he was fearful might be practised amongst 'em. It sometimes

[28] *mumpers*: Beggars.

proved the adventurer had mistaken his number or the number that
was drawn to the benefit, which proved such a disappointment to 'em
that their silly looks would render 'em a laughing-stock to the whole
congregation of Fortune's courtiers, every one equally big with the
hopes of being the only favourite.

My friend and I, having no pretence or title to be ranked, by any
accident, in the number of the fortunate, having ventured nothing in
their plausible piece of uncertainty, thought it not worth our while to
spend any further time amongst 'em, but concluded to march about
our business, and leave the numerous sons and daughters of Fortune
to flatter themselves with the vain hopes of their mother's kindness.
So we came out to go to a neighbouring coffee-house, where we
smoked a pipe and consulted of some new measures to take in our
next *Spy*. This being done, we retired home, where I scribbled the following lines upon lotteries, with which I shall conclude:

> What sundry projects the ingenious find
>   T' allure and cozen avaricious fools;
> And draw the common people, who are blind
>   In all their stratagems to be their tools.
>
> The hope of sudden wealth does most deceive
>   When 'tis from labour and from danger free;
> Let but the hopes be plausible you give,
>   And most men will with your designs agree.
>
> For all men love prosperity and ease,
>   And when its prospect they with safety have,
> Though at a vast long distance, yet 'twill please
>   The silly wretch whom want does most enslave.
>
> This made the lott'ries with the crowd prevail;
>   The odds, though great, they never mind to scan
> As long as each among the num'rous all
>   Has equal hopes to be the happy man.
>
> The vast deduction for the pains and charge
>   Of ten per cent, in reason, is too great;
> And where the gain in justice is too large,
>   The very profit is alone a cheat.
>
> Thousands, 'tis plain, would soon have been undone
>   Had the late Act[29] much longer been delayed.

[29] *the late Act:* In 1699 the government passed a law forbidding lotteries; in
1709–10 the government reestablished state lotteries.

Where many suffer to enrich but one,
   All such designs are in their nature bad.

All loose vain projects ought to be debarred
   Which are of evil to the public known,
Wherein projectors have a large reward
   For doing what had better ne'er been done.

This is enough to prove they hurtful are,
   Since among all the adventurers you meet,
To one who's reason to believe 'em fair
   A thousand shall cry out, 'A cheat, a cheat'.

He that projects or models the design,
   Like the box-keeper, certain is to win:
In lott'ries 'tis the same as 'tis in play:
   The knaves are vultures and the fools their prey.

[Jonathan's Coffee-house]

From thence I took a turn into the City, where people were running about with as much concern in their countenances as if they had received news of the French landing, or that an army of Irish Papists had taken possession of Stocks Market, in order to massacre the Protestants, and plunder the City.

At last I went to Jonathan's Coffee-house[30] by the 'Change, to enquire into the meaning of this strange disorder. There I saw a parcel of men at one table consulting together with as much malice, horror, anger and despair in their looks, as if a new pestilence had sprung up in their families, and their wives had run away with their journeymen to avoid the infection. And at another table was a parcel of merry, hawked-looked blades, laughing and pointing at the rest, as if, with abundance of satisfaction, they triumphed over the others' afflictions. At last, upon a little enquiry into the matter, I found the honest brotherhood of the stockjobbers were in a lamentable confusion, and had divided themselves in two parts, fools and knaves. A few of the latter (having been too cunning for a great many of the former) had drawn in the fools, some two, some three, some four or five hundred pounds deep, to the ruin of many and the great disadvantage of more; who having been under the reputation of knaves all their lives' time, have at last, by the unexpected ill-success of an unlucky project,

---

[30] *Jonathan's Coffee-house:* Near the Royal Exchange, this was a popular meeting place for businessmen and especially stockbrokers. See *Spectator* No.1 (p. 81).

undeceived the world at once, and proved themselves the arrantest
fools in the whole City. And for the reader's better information I have
drawn one of these sublunary busybodies into a brief character, with
which I shall conclude.

A Stockjobber

He is a compound of knave, fool, shopkeeper, merchant, and
gentleman. His whole business is tricking. When he cheats another
he's a knave; when he suffers himself to be outwitted he's a fool. He
most commonly keeps a visible trade going, and with whatsoever he
gets in his shop he makes himself a domestic merchant upon 'Change
by turning stock-adventurer, led on by the mighty hopes of advancing
himself to a coach and horses, so that he might lord it over his neighbouring mechanics. He's as great a lover of uncertainty as some fools
are of the Royal Oak lottery,[31] and would not give a farthing for an
estate got without a great deal of hazard. He's a kind of speculum
wherein you may behold the passions of mankind and the vanity of
human life. Today he laughs, and tomorrow he grins; is the third day
mad, and always labours under those twin passions, hope and fear,
rising one day, and falling the next, like mercury in a weather-glass,[32]
and cannot arrive to that pitch of wisdom as to know one day what
he shall be the next. He is never under the prospect of growing rich
but at the same time under the danger of being poor, and is always to
be found between hawk and buzzard. He spins out his life between
Faith and Hope, but has nothing to do with Charity because there's
little to be got by't. He's a man whose great ambition is to ride over
others, in order to which, he resolves to win the horse, or lose the
saddle.

[Shopgirls at the New Exchange]

We moved on along the Strand, as leisurely as a couple of *valets-
de-chambres*[33] out of places, in search of a dinner, meeting nothing
remarkable till we came to the New Exchange,[34] into which seraglio
of fair ladies we made our entrance, to take a pleasing view of the
cherubimical lasses, who, I suppose, had dressed themselves up for

[31] *Royal Oak lottery:* A state lottery run in 1698.
[32] *weather-glass:* A barometer.
[33] *valets-de-chambres:* A man's male personal servant.
[34] *the New Exchange:* An emporium of stalls in the Strand where fashionable
goods were sold.

sale to the best advantage, as well as the fopperies and toys[35] they
dealt in. And indeed, many of them looked so very amiable, so enticing fair, that had I been happily furnished with some superfluous angels, I could willingly have dealt among the charming witches for
some of their commodities; but as cursed cows have short horns, I
could only walk by, and lick my lips at their handsome faces, as a
hungry beggar when he stares into a cook's shop, and was forced so
to content myself. The chiefest customers that I observed they had,
were beaus, who, I imagined, were paying a double price for linen,
gloves, or sword-knots, to the prettiest of the women, that they might
go from thence and boast among their brother fops what singular
favours and great encouragements they had received from the fair
lady that sold 'em.

Finding nothing else amongst 'em worth observing, I digested a
little of their shop language into a song, and so proceeded.

> 'Fine lace or linen, sir,
> Good gloves or ribbons here —
>   What is't you please to buy, sir?'
> "Pray what d'ye ask for this?"
> 'Ten shilling is the price;
> It cost me, sir, no less,
>   I scorn to tell a lie, sir.
>
> 'Madam, what is't you want?
> Rich fans of India paint?
>   Fine hoods or scarves, my lady?
> Silk stockings will you buy,
> In grain or other dye?
> Pray, madam, please your eye,
>   I've good as e'er was made ye.
>
> 'My lady, feel the weight —
> They're fine, and yet not slight,
>   I'd with my mother trust 'em
> For goodness and for wear.
> Madam, I vow and swear
> I showed you this same pair,
>   In hopes to gain your custom.'
>
> "Pray, tell me in a word,
> At what you can afford,
>   With living gain to sell 'em?"

---

[35] *toys:* Not necessarily children's playthings, but fashionable knickknacks and ornaments.

'The price is one pound five,
And, as I hope to live,
I do my profit give,
     Your Honour's very welcome.

'Knives, penknives, combs or scissors,
Tooth-pickers, sirs; or tweezers,
     Or walking canes to ease ye.
Ladies, d'ye want fine toys,
For misses, or for boys?
Of all sorts I have choice,
     And pretty things to please ye.

'I want a little baby[36]
As pretty a one as may be,
     With head-dress made of feather.
And now I think again,
I want a toy from Spain[37] —
You know what 'tis I mean.
     Pray send 'em home together.'

Having taken a satisfactory survey of this jilts' academy, where
girls are admitted at nine years old, and taught by eleven to out-
chatter a magpie, outwit their parents, and by the improving instructions and example of their kind mistresses and neighbouring correspondents, are made as forward and as ripe in thought before they
are out of their hanging-sleeves[38] as a country wench is at five-and-
twenty.

ALEXANDER POPE

From Windsor-Forest

Alexander Pope (1688–1744) published *Windsor-Forest* in 1713 to
celebrate the Treaty of Utrecht, which ended the War of the Spanish
Succession (1701–14). Like *Coopers Hill*, which it takes as its model,
Windsor-Forest is a topographical poem that surveys the English landscape and English history to frame a meditation on legitimate and benefi-

---

[36] *baby:* A fashion doll.
[37] *a toy from Spain:* Perhaps a dildo.
[38] *hanging-sleeves:* Loose, open sleeves worn by children.

cial sovereignty. The poem figures the Treaty of Utrecht as a kind of Pax Britannica: right rule will be restored to the world, old and new, through England's just dominion — political, military, and commercial. The peace commemorated in the poem is manifest in the riches that now flow up the Thames from the world's oceans: "The figur'd Streams in Waves of Silver roll'd, / And on their Banks *Augusta* rose in Gold" (ll. 335–36). The Treaty of Utrecht brought England Gibraltar; a number of North American territories (New Brunswick, Nova Scotia, and Prince Edward Island); and the coveted Asiento, the contract to provide slaves to the Spanish Americas. In *Windsor-Forest* the violence of England's commercial imperialism and the nation's newly intensified participation in the slave trade are displaced and obscured by a vision of global harmony, which Pope posits as the outcome of the treaty. Under English rule, the poem asserts, justice will be established throughout the New World: "Till Conquest cease, and Slav'ry be no more" (l. 407).

The lines reprinted here are taken from *The Poems of Alexander Pope*, ed. John Butt (New Haven, CT: Yale UP, 1963), 202–10.

Thou too, great Father of the *British* Floods°!
With joyful Pride survey'st our lofty Woods,   220
Where tow'ring Oaks their growing Honours rear,
And future Navies on thy Shores appear.
Not *Neptune*'s° self from all his Streams receives
A wealthier Tribute, than to thine he gives.
No Seas so rich, so gay no Banks appear,   225
No Lake so gentle, and no Spring so clear.
Nor *Po*° so swells the fabling Poet's Lays,
While led along the Skies his Current strays,
As thine, which visits *Windsor*'s fam'd Abodes,
To grace the Mansion of our earthly Gods.   230
Nor all his Stars above a Lustre show,
Like the bright Beauties on thy Banks below;
Where *Jove*, subdu'd by mortal Passion still,
Might change *Olympus*° for a nobler Hill.

219. *great Father of the British Floods:* The Thames River.
223. *Neptune's:* Roman god of the sea (Greek Poseidon).
227. *Po:* A river in Italy.
233–34. *Jove . . . Olympus:* Jove (Jupiter) is the chief god in the Roman pantheon (Greek Zeus). Mount Olympus is the mythical home of the gods.

Happy the Man whom this bright Court approves,   235
His Sov'reign favours, and his Country loves;
Happy next him who to these Shades retires,
Whom Nature charms, and whom the Muse inspires,
Whom humbler Joys of home-felt Quiet please,
Successive Study, Exercise and Ease.   240
He gathers Health from Herbs the Forest yields,
And of their fragrant Physick spoils the Fields:
With Chymic Art° exalts the Min'ral Pow'rs,
And draws the Aromatick Souls of Flow'rs.
Now marks the Course of rolling Orbs on high;   245
O'er figur'd Worlds now travels with his Eye.
Of ancient Writ unlocks the learned Store,
Consults the Dead, and lives past Ages o'er.
Or wandring thoughtful in the silent Wood,
Attends the Duties of the Wise and Good,   250
T'observe a Mean, be to himself a Friend,
To follow Nature, and regard his End.
Or looks on Heav'n with more than mortal Eyes,
Bids his free Soul expatiate in the Skies,
Amid her Kindred Stars familiar roam,   255
Survey the Region, and confess her Home!
Such was the Life great *Scipio* once admir'd,
Thus *Atticus*, and *Trumbal* thus retir'd.°
    Ye sacred Nine!° that all my Soul possess,
Whose Raptures fire me, and whose Visions bless,   260
Bear me, oh bear me to sequester'd Scenes,
The Bow'ry Mazes and surrounding Greens;
To *Thames*'s Banks which fragrant Breezes fill,
Or where ye Muses sport on *Cooper*'s Hill.°
(On *Cooper*'s Hill eternal Wreaths shall grow,   265

243. *Chymic Art:* Alchemy.
257–58. *Scipio . . . Atticus . . . Trumbal thus retir'd:* Scipio Africanus (237–183
B.C.) was a Roman general who defeated the Carthaginian Hannibal in the second
Punic War. After his victory, he refused the political distinctions offered to him. Titus
Pomponius, or Atticus (109–32 B.C.), was the friend and correspondent of the orator
and statesman Cicero; he withdrew from political life and retired to a country estate.
Sir William Trumball (1639–1716) was Secretary of State under William III; he was
born in Windsor Forest and retired there when he resigned from public office.
259. *sacred Nine:* The nine Muses of classical mythology.
264. *Cooper's Hill:* See headnote to *Coopers Hill* and note to line 159 (pp. 243–44).

While lasts the Mountain, or while *Thames* shall flow)
I seem thro' consecrated Walks to rove,
I hear soft Musick dye along the Grove;
Led by the Sound I roam from Shade to Shade,
By God-like Poets Venerable made: 270
Here his first Lays Majestick *Denham*° sung;
There the last Numbers flow'd from *Cowley*'s° Tongue.
O early lost! what Tears the River shed
When the sad Pomp along his Banks was led?
His drooping Swans on ev'ry Note expire,   275
And on his Willows hung each Muse's Lyre.

    Since Fate relentless stop'd their Heav'nly Voice,
No more the Forests ring, or Groves rejoice;
Who now shall charm the Shades where *Cowley* strung
His living Harp, the lofty *Denham* sung?   280
But hark! the Groves rejoice, the Forest rings!
Are these reviv'd? or is it *Granville*° sings?

    'Tis yours, my Lord, to bless our soft Retreats,
And call the Muses to their ancient Seats,
To paint anew the flow'ry Sylvan Scenes,   285
To crown the Forests with Immortal Greens,
Make *Windsor* Hills in lofty Numbers rise,
And lift her Turrets nearer to the Skies;
To sing those Honours you deserve to wear,
And add new Lustre to her Silver *Star*.°   290

    Here noble *Surrey*° felt the sacred Rage,
Surrey, the *Granville* of a former Age:
Matchless his Pen, victorious was his Lance;
Bold in the Lists, and graceful in the Dance:
In the same Shades the *Cupids* tun'd his Lyre,   295

---

271. *Denham:* See headnote to *Coopers Hill* (p. 243).

272. *Cowley's:* The poet Abraham Cowley (1618–1667) died in Chertsey, at the edge of Windsor Forest, and his funeral bier was floated down the Thames to London.

282. *Granville:* George Granville, Lord Landsdowne, Secretary of War under Queen Anne. Pope dedicated *Windsor-Forest* to Granville, who was also a minor poet and playwright.

290. *Silver Star:* The Star emblem of the Order of the Garter, instituted in 1348 at Windsor Castle by Edward III (1312–1377). Membership in the Order is considered the highest English civil and military honor.

291. *Surrey:* Henry Howard, Earl of Surrey (1517–1547), the poet who, with Sir Thomas Wyatt (1503–1542), introduced Italian poetic styles and meters into England.

To the same Notes, of Love, and soft Desire:
Fair *Geraldine*, bright Object of his Vow,
Then fill'd the Groves, as heav'nly *Myra* now.°
   Oh wou'dst thou sing what Heroes *Windsor* bore,
What Kings first breath'd upon her winding Shore,   300
Or raise old Warriors whose ador'd Remains
In weeping Vaults her hallow'd Earth contains!
With *Edward*'s Acts adorn the shining Page,
Stretch his long Triumphs down thro' ev'ry Age,
Draw Monarchs chain'd, and *Cressi*'s glorious Field,°   305
The Lillies blazing on the Regal Shield.
Then, from her Roofs when *Verrio*'s° Colours fall,
And leave inanimate the naked Wall;
Still in thy Song shou'd vanquish'd *France* appear,
And bleed for ever under *Britain*'s Spear.   310
   Let softer Strains Ill-fated *Henry*° mourn,
And Palms Eternal flourish round his Urn.
Here o'er the Martyr-King° the Marble weeps,
And fast beside him, once-fear'd *Edward*° sleeps:
Whom not th'extended *Albion*° could contain,   315
From old *Belerium*° to the *Northern* Main,
The Grave unites; where ev'n the Great find Rest,
And blended lie th' Oppressor and th' Opprest!
   Make sacred *Charles*'s Tomb° for ever known,
(Obscure the Place, and uninscrib'd the Stone)   320
Oh Fact accurst! What Tears has *Albion* shed,

297–98. *Geraldine . . . Myra:* The fictitious names of the women to whom Surrey and Granville addressed their poetry.

305. *Cressi's glorious Field:* Edward III defeated the French at Crécy. In 1340, he took the title King of France and put the lilies of France on his coat of arms.

307. *Verrio's:* Antonio Verrio (1639–1707) was a painter whose murals adorned parts of Windsor Castle.

311. *Henry:* Henry VI (1421–1471) ruled from 1422 to 1461 and again from 1470 to 1471. Henry's throne was challenged by Edward (1442–1482), Duke of York, who proclaimed himself King Edward IV in 1461.

313. *the Martyr-King:* Henry VI was murdered in the Tower of London in 1471, after which he was revered as a saint and martyr.

314. *Edward:* See note to line 311. The two kings were buried near one another in St. George's Chapel in Windsor Castle.

315. *Albion:* Latin name for England.

316. *old Belerium: Belerium promontorium* was the Latin name for Land's End, a peninsula of southwest England on the coast of Cornwall.

319. *Charles's Tomb:* Charles I (1600–1649) was buried in St. George's Chapel in Windsor Castle in the same tomb as Henry VIII (1491–1547).

Heav'ns! what new Wounds, and how her old have bled?
She saw her Sons with purple Deaths expire,
Her sacred Domes involv'd in rolling Fire,
A dreadful Series of Intestine Wars,°   325
Inglorious Triumphs, and dishonest Scars.
At length great *ANNA*° said — Let Discord cease!
She said, the World obey'd, and all was *Peace!*
     In that blest Moment, from his Oozy Bed
Old Father *Thames* advanc'd his rev'rend Head.   330
His Tresses dropt with Dews, and o'er the Stream
His shining Horns° diffus'd a golden Gleam;
Grav'd on his Urn appear'd the Moon, that guides
His swelling Waters, and alternate Tydes;
The figur'd Streams in Waves of Silver roll'd,   335
And on their Banks *Augusta*° rose in Gold.
Around his Throne the Sea-born Brothers stood,
Who swell with Tributary Urns his Flood.
First the fam'd Authors of his ancient Name,
The winding *Isis*, and the fruitful *Tame*:   340
The *Kennet* swift, for silver Eels renown'd;
The *Loddon* slow, with verdant Alders crown'd:
Cole, whose dark Streams his flow'ry Islands lave;
And chalky *Wey*, that rolls a milky Wave:
The blue, transparent *Vandalis* appears;   345
The gulphy *Lee* his sedgy Tresses rears:
And sullen *Mole*, that hides his diving Flood;
And silent *Darent*, stain'd with *Danish* Blood.
     High in the midst, upon his Urn reclin'd,
(His Sea-green Mantle waving with the Wind)   350
The God appear'd; he turn'd his azure Eyes
Where *Windsor*-Domes and pompous Turrets rise,
Then bow'd and spoke; the Winds forget to roar,
And the hush'd Waves glide softly to the Shore.

323–25. *purple Deaths . . . rolling Fire . . . Intestine Wars:* The plague of 1665 and
the Great Fire in 1666 are here seen as effects of Charles I's execution. The "Intestine
Wars" may refer to both the Civil Wars (1642–48) and to the Glorious Revolution in
1688.

327. *great ANNA:* Queen Anne (1655–1714) ruled 1702–14; she was the last Stuart monarch.

332. *Horns:* A conventional attribute of river gods.

336. *Augusta:* A Roman name for London.

Hail Sacred *Peace!* hail long-expected Days,   355
That *Thames*'s Glory to the Stars shall raise!
Tho' *Tyber*'s Streams immortal *Rome* behold,
Tho' foaming *Hermus* swells with Tydes of Gold,
From Heav'n it self tho' sev'nfold *Nilus* flows,
And Harvests on a hundred Realms bestows;   360
These now no more shall be the Muse's Themes,
Lost in my Fame, as in the Sea their Streams.
Let *Volga*'s Banks with Iron Squadrons shine,
And Groves of Lances glitter on the *Rhine*,
Let barb'rous *Ganges* arm a servile Train;   365
Be mine the Blessings of a peaceful Reign.
No more my Sons shall dye with *British* Blood
Red *Iber*'s Sands, or *Ister*'s foaming Flood;
Safe on my Shore each unmolested Swain
Shall tend the Flocks, or reap the bearded Grain;   370
The shady Empire shall retain no Trace
Of War or Blood, but in the Sylvan Chace,
The Trumpets sleep, while chearful Horns are blown,
And Arms employ'd on Birds and Beasts alone.
Behold! th'ascending *Villa*'s on my Side   375
Project long Shadows o'er the Chrystal Tyde.
Behold! *Augusta*'s glitt'ring Spires increase,
And Temples rise, the beauteous Works of Peace.
I see, I see where two fair Cities bend
Their ample Bow, a new *White-Hall*° ascend!   380
There mighty Nations shall inquire their Doom,
The World's great Oracle in Times to come;
There Kings shall sue, and suppliant States be seen
Once more to bend before a *British* QUEEN.
    Thy Trees, fair *Windsor*! now shall leave their Woods,   385
And half thy Forests rush into my Floods,
Bear *Britain*'s Thunder, and her Cross° display,
To the bright Regions of the rising Day;
Tempt Icy Seas, where scarce the Waters roll,
Where clearer Flames glow round the frozen Pole;   390

---

380. *White-Hall:* Whitehall Palace, off St. James's Park, served as a residence for
English monarchs until it burned down in 1698. The banqueting hall designed by Inigo
Jones survived the fire.
    387. *her Cross:* The red cross of St. George on the Union Jack.

Or under Southern Skies exalt their Sails,
Led by new Stars, and born by spicy Gales!
For me the Balm shall bleed, and Amber flow,
The Coral redden, and the Ruby glow,
The Pearly Shell its lucid Globe infold,   395
And *Phœbus*° warm the ripening Ore to Gold.
The Time shall come, when free as Seas or Wind
Unbounded *Thames* shall flow for all Mankind,
Whole Nations enter with each swelling Tyde,
And Seas but join the Regions they divide;   400
Earth's distant Ends our Glory shall behold,
And the new World launch forth to seek the Old.
Then Ships of uncouth Form shall stem the Tyde,
And Feather'd People° crowd my wealthy Side,
And naked Youths and painted Chiefs admire   405
Our Speech, our Colour, and our strange Attire!
Oh stretch thy Reign, fair *Peace!* from Shore to Shore,
Till Conquest cease, and Slav'ry be no more:
Till the freed *Indians* in their native Groves
Reap their own Fruits, and woo their Sable Loves,   410
Peru once more a Race of Kings behold,
And other *Mexico*'s be roof'd with Gold.
Exil'd by Thee from Earth to deepest Hell,
In Brazen Bonds shall barb'rous *Discord* dwell:
Gigantick *Pride*, pale *Terror*, gloomy *Care*,   415
And mad *Ambition*, shall attend her there.
There purple *Vengeance* bath'd in Gore retires,
Her Weapons blunted, and extinct her Fires:
There hateful *Envy* her own Snakes shall feel,
And *Persecution* mourn her broken Wheel: 420
There *Faction* roar, *Rebellion* bite her Chain,
And gasping Furies thirst for Blood in vain.
    Here cease thy Flight, nor with unhallow'd Lays
Touch the fair Fame of *Albion*'s Golden Days.
The Thoughts of Gods let *Granville*'s° Verse recite, 425
And bring the Scenes of opening Fate to Light.
My humble Muse, in unambitious Strains,

---

396. *Phœbus:* Phoebus Apollo, the Greek god of light, here as a sun god.
404. *Feather'd People:* North American natives.
425. *Granville's:* See note to line 282.

Paints the green Forests and the flow'ry Plains,
Where Peace descending bids her Olives spring,
And scatters Blessings from her Dove-like Wing.   430
Ev'n I more sweetly pass my careless Days,
Pleas'd in the silent Shade with empty Praise;
Enough for me, that to the listning Swains
First in these Fields I sung the Sylvan Strains.

ALEXANDER POPE

From *Epistle to Allen Lord Bathurst*

Taking up some of the issues Isaac Bickerstaff addresses in *Tatler*
No. 25 in his description of Paulo and Avaro, in his *Epistle to Allan
Lord Bathurst*, Pope moralizes on the proper use of riches. As Nicholas
Barbon does in his chapter "Of the Chief Causes that Promote Trade,"
Pope warns against both extremes of avarice and prodigality. Looking
for "the due Medium and true use of Riches," Pope finds it in the life of
his friend Allen Lord Bathurst, who is able "To balance Fortune by a just
expence, / Join with Oeconomy, Magnificence" (ll. 223–24). Allen
Bathurst (1685–1775), a Tory M.P., was made a baron in 1712. He was
a close friend of Congreve, Prior, and Swift and a dedicated landscape
gardener at his country houses in Cirencester and Riskins. First published
independently in 1733, the *Epistle to Allen Lord Bathurst* was later collected as the third of four moral essays in Pope's *Epistles to Several Persons* (1735).

The lines reprinted here are excerpted from *The Poems of Alexander
Pope*, ed. John Butt (New Haven, CT: Yale UP, 1963), 570–81.

Argument

Of the Use *of* Riches. *That it is known to few, most falling into one
of the extremes,* Avarice *or* Profusion, *v. 1, &c. The Point discuss'd, whether the invention of Money has been more commodious, or pernicious to Mankind, v. 21 to 78. That Riches, either to
the* Avaricious *or the* Prodigal, *cannot afford Happiness, scarcely*

Necessaries, v. 81 to 108. *That Avarice is an absolute Frenzy, without an End or Purpose,* v. 109 &c. *Conjectures about the Motives of Avaricious men,* v. 113 to 152. *That the conduct of men, with respect to Riches, can only be accounted for by the* ORDER OF PROVIDENCE, *which works the general Good out of Extremes, and brings all to its great End by perpetual Revolutions,* v. 161 to 178. *How a* Miser *acts upon Principles which appear to him reasonable,* v. 179. *How a* Prodigal *does the same,* v. 199. *The due Medium, and true use of Riches,* v. 219. *The* Man *of* Ross, v. 250. *The fate of the* Profuse *and the* Covetous, *in two examples; both miserable in Life and in Death,* v. 301, &c. *The Story of Sir* Balaam, v. 341 to the end.

Who shall decide, when Doctors° disagree,
And soundest Casuists° doubt, like you and me?
You hold the word, from Jove to Momus° giv'n,
That Man was made the standing jest of Heav'n;
And Gold but sent to keep the fools in play,   5
For some to heap, and some to throw away.
 But I, who think more highly of our kind,
(And surely, Heav'n and I are of a mind)
Opine, that Nature, as in duty bound,
Deep hid the shining mischief under ground: 10
But when by Man's audacious labour won,
Flam'd forth this rival to, its Sire, the Sun,
Then careful Heav'n supply'd two sorts of Men,
To squander these, and those to hide agen.
 Like Doctors thus, when much dispute has past,   15
We find our tenets just the same at last.
Both fairly owning, Riches in effect
No grace of Heav'n or token of th' Elect;
Giv'n to the Fool, the Mad, the Vain, the Evil,
To Ward, to Waters, Chartres,° and the Devil.   20

1. *Doctors:* Learned men.
2. *Casuists:* Men trained in deliberations of morals and conscience.
3. *Jove to Momus:* Jove is the god at the head of the Roman pantheon; Momus is the god of derision and mockery.
20. *To Ward, to Waters, Chartres:* John Ward (d. 1755) was an M.P. convicted of forgery and expelled from the House of Commons in 1727. Peter Waters (1664–1746) was an M.P. and a corrupt moneylender. Francis Chartres (1675–1732) was an infamously vicious man, a gambler, a moneylender, and a rapist.

What Nature wants, commodious Gold bestows,
'Tis thus we eat the bread another sows:
But how unequal it bestows, observe,
'Tis thus we riot, while who sow it, starve.
What Nature wants (a phrase I much distrust)   25
Extends to Luxury, extends to Lust:
And if we count among the Needs of life
Another's Toil, why not another's Wife?
Useful, I grant, it serves what life requires,
But dreadful too, the dark Assassin hires: 30
Trade it may help, Society extend;
But lures the Pyrate, and corrupts the Friend:
It raises Armies in a Nation's aid,
But bribes a Senate, and the Land's betray'd.
   Oh! that such bulky Bribes as all might see,   35
Still, as of old, incumber'd Villainy!
In vain may Heroes fight, and Patriots rave;
If secret Gold saps on from knave to knave.
Could France or Rome divert our brave designs,
With all their brandies or with all their wines?   40
What could they more than Knights and Squires confound,
Or water all the Quorum° ten miles round?
A Statesman's slumbers how this speech would spoil!
'Sir, Spain has sent a thousand jars of oil;
Huge bales of British cloth blockade the door;   45
A hundred oxen at your levee° roar.'
   Poor Avarice one torment more would find;
Nor could Profusion squander all in kind.
Astride his cheese Sir Morgan° might we meet,
And Worldly crying coals from street to street,   50
(Whom with a wig so wild, and mien so maz'd,
Pity mistakes for some poor tradesman craz'd).
Had Colepepper's° whole wealth been hops and hogs,
Could he himself have sent it to the dogs?

42. *the Quorum:* The Justices of the Peace.
46. *levee:* A morning assembly where statesmen and politicians would meet with their clients.
49. *Sir Morgan:* A fictitious name.
53. *Colepepper's:* Sir William Colepepper (1668–1740), according to Pope's note, was "a person of an ancient family, and ample fortune, without one other quality of a Gentleman." He gambled his estate away.

His Grace will game: to White's° a Bull be led,   55
With spurning heels and with a butting head.
To White's be carried, as to ancient games,°
Fair Coursers, Vases, and alluring Dames.
Shall then Uxorio,° if the stakes he sweep,
Bear home six Whores, and make his Lady weep?   60
Or soft Adonis,° so perfum'd and fine,
Drive to St. James's° a whole herd of swine?
Oh filthy check on all industrious skill,
To spoil the nation's last great trade, Quadrille!°
    Once, we confess, beneath the Patriot's cloak,°   65
From the crack'd bag the dropping Guinea spoke,
And gingling down the back-stairs, told the crew,
'Old Cato° is as great a Rogue as you.'
Blest paper-credit! last and best supply!
That lends Corruption lighter wings to fly!   70
Gold imp'd° by thee, can compass hardest things,
Can pocket States, can fetch or carry Kings;
A single leaf shall waft an Army o'er,
Or ship off Senates to a distant Shore;
A leaf, like Sibyl's,° scatter to and fro   75
Our fates and fortunes, as the winds shall blow:
Pregnant with thousands flits the Scrap unseen,
And silent sells a King, or buys a Queen.

    55. *White's:* A fashionable chocolate house in St. James's Street. Notorious as the haunt of heavy gamblers, White's was established as a private club in 1730 in order to keep out professional cardsharps.
    57. *ancient games:* The Olympic competitions of ancient Greece.
    59. *Uxorio:* A doting husband.
    61. *Adonis:* In Greek mythology, a beautiful young man beloved by the goddess Aphrodite. Here, an effeminate fop.
    62. *St. James's:* St. James's Palace, the royal residence.
    64. *Quadrille:* A fashionable card game.
    65. *the Patriot's cloak:* Pope's note tells us that "this is a true story, which happened in the reign of William III, to an unsuspected old Patriot, who coming out at the back-door from having been closeted by the King, where he had received a large bag of Guineas [pieces of money worth 21 shillings], the bursting of the bag discovered his business there."
    68. *Old Cato:* Cato the Elder (234–149 B.C.) known for his moral severity and uncompromised patriotism.
    71. *imp'd:* In falconry, to engraft new feathers onto the wing of a bird to improve its flight.
    75. *like Sibyl's:* In ancient Rome, a female prophet who wrote her prophecies on leaves, which were then put at the entrance to her cave. The cave of the most renowned sibyl was at Cumae in Campania.

Since then, my Lord, on such a World we fall,
What say you? 'Say? Why take it, Gold and all.'   80
    What Riches give us let us then enquire:
Meat, Fire, and Cloaths. What more? Meat, Cloaths, and Fire.
Is this too little? would you more than live?
Alas! 'tis more than Turner° finds they give.
Alas! 'tis more than (all his Visions past)   85
Unhappy Wharton,° waking, found at last!
What can they give? to dying Hopkins° Heirs;
To Chartres, Vigour; Japhet,° Nose and Ears?
Can they, in gems bid pallid Hippia° glow,
In Fulvia's buckle ease the throbs below,   90
Or heal, old Narses,° thy obscener ail,
With all th' embroid'ry plaister'd at thy tail?
They might (were Harpax° not too wise to spend)
Give Harpax self the blessing of a Friend;
Or find some Doctor that would save the life   95
Of wretched Shylock,° spite of Shylock's Wife:
But thousands die, without or this or that,
Die, and endow a College, or a Cat:
To some, indeed, Heav'n grants the happier fate,
T' enrich a Bastard, or a Son they hate.   100
    Perhaps you think the Poor might have their part?
Bond damns the Poor, and hates them from his heart:

---

    84. *Turner:* Richard Turner (d. 1733) was a merchant who lost £70,000 in a bad
investment. Pope's note says that he took this loss "so much to heart, that he kept his
chamber ever after." By living entirely in private "he sav'd both cloaths and all other
expences."
    86. *Wharton:* Philip, Duke of Wharton (1698–1731) was a fashionable profligate
who went to France, converted to Catholicism, and fought with the Spanish against the
English at the siege of Gibraltar; he died in a Spanish convent.
    87. *Hopkins:* John Hopkins (d. 1732) who, according to Pope's note, was "a Citi-
zen, whose rapacity obtained him the name of *Vultur Hopkins.*"
    88. *Chartres . . . Japhet:* For Chartres, see note to line 20. Japhet Crook (1662–
1734) had his nose and ears cut off as punishment for forgery.
    89. *Hippia:* A name for a type of hypochondriacal woman. Hypochondria was a
fashionable nervous disorder characterized by ennui, fainting fits, and weakness.
    91. *Narses:* A eunuch (d. 568 A.D.) who served as a private treasurer and general
soldier under the emperor Justinian I. Pope may have chosen the name merely for its
sound (see note 91, Aubrey Williams's edition).
    93. *Harpax:* Greek for robber.
    96. *Shylock:* In William Shakespeare's play *The Merchant of Venice*, published in
1600, Shylock is an unsavory Jewish usurer. A ruthless moneylender, a loan shark.

The grave Sir Gilbert° holds it for a rule,
That 'every man in want is knave or fool:'
'God cannot love (says Blunt,° with tearless eyes)   105
The wretch he starves' — and piously denies:
But the good Bishop, with a meeker air,
Admits, and leaves them Providence's care.
    Yet, to be just to these poor men of pelf,°
Each does but hate his Neighbour as himself: 110
Damn'd to the Mines, an equal fate betides
The Slave that digs it, and the Slave that hides.
Who suffer thus, mere Charity should own,
Must act on motives pow'rful, tho' unknown:
Some War, some Plague, or Famine they foresee,   115
Some Revelation hid from you and me.
Why Shylock wants a meal, the cause is found,
He thinks a Loaf will rise to fifty pound.
What made Directors cheat in South-sea year?°
To live on Ven'son when it sold so dear.   120
Ask you why Phryne° the whole Auction buys?
Phryne foresees a general Excise.
Why she and Sappho° raise that monstrous sum?
Alas! they fear a man will cost a plum.°
. . . .

    The Sense to value Riches, with the Art
T'enjoy them, and the Virtue to impart,   220
Not meanly, nor ambitiously pursu'd,
Not sunk by sloth, nor rais'd by servitude;
To balance Fortune by a just expence,

---

103. *Sir Gilbert:* Sir Gilbert Heathcote (1652–1733), a founder and governor of the Bank of England. He was very rich and very parsimonious.
    105. *Blunt:* Sir John Blunt (1665–1733) was a director of the South Sea Company, a monopoly founded for trade, especially in slaves, with South America and the Pacific Islands. In 1720 the company's stock went from £128 to £1,000 per share. This inflation sparked a fury of speculative buying; the resulting decline in the stock's value then brought financial ruin to thousands of shareholders.
    109. *pelf:* Riches.
    119. *South-sea year:* See note to line 105.
    121. *Phryne:* Phryne was a famously wealthy courtesan in ancient Athens.
    123. *Sappho:* A Greek poet born in the late seventh century B.C. on the island of Lesbos. Here, an unchaste woman poet or wit.
    124. *plum:* The sum of £100,000.

Join with Oeconomy, Magnificence;
With Splendour, Charity; with Plenty, Health;   225
Oh teach us, BATHURST!° yet unspoil'd by wealth!
That secret rare, between th' extremes to move
Of mad Good-nature, and of mean Self-love.
    To Want or Worth well-weigh'd, be Bounty giv'n,
And ease, or emulate, the care of Heav'n,   230
Whose measures full o'erflows on human race;
Mend Fortune's fault, and justify her grace.
Wealth in the gross is death, but life diffus'd,
As Poison heals, in just proportion us'd:
In heaps, like Ambergrise, a stink it lies   235
But well-dispers'd, is Incense to the Skies.

DANIEL DEFOE

On Credit
(From Review *Vol. 3, No. 5, and Vol. 7, No. 134)*

Daniel Defoe (1661?–1731) began writing *A Review of the State of the English Nation* while imprisoned at Newgate for libeling the church in his pamphlet "The Shortest Way with the Dissenters" (1702). In this tract he satirically suggests that the English government pursue the same course of harassment, massacre, and extermination toward Dissenters (Protestants who refused to conform to the Anglican Church) as the French government had toward the Huguenots. The first number of the *Review* came out on February 17, 1704, and Defoe continued to publish it single-handedly for nine more years until the last number on June 11, 1713. The paper thus covers almost the entire period of Queen Anne's reign (1702–14). At first it appeared weekly, then twice a week, and finally, three times a week.

The *Review* takes on the major political issues of its day. It is preoccupied during the War of the Spanish Succession by England's embroilments with France. As the author of a number of tracts and books on trade, commerce, and finance, Defoe frequently engages questions of political economy, especially in relation to political wrangles at home and England's military status abroad. In the two papers selected here, Defoe

226. BATHURST: See headnote (p. 266).

addresses the issue of credit in the commercial and national economies. Like Addison in *Spectator* No. 3 (1711), Defoe portrays credit in the female figure of Lady Credit, who is subject to the fits and starts characteristic of a vaporish, hypochondriacal woman. Such an allegorization is conventional at this time and is used by both Tory and Whig writers. (For more information on Defoe, see *Mercure Scandale*, p. 122.)

From Vol. 3, No. 5
Thursday, January 10. 1706.
Of Credit in T R A D E.

Money has a younger Sister, a very useful and officious Servant in Trade, which in the absence of her senior Relation, but with her Consent, and on the Supposition of her Confederacy, is very assistant to her; frequently supplies her place for a Time, answers all the Ends of Trade perfectly, and to all Intents and Purposes, as well as Money her self; only with one Proviso, That her Sister constantly and punctually relieves her, keeps time with her, and preserves her good Humour: but if she be never so little disappointed, she grows sullen, sick, and ill-natur'd, and will be gone for a great while together: Her Name in our Language is call'd *CREDIT*, in some Countries Honour, and in others, I know not what.

This is a coy Lass, and wonderful chary of her self; yet a most necessary, useful, industrious Creature: she has some Qualification so peculiar, and is so very nice in her Conduct, that a World of good People lose her Favour, before they well know her Name; others are courting her all their days to no purpose, and can never come into her Books.

If once she be disoblig'd, she's the most difficult to be Friends again with us, of any thing in the World; and yet she will court those most, that have no occasion for her; and will stand at their Doors neglected and ill-us'd, scorn'd, and rejected, like a Beggar, and never leave them: But let such have a Care of themselves, and be sure they never come to want her; for, if they do, they may depend upon it, she will pay them home, and never be reconcil'd to them, but upon a World of Entreaties, and the severe Penance of some years Prosperity.

'Tis a strange thing to think, how absolute this Lady is; how despotickly she governs all her Actions: If you court her, you lose her, or must buy her at unreasonable Rates; and if you do, she is always jealous of you, and Suspicious; and if you don't discharge her to a Tittle of your Agreement, she is gone, and perhaps may never come again as long as you live; and if she does, 'tis with long Entreaty and abundance of Difficulty.

Nor is she to be won by the greatest Powers; Kings cannot bribe her; Parliaments cannot force her; as has been seen by manifold Experience, among a great Variety of Ladies. King *Charles* II[1] had got her once for his Mistress, and she was very kind to him a great while; what vast Anticipations did she bring him, upon every Act of Parliament: what a Heighth did she run up his *Exchequer*[2] too? that, had he gone on, he might in time, meerly by this jades Assistance, have got all the Mony in the Nation into it: But he, *like the old Woman in the Fable, that had a Hen laid every day a golden Egg*, was for killing the Hen to have all the Eggs at once; thinking he had got her fast in his *Exchequer*, claps upon her, and shut up the Place;[3] but she was too nimble for him: he got the Money indeed, *but he lost the CREDIT*; away she flew, and she never came near him again as long as he liv'd.

In King *James* his Time,[4] by pretty good Management, punctual Dealing, and exact Compliance, she began to come to hand in a few Matters, but never to be wholly at his Devotion, as she was before at his Brother's: Nor indeed has she been heartily a Friend to the Publick Funds ever since, till very lately.

In the last Reign[5] she stood at some distance; for the King being embarrass'd at first, stood Neuter; she was very good Friends with his Majesty before he came over; but as King of *England*, she had been so ill used here, she would not treat with him; so his Majesty referr'd her to the Parliament.

---

[1] *King Charles II:* In 1660, after the period of Civil Wars and Interregnum, Charles II (1630–1685) was restored to the English throne and ruled until his death in 1685. His financial problems were notorious, and he was (rightly) suspected of receiving money from the French monarch, Louis XIV (1638–1715).

[2] *Exchequer:* The bureau of the English government that received and dispensed public funds. Charles II was voted an annual income of £1,200,000, but his revenues could never bring in this much at once, so he borrowed heavily and damaged his government severely with the debt.

[3] *shut up the Place:* In 1672 Charles suspended the interest payments on all his loans to the great discredit of his administration.

[4] *King James his Time:* James II (1633–1701) ruled from his brother Charles II's death in 1685 until his own extradition in 1688.

[5] *the last Reign:* That of William III (1650–1702), who ruled from 1688 to 1702.

The Parliament treated with her a long time, and brought her to some good Terms of Agreement, and we were in mighty hopes she would have come and settled among us again: In pursuance of this Treaty, they establish'd several very considerable Parliamentary Funds and Securities; and she seem'd very well pleased; having Duties on Salt, and Coles, and Glass, Pole-Taxes, and Land-Taxes, and a hundred Schemes; the abortive Births of gaping Projectors,[6] that in those days besieg'd the Government with their empty Unperforming Proposals.

The Government however meaning well, gave her whole Bundles of Tallies,[7] like *Bath-Faggots*, upon these Funds; but Deficiencies happening, and the Supply not coming in, she was fain to make vast Discounts with the greedy Banks and Brokers, to answer her Foreign Demands; and having no Satisfaction, she took it so ill, that she made a second Elopement, and away she run and left us.

To retrieve this Disaster, and, if possible, Court her Ladyship's Company, and procure her Return, a Knot of her Friends got together, and invited her to come and live with them, and promised, that for her Security they would establish a General Fund for running Cash, that should at any time furnish what quantity of Money she should have occasion for, and supply either Government or private Persons upon reasonable Terms; and this they call'd, A BANK.[8]

She had been jilted indeed by Proposals of like Nature, and under the same Name, before; such as *Land-Banks*, *Chamberlain's Bank*, *Chamber of* London, *Million Bank*,[9] and the like, and was therefore shye, and not ve-well pleased with this Proposal at first; and tho' the particular Men in their private Capacity had some Interest in her Favour; yet they had a great hand with her, before they could bring her to accept of being one of their Directors.

At last they got her among them, and mighty joyful they were; but all of a suddain, whether it was the Fate of the Times, or the Alteration of the Coin, or the Knavery of the Stock-Jobbers; they Disoblig'd her upon a suddain, and away she went in a Huff ——— 'Twas a strange thing, not all the Entreaty they could make, not

[6] *Projectors:* Here, devisers of schemes for financial gain.
[7] *Tallies:* Notched sticks used to record debt or payment (the creditor and debtor each kept half of the stick).
[8] *A BANK:* In 1694 the English government passed an act establishing the Bank of England. It provided loans to the government to finance the French-Dutch war.
[9] *... Million Bank:* Before the establishment of the Bank of England, a number of other banking schemes had been proposed to and contemplated by the government.

buying up their own Notes at large Discount, not offering larger Interest, not a hundred Tricks and Shams of the Directors, could bring her back; the Consequence of which was, their Bills coming to the Scandalous Discount of 20 *per Cent*, paying a little and a little in part of their Notes Alphabetically, and at last none at all, or in the Language of Trade quite broke; till a Cure was found out by Parliament, by making a New Settlement, and this has put them into such a Posture, that Madam CREDIT, has sometimes seem'd to be Reconcil'd to them again, and their Actions have been very forward and high, and they have valued themselves very much upon her Friendship; but by continual dividing their Capital, lessening their Stock, aud some other remarkable pieces of Management, a more particular Account of which, may perhaps in time be expected, this Gentlewoman and they seem to be bickering, and her Kindness to them declines again, and must do more so, unless they call to the National Assistance again to Re-establish them.

At present the likelyest place for her, to take up her Abode now, is in the Exchequer; the Knavery and ill Conduct of the *R———n*[10] Administration has been so long forgot, and the Punctual Management of Affairs there, has of late so well pleas'd her, that she comes pretty often to Court, and has lately offer'd a great Summ of Money in her own Name at 4 *per Cent*.

Indeed, she had frequently, as I have been told, tender'd Money at the Treasury, upon *Loan* at Interest, on the Common Reputation of the Exchequer, and it has been refus'd; if that be true, she certainly comes again; for she always loves to give her Attendance, when People have no need of her.

Indeed the Management of our Treasury in *England*, has of Course retriev'd the Favour of this Coy Dame, by that very Method, *viz. Not having occasion of her*; and the way to keep her, is to keep up that Condition; that not having any need of her Assistance, you may always have her at Command.

I cannot but Remark here, how these Gentlemen are baulk'd in their Pretences; who Cry out, our Funds are Exhausted, our Money is gone, and we are not able to carry on the War[11] three Years more; To these I Answer in short here, but may take occasion to say more to it hereafter; but for the present, Thus if Parliamentary and Exchequer Credit comes to join, or to carry the Allegory on, if the Parliament

---

[10] *R———n:* The Restoration Administration under Charles II; see note 3.
[11] *the War:* The War of the Spanish Succession against the French.

and Treasury join their Powerful Solicitations, to Engage this Nice Lady to come again, and heartily Espouse them, they are able meerly upon Credit, without any such thing as an extraordinary Fund, to carry on the Expence of War these 20 Years.

By an extraordinary Fund, I mean without any more than are Current and usual, Punctual Discharge of Interest, and Principal at Demand; and Parliamentary Authority to make good a Running Cash, would soon make the Exchequer of *England*, the best and Greatest Bank in the World, and Revive the Old Proverb, *as sure as Check* — which there has been too much Cause to let be almost forgotten.

I cannot confess but acknowledge, that to recover Credit to any place, where she has been ill Treated, and perswade her to return, is almost as Difficult as to restore Virginity, or to make a W——re[12] an Honest Woman; and therefore, tho' I am but a very indifferent maker of Panegyricks, yet I think I say too little, if I say, 'tis Superiour to all the Conquests of *Hochstette*, and *Catalonia*; tho' those Articles are also Prodigies in their kind too.

Nothing but punctual honourable dealing can restore Credit, *nor that*, without a Series, a continued Practice of such dealing; how to do this under Difficulties, Disappointments, and Deficiencies, I must own is the Miracle; and I take these things to be the Misfortune, rather than the Error of the late Management; but as Her Majesty has been the first, that for many Years has been able to say, the Funds answer'd beyond themselves; so that Success, join'd to Good Husbandry and Vigilance, has added that thing call'd CREDIT, to the Affairs of the Exchequer; a thing of that Immense Value and Infinite Consequence, that I dare not Write, what to me seems contain'd in the Teeming Womb, of this Mother of Great Designs.

What cannot CREDIT do, when built on the National Probity, when every End is fully Answer'd, every reasonable Demand satisfi'd, and when she is Establish'd, on the inexhaustible Fund of Wisdom and Integrity?

I Confess these are things too great to be Talk'd of in this Paper; and it deserves a Large Book, to Describe all the Windings and Meanders of this growing Article of CREDIT; nor did I design to have pursu'd the meer Allegory of CREDIT to the National Affairs; but I see such room for Publick Service in it, that I thought it my Duty to make this mention of it; which the Wife Heads, to whom the matter belongs, knows better than I, how to improve to the Publick Advantage.

[12] *W——re:* Whore.

'Tis plain, if any Summ of Money be wanting on suited Advantage, it is to be had; and I shall in a little time Demonstrate it; if a National CREDIT can be so form'd, as to be as safe as a National Fund, I think 'tis easie to see, that the same Flux of Money will follow one, as will follow the other. That this Credit is to be rais'd, is very plain and easie; and I think 'tis needless to make the Essay here; I leave it to the Conduct of those above me.

From Vol. 7, No. 134
Thursday, February 1. 1711.

. . . But come we next to the Point of Credit, which I have too long let fall; POOR CREDIT! sunk and dejected, sighing and walking alone; I met her t'other Day in the Fields, I hardly knew her, she was so lean, so pale; look'd so sickly, so faint, and was so meanly dress'd; but when I came nearer to her, and saw the Old Air of Honesty that sat always upon her Face, I worship'd her Immediately, and paid all the Homage a Friend to Commerce ow'd her.

She vouchsafed to own her humble Votary,[13] and smiling a little, told me, she was in a Condition only to acknowledge I was her Friend —— And so attempted to go on — I would have interrupted her with speaking something, but she told me she could not stay to say any more to me now, if ever she return'd to *England* again, she would ——— [14] I startled at the Word, threw my self at her Feet, and beg'd I might have the Liberty to speak to her — Which having obtain'd, I told her I was exceedingly surprized to hear her speak of returning to *England*, &c. which imply'd she was going away from us; I was going on, when she return'd short upon me, why, What should I do here? I have staid too long here already; you know how I have been us'd, how I have been Mob'd on one Side, and Mob'd on t'other Side; Bully'd and Insulted by Parties and Factions, and yet I have born it all with more Patience than I used to hear such Treatment with; I have, in short, stay'd till I am quite Ruin'd; I have neither Money, nor Trade, or Fund, to Act upon; and if I had, till you are better Friends with one another here, I can have no Satisfaction among you, and therefore I am just a going to take Shipping for another Country — I beg'd she would tell me where she design'd to go, that I might follow her, for having still a Trading Inclination, I resolv'd to begin again somewhere, but it should be no where but

---

[13] *her humble Votary:* Defoe.
[14] *she would* ——— : Probably "expire" or "perish."

where she was pleas'd to appear; for What is Commerce? What Invention? What Stock? What Industry, without Credit? —

She made no Scruple to tell me, she resolv'd to go directly for *France* —— She had not been there she said, for a long Time, and they had Succeeded accordingly; she was sure they had such a Sense of the Loss and of the Service she was able to do them, that she would meet with very good Usage, and might find out some Ways and Means, to let *England* know they ought to have us'd her better.

I was too sensible of the Truth of what she said, not to be deeply concern'd at her Resolution of leaving the Island, but much more of her going over to the Enemy,[15] and beg'd she would give me leave to make one Proposal to her, and to offer some Things to her Consideration, that perhaps might give her some Reason, at least, to delay so fatal a Resolution, till she had look'd a little farther into Matters, and that if she found any Room to Hope that Matters might be Retreiv'd, and she might meet with better Usage, she might not repent the Changeing her Resolution —— She told me it was impossible I could offer any Thing that she had not consider'd; that she saw no Disposition in the People to be easie with one another, or with their Rulers, or that those in whose Hands the Remedy lay, seem'd sensible of the Cafe —— She rather found People took her for a Bond-Woman,[16] or a Fool, that had no Power to remove her Situation, or no Capacity to Resent; and she thought Absence, as it would be her Honour and Safety, so it would be the best Physick to bring the Nation to their Senses again.

DANIEL DEFOE

On Trade (From The Complete English Tradesman*)*

Defoe (1661?–1731) was a great advocate of trade and of the commercial classes, and in his *Complete English Tradesman* he writes a kind of conduct book for tradesmen. This text is one of a number of didactic works, some of which, such as *The Family Instructor* (1727) and *Treatise Concerning the Use and Abuse of the Marriage Bed* (1727), were

[15] *the Enemy:* England was at war with France in the War of the Spanish Succession (1701–14).

[16] *a Bond-Woman:* An indentured servant who is bonded to work for her master without wages for a certain number of years.

chiefly religious and moral in orientation. Although not overtly religious, *The Complete English Tradesman* conveys a strong Puritan ethic that informs its prescriptions for the tradesman's conduct of life and conduct of business; indeed the two are inseparable. In Letter XIX, Defoe translates this ethic into material-aesthetic terms as he hands out advice on outfitting a respectable retail shop. Reflecting on the rising social status of the trading classes in Letter XXII, Defoe argues for their central place in England's national identity.

Letter XIX.
Of Fine Shops, and Fine Shews.

SIR,

It is a modern custom, and wholly unknown to our ancestors, who yet understood trade, in proportion to the Business they carried on, as well as we do, to have tradesmen lay out two thirds of their fortune in fitting up their shops.

By fitting up, I do not mean furnishing their shops with wares and goods to sell; for in that they came up to us in every particular, and perhaps went beyond us too; but in painting and gilding, in fine shelves, shutters, boxes, glass-doors, sashes and the like, in which they tell us now, 'tis a small matter to lay out two or three hundred pounds, nay five hundred pounds to fit up a Pastry-Cook's, or a Toy-shop.[1]

The first inference to be drawn from this must necessarily be, that this age must have more fools than the last, for certainly fools only are most taken with shews and outsides.

It is true, that a fine shew of goods will bring customers; and it is not a new custom, but a very old one, that a new shop very well furnished goes a great way to bringing a trade; for the proverb was, and still is, very true, *that every body has a penny for a new shop*; but that a fine shew of shelves and glass windows should bring customers, that was never made a rule in trade till now.

And yet even now I should not except so much against it, if it was not carried on to such an excess, as is too much for a middling Tradesman to bear the expence of; in this therefore it is made not a

---

[1] *Toy-shop:* A store selling knickknacks and ornamental articles of personal adornment, not children's playthings.

grievance only, but really scandalous to trade, for now a young beginner has such a tax upon him before he begins, that he must sink perhaps a third part, nay, a half part of his stock, in painting and gilding, winscoting and glazing, before he begins to trade, nay, before he can open his shop; As they say of building a water-mill, two thirds of the expence lies under the water; and when the poor Tradesman comes to furnish his shop, and lay in his stock of goods, he finds a great hole made in his cash to the workmen, and his shew of goods, on which the life of his trade depends, is fain to be lessen'd to make up his shew of boards, and glass to lay them in.

Nor is this heavy article to be abated upon any account; for if he does not make a good shew, he comes abroad like a mean ordinary fellow, and no body of fashion comes to his shop; the customers are drawn away by the pictures and painted shelves, tho' when they come there, they are not half so well fill'd, as in other places, with goods fit for a trade; and how indeed should it be otherwise? the Joiners and Painters, Glasiers and Carvers, must have all ready money; the Weavers and Merchants may give credit, their goods are of so much less moment to the shop-keeper, that they must trust, but the more important shew must be finish'd first; and paid first; and when that has made a deep hole in the Tradesman's stock, then the remainder may be spar'd to furnish the shop with goods, and the merchant must trust for the rest.

It will hardly be believ'd in ages to come, when our posterity shall be grown wiser by our loss, and, as I may truly say, at our expence, that a Pastry-Cook's shop, which twenty pounds would effectually furnish at a time, with all needful things for sale; nay, except on an extraordinary shew, as on Twelfth-day[2] at night for cakes, or upon some great Feast, twenty pounds can hardly be laid out at one time in goods for sale, yet that fitting up one of these shops should cost upwards of 300 *l. Anno Domini*,[3] 1710. Let the year be recorded: The fitting up of a shop for Pastry ware in *London* to consist of the following particulars;

1. Sash windows, all of looking-glass plates, 12 inches by 16 inches in measure.

---

[2] *Twelfth-day:* Twelve days after Christmas, January 6, the Feast of the Epiphany which commemorates the manifestation of the Christ child's divine nature before the Magi, or Three Wise Men.

[3] *Anno Domini:* In the year of the Lord.

2. All the walks of the shop lin'd up with galley-tiles,[4] and the Black-shop with galley-tiles in pannels, finely pained in forest-work[5] and figures.

3. Two large Peir looking-glasses and one chimney glass in the shop, and one very large Peir-glass seven foot high in the Back-shop.

4. Two large branches of Candlesticks, one in the shop and one in the back-room.

5. Three great glass lanthorns in the shop, and eight small ones.

6. Twenty five sconces against the wall, with a large pair of silver standing candlesticks in the back room, value 25 *l.*

7. Six fine large silver salvers to serve sweet-meats.

8. Twelve large high stands of rings, whereof three silver, to place small dishes for tarts, jelleys, &c. at a Feast.

9. Painting the cieling, and gilding the lanthorns, the sashes, and the carv'd work, 55 *l.*

These with some odd things to set forth the shop, and make a shew, besides small plate,[6] and besides China basons and cups, amounted to, as I am well inform'd, above 300 *l.*

Add to this the more necessary part, which was,

1. Building two ovens, about twenty five pounds.
2. Twenty pounds in stock for pies, and cheese-cakes, &c.

So that in short here was a trade, which might be carried on for about 30 or 40 *l.* stock, requir'd 300 *l.* expence to fit up the shop, and make a shew to invite customers.

I might give something of a like example of extravagance in fitting up a Cutler's shop, *Anglicè* a Toy-man,[7] which are now come up to such a ridiculous expence, as is hardly to be thought of without the utmost contempt; let any one stop at the Temple,[8] or at *Paul's* corner,[9] or in many other places.

[4] *galley-tiles:* Ceramic tiles.
[5] *forest-work:* Decorative representation of sylvan scenery.
[6] *small plate:* Small pieces of silver-plated serving ware.
[7] *Anglicè a Toy-man:* "In English, a Toy-man"; see note 1.
[8] *Temple:* The four Inns of Court housed along Fleet Street in London. Originally owned by the medieval religious and military order the Knights Templar, who built their residence there in the twelfth century, this series of buildings, known collectively as the Temple, was presented by James I to lawyers for their professional use. It housed both residential and professional legal apartments.
[9] *Paul's corner:* A corner on the block where St. Paul's Cathedral stands.

As to the shops of the more considerable trades, they all bear a proportion of the humour of the times, but do not call for so loud a remark; leaving therefore the just reflection which such things call for, let me bring it home to the young Tradesman, to whom I am directing this discourse, and to whom I am desirous to give solid and useful hints for his instruction; I would recommend it to him to avoid all such needless expences, and rather endeavor to furnish his shop with goods, than to paint and gild it over, to make it fine and gay; let it invite customers rather by the well-fill'd presses[10] and shelves, and the great choice of rich and fashionable goods, that one customer being well serv'd may bring another; and let him study to bring his shop into reputation for good choice of wares, and good attendance on his customers; and this shall bring a throng to him much better, and of much better people, than those that *go* in merely for a gay shop.

Let the shop be decent and handsome, spacious as the place will allow, and let something like the face of a master be always to be seen in it; and, if possible, be always busy, and doing something in it, that may look like being employ'd; this takes as much with the wiser observer of such things, as any other appearance can do.

I have heard of a young Apothecary, who setting up in a part of the Town, where he had not much acquaintance, and fearing much, whether he should get into business, hir'd a man acquainted with such business, and made him be every morning between five and six, and often late in the evenings, working very hard at the great mortar; pounding and beating, tho' he had nothing to do with it, but beating some very needless thing, that all his neighbours might hear it, and find that he was in full employ, being at work early and late, and that consequently he must be a man of vast business, and have a great practice; the thing was well laid, and took accordingly; for the neighbours believing he had business, brought business to him; and the reputation of having a trade, made a trade for him.

The observation is just; a shew may bring some people to a shop, but 'tis the fame of Business that brings Business; nothing raises the fame of a shop like its being a shop of good trade already; then people go to it, because they think other people go to it, and because they think there is good choice; their gilding and painting may go a little way, but 'tis the having a shop well fill'd with goods, having good choice to sell, and selling reasonable, these are the things that

[10] *presses:* Upright closets for storing goods.

bring a trade, and a trade thus brought will stand by you, and last; for fame of trade brings trade any where.

It is a sign of barrenness of the peoples fancy, when they are so easily taken with shews and outsides of things: Never was such painting and gilding, such sashings and looking-glasses among the shop-keepers, as there is now; and yet trade flourish'd more in former times by a great deal than it does now, if we may believe the report of very hory honest and understanding men; the reason, I think, cannot be to the credit of the present age, nor is it to the discredit of the former; for they carried on their trade with less gaiety, and with less expence than we do now.

My advice to a young Tradesman is to keep the safe middle between these extremes; something the times must be humour'd in, because fashion and custom must be follow'd; but let him consider the depth of his stock, and not lay out half his estate upon fitting up his shop, and then leave but the other half to furnish it; 'tis much better to have a Full shop, than a Fine shop; and a hundred pounds in goods will make a much better shew than a hundred pounds worth of painting and carv'd work; 'tis good to make a shew, but not to be All shew.

It is true, that painting and adorning a shop seems to intimate, that the Tradesman has a large stock to begin with, or else they suggest he would not make such a shew; hence the young shop-keepers are willing to make a great shew, and beautify, and paint, and gild, and carve, because they would be thought to have a great stock to begin with; but let me tell you, the reputation of having a great stock is ill purchas'd, when half your stock is laid out to make the world believe it; that is, *in short*, reducing yourself to a small stock to have the world believe you have a great one; in which by the way, you do no less than barter the real stock for the imaginary, and give away your stock to keep the name of it only.

I take this indeed to be a *French* humour, or a spice of it turn'd *English*, and indeed we are famous for this, that when we do mimick the *French*, we generally do it to our hurt, and over-do the *French* themselves.

The *French* nation are eminent for making a fine outside, when perhaps within they want necessaries; and indeed a gay shop and a mean stock is something like the *Frenchman* with his laced ruffles, without a shirt: I cannot but think a well furnish'd shop with a moderate outside is much better to a Tradesman, than a fine shop and few goods; I am sure it will be much more to his satisfaction, when he casts up his year's account, for his fine shop will weigh but sorrily in his account of profit and loss; 'tis all a dead article, 'tis sunk out of his first money, before he makes a shilling profit, and may be some years a recovering, as trade may go with him.

It is true that all these notions of mine in trade are founded upon the principle of frugality and good husbandry; and this is a principle so disagreeable to the times, and so contrary to the general practice, that we shall find very few people to whom it is agreeable: But let me tell my young tradesmen, that if they must banish frugality and good husbandry, they must at the same time banish all expectation of growing rich by their trade: It is a maxim in commerce, that money gets money, and they that will not frugally lay up their gain, in order to encrease their gain, must not expect to gain as they might otherwise do; frugality may be out of fashion among the gentry, but if it comes to be so among tradesmen, we shall soon see that wealthy tradesmen will be hard to find; for they who will not save as well as gain must expect to go out of trade as lean as they began.

Some people tell us indeed in many cases, especially in trade, that putting a good face upon things goes as far as the real merit of the things themselves; and that a fine, painted, gilded shop, among the rest, has a great influence upon the people, draws customers, and brings trade; and they run a great length in this discourse by satyrising on the blindness and folly of mankind, and how the world are to be taken in their own way; and seeing they are to be deluded and imposed upon in such an innocent way, they ought to be so far deluded and imposed upon, alluding to the old proverbial saying, *Si populus, vult docipi, decipiatur*;[11] that 'tis no fraud, no crime, and can neither be against conscience or prudence; for if they are pleas'd with a shew, why should they not have it? *and the like.*

This way of talking is indeed plausible; and were the fact true, there might be more in it, than I think there is: But I do not grant that the world is thus to be deluded; and that the people do follow this rule in general, I mean, to go always to a fine shop to lay out their money; perhaps in some cases it may be so, where the women, and weakest of the sex too, are chiefly concern'd; or where the fops and fools of the age resort; and as to those few, that they are willing to be so impos'd upon, let them have it.

But I do not see, that even this extends any farther than to a few Toy-shops,[12] and Pastry-Cooks; and the customers of both these are

[11] *Si . . . decipiatur:* "If the people want to be deceived, they will be deceived."
[12] *Toy-shops:* See note 1.

not of credit sufficient, I think, to weigh in this case; we may as well argue for the fine habits at a *Puppet-shew* and a *Rope-dancing*,[13] because they draw the Mob about them; but I cannot think, after you go but one degree above these, the thing is of any weight, much less does it bring credit to the Tradesman, whatever it may do to the shop.

The credit of a Tradesman respects two sorts of people, *first*, the merchants, or wholesale men, or *makers*, who sell him his goods, or the customers, who come to his shop to buy.

The first of these are so far from valuing him upon the gay appearance of his shop, that they are often the first that take an offence at it, and suspect his credit upon that account; their opinion upon a Tradesman, and his credit with them, is rais'd quite another way, namely, by his current pay, diligent attendance, and honest figure; *the gay shop* does not help him at all there, but rather the contrary.

As to *the latter*, though some customers may *at first* be drawn by the gay appearance and fine gilding and painting of a shop, yet it is the well sorting a shop with goods, and the selling good pennyworths that will bring trade, especially after the shop has been open some time; this, and this only, establishes the man and the credit of the shop.

To conclude; the credit rais'd by the fine shew of things is also of a different kind from the substantial reputation of a Tradesman; 'Tis rather the credit of the shop, than of the man; and in a word, it is no more or less than a net spread to catch fools; 'tis a bait to allure and deceive, and the Tradesman generally intends it so; He intends that the customers shall pay for the gilding and painting his shop, and 'tis the use he really makes of it, *viz.* that his shop looking like something eminent, he may sell dearer than his neighbours: who, and what kind of fools can so be drawn in, it is easy to describe; but satyr is none of our business here.

On the contrary, the customers, who are the substantial dependence of a Tradesman's shop, are such as are gain'd and preserv'd by good usage, good pennyworths, good wares, and good choice; and a shop that has the reputation of these four, like good wine that needs no bush, needs no painting or gilding, no carv'd works and ornaments; it requires only a diligent master and a faithful servant, and it will never want a trade.

I am, &c.

---

[13] *Rope-dancing:* Tightrope walking.

Letter XXII.

Of the Dignity of Trade in England
more than in other Countries.

SIR,

It is said of *England* by way of distinction, and we all value our selves upon it, that it is a trading country; and King *Charles* II[14] who was perhaps the Prince of all the Kings that ever reign'd in *England*, that best understood the country and the people that he govern'd, us'd to say, *That the Tradesmen were the only Gentry in* England: His Majesty spoke it merrily, but it had a happy signification in it, such as was peculiar to the best Genius of that Prince, who, tho' he was not the bright governour, was the best acquainted with the world, of all the Princes of his age, if not of all the men in it; and tho' it be a digression give me leave, after having quoted the King, to add three short observations of my own, in favour of *England*, and of the people and trade of it, and yet without the least partiality to our own country.

I. We are not only a trading country, but the greatest trading country in the world.

II. Our climate is the most agreeable climate in the world to live in.

III. Our *Englishmen* are the stoutest and best men (I mean what we call men of their hands) in the world.

These are great things to advance in our own favour, and yet to pretend not to be partial too; and therefore I shall give my reasons, which I think support my opinion, and they shall be as short as the heads themselves, that I may not go too much off from my subject.

1. We are the greatest trading country in the world, because we have the greatest exportation of the growth and product of our land, and of the manufacture and labour of our people; and the greatest importation and consumption of the growth, product, and manufactures of other countries from abroad, of any nation in the world.

2. Our climate is the best and most agreeable, because a man can be more out of doors in *England* than in other countries. This was King *Charles* the second's reason for it; and I cannot name it, without doing justice to his Majesty in it.

[14] *King Charles II:* Charles II (1630–1685) reigned from 1660 to 1685.

3. Our men are the *stoutest* and *best*, because strip them naked from the wast upwards, and give them no weapons at all but their Hands and Heels, and turn them into a room, or stage, and lock them in with the like number of other men of any nation, man for man, and they shall beat the best men you shall find in the world.

From this digression, which I hope will not be disagreeable, as it is not very tedious, I come back to my first observation, that *England* is a trading country; and two things I offer from that head.

> *First*, Our tradesmen are not, as in other countries, the meanest of our people.
> *Secondly*, Some of the greatest and best, and most flourishing families among not the gentry only, but even the nobility, have been rais'd from trade, owe their beginning, their wealth, and their estates to trade; and I may add,
> *Thirdly*, Those families are not at all ashamed of their original, and indeed have no occasion to be ashamed of it.

It is true, that in *England* we have a numerous and an illustrious Nobility and Gentry; and it is true also, that not so many of those families have rais'd themselves by the sword as in other nations, though we have not been without men of fame in the field too.

But *Trade* and *Learning* has been the two chief steps, by which our gentlemen have rais'd their relations, and have built their fortunes; and from which they have ascended up to the prodigious height, both in wealth and number, which we see them now risen to.

As so many of our noble and wealthy families are rais'd by, and derive from trade, so it is true, and indeed it cannot well be otherwise, that many of the younger branches of our gentry, and even of the nobility it self, have descended again into the spring from whence they flow'd, and have become tradesmen; and thence it is, that, as I said above, our tradesmen in *England* are not, *as it generally is in other countries*, always of the meanest of our people.

Indeed I might have added here, that trade it self in England is not, as it generally is in other countries, the meanest thing the men can turn their hand to; but on the contrary trade is the readiest way for men to raise their fortunes and families; and therefore it is a field of men of figure and of good families to enter upon.

N.B. By trade we must be understood to include Navigation, and
foreign discoveries, because they are generally speaking all promoted and carried on by trade, and even by tradesmen, as well
as merchants; and the tradesmen are at this time as much concern'd in shipping (as Owners) as the merchants, only the latter
may be said to be the chief employers of the shipping.

Having thus done a particular piece of justice to ourselves, in the
value we put upon trade and tradesmen in *England*, it reflects very
much upon the understandings of those refin'd heads, who *pretend to*
depreciate that part of the nation, which is so infinitely superior in
number and in wealth to the families who call themselves gentry, and
so infinitely more numerous.

As to the wealth of the nation, that undoubtedly lies chiefly among
the trading part of the people; and tho' there are a great many families rais'd within a few years, in the late war by great employments,
and by great actions abroad, to the honour of the *English* Gentry; yet
how many more families among the tradesmen have been rais'd to
immense estates, even during the same time, by the attending circumstances of the war?[15] such as the cloathing, the paying, the victualling[16] and furnishing, *&c.* both army and navy? And by whom
have the prodigious taxes been paid, the loans supplied, and money
advanced upon all occasions? By whom are the Banks and Companies carried on? And on whom are the Customs and Excises levied?
Has not the trade and tradesmen born the burthen of the war? And
do they not still pay four millions a year interest for the publick
debts? On whom are the funds levied, and by whom the publick
credit supported? Is not trade the inexhausted fund of all funds, and
upon which all the rest depend?

As is the trade, so in proportion are the tradesmen; and how
wealthy are tradesmen in almost all the several parts of *England*,
as well as in *London*? How ordinary is it to see a tradesman go
off of the stage, even but from mere shop-keeping, with, from ten
to forty thousand pounds estate, to divide among his family? when,
on the contrary, take the gentry in *England* from one end to the
other, except a few here and there, what with excessive high living,
which is of late grown so much into a disease, and the other ordinary

[15] *the war:* The War of the Spanish Succession (1701–14).
[16] *victualling:* Providing food.

circumstances of families, we find few families of the lower gentry, that is to say, from six or seven hundred a year downwards, but they are in debt and in necessitous circumstances, and a great many of greater estates also.

On the other hand, let any one who is acquainted with *England*, look but abroad into the several counties, especially near *London*, or within fifty miles of it: How are the antient families worn out by time and family misfortunes, and the estates possess'd by a new race of tradesmen, grown up into families of gentry, and establish'd by the immense wealth, gain'd, as I may say, behind the counter; that is, in the shop, the warehouse, and the compting-house?[17] How are the sons of tradesmen rank'd among the prime of the gentry? How are the daughters of tradesmen at this time adorn'd with the ducal coronets, and seen riding in the coaches of the best of the nobility? Nay, many of our trading gentlemen at this time refuse to be Ennobled, scorn being knighted, and content themselves with being known to be rated among the richest Commoners in the nation: And it must be acknowledg'd, that whatever they be as to court-breeding, and to manners, they, generally speaking, come behind none of the gentry in knowledge of the world.

• • •

It was a smart, but just repartee of a *London* Tradesman, when a gentleman *who had a good estate too*, rudely reproach'd him in company and bad him hold his tongue, for he was no gentleman; *No, Sir,* says he, *but I can buy a gentleman,* and therefore I claim a liberty to speak among gentlemen.

Again, in how superior a port or figure (as we now call it) do our tradesmen live to what the middling gentry either do or can support? An ordinary Tradesman now, not in the city only, but in the country, shall spend more money by the year, than a gentleman of four or five hundred pounds a Year can do; and shall encrease and lay up every year too; whereas the gentleman shall at the best stand stock still, just where he began, nay, perhaps decline; and as for the lower gentry, from an hundred pounds a year to three hundred, or thereabouts, *though they are often as proud and high in their appearance as the other*; as to them, I say, a *Shoemaker* in *London* shall keep a better house, spend more money, cloath his family better, and yet grow rich

---

[17] *compting-house:* Accounting firm.

too: It is evident where the difference lies, *an Estate's a pond*, but *a Trade's a spring*; The first, if it keeps full, and the water wholesom, by the ordinarry supplies and dreins from the neighbouring grounds, 'tis well, and 'tis all that is expected; but the other is an inexhausted current, which not only fills the pond, and keeps it full, but is continually running over, and fills all the lower ponds and places about it.

This being the case in *England*, and our trade being so vastly great, it is no wonder that the tradesmen in *England* fill the lifts of our nobility and gentry; no wonder that the gentlemen of the best families marry tradesmen's daughters, and put their younger sons apprentices to tradesmen; and how often do these younger sons come to buy the elder sons estates, and restore the family, when the elder, and head of the house, proving rakish and extravagant, has wasted his patrimony, and is obliged to make out the blessing of *Israel*'s family,[18] where the younger son bought the birth-right, and the elder was doomed to serve him?

Trade is so far *here* from being inconsistent with a Gentleman, that *in short* trade in *England* makes Gentlemen, and has peopled this nation with Gentlemen; for after a generation or two the tradesmen's children, or at least their grand-children, come to be as good Gentlemen, Statesmen, Parliament-men, Privy-Counsellors, Judges, Bishops, and Noblemen, as those of the highest birth and the most ancient families; and nothing too high for them: Thus the late Earl of *Haversham*[19] was originally a Merchant, the late Secretary *Craggs*[20] was the son of a *Barber*; the present Lord *Castlemain*'s father was a Tradesman; the great grandfather of the present Duke of *Bedford* the same, and so of several others: Nor do we find any defect either in the genius or capacities of the posterity of tradesmen, arising from any remains of mechanick blood, which 'tis pretended should influence them; but all the gallantry of spirit, greatness of soul, and all the generous principles that can be found in any of the ancient families, whose blood is the most untainted, as they call it, with the low mixtures of a mechanick race, are found in these; and, as is said before,

---

[18] *Israel's family:* Jacob (Israel) tricked his father, Isaac, into giving the birthright to him rather than to his elder brother, Esau (Gen. 27).

[19] *Earl of Haversham:* Sir John Thompson, First Baron Haversham (1647–1710), was created a baronet in 1673 and served as M.P. for Surrey in 1684–85. He was elevated to the peerage as Baron Haversham in 1696.

[20] *Secretary Craggs:* James Cragg (1686–1721) was appointed secretary of war in 1711; a year later, on Joseph Addison's retirement, he was made one of the chief secretaries of state.

they generally go beyond them in knowledge of the world, which is the best education.

We see the tradesmen of *England*, as they grow wealthy, coming every day to the Herald's office, to search for the Coats of Arms of their ancestors, in order to paint them upon their coaches, and engrave them upon their plate, embroider them upon their furniture, or carve them upon the pediments of their new houses; and how often do we see them trace the registers of their families up to the prime nobility, or the most ancient gentry of the kingdom?

In this search we find them often qualified to raise new families, if they do not descend from old; as was said of a certain Tradesman of *London*, that if he could not find the ancient race of Gentlemen, from which he came, he would begin a new race, who should be as good Gentlemen as any that went before them.

On Shopping
(From The Female Tatler Nos. 9 and 67)

In these papers, the narrator Mrs. Crackenthorpe focuses on several social types — the fashionable mercer; the pretentious, affected City merchant; and the hypocritical Quaker lady — through their habits of consumption and personal display. The shopping expeditions show that shopping, rather than a necessary chore, was a favorite leisure activity of upper-middle-class women with little else to occupy their time.

For more information on *The Female Tatler,* see Chapter 1, page 129.

Both papers are reprinted from *The Female Tatler,* ed. Fidelis Morgan (Rutland, VT: Charles Tuttle/Everyman's, 1992), 17–18 and 135–37.

No. 9
Monday, July 25, to Wednesday, July 27

This afternoon, some ladies, having an opinion of my fancy in clothes, desir'd me to accompany 'em to Ludgate-Hill,[1] which I take to be as agreeable an amusement as a lady can pass away three or four hours in; the shops are perfect gilded theatres. The variety of

---

[1] *Ludgate-Hill:* A shopping street in the City, to the west of St. Paul's.

wrought silks, so many changes of fine scenes; and the mercers[2] are the performers in the opera, and instead of 'Viviture Ingenio',[3] you have in gold capitals 'No Trust by Retail'. They are the sweetest, fairest, nicest dish'd out creatures, and by their elegant address and soft speeches, you would guess 'em to be Italians.[4] As people glance within their doors, they salute 'em with: 'garden silks, ladies, Italian silks, brocades, tissues, cloth of silver, or cloth of gold, very fine Mantua silks, any right Geneva velvet, English velvet, velvets emboss'd' — and to the meaner sort — 'fine thread satins, both strip'd and plain, fine mohairs, silk satinets, burdets, perfianets, Norwich crepes, auterines, silks for hoods and scarves — any camlets, drudgets,[5] or sagathies; gentlemen, nightgowns ready made, shalloons,[6] durances and right Scotch plaids'.

We went into a shop which had three partners, two of 'em were to flourish out their silks and, after an obliging smile and a pretty mouth made, Cicero-like,[7] to expatiate on their goodness; and the other's sole business was to be gentleman-usher of the shop, to stand completely dress'd at the door, bow to all the coaches that pass by, and hand ladies out and in.

We saw abundance of gay fancies fit for sea captains wives, sheriffs feasts, and Taunton-Dean Ladies — 'This madam, is wonderful charming' — 'This madam is so diverting a silk' — 'This madam — my stars! how cool it looks'. 'But this, madam, ye gods, would I had ten thousand yards of it' (then gathers up a sleeve and places it to our shoulders), 'It suits your ladyship's face wonderfully well.' When we had pleas'd ourselves, and bid him ten shillings a yard for what he ask'd fifteen. 'Fan me, ye winds, your ladyship rallies me! Shou'd I part with it at such a price, the weavers wou'd rise upon the very shop — Was you at the park last night, madam? — Your ladyship shall abate me sixpence — Have you read *The Tatler* today, pretty lady? A smart fellow I'll assure you.'

But being tir'd with his impertinence, as very ridiculous things soon cloy people, we agreed the point. He whipp'd us off twenty-

---

[2] *mercers:* Men that run shops selling fabric.

[3] *'Viviture Ingenio':* "Long live genius."

[4] *Italians:* Refers to the castrati of the Italian opera, suggesting that these mercers are effeminate sodomites.

[5] *camlets, drudgets:* Camlet is a rich cloth made of goat's hair and silk. Drugget is a kind of felted wool.

[6] *shalloons:* Shalloon is a lightweight wool or worsted twill fabric.

[7] *Cicero-like:* In an elaborate periodic rhetorical style like that of the Roman orator Cicero (106–43 B.C.).

eight yards with as much dexterity as Young G——y shall dash you out glasses of wine, and Mr Fantast at the door reconvey'd us into the coach.

These fellows are positively the greatest fops in the kingdom; they have their toilets,[8] and their fine night-gowns, their chocolate in a morning, and their green-tea two hours after, turkey polts for their dinner, and then perfumes, washes and clean linen equip 'em for the parade. 'Tis fit those whose professions invite the ladies shou'd appear decent before 'em. But if some women of note wou'd not countenance their foppery, and cry, 'Really Mr Farendine, you are too well bred, and have too good an air for a tradesman, but a mercer is a genteel calling. Suppose you had been bred a soap-boiler' . . . 'Fogh!', says he. 'Oh filthy!', says she, nor invite 'em to collations,[9] and be seen in a hackney coach with 'em, they'd leave off their conceited niceties and keep within the sphere of industry, for sure, no composition can be more ridiculous, than a creature made up of beau and business. Our sex indeed have a might ascendant, and those poor animals may be a little excus'd, when some women shall have power to coin fops and fools out of the greatest statesmen and politicians.

No. 67
Wednesday, December 7, to Friday, December 9
Arabella's Day

Emilia and I having at an India house[10] muddled away a little of our own money, were sitting to observe the variety of the company that frequent those places, and how different their fancies[11] were in pictures, fans, china, and such fashionable impertinences. Lady Praise-All surveyed the nick-nackatory, with an amazement, as if she had received a new sense — these cups were charming, those stones unparalleled, and such prodigious jars were never heard of — everything was displaced to oblige her ladyship's curiosity, who protested she shouldn't grudge to spend an estate on things so prodigiously fine, drank a gallon of tea, and marched off without laying out a sixpence. Mrs Trifleton came so full of commissions from ladies in the country that we thought she would have emptied the warehouse, and stared at the handsome 'prentice as if she expected to have him into

---

[8] *toilets:* Dressing tables.
[9] *collations:* Meals.
[10] *India house:* A shop selling wares imported from the East Indies.
[11] *fancies:* Tastes, preferences.

the bargain. She wanted finer things than were ever made, and, could they have been had, would have demanded them cheaper than they were bought. She bid three half crowns for a two guinea fan, wanted chocolate, all nut, for eighteen pence a pound, and beat down the best Imperial tea to the price of Sage o' Virtue.[12] Japan work[13] she thought at an excessive rate, China images were idolatrous, India pictures were the foolishest things, she'd have had them given her a dozen. At last, having positive orders from my Lady Smoak and Sot of Exeter, to buy her a stone spitting-pot, she shook her head at the dearness of it, and ordered them to set it down to her.

Mrs Honeysuckle was two hours pleasing herself in a paper nosegay, and Mrs Delf employed five people to match her grout[14] cup. On a sudden, stops a leathern conveniency[15] at the door, with four fellows of the world behind it, in the gayest liveries I ever saw, out of which comes a couple of quality Quakers.[16] They moved in, like disdainful duchesses who complain of corns if they walk but cross a room, rolled about their sanctified eyes, as if it were condescension in them to appear upon earth, and with abundance of reluctancy, one of them vouchsafed us a bow, instead of a curtsey. Emilia and I were not a little pleased to remark the pride and singularity in dress, speech and behaviour in that sect of people summed up in these two statues. Their clothes were costly without making any show, and though they abominate profane pinners and topknots,[17] yet, by the disposition of their locks and the artful crimping of their hoods upon wires, they showed themselves equally vain, and that they had taken as much pains to be particular as other ladies do to appear like the rest of the world, yet notwithstanding all their seeming plainness, the old man had crept in among them for watches, tweezer cases, and gold chains, and a patch[18] or two to cover pretended pimples. When

---

[12] *Sage o' Virtue:* An inexpensive herb tea.

[13] *Japan work:* Lacquerware.

[14] *grout:* Beer.

[15] *conveniency:* A small carriage.

[16] *Quakers:* Members of the Society of Friends, a radical Protestant religious and social sect established by George Fox in England in the mid–seventeenth century. The Friends rejected the ordained ministry and the outward rules and trappings of conventional religious orders. Although they spurned worldly vanities and cultivated a plain style of dress, the Friends were often quite prosperous businessmen. They acquired the name "Quakers" from the way they reputedly shook with religious enthusiasm at their meetings.

[17] *pinners and topknots:* Fashions in hairdressing, pinners were pieces of lace attached to the head, and topknots a way of arranging the hair on top of the head.

[18] *patch:* Patches of black silk were pasted on the face, neck, shoulders, and breast as supplementary "beauty marks."

they had with secret satisfaction received all the ceremonious address
of 'Ladies, your most obedient, do me the honour, etc.' which they
expect from people of the world without vouchsafing any other return than a precise nod, in a sighing tone, they enquired for fine tea-
tables, gilded cabinets, glass sconces, and all the richest things more
proper to adorn the palace of a prince than to dizen out a yea and
nay parlour in Hand Alley. Whatever bore a moderate price was
trash and trumpery. 'Does thee think my Ananias can eat his barley
gruel out of such coarse ware?' But a Japan basin of ten guineas is fit
for the pure ones to make gooseberry fool in, and the pieces moved as
gradually out of their pockets as if the spirit had directed each in its
proper place, according to the seniority of their being coined.

Susanna, having drunk too much green tea, was seized with a violent fit of the colic, so that the creature *Rosa Solis*[19] was forced to be
called for. Rachel too, being an apprehensive of that diabolical distemper, by way of prevention, tasted of that tempting liquor, which
they say, those carnal women called Duchesses guzzle. At that abominable rate, the demure sisters sipped up a whole quart, but their
heads not being the least intoxicated with the pomps and vanities of
the world, it only made them cheerful, and being pure in spirit they
were very much rejoiced.

But, as in this wicked age misfortunes will happen to afflict the upright, Colonel Sturdy, one of the greatest rakes that ever kept basset
bank[20] or carried doxy[21] out of the side box, happened to reel in,
seized upon Susanna, smuggled her as if she had been a beastly orange wench[22] and swore so prodigiously that Rachel staggered, and
was falling into a swoon, had not the Colonel left Susanna, and taken
her into his arms. Rachel, though in wondrous confusion, had the
presence of mind to say, 'Dear man, who art called Colonel, do anything to me, but don't swear.' Susanna, with robust zeal, divides
Rachel and the Colonel, and told him that though he had the assurance to accost her in that lustful manner, he ought to have shown
more reverence to Rachel, who had been a speaker[23] these seven
years. Rachel accused Susanna of incivility, and said, 'What the man
did to thee, sister, was blame worthy, and thou ought'st to chide him

[19] *Rosa Solis:* An alcoholic cordial.
[20] *basset bank:* Acted as a banker during the card game basset.
[21] *doxy:* A prostitute.
[22] *orange wench:* A girl who sold oranges in the playhouses, assumed to be a prostitute.
[23] *speaker:* An official at a Friend's meeting.

for't, but 'twas kind and tender in him to support my weakness, or I had stumbled and fell.'

In short, the sanctified sisters quarrelled so about a libertine, whom even loose women that sin with some restraint abominate for his inconstancy, that 'twas with no small struggling they concealed their enmity from the servants, and went home together in the same coach. Emilia and I were so crowded with reflections on what we had seen, that we had hardly patience to vent them without interrupting each other, but at length our sentiments appeared to be much the same, that Quakers are the most designing, deceitful sect of creatures in the world, who assume more pride and exact more homage from their seeming sanctity, than the truly pious, who are always easy and unconstrained.

Their houses are as richly and gaily furnished as those of quality, their equipages as glaring, and though they affect a ridiculous habit, a primness of air, and screw themselves up like trussed rabbits, yet they are as foppish their way, and by little and little wink at one another in those modes and fancies, which they term Babylonish, idolatrous, and diabolical. They love music and dancing, though they won't practice it themselves, read plays though they won't see them, will sneak into a tavern at the back door, fornicate with a Holy Sister, and if, by subtlety in trade, they can over-reach their neighbours, 'tis but engrossing to themselves the spoils of the wicked. The young Quakers of both sexes are so far gone from the truth, as to arrive at most libertines of the age. The men play as high at Roly-Poly[24] and the women coquet as much upon the walks, and 'tis no novelty nowadays to see, a Fleet Street Sylvia whip into a tavern with a Damon that has no button holes[25] behind.

[24] *play as high at Roly-Poly:* Wager as heavily on the ball game of roly-poly.
[25] *no button holes:* The Friends did not use buttons on their clothing.

BERNARD MANDEVILLE

"The Grumbling Hive" and
"A Search into the Nature of Society"
(From The Fable of the Bees)

Bernard Mandeville (1670–1733) was a Dutch physician, prose writer, and social philosopher. After receiving his medical degree at the University of Leyden, Mandeville went to England, where he married and lived for the rest of his life. His best known work, *The Fable of the Bees; or, Private Vices, Publick Benefits* (1728), grew up as an extensive commentary on an earlier verse fable, *The Grumbling Hive: or, Knaves Turn'd Honest* (1705). In this poem, Mandeville explores the thesis that the subtitle of *The Fable of the Bees* proposes: private vices generate public benefits. The satisfaction of desires, the pursuit of selfish interests, the indulgence of appetites — these are the energies that fuel an active, productive society. In his own time, Mandeville was widely reviled as an advocate of "beneficial" vices such as pride, luxury, prodigality, and vanity. But he did not so much promote vice as satirize the hypocrisy that ignores the connection between what, within an ethical context, conventional morality denounces and, within an economic context, it celebrates. He explicates his propositions about society and human nature in "The Grumbling Hive," and in *The Fable of the Bees* analyzes society within a range of contexts: economic, sociological, and psychological. In the selection from "A Search into the Nature of Society" excerpted here, Mandeville explains, with characteristic skepticism, the psychosocial logic of an exchange between a mercer and his customer.

The text reprinted here is taken from *The Fable of the Bees*, with commentary by F. B. Kaye (Oxford, Eng.: Clarendon Press, 1925), vol. 1, 17–37 and 349–53.

The Grumbling Hive: or, Knaves *turn'd Honest.*

A Spacious Hive well stockt with Bees,
That liv'd in Luxury and Ease;
And yet as fam'd for Laws and Arms,
As yielding large and early Swarms;
Was counted the great Nursery   5
Of Sciences and Industry.

No Bees had better Government,
More Fickleness, or less Content:
They were not Slaves to Tyranny,
Nor rul'd by wild *Democracy*;   10
But Kings, that could not wrong, because
Their Power was circumscrib'd by Laws.

    These Insects liv'd like Men, and all
Our Actions they perform'd in small:
They did whatever's done in Town,   15
And what belongs to Sword or Gown:°
Tho' th' Artful Works, by nimble Slight
Of minute Limbs, 'scap'd Human Sight;
Yet we've no Engines, Labourers,
Ships, Castles, Arms, Artificers,   20
Craft, Science, Shop, or Instrument,
But they had an Equivalent:
Which, since their Language is unknown,
Must be call'd, as we do our own.
As grant, that among other Things,   25
They wanted Dice, yet they had Kings;
And those had Guards; from whence we may
Justly conclude, they had some Play;
Unless a Regiment be shewn
Of Soldiers, that make use of none.   30

    Vast Numbers throng'd the fruitful Hive;
Yet those vast Numbers made 'em thrive;
Millions endeavouring to supply
Each other's Lust and Vanity;
While other Millions were employ'd,   35
To see their Handy-works destroy'd;
They furnish'd half the Universe;
Yet had more Work than Labourers.
Some with vast Stocks, and little Pains,
Jump'd into Business of great Gains;   40
And some were damn'd to Sythes and Spades,
And all those hard laborious Trades;
Where willing Wretches daily sweat,
And wear our Strength and Limbs to eat:

16. *Sword or Gown:* To the military or to the learned professions.

(*A.*)° While others follow'd Mysteries,   45
To which few Folks bind 'Prentices;
That want no Stock, but that of Brass,
And may set up without a Cross;°
As Sharpers,° Parasites, Pimps, Players,
Pick-pockets, Coiners, Quacks, South-sayers,   50
And all those, that in Enmity,
With downright Working, cunningly
Convert to their own Use the Labour
Of their good-natur'd heedless Neighbour.
(*B.*) These were call'd Knaves, but bar the Name,   55
The grave Industrious were the same:
All Trades and Places knew some Cheat,
No Calling was without Deceit.

   The Lawyers, of whose Art the Basis
Was raising Feuds and splitting Cases,   60
Oppos'd all Registers, that Cheats
Might make more Work with dipt Estates;°
As wer't unlawful, that one's own,
Without a Law-Suit, should be known.
They kept off Hearings wilfully,   65
To finger the refreshing Fee;
And to defend a wicked Cause,
Examin'd and survey'd the Laws,
As Burglars Shops and Houses do,
To find out where they'd best break through.   70

   Physicians valu'd Fame and Wealth
Above the drooping Patient's Health,
Or their own Skill: The greatest Part
Study'd, instead of Rules of Art,
Grave pensive Looks and dull Behaviour,   75
To gain th' Apothecary's Favour;
The Praise of Midwives, Priests, and all
That serv'd at Birth or Funeral.
To bear with th' ever-talking Tribe,
And hear my Lady's Aunt prescribe;   80

    45. (*A.*): These letters are intended to direct the reader to Mandeville's explications
in various sections of the *Fable of the Bees* that follow the poem.
    48. *without a Cross:* Without money; a cross was a small coin.
    49. *Sharpers:* Cardsharps, con artists.
    62. *dipt Estates:* Mortgaged estates.

With formal Smile, and kind How d'ye,
To fawn on all the Family;
And, which of all the greatest Curse is,
T' endure th' Impertinence of Nurses.

    Among the many Priests of *Jove*,°   85
Hir'd to draw Blessings from Above,
Some few were Learn'd and Eloquent,
But thousands Hot and Ignorant:
Yet all pass'd Muster that could hide
Their Sloth, Lust, Avarice and Pride;   90
For which they were as fam'd as Tailors
For Cabbage, or for Brandy Sailors:
Some, meagre-look'd, and meanly clad,
Would mystically pray for Bread,
Meaning by that an ample Store,   95
Yet lit'rally received no more;
And, while these holy Drudges starv'd,
The lazy Ones, for which they serv'd,
Indulg'd their Ease, with all the Graces
Of Health and Plenty in their Faces.   100

    (C.) The Soldiers, that were forc'd to fight,
If they surviv'd, got Honour by't;
Tho' some, that shunn'd the bloody Fray,
Had Limbs shot off, that ran away:
Some valiant Gen'rals fought the Foe;   105
Others took Bribes to let them go:
Some ventur'd always where 'twas warm,
Lost now a Leg, and then an Arm;
Till quite disabled, and put by,
They liv'd on half their Salary;   110
While others never came in Play,
And staid at Home for double Pay.

    Their Kings were serv'd, but Knavishly,
Cheated by their own Ministry;
Many, that for their Welfare slaved,   115
Robbing the very Crown they saved:
Pensions were small, and they liv'd high,
Yet boasted of their Honesty.

---

85. *Jove:* The chief god in the Roman pantheon (Zeus in Greek mythology).

Calling, whene'er they strain'd their Right,
The slipp'ry Trick a Perquisite;   120
And when Folks understood their Cant,°
They chang'd that for Emolument;
Unwilling to be short or plain,
In any thing concerning Gain;
(D.) For there was not a Bee but would   125
Get more, I won't say, than he should;
But than he dar'd to let them know,
(E.) That pay'd for't; as your Gamesters do,
That, tho' at fair Play, ne'er will own
Before the Losers what they've won.   130

    But who can all their Frauds repeat?
The very Stuff, which in the Street
They sold for Dirt t'enrich the Ground,
Was often by the Buyers found
Sophisticated with a quarter   135
Of good-for-nothing Stones and Mortar;
Tho' *Flail* had little Cause to mutter,
Who sold the other Salt for Butter.

    Justice her self, fam'd for fair Dealing,
By Blindness had not lost her Feeling;   140
Her Left Hand, which the Scales should hold,
Had often dropt 'em, brib'd with Gold;
And, tho' she seem'd Impartial,
Where Punishment was corporal,
Pretended to a reg'lar Course,   145
In Murther, and all Crimes of Force;
Tho' some, first pillory'd for Cheating,
Were hang'd in Hemp of their own beating;°
Yet, it was thought, the Sword she bore
Check'd but the Desp'rate and the Poor;   150
That, urg'd by meer Necessity,
Were ty'd up to the wretched Tree
For Crimes, which not deserv'd that Fate,
But to secure the Rich and Great.

---

   121. *Cant:* Slang or jargon.
   148. *Hemp of their own beating:* Prisoners were put to work beating hemp to make ropes.

Thus every Part was full of Vice,   155
Yet the whole Mass a Paradise;
Flatter'd in Peace, and fear'd in Wars,
They were th' Esteem of Foreigners,
And lavish of their Wealth and Lives,
The Balance of all other Hives.   160
Such were the Blessings of that State;
Their Crimes conspir'd to make them Great:
(F.) And Virtue, who from Politicks
Had learn'd a Thousand Cunning Tricks,
Was, by their happy Influence,   165
Made Friends with Vice: And ever since,
(G.) The worst of all the Multitude
Did something for the Common Good.

This was the State's Craft, that maintain'd
The Whole of which each Part complain'd: 170
This, as in Musick Harmony,
Made Jarrings in the main agree;
(H.) Parties directly opposite,
Assist each other, as 'twere for Spight;
And Temp'rance with Sobriety,   175
Serve Drunkenness and Gluttony.

(I.) The Root of Evil, Avarice,
That damn'd ill-natur'd baneful Vice,
Was Slave to Prodigality,
(K.) That noble Sin; (L.) whilst Luxury   180
Employ'd a Million of the Poor,
(M.) And odious Pride a Million more:
(N.) Envy it self, and Vanity,
Were Ministers of Industry;
Their darling Folly, Fickleness,   185
In Diet, Furniture and Dress,
That strange ridic'lous Vice, was made
The very Wheel that turn'd the Trade.
Their Laws and Clothes were equally
Objects of Mutability;   190
For, what was well done for a time,
In half a Year became a Crime;
Yet while they alter'd thus their Laws,
Still finding and correcting Flaws,

They mended by Inconstancy   195
Faults, which no Prudence could foresee.

   Thus Vice nurs'd Ingenuity,
Which join'd with Time and Industry,
Had carry'd Life's Conveniencies,
(O.) It's real Pleasures, Comforts, Ease,   200
(P.) To such a Height, the very Poor
Liv'd better than the Rich before,
And nothing could be added more.

   How Vain is Mortal Happiness!
Had they but known the Bounds of Bliss;   205
And that Perfection here below
Is more than Gods can well bestow;
The Grumbling Brutes had been content
With Ministers and Government.
But they, at every ill Success,   210
Like Creatures lost without Redress,
Curs'd Politicians, Armies, Fleets;
While every one cry'd, *Damn the Cheats*,
And would, tho' conscious of his own,
In others barb'rously bear none.   215

   One, that had got a Princely Store,
By cheating Master, King and Poor,
Dar'd cry aloud, *The Land must sink
For all its Fraud*; And whom d'ye think
The Sermonizing Rascal chid?   220
A Glover that sold Lamb for Kid.°

   The least thing was not done amiss,
Or cross'd the Publick Business;
But all the Rogues cry'd brazenly,
Good Gods, Had we but Honesty!   225
Merc'ry° smil'd at th' Impudence,
And others call'd it the want of Sense,
Always to rail at what they lov'd:
But *Jove* with Indignation mov'd,
At last in Anger swore, *He'd rid*   230

---

   221. *sold Lamb for Kid*: The merchant sold gloves made out of lambskin at the
price of the more costly kidskin.
   226. *Merc'ry*: Mercury, the Roman messenger god, a trickster god of the cross-
roads, of travel, thievery, and commerce (in Greek myth, Hermes).

The bawling Hive of Fraud; and did.
The very Moment it departs,
And Honesty fills all their Hearts;
There shews 'em, like th' Instructive Tree,
Those Crimes which they're asham'd to see;   235
Which now in Silence they confess,
By blushing at their Ugliness:
Like Children, that would hide their Faults,
And by their Colour own their Thoughts:
Imag'ning, when they're look'd upon,   240
That others see what they have done.

But, Oh ye Gods! What Consternation,
How vast and sudden was th' Alteration!
In half an Hour, the Nation round,
Meat fell a Peny in the Pound.   245
The Mask Hypocrisy's flung down,
From the great Statesman to the Clown:
And some in borrow'd Looks well known,
Appear'd like Strangers in their own.
The Bar° was silent from that Day;   250
For now the willing Debtors pay,
Ev'n what's by Creditors forgot;
Who quitted them that had it not.
Those, that were in the Wrong, stood mute,
And dropt the patch'd vexatious Suit: 255
On which since nothing less can thrive,
Than Lawyers in an honest Hive,
All, except those that got enough,
With Inkhorns by their sides troop'd off.

Justice hang'd some, set others free;   260
And after Goal delivery,
Her Presence being no more requir'd,
With all her Train and Pomp retir'd.
First march'd some Smiths with Locks and Grates,
Fetters, and Doors with Iron Plates: 265
Next Goalers, Turnkeys and Assistants:
Before the Goddess, at some distance,
Her chief and faithful Minister,

---

250. *The Bar:* The legal profession.

'Squire CATCH,° the Law's great Finisher,
Bore not th' imaginary Sword,   270
But his own Tools, an Ax and Cord:
Then on a Cloud the Hood-wink'd Fair,
JUSTICE her self was push'd by Air:
About her Chariot, and behind,
Were Serjeants, Bums° of every kind,   275
Tip-staffs,° and all those Officers,
That squeeze a Living out of Tears.

   Tho' Physick liv'd, while Folks were ill,
None would prescribe, but Bees of skill,
Which through the Hive dispers'd so wide,   280
That none of them had need to ride;
Wav'd vain Disputes, and strove to free
The Patients of their Misery;
Left Drugs in cheating Countries grown,
And us'd the Product of their own;   285
Knowing the Gods sent no Disease
To Nations without Remedies.

   Their Clergy rous'd from Laziness,
Laid not their Charge on Journey-Bees;°
But serv'd themselves, exempt from Vice,   290
The Gods with Pray'r and Sacrifice;
All those, that were unfit, or knew
Their Service might be spar'd, withdrew:
Nor was there Business for so many,
(If th' Honest stand in need of any,)   295
Few only with the High-Priest staid,
To whom the rest Obedience paid:
Himself employ'd in Holy Cares,
Resign'd to others State-Affairs.
He chas'd no Starv'ling from his Door,   300
Nor pinch'd the Wages of the Poor;
But at his House the Hungry's fed,

269. *'Squire* CATCH: For almost two hundred years after his death in 1686, Jack
Ketch was used as a generic name for any public executioner. The historic Jack Ketch
was notorious for his blundering inefficiency.
   275. *Bums:* Bumbailiff, an assistant to a sheriff who has the power of arrest.
   276. *Tip-staffs:* Bailiffs or constables, who carried a staff with a metal tip as a sign
of office.
   289. *Journey-Bees:* Bee analogues to journeyman parsons or curates.

The Hireling finds unmeasur'd Bread,
The needy Trav'ler Board and Bed.

   Among the King's great Ministers,   305
And all th' inferior Officers
The Change was great; (*Q.*) for frugally
They now liv'd on their Salary:
That a poor Bee should ten times come
To ask his Due, a trifling Sum,   310
And by some well-hir'd Clerk be made
To give a Crown, or ne'er be paid,
Would now be call'd a downright Cheat,
Tho' formerly a Perquisite.
All Places manag'd first by Three,   315
Who watch'd each other's Knavery,
And often for a Fellow-feeling,
Promoted one another's stealing,
Are happily supply'd by One,
By which some thousands more are gone.   320

   (*R.*) No Honour now could be content,
To live and owe for what was spent;
Liv'ries in Brokers Shops° are hung,
They part with Coaches for a Song;
Sell stately Horses by whole Sets;   325
And Country-Houses, to pay Debts.

   Vain Cost is shunn'd as much as Fraud;
They have no Forces kept Abroad;
Laugh at th' Esteem of Foreigners,
And empty Glory got by Wars;   330
They fight, but for their Country's sake,
When Right or Liberty's at Stake.

   Now mind the glorious Hive, and see
How Honesty and Trade agree.
The Shew is gone, it thins apace;   335
And looks with quite another Face.
For 'twas not only that They went,
By whom vast Sums were Yearly spent;
But Multitudes that liv'd on them,
Were daily forc'd to do the same.   340

---

323. *Brokers Shops:* Pawn shops.

In vain to other Trades they'd fly;
All were o'er-stock'd accordingly.

   The Price of Land and Houses falls;
Mirac'lous Palaces, whose Walls,
Like those of *Thebes*, were rais'd by Play,°   345
Are to be let; while the once gay,
Well-seated Houshold Gods would be
More pleas'd to expire in Flames, than see
The mean Inscription on the Door
Smile at the lofty ones they bore.   350
The building Trade is quite destroy'd,
Artificers are not employ'd;
(*S.*) No Limner for his Art is fam'd,
Stone-cutters, Carvers are not nam'd.

   Those, that remain'd, grown temp'rate, strive,   355
Not how to spend, but how to live,
And, when they paid their Tavern Score,°
Resolv'd to enter it no more:
No Vintner's Jilt° in all the Hive
Could wear now Cloth of Gold, and thrive;   360
Nor *Torcol* such vast Sums advance,
For *Burgundy* and *Ortelans*;°
The Courtier's gone, that with his Miss
Supp'd at his House on *Christmas* Peas;
Spending as much in two Hours stay,   365
As keeps a Troop of Horse a Day.

   The haughty *Chloe*, to live Great,
Had made her (*T.*) Husband rob the State:
But now she sells her Furniture,
Which th' *Indies*° had been ransack'd for;   370
Contracts th' expensive Bill of Fare,
And wears her strong Suit a whole Year:
The slight and fickle Age is past;

---

345. *rais'd by Play:* In Greek legend, the walls of the city Thebes were raised by lyre music played by Amphion. Mandeville puns on "play" here, referring both to playing music and to gambling.
   357. *Tavern Score:* The bill, or tab, run up at a tavern.
   359. *Jilt:* Mistress.
   362. *Burgundy and Ortelans:* Types of wine.
   370. *th' Indies:* Either the West Indies (the Caribbean) or the East Indies (Asia). Jamaican mahogany was highly prized for furniture, and Japanese and Chinese lacquered goods were very fashionable.

And Clothes, as well as Fashions, last.
Weavers, that join'd rich Silk with Plate,   375
And all the Trades subordinate,
Are gone. Still Peace and Plenty reign,
And every Thing is cheap, tho' plain:
Kind Nature, free from Gard'ners Force,
Allows all Fruits in her own Course;   380
But Rarities cannot be had,
Where Pains to get them are not paid.

   As Price and Luxury decrease,
So by degrees they leave the Seas.
Not Merchants now, but Companies   385
Remove whole Manufactories.
All Arts and Crafts neglected lie;
(V.) Content, the Bane of Industry,
Makes 'em admire their homely Store,
And neither seek nor covet more.   390

   So few in the vast Hive remain,
The hundredth Part they can't maintain
Against th' Insults of numerous Foes;
Whom yet they valiantly oppose:
'Till some well-fenc'd Retreat is found,   395
And here they die or stand their Ground.
No Hireling in their Army's known;
But bravely fighting for their own,
Their Courage and Integrity
At last were crown'd with Victory.   400

   They triumph'd not without their Cost,
For many Thousand Bees were lost.
Hard'ned with Toils and Exercise,
They counted Ease it self a Vice;
Which so improv'd their Temperance;   405
That, to avoid Extravagance,
They flew into a hollow Tree,
Blest with Content and Honesty.

The Moral.

Then leave Complaints: Fools only strive
(X.) To make a Great an Honest Hive
(Y.) T' enjoy the World's Conveniencies,
Be fam'd in War, yet live in Ease,

Without great Vices, is a vain   5
EUTOPIA° *seated in the Brain.*
Fraud, Luxury and Pride must live,
While we the Benefits receive:
Hunger's a dreadful Plague, no doubt,
Yet who digests or thrives without?   10
Do we not owe the Growth of Wine
To the dry shabby crooked Vine?
Which, while its Shoots neglected stood,
Chok'd other Plants, and ran to Wood;
But blest us with its noble Fruit,   15
As soon as it was ty'd and cut:
So Vice is beneficial found,
When it's by Justice lopt and bound;
Nay, where the People would be great,
As necessary to the State,   20
As Hunger is to make 'em eat.
Bare Virtue can't make Nations live
In Splendor; they, that would revive
A Golden Age, must be as free,
For Acorns,° as for Honesty.   25

From "A Search into the Nature of Society"

To me it is a great Pleasure, when I look on the Affairs of human
Life, to behold into what various and often strangely opposite Forms
the hope of Gain and thoughts of Lucre shape Men, according to the
different Employments they are of, and Stations they are in. How gay
and merry does every Face appear at a well-ordered Ball, and what a
solemn Sadness is observ'd at the Masquerade of a Funeral! But the
Undertaker is as much pleas'd with his Gains as the Dancing-Master:
Both are equally tired in their Occupations, and the Mirth of the one
is as much forced as the Gravity of the other is affected. Those who
have never minded the Conversation of a spruce Mercer,[1] and a
young Lady his Customer that comes to his Shop, have neglected a
Scene of Life that is very Entertaining. I beg of my serious Reader,
that he would for a while abate a little of his Gravity, and suffer me

---

6. EUTOPIA: In Greek, literally "nowhere"; an ideal place.
25. *For Acorns:* Acorns are a conventional staple in the diet of the mythical Golden
Age, a time before the corruptions of agriculture, industry, agriculture, and commerce.
[1] *Mercer:* A shopkeeper who sells fine fabrics.

to examine these People separately, as to their Inside and the different Motives they act from.

His Business is to sell as much Silk as he can at a Price by which he shall get what he proposes to be reasonable, according to the Customary Profits of the Trade. As to the Lady, what she would be at is to please her Fancy, and buy cheaper by a Groat or Sixpence *per* Yard than the Things she wants are commonly sold at. From the Impression the Gallantry of our Sex has made upon her, she imagines (if she be not very deform'd) that she has a fine Mien and easy Behaviour, and a peculiar Sweetness of Voice; that she is handsome, and if not beautiful at least more agreeable than most young Women she knows. As she has no Pretensions to purchase the same Things with less Money than other People, but what are built on her good Qualities, so she sets her self off to the best Advantage her Wit and Discretion will let her. The thoughts of Love are here out of the Case; so on the one hand she has no room for playing the Tyrant, and giving herself Angry and Peevish Airs, and on the other more liberty of speaking kindly, and being affable than she can have almost on any other occasion. She knows that abundance of well-bred People come to his Shop, and endeavours to render her self as Amiable as Virtue and the Rules of Decency allow of. Coming with such a Resolution of Behaviour she cannot meet with any thing to ruffle her Temper.

Before her Coach is yet quite stopp'd, she is approach'd by a Gentleman-like Man, that has every thing Clean and Fashionable about him, who in low obeisance pays her Homage, and as soon as her Pleasure is known that she has a mind to come in, hands her into the Shop, where immediately he slips from her, and through a by-way that remains visible only for half a Moment with great address entrenches himself behind the Counter: Here facing her, with a profound Reverence and modish Phrase he begs the favour of knowing her Commands. Let her say and dislike what she pleases, she can never be directly contradicted: She deals with a Man in whom consummate Patience is one of the Mysteries of his Trade, and whatever trouble she creates, she is sure to hear nothing but the most obliging Language, and has always before her a chearful Countenance, where Joy and Respect seem to be blended with Good-humour, and altogether make up an Artificial Serenity more engaging than untaught Nature is able to produce.

When two Persons are so well met, the Conversation must be very agreeable, as well as extremely mannerly, tho' they talk about trifles. While she remains irresolute what to take he seems to be the same in advising her; and is very cautious how to direct her Choice; but when once she has made it and is fix'd, he immediately becomes positive, that it is the best of the sort, extols her Fancy, and the more he looks upon it, the more he wonders he should not before have discovered the preeminence of it over any thing he has in his Shop. By Precept, Example and great Application he has learn'd unobserv'd to slide into the inmost Recesses of the Soul, sound the Capacity of his Customers, and find out their blind Side unknown to them: By all which is he instructed in fifty other Stratagems to make her over-value her own Judgment as well as the Commodity she would purchase. The greatest Advantage he has over her, lies in the most material part of the Commerce between them, the debate about the Price, which he knows to a Farthing, and she is wholly Ignorant of: Therefore he no where more egregiously imposes on her Understanding; and tho' here he has the liberty of telling what Lies he pleases, as to the Prime Cost and the Money he has refus'd, yet he trusts not to them only; but attacking her Vanity makes her believe the most incredible Things in the World, concerning his own Weakness and her superior Abilities; He had taken a Resolution, he says, never to part with that Piece under such a Price, but she has the power of talking him out of his Goods beyond any body he ever sold to: He protests that he loses by his Silk, but seeing that she has a Fancy for it, and is resolv'd to give no more, rather than disoblige a Lady he has such an uncommon value for, he'll let her have it, and only begs that another time she will not stand so hard with him. In the mean time the Buyer, who knows that she is no Fool and has a voluble Tongue, is easily persuaded that she has a very winning way of Talking, and thinking it sufficient for the sake of Good-breeding to disown her Merit, and in some witty Repartee retort the Compliment, he makes her swallow very contentedly the Substance of every thing he tells her. The upshot is, that with the Satisfaction of having saved Ninepence *per* Yard, she has bought her Silk exactly at the same Price as any body else might have done, and often gives Sixpence more, than, rather than not have sold it, he would have taken.

It is possible that this Lady for want of being sufficiently flatter'd, for a Fault she is pleased to find in his Behaviour, or perhaps the tying of his Neckcloth, or some other dislike as Substantial, may be lost, and her Custom bestow'd on some other of the Fraternity. But where many of them live in a Cluster, it is not always easily determin'd which Shop to go to, and the Reasons some of the Fair Sex have for their choice are often very whimsical and kept as a great

Secret. We never follow our Inclinations with more freedom, than where they cannot be traced, and it is unreasonable for others to suspect them. A Virtuous Woman has preferr'd one House to all the rest, because she had seen a handsome Fellow in it, and another of no bad Character for having receiv'd greater Civility before it, than had been paid her any where else, when she had no thoughts of buying and was going to *Paul*'s Church: for among the fashionable Mercers the fair Dealer must keep before his own Door, and to draw in random Customers make use of no other Freedom or Importunities than an obsequious Air, with a submissive Posture, and perhaps a Bow to every well-dress'd Female that offers to look towards his Shop.

The Story of Inkle and Yarrico

One of a number of Inkle and Yarrico poems, plays, songs, ballets, novels, and operas composed in England, France, and Germany during the eighteenth and nineteenth centuries, this short poem illustrates the sentimentalization of slavery that begins with Steele's retelling of Richard Ligon's short anecdote (*True and Exact History . . . of Barbadoes*, 1674) in *Spectator* No. 11 (see p. 192). Although there was not as yet anything like an abolitionist movement in England, this sentimental discourse becomes a key propaganda tool for that movement in the last decades of the eighteenth century, largely under the auspices of William Wilberforce (1759–1833). Slavery was abolished in England's colonies in 1834. In this early verse narration, sentimentality is used chiefly as an ethical weapon against Inkle's perfidious betrayal of the woman who loved him, rather than against the condition of slavery itself.

A most moving TALE from the *Spectator*.[1]
Attempted in VERES by
The Right Hon. the Countess of * * * *[2]

A Youth there was possess'd of every charm,
Which might the coldest heart with passion warm;
His blooming cheeks with ruddy beauty glow'd,

[1] *Spectator:* No. 11 (see p. 192).
[2] *Countess of * * * *:* The identity of this author is not known.

His hair in waving ringlets graceful flow'd;
Thro' all his person an attractive mein,   5
Just symmetry, and elegance were seen:
But niggard Fortune had her aid witheld,
And poverty th'unhappy Boy compell'd
To distant climes to fail, in search of gain,
Which might in ease his latter days maintain.   10
By chance, or rather the decree of Heaven,
The vessel on a barbarous coast was driven;
He, with a few unhappy Striplings° more,
Ventur'd too far upon the fatal shore:
The cruel natives thirsted for their blood,   15
And issued furious from a neighb'ring wood.
His friends all fell by brutal Rage o'erpowr'd,
Their flesh the horrid *Cannibals* devour'd;
Whilst he alone escap'd by speedy flight,
And in a thicket lay conceal'd from sight!   20
Now he reflects on his companions fate,
His threat'ning danger, and abandon'd state.
Whilst thus in fruitless grief he spent the day,
A *Negro*° Virgin chanc'd to pas that way;
He view'd her naked beauties with surprise,   25
Her well proportion'd limbs and sprightly eyes!
With his complexion and gay dress amaz'd,
The artless Nymph upon the Stranger gaz'd;
Charm'd with his features and alluring grace,
His flowing locks and his enliven'd face.   30
His safety now became her tend'rest care,
A vaulted rock she knew and hid him there;
The choicest fruits the isle produc'd she sought,
And kindly to allay his hunger brought;
And when his thirst requir'd, in search of drink,   35
She led him to a chrystal fountain's brink.
Mutually charm'd by various arts they strove,
To inform each other of their mutual love;
A language soon they form'd, which might express
Their pleasing care and growing tenderness.   40

13. *Striplings:* Young men, Inkle's shipmates.
24. *Negro:* Here Yarrico is described as an African Caribbean, and later as an Amerindian (see note to line 46). In Ligon's account she is an Amerindian.

With tygers speckled skins she deck'd his bed,
O'er which the gayest plumes of birds were spread;
And every morning, with the nicest care,
Adorn'd her well turn'd neck and shining hair,
With all the glittering shells and painted flowers, 45
That serve to deck the *Indian*° Virgins bowers.
And when the sun descended in the sky,
And length'ning shades foretold the ev'ning nigh,
Beneath some spreading palm's delightful shade,
Together sat the Youth and lovely Maid; 50
Or, where some bubbling river gently crept,
She in her arms secur'd him while he slept.
When the bright moon in midnight pomp was seen,
And star-light glitter'd o'er the dewy green,
In some close arbor, or some fragrant grove, 55
He whisper'd vows of everlasting love.
Then, as upon the verdant turf he lay,
He oft would to th' attentive Virgin say,
"Oh could I but, my YARRICO, *with thee*
"Once more my dear, my native country see! 60
"In softest silks thy limbs should be array'd,
"Like that of which the cloaths I wear are made;
"What different ways my grateful Soul would find,
"To indulge thy person and divert thy mind"?
While she on the enticing accents hung, 65
That smoothly fell from his persuasive tongue;
One evening, from a rock's impending side,
An *European* vessel she describ'd,
And made them signs to touch upon the shore,
Then to her Lover she bad tidings bore; 70
Who with his Mistress to the ship descends,
And found the crew were country-men and friends.
Reflecting now upon the time he past,
Deep melancholy all his thoughts o'ercast,
"Was it for this, said he, I cross'd the Main 75
"Only a doating Virgin's heart to gain?
"I needed not for such a prize to roam,
"There are a thousand doating maids at home.

46. *Indian:* Compare note to line 24.

While thus his disappointed mind was toss'd,
The Ship arriv'd on the *Barbarian*° coast;   80
Immediately the Planters from the town,
Who trade for goods and *Negro* Slaves, came down;
And now his mind, by sordid int'rest sway'd,
Resolv'd to sell his faithful *Indian* Maid.
Soon at his feet for mercy she implor'd,   85
And thus in moving strains her fate deplor'd:
"*O whither can I turn to seek redress,*
"*When thou'rt the cruel cause of my distress!*
"*If the remembrance of our former love,*
"*And all thy plighted vows want force to move;*   90
"*Yet, for the helpless Infant's sake I bear,*
"*Listen with pity to my just despair,*
"*Oh let me not in slavery remain,*
"*Doom'd all my life to drag a servile chain!*
"*It cannot surely be! thy generous breast*   95
"*An act so vile, so sordid must detest:*
"*But, if thou hate me, rather let me meet*
"*A gentler fate, and stab me at thy feet;*
"*Then will I bless thee with my dying breath,*
"*And sink contended in the shades of death.*   100
Not all she said could his compassion move,
Forgetful of his vows and promis'd love;
The weeping Damsel from his knees he spurn'd,
And with her price pleas'd to the ship return'd.

80. *Barbarian:* Probably a misprint for "Barbadian."

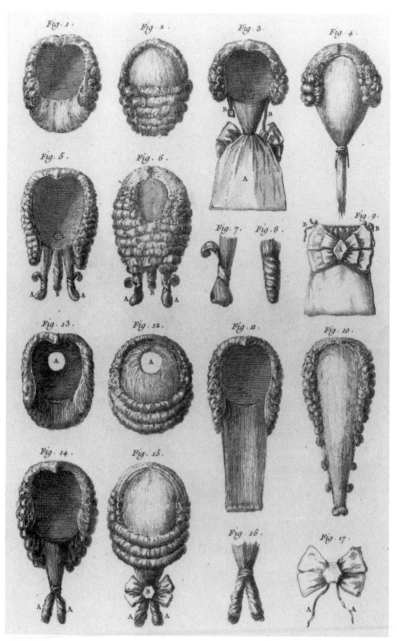

"Perruques" (Wigs), from *Encyclopedie, Recuiel de Planches.*

3

Fashioning Taste
on the Culture Market

This section includes papers from the *Tatler* and *Spectator* whose major theme is the reform of genteel taste. These debates about taste, the imagination, sense, wit, and judgment focus on the critical vocabularies and aesthetic-cultural concerns of the eighteenth century. The texts deliberate proper and improper modes of conversation, of entertainment, of poetic production, of criticism itself. Unlike the more formal and extrinsic aesthetic "rules," which it to some extent displaces, taste, according to Addison's formulation in *Spectator* No. 409, is an intrinsic, subjective element in the human psyche: it inheres not in the cultural object but in the person perceiving that object. To some degree inborn, taste is an ethical as well as an aesthetic faculty, an aspect of character and sensibility. Although some are born with a more refined sensibility than others, everyone may develop and improve this natural faculty. Indeed, without proper cultivation, even the best natural sense of taste will be "of little use to the Person that possesses it" (*Spectator* No. 409, see p. 385). By providing the sensual and conceptual capacities for enjoying aesthetic beauty, taste is at once an affective faculty of pleasure and an intellectual faculty of discrimination. It allows us to enjoy fine writing and other forms of cultural production, but it also enables us to distinguish between the varying quality of cultural forms, to tell the good from the bad. Taste thus becomes the repository of qualitative value in a social milieu where values are becoming increasingly quantified under the pressure of the commercial market.

As noted in the Introduction, the early eighteenth century witnessed the emergence of a commercial market in the arts and entertainment. The commercialization of culture, and its attendant quantification of value, is widely perceived at this time as a threat to social and aesthetic values. In *Peri Bathous: or, Martinus Scriblerus His Treatise of the Art of Sinking in Poetry*, a parody of Longinus' *On the Sublime*, Alexander Pope locates the taste for bathetic poetry in the conditions of the commercial literary market, where monetary "*Gain*" is "the principal end of our Art" (see p. 452).

Monetary gain proved a great impetus not only to the burgeoning literary marketplace but also to the development in London of all sorts of popular diversions. Once financed by court patronage, such spectacular entertainments now fall into the hands of entrepreneurs like Martin Heidegger, a great promoter of commercial masquerade parties. Open to all who could afford a ticket, these public parties enjoyed great popularity. But as we see in the letters to *Spectator* No. 8, the delights of the masquerade were not unanimously celebrated. Indeed, because it promoted counterfeit identities, it was often viewed as an affront to moral and social stability.

Masquerades were only one pastime among the many that were emerging in the assembly halls, in the theaters, on the streets, and in the taverns of London in the early eighteenth century. Citizens enjoyed a rich variety of performances and exhibitions: the opera, puppet shows, gymnastic displays, lions and dancing monkeys, raree shows, mechanical waterworks and waxworks, and public displays of exotic curiosities in museums, coffeehouses, and retail shops. Alongside notices for books, plays, cosmetics, medicines, and clothing in the back pages of *The Tatler* and *The Spectator* were advertisements for many of these events. Like other commodities, cultural productions contended for their audience in a competitive cultural marketplace through promotion and advertisement.

To further their broad reform, *The Tatler* and *The Spectator* join contemporary publications in a critical examination of the state of these "publick Diversions," which, as Steele laments in *Tatler* No. 12, have declined into a lamentably barbaric state (see p. 324). As leading agents in the definition of the standards of middle-brow culture, both papers engage in an ongoing struggle to purge their genteel audiences of the taste for "low" and "vulgar" entertainments like contortionist acts, puppet shows, ladder-dancing, emblem poems, and even, though with some equivocation, the opera.

But the papers by no means eschew all aspects of the popular. Accessibility, ease, lack of artifice and pedantry, common sense in a common language: these are the aesthetic qualities valued by *The Tatler* and *The Spectator*. Against, though always in relation to, a literary elitism based on the Greek and Roman classics, Addison promotes the literary and sentimental merits of the popular folk ballad, *Two Children in the Wood* (*Spectator* No. 85; see p. 368). By refusing the superficial sparkle and moral insensibility of Etherege's *Man of Mode* and by censuring the faulty taste for flash and spectacle cultivated among some people of high degree, the papers disavow many of the cultural standards associated with the fashionable elite. Transcending the at once economic and status-linked qualifications of property ownership, the pleasures of Addison's realm of the imagination are available to all simply for the looking. Pioneers in the founding of the modern aesthetic, *The Tatler* and even more *The Spectator* begin to draw up a map of culture and its modern territories of "high," "middle," and "low" and to stake out a middle ground for envisioning and evaluating these levels. Mediating between the high and the low, this middle-brow culture embraces both the refinement and the gentility formerly the provenance of elite culture and the broad accessibility identified with more popular cultural forms.

The materials collected here reflect regulative responses to the increasing proliferation of cultural forms in a commercialized market in the form of prescriptions for proper standards of taste. The critical discourse of taste, along with the forms of production it would govern, becomes a popular, public interest. Indeed, alongside financial and commercial schemes are public projects for ethical and cultural improvement. In Chapter 1 we looked at the Society for the Reformation of Manners and Morals; here we have Swift's project for founding a society to oversee the improvement of the English tongue, a letter in *Spectator* No. 175 calling for the establishment of a Society for the Inspection of Modes and Fashions, and a proposal for a national Repository of Fashion by a correspondent in *Spectator* No. 478. Clearly, these are responses to a felt need for cultural gatekeeping in a society where manners and morals all seem dangerously unregulated. The drive to control these forces of proliferation, change, and instability motivates the entire reformative design of *The Tatler* and *The Spectator*.

In *The Tatler* and *The Spectator* the reform of taste, an intrinsic strand in the fabric of moral correction, works through the formulation of critical precepts that direct choices at once ethical and aesthetic. Their standard of taste is applicable across the broad spectrum of cultural production and social practices. The same ideal standard of ornamental simplicity contained in the Horatian tag *simplex munditiis* governs correct taste in wit, conversation, and dress (*Tatler* No. 62; see p. 327). Metaphors are easily transported across the boundaries of genre and media: the gardener who writes in to *Spectator* No. 478 describes modes of horticulture in literary terms, and in almost every critical treatise on verbal wit, the metaphor of dress is imported to describe rhetorical effect. As the proposals for a Society for the Inspection of Modes and Fashions and for a Repository of Fashion dramatically reveal, fashion embodies exactly those forces of change that most threaten sociocultural stability (*Spectator* No. 175). Throughout the period, fashion serves as a discursive category through which change and stability, the superficial and the essential, are represented and weighed. Pope's *Essay on Criticism* reaches almost automatically into the discourse of fashion, borrowing its metaphors to articulate the difference between nature and artifice, mere ornament and true signification. For while "Expression," in Pope's phrase, "is the Dress of Thought," dress itself is identified with the forces of dissimulation and disguise that threaten the more straightforward communicative and representative operations of language.

As the central conduit of significance and communication, language occupies a pivotal position in critical discussion. Threatened in its integrity by the "Fashion of false Wit" (see p. 358) to which Addison refers in *Spectator* No. 58, and by the fashionably slangy and abbreviated English Swift parodies in *Tatler* No. 230, language lies at the heart of the reform of wit and taste in early-eighteenth-century England. As Addison points out in *Spectator* No. 409, it is largely through reading and conversation that taste is developed and manifested. The selections emphasize the agency of oral as well as verbal culture in the development of taste and wit. We see in these texts, and more generally in the intimate affiliation of the popular periodical with coffeehouse society and town talk, an ongoing dialectical interplay between literary and oral culture. In the reading rooms of public coffeehouses and clubs, as at the private family breakfast and tea table, *The Tatler* and *The Spectator* were talked about. They were written to be talked about and to reform the talk of the town, through which cultural standards were debated and cultural trends established.

By considering how their contemporaries should talk and by striving to correct the terms and aims of critical discourse, the *Tatler* and *Spectator* papers, like Pope's *Essay on Criticism* and Swift's "A Digression Concerning Critics," serve a metacritical function. They are engaged in a critique of criticism itself, its standards, categories, objects, ends, and the quality of its language. The satires on critics collected here highlight the central impulse that drives the prolific critical debate of the eighteenth century: the desire to gain ascendancy as the ultimate cultural arbiter. Critical discourse flourishes in free nations, where tyrannical force is replaced by rhetorical persuasion and many voices publicly contend for preeminence. When cultural production is freed from the exclusive purview of the aristocratic elite and the church, the secular public critic becomes the watchdog of standards of taste. Within many genres and media — prose, verse, the periodical essay, painting, engraving, drama, and popular operas — sociocultural criticism is the dominant mode. Growing up alongside and in response to an ever more commercial cultural marketplace, eighteenth-century criticism, with its self-reflexive attitudes, is an emphatically modern discourse. It is indeed the discourse of modernity, shaped by the political liberalism, social mobility, market-driven economic imperatives, and secular attitudes that characterize capitalist society in the West.

Modern criticism, as is especially apparent in Swift's venomous attacks, is itself a critique of modernity. Its target is the cultural and ethical destabilization brought on by the ongoing revolutions in political, economic, and social institutions. Change and permanence are its polar guides. In the critical discourse of the later seventeenth and early eighteenth centuries, stabilization is always *re*-stabilization and improvement, *re*-form. There is throughout a sense of an inalterable rupture with the past and with permanent standards and values. The rhetoric of *re*-storation is strong well into the eighteenth century. In contrast to the more severe and pessimistic outlook of Swift and the later Pope, Addison and Steele succeed in their quest for a balanced restoration of cultural and social norms by accommodating their standards to changing social, political, and economic conditions. In *The Tatler* and *The Spectator*, change is understood less as a falling away from ancient order and stability than as a promise of future progress and restabilization. Change, if carefully managed, may be for the better. With their measured progressivism, tolerant social attitudes, advocacy of commerce, and (sometimes equivocal) acceptance of their own dependence on the commercial literary market, *The*

Tatler and *The Spectator* embody attitudes that remain current throughout the eighteenth century and, to some extent, well into the twentieth.

The Tatler

No. 12
Saturday, May 7, 1709
[Steele on the Barbaric State of "Publick Diversions"]

May 5.

When a Man has engag'd to keep a Stage-Coach, he is oblig'd, whether he has Passengers or not, to set out: Thus it fares with us Weekly Historians; but indeed, for my Particular, I hope I shall soon have little more to do in this Work, than to Publish what is sent me from such as have Leisure and Capacity for giving Delight, and being pleas'd in an elegant Manner. The present Grandeur of the *British* Nation might make us expect, that we should rise in our Publick Diversions, and Manner of enjoying Life, in Proportion to our Advancement in Glory and Power. Instead of that, take and survey this Town, and you'l find, Rakes and Debauchees are your Men of Pleasure; Thoughtless Atheists, and Illiterate Drunkards, call themselves Free Thinkers;[1] and Gamesters, Banterers, Biters,[2] Swearers, and Twenty new-born Insects more, are, in their several Species, the modern Men of Wit. Hence it is, that a Man who has been out of Town but one half Year, has lost the Language, and must have some Friend to stand by him, and keep him in Countenance for talking common Sense. To Day I saw a short Interlude at *White*'s[3] of this Nature, which I took Notes of, and put together as well as I could in a Publick Place. The Persons of the *Drama* are, *Pip*,[4] the last Gentleman that has been

---

[1] *Free Thinkers:* People who refuse to submit their reason to the control of authority in matters of religious belief. The word refers to Deists and others who dissented from the dogmas of Christianity.

[2] *Biters:* To "bite" is to deceive verbally, as in the narrative that follows here.

[3] *White's:* A fashionable chocolate house in St. James's Street. Notorious as the haunt of heavy gamblers, White's was established as a private club in 1730 in order to keep out professional cardsharps.

[4] *Pip:* One of the spots on a playing card.

made so at Cards; *Trimmer*,[5] a Person half undone at 'em, and is now between a Cheat and a Gentleman; *Acorn*, an honest *English* Man, of good plain Sense and Meaning; and Mr. *Friendly*, a reasonable Man of the Town.

White's Chocolate-house, May 5.
Enter *Pip*, *Trim*, and *Acorn*.

Ac. What's the Matter Gentlemen? What! Take no Notice of an old Friend?

Pip. Pox on it! don't talk to me, I am Vowel'd[6] by the Count, and cursedly out of Humour.

Ac. Vowel'd! Prithee, *Trimmer*, What does he mean by that?

Trim. Have a Care, *Harry*, speak softly; don't show your Ignorance: — If you do, they'l Bite you where-e'er they meet you; they are such cursed Curs, — the present Wits.

Ac. Bite me! What do you mean?

Pip. Why! Don't you know what Biting is? Nay, you are in the right on't. However, one would learn it only to defend one's self against Men of Wit, as one would know the Tricks of Play, to be secure against the Cheats. But don't you hear, *Acorn*, that Report, That some Potentates of the Alliance[7] have taken Care of themselves, exclusive of us?

Ac. How! Heav'n forbid! After all our Glorious Victories; all this Expence of Blood and Treasure!

Pip. Bite —

Ac. Bite! How?

Trim. Nay, he has Bit you fairly enough; that's certain.

Ac. Pox! I don't feel it — How? Where?

Exit *Pip*, and *Trimmer*, laughing.

Ac. Ho! Mr. *Friendly*, your most humble Servant; you heard what pass'd between those fine Gentlemen and me. *Pip* complain'd to me, That he has been Vowel'd; and they tell me, I am Bit.

Friend. You are to understand, Sir, That Simplicity of Behaviour, which is the Perfection of good Breeding and good Sense, is utterly lost in the World; and in the Room of it, there are started a Thousand

---

[5] *Trimmer:* One who "trims between" opposing sides in an argument, taking up either as self-interest dictates (*OED*).

[6] *Vowel'd:* To be presented with an IOU.

[7] *Potentates of the Alliance:* In 1701, early on in the War of the Spanish Succession, the Grand Alliance against France was established; it consisted of England, the Netherlands, Austria, Prussia, most other German states, and (later) Portugal.

little Inventions, which Men, barren of better Things, take up in the
Place of it. Thus, for every Character in Conversation that us'd to
please, there is an Impostor put upon you. Him whom we allow'd
formerly for a certain pleasant Subtilty, and natural Way of giving
you an unexpected Hit, call'd a *Droll*, is now mimick'd by a *Biter*,
who is a dull Fellow, that tells you a Lye with a grave Face, and
laughs at you for knowing him no better than to believe him. Instead
of that Sort of Companion, who could rally you, and keep his Countenance, 'till he made you fall into some little Inconsistency of Behaviour, at which you your self could laugh with him, you have the
Snearer, who will keep you Company from Morning to Night, to
gather your Follies of the Day, (which perhaps you commit out of
Confidence in him) and expose you in the Evening to all the Scorners
in Town. For your Man of Sense and free Spirit, whose Set of
Thoughts were built upon Learning, Reason, and Experience, you
have now an impudent Creature made up of Vice only, who supports
his Ignorance by his Courage, and Want of Learning by Contempt
of it.

Ac. Dear Sir, hold: What you have told me already of this Change
in Conversation, is too miserable to be heard with any Delight; but,
methinks, as these new Creatures appear in the World, it might give
an excellent Field to Writers for the Stage, to divert us with the Representation of them there.

Friend. No, No: As you say, there might be some Hopes of Redress of these Grievances, if there were proper Care taken of the Theatre; but the History of that is yet more lamentable than that of the
Decay of Conversation I gave you.

Ac. Pray, Sir, a little: I han't been in Town these Six Years, 'till
within this Fortnight.

Friend. It is now some Years, since several Revolutions in the Gay
World, had made the Empire of the Stage subject to very fatal Convulsions, which were too dangerous to be cured by the Skill of little
King *Oberon*,[8] who then sat in the Throne of it. The Laziness of this
Prince threw him upon the Choice of a Person who was fit to spend
his Life in Contentions, an able and profound Attorney, to whom he
mortgag'd his whole Empire. This *Divito* is the most skilful of all
Politicians: He has a perfect Art in being unintelligible in Discourse,
and uncomeatable in Business. But he having no Understanding in

---

[8] *King Oberon:* Oberon is the king of the fairies in William Shakespeare's play *A
Midsummer Night's Dream* (1595–96).

this polite Way, brought in upon us, to get in his Money, Ladder-dancers, Rope-dancers,[9] Juglers, and Mountebanks, to strut in the Place of *Shakespear*'s Heroes, and *Johnson*'s Humourists. When the Seat of Wit was thus mortgag'd, without Equity of Redemption, an Architect arose, who has built the Muse a new Palace, but secur'd her no Retinue; so that instead of Action there, we have been put off by Song and Dance. This latter Help of Sound has also began to fail for want of Voices; therefore the Palace has since been put into the Hands of a Surgeon, who cuts any Foreign Fellow into an Eunuch, and passes him upon us for a Singer of *Italy*.[10]

Ac. I'll go out of Town to Morrow.

Trim. Things are come to this pass, and yet the World will not understand, that the Theatre has much the same Effect on the Manners of the Age, as the Bank on the Credit of the Nation. Wit and Spirit, Humour and good Sense, can never be reviv'd, but under the Government of those who are Judges of such Talents, who know, that whatever is put up in their stead, is but a short and trifling Expedient, to support the Appearance of 'em for a Season. It is possible a Peace will give leisure to put these Matters under new Regulations; but at present, all the Assistance we can see towards our Recovery, is as far from giving us Help, as a Poultice is from performing what can be done only by the Grand Elixir.

No. 62
Thursday, September 1, 1709
[Steele on Correct Taste Governed
by the Principle "Simplex Munditiis"]

Will's Coffee-house, August 31.

This Evening was spent at our Table in Discourse of Propriety of Words and Thoughts, which is Mr. *Dryden*'s Definition of Wit;[1] but a very odd Fellow, who would intrude upon us, and has a Briskness of Imagination more like Madness than regular Thought, said, that

---

[9] *Rope-dancers:* Tightrope walkers, as in today's circus.

[10] *Singer of Italy:* Refers to the *castrati* who sang in the Italian opera.

[1] *Definition of Wit:* John Dryden (1631–1700) was a poet, playwright, essayist, and translator. His definition of wit appears in the *Apology* prefixed to his play *The State of Innocence.*

Harry Jacks was the first who told him of the taking of the Citadel of
Tournay, and (says he) *Harry* deserves a Statue more than the Boy
who ran to the Senate with a Thorn in his Foot to tell of a Victory.
We were astonish'd at the Assertion, and *Spondee* ask'd him, What
Affinity is there between that Boy and *Harry*, that you say their Merit
resembles so much as you just now told us? Why (says he) *Harry* you
know is in the *French* Interest, and it was more Pain to him to tell the
Story of *Tournay*, than to the Boy to run upon a Thorn to relate a
Victory which he was glad of. The Gentleman who was in the Chair
upon the Subject of Propriety of Words and Thoughts, would by no
means allow, that there was Wit in this Comparison; and urg'd, that
to have any Thing gracefully said, it must be natural; but that whatsoever was introduc'd in common Discourse with so much Premedi-
tation, was insufferable. That Critick went on: Had Mr. *Jacks* (said
he) told him the Citadel was taken, and another had answer'd, He deserves a Statue as well as the *Roman* Boy, for he told it with as much
Pain; it might have pass'd for a sprightly Expression: But there is a
Wit for Discourse, and a Wit for Writing. The Easiness and Familiarity of the first, is not to savour in the least of Study; but the Exactness
of the other, is to admit of something like the Freedom of Discourse,
especially in Treatises of Humanity, and what regards the *Belles Lettres*. I do not in this allow, that *Bickerstaff*'s *Tatlers*, or Discourses of
Wit by Retail, and for the Penny, should come within the Description
of *Writing*. I bow'd at his Compliment, and — But he would not let
me proceed.

  You see in no Place of Conversation the Perfection of Speech so
much as in an accomplish'd Woman. Whether it be, that there is a
Partiality irresistible when we judge of that Sex, or whatever it is, you
may observe a wonderful Freedom in their Utterance, and an easy
Flow of Words, without being distracted (as we often are who read
much) in the Choice of Dictions and Phrases. My Lady *Courtly* is an
Instance of this: She was talking the other Day of Dress, and did it
with so excellent an Air and Gesture, that you would have sworn she
had learn'd her Action from our *Demosthenes*.[2] Besides which, her
Words were so particularly well adapted to the Matter she talk'd of,
that tho' Dress was a new Thing to us Men, she avoided the Terms of
Art in it, and describ'd an unaffected Garb and Manner in so proper
Terms, that she came up to that of *Horace*'s *Simplex Munditiis*;[3]

---

[2] *Demosthenes:* A famous Athenian orator (384–322 B.C.).

[3] *Horace's Simplex Munditiis:* Horace (65–8 B.C.) was a renowned Roman lyric
poet. This tag means simple neatness, or elegance (*Odes* 1.5.5).

which, whoever can translate in Two Words, has as much Eloquence as Lady *Courtly*. I took the Liberty to tell her, That all she had said with so much good Grace, was spoken in Two Words in *Horace*, but would not undertake to translate them; upon which she smil'd, and told me, She believ'd me a very great Scholar, and I took my Leave.

No. 99
Saturday, November 26, 1709
[Steele on Ladder-Dancers]

—— *Spirat Tragicum satis & feliciter audet.*[1]

Will's Coffee-house, November 25.

I have been this Evening recollecting what Passages (since I could first think) have left the strongest Impressions upon my Mind; and after strict Enquiry, I am convinced, that the Impulses I have received from Theatrical Representations, have had a great Effect, than otherwise would have been wrought in me by the little Occurrences of my private Life. My old Friends, *Hart* and *Mohun*;[2] the one by his natural and proper Force, the other by his great Skill and Art, never failed to send me Home full of such Idea's as affected my Behaviour, and made me insensibly more courteous and humane to my Friends and Acquaintance. It is not the Business of a good Play to make every Man an Hero; but it certainly gives him a livelier Sense of Virtue and Merit than he had when he entered the Theatre.

This rational Pleasure (as I always call it) has for many Years been very little tasted: But I am glad to find, that the true Spirit of it is reviving again amongst us, by a due Regard to what is presented, and by supporting only one Playhouse. It has been within the Observation of the youngest amongst us, That while there were Two Houses, they did not outvie each other by such Representations as tended to the Instruction and Ornament of Life, but by introducing mimical Dances, and fulsom Buffoonries. For when an excellent Tragedy was to be acted in one House, the Ladder-Dancer[3] carried the whole Town to

---

[1] *Spirat . . . audet:* From Horace, *Epistles* 2.1.166: "By Nature great and fit for Tragedy" [Bond].

[2] *Hart and Mohun:* Charles Hart (d. 1683) and Michael Mohun (1620?–1684) were chief actors in Charles Killigrew's company at the Theatre Royal (later the Drury Lane Theatre at Haymarket).

[3] *Ladder-Dancer:* Someone who performs a feat of skill on a ladder. In the ladder dance, the performer stands on a ladder, shifting it from place to place as he goes up and down the rungs without losing his balance.

the other: And indeed such an Evil as this, must be the natural Consequence of Two Theatres, as certainly as that there are more who can
see than can think. Every one is sensible of the Danger of the Fellow
on the Ladder, and can see his Activity in coming down safe; but very
few are Judges of the Distress of an Hero in a Play, or of his Manner
of Behaviour in those Circumstances. Thus, to please the People, Two
Houses must entertain them with what they can understand, and not
with Things which are designed to improve their Understanding: And
the readiest Way to gain good Audiences, must be to offer such
Things as are most relished by the Crowd; that is to say, immodest
Action, empty Show, or impertinent Activity. In short, Two Houses
cannot hope to subsist, but by Means which are contradictory to the
very Institution of a Theatre in a well-govern'd Kingdom.

No. 108
Saturday, December 17, 1709
[Addison on a Contortionist Show]

Pronaque cum spectant Animalia caetera Terram,
Os Homini sublime dedit, Coelumque tueri
Jussit.[1]
— Ovid. Met.

Sheer-Lane, December 16.

It is not to be imagined, how great an Effect well-disposed Lights,
with proper Forms and Orders in Assemblies, have upon some Tempers. I am sure I feel it in so extraordinary a Manner, that I cannot in
a Day or Two get out of my Imagination any very beautiful or disagreeable Impression which I receive on such Occasions. For this
Reason I frequently look in at the Playhouse, in order to enlarge my
Thoughts, and warm my Mind with some new Idea's, that may be
serviceable to me in my Lucubrations.

In this Disposition I entered the Theatre the other Day, and placed
my self in a Corner of it, very convenient for seeing, without being
my self observed. I found the Audience hushed in a very deep Atten-

---

[1] *Pronaque . . . Jussit:* From Ovid, *Metamorphoses* i.84–88 (altered):

> Thus, while the mute creation downward bend,
> Their Sight, and to their Earthy Mother tend,
> Man looks aloft; and with erected Eyes
> Beholds his own Hereditary Skies.
> — DRYDEN [Bond]

tion, and did not question but some noble Tragedy was just then in its Crisis, or that an Incident was to be unravelled which would determine the Fate of an Hero. While I was in this Suspence, expecting every Moment to see my old Friend Mr. *Betterton*[2] appear in all the Majesty of Distress, to my unspeakable Amazement, there came up a Monster with a Face between his Feet; and as I was looking on, he raised himself on one Leg in such a perpendicular Posture, that the other grew in a direct Line above his Head.[3] It afterwards twisted it self into the Motions and Wreathings of several different Animals, and after great Variety of Shapes and Transformations, went off the Stage in the Figure of an human Creature. The Admiration, the Applause, the Satisfaction, of the Audience, during this strange Entertainment, is not to be expressed. I was very much out of Countenance for my dear Countrymen, and looked about with some Apprehension for Fear any Foreigner should be present. Is it possible (thought I) that human Nature can rejoice in its Disgrace, and take Pleasure in seeing its own Figure turned to Ridicule, and distorted into Forms that raise Horror and Aversion? There is something disingenuous and immoral in the being able to bear such a Sight. Men of elegant and noble Minds, are shocked at seeing the Characters of Persons who deserve Esteem for their Virtue, Knowledge, or Services to their Country, placed in wrong Lights, and by Misrepresentation made the Subject of Buffoonry. Such a nice Abhorrence is not indeed to be found among the Vulgar; but methinks it is wonderful, that these who have nothing but the outward Figure to distinguish them as Men, should delight in seeing it abused, vilified, and disgraced.

I must confess, there is nothing that more pleases me, in all that I read in Books, or see among Mankind, than such Passages as represent Human Nature in its proper Dignity. As Man is a Creature made up of different Extremes, he has something in him very great and very mean: A skilful Artist may draw an excellent Picture of him in either of these Views. The finest Authors of Antiquity have taken him on the more advantagious Side. They cultivate the natural Grandeur of the Soul, raise in her a generous Ambition, feed her with Hopes of Immortality and Perfection, and do all they can to widen the Partition between the Virtuous and the Vicious, by making the Difference betwixt them as great as between Gods and Brutes. In short, it is

---

[2] *Mr. Betterton:* Thomas Betterton (1635–1710) was the greatest Restoration actor and appeared in 180 roles. For Betterton's performance in *Hamlet* see *Tatler* No. 71. Betterton died in the following April, and Steele published a eulogy for him in *Tatler* No. 167.

[3] *. . . above his Head:* Addison is describing a contortionist.

impossible to read a Page in *Plato, Tully,*[4] and a Thousand other ancient Moralists, without being a greater and a better Man for it. On
the contrary, I could never read any of our modish *French* Authors,
or those of our own Country who are the Imitators and Admirers of
that trifling Nation, without being for some Time out of Humour
with my self, and at every Thing about me. Their Business is, to depreciate human Nature, and consider it under its worst Appearances.
They give mean Interpretations and base Motives to the worthiest
Actions: They resolve Virtue and Vice into Constitution. In short,
they endeavour to make no Distinction between Man and Man, or
between the Species of Men and that of Brutes. As an Instance of this
kind of Authors, among many others, let any one examine the celebrated *Rochefaucault,*[5] who is the great Philosopher for administring
of Consolation to the Idle, the Envious, and worthless Part of
Mankind.

I remember a young Gentleman of moderate Understanding, but
great Vivacity, who by dipping into many Authors of this Nature,
had got a little Smattering of Knowledge, just enough to make an
Atheist or a Free-thinker,[6] but not a Philosopher or a Man of Sense.
With these Accomplishments, he went to visit his Father in the Country, who was a plain, rough, honest Man, and wise, tho' not learned.
The Son, who took all Opportunities to show his Learning, began to
establish a new Religion in the Family, and to enlarge the Narrowness of their Country Notions; in which he succeeded so well, that he
had seduced the Butler by his Table-Talk, and staggered his eldest
Sister. The old Gentleman began to be alarmed at the Schisms that
arose among his Children, but did not yet believe his Son's Doctrine
to be so pernicious as it really was, 'till one Day talking of his Setting-
Dog, the Son said, He did not question but *Trey* was as immortal as
any one of the Family; and in the Heat of the Argument told his Father, That for his own Part, he expected to die like a Dog. Upon
which the old Man, starting up in a very great Passion, cried out,
Then, Sirrah, you shall live like one; and taking his Cane in his Hand,

[4]*Plato, Tully:* Plato (427?–347? B.C.) was the Athenian philosopher, a disciple of
Socrates and founder of the Academy (386) where he taught and wrote. Tully is Marcus Tullius Cicero (106–43 B.C.), the famous Roman orator, philosopher, and statesman.
[5]*Rochefaucault:* François VI, Duc de La Rochefoucauld (1613–1680), was a
prominent French aristocrat, active in political, military, and literary enterprises; his
book of epigrams, *The Maxims of La Rochefoucauld* (1655), appeared in translation
in England by 1670.
[6]*Free-thinker:* See *Tatler* No. 12, note 1 (p. 324).

cudgelled him out of his System. This had so good an Effect upon him, that he took up[7] from that Day, fell to reading good Books, and is now a Bencher in the *Middle-Temple*.[8]

I do not mention this Cudgelling Part of the Story with a Design to engage the secular Arm in Matters of this Nature; but certainly, if it ever exerts it self in Affairs of Opinion and Speculation, it ought to do it on such shallow and despicable Pretenders to Knowledge, who endeavour to give Man dark and uncomfortable Prospects of his Being, and destroy those Principles which are the Support, Happiness, and Glory, of all publick Societies, as well as private Persons.

I think it is one of *Pythagoras*'s golden Sayings, *That a Man should take Care above all Things to have a due Respect for himself*.[9] And it is certain, that this licentious Sort of Authors, who are for depreciating Mankind, endeavour to disappoint and undo what the most refined Spirits have been labouring to advance since the Beginning of the World. The very Design of Dress, Good-breeding, outward Ornaments, and Ceremony, were to lift up human Nature, and set it off to an Advantage. Architecture, Painting, and Statuary, were invented with the same Design; as indeed every Art and Science contributes to the Embellishment of Life, and to the wearing off or throwing into Shades the mean and low Parts of our Nature. Poetry carries on this great End more than all the rest, as may be seen in the following Passage, taken out of Sir *Francis Bacon*'s *Advancement of Learning*,[10] which gives a truer and better Account of this Art than all the Volumes that were ever written upon it.

'Poetry, especially Heroical, seems to be raised altogether from a noble Foundation, which makes much for the Dignity of Man's

---

[7] *took up:* To reform, mend one's ways.

[8] *Middle-Temple:* The Middle Temple is one section of the Temple Bar, one of the four Inns of Court housed along Fleet Street in London. Originally owned by the medieval religious and military order the Knights Templar, who built their residence there in the twelfth century, this series of buildings, known collectively as the Temple, was presented by James I to lawyers for their professional use. It housed both residential and professional legal apartments. A bencher is a member of the inner or higher bar who acts as a governor of one of the Inns of Court.

[9] *... for himself:* No. 12 of Pythagoras's *Golden Verses*. These were published in 1707 in André Dacier's *Life of Pythagoras, with his Symbols and Golden Verses* [Bond]. Pythagoras was a sixth-century B.C. Greek mathematician, philosopher, and mystic.

[10] *Advancement of Learning:* Sir Francis Bacon (1561–1626) was an early empirical philosopher and essayist whose *Great Instauration* probed the workings of nature and the mysteries of science. This passage is from the first part of that work, *The Advancement of Learning* (1605), book 2, part 4, section 2 [Bond].

Nature. For seeing this sensible World is in Dignity inferior to the Soul of Man, Poesy seems to endow human Nature with that which History denies; and to give Satisfaction to the Mind, with at least the Shadow of Things, where the Substance cannot be had. For if the Matter be throughly considered, a strong Argument may be drawn from Poesy, that a more stately Greatness of Things, a more perfect Order, and a more beautiful Variety, delights the Soul of Man, than any Way can be found in Nature since the Fall. Wherefore seeing the Acts and Events, which are the Subject of true History, are not of that Amplitude as to content the Mind of Man; Poesy is ready at Hand to feign Acts more Heroical. Because true History reports the Successes of Business not proportionable to the Merit of Virtues and Vices, Poesy corrects it, and presents Events and Fortunes according to Desert, and according to the Law of Providence: Because true History, thro' the frequent Satiety and Similitude of Things, works a Distast and Misprision in the Mind of Man, Poesy cheareth and refresheth the Soul, chanting Things rare and various, and full of Vicissitudes. So as Poesy serveth and conferreth to Delectation, Magnanimity, and Morality; and therefore it may seem deservedly to have some Participation of Divineness, because it doth raise the Mind, and exalt the Spirit with high Raptures, by proportioning the Shews of Things to the Desires of the Mind; and not submitting the Mind to Things, as Reason and History do. And by these Allurements and Congruities, whereby it cherisheth the Soul of Man, joined also with Consort of Musick, whereby it may more sweetly insinuate it self; it hath won such Access, that it hath been in Estimation even in rude Times, and barbarous Nations, when other Learning stood excluded.'

But there is nothing which favours and falls in with this natural Greatness and Dignity of human Nature so much as Religion, which does not only promise the entire Refinement of the Mind, but the glorifying of the Body, and the Immortality of both.

No. 163
Tuesday, April 25, 1710
[Addison on Ned Softly's Poem]

Idem Inficeto est inficetior Rure
Simul Poemata attigit; neque idem unquam
Aequè est beatus, ac Poema cum scribit:
Tam gaudet in se, tamque se ipse miratur.
Nimirum idem omnes fallimur; neque est quisquam
Quem non in aliqua re videre Suffenum
Possis.[1]

— Catul. de Suffeno.

Will's Coffee-house, April 24.

I Yesterday came hither about Two Hours before the Company generally make their Appearance, with a Design to read over all the News-Papers; but upon my sitting down, I was accosted by *Ned Softly*, who saw me from a Corner in the other End of the Room, where I found he had been writing something. Mr. *Bickerstaff*, says he, I observe by a late Paper[2] of yours, that you and I are just of a Humour; for you must know, of all Impertinencies, there is nothing which I so much hate as News. I never read a *Gazette*[3] in my Life; and never trouble my Head about our Armies, whether they win or lose, or in what Part of the World they lie encamped. Without giving me Time to reply, he drew a Paper of Verses out of his Pocket, telling me, That he had something which would entertain me more agreeably, and that he would desire my Judgment upon every Line, for that we had Time enough before us till the Company came in.

Ned Softly is a very pretty Poet, and a great Admirer of easy Lines. *Waller*[4] is his Favourite: And as that admirable Writer has the best and worst Verses of any among our great *English* Poets, *Ned Softly* has got all the bad Ones without Book, which he repeats upon Occasion, to show his Reading, and garnish his Conversation. *Ned* is

---

[1] *Idem . . . Possis:* From Catullus 22.14–20: "Suffenus has no more wit than a mere clown when he attempts to write verses; and yet he is never happier than when he is scribbling: so much does he admire himself and his compositions. And, indeed, this is the foible of every one of us; for there is no man living who is not a Suffenus in one thing or other" — NICHOLS [Bond].

[2] *a late Paper: Tatler* No. 160.

[3] *Gazette:* The official newspaper of the English government.

[4] *Waller:* Edmund Waller (1608–1687) was a Royalist poet. His *Poems* appeared in 1645 and his *Divine Poems* in 1685. Along with John Denham, Waller is credited with the development of the closed rhymed couplet.

indeed a true *English* Reader, incapable of relishing the great and masterly Strokes of this Art; but wonderfully pleased with the little *Gothick* Ornaments of Epigrammatical Conceits, Turns, Points, and Quibbles, which are so frequent in the most admired of our *English* Poets, and practised by those who want Genius and Strength to represent, after the Manner of the Ancients, Simplicity in its natural Beauty and Perfection.

Finding my self unavoidably engaged in such a Conversation, I was resolved to turn my Pain into a Pleasure, and to divert my self as well as I could with so very odd a Fellow. You must understand, says *Ned*, that the Sonnet I am going to read to you was written upon a Lady, who showed me some Verses of her own making, and is perhaps the best Poet of our Age. But you shall hear it. Upon which he begun to read as follows:

To Mira *on her incomparable Poems.*

1.

When dress'd in Lawrel Wreaths you shine,
And tune your soft melodious Notes,
You seem a Sister of the Nine[5]
Or Phoebus[6] *self in Petticoats.*

2.

I fancy, when your Song you sing,
(Your Song you sing with so much Art)
Your Pen was pluck'd from Cupid's *Wing;*
For ah! it wounds me like his Dart.

Why, says I, this is a little Nosegay of Conceits, a very Lump of Salt: Every Verse hath something in it that piques; and then the Dart in the last Line is certainly as pretty a Sting in the Tail of an Epigram (for so I think your Criticks call it) as ever entered into the Thought of a Poet. Dear Mr. *Bickerstaff*, says he, shaking me by the Hand, every Body knows you to be a Judge of these Things; and to tell you truly, I read over *Roscommon*'s Translation of *Horace*'s *Art of Poetry*[7] Three several Times, before I sat down to write the Sonnet which I have shown you. But you shall hear it again, and pray observe every Line of it, for not one of them shall pass without your Approbation.

[5] *the Nine:* The nine Muses of classical myth.
[6] *Phoebus:* Phoebus Apollo, Greek god of music, medicine, prophecy, and poetry.
[7] *Horace's Art of Poetry:* Horace's (65–8 B.C.) *Ars Poetica* is an influential verse guide for the poet. Wentworth Dillon, fourth Earl of Roscommon (1635?–1685), translated Horace's *Art of Poetry* into blank verse (1680, 1684, 1709).

When dress'd in Lawrel Wreaths you shine.

That is, says he, when you have your Garland on; when you are writing Verses. To which I replied, I know your Meaning: A Metaphor! The same, said he, and went on.

And tune your soft melodious Notes.

Pray observe the Gliding of that Verse; there is scarce a Consonant in it: I took Care to make it run upon Liquids. Give me your Opinion of it. Truly, said I, I think it as good as the former. I am very glad to hear you say so, says he; but mind the next.

You seem a Sister of the Nine.

That is, says he, you seem a Sister of the *Muses*; for if you look into ancient Authors, you will find it was their Opinion, that there were Nine of them. I remember it very well, said I; put pray proceed.

Or Phoebus *self in Petticoats.*

Phoebus, says he, was the God of Poetry. These little Instances, Mr. *Bickerstaff*, show a Gentleman's Reading. Then to take off from the Air of Learning, which *Phoebus* and the Muses have given to this First Stanza, you may observe, how it falls all of a sudden into the Familiar; *in Petticoats*!

Or Phoebus *self in Petticoats.*

Let us now, says I, enter upon the Second Stanza. I find the First Line is still a Continuation of the Metaphor.

I fancy, when your Song you sing.

It is very right, says he; but pray observe the Turn of Words in those Two Lines. I was a whole Hour in adjusting of them, and have still a Doubt upon me, Whether in the Second Line it should be, *Your Song you sing*; or, *You sing your Song*? You shall hear them both.

I fancy, when your Song you sing,
   (Your Song you sing with so much Art).

OR,

I Fancy, when your Song you sing,
   You sing your Song with so much Art.

Truly, said I, the Turn is so natural either Way, that you have made me almost giddy with it. Dear Sir, said he, grasping me by the

Hand, you have a great deal of Patience; but pray what do you think of the next Verse?

> *Your Pen was pluck'd from* Cupid's *Wing.*

Think! says I, I think you have made *Cupid* look like a little Goose. That was my Meaning, says he: I think the Ridicule is well enough hit off. But we now come to the last, which sums up the whole Matter:

> *For Ah! it wounds me like his Dart.*

Pray how do you like that *Ah!* Doth it not make a pretty Figure in that Place? *Ah!* It looks as if I felt the Dart, and cried out at being pricked with it.

> *For Ah! it wounds me like his Dart.*

My friend *Dick Easy*, continued he, assured me, he would rather have written that *Ah!* than to have been the Author of the *Aeneid.*[8] He indeed objected, that I made *Mira*'s Pen like a Quill in one of the Lines, and like a Dart in the other. But as to that — Oh! as to that, says I, it is but supposing *Cupid* to be like a Porcupine, and his Quills and Darts will be the same thing. He was going to embrace me for the Hint; but half a Dozen Criticks coming into the Room, whose Faces he did not like, he conveyed the Sonnet into his Pocket, and whispered me in the Ear, he would show it me again as soon as his Man had written it over fair.[9]

No. 165
Saturday, April 29, 1710
[Addison on Sir Timothy Tittle, Critic]

From my own Apartment, April 28.

It has always been my Endeavour to distinguish between Realities and Appearances, and to separate true Merit from the Pretence to it. As it shall ever be my Study to make Discoveries of this Nature in human Life, and to settle the proper Distinctions between the Virtues

---

[8] *Aeneid:* Virgil's (70–19 B.C.) epic of the founding of Rome.
[9] *. . . fair:* Written it out neatly and with no corrections.

and Perfections of Mankind, and those false Colours and Resemblances of them that shine alike in the Eyes of the Vulgar; so I shall be more particularly careful to search into the various Merits and Pretences of the learned World. This is the more necessary, because there seems to be a general Combination among the Pedants to extol one another's Labours, and cry up one another's Parts; while Men of Sense, either through that Modesty which is natural to them, or the Scorn they have for such trifling Commendations, enjoy their Stock of Knowledge like a hidden Treasure, with Satisfaction and Silence. Pedantry indeed in Learning is like Hypocrisy in Religion, a Form of Knowledge without the Power of it, that attracts the Eyes of the Common People, breaks out in Noise and Show, and finds its Reward not from any inward Pleasure that attends it, but from the Praises and Approbations which it receives from Men.

Of this shallow Species there is not a more importunate, empty, and conceited Animal than that which is generally known by the Name of a Critick. This, in the common Acceptation of the Word, is one that, without entering into the Sense and Soul of an Author, has a few general Rules, which, like mechanical Instruments, he applies to the Works of every Writer, and as they quadrate with them, pronounces the Author perfect or defective. He is Master of a certain Set of Words, as Unity, Style, Fire, Flegm, Easy, Natural, Turn, Sentiment, and the like; which he varies, compounds, divides, and throws together, in every Part of his Discourse, without any Thought or Meaning. The Marks you may know him by are, an elevated Eye, and dogmatical Brow, a positive Voice, and a Contempt for every Thing that comes out, whether he has read it or not. He dwells altogether in Generals. He praises or dispraises in the Lump. He shakes his Head very frequently at the Pedantry of Universities, and bursts into Laughter when you mention an Author that is not known at *Will's*. He hath formed his Judgment upon *Homer*, *Horace*, and *Virgil*, not from their own Works, but from those of *Rapin* and *Bossu*.[1] He

---

[1] *Homer, Horace, and Virgil . . . Rapin and Bossu:* Homer (fl. 850 B.C.) was the author of the ancient Greek epics the *Iliad* and the *Odyssey*; Horace was a Roman lyric poet; Virgil was a Roman poet, author of the epic *Aeneid*. Paul de Rapin (1661–1725) was a historian; his great work was *L'Histoire d'Angleterre* (*The History of England*) (1724). Rapin's *Comparison of Homer and Virgil* was a standard critical text. René Le Bossu (1631–1680) was another renowned and familiar French critic; he wrote *Traite du poeme epique* (*The Nature of an Epic Poem*).

knows his own Strength so well, that he never dares praise any Thing in which he has not a *French* Author for his Voucher.

With these extraordinary Talents and Accomplishments, Sir *Timothy Tittle* puts Men in Vogue, or condemns them to Obscurity, and sits as Judge of Life and Death upon every Author that appears in Publick. It is impossible to represent the Pangs, Agonies, and Convulsions, which Sir *Timothy* expresses in every Feature of his Face, and Muscle of his Body, upon the reading of a bad Poet.

About a Week ago I was engaged at a Friend's of mine in an agreeable Conversation with his Wife and Daughters, when in the Height of our Mirth, Sir *Timothy*, who makes Love to my Friend's eldest Daughter, came in amongst us puffing and blowing as if he had been very much out of Breath. He immediately called for a Chair, and desired Leave to sit down, without any further Ceremony. I ask'd him, Where he had been? Whether he was out of Order? He only reply'd, That he was quite spent, and fell a cursing in Soliloquy. I could hear him cry, *A Wicked Rogue — An Execrable Wretch — Was there ever such a Monster —* The young Ladies upon this began to be affrighted, and asked, Whether any one had hurt him? He answered nothing, but still talked to himself. *To lay the first Scene*, says he, *in St.* James's Park[2] *and the last* in Northamptonshire! Is that all, says I? Then I suppose you have been at the Rehearsal of a Play this Morning. *Been!* says he, I have been at *Northampton*, in the *Park*, in a Lady's Bed-Chamber, in a Dining-Room, every where; the Rogue has led me such a Dance — Tho' I could scarce forbear laughing at his Discourse, I told him I was glad it was no worse, and that he was only Metaphorically weary. In short, Sir, says he, the Author has not observed a single Unity in his whole Play; the Scene shifts in every Dialogue; the Villain has hurried me up and down at such a Rate, that I am tired off my Legs. I could not but observe with some Pleasure, that the young Lady whom he made Love to, conceived a very just Aversion towards him, upon seeing him so very passionate in Trifles. And as she had that natural Sense which makes her a better Judge than a Thousand Criticks, she began to rally him upon this foolish Humour. For my Part, says she, I never knew a Play take that was written up to your Rules, as you call them. How Madam! says he, Is that your Opinion? I am sure you have a better Tast. It is a pretty

---

[2] *St. James's Park:* The oldest of London's royal parks and a resort of the sovereigns and their courts through the Restoration.

Kind of Magick, says she, the Poets have, to transport an Audience from Place to Place without the Help of a Coach and Horses. I could travel round the World at such a Rate. It is such an Entertainment as an Enchantress finds when she fancies her self in a Wood, or upon a Mountain, at a Feast, or a Solemnity; though at the same Time she has never stirred out of her Cottage. Your Simile, Madam, says Sir *Timothy*, is by no Means just. Pray, says she, let my Simile's pass without a Criticism. I must confess, continued she, (for I found she was resolved to exasperate him) I laughed very heartily at the last New Comedy which you found so much Fault with. But Madam, says he, you ought not to have laughed; and I defy any one to show me a single Rule that you could laugh by. Ought not to laugh! says she: Pray who should hinder me. Madam, says he, there are such People in the World as *Rapin, Dacier*,[3] and several others, that ought to have spoiled your Mirth. I have heard, says the young Lady, That your great Criticks are always very bad Poets: I fancy there is as much Difference between the Carriage of a Dancing-Master and a Gentleman. I must confess, continued she, I would not be troubled with so fine a Judgment as yours is; for I find you feel more Vexation in a bad Comedy than I do in a deep Tragedy. Madam, says Sir *Timothy*, That is not my Fault, they should learn the Art of Writing. For my Part, says the young Lady, I should think the greatest Art in your Writers of Comedies is to please. To please! Sir *Timothy*, and immediately fell a laughing. Truly, says she, that is my Opinion. Upon this, he composed his Countenance, looked upon his Watch, and took his Leave.

I hear that Sir *Timothy* has not been at my Friend's House since this notable Conference, to the great Satisfaction of the young Lady, who by this Means has got rid of a very impertinent Fop.

I must confess, I could not but observe, with a great deal of Surprize, how this Gentleman, by his ill Nature, Folly, and Affectation, hath made himself capable of suffering so many imaginary Pains, and looking with such a senseless Severity upon the common Diversions of Life.

---

[3] *Rapin, Dacier:* For Rapin see note 1. André Dacier (1651–1722) was a French classical scholar. He is most noted for his translations and editions of classical texts.

No. 225
Saturday, September 16, 1710
[Steele on Polite Conversation]

—— Si quid novisti rectius istis
Candidus imperti, si non, his utere mecum.[1]
— Hor.

From my own Apartment, September 15.

The Hours which we spend in Conversation are the most pleasing
of any which we enjoy; yet, methinks, there is very little Care taken
to improve our selves for the frequent Repetition of them. The common Fault in this Case, is that of growing too intimate, and falling
into displeasing Familiarities: For it is a very ordinary Thing for Men
to make no other Use of a close Acquaintance with each other's Affairs, but to teaze one another with unacceptable Allusions. One
would pass over patiently such as converse like Animals, and salute
each other with Bangs on the Shoulder, sly Raps with Canes, or other
robust Pleasantries practised by the rural Gentry of this Nation: But
even among those who should have more polite Idea's of Things, you
see a Set of People who invert the Design of Conversation, and make
frequent Mention of ungrateful Subjects, nay, mention them because
they are ungrateful; as if the Perfection of Society were in knowing
how to offend on the one Part, and how to bear an Offence on the
other. In all Parts of this populous Town you find the Merry World
made up of an active and a passive Companion; one who has Good-
nature enough to suffer all his Friend shall think fit to say, and one
who is resolved to make the most of his Good-Humour to show his
Parts. In the trading Part of Mankind, I have ever observed the Jest
went by the Weight of Purses, and the Ridicule is made up by the
Gains which arise from it. Thus the Packer allows the Clothier to say
what he pleases, and the Broker has his Countenance ready to laugh
with the Merchant, though the Abuse is to fall on himself, because he
knows that, as a Go-between, he shall find his Account in being in the
good Graces of a Man of Wealth. Among these just and punctual
People, the richest Man is ever the better Jester; and they know no
such Thing as a Person who shall pretend to a superior Laugh at a
Man, who does not make him Amends by Opportunities of Advantage in another Kind: But among People of a different Way, where

---

[1] *Si . . . mecum:* From Horace, *Epistles* 1.6.67–68: "If you know better rules than
these be free, / Impart them, but if not, use these with me" [Bond].

the pretended Distinction in Company is only what is raised from Sense and Understanding, it is very absurd to carry on a rough Raillery so far, as that the whole Discourse should turn upon each other's Infirmities, Follies, or Misfortunes.

I was this Evening with a Set of Wags of this Class. They appear generally by Two and Two; and what is most extraordinary, is, that those very Persons who are most together, appear least of a Mind when joined by other Company. This Evil proceeds from an indiscreet Familiarity, whereby a Man is allowed to say the most grating Thing imaginable to another, and it shall be accounted Weakness to show an Impatience for the Unkindness. But this and all other Deviations from the Design of pleasing each other when we meet, are derived from Interlopers in Society, who want Capacity to put in a Stock among regular Companions, and therefore supply their Wants by stale Histories, sly Observations, and rude Hints, which relate to the Conduct of others. All Cohabitants in general run into this unhappy Fault; Men and their Wives break into Reflections which are like so much *Arabick* to the rest of the Company; Sisters and Brothers often make the like Figure from the same unjust Sense of the Art of being intimate and familiar. It is often said, such a one cannot stand the Mention of such a Circumstance: If he cannot, I am sure it is for Want of Discourse, or a worse Reason, that any Companion of his touches upon it.

Familiarity, among the truly Well-bred, never gives Authority to trespass upon one another in the most minute Circumstance, but it allows to be kinder than we ought otherwise presume to be. *Eusebius* has Wit, Humour, and Spirit; but there never was a Man in his Company who wished he had less, for he understands Familiarity so well, that he knows how to make Use of it in a Way that neither makes himself or his Friend contemptible; but if any one is lessened by his Freedom, it is he himself, who always likes the Place, the Diet, and the Reception, when he is in the Company of his Friends. Equality is the Life of Conversation; and he is as much out who assumes to himself any Part above another, as he who considers himself below the rest of the Society. Familiarity in Inferiors is Sauciness; in Superiors, Condescension; neither of which are to have Being among Companions, the very Word implying that they are to be equal. When therefore we have abstracted the Company from all Considerations of their Quality or Fortune, it will immediately appear, that to make it happy and polite, there must nothing be started which shall discover that our Thoughts run upon any such Distinctions. Hence it will arise, that Benevolence must become the Rule of Society, and he that is most obliging must be most diverting.

This Way of Talking I am fallen into from the Reflection that I am wherever I go entertained with some Absurdity, Mistake, Weakness, or ill Luck of some Man or other whom not only I, but the Person who makes me those Relations has a Value for. It would therefore be a great Benefit to the World if it could be brought to pass that no Story should be a taking one, but what was to the Advantage of the Person of whom it is related. By this Means, he that is now a Wit in Conversation, would be considered as a Spreader of false News is in Business.

But above all, to make a Familiar fit for a Bosom Friend, it is absolutely necessary that we should always be inclined rather to hide than rally each others Infirmities. To suffer for a Fault, is a Sort of Attonement; and no Body is concerned for the Offence for which he has made Reparation.

The Spectator

No. 8
Friday, March 9, 1711
[Addison on Letters — One from a Director of the Society for the Reformation of Manners; Another on the Masquerade]

> *At* Venus *obscuro gradientes aere sepsit,*
> *Et multo Nebulæ circum Dea fudit amictu,*
> *Cernere ne quis eos . . .*[1]
>
> —Virg.

I shall here communicate to the World a couple of Letters, which I believe will give the Reader as good an Entertainment as any that I am able to furnish him with, and therefore shall make no Apology for them.

---

[1]*At . . . eos:* From Virgil, *Aeneid* 1.411–13: "They march obscure, for *Venus* kindly shrowds, / With Mists, their Persons, and involves in Clouds: / That, thus unseen, their Passage none might stay, / Or force to tell the Causes of their Way" — DRYDEN [Bond].

To the SPECTATOR, &c.

SIR,

'I am one of the Directors of the Society for the Reformation of Manners,[2] and therefore think my self a proper Person for your Correspondence. I have thoroughly examined the present State of Religion in *Great-Britain*, and am able to acquaint you with the predominant Vice of every Market-Town in the whole Island. I can tell you the Progress that Virtue has made in all our Cities, Boroughs, and Corporations; and know as well the evil Practices that are committed in *Berwick* or *Exeter*, as what is done in my own Family. In a Word, Sir, I have my Correspondents in the remotest Parts of the Nation, who send me up punctual Accounts from time to time of all the little Irregularities that fall under their Notice in their several Districts and Divisions.

'I am no less acquainted with the particular Quarters and Regions of this great Town, than with the different Parts and Distributions of the whole Nation. I can describe every Parish by its Impieties, and can tell you in which of our Streets Lewdness prevails, which Gaming has taken the Possession of, and where Drunkenness has got the better of them both. When I am disposed to raise a Fine for the Poor, I know the Lanes and Allies that are inhabited by common Swearers. When I would encourage the Hospital of *Bridewell*[3] and improve the Hempen Manufacture, I am very well acquainted with all the Haunts and Resorts of Female Nightwalkers.

'After this short Account of my self, I must let you know, that the Design of this Paper is to give you Information of a certain irregular Assembly which I think falls very properly under your Observation, especially since the Persons it is composed of are Criminals too con-

---

[2] *Society for the Reformation of Manners:* Compromising Low Church Anglicans and Dissenters (radical Protestant sects outside the official Anglican church), these societies were active in London and in provincial towns from 1690–1738. They campaigned for stricter enforcement by magistrates of moral legislation, pursuing prosecutions for drunkenness, swearing, prostitution, and other criminal vices. Josiah Woodward's *Account of the Societies for Reformation of Manners in England and Ireland* was published in 1699 and is excerpted in Chapter 1's Cultural Contexts (p. 115).

[3] *Bridewell:* Originally a royal palace built in 1515–20 for Henry VIII, Bridewell was named after a holy well dedicated to St. Bride. In 1553, Edward VI gave the palace to the city of London to house vagrants and homeless children and as a correctional institution for petty offenders and wayward women. In 1556 the city took possession and with the confirmation of Queen Mary turned the palace into a prison, hospital, and workhouse.

siderable for the Animadversions of our Society. I mean, Sir, the Midnight Masque,[4] which has of late been very frequently held in one of the most conspicuous Parts of Town, and which I hear will be continued with Additions and Improvements. As all the Persons who compose this lawless Assembly are masqued, we dare not attack any of them in *our Way*, lest we should send a Woman of Quality to *Bridewell* or a Peer of *Great-Britain* to the *Counter*:[5] Besides, that their Numbers are so very great, that I am afraid they would be able to rout our whole Fraternity, tho' we were accompanied with all our Guard of Constables. Both these Reasons which secure them from our Authority, make them obnoxious to yours; As both their Disguise and their Numbers will give no particular Person Reason to think himself affronted by you.

'If we are rightly inform'd, the Rules that are observed by this new Society are wonderfully contriv'd for the Advancement of Cuckoldom. The Women either come by themselves or are introduced by Friends, who are obliged to quit them upon their first Entrance, to the Conversation of any Body that addresses himself to them. There are several Rooms where the Parties may retire, and, if they please, show their Faces by Consent. Whispers, Squeezes, Nods, and Embraces, are the innocent Freedoms of the Place. In short, the whole Design of this libidinous Assembly seems to terminate in Assignations and Intrigues; and I hope you will take effectual Methods by your publick Advice and Admonitions, to prevent such a promiscuous Multitude of both Sexes from meeting together in so clandestine a Manner

I am,

Your humble Servant,

And Fellow-Labourer,

T. B.'

Not long after the Perusal of this Letter I received another upon the same Subject; which by the Date and Stile of it, I take to be written by some young Templer.[6]

---

[4] *Masque:* Masques were large public masked balls (masquerades) and were the object of much scandalized criticism in the eighteenth century. It was widely feared that, concealed under their costumes, assuming identities not their own, people would indulge in unrestrained sexual license.

[5] *Counter:* The prison attached to a city court, especially a debtor's court.

[6] *Templer:* Men in the legal professions housed in the Temple. The Temple Bar consisted of the four Inns of Court housed along Fleet Street in London. Originally owned by the medieval religious and military order the Knights Templar, who built

SIR,   *Middle-Temple*, 1710–11.

'When a Man has been guilty of any Vice or Folly, I think the best Attonement he can make for it is to warn others not to fall into the like. In order to this I must acquaint you, that some Time in *February* last I went to the *Tuesday's* Masquerade. Upon my first going in I was attacked by half a Dozen female Quakers, who seem'd willing to adopt me for a Brother; but upon a nearer Examination I found they were a Sisterhood of Coquets disguised in that precise Habit. I was soon after taken out to dance, and as I fancied, by a Woman of the first Quality, for she was very tall, and moved gracefully. As soon as the Minuet was over, we ogled one another through our Masques; and as I am very well read in *Waller*,[7] I repeated to her the four following Verses out of his Poem to *Vandike*.

> *The heedless Lover does not know*
> *Whose Eyes they are that wound him so;*
> *But confounded with thy Art,*
> *Enquires her Name that has his Heart.*[8]

I pronounced these Words with such a languishing Air, that I had some Reason to conclude I had made a Conquest. She told me that she hoped my Face was not akin to my Tongue; and looking upon her Watch, I accidentally discovered the Figure of a Coronet on the back Part of it. I was so transported with the Thought of such an Amour, that I plied her from one Room to another with all the Gallantries I could invent; and at length brought things to so happy an Issue, that she gave me a private Meeting the next Day, without Page or Footman, Coach or Equipage. My Heart danced in Raptures; but I had not lived in this golden Dream above three Days, before I found good Reason to wish that I had continued true to my Landress. I have since heard by a very great Accident, that this fine Lady does not live far from *Covent-Garden*,[9] and that I am not the first Cully whom she has pass'd her self upon for a Countess.

---

their residence there in the twelfth century, this series of buildings, known collectively as the Temple, was presented by James I to lawyers for their professional use. It housed both residential and professional legal apartments.

[7] *Waller:* Edmund Waller (1608–1687) was a Royalist poet. His *Poems* appeared in 1645 and his *Divine Poems* in 1685. Along with John Denham, Waller is credited with the development of the closed rhyme couplet.

[8] *. . . Heart:* These are lines 5–8 of Waller's poem *To Vandyck* [Bond].

[9] *Covent-Garden:* Established in 1670, Covent Garden was the chief flower, fruit, and vegetable market in London. In the midst of the theater district, Covent Garden acquired its reputation as a center of dissipated pleasures.

'Thus, Sir, you see how I have mistaken a *Cloud* for a *Juno*,[10] and if you can make any use of this Adventure, for the Benefit of those who may possibly be as vain young Coxcombs as my self, I do most heartily give you Leave.

I am,

SIR,

Your most humble Admirer,

B. L.'

I design to visit the next Masquerade my self, in the same Habit I wore at *Grand Cairo*; and till then shall suspend my Judgment of this Midnight Entertainment.

No. 18
Wednesday, March 21, 1711
[Addison on the History of the Italian Opera on the English Stage]

. . . Equitis quoque jam migravit ab aure voluptas
Omnis ad incertos oculos & gaudia vana.[1]

— Hor.

It is my Design in this Paper to deliver down to Posterity a faithful Account of the *Italian* Opera, and of the gradual Progress which it has made upon the *English* Stage: For there is no Question but our great Grand-children will be very curious to know the Reason why their Forefathers used to sit together like an Audience of Foreigners in their own Country, and to hear whole Plays acted before them in a Tongue which they did not understand.

Arsinoe[2] was the first Opera that gave us a Taste of *Italian* Musick. The great Success this Opera met with, produced some Attempts

---

[10] *Cloud for a Juno:* In Greek mythology, Ixion murdered his father-in-law and could obtain purification for the sin only from Jove. When Jove invited Ixion to Olympus for the ritual of purification, Ixion tried to seduce Zeus's wife Juno. She complained to Zeus, who trapped Ixion by forming a cloud, also a goddess Nephele, in the shape of Juno.

[1] *Equitis . . . vana:* From Horace, *Epistles* 2.1.187–88: "But now our *Nobles* too are Fops and Vain, / Neglect the Sense, but love the Painted Scene" — CREECH [Bond].

[2] *Arsinoe:* Arsinoe, Queen of Cyprus was first produced at Drury Lane on January 16, 1705 [Bond].

of forming Pieces upon *Italian* Plans, which should give a more natural and reasonable Entertainment than what can be met with in the
elaborate Trifles of that Nation. This alarm'd the Poetasters and
Fidlers of the Town, who were used to deal in a more ordinary Kind
of Ware; and therefore laid down an establish'd Rule, which is receiv'd as such to this Day, *That nothing is capable of being well set to
Musick, that is not Nonsense.*

This Maxim was no sooner receiv'd, but we immediately fell to
translating the *Italian* Operas; and as there was no great Danger of
hurting the Sense of those extraordinary Pieces, our Authors would
often make Words of their own which were entirely foreign to the
Meaning of the Passages they pretended to translate; their chief Care
being to make the Numbers of the *English* Verse answer to those of
the *Italian*, that both of them might go to the same Tune. Thus the
famous Song in *Camilla*,[3]

> *Barbara si t'intendo, &c.*
> *Barbarous Woman, yes, I know your Meaning,*

which expresses the Resentments of an angry Lover, was translated
into that *English* Lamentation

> *Frail are a Lover's Hopes, &c.*

And it was pleasant enough to see the most refined Persons of the
British Nation dying away and languishing to Notes that were filled
with a Spirit of Rage and Indignation. It happen'd also very frequently, where the Sense was rightly translated, the necessary Trans-
position of Words which were drawn out of the Phrase of one
Tongue into that of another, made the Musick appear very absurd in
one Tongue that was very natural in the other. I remember an *Italian*
Verse that ran thus Word for Word,

> *And turn'd my Rage into Pity;*

which the *English* for Rhime sake translated,

> *And into Pity turn'd my Rage.*

By this Means the soft Notes that were adapted to *Pity* in the *Italian*,
fell upon the Word *Rage* in the *English*; and the angry Sounds that
were tuned to *Rage* in the Original, were made to express *Pity* in the

---

[3] *Camilla*: An Italian opera rewritten with an English libretto and performed at
Drury Lane in March 1706 [Bond].

Translation. It oftentimes happen'd likewise, that the finest Notes in
the Air fell upon the most insignificant Words in the Sentence. I have
known the Word *And* pursu'd through the whole Gamut, have been
entertain'd with many a melodious *The*, and have heard the most
beautiful Graces, Quavers and Divisions bestow'd upon *Then*, *For*,
and *From*; to the eternal Honour of our *English* Particles.

The next Step to our Refinement, was the introducing of *Italian*
Actors into our Opera; who sung their Parts in their own Language,
at the same Time that our Countrymen perform'd theirs in our native
Tongue. The King or Hero of the Play generally spoke in *Italian*, and
his Slaves answer'd him in *English*: The Lover frequently made his
Court, and gain'd the Heart of his Princess in a Language which she
did not understand. One would have thought it very difficult to have
carry'd on Dialogues after this Manner, without an Interpreter between the Persons that convers'd together; but this was the State of
the *English* Stage for about three Years.

At length the Audience grew tir'd of understanding Half the
Opera, and therefore to ease themselves intirely of the Fatigue of
Thinking, have so order'd it at Present that the whole Opera is perform'd in an unknown Tongue. We no longer understand the Language of our own Stage; insomuch that I have often been afraid,
when I have seen our *Italian* Performers chattering in the Vehemence
of Action, that they have been calling us Names, and abusing us
among themselves; but I hope, since we do put such an entire Confidence in them, they will not talk against us before our Faces, though
they may do it with the same Safety as if it were behind our Backs. In
the mean Time I cannot forbear thinking how naturally an Historian,
who writes Two or Three hundred Years hence, and does not know
the Taste of his wise Fore-fathers, will make the following Reflection,
In the Beginning of the Eighteenth Century the Italian *Tongue was so
well understood in* England, *that Opera's were acted on the publick
Stage in that Language.*

Once scarce knows how to be serious in the Confutation of an Absurdity that shews itself at the first Sight. It does not want any great
Measure of Sense to see the Ridicule of this monstrous Practice; but
what makes it the more astonishing, it is not the Taste of the Rabble,
but of Persons of the greatest Politeness, which has establish'd it.

If the *Italians* have a Genius for Musick above the *English*, the
English have a Genius for other Performances of a much higher Na-
ture, and capable of giving the Mind a much nobler Entertainment.
Would one think it was possible (at a Time when an Author lived

that was able to write the *Phaedra* and *Hippolitus*)[4] for a People to be so stupidly fond of the *Italian* Opera, as scarce to give a Third Days Hearing to that admirable Tragedy? Musick is certainly a very agreeable Entertainment, but if it would take the entire Possession of our Ears, if it would make us incapable of hearing Sense, if it would exclude Arts that have a much greater Tendency to the Refinement of humane Nature: I must confess I would allow it no better Quarter than *Plato* has done, who banishes it out of his Commonwealth.

At present, our Notions of Musick are so very uncertain, that we do not know what it is we like; only, in general, we are transported with any thing that is not *English*: So it be of a foreign Growth, let it be *Italian*, *French*, or *High-Dutch*, it is the same thing. In short, our *English* Musick is quite rooted out, and nothing yet planted in its stead.

When a Royal Palace is burnt to the Ground, every Man is at Liberty to present his Plan for a new one; and tho' it be but indifferently put together, it may furnish several Hints that may be of Use to a good Architect. I shall take the same Liberty in a following Paper, of giving my Opinion upon the Subject of Musick, which I shall lay down only in a problematical Manner to be considered by those who are Masters in the Art.

No. 31
Thursday, April 5, 1711
[Addison on a Project for an Opera]

Sit mihi fas audita loqui! . . .[1]
     — Vir.

Last Night, upon my going into a Coffee-House not far from the *Hay-Market* Theatre,[2] I diverted my self for above half an Hour with overhearing the Discourse of one, who, by the Shabbiness of his Dress, the Extravagance of his Conceptions, and the Hurry of his

[4] *the Phaedra and Hippolitus: Phaedra and Hippolitus*, by Addison's friend Edmund Smith, was produced at the Haymarket on April 21, 1707 . . . and published on June 19, 1707. The Prologue [was] written by Addison [Bond].

[1] *Sit mihi fas audita loqui! . . .*: Virgil, *Aeneid* 6.266: "May I be allowed to tell what I have heard!" [Bond].

[2] *Hay-Market Theatre:* Haymarket was a market area that ran south from Coventry Street to Pall Mall east. Because it was close to the Royal Mews, in the seventeenth

Speech, I discovered to be of that Species who are generally distin-guished by the Title of Projectors.[3] This Gentleman, for I found he was treated as such by his Audience, was entertaining a whole Table of Listners with the Project of an Opera, which he told us had not cost him above two or three Mornings in the Contrivance, and which he was ready to put in Execution, provided he might find his Account in it. He said, that he had observed the great Trouble and Inconve-nience which Ladies were at, in travelling up and down to the several Shows that are exhibited in different Quarters of the Town. The dancing Monkies are in one Place; the Puppet Show in another; the Opera in a third; not to mention the Lions,[4] that are almost a whole Day's Journey from the Politer Part of the Town. By this means People of Figure are forced to lose half the Winter after their coming to Town, before they have seen all the strange Sights about it. In order to remedy this great Inconvenience, our Projector drew out of his Pocket the Scheme of an Opera, Entitled, *The Expedition of* Alexander *the Great;*[5] in which he had disposed all the remarkable Shows about Town, among the Scenes and Decorations of his Piece. The Thought, he confest, was not originally his own, but that he had taken the Hint of it from several Performances which he had seen upon our Stage: In one of which there was a Rary-Show; in another, a Ladder-dance;[6] and in others a Posture-Man, a moving Picture,[7] with many Curiosities of the like nature.

This *Expedition of Alexander* opens with his consulting the Oracle at *Delphos*,[8] in which the dumb Conjurer, who has been visited by so many Persons of Quality of late Years, is to be introduced as telling

---

century a market was established here for hay and straw. In 1705 Thomas Betterton brought his company from Lincoln's Inn Fields to a new theater in Haymarket. Within a few years this new Queen's Theatre had become the venue for opera performances.

[3] *Projectors:* Men who employ themselves in thinking up adventurist schemes for financial or social improvement; entrepreneurs.

[4] *Lions:* Lions and other animals were kept in cages at the tower of London where the public could view them.

[5] *The Expedition of Alexander the Great:* Lee's *The Rival Queen, or the Death of Alexander the Great,* first produced in 1677, was still a standard piece of the repertory at Drury Lane Theatre [Bond].

[6] *Rary-Show . . . Ladder-dance:* A rary-show was a peep show carried on a man's back. In the ladder dance, the performer stands on a ladder, shifting it from place to place as he goes up and down the rungs without losing his balance.

[7] *Posture-Man, a moving Picture:* Posture men were contortionists. A moving pic-ture was another sort of popular entertainment, often displayed in London taverns. It seems to have been a sort of mechanized sequence of illustrative scenes.

[8] *Oracle at Delphos:* The god Apollo's oracle was located at Delphi near Mt. Par-nassus in central Greece.

him his Fortune: At the same time *Clench* of *Barnet*[9] is represented in another Corner of the Temple, as ringing the Bells of *Delphos*, for joy of his Arrival. The Tent of *Darius*[10] is to be Peopled by the Ingenious Mrs. *Salmon*,[11] where *Alexander* is to fall in Love with a Piece of Wax-Work, that represents the beautiful *Statira*. When *Alexander* comes into that Country, in which *Quintus Curtius*[12] tells us the Dogs were so exceeding fierce that they would not loose their Hold, tho' they were cut to pieces Limb by Limb, and that they would hang upon their Prey by their Teeth when they had nothing but a Mouth left, there is to be a Scene of *Hockley in the Hole*,[13] in which is to be represented all the Diversions of that Place, the Bull-baiting only excerpted, which cannot possibly be exhibited in the Theatre, by Reason of the Lowness of the Roof. The several Woods in *Asia*, which *Alexander* must be supposed to pass through, will give the Audience a Sight of Monkies dancing upon Ropes, with the many other Pleasantries of that ludicrous Species. At the same time, if there chance to be any Strange Animals in Town, whether Birds or Beasts, they may be either let loose among the Woods, or driven across the Stage by some of the Country People of *Asia*. In the last great Battel, *Pinkethman* is to personate King *Porus*[14] upon an Elephant, and is to be encounter'd by *Powell*, representing *Alexander* the Great upon a Dromedary, which nevertheless Mr. *Powell* is desired to call by the Name of *Bucephalus*.[15] Upon the Close of this great decisive Battel, when the two Kings are thoroughly reconciled, to shew the mutual Friendship and good Correspondence that reigns between them, they both

[9] *Clench of Barnet:* A popular entertainer who mimicked nonhuman sounds. In *Tatler* No. 51 Bickerstaff describes his act: "A good Company of us were this Day to see, or rather to hear, an artful Person do several Feats of Activity with his Throat and Wind-pipe. The first Thing wherewith he presented us, was a Ring of Bells, which he imitated in a most miraculous Manner; after that he gave us all the different Notes of a Pack of Hounds, to our great Delight and Astonishment."

[10] *Darius:* Darius III Codomanus (c. 380–330 B.C.), the king of Persia overthrown by Alexander the Great.

[11] *Mrs. Salmon:* Mrs. Salmon kept a popular waxworks. Her shop is referred to in *Spectator* No. 28, which describes the signs of London shops.

[12] *Quintus Curtius:* Quintus Curtius Rufus was a Roman historian of the first century A.D. who wrote a history of Alexander the Great.

[13] *Hockley in the Hole:* The site of a popular bear garden where the sports of bear-baiting and prizefighting were pursued.

[14] *Pinkethman . . . King Porus:* William Pinkethman (d. 1725) was an actor who worked at various times with the companies at the Theatre Royal, Drury Lane, and the Haymarket. King Porus was an Indian king who fought Alexander the Great with a cavalry on elephants in 326 B.C.

[15] *Mr. Powell . . . Bucephalus:* George Powell (1658?–1714) was an actor and dramatist. Bucephalus was Alexander the Great's prized horse.

of them go together to a Puppet Show, in which the ingenious Mr. *Powell, Junior*,[16] may have an Opportunity of displaying his whole Art of Machinery, for the Diversion of the two Monarchs. Some at the Table urged that a Puppet Show was not a suitable Entertainment for *Alexander* the Great; and that it might be introduced more properly, if we suppose the Conqueror touched upon that Part of *India* which is said to be inhabited by the Pigmies. But this Objection was looked upon as frivolous, and the Proposal immediately over-ruled. Our Projector further added, that after the Reconciliation of these two Kings they might invite one another to Dinner, and either of them entertain his Guest with the *German* Artist,[17] Mr. *Pinkethman's* Heathen Gods,[18] or any of the like Diversions, which shall then chance to be in vogue.

This Project was receiv'd with very great Applause by the whole Table. Upon which the Undertaker told us, that he had not yet communicated to us above half his Design; for that *Alexander* being a *Greek*, it was his Intention that the whole Opera should be acted in that Language, which was a Tongue he was sure would wonderfully please the Ladies, especially when it was a little raised and rounded by the *Ionick* Dialect;[19] and could not but be acceptable to the whole Audience, because there are fewer of them who understand *Greek* than *Italian*. The only Difficulty that remained, was, how to get Performers, unless we could persuade some Gentlemen of the Universities to learn to Sing, in order to qualify themselves for the Stage; but this Objection soon vanished, when the Projector informed us that the *Greeks* were at present the only Musicians in the *Turkish* Empire, and that it would be very easy for our Factory[20] at *Smyrna* to furnish us every Year with a Colony of Musicians, by the Opportunity of the *Turkey* Fleet; besides, says he, if we want any single Voice for any

[16] *Mr. Powell, Junior:* Martin Powell (fl. 1709–1729) was a puppet showman. In 1710 he established his puppet show in Covent Garden.

[17] *the German Artist:* This may refer to the operator of the moving picture mentioned in the preceding paragraph, but more likely to the posture-master [Bond].

[18] *Heathen Gods:* "Mr. Penkethman's Wonderful Invention, call'd the Pantheon: Or, the Temple of the Heathen-gods" is advertised in No. 43, to be seen "in the Little Piazza's Covent-Garden, in the same House where Punch's Opera is." It is described more fully in advertisements in *Spectator* Nos. 181, 184, and 192 [Bond].

[19] *Ionick Dialect:* The ancient Greek dialect spoken in most of the Aegean islands and in Ionia, an area of Greek settlement in western Asia Minor along the coast of the Aegean Sea. It was noted for its more fluid, "feminine" qualities. Old Ionic was the chief component in the literary dialect of Homer's *Iliad* and *Odyssey*.

[20] *Factory:* A business establishment for commercial agents or factors in a foreign country.

lower part in the Opera, *Lawrence*[21] can learn to speak *Greek*, as well as he does *Italian*, in a Fortnight's time.

The Projector having thus settled Matters, to the good liking of all that heard him, he left his Seat at the Table, and planted himself before the Fire, where I had unluckily taken my Stand for the Convenience of over-hearing what he said. Whether he had observed me to be more attentive than ordinary, I cannot tell, but he had not stood by me above a quarter of a Minute, but he turned short upon me on a sudden, and catching me by a Button of my Coat, attack'd me very abruptly after the following manner. Besides, Sir, I have heard of a very extraordinary Genius for *Musick*[22] that lives in *Switzerland*, who has so strong a Spring in his Fingers, that he can make the Board of an Organ sound like a Drum, and if I could but procure a Subscription of about Ten Thousand Pound every Winter, I would undertake to fetch him over, and oblige him by Articles to set every thing that should be sung upon the *English* Stage. After this he looked full in my Face, expecting I wou'd make an Answer, when, by good Luck, a Gentleman that had entered the Coffee-House since the Projector applied himself to me, hearing him talk of his *Swiss* Compositions, cry'd out with a kind of Laugh, Is our Musick then to receive further Improvements from *Switzerland*? This alarm'd the Projector, who immediately let go my Button, and turned about to answer him. I took the Opportunity of the Diversion, which seemed to be made in favour of me, and laying down my Penny upon the Bar, retired with some Precipitation.

---

[21] *Lawrence:* A tenor singer in the Italian opera. He . . . appeared as the Messenger in Addison and Clayton's *Rosamond* (1707) [Bond].

[22] *Genius for Musick:* John Heidegger (1659?–1749), a Swiss émigré who managed the Italian opera at Haymarket, and then for the Royal Academy of Music. He was an entertainment entrepreneur and also produced large public masquerades and ridottos. His ugliness is often noted.

No. 58
Monday, May 7, 1711
[Addison on True and False Wit]

Ut pictura poesis erit . . .[1]
— Hor.

Nothing is so much admired and so little understood as Wit. No
Author that I know of has written professedly upon it; and as for
those who make any Mention of it, they only treat on the Subject as
it has accidentally fallen in their Way, and that too in little short Reflections, or in general declamatory Flourishes, without entering into
the Bottom of the Matter. I hope therefore I shall perform an acceptable Work to my Countrymen if I treat at large upon this Subject;
which I shall endeavour to do in a Manner suitable to it, that I may
not incur the Censure which a famous Critick bestows upon one who
had written a Treatise upon *the Sublime* in a low groveling Stile. I intend to lay aside a whole Week for this Undertaking, that the Scheme
of my Thoughts may not be broken and interrupted; and I dare
promise my self, if my Readers will give me a Week's Attention, that
this great City will be very much changed for the better by next *Satur-*
day Night. I shall endeavour to make what I say intelligible to ordinary
Capacities; but if my Readers meet with any Paper that in some Parts
of it may be a little out of their Reach, I would not have them discouraged, for they may assure themselves the next shall be much clearer.

As the great and only End of these my Speculations is to banish
Vice and Ignorance out of the Territories of *Great Britain*, I shall endeavour as much as possible to establish among us a Taste of polite
Writing. It is with this View that I have endeavoured to set my Readers right in several Points relating to Operas and Tragedies; and shall
from Time to Time impart my Notions of Comedy, as I think they
may tend to its Refinement and Perfection. I find by my Bookseller
that these Papers of Criticism, with that upon Humour, have met
with a more kind Reception than indeed I could have hoped for from
such Subjects; for which Reason I shall enter upon my present Undertaking with greater Chearfulness.

In this and one or two following Papers I shall trace out the History of false Wit, and distinguish the several Kinds of it as they have
prevailed in different Ages of the World. This I think the more neces-

---

[1] *Ut . . . erit:* From Horace, *Ars Poetica* 361: "A poem will be like a picture" [Bond].

sary at present, because I observed there were Attempts on foot last Winter to revive some of those antiquated Modes of Wit that have been long exploded out of the Common-wealth of Letters. There were several Satyrs and Panegyricks handed about in Acrostick, by which Means some of the most arrant undisputed Block-heads about the Town began to entertain ambitious Thoughts, and to set up for polite Authors. I shall therefore describe at length those many Arts of false Wit, in which a Writer does not shew himself a Man of a beautiful Genius, but of great Industry.

The first Species of false Wit which I have met with is very venerable for its Antiquity, and has produced several Pieces which have lived very near as long as the *Iliad* it self: I mean those short Poems printed among the minor *Greek* Poets, which resemble the Figure of an Egg, a Pair of Wings, an Ax, a Shepherd's Pipe, and an Altar.

As for the first, it is a little oval Poem, and may not improperly be called a Scholar's Egg. I would endeavour to hatch it, or, in more intelligible Language, to translate it into *English*, did not I find the Interpretation of it very difficult; for the Author seems to have been more intent upon the Figure of his Poem, than upon the Sense of it.

The Pair of Wings consist of twelve Verses, or rather Feathers, every Verse decreasing gradually in its Measure according to its Situation in the Wing. The Subject of it (as in the rest of the Poems which follow) bears some remote Affinity with the Figure, for it describes a God of Love, who is always painted with Wings.

The Ax methinks would have been a good Figure for a Lampoon, had the Edge of it consisted of the most satyrical Parts of the Work; but as it is in the Original, I take it to have been nothing else but the Posy of an Ax which was consecrated to *Minerva*[2] and was thought to have been the same that *Epeus*[3] made use of in the building of the *Trojan* Horse; which is a Hint I shall leave to the Consideration of the Criticks. I am apt to think that the Posy was written originally upon the Ax, like those which our modern Cutlers inscribe upon their Knives; and that therefore the Posy still remains in its ancient Shape, though the Ax it self is lost.

---

[2] *Minerva:* Roman goddess of wisdom, invention, the arts, and military science (Greek, Athena).

[3] *Epeus:* In Greek legend, a large wooden horse was used by the Greeks to capture Troy during the Trojan War. The horse was made by the Greek Epeius, and the Trojans were told that the horse was an offering to Athena and that it would make the city impregnable if brought inside the walls. The Greeks hid inside the hollow horse, were brought inside Troy, and sacked the city.

The Shepherd's Pipe may be said to be full of Musick, for it is composed of nine different Kinds of Verses, which by their several Lengths resemble the nine Stops of the old musical Instrument, that is likewise the Subject of the Poem.

The Altar is inscribed with the Epitaph of *Troilus* the Son of *Hecuba*;[4] which, by the Way, makes me believe, that these false Pieces of Wit are much more ancient than the Authors to whom they are generally ascribed; at least I will never be perswaded, that so fine a Writer as *Theocritus*[5] could have been the Author of any such simple Works.

It was impossible for a Man to succeed in these Performances who was not a kind of Painter, or at least a Designer: He was first of all to draw the Out-line of the Subject which he intended to write upon, and afterwards conform the Description to the Figure of his Subject. The Poetry was to contract or dilate itself according to the Mould in which it was cast. In a Word, the Verses were to be cramped or extended to the Dimensions of the Frame that was prepared for them; and to undergo the Fate of those Persons whom the Tyrant *Procrustes* used to lodge in his Iron Bed; if they were too short he stretched them on a Rack, and if they were too long chopped off a Part of their Legs, till they fitted the Couch which he had prepared for them.

Mr. *Dryden* hints at this obsolete kind of Wit in one of the following Verses, in his *Mac Fleckno*;[6] which an *English* Reader cannot understand, who does not know that there are those little Poems abovementioned in the Shape of Wings and Altars.

> . . . *Chuse for thy Command*
> *Some peaceful Province in Acrostick Land;*
> *There may'st thou* Wings *display and* Altars *raise,*
> *And torture one* Poor Word *a thousand Ways.*

This Fashion of false Wit was revived by several Poets of the last Age, and in particular may be met with among Mr. *Herbert's* Poems;[7]

---

[4] *Troilus the Son of Hecuba:* In Greek legend, Troilus was the son of Priam, king of Troy, and Hecuba.

[5] *Theocritus:* Theocritus was a third-century B.C. Hellenistic Greek poet. He is known as the originator of pastoral, or bucolic, poetry. His *Idylls* depict pastoral life in the hills of Sicily and south Italy.

[6] *Mac Fleckno:* John Dryden's satiric poem (1682) that parodies the coronation of the dunce poet laureate. The passage cited is lines 205–08.

[7] *Mr. Herbert's Poems:* George Herbert (1593–1633) was a divine and a poet. His *The Temple* (1633) was widely read and influential and went into a number of editions through the seventeenth and eighteenth centuries.

and if I am not mistaken, in the Translation of *Du Bartas*.[8] I do not remember any other Kind of Work among the Moderns which more resembles the Performances I have mentioned, than that famous Picture of King *Charles* the First,[9] which has the whole Book of *Psalms* written in the Lines of the Face and the Hair of the Head. When I was last at *Oxford* I perused one of the Whiskers; and was reading the other, but could not go so far in it as I would have done, by reason of the Impatience of my Friends and Fellow-Travellers, who all of them pressed to see such a Piece of Curiosity. I have since heard, that there is now an eminent Writing-Master in Town, who has transcribed all the *Old Testament* in a full-bottom'd Perriwig; and if the Fashion should introduce the thick Kind of Wigs which were in Vogue some few Years ago, he promises to add two or three supernumerary Locks that shall contain all the *Apocrypha*.[10] He designed this Wig originally for King *William*,[11] having disposed of the two Books of *Kings* in the two Forks of the Foretop; but that glorious Monarch dying before the Wig was finished, there is a Space left in it for the Face of any one that has a mind to purchase it.

But to return to our ancient Poems in Picture, I would humbly propose, for the Benefit of our modern Smatterers in Poetry, that they would imitate their Brethren among the Ancients in those ingenious Devices. I have communicated this Thought to a young Poetical Lover of my Acquaintance, who intends to present his Mistress with a Copy of Verses made in the Shape of her Fan; and if he tells me true, has already finished the three first Sticks of it. He has likewise promised me to get the Measure of his Mistress's Marriage-Finger, with a Design to make a Posie in the Fashion of a Ring which shall exactly fit it. It is so very easy to enlarge upon a good Hint, that I do not question but my ingenious Readers will apply what I have said to many other Particulars; and that we shall see the Town filled in a very little Time with Poetical Tippets, Handkerchiefs, Snuff-Boxes, and

[8] *Du Bartas:* Guillaume de Salluste du Bartas (1544–1590) was an important French Protestant poet. Joshua Sylvester (1563–1618), an English poet, published translations of du Bartas's "Canticle" in 1590, "La Semaine" in 1592, and a collected edition of du Bartas's poems in 1606.

[9] *Picture of King Charles the First:* There was a portrait of Charles I (1630–1683) in a gallery at St. John's College, Oxford, in which the hair of his head was made up of lines of scripture [Bond].

[10] *Apocrypha:* The fourteen books of the Septuagint included in the Vulgate Bible but considered uncanonical by Protestants because they are not part of Hebrew Scripture.

[11] *King William:* William III (1650–1702) reigned in England from 1689–1702.

the like Female Ornaments. I shall therefore conclude with a Word of Advice to those admirable *English* Authors who call themselves Pindarick Writers,[12] that they would apply themselves to this Kind of Wit without Loss of Time, as being provided better than any other Poets with Verses of all Sizes and Dimensions.

No. 63
Saturday, May 12, 1711
[Addison on True and False Wit]

Humano Capiti cervicem pictor Equinam
Jungere si velit & varias inducere plumas
Undique collatis membris, ut turpiter atrum
Desinat in piscem mulier formosa supernè;
Spectatum admissi risum teneatis, amici?
Credite, Pisones, isti tabulæ fore librum
Persimilem, cujus, velut ægri somnia, vanæ
Finguntur species . . .[1]

— Hor.

It is very hard for the Mind to disengage it self from a Subject in which it has been long employed. The Thoughts will be rising of themselves from time to time, tho' we give them no Encouragement; as the Tossings and Fluctuations of the Sea continue several hours after the Winds are laid.

It is to this that I impute my last Night's Dream or Vision, which formed into one Continued Allegory the several Schemes of Wit,

---

[12] *Pindarick Writers:* Pindar (518–post-446 B.C.) was a Greek lyric poet famous for his Victory Odes written in honor of the winners at the four Panhellenic games (Olympian, Pythian, Nemean, and Isthmian). The style is lofty, full of strong metaphors and classical reference. Cowley, Dryden, and Pope all wrote Pindarics.

[1] *Humano . . . species . . . :* From Horace, *Ars Poetica* 1–8:

If in a Picture (*Piso*) you should see,
A handsom Woman with a Fishes Tail,
Or a Man's Head upon a Horse's Neck,
Or Limbs of Beasts of the most diff'rent kinds,
Cover'd with Feathers of all sorts of Birds,
Would you not laugh, and think the Painter mad?
Trust me, that Book is as ridiculous,
Whose incoherent Stile (like sick Mens Dreams)
Varies all Shapes, and mixes all Extremes."

— ROSCOMMON [Bond]

whether False, Mixed, or True, that have been the Subject of my late Papers.

Methoughts I was transported into a Country that was filled with Prodigies and Enchantments, Governed by the Goddess of FALSE-HOOD, and entitled the *Region of false Wit*. There was nothing in the Fields, the Woods, and the Rivers, that appeared natural. Several of the Trees blossom'd in Leaf-Gold, some of them produced Bone-Lace, and some of them precious Stones. The Fountains bubbled in an Opera Tune, and were filled with Stags, Wild-Boars, and Mermaids, that lived among the Waters, at the same time that Dolphins and several kinds of Fish played upon the Banks, or took their Pastime in the Meadows. The Birds had many of them Golden Beaks, and human Voices. The Flowers perfumed the Air with Smells of Incense, Amber-Greese and Pulvillios,[2] and were so interwoven with one another, that they grew up in Pieces of Embroidery. The Winds were fill'd with Signs and Messages of distant Lovers. As I was walking to and fro in this enchanted Wilderness, I could not forbear breaking out into Soliloquies upon the several Wonders which lay before me, when to my great Surprise I found there were artificial Ecchoes in every Walk, that by Repetitions of certain Words which I spoke, agreed with me, or contradicted me, in every thing I said. In the midst of my Conversation with these invisible Companions, I discover'd in the Center of a very dark Grove a Monstrous Fabrick built after the *Gothick* manner, and covered with innumerable Devices in that barbarous kind of Sculpture. I immediately went up to it, and found it to be a kind of Heathen Temple consecrated to the God of *Dullness*. Upon my Entrance I saw the Deity of the Place dressed in the Habit of a Monk, with a Book in one Hand and a Rattle in the other. Upon his right Hand was *Industry*, with a Lamp burning before Her; and on his left *Caprice*, with a Monky sitting on her Shoulder. Before his Feet there stood an Altar of a very odd Make, which, as I afterwards found, was shaped in that manner, to comply with the Inscription that surrounded it. Upon the *Altar* there lay several Offerings of *Axes*, *Wings*, and *Eggs*, cut in Paper, and inscribed with Verses. The Temple was filled with Votaries, who applied themselves to different Diversions, as their Fancies directed them. In one Part of it I saw a Regiment of *Anagrams*,[3] who were continually in motion, turning to the Right or to the Left, facing about, doubling their

[2] *Pulvillios:* Perfumed powders used as on the body and on wigs.

[3] *Anagrams:* Anagrams are words or phrases formed by rearranging the letters of another word or phrase.

Ranks, shifting their Stations, and throwing themselves into all the
Figures and Counter-marches of the most changeable and perplexed
Exercise.

Not far from these was a Body of *Acrosticks*[4] made up of very dis-
proportioned Persons. It was disposed into three Columns, the Officers planting themselves in a Line on the left Hand of each Column.
The Officers were all of them at least Six Foot high, and made three
Rows of very proper Men; but the Common Soldiers, who filled up
the Spaces between the Officers, were such Dwarfs, Cripples, and
Scare-Crows, that one could hardly look upon them without laughing. There were behind the *Acrosticks* two or three files of *Chrono-
grams*, which differed only from the former, as their Officers were
equipped (like the Figure of Time) with an Hourglass in one Hand,
and a Scythe in the other, and took their Posts promiscuously among
the Private Men whom they commanded.

In the Body of the Temple, and before the very Face of the Deity,
methoughts I saw the Phantom of *Tryphiodorus*[5] the *Lipo-grammatist*,
engaged in a Ball with four and twenty Persons, who pursued him by
turns through all the Intricacies and Labyrinths of a Country Dance,
without being able to overtake him.

Observing several to be very busie at the Western end of the
Temple, I enquired into what they were doing, and found there was
in that Quarter the great Magazine of *Rebus*'s. These were several
things of the most different Natures tied up in Bundles, and thrown
upon one another in heaps like Faggots. You might behold an An-
chor, a Night-rail,[6] and an Hobby-horse bound up together. One of
the Workmen seeing me very much surprized, told me, there was an
infinite deal of Wit in several of those Bundles, and that he would explain them to me if I pleased: I thanked him for his Civility, but told

---

[4] *Acrosticks:* Acrostics are poems or series of lines in which certain letters, usually
the first in each line, form a name, motto, or message.

[5] *Tryphiodorus:* In *Spectator* No. 89 Addison discusses this fifth-century Greek
grammarian and epic writer, and his lipogrammatic text, at more length: "the *Lipo-
grammatists*, or *Letter-droppers* of Antiquity, that would take an Exception, without
any Reason, against some particular letter in the Alphabet, so as not to admit it once
into the whole Poem. One *Tryphiodorus* was a great Master in this kind of Writing.
He composed an *Odissey* of Epic Poem on the Adventures of *Ulysses*, consisting of
four and twenty Books, having entirely banished the Letter *A* from his first Book,
which was called *Alpha* . . . because there was not an *Alpha* in it. His Second Book was
inscribed *Beta*, for the same reason. In short, the Poet excluded the whole four and
twenty Letters in their turns."

[6] *Night-rail:* A dressing gown.

him I was in very great haste at that time. As I was going out of the Temple, I observed in one Corner of it a Cluster of Men and Women laughing very heartily, and diverting themselves at a Game of *Crambo.*[7] I heard several *double Rhymes* as I passed by them, which raised a great deal of Mirth.

Not far from these was another Set of Merry People engaged at a Diversion, in which the whole Jest was to mistake one Person for another. To give occasion for these ludicrous Mistakes, they were divided into Pairs, every Pair being covered from Head to Foot with the same kind of Dress, though, perhaps, there was not the least Resemblance in their Faces. By this means an old Man was sometimes mistaken for a Boy, a Woman for a Man, and a Black-a-moor for an *European*, which very often produced great Peals of Laughter. These I guess'd to be a Party of *Punns*. But being very desirous to get out of this World of Magick, which had almost turned my Brain, I left the Temple, and crossed over the Fields that lay about it with all the speed I could make. I was not gone far before I heard the Sound of Trumpets and Alarms, which seemed to proclaim the March of an Enemy; and, as I afterwards found, was in reality what I apprehended it. There appear'd at a great distance a very shining Light, and in the midst of it a Person of a most beautiful Aspect; her Name was Truth. On her Right Hand there marched a Male Deity, who bore several Quivers on his Shoulders, and grasped several Arrows in his Hand. His Name was *Wit*. The Approach of these two Enemies filled all the Territories of *False Wit* with an unspeakable Consternation, insomuch that the Goddess of those Regions appear'd in Person upon her Frontiers with the several inferior Deities, and the different Bodies of Forces which I had before seen in the Temple, who were now drawn up in Array, and prepared to give their Foes a warm Reception. As the March of the Enemy was very slow, it gave time to the several Inhabitants who border'd upon the *Regions of* Falsehood to draw their Forces into a Body, with a Design to stand upon their Guard as Neuters, and attend the Issue of the Combat.

I must here inform my Reader, that the Frontiers of the Enchanted Region, which I have before described, were inhabited by the Species of Mixed Wit, who made a very odd Appearance when they were Mustered together in an Army. There were Men whose Bodies were stuck full of Darts, and Women whose Eyes were burning Glasses:

---

[7] *Crambo:* A word game in which one player gives a line of verse for which the next has to find a rhyme.

Men that had Hearts of Fire, and Women that had Breasts of Snow. It would be endless to describe several Monsters of the like Nature, that composed this great Army; which immediately fell asunder, and divided it self into two Parts; the one half throwing themselves behind the Banners of TRUTH, and the others behind those of FALSEHOOD.

The Goddess of FALSEHOOD was of a Gigantick Stature, and advanced some Paces before the Front of her Army; but as the dazling Light, which flowed from TRUTH, began to shine upon her, she faded insensibly; insomuch that in a little space she looked rather like an huge Phantom, than a real Substance. At length, as the Goddess of TRUTH, approached still nearer to her, she fell away entirely, and vanish'd amidst the Brightness of her Presence; so that there did not remain the least Trace or Impression of her Figure in the Place where she had been seen.

As at the rising of the Sun the Constellations grow thin, and the Stars go out one after another, 'till the whole Hemisphere is extinguish'd; such was the vanishing of the Goddess; and not only of the Goddess her self, but of the whole Army that attended her, which sympathized with their Leader, and shrunk into Nothing, in Proportion as the Goddess disappeared. At the same time the whole Temple sunk, the Fish betook themselves to the Streams, and the wild Beasts to the Woods: The Fountains recovered their Murmurs, the Birds their Voices, the Trees their Leaves, the Flowers their Scents, and the whole Face of Nature its true and genuine Appearance. Tho' I still continued asleep, I fancy'd my self as it were awaken'd out of a Dream, when I saw this Region of Prodigies restor'd to Woods and Rivers, Fields and Meadows.

Upon the Removal of that wild Scene of Wonders, which had very much disturbed my Imagination, I took a full Survey of the Persons of WIT and TRUTH, for indeed it was impossible to look upon the first, without seeing the other at the same time. There was behind them a strong and compact Body of Figures. The Genius of *Heroic Poetry* appeared with a Sword in her Hand, and a Lawrel on her Head. *Tragedy* was crowned with Cypress, and covered with Robes dipped in Blood. *Satyr* had Smiles in her Look, and a Dagger under her Garment. *Rhetorick* was known by her Thunderbolt; and *Comedy* by her Mask. After several other Figures, *Epigram* marched up in the Rear, who had been posted there at the beginning of the Expedition, that he might not revolt to the Enemy, whom he was suspected to favour in his Heart. I was very much awed and delighted with the Appearance of the God of *Wit*; there was something so amiable and yet so piercing in his Looks, as inspired me at once with Love and Terrour. As I was gazing on him to my unspeakable Joy, he took a Quiver of Arrows from his Shoulder, in order to make me a Present of it, but as I was reaching out my Hand to receive it of him, I knocked it against a Chair, and by that means awaked.

No. 65
Tuesday, May 15, 1711
[Steele on Etherege's Man of Mode]

> . . . Demetri, teque, Tigelli,
> Discipularum inter Jubeo plorare cathedras.[1]
> — Hor.

After having at large explained what Wit is, and described the false Appearances of it, all that Labour seems but an useless Enquiry, without some Time be spent in considering the Application of it. The Seat of Wit, when one speaks as a Man of the Town and the World, is the Play-house; I shall therefore fill this Paper with Reflections upon the Use of it in that Place. The Application of Wit in the Theatre has as strong an Effect upon the Manners of our Gentlemen, as the Taste of it has upon the Writings of our Authors. It may, perhaps, look like a very Presumptuous Work, tho' not Foreign from the Duty of a SPECTATOR, to tax the Writings of such as have long had the general Applause of a Nation: But I shall always make Reason, Truth, and Nature the Measure of Praise and Dispraise; if those are for me, the Generality of Opinion is of no Consequence against me; if they are against me, the General Opinion cannot long support me.

Without further Preface, I am going to look into some of our most Applauded Plays, and see whether they deserve the Figure they at present bear in the Imaginations of Men, or not.

In reflecting upon these Works, I shall chiefly dwell upon that for which each respective Play is most celebrated. The present Paper shall be employed upon Sir *Foplin Flutter*.[2] The Received Character of this

---

[1] *Demetri . . . cathedras:* From Horace, *Satires* 1.10.90–91: "Demetrius and Tigellius, Know your place; / Go hence, and whine among the school-boy race" [Bond].

[2] *Sir Foplin Flutter:* Sir Fopling Flutter is a major character in Etherege's Restoration comedy *The Man of Mode*. Sir George Etherege (1635?–1691) was a successful playwright and a regular among the group of court wits of the Restoration court.

Play is, That it is the Pattern of Gentile Comedy. *Dorimant* and *Harriot*[3] are the Characters of Greatest Consequence, and if these are Low and Mean, the Reputation of the Play is very Unjust.

I will take for granted, that a fine Gentleman should be honest in his Action, and refined in his Language. Instead of this, our Hero, in this Piece, is a direct Knave in his Designs, and a Clown in his Language. *Bellair* is his Admirer and Friend, in return for which, because he is forsooth a greater Wit than his said Friend, he thinks is reasonable to perswade him to Marry a young Lady, whose Virtue, he thinks, will last no longer than 'till she is a Wife, and then she cannot but fall to his Share, as he is an irresistible fine Gentleman. The Falshood to Mrs. *Loveit*, and the Barbarity of Triumphing over her Anguish for losing him, is another Instance of his Honesty, as well as his good Nature. As to his fine Language; he calls the Orange Woman, who, it seems, is inclined to grow Fat, *An Over-grown Jade, with a Flasket of Guts before her*; and salutes her with a pretty Phrase of, *How now, Double Tripe?* Upon the Mention of a Country Gentlewoman, whom he knows nothing of, (no one can imagine why) he *will lay his Life she is some awkard, ill-fashioned Country Toad, who not having above four Dozen of Hairs on her Head, has adorned her Baldness with a large white Fruz, that she may look Sparkishly in the Fore-front of the King's Box at an old Play.* Unnatural Mixture of senseless Common Place!

As to the Generosity of his Temper, he tells his poor Footman, *If he did not wait better*—he would turn him away, in the insolent Phrase of, *I'll Uncase you.*

Now for Mrs. *Harriot*: She laughs at Obedience to an absent Mother, whose Tenderness *Busie* describes to be very exquisite, for *that she is so pleased with finding* Harriot *again, that she cannot chide her for being out of the Way.* This Witty Daughter, and Fine Lady, has so little Respect for this good Woman, that she Ridicules her Air in taking Leave, and cries, *In what Struggle is my poor Mother yonder? See, See, her Head tottering, her Eyes staring, and her under Lip trembling.* But all this is atoned for, because *she has more Wit than is usual in her Sex, and as much Malice, tho' she is as Wild as you would wish her, and has a Demureness in her Looks that*

Etherege wrote satirical comedies of manners, including *The Comical Revenge, or, Love in a Tub* (1664); *She Would If She Could* (1667); and his best-known play, *The Man of Mode, or, Sir Fopling Flutter* (1676). See Introduction (p. 11).

[3] *Dorimant and Harriot:* The other protagonists in *The Man of Mode.*

makes it so surprising! Then to recommend her as a fit Spouse for his Hero, the Poet makes her speak her Sense of Marriage very ingeniously. *I think,* says she, *I might be brought to endure him, and that is all a reasonable Woman should expect in an Husband.* It is, methinks, unnatural that we are not made to understand how she that was bred under a silly pious old Mother, that would never trust her out of her Sight, came to be so Polite.

It cannot be denied, but that the Negligence of every thing, which engages the Attention of the sober and valuable Part of Mankind, appears very well drawn in this Piece: But it is denied, that it is necessary to the Character of a Fine Gentleman, that he should in that manner Trample upon all Order and Decency. As for the Character of *Dorimant,* it is more of a Coxcomb than that of *Foplin.* He says of one of his Companions,[4] that a good Correspondence between them is their mutual Interest. Speaking of that Friend, he declares, their being much together *makes the Women think the better of his Understanding, and judge more favourably of my Reputation. It makes him pass upon some for a Man of very good Sense, and me upon others for a very civil Person.*

This whole celebrated Piece is a perfect Contradiction to good Manners, good Sense, and common Honesty; and as there is nothing in it but what is built upon the Ruin of Virtue and Innocence, according to the Notion of Merit in this Comedy, I take the Shoomaker to be, in reality, the fine Gentleman of the Play: For it seems he is an Atheist, if we may depend upon his Character as given by the Orange-Woman, who is her self far from being the lowest in the Play. She says of a Fine Man, who is *Dorimant's* Companion, There *is not such another Heathen in the Town, except the Shoe-maker.* His Pretention to be the Hero of the *Drama* appears still more in his own Description of his way of Living with his Lady. *There is,* says he, *never a Man in Town lives more like a Gentleman with his Wife than I do; I never mind her Motions; she never enquires into mine. We speak to one another civilly, hate one another heartily; and because it is Vulgar to Lye and Soak together, we have each of us our several Settle-Bed.* That of *Soaking together* is as good as if *Dorimant* had spoken it himself; and, I think, since he puts Human Nature in as ugly a Form as the Circumstance will bear, and is a staunch Unbeliever, he is very much Wronged in having no part of the good Fortune bestowed in the last Act.

[4] *one of his Companions:* The character Bellair, a much less rakish and libertine man than Dorimant.

To speak plainly of this whole Work, I think nothing but being lost to a Sense of Innocence and Virtue can make any one see this Comedy, without observing more frequent Occasion to move Sorrow and Indignation, than Mirth and Laughter. At the same time I allow it to be Nature, but it is Nature in its utmost Corruption and Degeneracy.

No. 85
Thursday, June 7, 1711
[Addison on Two Children in the Wood]

> *Interdum speciosa locis, morataque rectè*
> *Fabula nullius Veneris, sine pondere & Arte,*
> *Valdiùs oblectat populum, meliusque moratur,*
> *Quàm versus inopes rerum, nugæque canoræ.*[1]
> — Hor.

It is the Custom of the *Mahometans*, if they see any printed or written Paper upon the Ground, to take it up and lay it aside carefully, as not knowing but it may contain some Piece of their *Alcoran*.[2] I must confess I have so much of the *Mussulman* in me, that I cannot forbear looking into every Printed Paper which comes in my way, under whatsoever despicable Circumstances it may appear; for as no Mortal Author, in the ordinary Fate and Vicissitude of Things, knows to what use his Works may, some time or other, be applied, a Man may often meet with very celebrated Names in a Paper of Tobacco. I have lighted my Pipe more than once with the Writings of a Prelate, and know a Friend of mine who, for these several Years, has converted the Essays of a Man of Quality into a kind of Fringe for his Candlesticks. I remember, in particular, after having read over a Poem of an Eminent Author on a Victory, I met with several Fragments of it upon the next Rejoycing-day, which had been employed in Squibs and Crackers, and by that means celebrated its Subject in a

---

[1] *Interdum . . . canoræ*: From Horace, *Ars Poetica* 319–22: "Sometimes in rough and undigested Plays / We meet with such a lucky Character, / As being humor'd right and well persu'd, / Succeeds much better, than the shallow Verse, / And chiming Trifles, of more studious Pens" — ROSCOMMON [Bond].

[2] *Alcoran*: The Koran, the sacred book of Islam.

double Capacity. I once met with a Page of Mr. ˙*Baxter*[3] under a *Christmas* Pye. Whether or no the Pastry-Cook had made use of it through Chance, or Waggery, for the defence of that Superstitious *Viande*, I know not; but, upon the Perusal of it, I conceived so good an Idea of the Author's Piety, that I bought the whole Book. I have often profited by these accidental Readings, and have sometimes found very Curious Pieces that are either out of Print, or not to be met with in the Shops of our *London* Booksellers. For this Reason, when my Friends take a Survey of my Library, they are very much surprised to find, upon the Shelf of Folio's,[4] two long Band-boxes standing upright among my Books, till I let them see that they are both of them lined with deep Erudition and abstruse Literature. I might likewise mention a Paper Kite, from which I have received great Improvement; and a Hat-Case, which I would not exchange for all the Beavers[5] in *Great Britain*. This my inquisitive Temper, or rather impertinent Humour of prying into all sorts of Writing, with my natural Aversion to Loquacity, give me a good deal of Employment when I enter any House in the Country; for I can't, for my Heart, leave a Room before I have thoroughly studied the Walls of it, and examined the several printed Papers which are usually pasted upon them. The last Piece that I met with upon this Occasion, gave me a most exquisite Pleasure. My Reader will think I am not serious, when I acquaint him that the Piece I am going to speak of was the old Ballad of the *Two Children in the Wood*,[6] which is one of the Darling Songs of the Common People, and has been the Delight of most *Englishmen* in some Part of their Age.

This Song is a plain simple Copy of Nature, destitute of all the Helps and Ornaments of Art. The Tale of it is a pretty Tragical Story, and pleases for no other Reason, but because it is a Copy of Nature. There is even a despicable Simplicity in the Verse; and yet, because the Sentiments appear genuine and unaffected, they are able to move the Mind of the most polite Reader with inward Meltings of Humanity and Compassion. The Incidents grow out of the Subject, and are such as are the most proper to excite Pity. For which Reason the whole Narration has something in it very moving; notwithstanding

---

[3] *Mr. Baxter:* Richard Baxter (1615–1691), [was] the celebrated Puritan divine and controversialist [Bond].

[4] *Folio's:* The largest common size of book, usually about fifteen inches high.

[5] *Beavers:* A man's hat made of beaver's fur.

[6] *Two Children in the Wood:* Also known as *The Babes in the Wood*, this is one of the best-known broadside "vulgar" ballads [Bond].

the Author of it (whoever he was) has delivered it in such an abject Phrase, and poorness of Expression, that the quoting any part of it would look like a Design of turning it into Ridicule. But though the Language is mean, the Thoughts, as I have before said, from one end to the other are natural; and therefore cannot fail to please those who are not Judges of Language, or those who notwithstanding they are Judges of Language, have a true and unprejudiced Taste of Nature. The Condition, Speech and Behaviour of the dying Parents, with the Age, Innocence and Distress of the Children, are set forth in such tender Circumstances, that it is impossible for a Reader of common Humanity not to be affected with them. As for the Circumstance of the *Robin-red-breast*, it is indeed a little Poetical Ornament; and to shew the Genius of the Author amidst all his Simplicity, it is just the same kind of Fiction which one of the greatest of the *Latin* Poets has made use of upon a Parallel Occasion; I mean that Passage in *Horace*, where he describes himself when he was a Child, fallen asleep in a Desart Wood, and covered with Leaves by the Turtles that took pity on him.

> *Me fabulosæ Vulture in Appulo,*
> *Altricis extra limen Apuliæ*
> *Ludo fatigatumque somno*
> *Fronde novâ puerum palumbes*
> *Texere . . .*[7]

I have heard that the late Lord DORSET,[8] who had the greatest Wit tempered with the greatest Candour, and was one of the finest Criticks as well as the best Poets of his Age, had a numerous Collection of old *English* Ballads, and took a particular Pleasure in the Reading of them. I can affirm the same of Mr. DRYDEN, and know several of the most refined Writers of our present Age, who are of the same Humour.

I might likewise refer my Reader to *Moliere*'s Thoughts[9] on this Subject, as he has expressed them in the Character of the *Misanthrope*; but those only who are endowed with a true Greatness of Soul and Genius, can divest themselves of the little Images of Ridicule, and admire Nature in her Simplicity and Nakedness. As for

---

[7] *Me . . . Texere:* From Horace, *Odes* 3.4.9–13 [Bond]: "On the famed Appulian Vultur [a hill], outside the bounds of my Nurse Apulia, I slept tired with play and the doves covered me with fresh leaves."

[8] *Lord Dorset:* Charles Sackville, sixth Earl of Dorset (1643–1706).

[9] *Moliere's Thoughts:* Jean-Baptiste Poquelin, known as Molière (1622–1673), the French comic playwright. Addison refers to Molière's play *The Misanthrope* (1666).

the little conceited Wits of the Age, who can only show their Judgment by finding Fault, they cannot be supposed to admire these Productions which have nothing to recommend them but the Beauties of Nature, when they do not know how to relish even those Compositions that, with all the Beauties of Nature, have also the additional Advantages of Art.

No. 105
Saturday, June 30, 1711
[Addison on the "Pedantry" of the "Meer Man of the Town"]

> *. . . Id arbitror*
> *Adprime in vita esse utile, ne quid nimis.*[1]
> — Ter. *Andr.*

My Friend, WILL. HONEYCOMB,[2] values himself very much upon what he calls the Knowledge of Mankind, which has cost him many Disasters in his Youth; for WILL. reckons every Misfortune that he has met with among the Women, and every Rencounter among the Men, as Parts of his Education, and fancies he should never have been the Man he is, had not he broke Windows, knocked down Constables, disturbed honest People with his Midnight Serenades, and beat up a Lewd Woman's Quarters, when he was a young Fellow. The engaging in Adventures of this nature WILL. calls the studying of Mankind, and terms this Knowledge of the Town the Knowledge of the World. WILL. ingenuously confesses that for half his Life his Head ached every Morning with reading of Men over-night, and at present Comforts himself under certain Pains which he endures from time to time, that without them he could not have been acquainted with the Gallantries of the Age. This WILL. looks upon as the Learning of a Gentleman, and regards all other kinds of Science as the Accomplishments of one whom he calls a Scholar, a Bookish Man, or a Philosopher.

---

[1] *Id . . . nimis:* From Terence, *Andira* 60–61 (altered): "Not to be addicted too much to any one thing, I take to be the most excellent rule of life" [Bond].

[2] *Will. Honeycomb:* An aging relic of the Restoration, the rakish man-about-town Will Honeycomb is a member of the Spectator Club introduced in *Spectator* No. 2 (see p. 83).

For these Reasons WILL. shines in mixt Company, where he has the Discretion not to go out of his Depth, and has often a certain way of making his real Ignorance appear a seeming one. Our Club however has frequently caught him tripping, at which times they never spare him. For as WILL. often insults us with the Knowledge of the Town, we sometimes take our Revenge upon him by our Knowledge of Books.

He was last Week producing two or three Letters which he writ in his Youth to a Coquet Lady. The Raillery of them was natural, and well enough for a meer Man of the Town; but, very unluckily, several of the Words were wrong spelt. WILL. laught this off at first as well as he could, but finding himself pushed on all sides, and especially by the *Templar*,[3] he told us, with a little Passion, that he never liked Pedantry in Spelling, and that he spelt like a Gentleman, and not like a Scholar; Upon this WILL. had Recourse to his old Topick of showing the narrow Spiritedness, the Pride and Ignorance of Pedants; which he carried so far, that upon my retiring to my Lodgings, I could not forbear throwing together such Reflections as occurred to me upon that Subject.

A Man who has been brought up among Books, and is able to talk of nothing else, is a very indifferent Companion, and what we call Pedant. But, methinks, we should enlarge the Title, and give it every one that does not know how to think out of his Profession, and particular way of Life.

What is a greater Pedant than a meer Man of the Town? Barr him the Play-houses, a Catalogue of the reigning Beauties, and an Account of a few fashionable Distempers that have befallen him, and you strike him Dumb. How many a pretty Gentleman's Knowledge lies all within the Verge of the Court? He will tell you the Names of the Principal Favourites, repeat the shrewd Sayings of a Man of Quality, whisper an Intriegue that is not yet blown upon by common Fame; or, if the Sphere of his Observations is a little larger than ordinary, will perhaps enter into all the Incidents, Turns and Revolutions in a Game of Ombre.[4] When he has gone thus far he has shown you the whole Circle of his Accomplishments, his Parts are drained, and he is disabled from any further Conversation. What are these but

---

[3] *Templar:* A law student, also a member of the club. England's law offices were housed in a group of buildings called the Inns of Court, collectively known as the Temple.
[4] *Game of Ombre:* A popular card game.

rank Pedants? and yet these are the Men who value themselves most on their Exemption from the Pedantry of Colleges.

I might here mention the Military Pedant, who always talks in a Camp, and is storming Towns, making Lodgments, and fighting Battels from one end of the Year to the other. Every thing he speaks smells of Gunpowder; if you take away his Artillery from him, he has not a Word to say for himself. I might likewise mention the Law Pedant, that is perpetually putting Cases, repeating the Transactions of *Westminster-Hall*,[5] wrangling with you upon the most indifferent Circumstances of Life, and not to be convinced of the Distance of a Place, or of the most trivial Point in Conversation, but by dint of Argument. The State-Pedant is wrapt up in News, and lost in Politicks. If you mention either of the Kings of *Spain* or *Poland*, he talks very notably, but if you go out of the *Gazette*[6] you drop him. In short, a meer Courtier, a meer Soldier, a meer Scholar, a meer any thing, is an insipid Pedantick Character, and equally ridiculous.

Of all the Species of Pedants, which I have mentioned, the Book-Pedant is much the most supportable; he has at least an exercised Understanding, and a Head which is full though confused, so that a Man who converses with him may often receive from him hints of things that are worth knowing, and what he may possibly turn to his own Advantage, tho' they are of little use to the Owner. The worst kind of Pedants among Learned Men are such as are naturally endued with a very small Share of common Sense, and have read a great number of Books without Taste or Distinction.

The Truth of it is, Learning, like Travelling, and all other Methods of Improvement, as it finishes good Sense, so it makes a silly Man ten thousand times more insufferable, by supplying variety of Matter to his Impertinence, and giving him an Opportunity of abounding in Absurdities.

Shallow Pedants cry up one another much more than Men of solid and useful Learning. To read the Titles they give an Editor, of Collator of a Manuscript, you would take him for the Glory of the Common Wealth of Letters, and the Wonder of his Age; when perhaps

---

[5] *Westminster-Hall:* The surviving remnant of the original palace of Westminster, built as an extension of Edward the Confessor's palace in 1097, Westminster Hall served as the center of administrative life outside the city walls (Westminster is west of the city). From the thirteenth century until 1882, the building contained the courts of law. During the seventeenth and eighteenth centuries the hall also served as an emporium for books, gewgaws, and clothes.

[6] *the Gazette:* The official newspaper of the English government.

upon Examination you find that he has only Rectify'd a *Greek Particle*, or laid out a whole Sentence in proper Comma's.

They are obliged indeed to be thus lavish of their Praises, that they may keep one another in Countenance; and it is no wonder if a great deal of Knowledge, which is not capable to making a Man Wise, has a natural Tendency to make him Vain and Arrogant.

No. 175
Thursday, September 20, 1711
[Budgell on a Letter Calling for the Establishment
of a Society for the Inspection of Modes and Fashions]

I have, indeed, seen and heard of several young Gentlemen under the same Misfortune with my present Correspondent. The best Rule I can lay down for them to avoid the like Calamities for the future, is throughly to consider not only *Whether their Companions are weak*, but *Whether themselves are Wits*.

The following Letter comes to me from *Exeter*, and being credibly informed that what it contains is Matter of Fact, I shall give it my Reader as it was sent me.

Mr. SPECTATOR,   *Exeter, Sept. 7.*

'You were pleas'd in a late Speculation[1] to take notice of the Inconvenience we lie under in the Country, in not being able to keep pace with the Fashion; but there is another Misfortune which we are subject to, and is no less grievous than the former, which has hitherto escaped your Observation. I mean the having things palmed upon us for *London* Fashions, which were never once heard of there.

'A Lady of this Place had some time since a Box of the newest Ribbons sent down by the Coach: Whether it was her own malicious Invention, or the Wantonness of a *London* Milliner, I am not able to inform you; but, among the rest, there was one Cherry-coloured Ribbon, consisting of about half a Dozen Yards, made up in the Figure of a Small Head-dress. The foresaid Lady had the Assurance to affirm amidst a Circle of Female Inquisitors, who were present at the open-

---

[1] *a late Speculation:* *Spectator* No. 119.

ing of the Box, that this was the newest Fashion worn at Court. Accordingly the next *Sunday* we had several Females, who came to Church with their Heads dress'd wholly in Ribbons, and looked like so many Victims ready to be Sacrificed.[2] This is still a reigning Mode among us. At the same time we have a Sett of Gentlemen, who take the Liberty to appear in all Publick Places without any Buttons to their Coats, which they supply with several little Silver Hasps; tho' our freshest Advices from *London* make no mention of any such Fashion; and we are something shy of affording Matter to the Button-makers for a second Petition.

'What I would humbly propose to the Publick is, that there may be a Society erected in *London*, to consist of the most skilful Persons of both Sexes, for the *Inspection of Modes and Fashions*; and that hereafter no Person or Persons shall presume to appear singularly habited in any Part of the Country, without a Testimonial from the foresaid Society that their Dress is answerable to the Mode at *London*. By this means, Sir, we shall know a little where about we are.

'If you could bring this Matter to bear, you would very much oblige great Numbers of your Country Friends, and among the rest,

Your very Humble Servant,

Jack Modish.'

No. 226
Monday, November 19, 1711
[Steele on Painting as a Tool for Moral Education]

. . . *mutum est pictura poema.*[1]
— Hor.

I have very often lamented and hinted my Sorrow in several Speculations,[2] that the Art of Painting is made so little Use of to the Improvement of our Manners. When we consider that it places the Action of the Person represented in the most agreeable Aspect

---

[2] *Victims ready to be Sacrificed:* In ancient Greek and Roman rituals, animals were bedecked with garlands before being sacrificed to the gods.

[1] *mutum . . . poema:* Possibly adapted from the *Rhetorica ad Herennium* (formerly attributed to Cicero), 4.28.39: "A painting is a silent poem" [Bond].

[2] *several Speculations:* In *Spectator* Nos. 172 and 142.

imaginable, that it does not only express the Passion or Concern as it sits upon him who is drawn, but has under those Features the Height of the Painter's Imagination, What strong Images of Virtue and Humanity might we not expect would be instilled into the Mind from the Labours of the Pencil? This is a Poetry which would be understood with much less Capacity, and less Expence of Time, than what is taught by Writing; but the Use of it is generally perverted, and that admirable Skill prostituted to the basest and most unworthy Ends. Who is the better Man for beholding the most beautiful *Venus*, the best wrought *Bacchanal*,[3] the Images of sleeping Cupids, Languishing Nymphs, or any of the Representations of Gods, Goddesses, Demygods, Satyrs, *Polyphemes*,[4] Sphinxes or Fauns? But if the virtues and Vices which are sometimes pretended to be represented under such Draughts, were given us by the Painter in the Characters of real Life, and the Persons of Men and Women whose Actions have rendered them laudable or infamous; we should not see a good History-Piece without receiving an instructive Lecture. There needs no other Proof of this Truth, than the Testimony of every reasonable Creature who has seen the Cartons in Her Majesty's Gallery at *Hampton-Court*:[5] These are Representations of no less Actions than those of our Blessed Saviour and his Apostles.[6] As I now sit and recollect the warm Images which the admirable *Raphael* has raised, it is impossible, even from the faint Traces in one's Memory of what one has not seen these two Years, to be unmoved at the Horrour and Rever-

---

[3] *Venus . . . Bacchanal:* Venus is the Roman goddess of love (Greek, Aphrodite); a bacchanal is an orgiastic ritual celebrating the god of wine Bacchus, or Dionysus.

[4] *Polyphemes:* In Greek mythology, Polyphemus was a Cyclops, the son of Poseidon. In Homer's *Odyssey*, Polyphemus is one of a race of monstrous, one-eyed giants (Book 9).

[5] *Hampton-Court:* Hampton Court Palace is situated on the Thames, about fifteen miles southwest from London. Thomas Wolsey bought the site in 1514 from the Order of St. John of Jerusalem and later presented it to Henry VIII. After the Restoration, Charles II redecorated the palace and after 1688 William and Mary employed Christopher Wren in a second rebuilding. George II (1683–1760) was the last English monarch to live at Hampton Court.

[6] *our Blessed Saviour and his Apostles:* Steele is discussing seven tapestry cartoons by the Italian artist Raphael (1483–1520), originally commissioned by Pope Leo X for tapestries in the Sistine Chapel at the Vatican in Rome, and purchased by King James I (1566–1625) after they had been used at Brussels for making tapestries. When Hampton Court was rebuilt by Sir Christopher Wren, the cartoons were set up there in a special gallery, where Steele saw them. Since 1865 they have been exhibited on loan at the Victoria and Albert Museum in London. The subjects of the cartoons are (1) Christ's Charge to Peter, (2) The Miraculous Draught of Fishes, (3) The Death of Ananias, (4) The Healing of the Lame Man, (5) The Blinding of Elymas, (6) The Sacrifice at Lystra, and (7) St. Paul Preaching at Athens [Bond].

ence which appear in the whole Assembly when the mercenary Man
fell down dead; at the Amazement of the Man born blind, when he
first receives Sight; or at the graceless Indignation of the Sorcerer,
when he is struck blind. The Lame, when they first find Strength in
their Feet, stand doubtful of their new Vigour. The heavenly Apostles
appear acting these great things, with a deep Sense of the Infirmities
which they relieve, but no Value of themselves who administer to
their Weakness. They know themselves to be but Instruments; and
the generous Distress they are painted in when divine Honours are
offered to them, is a Representation in the most exquisite Degree of
the Beauty of Holiness. When St. *Paul*[7] is preaching to the *Athenians*,
with what wonderful Art are almost all the different Tempers of
Mankind represented in that elegant Audience? You see one credu-
lous of all that is said, another wrapt up in deep Suspence, another
saying there is some Reason in what he says, another angry that the
Apostle destroys a favourite Opinion which he is unwilling to give
up, another wholly convinced and holding out his Hands in Rapture;
while the Generality attend, and wait for the Opinion of those who
are of leading Characters in the Assembly. I will not pretend so much
as to mention that Chart on which is drawn the Appearance of our
Blessed Lord after his Resurrection. Present Authority, late Suffering,
Humility and Majesty, Despotick Command and Divine Love, are at
once seated in his Celestial Aspect. The Figures of the Eleven Apostles
are all in the same Passion of Admiration, but discover it differently
according to their Characters. *Peter*[8] receives his Master's Orders on
his Knees with an Admiration mixed with a more particular Attention: The two next with a more open Extasie, though still constrained
by the Awe of the Divine Presence: The beloved Disciple, whom I
take to be the Right of the two first Figures, has in his Countenance
Wonder drowned in Love; and the last Personage, whose Back is towards the Spectator and his Side towards the Presence, one would

[7] *St. Paul:* St. Paul (A.D. 5?–67?) was a first-century Christian apostle to the Gen-
tiles and author of the oldest writing in the New Testament. About the year 32, two
years after the crucifixion of Jesus Christ, Paul was converted and baptized. His teachings are contained in the Acts of the Apostles and in his letters to the Romans, Corinthi-
ans, Galatians, Philippians, Colossians, and Thessalonians.

[8] *Peter:* St. Peter (d. A.D. 64) was an apostle of Jesus Christ. Originally a fisherman
from Galilee named Simon, he was renamed Peter (Greek, *petros*, "rock") by Christ
who charged him with the founding of his church: "And I say also unto thee, That
thou art Peter, and upon this rock I will build my church; and the gates of hell shall not
prevail against it. And I will give unto thee the keys of the kingdom of heaven"
(Matthew 16:18–19).

fancy to be St. *Thomas*,[9] as abashed by the Conscience of his former Diffidence; which perplexed Concern it is possible *Raphael* thought too hard a Task to draw but by this Acknowledgement of the Difficulty to describe it.

The whole Work is an Exercise of the highest Piety in the Painter; and all the Touches of a religious Mind are expressed in a Manner much more forcible than can possibly be performed by the most moving Eloquence. These invaluable Pieces are very justly in the Hands of the greatest and most pious Soveraign in the World; and cannot be the frequent Object of every one at their own Leisure: But as an Engraver is to the Painter, what a Printer is to an Author, it is worthy Her Majesty's Name, that she has encouraged that noble Artist, Monsieur *Dorigny*, to publish these Works of *Raphael*. We have of this Gentleman a Piece of the Transfiguration, which, I think, is held a Work second to none in the World.

Methinks it would be ridiculous in our People of Condition, after their large Bounties to Foreigners of no Name or Merit, should they overlook this Occasion of having for a trifling Subscription, a Work which it is impossible for a Man of Sense to behold, without being warmed with the noblest Sentiments that can be inspired by Love, Admiration, Compassion, Contempt of this World, and Expectation of a Better.

It is certainly the greatest Honour we can do our Country, to distinguish Strangers of Merit who apply to us with Modesty and Diffidence, which generally accompanies Merit. No Opportunity of this Kind ought to be neglected; and a modest Behaviour should alarm us to examine whether we do not lose something excellent under that Disadvantage in the Possessor of that Quality. My Skill in Paintings, where one is not directed by the Passion of the Pictures, is so inconsiderable, that I am in very great Perplexity when I offer to speak of any Performances of Painters of Landskips, Buildings, or single Figures. This makes me at a Loss how to mention the Pieces which Mr. *Boul* exposes to Sale by Auction on *Wednesday* next in *Shandois-street*: But having heard him commended by those who have bought of him heretofore for great Integrity in his Dealing, and over-heard him himself (tho' a laudable Painter) say nothing of his own was fit to

---

[9] *St. Thomas:* Thomas was one of Christ's apostles. His "Diffidence" refers to the story that Thomas would not believe in Christ's resurrection until he saw the twelve wounds from the crucifixion, hence the term "doubting Thomas."

come into the Room with those he had to sell, I feared I should lose an Occasion of serving a Man of Worth in omitting to speak of his Auction.

ADVERTISEMENT.

There is arrived from Italy a Painter who acknowledges himself the greatest Person of the Age in that Art, and is willing to be as renowned in this Island as he declares he is in foreign Parts.

The Doctor paints the Poor for nothing.

No. 291
Saturday, February 2, 1712
[Addison on Criticism]

> . . . *Ubi plura nitent in carmine, non ego paucis*
> *Offendar maculis, quas aut Incuria fudit,*
> *Aut Humana parum cavit Natura . . .*[1]
> — Hor.

I have now consider'd *Milton's Paradise Lost*[2] under those four great Heads of the Fable, the Characters, the Sentiments, and the Language; and have shewn that he excels, in general, under each of these Heads. I hope that I have made several Discoveries which may appear new, even to those who are versed in Critical Learning. Were I indeed to chuse my Readers, by whose Judgment I would stand or fall, they should not be such as are acquainted only with the *French* and *Italian* Criticks, but also with the Ancient and Modern who have written in either of the learned Languages. Above all, I would have them well versed in the *Greek* and *Latin* Poets, without which a Man

[1] *Ubi . . . Natura:* From Horace, *Ars Poetica* 351–53: "If numerous Graces shine in what he writes, / I'le not condemn tho some few Faults appear, / Which common frailty leaves, or want of Care"— CREECH [Bond].

[2] *Milton's Paradise Lost:* John Milton (1608–1674) was an English poet, radical Protestant thinker, and scholar. He is best known for his Christian epic *Paradise Lost* (1667). Addison's papers on *Paradise Lost* ran once a week, every Saturday through Nos. 267–369.

very often fancies that he understands a Critick, when in reality he does not comprehend his Meaning.

It is in Criticism, as in all other Sciences and Speculations; one who brings with him any implicit Notions and Observations which he has made in his reading of the Poets, will find his own Reflections methodized and explained, and perhaps several little Hints that had passed in his Mind, perfected and improved in the Works of a good Critick; whereas one who has not these previous Lights, is very often an utter Stranger to what he reads, and apt to put a wrong Interpretation upon it.

Nor is it sufficient, that a Man who sets up for a Judge in Criticism, should have perused the Authors above-mentioned, unless he has also a clear and Logical Head. Without this Talent he is perpetually puzzled and perplexed amidst his own Blunders, mistakes the Sense of those he would confute, or if he chances to think right, does not know how to convey his Thoughts to another with Clearness and Perspicuity. *Artistotle*,[3] who was the best Critick, was also one of the best Logicians that ever appeared in the World.

Mr. *Lock*'s Essay[4] on Human Understanding would be thought a very odd Book for a Man to make himself Master of, who would get a Reputation by Critical Writings; though at the same time it is very certain, that an Author who has not learn'd the Art of distinguishing between Words and Things, and of ranging his Thoughts, and setting them in proper Lights, whatever notions he may have, will lose himself in Confusion and Obscurity. I might further observe, that there is not a *Greek* or *Latin* Critick who has not shewn, even in the stile of his Criticisms, that he was a Master of all the Elegance and Delicacy of his Native Tongue.

The truth of it is, there is nothing more absurd, than for a Man to set up for a Critick, without a good Insight into all the Parts of Learning; whereas many of those who have endeavoured to signalize themselves by Works of this Nature among our *English* Writers, are not only defective in the above-mentioned Particulars, but plainly discover by the Phrases which they make use of, and by their confused

---

[3] *Aristotle:* Aristotle (384–322 B.C.) was the student of Plato and with him one of the greatest Greek philosophers. His *Poetics*, a series of what seem to be lecture notes on epic, dramatic (the genre most thoroughly treated), and lyrical poetry, was a cornerstone of dramatic and poetic theory in the seventeenth and eighteenth centuries.\

[4] *Mr. Lock's Essay:* John Locke (1632–1704), an English philosopher, published his *Essay Concerning Human Understanding* in 1690.

way of thinking, that they are not acquainted with the most common and ordinary Systems of Arts and Sciences. A few general Rules extracted out of the *French* Authors, with a certain Cant of Words, has sometimes set up an Illiterate heavy Writer for a most judicious and formidable Critick.

One great Mark, by which you may discover a Critick who has neither Taste nor Learning, is this, that he seldom ventures to praise any Passage in an Author which has not been before received and applauded by the Publick, and that his Criticism turns wholly upon little Faults and Errors. This part of a Critick is so very easie to succeed in, that we find every ordinary Reader, upon the publishing of a new Poem, has Wit and Ill-nature enough to turn several Passages of it into Ridicule, and very often in the right Place. This Mr. *Dryden* has very agreeably remarked in those two celebrated Lines,

> *Errors, Like Straws, upon the Surface flow;*
> *He who would search for Pearls must dive below.*[5]

A true Critick ought to dwell rather upon Excellencies than Imperfections, to discover the concealed Beauties of a Writer, and communicate to the World such things as are worth their Observation. The most exquisite Words and finest Strokes of an Author are those which very often appear the most doubtful and exceptionable, to a Man who wants a Relish for polite Learning; and they are these, which a sower undistinguishing Critick generally attacks with the greatest Violence. *Tully*[6] observes, that it is very easie to brand or fix a Mark upon what he calls *Verbum ardens*, or, as it may be rendered into *English, a glowing bold Expression*, and to turn it into Ridicule by a cold ill-natured Criticism. A little Wit is equally capable of exposing a Beauty, and of aggravating a Fault; and though such a Treatment of an Author naturally produces indignation in the Mind of an understanding Reader, it has however its effect among the generality of those whose Hands it falls into, the Rabble of Mankind being very apt to think that every thing which is laughed at with any mixture of Wit, is ridiculous in it self.

Such a Mirth as this, is always unseasonable in a Critick, as it rather prejudices the Reader than convinces him, and is capable of

---

[5] *Errors . . . must dive below:* Dryden, *All for Love, Prologue*, 25–26 [Bond].

[6] *Tully:* Tully is Marcus Tullius Cicero (106–43 B.C.), the famous Roman orator, philosopher, and statesman. This reference is to his *Ad Marcum Brutum Orator*, 8.27 [Bond].

making a Beauty, as well as a Blemish, the Subject of Derision. A Man, who cannot write with Wit on a proper Subject, is dull and stupid, but one who shews it in an improper place, is as impertinent and absurd. Besides, a Man who has the Gift of Ridicule is apt to find Fault with any thing that gives him an Opportunity of exerting his beloved Talent, and very often censures a Passage, not because there is any Fault in it, but because he can be merry upon it. Such kinds of Pleasantry are very unfair and disingenuous in Works of Criticism, in which the greatest Masters, both Ancient and Modern, have always appeared with a serious and instructive Air.

As I intend in my next Paper to shew the Defects in *Milton*'s *Paradise Lost*, I thought fit to premise these few Particulars, to the End that the Reader may know I enter upon it, as on a very ungrateful Work, and that I shall just point at the Imperfections, without endeavouring to enflame them with Ridicule. I must also observe with *Longinus*,[7] that the Productions of a great Genius, with many Lapses and Inadvertencies, are infinitely preferable to the Works of an inferior kind of Author, which are scrupulously exact and conformable to all the Rules of correct Writing.

I shall conclude my Paper with a story out of *Boccalini*,[8] which sufficiently shews us the Opinion that Judicious Author entertained of the sort of Criticks I have been here mentioning. A famous Critick, says he, having gathered together all the Faults of an Eminent Poet, made a Present of them to *Apollo*,[9] who received them very graciously, and resolved to make the Author a suitable Return for the Trouble he had been at in collecting them. In order to this, he set before him a Sack of Wheat, as it had been just threshed out of the Sheaf. He then bid him pick out the Chaff from among the Corn, and lay it aside by it self. The Critick applied himself to the Task with great Industry and Pleasure, and after having made the due Separation, was presented by *Apollo* with the Chaff for his Pains.

---

[7] *Longinus:* Dionysus Cassius Longinus (210?–273) was a Greek philosopher and the critic to whom is ascribed the rhetorical text *On the Sublime* (*Peri Hypsos*). Addison refers to Chapter 33 of this text where the author discusses the character of genius.

[8] *Boccalini:* Boccalini (1556–1613) was an Italian prose satirist and anti-Spanish political writer known for his satire *Ragguagli di Parnaso* (Reports from Parnassus), to which Addison refers here.

[9] *Apollo:* The Greek god of music, medicine, and poetry.

No. 409
Thursday, June 19, 1712
[Addison on Good Taste]

. . . Musæo contingere cuncta lepore.[1]
— Lucr.

Gratian[2] very often recommends the *fine Taste*, as the utmost Perfection of an accomplished Man. As this Word arises very often in Conversation, I shall endeavour to give some Account of it, and to lay down Rules how we may know whether we are possessed of it, and how we may acquire that fine Taste of Writing, which is so much talked of among the Polite World.

Most Languages make use of this Metaphor, to express that Faculty of the Mind, which distinguishes all the most concealed Faults and nicest Perfections in Writing. We may be sure this Metaphor would not have been so general in all Tongues, had there not been a very great Conformity between that Mental Taste, which is the Subject of this Paper, and that Sensitive Taste which gives us a Relish of very different Flavour that affects the Palate. Accordingly we find, there are as many Degrees of Refinement in the intellectual Faculty, as in the Sense, which is marked out by this common Denomination.

I knew a Person who possessed the one in so great a Perfection, that after having tasted ten different Kinds of Tea, he would distinguish, without seeing the Colour of it, the particular Sort which was offered him; and not only so, but any two sorts of them that were mixt together in an equal Proportion; nay, he has carried the Experiment so far, as upon tasting the Composition of three different sorts, to name the Parcels from whence the three several Ingredients were taken. A Man of a fine Taste in Writing will discern, after the same manner, not only the general Beauties and Imperfections of an Author, but discover the several Ways of thinking and expressing himself, which diversify him from all other Authors, with the several Foreign Infusions of Thought and Language, and the particular Authors from whom they were borrowed.

---

[1] *Musæo . . . lepore:* From Lucretius, *De rerum natura* 1.934 (altered): "To grace each subject with wit" [Bond].
[2] *Gratian:* Baltasar Gracián (1601–1658), Spanish philosopher and writer.

After having thus far explained what is generally meant by a fine Taste in Writing, and shown the Propriety of the Metaphor which is used on this Occasion, I think I may define it to be *that Faculty of the Soul, which discerns the Beauties of an Author with Pleasure, and the Imperfections with Dislike.* If a Man would know whether he is possessed of this Faculty, I would have him read over the celebrated Works of Antiquity, which have stood the Test of so many different Ages and Countries; or those Works among the Moderns, which have the Sanction of the Politer Part of our Contemporaries. If upon the Perusal of such Writings he does not find himself delighted in an extraordinary manner, or, if upon reading the admired Passages in such Authors, he finds a Coldness and Indifference in his Thoughts, he ought to conclude, not (as is too usual among tasteless Readers) that the Author wants those Perfections which have been admired in him, but that he himself wants the Faculty of discovering them.

He should, in the second place, be very careful to observe, whether he tastes the distinguishing Perfections, or, if I may be allowed to call them so, the Specifick Qualities of the Author whom he peruses; whether he is particularly pleased with *Livy* for his manner of telling a Story, with *Sallust* for his entering into those internal Principles of Action which arise from the Characters and Manners of the Persons he describes, or with *Tacitus* for his displaying those outward Motives of Safety and Interest, which give birth to the whole Series of Transactions which he relates.

He may likewise consider, how differently he is affected by the same Thought, which presents it self in a great Writer, from what he is when he finds it delivered by a Person of an ordinary Genius. For there is as much difference in apprehending a Thought cloathed in *Cicero*'s Language, and that of a common Author, as in seeing an Object by the Light of a Taper, or by the Light of the Sun.

It is very difficult to lay down Rules for the acquirement of such a Taste as that I am here speaking of. The Faculty must in some degree be born with us, and it very often happens, that those who have other Qualities in Perfection are wholly void of this. One of the most eminent Mathematicians of the Age[3] has assured me, that the greatest Pleasure he took in reading *Virgil*, was in examining *Æneas* his Voyage by the Map; as I question not but many a Modern Compiler of History would be delighted with little more in that Divine Author, than in the bare matters of Fact.

---

[3] *Mathematicians of the Age:* Perhaps Sir Isaac Newton.

But notwithstanding this Faculty must in some measure be born with us, there are several Methods for Cultivating and Improving it, and without which it will be very uncertain, and of little use to the Person that possesses it. The most natural Method for this Purpose is to be conversant among the Writings of the most Polite Authors. A Man who has any Relish for fine Writing, either discovers new Beauties, or receives stronger Impressions from the Masterly Stroaks of a great Author every time he peruses him: Besides that he naturally wears himself into the same manner of Speaking and Thinking.

Conversation with Men of a Polite Genius is another Method for improving our Natural Taste. It is impossible for a Man of the greatest Parts to consider any thing in its whole Extent, and in all its variety of Lights. Every Man, besides those general Observations which are to be made upon an Author, forms several Reflections that are peculiar to his own manner of Thinking; so that Conversation will naturally furnish us with Hints which we did not attend to, and make us enjoy other Mens Parts and Reflections as well as our own. This is the best Reason I can give for the Observation which several have made, that Men of great Genius in the same way of Writing seldom rise up singly, but at certain Periods of Time appear together, and in a Body; as they did at *Rome* in the Reign of *Augustus*, and in *Greece* about the Age of *Socrates*.[4] I cannot think that *Corneille, Racine, Moliere, Boileau, la Fontaine, Bruyere, Bossu,* or the *Daciers,*[5] would have written so well as they have done, had they not been Friends and Contemporaries.

---

[4] *Reign of Augustus . . . Age of Socrates:* Gaius Octavius Augustus (963 B.C.–A.D. 14) was Roman emperor from 31 B.C. until A.D. 14. More than any other emperor, he won the support of poets and writers. The Age of Socrates (469?–399 B.C.) in fifth-century Athens was famed as a Golden Age of Western poetic, dramatic, historical, and philosophical cultural production.

[5] *Corneille . . . Daciers:* All seventeenth-century neoclassical French writers and critics. Pierre Corneille (1606–1684), Jean Racine (1639–1699), and Jean-Baptiste Poquelin, known as Molière (1622–1673), were dramatists. Nicolas Boileau (1636–1711) was a French poet and literary critic who shaped the neoclassical standards for French and English literature in *L'Art Poetique* (The Poetic Art) (1674). Jean de La Fontaine (1621–1695) collected the stories of the ancient Greek writer Aesop in his *Fables* (1668–1694). Jean de La Bruyère (1645–1696) was a moral satirist and published a translation of Theophrastus' *Characters* (1688). René Le Bossu (1631–1680) was a renowned French critic of the epic. André Dacier (1651–1722) was a French classical scholar. He is most noted for his translations and editions of classical texts. His wife, Anne Dacier (1654–1720), was famous for her translations of the *Iliad* (1699) and the *Odyssey* (1708), and she worked with her husband on the Delphins Series of editions of Latin texts.

It is likewise necessary for a Man who would form to himself a finished Taste of good Writing, to be well versed in the Works of the best *Criticks* both Ancient and Modern. I must confess that I could wish there were Authors of this kind, who, beside the Mechanical Rules which a Man of very little Taste may discourse upon, would enter into the very Spirit and Soul of fine Writing, and shew us the several Sources of that Pleasure which rises in the Mind upon the Perusal of a noble Work. Thus altho' in Poetry it be absolutely necessary that the Unities of Time, Place and Action, with other Points of the same Nature should be thoroughly explained and understood; there is still something more essential, to the Art, something that elevates and astonishes the Fancy, and gives a Greatness of Mind to the Reader, which few of the Criticks besides *Longinus* have consider'd.

Our general Taste in *England* is for Epigram, turns of Wit, and forced Conceits, which have no manner of Influence, either for the bettering or enlarging the Mind of him who reads them, and have been carefully avoided by the greatest Writers, both among the Ancients and Moderns. I have endeavoured in several of my Speculations to banish this *Gothic* Taste which has taken Possession among us. I entertained the Town for a Week together with an Essay upon Wit, in which I endeavoured to detect several of those false kinds which have been admir'd in the different Ages of the World; and at the same time to shew wherein the nature of true Wit consists. I afterwards gave an instance of the great force which lies in a natural Simplicity of Thought to affect the Mind of the Reader, from such Vulgar Pieces as have little else besides this single Qualification to recommend them. I have likewise examined the Works of the greatest Poet which our Nation or perhaps any other has produced, and particularized most of those rational and manly Beauties which give a value to that Divine Work. I shall next *Saturday* enter upon an Essay *on the Pleasures of the Imagination*, which though it shall consider that Subject at large, will perhaps suggest to the Reader what it is that gives a Beauty to many Passages of the finest Writers both in Prose and Verse. As an Undertaking of this nature is entirely new, I question not but it will be receiv'd with Candour.

No. 411
Saturday, June 21, 1712
[Addison on the Pleasures of the Imagination]

Avia Pieridum peragro loca, nullius ante
Trita solo; juvat integros accedere fonteis;
Atque haurire: . . .[1]

— Lucr.

Our Sight is the most perfect and most delightful of all our Senses. It fills the Mind with the largest Variety of Ideas converses with its Objects at the greatest Distance, and continues the longest in Action without being tired or satiated with its proper Enjoyments. The Sense of Feeling can indeed give us a Notion of Extension, Shape, and all other Ideas that enter at the Eye, except Colours; but at the same time it is very much streightned and confined in its Operations, to the number, bulk, and distance of its particular Objects. Our Sight seems designed to supply all these Defects, and may be considered as a more delicate and diffusive kind of Touch, that spreads it self over an infinite Multitude of Bodies, comprehends the largest Figures, and brings into our reach some of the most remote Parts of the Universe.

It is this Sense which furnishes the Imagination with its Ideas; so that by the Pleasures of the Imagination or Fancy (which I shall use promiscuously) I here mean such as arise from visible Objects, either when we have them actually in our view, or when we call up their ideas into our Minds by Paintings, Statues, Descriptions, or any the like Occasion. We cannot indeed have a single Image in the Fancy that did not make its first Entrance through the Sight; but we have the Power of retaining, altering and compounding those Images, which we have once received, into all the varieties of Picture and Vision that are most agreeable to the Imagination; for by this Faculty a Man in a Dungeon is capable of entertaining himself with Scenes and Landskips more beautiful than any that can be found in the whole Compass of Nature.

There are few Words in the *English* Language which are employed in a more loose and uncircumscribed Sense than those of the *Fancy* and the *Imagination*. I therefore thought it necessary to fix and

[1] *Avia . . . haurire: . . .* : From Lucretius, *De rerum natura* 1.926–28: "The Muses close Retreat I wander o'er, / Their unacquainted Solitudes explore, / At the Spring-head it charms me to be first, / And in th' untainted Stream to quench my Thirst" [Bond].

determine the Notion of these two Words, as I intend to make use of them in the Thread of my following Speculations, that the Reader may conceive rightly what is the Subject which I proceed upon. I must therefore desire him to remember, that by the Pleasures of the Imagination, I mean only such Pleasures as arise originally from Sight, and that I divide these Pleasure into two kinds: My Design being first of all to Discourse of those Primary Pleasures of the Imagination, which entirely proceed from such Objects as are before our Eyes; and in the next place to speak of those Secondary Pleasures of the Imagination which flow from the Ideas of visible Objects, when the Objects are not actually before the Eye, but are called up into our Memories, or form'd into agreeable Visions of Things that are either Absent or Fictitious.

The Pleasures of the Imagination, taken in their full Extent, are not so gross as those of Sense, nor so refined as those of the Understanding. The last are, indeed, more preferable, because they are founded on some new Knowledge or Improvement in the Mind of Man; yet it must be confest, that those of the Imagination are as great and as transporting as the other. A beautiful Prospect delights the Soul, as much as a Demonstration; and a Description in *Homer* has charmed more Readers than a Chapter in *Aristotle*.[2] Besides, the Pleasures of the Imagination have this Advantage, above those of the Understanding, that they are more obvious, and more easie to be acquired. It is but opening the Eye, and the Scene enters. The Colours paint themselves on the Fancy, with very little Attention of Thought or Application of Mind in the Beholder. We are struck, we know not how, with the Symmetry of any thing we see, and immediately assent to the Beauty of an Object, without enquiring into the particular Causes and Occasions of it.

A Man of a Polite Imagination, is let into a great many Pleasures that the Vulgar are not capable of receiving. He can converse with a Picture, and find an agreeable Companion in a Statue. He meets with a secret Refreshment in a Description, and often feels a greater Satisfaction in the Prospect of Fields and Meadows, than another does in the Possession. It gives him, indeed, a kind of Property in every thing he sees, and makes the most rude uncultivated parts of Nature ad-

---

[2] *Homer . . . Aristotle:* Homer (fl. 850 B.C.), author of the ancient Greek epics the *Iliad* and the *Odyssey*, wrote fictional, narrative, and descriptive poetry. Aristotle (384–322 B.C.) wrote analytical, philosophical prose.

minister to his Pleasure: So that he looks upon the World, as it were, in another Light, and discovers in it a Multitude of Charms, that conceal themselves from the generality of Mankind.

There are, indeed, but very few who know how to be idle and innocent, or have a Relish of any Pleasures that are not Criminal; every Diversion they take is at the Expence of some one Virtue or another, and their very first Step out of Business is into Vice or Folly. A Man should endeavour, therefore, to make the Sphere of his innocent Pleasures as wide as possible, that he may retire into them with Safety, and find in them such a Satisfaction as a wise Man would not blush to take. Of this Nature are those of the Imagination, which do not require such a Bent of Thought as is necessary to our more serious Employments, nor, at the same time, suffer the Mind to sink into that Negligence and Remissness, which are apt to accompany our more sensual Delights, but, like a gentle Exercise to the Faculties, awaken them from Sloth and Idleness, without putting them upon any Labour or Difficulty.

We might here add, that the Pleasures of the Fancy are more conducive to Health, than those of the Understanding, which are worked out by Dint of Thinking, and attended with too violent a Labour of the Brain. Delightful Scenes, whether in Nature, Painting, or Poetry, have a kindly Influence on the Body, as well as the Mind, and not only serve to clear and brighten the Imagination, but are able to disperse Grief and Melancholly, and to set the Animal Spirits in pleasing and agreeable Motions. For this reason Sir *Francis Bacon*,[3] in his Essay upon Health, has not thought it improper to prescribe to his Reader a Poem or a Prospect, where he particularly dissuades him from knotty and subtile Disquisitions, and advises him to pursue Studies, that fill the Mind with splendid and illustrious Objects, as Histories, Fables, and Contemplations of Nature.

I have in this Paper, by way of Introduction, settled the Notion of those Pleasures of the Imagination, which are the Subject of my present Undertaking, and endeavoured, by several Considerations, to recommend to my Reader the Pursuit of those Pleasures. I shall, in my next Paper, examine the several Sources from whence these Pleasures are derived.

---

[3] *Sir Francis Bacon:* Sir Francis Bacon (1561–1626) was an early empirical philosopher and essayist. Bacon's *Essays* were published in 1597; here Addison refers to Essay 30, "Of Regiment of Health."

No. 412
Monday, June 23, 1712
[Addison on the Pleasures of the Imagination]

. . . Divisum sic breve fiet Opus.[1]
— Mart.

I shall first consider those Pleasures of the Imagination, which arise from the actual View and Survey of outward Objects: And these, I think, all proceed from the Sight of what is *Great, Uncommon,* or *Beautiful.* There may, indeed, be something so terrible or offensive, that the Horrour or Loathsomness of an Object may over-bear the Pleasure which results from its *Greatness, Novelty,* or *Beauty*; but still there will be such a Mixture of Delight in the very Disgust it gives us, as any of these three Qualifications are most conspicuous and prevailing.

By *Greatness,* I do not only mean the Bulk of any single Object, but the Largeness of a whole View, considered as one entire Piece. Such are the Prospects of an open Champian Country, a vast uncultivated Desart, of huge Heaps of Mountains, high Rocks and Precipices, or a wide Expanse of Waters, where we are not struck with the Novelty or Beauty of the Sight, but with that rude kind of Magnificence which appears in many of these stupendous Works of Nature. Our Imagination loves to be filled with an Object, or to graspe at any thing that is too big for its Capacity. We are flung into a pleasing Astonishment at such unbounded Views, and feel a delightful Stillness and Amazement in the Soul at the Apprehension of them. The Mind of Man naturally hates every thing that looks like a Restraint upon it, and is apt to fancy it self under a sort of Confinement, when the Sight is pent up in a narrow Compass, and shortned on every side by the Neighbourhood of Walls or Mountains. On the contrary, a spacious Horison is an Image of Liberty, where the Eye has Room to range abroad, to expatiate at large on the Immensity of its Views, and to lose it self amidst the Variety of Objects that offer themselves to its Observation. Such wide and undetermined Prospects are as pleasing to the Fancy, as the Speculations of Eternity or Infinitude are to the Understanding. But if there be a Beauty or Uncommonness joyned

---

[1] *Divisum . . . Opus:* From Martial, *Epigrams* 4.82.8: "The work thus divided will become brief" [Bond].

with this Grandeur, as in a troubled Ocean, a Heaven adorned with Stars and Meteors, or a spacious Landskip cut out into Rivers, Woods, Rocks, and Meadows, the Pleasure still grows upon us, as it arises from more than a single Principle.

Every thing that is *new* or *uncommon* raises a Pleasure in the Imagination, because it fills the Soul with an agreeable Surprise, gratifies its Curiosity, and gives it an Idea of which it was not before possest. We are, indeed, so often conversant with one Sett of Objects, and tired out with so many repeated Shows of the same Things, that whatever is *new* or *uncommon* contributes a little to vary Human Life, and to divert our Minds, for a while, with the Strangeness of its Appearance: It serves us for a kind of Refreshment, and takes off from that Satiety we are apt to complain of in our usual and ordinary Entertainments. It is this that bestows Charms on a Monster, and makes even the Imperfections of Nature please us. It is this that recommends Variety, where the Mind is every Instant called off to something new, and the Attention not suffered to dwell too long, and waste it self on any particular Object. It is this, likewise, that improves what is great or beautiful, and makes it afford the Mind a double Entertainment. Groves, Fields, and Meadows, are at any Season of the Year pleasant to look upon, but never so much as in the opening of the Spring, when they are all new and fresh, with their first Gloss upon them, and not yet too much accustomed and familiar to the Eye. For this reason there is nothing that more enlivens a Prospect than Rivers, Jetteaus,[2] or Falls of Water, where the Scene is perpetually shifting, and entertaining the Sight every Moment with something that is new. We are quickly tired with looking upon Hills and Valleys, where every thing continues fixt and settled in the same Place and Posture, but find our Thoughts a little agitated and relieved at the sight of such Objects as are ever in Motion, and sliding away from beneath the Eye of the Beholder.

But there is nothing that makes its way more directly to the Soul than *Beauty*, which immediately diffuses a secret Satisfaction and Complacency thro' the Imagination, and gives a Finishing to any thing that is Great or Uncommon. The very first Discovery of it strikes the Mind with an inward Joy, and spreads a Chearfulness and Delight through all its Faculties. There is not perhaps any real Beauty or Deformity more in one piece of Matter than another, because we

---

[2] *Jetteaus:* Fountains.

might have been so made, that whatsoever now appears loathsom to us, might have shewn it self agreeable; but we find by Experience, that there are several Modifications of Matter which the Mind, without any previous Consideration, pronounces at first sight Beautiful or Deformed. Thus we see that every different Species of sensible Creatures has its different Notions of Beauty, and that each of them is most affected with the Beauties of its own kind. This is no where more remarkable than in Birds of the same Shape and Proportion, where we often see the Male determined in his Courtship by the single Grain or Tincture of a Feather, and never discovering any Charms but in the Colour of its Species.

> *Scit thalamo servare fidem, sanctasque veretur*
> *Connubii leges, non illum in pectore candor*
> *Sollicitat niveus; neque pravum accendit amorem*
> *Splendida Lanugo, vel honesta in vertice crista,*
> *Purpureusve nitor pennarum; ast agmina latè*
> *Fœminea explorat cautus, maculasque requirit*
> *Cognatas, paribusque interlita corpora guttis:*
> *Ni faceret, pictis sylvam circum undique monstris*
> *Confusam aspiceres vulgò, partusque biformes,*
> *Et genus ambiguum, & Veneris monumenta nefandæ.*
>   *Hinc merula in nigro se oblectat nigra marito,*
> *Hinc socium lasciva petit Philomela canorum,*
> *Agnoscitque pares sonitus, hinc Noctua tetram*
> *Canitiem alarum, & Glaucos miratur ocellos.*
> *Nempe sibi semper constat, crescitque quotannis*
> *Lucida progenies, castos confessa parentes;*
> *Dum virides inter saltus lucosque sonoros*
> *Vere novo exultat, plumasque decora Juventus*
> *Explicat ad solem, patriisque coloribus ardet.*[3]

---

[3] *. . . coloribus ardet:* These Latin verses are by Addison. There is a translation in the 1744 edition of the *Spectator*:

> The feather'd Husband, to his Partner true,
> Preserves connubial Rites inviolate.
> With cold Indifference every Charm he sees,
> The milky Whiteness of the stately Neck,
> The shining Down, proud Crest, and purple Wings:
> But cautious with a searching Eye explores
> The female Tribes, his proper Mate to find,
> With kindred Colours mark'd: Did he not so,
> The Grove with painted Monsters wou'd abound,

There is a second kind of *Beauty* that we find in the several Products of Art and Nature, which does not work in the Imagination with that Warmth and Violence as the Beauty that appears in our proper Species, but is apt however to raise in us a secret Delight, and a kind of Fondness for the Places or Objects in which we discover it. This consists either in the Gaiety or Variety of Colours, in the Symmetry and Proportion of Parts, in the Arrangement and Disposition of Bodies, or in a just Mixture and Concurrence of all together. Among these several kinds of Beauty the Eye takes most Delight in Colours. We no where meet with a more glorious or pleasing Show in Nature, than what appears in the Heavens at the rising and setting of the Sun, which is wholly made up of those different Stains of Light that shew themselves in Clouds of a different Situation. For this Reason we find the Poets, who are always addressing themselves to the Imagination, borrowing more of their Epithets from Colours than from any other Topic.

As the Fancy delights in every thing that is Great, Strange, or Beautiful, and is still more pleased the more it finds of these Perfections in the same Object, so is it capable of receiving a new Satisfaction by the Assistance of another Sense. Thus any continued Sound, as the Musick of Birds, or a Fall of Water, awakens every moment the Mind of the Beholder, and makes him more attentive to the several Beauties of the Place that lie before him. Thus if there arises a Fragrancy of Smells or Perfumes, they heighten the Pleasures of the Imagination, and make even the Colours and Verdure of the Landskip appear more agreeable; for the Ideas of both Senses recommend each other, and are pleasanter together than when they enter the Mind separately: As the different Colours of a Picture, when they are well disposed, set off one another, and receive an additional Beauty from the Advantage of their Situation.

Th' ambiguous Product of unnatural Love.
The Black-bird hence selects her sooty Spouse;
The Nightingale her musical Compeer,
Lur'd by the well-known Voice: the Bird of Night,
Smit with his dusky Wings, and greenish Eyes,
Wo[o]s his dun Paramour. The beauteous Race
Speak the chaste Loves of their Progenitors;
When, by the Spring invited, they exult
In Woods and Fields, and to the Sun unfold
Their Plumes, that with paternal Colours glow.

No. 414
Wednesday, June 25, 1712
[Addison on the Pleasures of the Imagination]

. . . *Alterius sic*
Altera poscit opem res & conjurat amicè.[1]
— Hor.

If we consider the Works of *Nature* and *Art*, as they are qualified to entertain the Imagination, we shall find the last very defective, in Comparison of the former; for though they may sometimes appear as Beautiful or Strange, they can have nothing in them of that Vastness and Immensity, which afford so great an Entertainment to the Mind of the Beholder. The one may be as Polite and Delicate as the other, but can never shew her self so August and Magnificent in the Design. There is something more bold and masterly in the rough careless Strokes of Nature, than in the nice Touches and Embellishments of Art. The Beauties of the most stately Garden or Palace lie in a narrow Compass, the Imagination immediately runs them over, and requires something else to gratifie her; but, in the wide Fields of Nature, the Sight wanders up and down without Confinement, and is fed with an infinite variety of Images, without any certain Stint or Number. For this Reason we always find the Poet in love with a Country-Life, where Nature appears in the greatest Perfection, and furnishes out all those Scenes that are most apt to delight the Imagination.

Scriptorum chorus omnis amat nemus & fugit Urbes. Hor.[2]

Hic Secura quies, & nescia fallere vita,
Dives opum variarum; hic latis otia fundis,
Speluncæ, vivique lacus, hic frigida Tempe,
Mugitusque boum, mollesque sub arbore somni. Vir.[3]

But tho' there are several of these wild Scenes, that are more delightful than any artificial Shows; yet we find the Works of Nature still more pleasant, the more they resemble those of Art: For in this

---

[1] *Alterius . . . amicè*: From Horace, *Ars Poetica* 410–11: "Each by it self is vain, I'm sure, but join'd, / Their Force is strong, each proves the others Friend" — CREECH [Bond].

[2] *Hor.*: From Horace, *Epistles* 2.2.77 [Bond]: "The whole troop of writers loves the woods and flees the city."

[3] *Vir.*: From Virgil, *Georgics* 2.467–70: "Unvex'd with Quarrels, undisturb'd with Noise / The Country King his peaceful Realm enjoys: / Cool grits, and living Lakes, the Flow'ry Pride / Of Meads, and Streams that thro' the Valley glide / And shady groves that easie Sleep invite, / And after toilsome Days, a soft repose at Night." — DRYDEN [Bond].

case our Pleasure arises from a double Principle; from the Agreeableness of the Objects to the Eye, and from their Similitude to other Objects: We are pleased as well with comparing their Beauties, as with surveying them, and can represent them to our Minds, either as Copies or Originals. Hence it is that we take Delight in a Prospect which is well laid out, and diversified with Fields and Meadows, Woods and Rivers, in those accidental Landskips of Trees, Clouds and Cities, that are sometimes found in the Veins of Marble, in the curious Fret-work of Rocks and Grottos, and, in a Word, in any thing that hath such a Variety or Regularity as may seem the Effect of Design, in what we call the Works of Chance.

If the Products of Nature rise in Value, according as they more or less resemble those of Art, we may be sure that artificial Works receive a greater Advantage from their Resemblance of such as are natural; because here the Similitude is not only pleasant, but the Pattern more perfect. The prettiest Landskip[4] I ever saw, was one drawn on the Walls of a dark Room, which stood opposite on one side to a navigable River, and on the other to a Park. The Experiment is very common in Opticks. Here you might discover the Waves and Fluctuations of the Water in strong and proper Colours, with the Picture of a Ship entering at one end, and sailing by Degrees through the whole Piece. On another there appeared the Green Shadows of Trees, waving to and fro with the Wind, and Herds of Deer among them in Miniature, leaping about upon the Wall. I must confess, the Novelty of such a sight may be one occasion of its Pleasantness to the Imagination, but certainly the chief Reason is its near Resemblance to Nature, as it does not only, like other Pictures, give the Colour and Figure, but the Motion of the Things it represents.

We have before observed, that there is generally in Nature something more Grand and August, than what we meet with in the Curiosities of Art. When, therefore, we see this imitated in any measure, it gives us a nobler and more exalted kind of Pleasure than what we receive from the nicer and more accurate Productions of Art. On this Account our *English* Gardens are not so entertaining to the Fancy as those in *France* and *Italy*,[5] where we see a large Extent of Ground covered over with an agreeable mixture of Garden and Forest, which

[4] *Landskip:* Landscape. Addison probably has in mind the scene obtained by a camera obscura. . . . There was such a camera obscura at Greenwich Park [Bond].

[5] *English . . . France and Italy:* Addison here contrasts the formal gardens of England, owing something to the Dutch influence introduced at the time of William III (1689–1702), with the private gardens of France and Italy — not, of course, the great gardens of Le Notre at Versailles [Bond].

represent every where an artificial Rudeness, much more charming than that Neatness and Elegancy which we meet with in those of our own Country. It might, indeed, be of ill Consequence to the Publick, as well as unprofitable to private Persons, to alienate so much Ground from Pasturage, and the Plow, in many Parts of a Country that is so well peopled, and cultivated to a far greater Advantage. But why may not a whole Estate be thrown into a kind of Garden by frequent Plantations, that may turn as much to the Profit, as the Pleasure of the Owner? A Marsh overgrown with Willows, or a Mountain shaded with Oaks, are not only more beautiful, but more beneficial, than when they lie bare and unadorned. Fields of Corn make a pleasant Prospect, and if the Walks were a little taken care of that lie between them, if the natural Embroidery of the Meadows were helpt and improved by some small Additions of Art, and the several Rows of Hedges set off by Trees and Flowers, that the Soil was capable of receiving, a Man might make a pretty Landskip of his own Possessions.

Writers,[6] who have given us an Account of *China*, tell us, the Inhabitants of that Country laugh at the Plantations of our *Europeans*, which are laid out by the Rule and Line; because, they say, any one may place Trees in equal Rows and uniform Figures. They chuse rather to shew a Genius in Works of this Nature, and therefore always conceal the Art by which they direct themselves. They have a Word, it seems, in their Language, by which they express the particular Beauty of a Plantation that thus strikes the Imagination at first Sight, without discovering what it is that has so agreeable an Effect. Our *British* Gardeners, on the contrary, instead of humouring Nature, love to deviate from it as much as possible. Our Trees rise in Cones, Globes, and Pyramids. We see the Marks of the Scissars upon every Plant and Bush. I do not know whether I am singular in my Opinion, but, for my own part, I would rather look upon a Tree in all its Luxuriancy and Diffusion of Boughs and Branches, than when it is thus cut and trimmed into a Mathematical Figure; and cannot but fancy that an Orchard in Flower looks infinitely more delightful, than all the little Labyrinths of the most finished Parterre. But as our great Modellers of Gardens have their Magazines of Plants to dispose of, it is very natural for them to tear up all the Beautiful Plantations of Fruit Trees, and contrive a Plan that may most turn to their own Profit, in taking off their Evergreens, and the like Moveable Plants, with which their Shops are plentifully stocked.

[6] *Writers:* Here Addison refers to Sir William Temple's essay "Upon the Gardens of Epicurus; or, of Gardening, In the Year 1685," in *Miscellanea*, part 2, 1.186 [Bond].

No. 478
Monday, September 8, 1712
[Steele's Proposal for a Sphinx-Shaped Museum of Fashion]

... Usus
Quem penes Arbitrium est, & Jus & norma ...[1]

Mr. SPECTATOR,

'It happened lately, that a Friend of mine, who had many things to buy for his Family, wou'd oblige me to walk with him to the Shops. He was very nice in his Way, and fond of having every thing shewn, which at first made me very uneasy; but as his Humour still continu'd, the things which I had been staring at along with him began to fill my Head, and led me into a Set of amusing Thoughts concerning them.

'I fancy'd it must be very surprizing to any one who enters into a Detail of Fashions, to consider how far the Vanity of Mankind has laid it self out in Dress, what a prodigious Number of People it maintains, and what a Circulation of Money it occasions. Providence in this Case makes use of the Folly which we will not give up, and it becomes instrumental to the Support of those who are willing to labour. Hence it is, that Fringe-Makers, Lace-Men, Tire-Women, and a Number of other Trades, which would be useless in a simple State of Nature, draw their Subsistence; tho' it is seldom seen that such as these are extremely rich, because their original Fault of being founded upon Vanity, keeps them poor by the light Inconstancy of its Nature. The Variableness of Fashion turns the Stream of Business, which flows from it now into one Channel, and anon into another; so that different Sets of People sink or flourish in their Turns by it.

'From the Shops we retir'd to the Tavern, where I found my Friend express so much Satisfaction for the Bargains he had made, that my moral Reflections (if I had told them,) might have pass'd for a Reproof; so I chose rather to fall in with him, and let the Discourse run upon the use of Fashions.

'Here we remembred how much Man is govern'd by his Senses, how livelily he is struck by the Objects which appear to him in an agreeable Manner, how much Cloaths contribute to make us agreeable Objects, and how much we owe it to our selves that we should appear so.

---

[1] *Usus ... norma ...* : From Horace, *Ars Poetica* 71–72: "Use is the Judge, the Law, and Rule of Speech" — ROSCOMMON [Bond].

'We considered Man as belonging to Societies; Societies as form'd of different Ranks, and different Ranks distinguished by Habits, that all proper Duty or Respect might attend their Appearance.

'We took notice of several Advantages which are met with in the Occurrences of Conversation. How the bashful Man has been sometimes so rais'd, as to express himself with an Air of Freedom, when he imagines that his Habit introduces him to Company with a becoming manner: And again, how a Fool in fine Cloaths shall be suddenly heard with Attention, till he has betrayed himself; whereas a Man of Sense appearing with a Dress of Negligence, shall be but coldly received, till he be prov'd by Time, and established in a Character. Such Things as these we cou'd recollect to have happen'd to our own Knowledge so very often, that we concluded the Author had his Reasons, who advises his Son to go in Dress rather above his Fortune than under it.

'At last the Subject seem'd so considerable, that it was propos'd to have a Repository builded for Fashions, as there are Chambers for Medals and other Rarities. The Building[2] may be shap'd as that which stands among the Pyramids, in the Form of a Woman's Head. This may be rais'd upon Pillars, whose Ornaments shall bear a just Relation to the Design. Thus there may be an Imitation of Fringe carv'd in the Base, a Sort of Appearance of Lace in the Frize;[3] and a Representation of curling Locks, with Bows of Riban sloping over them, may fill up the Work of the Cornish.[4] The Inside may be divided into two Apartments, appropriated to each Sex. The Apartments may be fill'd with Shelves, on which Boxes are to stand as regularly as Books in a Library. These are to have Folding-Doors, which being open'd, you are to behold a Baby[5] dress'd out in some Fashion which has flourish'd, and standing upon a Pedestal, where the Time of its Reign is mark'd down. For its further Regulation let it be order'd, that every one who invents a Fashion shall bring in his Box, whose Front he may at Pleasure have either work'd or painted with some amorous or gay Device, that, like Books with gilded Leaves and

---

[2] *The Building:* This fashion repository is to take the shape of the Great Sphinx that stands near the pyramid of El-Gizeh in Egypt. A mythical, monstrous creature, the sphinx has a human head and a lion's body. Sphinxes appear in Egyptian and Greek mythology.

[3] *Frize:* Frieze, a decorative part of the entablature, the panel above the columns in a classical building.

[4] *Cornish:* Cornice, a horizontal molded projection that attached above the frieze.

[5] *Baby:* A fashion doll, or miniature mannequin. At this time new fashions were sent from France to England on dolls, as in *Spectator* No. 277.

Covers, it may the sooner draw the Eyes of the Beholders. And to the End that these may be preserv'd with all due Care, let there be a Keeper appointed, who shall be a Gentleman qualify'd with a competent Knowledge in Cloaths; so that by this Means the Place will be a comfortable Support for some Beau who has spent his Estate in dressing.

'The Reasons offer'd by which we expected to gain the Approbation of the Publick, were are follows.

'First, That every one who is considerable enough to be a Mode,[6] and has any Imperfection of Nature of Chance, which it is possible to hide by the Advantage of Cloaths, may, by coming to this Repository, be furnish'd her self, and furnish all who are under the same Misfortune, with the most agreeable Manner of concealing it; and that on the other Side, every one who has any Beauty in Face or Shape, may be also furnish'd with the most agreeable Manner of shewing it.

'Secondly, That whereas some of our young Gentlemen who Travel, give us great reason to suspect that they only go abroad to make or improve a fancy for Dress, a Project of this nature may be a means to keep them at Home, which is in effect the keeping of so much Money in the Kingdom. And perhaps the Ballance of fashion in *Europe*, which now leans upon the side of *France*, may be so alter'd for the future, that it may become as common with *Frenchmen* to come to *England* for their finishing stroke of Breeding, as it has been for *Englishmen* to go to *France* for it.

'Thirdly, Whereas several great Scholars, who might have been otherwise useful to the World, have spent their time in studying to describe the Dresses of the Ancients from dark Hints, which they are feign to interpret and support with much Learning, it will from henceforth happen that they shall be freed from the trouble, and the World from useless Volumes. This Project will be a Registry to which Posterity may have recourse for the clearing such obscure Passages as tend that way in Authors, and therefore we shall not for the future submit ourselves to the learning of Etymology, which might perswade the Age to come, that the Farthingal was worn for cheapness, or the Furbeloe for warmth.

'Fourthly, Whereas they who are old themselves, have often a way of railing at the extravagance of Youth, and the whole Age in which their Children live; it is hoped that this ill Humour will be much

---

[6] *a Mode:* Someone who sets the fashion.

suppress'd, when we can have Recourse to the Fashions of their Times, produce them in our Vindication, and be able to shew that it might have been as expensive in Queen *Elizabeth*'s Time[7] only to wash and quill a Ruff,[8] as it is now to buy Cravats or Neck-Handkerchiefs.

'We desire also to have it taken Notice of, That because we would shew a particular Respect to Foreigners, which may induce them to perfect their Breeding here in a Knowledge which is very proper for pretty Gentlemen, we have conceived the Motto for the House in the Learned Language. There is to be a Picture over the Door, with a Looking-Glass and a Dressing-Chair in the Middle of it: Then on one Side are to be seen, above one another, Patch-Boxes, Pin-Cushions, and little Bottles; on the other, Powder-Bags, Puffs, Combs, and Brushes; beyond these, Swords with fine Knots, whose Points are hidden, and Fans almost closed, with the Handles downward, are to stand out interchangeably from the Sides, till they meet at the Top, and form a Semi-circle over the rest of the Figures: Beneath all, the Writing is to run in this pretty sounding manner:

> *Adeste, o quotquot sunt, Veneres, Gratiæ, Cupidines,*
> *En vobis adsunt in promptu*
> *Faces, Vincula, Spicula,*
> *Hinc eligite, sumite, regite.*[9]
>   I am, Sir,
>   *Your most humble Servant,*
>   A.B.'

The Proposal of my Correspondent I cannot but look upon as an ingenious Method of placing Persons (whose Parts make them ambitious to exert themselves in frivolous Things) in a Rank by themselves. In order to this, I would propose, That there be a Board of Directors of the Fashionable Society; and because it is a Matter of too much Weight for a private Man to determine alone, I should be highly obliged to my Correspondents if they would give in Lists of Persons qualified for this Trust. If the chief Coffee-houses, the Conversations of which Places are carry'd on by Persons, each of whom

---

[7] *Queen Elizabeth's Time:* Elizabeth I reigned from 1558 to 1603.

[8] *quill a Ruff:* To set the pleats or folds in the stiffly pleated collar of lace, linen, or muslin called a ruff, which was fashionable in the sixteenth and seventeenth centuries.

[9] . . . *sumite, regite:* Attend, all Venuses, Graces, and Cupids, / There are ready at hand for you / Torches, bands, darts, / From these choose, take up these weapons and rule.

has his little Number of Followers and Admirers, would name from among themselves two or three to be inserted, they shou'd be put up with great Faithfulness. Old Beaus are to be preferr'd in the first Place; but as that Sect, with relation to Dress, is almost extinct, it will, I fear, be absolutely necessary to take in all Time-Servers, properly so deem'd; that is, such as, without any Conviction of Conscience, or View of Interest, change with the World, and that meerly from a Terror of being out of Fashion. Such, also, who from Facility of Temper, and too much Obsequiousness, are vitious against their Will, and follow Leaders whom they do not approve, for Want of Courage to go their own Way, are capable Persons for this Superintendency. Those who are loth to grow old, or would do any thing contrary to the Course and Order of Things out of Fondness to be in Fashion, are proper Candidates. To conclude, those who are in Fashion without apparent Merit, must be suppos'd to have latent Qualities, which would appear in a Post of Direction, and therefore are to be regarded in forming these Lists. Any who shall be pleas'd, according to these, or what further Qualifications may occur to himself, to send a List, is desired to do it within Fourteen Days after this Date.

N. B. *The Place of the Physician to this Society, according to the last mentioned Qualification, is already engaged.*

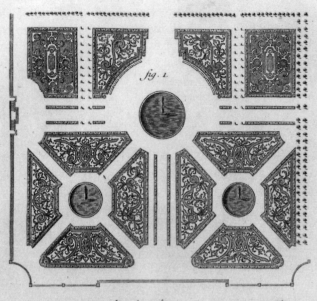

fig. 1.

10   20   30   40   50   100. *toises*.

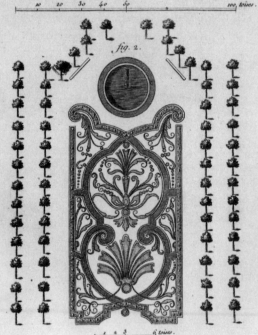

fig. 2.

1 2 3   6 *toises*.

Cultural Contexts

JONATHAN SWIFT

From *A Proposal for Correcting the English Tongue*

Jonathan Swift (1667–1745) was a prolific author of satiric narratives such as *A Tale of a Tub* and *Gulliver's Travels*, as well as poems and essays. An Anglican divine, Dean of St. Patrick's in Dublin, Swift was an intellectual fully engaged in the religious, social, literary, and political debates of his time. The selection here is from his *Proposal for Correcting, Improving and Ascertaining the English Tongue*, which appeared on May 17, 1713. It is one of the few texts that Swift ever published under his own name. While not overtly political in content, its Tory affiliations are readily apparent, for Swift was well known as the chief pamphleteer and political writer for the Tory ministry, and editor, from 1710, of the Tory paper *The Examiner*. In addition, Swift dedicates the work to Robert, Earl of Oxford and Mortimer, who was the leader of Queen Anne's Tory ministry and the Chancellor of the Exchequer. Swift

Left: "Agriculture Jardinage." *Below:* Woman's shoe, England, circa 1720. Los Angeles County Museum of Art, Alice Schott Bequest. Copyright © 1996 Museum Associates, Los Angeles County Museum of Art.

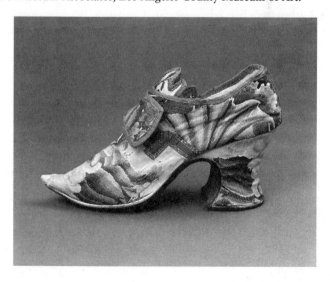

proposes the establishment of a Tory-based academy for correcting the English language. His anxiety about shifts in language usage, which he regarded as corruptions, persisted throughout his life and is a major topic in *A Tale of a Tub* and *Gulliver's Travels*. A few years before the appearance of the *Proposal,* Swift had published an essay in *The Tatler* (No. 230, September 28, 1710) voicing similar views.

The text excerpted here is taken from *A Proposal for Correcting the English Tongue, Polite Conversation, etc.,* ed. Herbert Davis (Oxford: Basil Blackwell, 1957), 9–16.

Having taken this Compass, I return to those Considerations upon our own Language, which I would humbly offer your Lordship. The Period wherein the *English* Tongue received most Improvement, I take to commence with the Beginning of Queen *Elizabeth*'s Reign,[1] and to conclude with the great Rebellion in Forty-two.[2] It is true, there was a very ill Taste both of Style and Wit, which prevailed under King *James* the First;[3] but that seems to have been corrected in the first Years of his Successor;[4] who, among many other Qualifications of an excellent Prince, was a great Patron of Learning. From that great Rebellion to this present Time, I am apt to doubt whether the Corruptions in our Language have not, at least, equalled the Refinements of it; and these Corruptions very few of the best Authors in our Age have wholly escaped. During the Usurpation,[5] such an Infusion of Enthusiastick Jargon prevailed in every Writing, as was not shaken off in many Years after. To this succeeded that Licentiousness

[1] *Queen Elizabeth's Reign:* Elizabeth I ruled from 1558 to 1603.
[2] *the great Rebellion in Forty-two:* The English Civil Wars between the Parliamentarians and the Royalists began in 1642 and continued until the utter defeat of the Royalists by Cromwell at the Battle of Worcester in 1651, after which Charles II fled England.
[3] *King James the First:* James I (1566–1625) ruled England from 1603 to 1625.
[4] *his Successor:* Charles I (1600–1649) ruled from 1625 until 1649, when he was executed for treason. His struggles with Parliament initiated the English Civil Wars.
[5] *the Usurpation:* The "usurpation" of the monarchy by Oliver Cromwell. Cromwell (1599–1658) was a soldier, a politician, and the Lord Protector during the Interregnum period 1653–58. Heading the army, Cromwell led the most successful opposition to the crown during the Civil Wars (see note 2 above), founding his Republic on military strength and dissolving the Parliament by force. In 1657, Cromwell turned down the offer of the Crown. He was briefly succeeded by his ineffectual son, Richard, before the Restoration of the Stuart monarchy with the return of Charles II in 1660.

which entered with the *Restoration*;[6] and from infecting our Religion and Morals, fell to corrupt our Language: Which last, was not like to be much improved by those, who, at that Time, made up the Court of King *Charles* the Second;[7] either such who had followed him in his Banishment, or who had been altogether conversant in the Dialect of those *Fanatick Times*; or young Men, who had been educated in the same Company; so that the *Court*, which used to be the Standard of Propriety, and Correctness of Speech, was then, and I think hath ever since continued the worst School in *England*, for that Accomplishment; and so will remain, till better Care be taken in the Education of our young Nobility; that they may set out into the World with some Foundation of Literature, in order to qualify them for Patterns of Politeness. The Consequence of this Defect upon our Language, may appear from the Plays, and other Compositions, written for Entertainment, within fifty Years past; filled with a Succession of affected Phrases, and new conceited Words, either borrowed from the current Style of the Court, or from those, who, under the Character of Men of Wit and Pleasure, pretended to give the Law. Many of these Refinements have already been long antiquated, and are now hardly intelligible; which is no Wonder, when they were the Product only of Ignorance and Caprice.

I have never known this great Town without one or more *Dunces* of Figure, who had Credit enough to give Rise to some new Word, and propagate it in most Conversations; although it had neither Humour nor Significancy. If it struck the present Taste, it was soon transferred into the Plays, and current Scribbles of the Week, and became an Addition to our Language; while the Men of Wit and Learning, instead of early obviating such Corruptions, were too often seduced to imitate and comply with them.

There is another Set of Men, who have contributed very much to the spoiling of the *English* Tongue; I mean the Poets, from the Time of the Restoration. These Gentlemen, although they could not be insensible how much our Language was already overstocked with Monosyllables, yet to save Time and Pains, introduced that barbarous Custom of abbreviating Words, to fit them to the Measure of their Verses; and this they have frequently done, so very injudiciously, as

---

[6] *the Restoration:* The Restoration of the Stuart monarchy with the return from France of Charles II (1630–1685) in 1660.

[7] *King Charles the Second:* Charles II ruled from 1660 to 1685; his court was noted for its license, crypto-Catholicism, and libertine sophistication.

to form such harsh unharmonious Sounds, that none but a *Northern Ear* could endure. They have joined the most obdurate Consonants, without one intervening Vowel, only to shorten a Syllable: And their Taste in Time became so depraved, that what was at first a poetical Licence, not to be justified, they made their Choice; alledging, that the Words pronounced at length, sounded faint and languid. This was a Pretence to take up the same Custom in Prose; so that most of the Books we see now-a-days, are full of those Manglings and Abbreviations. Instances of this Abuse are innumerable: What does your Lordship think of the Words, *Drudg'd, Disturb'd, Rebuk'd, Fledg'd*, and a Thousand others, every where to be met in Prose, as well as Verse? Where, by leaving out a Vowel to save a Syllable, we form so jarring a Sound, and so difficult to utter, that I have often wondered how it could ever obtain.

Another Cause (and perhaps borrowed from the former) which hath contributed not a little to the maiming of our Language, is a foolish Opinion, advanced of late Years, that we ought to spell exactly as we speak; which beside the obvious Inconvenience of utterly destroying our Etymology, would be a Thing we should never see an End of. Not only the several Towns and Counties of *England*, have a different Way of pronouncing; but even here in *London*, they clip their Words after one Manner about the Court, another in the City, and a third in the Suburbs; and in a few Years, it is probable, will all differ from themselves, as Fancy or Fashion shall direct: All which reduced to Writing, would entirely confound Orthography. [It would be just as wise as to shape our Bodies to our Cloathes and not our Cloaths to our bodyes.] Yet many People are so fond of this Conceit, that it is sometimes a difficult Matter to read modern Books and Pamphlets; where the Words are so curtailed, and varied from their original Spelling, that whoever hath been used to plain *English*, will hardly know them by Sight.

Several young Men at the Universities, terribly possessed with the Fear of Pedantry, run into a worse Extream; and think all Politeness to consist in reading the daily Trash sent down to them from hence: This they call *knowing the World*, and *reading Men and Manners*. Thus furnished, they come up to Town; reckon all their Errors for Accomplishments, borrow the newest Set of Phrases; and if they take a Pen into their Hands, all the odd Words they have picked up in a Coffee-House, or a Gaming Ordinary, are produced as Flowers of Style; and the Orthography refined to the utmost. To this we owe those monstrous Productions, which under the Names of *Trips, Spies*,

Amusements, and other conceited Appellations, have over-run us for some Years past. To this we owe that strange Race of Wits, who tell us they write to the *Humour of the Age*. And I wish I could say, these quaint Fopperies were wholly absent from graver Subjects. In short, I would undertake to shew your Lordship several Pieces, where the Beauties of this Kind are so predominant, that with all your Skill in Languages, you could never be able either to read or understand them.

But I am very much mistaken, if many of these false Refinements among us, do not arise from a Principle which would quite destroy their Credit, if it were well understood and considered. For I am afraid, my Lord, that with all the real good Qualities of our Country, we are naturally not very polite. This perpetual Disposition to shorten our Words, by retrenching the Vowels, is nothing else but a Tendency to lapse into the Barbarity of those *Northern* Nations from whom we are descended, and whose Languages labour all under the same Defect. For it is worthy our Observation, that the *Spaniards*, the *French*, and the *Italians*, although derived from the same *Northern* Ancestors with our selves, are, with the utmost Difficulty taught to pronounce our Words; which the *Swedes* and *Danes*, as well as the *Germans* and the *Dutch*, attain to with Ease, because our Syllables resemble theirs, in the Roughness and Frequency of Consonants. Now, as we struggle with an ill Climate to improve the nobler Kinds of Fruits; are at the Expence of Walls to receive and reverberate the faint Rays of the Sun, and fence against the *Northern* Blasts; we sometimes by the Help of a good Soil equal the Productions of warmer Countries, who have no need to be at so much Cost or Care: It is the same Thing with respect to the politer Arts among us; and the same Defect of Heat which gives a Fierceness to our Natures, may contribute to that Roughness of our Language, which bears some Analogy to the harsh Fruit of colder Countries. For I do not reckon, that we want a *Genius* more than the rest of our Neighbours: But your Lordship will be of my Opinion, that we ought to struggle with these natural Disadvantages as much as we can; and be careful whom we employ, whenever we design to correct them; which is a Work that hath hitherto been assumed by the least qualified Hands: So that if the Choice had been left to me, I would rather have trusted the Refinement of our Language, as far as it relates to Sound, to the Judgment of the Women, than of illiterate Court-Fops, half-witted Poets, and University-Boys. For, it is plain, that Women in their Manner of corrupting Words, do naturally discard the Consonants, as we do the Vowels. What I am going to tell your Lordship, appears very trifling; that more than once, where some of both Sexes were in Company, I have persuaded two or three of each to take a Pen, and write down a Number of Letters joined together, just as it came into their Heads; and upon reading this Gibberish we have found that which the Men had writ, by the frequent encountering of rough Consonants, to sound like *High-Dutch*; and the other by the Women, like *Italian*, abounded in Vowels and Liquids. Now, although I would by no Means give Ladies the Trouble of advising us in the Reformation of our Language; yet I cannot help thinking, that since they have been left out of all Meetings, except Parties at Play, or where worse Designs are carried on, our Conversation hath very much degenerated.

In order to reform our Language; I conceive, my Lord, that a free judicious Choice should be made of such Persons, as are generally allowed to be best qualified for such a Work, without any regard to Quality, Party, or Profession. These to a certain Number, at least, should assemble at some appointed Time and Place, and fix on Rules by which they design to proceed. What Methods they will take, is not for me to prescribe. Your Lordship, and other Persons in great Employment, might please to be of the Number: And I am afraid, such a Society would want your Instruction and Example, as much as your Protection: For I have, not without a little Envy, observed of late the Style of some great Ministers very much to exceed that of any other Productions.

The Persons who are to undertake this Work, will have the Example of the *French* before them, to imitate where these have proceeded right, and to avoid their Mistakes. Besides the Grammar-part, wherein we are allowed to be very defective, they will observe many gross Improprieties, which however authorized by Practice, and grown familiar, ought to be discarded. They will find many Words that deserve to be utterly thrown out of our Language; many more to be corrected, and perhaps not a few, long since antiquated, which ought to be restored, on Account of their Energy and Sound.

But what I have most at Heart, is, that some Method should be thought on for *Ascertaining* and *Fixing* our Language for ever, after such Alterations are made in it as shall be thought requisite. For I am of Opinion, that it is better a Language should not be wholly perfect, than that it should be perpetually changing; and we must give over at one Time or other, or at length infallibly change for the worse: As the *Romans* did, when they began to quit their Simplicity of Style for affected Refinements; such as we meet in *Tacitus* and other Authors, which ended by Degrees in many Barbarities, even before the *Goths* had invaded *Italy*.[8]

The Fame of our Writers is usually confined to these two Islands; and it is hard it should be limited in *Time* as much as *Place*, by the perpetual Variations of our Speech. It is your Lordship's Observation, that if it were not for the *Bible* and *Common-Prayer-Book*[9] in the vulgar Tongue, we should hardly be able to understand any thing that was written among us an Hundred Years ago; which is certainly true: For those Books being perpetually read in Churches, have proved a Kind of Standard for Language, especially to the common People. And I doubt whether the Alterations since introduced, have added much to the Beauty or Strength of the *English* Tongue, although they have taken off a great deal from that *Simplicity*, which is one of the greatest Perfections in any Language. You, my Lord, who are so conversant in the sacred Writings, and so great a Judge of them in their Originals, will agree, that no Translation our Country ever yet produced, hath come up to that of the *Old* and *New Testament*: And by the many beautiful Passages which I have often had the Honour to hear your Lordship cite from thence, I am persuaded that the Translators of the Bible were Masters of an *English* Stile much fitter for that Work, than any we see in our present Writings; which I take to be owing to the *Simplicity* that runs through the Whole. Then, as to the greatest Part of our *Liturgy*, compiled long before the Translation of the *Bible* now in use, and little altered since; there seem to be in it as great Strains of true sublime Eloquence, as are any where to be found in our Language; which every Man of good Taste will observe in the *Communion-Service*, that of *Burial*, and other Parts.

But, where I say that I would have our Language, after it is duly correct, always to last; I do not mean that it should never be enlarged: Provided, that no Word, which a Society shall give a Sanction to, be afterwards antiquated and exploded, they may have Liberty to receive whatever new ones they shall find Occasion for: Because then the old Books will yet be always valuable according to their intrinsick

---

[8] *the Goths had invaded Italy:* The Goths were a Germanic people who invaded Italy in A.D. 401, sacking Rome in 410.

[9] *Common-Prayer-Book:* The Book of Common Prayer, the liturgical book used in the Anglican church, was first authorized in 1549 and subsequently underwent several revisions. The 1662 version is now used in almost all Anglican services. A Protestant liturgy written in English ("the vulgar Tongue"), the Book of Common Prayer, along with King James I's authorized translation of the Bible in the early seventeenth century, set a standard for English usage.

Worth, and not thrown aside on Account of unintelligible Words and Phrases, which appear harsh and uncouth, only because they are out of Fashion. Had the *Roman* Tongue continued vulgar in that City till this Time; it would have been absolutely necessary, from the mighty Changes that have been made in Law and Religion; from the many Terms of Art required in trade and in War; from the new Inventions that have happened in the World; from the vast spreading of Navigation and Commerce; with many other obvious Circumstances, to have made great Additions to that Language; yet the Antients would still have been read, and understood with Pleasure and Ease. The *Greek* Tongue received many Enlargements between the Time of *Homer*, and that of *Plutarch*;[10] yet the former Author was probably as well understood in *Trajan*'s Time, as the latter. What *Horace* says of *Words going off, and perishing like Leaves, and new ones coming in their Place*, is a Misfortune he laments, rather than a Thing he approves: But I cannot see why this should be absolutely necessary, or if it were, what would have become of his *Monumentum ære perennius*.[11]

JONATHAN SWIFT

Hints towards an Essay on Conversation

As part of his program to correct the English language, Swift proposed measures to improve conversation in his tract *Hints towards an Essay on Conversation*. This text belongs to the same period as his essay on the corruption of English published in *Tatler* No. 230, September 17, 1710. Unlike the *Proposal* (1713) and *A Complete Collection of Polite and Ingenious Conversation* (1738), *Hints towards an Essay on Conversation* never appeared independently; it was first published in 1763 in Faulkner's collection of Swift's *Works* (vol. 10). The views it outlines are dramatized in *A Complete Collection of Polite and Ingenious Conversation*, a parody of the inane talk prevalent in polite circles. For more in-

[10] *between the Time of Homer, and that of Plutarch:* Homer (ninth century B.C.) was the author of the Greek epics the *Iliad* and the *Odyssey*; Plutarch (c. 46–after 119) was a first-century A.D. historical biographer. Trajan (53–117) ruled the Roman Empire from A.D. 98 to 117.

[11] *Monumentum ære perennius:* "A monument more enduring than bronze," Horace, *Odes* 3.30.1, a reference to Horace's own poetry.

formation on Jonathan Swift, see other headnotes (pp. 403, 418, 428, and 577).

The text excerpted here is taken from *A Proposal for Correcting the English Tongue, Polite Conversation, etc.*, ed. Herbert Davis (Oxford: Basil Blackwell, 1957), 87–95.

I have observed few obvious Subjects to have been so seldom, or, at least, so slightly handled as this; and, indeed, I know few so difficult, to be treated as it ought, nor yet upon which there seemeth to be so much to be said.

Most Things, pursued by Men for the Happiness of publick or private Life, our Wit or Folly have so refined, that they seldom subsist but in Idea; a true Friend, a good Marriage, a perfect Form of Government, with some others, require so many Ingredients, so good in their several Kinds, and so much Niceness in mixing them, that for some thousands of Years Men have despaired of reducing their Schemes to Perfection: But in Conversation, it is, or might be otherwise; for here we are only to avoid a Multitude of Errors, which, although a Matter of some Difficulty, may be in every Man's Power, for Want of which it remaineth as meer an Idea as the other. Therefore it seemeth to me, that the truest Way to understand Conversation, is to know the Faults and Errors to which it is subject, and from thence, every Man to form Maxims to himself whereby it may be regulated; because it requireth few Talents to which most Men are not born, or at least may not acquire without any great Genius or Study. For Nature hath left every Man a Capacity of being agreeable, though not of shining in Company, and there are an hundred Men sufficiently qualified for both, who by a very few Faults, that they might correct in half an Hour, are not so much as tolerable.

I was prompted to write my Thoughts upon this Subject by mere Indignation, to reflect that so useful and innocent a Pleasure, so fitted for every Period and Condition of Life, and so much in all Men's Power, should be so much neglected and abused.

And in this Discourse it will be necessary to note those Errors that are obvious, as well as others which are seldomer observed, since there are few so obvious or acknowledged, into which most Men, some Time or other, are not apt to run.

For Instance: Nothing is more generally exploded than the Folly of Talking too much, yet I rarely remember to have seen five People together, where some one among them hath not been predominant in that Kind, to the great Constraint and Disgust of all the rest. But among such as deal in Multitudes of Words, none are comparable to the sober deliberate Talker, who proceedeth with much Thought and Caution, maketh his Preface, brancheth out into several Digressions, findeth a Hint that putteth him in Mind of another Story, which he promiseth to tell you when this is done; cometh back regularly to his Subject, cannot readily call to Mind some Person's Name, holdeth his Head, complaineth of his Memory; the whole Company all this while in Suspence; at length says, it is no Matter, and so goes on. And, to crown the Business, it perhaps proveth at last a Story the Company hath heard fifty Times before; or, at best, some insipid Adventure of the Relater.

Another general Fault in Conversation is, That of those who affect to talk of themselves: Some, without any Ceremony, will run over the History of their Lives; will relate the Annals of their Diseases, with the several Symptoms and Circumstances of them; will enumerate the Hardships and Injustice they have suffered in Court, in Parliament, in Love, or in Law. Others are more dexterous, and with great Art will lie on the Watch to hook in their own Praise: They will call a Witness to remember, they always foretold what would happen in such a Case, but none would believe them; they advised such a Man from the Beginning, and told him the Consequences just as they happened; but he would have his own Way. Others make a Vanity of telling their Faults; they are the strangest Men in the World; they cannot dissemble, they own it is a Folly; they have lost Abundance of Advantages by it; but, if you would give them the World they cannot help it; there is something in their Nature that abhors Insincerity and Constraint; with many other unsufferable Topicks of the same Altitude.

Of such mighty Importance every Man is to himself, and ready to think he is so to others; without once making this easy and obvious Reflection, that his Affairs can have no more Weight with other Men, than theirs have with him; and how little that is, he is sensible enough.

Where Company hath met, I often have observed two Persons discover, by some Accident, that they were bred together at the same School or University; after which the rest are condemned to Silence, and to listen while these two are refreshing each other's Memory with the arch Tricks and Passages of themselves and their Comrades.

I know a Great Officer of the Army, who will sit for some time with a supercilious and impatient Silence, full of Anger and Contempt for those who are talking; at length of a sudden demand Audience, decide the Matter in a short dogmatical Way; then withdraw within himself again, and vouchsafe to talk no more, until his Spirits circulate again to the same Point.

There are some Faults in Conversation, which none are so subject to as the Men of Wit, nor ever so much as when they are with each other. If they have opened their Mouths, without endeavouring to say a witty Thing, they think it is so many Words lost; it is a Torment to the Hearers, as much as to themselves, to see them upon the Rack for Invention, and in perpetual Constraint, with so little Success. They must do something extraordinary, in order to acquit themselves, and answer their Character; else the Standers-by may be disappointed, and be apt to think them only like the rest of Mortals. I have known two Men of Wit industriously brought together, in order to entertain the Company, where they have made a very ridiculous Figure, and provided all the Mirth at their own Expence.

I know a Man of Wit, who is never easy but where he can be allowed to dictate and preside; he neither expecteth to be informed or entertained, but to display his own Talents. His Business is to be good Company, and not good Conversation; and, therefore, he chuseth to frequent those who are content to listen, and profess themselves his Admirers. And, indeed, the worst Conversation I ever remember to have heard in my Life, was that at *Will's* Coffee-house,[1] where the Wits (as they were called) used formerly to assemble; that is to say, five or six Men, who had writ Plays, or at least Prologues, or had Share in a Miscellany, came thither, and entertained one another with their trifling Composures, in so important an Air, as if they had been the noblest Efforts of human Nature, or that the Fate of Kingdoms depended on them; and they were usually attended with an humble Audience of young Students from the Inns of Courts,[2] or the Universities, who, at due Distance, listened to these Oracles, and returned Home with great Contempt for their Law and Philosophy, their Heads filled with Trash, under the Name of Politeness, Criticism and Belles Lettres.

---

[1] *Will's Coffee-house:* A coffeehouse associated with a literary clientele.

[2] *Inns of Courts:* The four Inns of Court were housed along Fleet Street in London. Originally owned by the medieval religious and military order the Knights Templar, who built a residence there in the twelfth century, this series of buildings, known collectively as the Temple, was presented by James I to lawyers for their professional use. It housed both residential and professional legal apartments. A bencher is a member of the inner or higher bar who acts as a governor of one of the Inns of Court.

By these Means the Poets, for many Years past, were all over-run with Pedantry. For, as I take it, the Word is not properly used; because Pedantry is the too frequent or unseasonable obtruding our own Knowledge in common Discourse, and placing too great a Value upon it; by which Definition Men of the Court or the Army may be as guilty of Pedantry as a Philosopher, or a Divine; and, it is the same Vice in Women, when they are over-copious upon the Subject of their Petticoats, or their Fans, or their China: For which Reason, although it be a Piece of Prudence, as well as good Manners, to put Men upon talking on Subjects they are best versed in, yet that is a Liberty a wise Man could hardly take; because, beside the Imputation of Pedantry, it is what he would never improve by.

This great Town is usually provided with some Player, Mimick, or Buffoon, who hath a general Reception at the good Tables; familiar and domestick with Persons of the first Quality, and usually sent for at every Meeting to divert the Company; against which I have no Objection. You go there as to a Farce, or a Puppet-Show; your Business is only to laugh in Season, either out of Inclination or Civility, while this merry Companion is acting his Part. It is a Business he hath undertaken, and we are to suppose he is paid for his Day's Work. I only quarrel, when in select and private Meetings, where Men of Wit and Learning are invited to pass an Evening, this Jester should be admitted to run over his Circle of Tricks, and make the whole Company unfit for any other Conversation, besides the Indignity of confounding Men's Talents at so shameful a Rate.

Raillery is the finest Part of Conversation; but, as it is our usual Custom to counterfeit and adulterate whatever is dear to us, so we have done with this, and turned it all into what is generally called Repartee, or being smart; just as when an expensive Fashion cometh up, those who are not able to reach it, content themselves with some paltry Imitation. It now passeth for Raillery to run a Man down in Discourse, to put him out of Countenance, and make him ridiculous, sometimes to expose the Defects of his Person, or Understanding; on all which Occasions he is obliged not to be angry, to avoid the Imputation of not being able to take a Jest. It is admirable to observe one who is dexterous at this Art, singling out a weak Adversary, getting the Laugh on his Side, and then carrying all before him. The *French*, from whom we borrow the Word, have a quite different Idea of the Thing, and so had we in the politer Age of our Fathers. Raillery was to say something that at first appeared a Reproach, or Reflection; but, by some Turn of Wit unexpected and surprising, ended always in a Compliment, and to the Advantage of the Person it was addressed to. And, surely, one of the best Rules in Conversation is, never to say a Thing which any of the Company can reasonably wish we had rather left unsaid; nor can there any Thing be well more contrary to the Ends for which People meet together, than to part unsatisfied with each other, or themselves.

There are two Faults in Conversation, which appear very different, yet arise from the same Root, and are equally blameable; I mean, an Impatience to interrupt others, and the Uneasiness at being interrupted ourselves. The two chief Ends of Conversation are to entertain and improve those we are among, or to receive those Benefits ourselves; which whoever will consider, cannot easily run into either of those two Errors; because when any Man speaketh in Company, it is to be supposed he doth it for his Hearer's Sake, and not his own; so that common Discretion will teach us not to force their Attention, if they are not willing to lend it; nor on the other Side, to interrupt him who is in Possession, because that is in the grossest Manner to give the Preference to our own good Sense.

There are some People, whose good Manners will not suffer them to interrupt you; but what is almost as bad, will discover Abundance of Impatience, and lye upon the Watch until you have done, because they have started something in their own Thoughts which they long to be delivered of. Mean Time, they are so far from regarding what passes, that their Imaginations are wholly turned upon what they have in Reserve, for fear it should slip out of their Memory; and thus they confine their Invention, which might otherwise range over a hundred Things full as good, and that might be much more naturally introduced.

There is a Sort of rude Familiarity, which some People, by practising among their Intimates, have introduced into their general Conversation, and would have it pass for innocent Freedom, or Humour, which is a dangerous Experiment in our Northern Climate, where all the little Decorum and Politeness we have are purely forced by Art, and are so ready to lapse into Barbarity. This among the *Romans*, was the Raillery of Slaves, of which we have many Instances in *Plautus*.[3] It seemeth to have been introduced among us by *Cromwell*, who, by preferring the Scum of the People, made it a Court Entertain-

---

[3] *Plautus*: Titus Maccius Plautus (254?–184 B.C.) was a Roman comic dramatist whose works, loosely adapted from Greek plays, established a Roman drama in the Latin language.

ment, of which I have heard many Particulars; and, considering all Things were turned upside down, it was reasonable and judicious; although it was a Piece of Policy found out to ridicule a Point of Honour in the other Extream, when the smallest Word misplaced among Gentlemen ended in a Duel.

There are some Men excellent at telling a Story, and provided with a plentiful Stock of them, which they can draw out upon Occasion in all Companies; and, considering how low Conversation runs now among us, it is not altogether a contemptible Talent; however, it is subject to two unavoidable Defects; frequent Repetition, and being soon exhausted; so that whoever valueth this Gift in himself, hath need of a good Memory, and ought frequently to shift his Company, that he may not discover the Weakness of his Fund; for those who are thus endowed, have seldom any other Revenue, but live upon the main Stock.

Great Speakers in Publick, are seldom agreeable in private Conversation, whether their Faculty be natural, or acquired by Practice and often venturing. Natural Elocution, although it may seem a Paradox, usually springeth from a Barrenness of Invention and of Words, by which Men who have only one Stock of Notions upon every Subject, and one Set of Phrases to express them in, they swim upon the Superficies, and offer themselves on every Occasion; therefore, Men of much Learning, and who know the Compass of a Language, are generally the worst Talkers on a sudden, until much Practice hath inured and emboldened them, because they are confounded with Plenty of Matter, Variety of Notions, and of Words, which they cannot readily chuse, but are perplexed and entangled by too great a Choice; which is no Disadvantage in private Conversation; where, on the other Side, the Talent of Haranguing is, of all others, most insupportable.

Nothing hath spoiled Men more for Conversation, than the Character of being Wits, to support which, they never fail of encouraging a Number of Followers and Admirers, who list themselves in their Service, wherein they find their Accounts on both Sides, by pleasing their mutual Vanity. This hath given the former such an Air of Superiority, and made the latter so pragmatical, that neither of them are well to be endured. I say nothing here of the Itch of Dispute and Contradiction, telling of Lies, or of those who are troubled with the Disease called the Wandering of the Thoughts, that they are never present in Mind at what passeth in Discourse; for whoever labours under any of these Possessions, is as unfit for Conversation as a Madman in Bedlam.

I think I have gone over most of the Errors in Conversation, that have fallen under my Notice or Memory, except some that are merely personal, and others too gross to need exploding; such as lewd or prophane Talk; but I pretend only to treat the Errors of Conversation in general, and not the several Subjects of Discourse, which would be infinite. Thus we see how human Nature is most debased, by the Abuse of that Faculty which is held the great Distinction between Men and Brutes; and how little Advantage we make of that which might be the greatest, the most lasting, and the most innocent, as well as useful Pleasure of Life: In Default of which, we are forced to take up with those poor Amusements of Dress and Visiting, or the more pernicious ones of Play, Drink and Vicious Amours, whereby the Nobility and Gentry of both Sexes are entirely corrupted both in Body and Mind, and have lost all Notions of Love, Honour, Friendship, Generosity; which, under the Name of Fopperies, have been for some Time laughed out of Doors.

This Degeneracy of Conversation, with the pernicious Consequences thereof upon our Humours and Dispositions, hath been owing, among other Causes, to the Custom arisen, for some Years past, of excluding Women from any Share in our Society, further than in Parties at Play, or Dancing, or in the Pursuit of an Amour. I take the highest Period of Politeness in *England* (and it is of the same Date in *France*) to have been the peaceable Part of King *Charles* the First's Reign;[4] and from what we read of those Times, as well as from the Accounts I have formerly met with from some who lived in that Court, the Methods then used for raising and cultivating Conversation, were altogether different from ours: Several Ladies, whom we find celebrated by the Poets of that Age, had Assemblies at their Houses, where Persons of the best Understanding, and of both Sexes, met to pass the Evenings in discoursing upon whatever agreeable Subjects were occasionally started; and, although we are apt to ridicule the sublime Platonic Notions they had, or personated, in Love and Friendship, I conceive their Refinements were grounded upon Reason, and that a little Grain of the Romance is no ill Ingredient to preserve and exalt the Dignity of human Nature, without which it is apt to degenerate into every Thing that is sordid, vicious and low. If there were no other Use in the Conversation of Ladies, it is sufficient that it would lay a Restraint upon those odious Topicks of Immodesty and Indecencies, into which the Rudeness of our

---

[4] *King Charles the First's Reign:* Charles I ruled from 1625 to 1649.

Northern Genius is so apt to fall. And, therefore, it is observable in those sprightly Gentlemen about the Town, who are so very dexterous at entertaining a Vizard Mask in the Park or the Playhouse, that, in the Company of Ladies of Virtue and Honour, they are silent and disconcerted, and out of their Element.

There are some People who think they sufficiently acquit themselves, and entertain their Company with relating of Facts of no Consequence, nor at all out of the Road of such common Incidents as happen every Day; and this I have observed more frequently among the *Scots* than any other Nation, who are very careful not to omit the minutest Circumstances of Time or Place; which Kind of Discourse, if it were not a little relieved by the uncouth Terms and Phrases, as well as Accent and Gesture peculiar to that Country, would be hardly tolerable. It is not a Fault in Company to talk much; but to continue it long, is certainly one; for, if the Majority of those who are got together be naturally silent or cautious, the Conversation will flag, unless it be often renewed by one among them, who can start new Subjects, provided he doth not dwell upon them, but leaveth Room for Answers and Replies.

JONATHAN SWIFT

A Digression Concerning Critics
(From A Tale of a Tub*)*

Written during the years 1696–99, while Swift was serving as secretary to Sir William Temple at Moor Park, *A Tale of a Tub* was first published in 1704 and again in final form in 1710. It is the central text in a group of three that also includes *The Battle of the Books* and *The Mechanical Operation of the Spirit.* The earliest of Swift's prose satires, *A Tale* takes as its object the corruption in religion and learning. Through the allegorical story of three brothers, Peter, Martin, and Jack, the tale proper narrates the splintering of Christianity into Catholicism and the Protestant sects established by Calvin and Luther. But this story is regularly interrupted by the digressions of the mad modern author, who serves as Swift's satiric persona. Ultimately, the distinction between the tale and the digressions breaks down as the mad author succumbs to the complete disordering of his senses.

In this excerpt, the "Digression Concerning Critics," Swift parodies a defense of modern criticism. Like *The Battle of the Books, A Tale of a Tub* participates in the debate between the ancients and moderns, a kind of seventeenth-century cultural war. Those, including Swift and Sir William Temple, who took up the side of the ancients, argued that the Greco-Roman classics provided unsurpassed models for contemporary literature. In their view, the abandonment of reason and common sense and the onslaught of a peculiarly modern form of pedantry rooted in an adherence to the empty letter of the text rather than to its spirit were corrupting learning. On the other side, proponents of the modern, often citing the example of the scientific progress achieved in the seventeenth century, affirmed that contemporary literature might well surpass that of the ancients and so provide its own standards of excellence. Moreover, like the great classical scholar Richard Bentley, the moderns asserted that ancient texts could be corrected and improved by contemporary editorial methodologies based on philological and historical research. For more information on Jonathan Swift, see other Swift headnotes (pp. 403, 410, 428, and 577).

The text reprinted here is taken from *Jonathan Swift's A Tale of a Tub, with Other Early Works 1696–1707*, ed. Herbert Davis (Oxford: Basil Blackwell, 1957), 56–64.

Tho' I have been hitherto as cautious as I could, upon all Occasions, most nicely to follow the Rules and Methods of Writing, laid down by the Example of our illustrious *Moderns*; yet has the unhappy shortness of my Memory led me into an Error, from which I must immediately extricate my self, before I can decently pursue my Principal Subject. I confess with Shame, it was an unpardonable Omission to proceed so far as I have already done, before I had performed the due Discourses, Expostulatory, Supplicatory, or Deprecatory with my *good Lords* the *Criticks*. Towards some Atonement for this grievous Neglect, I do here make humbly bold to present them with a short Account of themselves and their *Art*, by looking into the Original and Pedigree of the Word, as it is generally understood among us, and very briefly considering the antient and present State thereof.

By the Word, *Critick*, at this Day so frequent in all Conversations, there have sometimes been distinguished three very different Species of Mortal Men, according as I have read in *Antient Books and Pamphlets*. For first, by this Term were understood such Persons as invented or drew up Rules for themselves and the World, by observing which, a careful Reader might be able to pronounce upon the productions of the *Learned*, form his Taste to a true Relish of the *Sublime* and the *Admirable*, and divide every Beauty of Matter or of Style from the Corruption that Apes it: In their common perusal of Books, singling out the Errors and Defects, the Nauseous, the Fulsome, the Dull, and the Impertinent, with the Caution of a Man that walks thro' *Edenborough* Streets in a Morning, who is indeed as careful as he can, to watch diligently, and spy out the Filth in his Way, not that he is curious to observe the Colour and Complexion of the Ordure, or take its Dimensions, much less to be padling in, or tasting it: but only with a Design to come out as cleanly as he may. These men seem, tho' very erroneously, to have understood the Appellation of, *Critick* in a literal Sence; That one principal part of his Office was to Praise and Acquit; and, that a *Critick*, who sets up to Read, only for an Occasion of Censure and Reproof, is a Creature as barbarous as a *Judge*, who should take up a Resolution to hang all Men that came before him upon a Tryal.

Again; by the Word *Critick*, have been meant, the Restorers of Antient Learning from the Worms, and Graves, and Dust of Manuscripts.

Now, the Races of these two have been for some Ages utterly extinct; and besides, to discourse any farther of them would not be at all to my purpose.

The Third, and Noblest Sort, is that of the *TRUE CRITICK*, whose Original is the most Antient of all. Every *True Critick* is a Hero born, descending in a direct Line from a Celestial Stem, by *Momus* and *Hybris*, who begat *Zoilus*, who begat *Tigellius*,[1] who begat *Etcætera* the Elder, who begat *Bently*, and *Rymer*, and *Wotton*, and *Perrault*, and *Dennis*,[2] who begat *Etcætera* the Younger.

And these are the *Criticks* from whom the Commonwealth of Learning has in all Ages received such immense benefits, that the

---

[1] *Zoilus . . . Tigellius:* Ancient literary critics. Zoilus attacked the Greek epic poet Homer, and Tigellius the Roman lyrical poet Horace.

[2] *Bently . . . Rymer . . . Wotton . . . Perrault . . . Dennis:* The most influential critics of the day. Richard Bentley (1661–1742) was a classical scholar and critic. Thomas Rymer (1643–1713) was a literary critic who introduced into England the principles of French neoclassical criticism. Sir Henry Wotton (1568–1639), an English poet, diplo-

Gratitude of their Admirers placed their Origine in Heaven, among those of *Hercules, Theseus, Perseus,*[3] and other great Deservers of Mankind. But Heroick Virtue it self hath not been exempt from the Obloquy of Evil Tongues. For it hath been objected, that those Antient Heroes, famous for their Combating so many Giants, and Dragons, and Robbers, were in their own Persons a greater Nuisance to Mankind, than any of those Monsters they subdued; and therefore, to render their Obligations more Compleat, when all *other* Vermin were destroy'd, should in Conscience have concluded with the same Justice upon themselves: as *Hercules* most generously did, and hath upon that Score, procured to himself more Temples and Votaries than the best of his Fellows. For these Reasons, I suppose it is, why some have conceived, it would be very expedient for the Publick Good of Learning, that every *True Critick,* as soon as he had finished his Task assigned, should immediately deliver himself up to Ratsbane, or Hemp, or from some convenient *Altitude,* and that no Man's Pretensions to so illustrious a Character, should by any means be received, before That Operation were performed.

Now, from this Heavenly Descent of *Criticism,* and the close Analogy it bears to *Heroick Virtue,* 'tis easie to Assign the proper Employment of a *True Antient Genuine Critick*; which is, to travel thro' this vast World of Writings: to pursue and hunt those Monstrous Faults bred within them: to drag out the lurking Errors like *Cacus* from his Den;[4] to multiply them like *Hydra*'s Heads; and rake them together

---

mat, connoisseur, and friend of the seventeenth-century poets John Donne and John Milton, took the side of the ancients. Charles Perrault (1628–1703) was a French poet and prose writer and a leading member of the Académie française; he also played a prominent part in the debate between the ancients and moderns, taking up the cause of the moderns. John Dennis (1657–1734), an English critic and dramatist, was later embroiled in a debate with the poet Alexander Pope over the place of passion in poetry.

[3] *Hercules, Theseus, Perseus:* Legendary Greek heroes. Hercules was the son of Zeus and Alcmene and is famous for the twelve labors he performed in the service of King Eurystheus. Theseus, the great Attic hero, was the son of Aegeus, King of Athens, or of Poseidon, god of the sea. Theseus is renowned for consolidating the city-state of Attica and for killing the Cretan Minotaur, a monster half-man and half-bull. Perseus, the son of Zeus, killed the monstrous Gorgon Medusa.

[4] *like Cacus from his Den:* In Greek and Roman legend, Cacus, half-man and half-satyr, and the son of the fire god Vulcan, stole cattle from the hero Hercules and hid them in his cave in the Aventine hill in Rome. Hercules burst in, killed Cacus, and retrieved his cattle.

like *Augeas*'s Dung.[5] Or else to drive away a sort of *Dangerous Fowl*, who have a perverse Inclination to plunder the best Branches of the *Tree of Knowledge*, like those *Stymphalian* Birds[6] that eat up the Fruit.

These Reasonings will furnish us with an adequate Definition of a *True Critick*; that, He is *a Discoverer and Collector of Writers Faults.* Which may be farther put beyond Dispute by the following Demonstration: That whoever will examine the Writings in all kinds, wherewith this antient Sect has honour'd the World, shall immediately find, from the whole Thread and Tenour of them, that the Idea's of the Authors have been altogether conversant, and taken up with the Faults and Blemishes, and Oversights, and Mistakes of other Writers; and let the Subject treated on be whatever it will, their Imaginations are so entirely possess'd and replete with the Defects of other Pens, that the very Quintessence of what is bad, does of necessity distill into their own: by which means the Whole appears to be nothing else but an *Abstract* of the *Criticisms* themselves have made.

Having thus briefly consider'd the Original and Office of a *Critick*, as the Word is understood in its most noble and universal Acceptation, I proceed to refute the Objections of those who argue from the Silence and Pretermission of Authors; by which they pretend to prove, that the very Art of *Criticism*, as now exercised, and by me explained, is wholly *Modern*; and consequently, that the *Criticks* of *Great Britain* and *France*, have no Title to an Original so Antient and Illustrious as I have deduced. Now, If I can clearly make out on the contrary, that the most Antient Writers have particularly described, both the Person and the Office of a *True Critick*, agreeable to the Definition laid down by me; their Grand Objection, from the Silence of Authors, will fall to the Ground.

I confess to have for a long time born a part in this general Error; from which I should never have acquitted my self, but thro' the Assistance of our Noble *Moderns*; whose most edifying Volumes I turn indefatigably over Night and Day, for the Improvement of my Mind, and the good of my Country: These have with unwearied Pains made

---

[5] *Hydra's Heads . . . Augeas's Dung:* In Greek legend, the Hydra was a monster with nine heads, the central one of which was immortal. The destruction of the Hydra was one of Hercules' twelve labors. In Greek legend, King Augeus, ruler of the Epeians in Elis, had a huge stable, the cleaning of which was another of Hercules' twelve labors.

[6] *Stymphalian Birds:* In Greek legend, the man-eating birds of the Stymphalian marshes were killed by Hercules as one of his twelve labors.

many useful Searches into the weak sides of the *Antients*, and given us a comprehensive List of them. Besides, they have proved beyond contradiction, that the very finest Things delivered of old, have been long since invented, and brought to Light by much later Pens, and that the noblest Discoveries those *Antients* ever made, of Art or of Nature, have all been produced by the transcending Genius of the present Age. Which clearly shews, how little Merit those *Ancients* can justly pretend to; and takes off that blind Admiration paid them by Men in a Corner, who have the Unhappiness of conversing too little with *present Things*. Reflecting maturely upon all this, and taking in the whole Compass of Human Nature, I easily concluded, that these *Antients*, highly sensible of their many Imperfections, must needs have endeavoured from some Passages in their Works, to obviate, soften, or divert the Censorious Reader, by *Satyr*, or *Panegyrick* upon the *True Criticks*, in Imitation of their *Masters* the *Moderns*. Now, in the *Common-Places* of both these, I was plentifully instructed, by a long Course of useful Study in *Prefaces* and *Prologues*; and therefore immediately resolved to try what I could discover of either, by a diligent Perusal of the most Antient Writers, and especially those who treated of the earliest Times. Here I found to my great Surprize, that although they all entred, upon Occasion, into particular Descriptions of the *True Critick*, according as they were governed by their Fears or their Hopes: yet whatever they touch'd of that kind, was with abundance of Caution, adventuring no farther than *Mythology* and *Hieroglyphick*. This, I suppose, gave ground to superficial Readers, for urging the Silence of Authors, against the Antiquity of the *True Critick*; tho' the *Types* are so apposite, and the Applications so necessary and natural, that it is not easy to conceive, how any Reader of a *Modern Eye* and *Taste* could over-look them. I shall venture from a great Number to produce a few, which I am very confident, will put this Question beyond Dispute.

It well deserves considering, that these *Antient Writers* in treating Enigmatically upon the Subject, have generally fixed upon the very *same Hieroglyph*, varying only the Story according to their Affections or their Wit. For first; *Pausanias*[7] is of Opinion, that the Perfection of Writing correct was entirely owing to the Institution of *Criticks*; and, that he can possibly mean no other than the *True Critick*, is, I think, manifest enough from the following Description. He says, *They were*

---

[7] *Pausanias*: Pausanias (143–176) was a Greek traveler and geographer. His *Descriptions of Greece* provides a guide to ancient ruins.

*a Race of Men, who delighted to nibble at the Superfluities, and Ex-
crescencies of Books; which the Learned at length observing, took
Warning of their own Accord, to lop* the *Luxuriant,* the *Rotten,* the
Dead, the *Sapless,* and the *Overgrown Branches from their Works.*
But now, all this he cunningly shades under the following Allegory;
that the Nauplians *in* Argia,[8] *learned the Art of pruning their Vines,
by observing, that when an* ASS *had browsed upon one of them, it
thrived the better, and bore fairer Fruit.* But *Herodotus*[9] holding the
very same *Hieroglyph,* speaks much plainer, and almost *in terminis.*
He hath been so bold as to tax the *True Criticks,* of Ignorance and
Malice; telling us openly, for I think nothing can be plainer, that *in
the Western Part of* Libya, *there were* ASSES *with* HORNS: Upon
which Relation *Ctesias*[10] yet refines, mentioning the very same animal
about *India,* adding, *That whereas all other* ASSES *wanted a* Gall,
*these horned ones were so redundant in that Part, that their Flesh
was not to be eaten because of its extream* Bitterness.

Now, the Reason why those Antient Writers treated this Subject
only by Types and Figures, was, because they durst not make open
Attacks against a Party so Potent and so Terrible, as the *Criticks* of
those Ages were: whose very Voice was so Dreadful, that a Legion of
Authors would tremble, and drop their Pens at the Sound; For so
Herodotus tells us expresly in another Place, how *a vast Army of*
Scythians *was put to flight in a Panick Terror, by the Braying of an*
ASS. From hence it is conjectured by certain profound *Philologers,*
that the great Awe and Reverence paid to a *True Critick,* by the Writers of *Britain,* have been derived to Us, from those our *Scythian* Ancestors. In short, this Dread was so universal, that in process of Time,
those Authors who had a mind to publish their Sentiments more
freely, in describing the *True Criticks* of their several Ages, were
forced to leave off the use of the former *Hieroglyph,* as too nearly approaching the *Prototype,* and invented other Terms instead thereof
that were more cautious and mystical; so *Diodorus*[11] speaking to the

[8] *Nauplians in Argia:* Nauplia is the chief town of Argolis in the Greek Pelopon-
nese. Ancient Nauplia fell to the city-state Argos in about 625 B.C.
[9] *Herodotus:* Herodotus (c. 484–c. 430/20 B.C.) was the Greek author of the first
great Western historical narrative, *The History of the Greco-Persian Wars.* This passage alludes to Book 4.
[10] *Ctesias:* Ctesias was a fifth-century Greek physician and historian of Persia and
India. His *Persica* was the only historical writing of his time based on official Persian
sources.
[11] *Diodorus:* Diodorus Siculus, a first-century A.D. Greek historian, was the author
of the universal history *Bibliotheca Historica.*

same purpose, ventures no farther than to say, That *in the Mountains of* Helicon *there grows a certain* Weed, *which bears a Flower of so damned a Scent, as to poison those who offer to smell it.* Lucretius gives exactly the Same Relation,

> *Est etiam in magnis Heliconis montibus arbos,*
> *Floris odore hominem tetro consueta necare.*   Lib. 6.[12]

But *Ctesias*, whom we lately quoted, hath been a great deal bolder; He had been used with much severity by the *True Criticks* of his own Age, and therefore could not forbear to leave behind him, at least one deep Mark of his Vengeance against the whole Tribe. His Meaning is so near the Surface, that I wonder how it possibly came to be over-look'd by those who deny the Antiquity of the *True Criticks*. For pretending to make a Description of many strange Animals about *India*, he hath set down these remarkable Words. *Amongst the rest,* says he, *there is a* Serpent *that wants* Teeth, *and consequently cannot bite, but if its* Vomit *(to which it is much addicted) happens to fall upon any Thing, a certain Rottenness or Corruption ensues: These* Serpents *are generally found among the Mountains where* Jewels *grow, and they frequently emit a* poisonous Juice *whereof, whoever drinks, that Person's* Brains *flie out of his Nostrils.*

There was also among the *Antients* a sort of *Critick*, not distinguisht in *Specie* from the Former, but in Growth or Degree, who seem to have been only the *Tyro's* or *junior* Scholars; yet, because of their differing Employments, they are frequently mentioned as a Sect by themselves. The usual exercise of these younger Students, was to attend constantly at Theatres, and learn to Spy out the *worst Parts* of the Play, whereof they were obliged carefully to take Note, and render a rational Account, to their Tutors. Flesht at these smaller Sports, like young Wolves, they grew up in Time, to be nimble and strong enough for hunting down large Game. For it hath been observed both among Antients and Moderns, that a *True Critick* hath one Quality in common with a *Whore* and an *Alderman*, never to change his Title or his Nature; that a *Grey Critick* has been certainly a *Green* one, the Perfections and Acquirements of his Age being only the improved Talents of his Youth; like *Hemp*, which some Naturalists inform us, is bad for *Suffocations*, tho' taken but in the Seed. I esteem the

---

[12] *. . . Lib. 6:* A passage from Book 6 of the Roman poet Titus Lucretius Carus's (98–55 B.C.) *De rerum naturum* (*On the Nature of Things*) which outlines the physical system of the philosopher Epicurus. The substance of the Latin is given by Swift in the italicized passage.

Invention, or at least the Refinement of *Prologues*, to have been owing to these younger Proficients, of whom *Terence*[13] makes frequent and honourable mention, under the Name of *Malevoli*.[14]

Now, 'tis certain, the Institution of the *True Criticks*, was of absolute Necessity to the Commonwealth of Learning. For all Human Actions seem to be divided like *Themistocles*[15] and his Company; One Man can *Fiddle*, and another can make *a small Town a great City*, and he that cannot do either one or the other, deserves to be kick'd out of the Creation. The avoiding of which Penalty, has doubtless given the first Birth to the Nation of *Criticks*, and withal, an Occasion for their secret Detractors to report; that a *True Critick* is a sort of Mechanick, set up with a Stock and Tools for his Trade, at as little Expence as a *Taylor*; and that there is much Analogy between the Utensils and Abilities of both: That the *Taylor's Hell*[16] is the Type of a Critick's *Common-Place-Book*, and his Wit and Learning held forth by the *Goose*:[17] That it requires at least as many of these, to the making up of one Scholar, as of the others to the Composition of a Man: That the Valour of both is equal, and their *Weapons* near of a Size. Much may be said in answer to these invidious Reflections; and I can positively affirm the first to be a Falshood: For, on the contrary, nothing is more certain, than that it requires greater Layings out, to be free of the *Critick's* Company, than of any other you can name. For, as to be a *true Beggar*, it will cost the richest Candidate every Groat he is worth; so, before one can commence a *True Critick*, it will cost a man all the good Qualities of his Mind; which, perhaps, for a less Purchase, would be thought but an indifferent Bargain.

Having thus amply proved the Antiquity of *Criticism*, and described the Primitive State of it; I shall now examine the present Condition of this Empire, and shew how well it agrees with its antient self. A certain Author, whose Works have many Ages since been entirely lost, does in his fifth Book and eighth Chapter, say of *Criticks*,

---

[13] *Terence:* Terence (195?–159? B.C.) was a Roman comic dramatist whose plays provided a model for the modern comedy of manners.

[14] *Malevoli:* The spiteful.

[15] *Themistocles:* Themistocles (c. 528–462 B.C.), an Athenian democratic statesman and general who built the navy that saved Greece from the Persian invasion under Xerxes.

[16] *Taylor's Hell:* The area under a tailor's work table.

[17] *Common-Place-Book . . . Goose:* A commonplace book is a ledger in which students and authors jot down witty sayings or important passages from other writers. A goose is a tailor's crook-necked iron.

that *their Writings are the Mirrors of Learning*. This I understand in a literal Sense, and suppose our Author must mean, that whoever designs to be a perfect Writer, must inspect into the Books of *Criticks*, and correct his Invention there as in a Mirror. Now, whoever considers, that the *Mirrors* of the Antients were made of *Brass*, and *sine Mercurio*,[18] may presently apply the two Principal Qualifications of a *True Modern Critick*, and consequently, must needs conclude, that these have always been, and must be for ever the same. For, *Brass* is an Emblem of Duration, and when it is skilfully burnished, will cast *Reflections* from its own *Superficies*, without any Assistance of *Mercury* from behind. All the other Talents of a *Critick* will not require a particular Mention, being included, or easily deducible to these. However, I shall conclude with three Maxims, which may serve both as Characteristicks to distinguish a *True Modern Critick* from a Pretender, and will be also of admirable Use to those worthy Spirits, who engage in so useful and honourable an Art.

The first is, That *Criticism*, contrary to all other Faculties of the Intellect, is ever held the truest and best, when it is the very *first* Result of the *Critick's* Mind: As Fowlers reckon the first aim for the surest, and seldom fail of missing the Mark, if they stay for a Second.

Secondly; The *True Criticks* are known by their Talent of swarming about the noblest Writers, to which they are carried meerly by Instinct, as a Rat to the best Cheese, or a Wasp to the fairest Fruit. So, when the *King* is a Horse-back, he is sure to be the *dirtiest* Person of the Company, and they that make their Court best, are such as *bespatter* him most.

Lastly; A *True Critick*, in the Perusal of a Book, is like a *Dog* at a Feast, whose Thoughts and Stomach are wholly set upon what the Guests *fling away*, and consequently, is apt to *Snarl* most, when there are the fewest *Bones*.

Thus much, I think, is sufficient to serve by way of Address to my Patrons, the *True Modern Criticks*, and may very well atone for my past Silence, as well as That which I am like to observe for the future. I hope I have deserved so well of their whole *Body*, as to meet with generous and tender Usage at their *Hands*. Supported by which Expectation, I go on boldly to pursue those Adventures already so happily begun.

---

[18] *sine Mercurio:* Without mercury.

JONATHAN SWIFT

From "On Poetry: A Rapsody"

Appearing at the end of 1733, Swift's "On Poetry: A Rapsody" satirizes the poetic pretensions of the legions of hack writers that populate Grub Street. Real poets, Swift asserts, are of no use to "Court, city" or "country," where only those who can "bribe, betray, or plot" have a place. Far from maintaining the standards and ideals of civilization, literary culture, as Swift and Pope assert, is being corrupted, even annihilated, by the conditions of the modern literary marketplace and contemporary social and political institutions. Swift's writing betrays the vulnerability he felt as an author, which can be sensed here in the poem's depiction of the bleak and precarious life of the modern poet. For more information about Swift, see other headnotes (pp. 403, 410, 418, and 577).

Lines 1–140 of "On Poetry" are taken from *Jonathan Swift: The Complete Poems*, ed. Pat Rogers (New York: Penguin Books, 1983).

All Human Race wou'd fain be *Wits*,
And Millions miss, for one that hits.
Young's universal Passion,° *Pride*,
Was never known to spread so wide.
Say *Britain*, cou'd you ever boast, — 5
Three *Poets* in an Age at most?
Our chilling Climate hardly bears
A Sprig of Bays° in Fifty Years:
While ev'ry Fool his Claim alledges,
As if it grew in common Hedges. 10
What Reason can there be assign'd
For this Perverseness in the Mind?
Brutes find out where their Talents lie:
A *Bear* will not attempt to fly:
A founder'd *Horse* will oft debate, 15
Before he tries a five-barr'd Gate:

3. *Young's universal Passion*: Edward Young, author of *The Universal Passion: The Love of Fame* (1725–28), a series of satires.
8. *Sprig of Bays*: A crown of bay leaves was the traditional symbol of the poet laureate.

A *Dog* by Instinct turns aside,
Who sees the Ditch too deep and wide.
But *Man* we find the only Creature,
Who, led by *Folly*, fights with *Nature*;   20
Who, when *she* loudly cries, *Forbear*,
With Obstinacy fixes there;
And, where his *Genius* least inclines,
Absurdly bends his whole Designs.

    Not *Empire* to the Rising-Sun,   25
By Valour, Conduct, Fortune won;
Nor highest *Wisdom* in Debates
For framing Laws to govern States;
Nor Skill in Sciences profound,
So large to grasp the Circle round;   30
Such heavenly Influence require,
As how to strike the *Muses Lyre*.

    Not Beggar's Brat, on Bulk° begot;
Nor Bastard of a Pedlar *Scot*;
Nor Boy brought up to cleaning Shoes,   35
The Spawn of *Bridewell*, or the Stews°;
Nor Infants dropt, the spurious Pledges
Of *Gipsies* littering under Hedges,
Are so disqualified by Fate
To rise in *Church*, or *Law*, or *State*,   40
As he, whom *Phebus*° in his Ire
Hath *blasted* with poetick Fire.

    What hope of Custom in the *Fair*,
While not a Soul demands your Ware?
Where you have nothing to produce   45
For private Life, or publick Use?
Court, *City*, *Country* want you not;
You cannot bribe, betray, or plot.

---

33. *Bulk:* The stall in front of a shop under which or on which the poor and the homeless would sleep.
    36. *Bridewell, or the Stews:* Originally a royal palace built 1515–1520 for Henry VIII, Bridewell was named after a holy well dedicated to St. Bride. In 1533, Edward VII gave the palace to the city of London to house vagrants and homeless children and as a correctional institution for petty offenders and wayward women. In 1556 the city took possession and with the confirmation of Queen Mary turned the palace into a prison, hospital, and workhouse. Stews are brothels.
    41. *Phebus:* In Greek mythology, Phoebus Apollo is the god of light.

For Poets, Law makes no Provision:
The Wealthy have you in Derision.   50
Of State-Affairs you cannot smatter,
Are awkward when you try to flatter.
Your Portion, taking *Britain* round,
Was just one annual Hundred Pound.
Now not so much as in Remainder   55
Since *Cibber*° brought in an Attainder;
For ever fixt by Right Divine,
(A Monarch's Right) on *Grubstreet*° Line.
Poor starv'ling Bard, how small thy Gains!
How unproportion'd to thy Pains!   60

    And here a *Simile* comes Pat in:
Tho' *Chickens* take a Month to fatten,
The Guests in less than half an Hour
Will more than half a Score devour.
So, after toiling twenty Days,   65
To earn a Stock of Pence and Praise,
Thy Labours, grown the Critick's Prey,
Are swallow'd o'er a Dish of Tea;
Gone, to be never heard of more,
Gone, where the *Chickens* went before.   70

    How shall a new Attempter learn
Of diff'rent Spirits to discern,
And how distinguish, which is which,
The Poet's Vein, or scribling Itch?
Then hear an old experienc'd Sinner   75
Instructing thus a young Beginner.

    Consult yourself, and if you find
A powerful Impulse urge your Mind,
Impartial judge within your Breast
What Subject you can manage best;   80
Whether your Genius most inclines
To Satire, Praise, or hum'rous Lines;

---

    56. *Cibber:* Colley Cibber (1671–1757), actor, playwright, theater manager, and autobiographer who became poet laureate under George II (reigned 1727–60) and who serves as the protagonist in Alexander Pope's final version of *The Dunciad* (1743).
    58. *Grubstreet:* A street near Moorfields in London inhabited by professional freelance writers, Grub Street refers not only to an actual place but to the whole symbolic realm of "low" literary culture produced by "hack" writers purely for financial gain.

To Elegies in mournful Tone,
Or Prologue sent from Hand unknown.
Then rising with *Aurora*'s° Light,   85
The Muse invok'd, sit down to write;
Blot out, correct, insert, refine,
Enlarge, diminish, interline;
Be mindful, when Invention fails,
To scratch your Head, and bite your Nails.   90

    Your Poem finish'd, next your Care
Is needful, to transcribe it fair.
In modern Wit all printed Trash, is
Set off with num'rous *Breaks* ——— and *Dashes* —

    To Statesmen wou'd you give a Wipe,   95
You print it in *Italick Type*.
When Letters are in vulgar Shapes,
'Tis ten to one the Wit escapes;
But when in *Capitals* exprest,
The dullest Reader smoaks the Jest: 100
Or else perhaps he may invent
A better than the Poet meant,
As learned Commentators view
In *Homer* more than *Homer*° knew.

    Your Poem in its modish Dress,   105
Correctly fitted for the Press,
Convey by Penny-Post to *Lintot*,°
But let no Friend alive look into't.
If *Lintot* thinks 'twill quit the Cost,
You need not fear your Labour lost: 110
And, how agreeably surpriz'd
Are you to see it advertiz'd!
The Hawker shews you one in Print,
As fresh as Farthings from the Mint:
The Product of your Toil and Sweating;   115
A Bastard of your own begetting.

---

85. *Aurora's:* In Roman mythology, Aurora is the goddess of the dawn.
104. *Homer:* Ninth-century B.C. poet and author of the Greek epics the *Iliad* and the *Odyssey*.
107. *Lintot:* Bernard Lintot (1675–1736) was a bookseller and printer who published a miscellany containing Pope's *Rape of the Lock* as well as his translations of the *Iliad* and the *Odyssey*.

Be sure at *Will's*° the following Day,
Lie Snug, and hear what Criticks say.
And if you find the general Vogue
Pronounces you a stupid Rogue;   120
Damns all your Thoughts as low and little,
Sit still, and swallow down your Spittle.
Be silent as a Politician,
For talking may beget Suspicion:
Or praise the Judgment of the Town,   125
And help yourself to run it down.
Give up your fond paternal Pride,
Nor argue on the weaker Side;
For Poems read without a Name
We justly praise, or justly blame: 130
And Criticks have no partial Views,
Except they know whom they abuse.
And since you ne'er provok'd their Spight,
Depend upon't their Judgment's right:
But if you blab, you are undone;   135
Consider what a Risk you run.
You lose your Credit all at once;
The Town will mark you for a Dunce:
The vilest Doggrel *Grubstreet* sends,
Will pass for yours with Foes and Friends.   140
And you must bear the whole Disgrace,
'Till some fresh Blockhead takes your Place.

On Poets
(*From* The Female Tatler *No. 45)*

In this selection Mrs. Crackenthorpe recounts a polite debate about
the character of poets and their place in society. One focus of this dialogue is the tension between the classical ideal of the poet as the divine
mouthpiece of the gods (a characterization defended by Mrs. Tire-quill)
and the skeptical modern view of the poet as an opportunistic literary adventurer whose ethics are the same as those of the commercial, fashion-
oriented marketplace in which he sells his work (Colonel Florid's view).

---

117. *Will's:* A coffeehouse associated with a literary clientele.

For more information on *The Female Tatler,* see Chapter 1's Cultural Contexts (p. 129).

The text reprinted here is taken from *The Female Tatler,* ed. Fidelis Morgan (Rutland, VT: Charles Tuttle/Everyman's, 1992), 101–04.

No. 45
Monday, October 17, to Wednesday, October 19

There are a sort of whimsical people in the world called poets, whose delight, whose transports, nay, generally speaking, whose livelihoods proceed from satire and invective from maliciously observing the little failings of the rest of mankind, and from an unhappy genius, turned to scandal, improving them into the grossest ridicule; some do it in comedy, others by paraphrastical translations, some by downright libel, and others more by panegyric. Lady Fanciful, who had the vanity to think herself exposed in the *Memoirs from the New Atalantis,*[1] started the question, What kind of creatures are these Poets? They must be unparalleled in religion, loyalty, chastity, sobriety, all moral virtues, and correct qualifications as nice dress and address, a just and proper decorum, in different companies and conversations, but above all, in prompt payment. That they seem to take an assured freedom in lashing not only the imagined vices of the town, but the pretty, pleasing, harmless affectations of our sex, which divert ourselves, and give offence to nobody.

Colonel Florid, who so judiciously penetrates into mankind, and with so much modest ease and musical eloquence, delineates not only particular persons, but any sect of people, that he bewitches our attention, entered upon the subject. His notion of poets was that they are a chimerical tribe, but a few degrees removed from madmen, who ought not be trusted with themselves, but like heedless, rambling schoolboys, have everything provided for them, their bounds set them, and their pocket-money paid them every day. They have no more concern about their passing through the world than if they were not even in it, yet have a more refined taste of dress, equipage, buildings, furniture, and entertainments than all the world besides. They

---

[1] *Memoirs from the New Atalantis:* The scandalous *roman à clef* by Mary de la Rivière Manley (1663–1724). The text slandered many prominent figures, especially Whigs. In October 1709 Manley and her publishers were arrested, but they were discharged in 1710. In June 1711, Manley took Jonathan Swift's place as the editor of the Tory periodical *The Examiner.*

have clothes regardless at what price they buy them, and, as regardless of discharging it, ride in great men's chariots, are at great men's seats, and as their wit and humour are the spirit of the table, think the greatest men are obliged to them for their company. Stepping out of the room to give some directions, I happened to hear Mrs Loveless, my intimate acquaintance, and as I thought my friend, fleeringly cry, 'Why, what is Crackenthorpe but a poetess?' The company was alarmed at the aspersion, and Mrs Wiseman wondered how a serious, reforming paper, though larded with jests, epigrams, and pleasant tales, could bring me under that denomination; but when I found the dispute growing high, I bolted smilingly into the room, and told them supper was just ready.

The colonel proceeded that poets having a finer thread of understanding, a quicker apprehension, and more noble ideas of things than the generality, they are intoxicated with sublime conceptions, fancy their bodies, where their imaginations soar, and in the heat of their poetical flights, discover the lunatic in all his shapes and postures. A poem well-finished is to them beyond settling a nice Act of Parliament, they have no plots but in plays, and seldom any there, and a comedy once brought to a full third night, is to them coming to a vast estate. They have no notion of honour but in the hero of a tragedy, friendship but for those who lend them money, sobriety after a hard debauch, nor regularity either in thought, deed, time, behaviour or habitation; therefore, when their patrons bestow preferments upon them, knowing their disposition for business, they generally take care they shall be sinecures. 'And are these the creatures,' says Lady Fanciful, 'that set up for observators, that won't let one be a little particular in public places to be taken notice of, but one's character is in the new comedy, which perhaps is so beastly a thing one is not able to sit it out.' But Mrs Tire-quill, who has the indisposition of scribbling herself, would not allow poets to be so contemptibly treated, she said they were rather Demi-Gods than men, that their thoughts were Supernatural, and, though their mortal clay over-animated for so small a tenement obliged them sometimes to terrestrial confabulation, yet they more frequently conversed with Deities; Jupiter gave them majestic notions, Mars showed them a specimen of war, Venus told them pretty love-tales, and they had rather be inebriated with Bacchus[2] in imagination, than be really so with the most

---

[2] *Jupiter . . . Mars . . . Venus . . . Bacchus:* In Roman mythology, Jupiter is the supreme god, Mars the god of war, Venus the goddess of love, and Bacchus the god of wine.

distinguished animal below the spheres. That such persons, whose writings make mortals as immortal as themselves, ought not to grovel about worldly cares, nor subject their fancies, which are always up on the wing, to any manner of constraint. That she thought conversing with an author, and perusing his works, before they were blown upon by the ungrateful world, was, next to happy conceptions of her own, the greatest felicity on earth.

Mrs Tire-quill was so zealous for the reputation of the here-and-thereian-tribe, and grew so inspired on the subject, that she would have immediately talked in verse, had not Colonel Florid turned the discourse upon a sort of miserable creatures called Would-be-Poets. Wretches! That are in business, tradesmen, petty-foggers,[3] and notary publics, that might plod on in their thoughtless vocation, grow rich, keep coaches, and never think of the next world, yet fancying they have a genius, leave their prosperous knavery to write songs, madrigals, and damned plays, till they starve indeed, being shunned by their own tribe, and laughed at by the Kit-Kat Club.[4] These are an incorrigible crew, who, though they are punished with poverty and the utmost contempt, yet like branded malefactors who return to their old courses, they still run on in their convulsive strains, and endeavour to bring forth without conception. Upon the whole, 'twas agreed that poets were an unaccountable race, that they built castles in the air, and though they gave birth to a lady called fortune, could never make her their friend; for though they may every hour have a project to advance them in the world, yet, from a fluency of thought, things crowd so fast upon them, that they drive out one another. Sanguine dispositions can settle to nothing; whereas more sedate, considerate, and politic persons, embrace the first probable opportunity, proceed upon mature deliberation, and by a constant assiduity secure their happiness.

Lady Drivel, for we must suppose one fool in the company, wondered how poets could have such odd fancies and out-of-the-way sayings; were she to write a play, she was sure she should make horrid stuff in it, and, of all of the plays she ever saw, none frightened her so much as *Macbeth*,[5] nor made her laugh so much as the *Trip to the Jubilee*,[6] but when her ladyship began to prate, the company dispersed.

---

[3] *petty-foggers:* Petty, quibbling, unscrupulous lawyers.

[4] *Kit-Kat Club:* (Also spelled Kit-Cat Club) a famous Whig club. Addison and Steele were prominent members.

[5] *Macbeth:* A tragedy by William Shakespeare (1564–1616) first produced in 1606.

[6] *Trip to the Jubilee: The Constant Couple; or, a Trip to the Jubilee,* a comedy by the Irish playwright George Farquhar (1678–1707).

Mrs Crackenthorpe has received intelligence from several people that there is a scandalous fellow about town, that makes it his business to impose on people by extorting money from them, under the pretence of producing sham letters, etc. — that unless they deposit such sums of money as he villainously demands, they shall be exposed in this paper. This is to give notice that she is no way directly or indirectly privy to or concerned in those his rascally and knavish impositions, and that she desires all persons to whom he shall hereafter endeavour to impose on to apprehend him, and, upon carrying him before a magistrate and sending immediate notice thereof to the publisher of this paper, distinguished in the superscription with care and speed, he shall be confronted and secured, she being sensible of the prejudice she has, and may hereafter receive upon these his clandestine and unjust proceedings, and desires no one to suffer themselves to be imposed on by so notorious an impostor, she being ashamed of so insufferable a practice, knowing it to be an imposition on the public, which was never the design of this paper, it being only to expose vice and folly, and to commend justice and honesty, which last, 'tis hoped she has always done, and declares she will.

Note: it is desired anyone that has been so abused, to discover the person to whom they have paid any money on the aforesaid account, and he shall be prosecuted as the law directs, without any charge to them.

EDWARD WARD

The Wit's Coffee-House
(From The London Spy)

In this passage, the Spy and his companion visit the "Wit's Coffee-House," probably meant to represent Will's Coffeehouse, a famous gathering place of literary men. In his portrait of the Modern Critic, the Spy castigates the pedantry, narrowness, and unrelieved negativity of that breed. In contrast, his companion offers a description of the more constructive and useful criticism pursued by the true ancient critic. For more information on Edward Ward, see Chapter 1's Cultural Contexts (p. 144).

The text reprinted here is from Part X of The London Spy, ed. Paul Hyland (East Lansing: Colleagues Press, 1993), 171–75.

From thence we adjourned to the Wits' Coffee-house, in hopes that the powerful eloquence which drops from the silver tongues of the ingenious company that frequent this noted mansion, might inspire us with such a genius as would better fit the perfection of our renovated clay, now that it was purged of all impurities,[1] and rendered a proper receptacle for the most discerning and poetic spirits. Accordingly, upstairs we went, and found much company, and but little talk; as if everyone remembered the old proverb, that a close mouth makes a wise head, and so endeavoured by his silence to be counted a man of judgement, rather than by speaking to stand the censure of so many critics, and run the hazard of losing that character which by holding of his tongue he might be in hopes of gaining.

We shuffled through this moving crowd of philosophical mutes to the other end of the room, where three or four wits of the upper classes were rendezvoused at a table, and were disturbing the ashes of the old poets by perverting their sense, and making strange allegories and allusions never dreamt or thought of by the authors. Thus, they excused some faults, which were really the slips or oversights of the poet, but made others so very gross, through prejudice and misconstruction, that none but critics of very little judgement, or very much ill-nature, could have wrested the sense of the words so much to the injury of him that writ 'em.

When they had showed their learning, as they thought, by arraigning and condemning many of the old Roman muses,[2] they condescended so low as to call some of our modern poets to stand the test of their all-judging opinions, upon whom, in brief, they conferred these characters. One was a man of great judgement, learning, and fancy, but of no principle; another was one that had writ well, and could write well, but would not write; a third never writ but one good thing in his life, and that he recanted; a fourth had a poetical talent, but it was hid under a philosophical bushel; a fifth was a good Latin poet, but had sacrificed his muse to Bacchus, instead of dedicating her to Apollo;[3] a sixth had got a great deal of credit by writing plays, but lost it all by defending the stage; a seventh had got some reputation by turning old ditties into new songs, but lost it all by

---

[1] *purged of all impurities:* The Spy and his companion have just emerged from the baths.

[2] *old Roman muses:* The classical muses invoked in Latin poetry.

[3] *Bacchus ... Apollo:* Bacchus is the classical god of wine, and Apollo of poetry, music, prophecy, and medicine. Bacchus is associated with emotional and physical abandon, the loosening of inhibitions, and Apollo with order and control.

turning a Spanish romance into an English stage play; an eighth had got honour by a dull poem, which his brother medico envied, and vowed he'd outdo him in verse, as he hoped also to be knighted.

Thus the carping Momuses[4] proceeded according to the critics' custom, never to let anything, though well performed, escape their scrutiny, to the discovery of some colourable fault, nor any character pass their lips, though of the worthiest persons in the world, without being tagged with some calumny or other, on purpose to eclipse the brightness of those virtues for which they are chiefly eminent. And it may generally be observed of those who delight in criticism, that they are so curious in having the maidenhead of an error that if a better judgement finds a fault, which has had the good fortune to escape his censure, he will, if it be possible, find out a salve for that sore, and justify the author ever hereafter in that particular. And he will make it appear there is more sense lies hid in those words than in all the book besides, though he knows what he defends to be arrant nonsense. For he is usually so conceited in his own judgement, that rather than acknowledge he had overlooked an error, he will justify it not to be so. And of such a sort of critic, of which there are hundreds in this town, as well as some at the next table, I think it very proper in this place to give a character. Accordingly I dictated, and my friend writ.

A Modern Critic

Is a compound of some learning, little judgement, less wit, much conceit, and abundance of ill-nature. Wanting true merit, he aims to raise a reputation not by his own performances but by others' failings. These he takes more pleasure to expose than he does to mend, and reads an author as much in search of his faults as a wise man does for his knowledge. Whoever speaks Latin in his company must be as watchful of his words as a prince is of his actions, for if once he breaks Priscian's head[5] he must be forced to break the critic's too, or else suffer himself to be baited as bad as the tiger at the cockpit. True spelling and pointing[6] he admires as the chief ornaments of a poem, and always minds the sense much less than the orthography. Whenever he repeats any grave verse he has more turns in his voice and changes in his countenance than a young preacher in his sermon

[4] *Momuses:* In Greek mythology, Momus is the god of blame and ridicule.
[5] *Priscian's head:* Priscian (fl. A.D. 500) was the most renowned Latin grammarian.
[6] *pointing:* Punctuation.

upon Death and Judgement. And when he reads a tragedy he out-mouths a player and corrects the stage with his extravagant gestures. Whoever talks of an author within his reading shall be sure to be attacked with those places that remain doubtful and obscure. These riddles he expounds and renders as plain (if you'll depend upon his judgement) as that the candle eats the cat, or the coach draws the horses. He would not give a farthing to understand anything but difficulties which have puzzled much wiser heads than his own to truly find the meaning of.

He's a man that seldom writes anything, but when he does, he is so very nice that it's carried as often to the corrector as a lady's stays, or a beau's coat to the tailor, before the typography and orthography are according to his judgement. His talk is usually like a maze or labyrinth, for none but himself has the clue to find the beginning and ending of his tedious comments with which, in all companies, he is very troublesome. Whenever he undertakes to reconcile an absurdity or expound a mystery, he usually does it with as much success as physicians when they labour to unfold the nature of such medicines to the patient which work by occult qualities, only tiring their ears with a few uncommon words which serve among fools as well as an intelligible explication.

He is one that is not wise but would very fain be thought so, and takes as much pains to sit astraddle upon other men's shoulders as would raise his reputation to twice the height, had he wisdom enough to apply the same industry to a better purpose. His head is a mere house of correction, his brains are the register of other men's faults, and his tongue the unmerciful scourge that punishes them. He is the storehouse of other men's infirmities, where seldom anything is laid up but what the authors are ashamed of. They are the mere wasps of the age, who are furnished with unlucky stings, but yield no honey.

Says my friend, 'You have deviated much from the character of a true critic, whose business in the Roman time was to judge the actions and works of men as delivered to the public by historians, poets, philosophers, and the like; to examine the probability and reasonableness of former transactions as they are handed down to us by our ancestors, to prevent their imposition on posterity; to enquire into the truth and usefulness of all sorts of learning, and report their opinions to the world accordingly; and to expound and give their best sense of all ambiguities and obscure passages which they find in any author. These were very commendable and serviceable tasks; but yours is such a coniwable[7] of a critic, I know not what to make of him.'

'Why, then, I'll tell you,' said I. 'I give not this as the character of a real critic, but such a sort of a mongrel critic as he that you heard talk just now. He takes a pride in nothing but snapping and snarling at the little slips and unavoidable failings of authors, which are much beneath the notice of any judicious and good-natured reader, and would die were it not that these petty students in syntax, who handle men's faults in company as a juggler does his balls, till they have made as many as they please of 'em and think they cannot give greater demonstrations of their learning than in public to disparage such persons who have ten times the parts of themselves, foolishly believing that whatever they detract from others they add to their own reputation, and fancy every stain or blemish they can give to an ingenious man's character is a heightening of their own merit. These are the persons of whom I have given this rough sketch. They are only cavillers, or pretenders to criticism, and know nothing of the matter.'

'Nay,' says my friend, 'if it be those you aim at, you have said less than they deserve. I have observed, since I have sat here, that I have heard those gentlemen judge very severely of some modern authors who have not only merited but enjoy a general approbation and applause. And they have so rashly condemned some writings of an ancient worthy and honourable gentleman as if they had a commission to take away men's reputations without giving the least reason why, or an account wherein they have forfeited their credits.'

At another table were seated a parcel of young, raw, second-rate beaus and wits, who were conceited if they had but once the honour to dip a finger and thumb into Mr Dryden's[8] snuff-box; it was enough to inspire 'em with a true genius of poetry, and make 'em write verse as fast as a tailor takes his stitches. These, too, were communicating one to another the newest labours of their brains, wherein were such wondrous flights, unaccountable thoughts, strange figures, hyperboles and similies, and upon such notable subjects, that to hear 'em read their works is at any time sufficient to cure the hypochondria,[9] and turn the deepest melancholy into a fit of laugh-

---

[7] *coniwable:* Constable.

[8] *Mr Dryden's:* John Dryden (1631–1700) was a poet, playwright, essayist, and translator.

[9] *hypochondria:* In the eighteenth century the term "hypochondria," like "vapors" and "spleen," referred to a fashionable mood disorder characterized by depression, anxiety, and irritability.

ter. One plucks out a panegyric upon orange-flower water; another, a satire against dirty weather; a third produces a cleanly lampoon upon nasty tobacco smokers; a fourth a poem in praise of short puff-wigs, together with the excellence of paint, powder and patches.[10]

ALEXANDER POPE

From *An Essay on Criticism*

In *An Essay on Criticism*, published anonymously in 1711, Alexander Pope (1688–1744) draws on a number of ancient and modern critics, in particular Horace, Boileau, and Quintilian, in an attempt to resolve the critical debate that had raged throughout the previous century. Horace's *Ars Poetica*, an epistle addressed to aspiring poets, is the model for Pope's verse essay addressed to aspiring critics. Pope's career as a poet is inseparable from the course of his critical work; indeed, much of his poetry is criticism, as in this work, for instance, and as in his *Dunciad*. Pope also published prose criticism, in his "Discourse on Pastoral Poetry," in the essay printed as *Guardian* No. 30, also on pastoral, in the prefaces to his translations of Homer and his edition of Shakespeare, and in *Peri Bathous: or, Martinus Scriblerus His Treatise of the Art of Sinking in Poetry*, his satire on pedantry (see p. 449). In this selection from *An Essay on Criticism*, Pope defines and negotiates the categories to which all types of cultural production (not just literature) were submitted: taste, wit, judgment, sense, nature, and art.

The lines reprinted here are taken from *The Poems of Alexander Pope*, ed. John Butt (New Haven: Yale University Press, 1963).

'Tis hard to say, if greater Want of Skill
Appear in *Writing* or in *Judging* ill;
But, of the two, less dang'rous is th' Offence,
To tire our *Patience*, than mis-lead our *Sense*:
Some few in *that*, but Numbers err in *this*,   5
Ten Censure wrong for one who Writes amiss;

---

[10] *patches:* Small patches of black silk attached to the face, neck, and shoulders as supplementary beauty marks.

A *Fool* might once *himself* alone expose,
Now *One* in *Verse* makes many more in *Prose*.
   'Tis with our *Judgments* as our *Watches*, none
Go just *alike*, yet each believes his own.   10
In *Poets* as true *Genius* is but rare,
True *Taste* as seldom is the *Critick*'s Share;
Both must alike from Heav'n derive their Light,
These *born* to Judge, as well as those to Write.
Let such teach others who themselves excell,   15
And *censure freely* who have *written well*.
Authors are partial to their *Wit*, 'tis true,
But are not *Criticks* to their *Judgment* too?
   Yet if we look more closely, we shall find
Most have the *Seeds* of Judgment in their Mind;   20
Nature affords at least a *glimm'ring Light*;
The *Lines*, tho' touch'd but faintly, are drawn right.
But as the slightest Sketch, if justly trac'd, ⎫
Is by ill *Colouring* but the more disgrac'd, ⎬
So by *false Learning* is *good Sense* defac'd; ⎭   25
Some are bewilder'd in the Maze of Schools,
And some made *Coxcombs* Nature meant but *Fools*.
In search of *Wit* these lose their *common Sense*,
And then turn Criticks in their own Defence.
Each burns alike, who can, or cannot write,   30
Or with a *Rival*'s or an *Eunuch*'s spite.
All *Fools* have still an Itching to deride,
And fain *wou'd* be upon the *Laughing Side*:
If *Mævius* Scribble in *Apollo*'s° spight,
There are, who *judge* still *worse* than he can *write*.   35
   Some have at first for *Wits*, then *Poets* past,
Turn'd *Criticks* next, and prov'd plain *Fools* at last;
Some neither can for *Wits* nor *Criticks* pass,
As heavy Mules are neither *Horse* nor *Ass*.
Those half-learn'd Witlings, num'rous in our Isle,   40
As half-form'd Insects on the Banks of *Nile*;
Unfinish'd Things, one knows now what to call,
Their Generation's so *equivocal*:
To tell 'em, wou'd a *hundred Tongues* require,

---

34. *Apollo's:* In classical mythology, Apollo is the god of poetry, music, prophecy, and medicine.

Or *one vain Wit's*, that might a hundred tire.   45
   But *you* who seek to *give* and *merit* Fame,
And justly bear a Critick's noble Name,
Be sure *your self* and your own *Reach* to know,
How far your *Genius*, *Taste*, and *Learning* go;
Launch not beyond your Depth, but be discreet,   50
And mark *that Point* where Sense and Dulness *meet*.
   Nature to all things fix'd the Limits fit,
And wisely curb'd proud Man's pretending Wit:
As on the *Land* while *here* the *Ocean* gains,
In *other Parts* it leaves wide sandy Plains;   55
Thus in the *Soul* while *Memory* prevails,
The solid Pow'r of *Understanding* fails;
Where Beams of warm *Imagination* play,
The *Memory*'s soft Figures melt away.
One *Science* only will one *Genius* fit;   60
So *vast* is Art, so *narrow* Human Wit;
Not only bounded to *peculiar Arts*,
But oft in *those*, confin'd to *single Parts*.
Like Kings we lose the Conquests gain'd before,
By vain Ambition still to make them more: 65
Each might his *sev'ral Province* well command,
Wou'd all but *stoop* to what they *understand*.
   First follow NATURE, and your Judgment frame
By her just Standard, which is still the same:
Unerring Nature, still divinely bright,   70
One *clear*, *unchang'd*, and *Universal* Light,
Life, Force, and Beauty, must to all impart,
At once the *Source*, and *End*, and *Test* of Art.
Art from that Fund each *just Supply* provides,
Works *without Show*, and *without Pomp* presides: 75
In some fair Body thus th' informing Soul
With Spirits feeds, with Vigour fills the whole,
Each Motion guides, and ev'ry Nerve sustains;
It self unseen, but in th' *Effects*, remains.
Some, to whom Heav'n in Wit has been profuse,   80
Want as much more, to turn it to its use;
For *Wit* and *Judgment* often are at strife,
Tho' meant each other's Aid, like *Man* and *Wife*.
'Tis more to *guide* than *spur* the Muse's Steed;
Restrain his Fury, than provoke his Speed;   85

The winged Courser, like a gen'rous Horse,
Shows most true Mettle when you *check* his Course.
   Those RULES of old *discover'd*, not *devis'd*,
Are *Nature* still, but *Nature Methodiz'd*;
Nature, like *Liberty*, is but restrain'd   90
By the same Laws which first *herself* ordain'd.
   Hear how learn'd *Greece* her useful Rules indites,
When to repress, and when indulge our Flights:
High on *Parnassus'*° Top her Sons she show'd,
And pointed out those arduous Paths they trod,   95
Held from afar, aloft, th' Immortal Prize,
And urg'd the rest by equal Steps to rise;
Just *Precepts* thus from great *Examples* giv'n,
She drew from *them* what they deriv'd from *Heav'n*.
The gen'rous Critick *fann'd* the *Poet's Fire*,   100
And taught the World, *with Reason* to *Admire*.
Then Criticism the Muse's Handmaid prov'd,
To dress her Charms, and make her more belov'd;
But following Wits from that Intention stray'd;
Who cou'd not win the Mistress, woo'd the Maid;   105
Against the Poets *their own Arms* they turn'd,
Sure to hate most the Men from whom they *learn'd*.
So modern *Pothecaries*,° taught the Art
By *Doctor's Bills* to play the *Doctor's Part*,
Bold in the Practice of *mistaken Rules*,   110
Prescribe, apply, and call their *Masters Fools*.
Some on the Leaves of ancient Authors prey,
Nor Time nor Moths e'er spoil'd so much as they:
Some dryly plain, without Invention's Aid,
Write dull *Receits*° how Poems may be made: 115
These leave the Sense, their Learning to display,
And those explain the Meaning quite away.
   You then whose Judgment the right Course wou'd steer,
Know well each ANCIENT's proper *Character*,
His *Fable, Subject, Scope* in ev'ry *Page*,   120
Religion, Country, Genius of his *Age*:
Without all these at once before your Eyes,

---

94. *Parnassus'*: Parnassus is the mountain in Greece sacred to Apollo and the Muses, and thus the classical site of poetry.
108. *Pothecaries*: Apothecaries.
115. *Receits*: Recipes.

Cavil you may, but never *Criticize.*
Be *Homer's* Works° your *Study,* and *Delight,*
Read them by Day, and meditate by Night,   125
Thence form your Judgment, thence your Maxims bring,
And trace the Muses *upward* to their *Spring;*
Still with *It self compar'd,* his Text peruse;
And let your *Comment* be the *Mantuan Muse.*°
   When first young *Maro°* in his boundless Mind   130
A Work t' outlast Immortal *Rome* design'd,
Perhaps he seem'd *above* the Critick's Law,
And but from *Nature's Fountains* scorn'd to draw:
But when t'examine ev'ry Part he came,
Nature and *Homer* were, he found, the *same:*   135
Convinc'd, amaz'd, he checks the bold Design,⎫
And Rules as strict his labour'd Work confine, ⎬
As if the *Stagyrite°* o'erlook'd each Line.⎭
Learn hence for Ancient *Rules* a just Esteem;
To copy *Nature* is to copy *Them.*   140
   Some Beauties yet, no Precepts can declare,
For there's a *Happiness* as well as *Care.*
Musick resembles *Poetry,* in each⎫
Are *nameless Graces* which no Methods teach,⎬
And which a *Master-Hand* alone can reach. ⎭   145
If, where the *Rules* not far enough extend,
(Since Rules were made but to promote their End)
Some Lucky LICENCE answers to the full
Th' Intent propos'd, *that Licence* is a *Rule.*
Thus *Pegasus,°* a nearer way to take,   150
May boldly deviate from the common Track.
Great Wits sometimes may *gloriously offend,*
And *rise* to *Faults* true Criticks *dare not mend;*
From *vulgar Bounds* with *brave Disorder* part,
And *snatch* a *Grace* beyond the Reach of Art,   155

   124. *Homer's Works:* The *Iliad* and the *Odyssey,* by the ninth-century B.C. Greek epic poet.
   129. *Mantuan Muse:* Virgil, a first-century B.C. Latin poet born near Mantua, is the author of the *Georgics,* the *Eclogues,* and the epic poem, the *Aeneid.*
   130. *Maro:* Virgil, whose full Latin name is Publius Vergilius Maro.
   138. *the Stagyrite:* Aristotle (384–322 B.C.), a student of Plato and with him one of the greatest of the Greek philosophers, was born in Stagira, Greece.
   150. *Pegasus:* In Greek mythology, a winged horse that sprang from the blood of the Gorgon Medusa when she was beheaded by the hero Perseus.

Which, without passing thro' the *Judgment*, gains
The *Heart*, and all its End *at once* attains.
In *Prospects*, thus, some *Objects* please our Eyes,⎫
Which *out of* Nature's *common Order* rise,   ⎬
The shapeless *Rock*, or hanging *Precipice*.   ⎭   160
But tho' the *Ancients* thus their *Rules* invade,
(As *Kings* dispense with *Laws* Themselves have made)
Moderns, beware! Or if you must offend
Against the *Precept*, ne'er transgress its *End*,
Let it be *seldom*, and *compell'd by Need*,   165
And have, at least, *Their Precedent* to plead.
The Critick else proceeds without Remorse,
Seizes your Fame, and puts his Laws in force.
    I know there are, to whose presumptuous Thoughts
Those *Freer Beauties*, ev'n in *Them*, seem Faults: 170
Some Figures *monstrous* and *mis-shap'd* appear,
Consider'd *singly*, or beheld too *near*,
Which, but *proportion'd* to their *Light*, or *Place*,
Due Distance *reconciles* to Form and Grace.
A prudent Chief not always must display   175
His Pow'rs in *equal Ranks*, and *fair Array*,
But with th' *Occasion* and the *Place* comply,
Conceal his Force, nay seem sometimes to *Fly*.
Those oft are *Stratagems* which *Errors* seem,
Nor is it *Homer Nods*, but *We* that *Dream*.   180
    Still green with Bays each *ancient* Altar stands,
Above the reach of *Sacrilegious* Hands,
Secure from *Flames*, from *Envy's* fiercer Rage,
Destructive *War*, and all-involving *Age*.
See, from *each Clime* the Learn'd their Incense bring;   185
Hear, in *all Tongues* consenting *Pæans* ring!
In Praise so just, let ev'ry Voice be join'd,
And fill the *Gen'ral Chorus* of *Mankind*!
Hail *Bards Triumphant*! born in *happier Days*;
Immortal Heirs of *Universal* Praise!   190
Whose Honours with Increase of Ages *grow*,
As Streams roll down, *enlarging* as they flow!
Nations *unborn* your mighty Names shall sound,
And Worlds applaud that must not yet be *found*!
Oh may some Spark of *your* Cœlestial Fire   195
The last, the meanest of your Sons inspire,

(That on weak Wings, from far, pursues your Flights;
Glows while he *reads*, but *trembles* as he *writes*)
To teach vain Wits a Science *little known*,
T' *admire* Superior Sense, and *doubt* their own!　　　　200
· ·
　　A *little Learning* is a dang'rous Thing;　　　　215
Drink deep, or taste not the *Pierian* Spring:°
There *shallow Draughts* intoxicate the Brain,
And drinking *largely* sobers us again.
Fir'd at first Sight with what the *Muse* imparts,
In *fearless Youth* we tempt the Heights of Arts,　　　　220
While from the bounded *Level* of our Mind,
Short Views we take, nor see the *Lengths behind*,
But *more advanc'd*, behold with strange Surprize
New, distant Scenes of *endless* Science rise!
So pleas'd at first, the towring *Alps* we try,　　　　225
Mount o'er the Vales, and seem to tread the Sky;
Th' Eternal Snows appear already past,
And the first *Clouds* and *Mountains* seem the last:
But *those attain'd*, we tremble to survey
The growing Labours of the lengthen'd Way,　　　　230
Th' *increasing* Prospect *tires* our wandring Eyes,
Hills peep o'er Hills, and *Alps* on *Alps* arise!
　　A perfect Judge will *read* each Work of Wit
With the same Spirit that its Author *writ*,
Survey the *Whole*, nor seek slight Faults to find,　　　　235
Where *Nature moves*, and *Rapture warms* the Mind;
Nor lose, for that malignant dull Delight,
The *gen'rous Pleasure* to be charm'd with Wit.
But in such Lays as neither *ebb*, nor *flow*,
Correctly cold, and *regularly low*,　　　　240
That shunning Faults, one quiet *Tenour* keep;
We cannot *blame* indeed — but we may *sleep*.
In Wit, as Nature, what affects our Hearts
Is not th' Exactness of peculiar Parts;
'Tis not a *Lip*, or *Eye*, we Beauty call,　　　　245
But the joint Force and full *Result* of all.
Thus when we view some well-proportion'd Dome,

---

216. *Pierian Spring:* In Greek mythology, a spring in Macedonia sacred to the Muses and a source of poetic inspiration.

(The *World*'s just Wonder, and ev'n *thine* O *Rome*!)
No single Parts unequally surprize;
All comes *united* to th' admiring Eyes;   250
No monstrous Height, or Breadth, or Length appear;
The *Whole* at once is *Bold*, and *Regular*.
   Whoever thinks a faultless Piece to see,
Thinks what ne'er was, nor is, nor e'er shall be.
In ev'ry Work regard the *Writer's End*,   255
Since none can compass more than they *Intend*;
And if the *Means* be just, the *Conduct* true,
Applause, in spite of trivial Faults, is due.
As Men of Breeding, sometimes Men of Wit,
T' avoid *great Errors*, must the *less* commit,   260
Neglect the Rules each *Verbal Critick* lays,
For *not* to know some Trifles, is a Praise.
Most Criticks, fond of some subservient Art,
Still make the *Whole* depend upon a *Part*,
They talk of *Principles*, but Notions prize,   265
And All to one lov'd Folly Sacrifice.
. . . .

   Unhappy *Wit*, like most mistaken Things,
Attones not for that *Envy* which it brings.   495
In *Youth* alone its empty Praise we boast,
But soon the Short-liv'd Vanity is lost!
Like some fair *Flow'r* the early *Spring* supplies,
That gaily Blooms, but ev'n in blooming *Dies*.
What is this *Wit* which must our Cares employ?   500
The *Owner's Wife*, that *other Men* enjoy,
Then most our *Trouble* still when most *admir'd*,
And still the more we *give*, the more *requir'd*;
Whose Fame with *Pains* we guard, but lose with *Ease*,
Sure *some* to *vex*, but never *all* to *please*;   505
'Tis what the *Vicious fear*, the *Virtuous shun*;
By *Fools* 'tis *hated*, and by *Knaves undone*!
   If *Wit* so much from *Ign'rance* undergo,
Ah let not *Learning* too commence its Foe!
Of old, those met *Rewards* who cou'd *excel*,   510
And such were *Prais'd* who but *endeavour'd well*:
Tho' *Triumphs* were to *Gen'rals* only due,
Crowns were reserv'd to grace the *Soldiers* too.
Now, they who reached *Parnassus'* lofty Crown,
Employ their Pains to spurn some others down;   515

And while Self-Love each jealous Writer rules,
Contending Wits becomes the *Sport of Fools*:
But still the *Worst* with most Regret commend,
For each *Ill Author* is as bad a *Friend.*
To what base Ends, and by what abject Ways,⁣ 520
Are Mortals urg'd thro' *Sacred Lust of Praise*!
Ah ne'er so *dire* a *Thirst of Glory* boast,
Nor in the *Critick* let the *Man* be lost!
Good-Nature and *Good-Sense* must ever join;
To Err is *Humane*; to Forgive, *Divine.*⁣ 525

ALEXANDER POPE

From *Peri Bathous: or, Martinus Scriblerus His Treatise of the Art of Sinking in Poetry*

Martinus Scriblerus is the satiric persona of the pedant created by the Scriblerus Club, of which Pope, along with Jonathan Swift and Dr. Arbuthnot, was a member. A satire on false taste, pedantry, bad writing, and commercial values, *Peri Bathous* (*On the Depths*) is modeled on *Peri Hypsos* (*On the Sublime*), a rhetorical treatise generally ascribed to the third-century philosopher Longinus. For more information on Alexander Pope, see the headnote to *An Essay on Criticism* (p. 441).

Chap. I.

It hath been long (my dear Countrymen) the Subject of my Concern and Surprize, that whereas numberless Poets, Criticks and Orators have compiled and digested the Art of *Ancient Poesie*, there hath not arisen among us one Person so publick spirited, as to perform the like for the *Modern*. Altho' it is universally known, that our everyway-industrious Moderns, both in the Weight of their *Writings*, and in the Velocity of their *Judgments*, do so infinitely excel the said Ancients.

Nevertheless, too true it is, that while a plain and direct Road is pav'd to their ὕψος, or *sublime*; no Track has been yet chalk'd out, to arrive at our βάθος, or *profund*. The *Latins*, as they came between the *Greeks* and Us, make use of the Word *Altitudo*, which implies equally *Height* and *Depth*. Wherefore considering with no small Grief, how many promising Genius's of this Age are wandering (as I may say) in the dark without a Guide, I have undertaken this arduous but necessary Task, to lead them as it were by the hand, and step by step, the gentle downhill way to the *Bathos*; the Bottom, the End, the Central Point, the *non plus ultra*[1] of true Modern Poesie!

When I consider (my dear Countrymen) the Extent, Fertility, and Populousness of our *Lowlands* of *Parnassus*,[2] the flourishing State of our Trade, and the Plenty of our Manufacture; there are two Reflections which administer great Occasion of Surprize; the one, that all Dignities and Honours should be bestow'd upon the exceeding few meager Inhabitants at the Top of the Mountain; the other, that our own Nation should have arriv'd to that Pitch of Greatness it now possesses, without any regular *System of Laws*. As to the first, it is with great Pleasure I have observ'd of late the gradual Decay of Delicacy and Refinement among Mankind, who are become too reasonable to require that we should labour with infinite Pains to come up to the Taste of those Mountaineers, when they without any, may condescend to ours. But as we have now an *unquestionable Majority* on our side, I doubt not but we shall shortly be able to level the *Highlanders*, and procure a farther Vent for our own Product, which is already so much relish'd, encourag'd, and rewarded, by the Nobility and Gentry of *Great Britain*.

Therefore to supply our former Defect, I purpose to collect the scatter'd Rules of our Art into regular Institutes, from the Example and Practice of the deep Genius's of our Nation; imitating herein my Predecessors, the Master of *Alexander*, and the Secretary of the renown'd *Zenobia*[3]: And in this my Undertaking I am the more animated, as I expect more Success than has attended even those great Criticks, since their Laws (tho' they might be good) have ever been slackly executed, and their Precepts (however strict) obey'd only by Fits, and by a very small Number.

At the same time I intend to do justice upon our Neighbours, Inhabitants of the *upper Parnassus*; who taking advantage of the rising

---

[1] *non plus ultra:* That beyond which there is nothing, the ultimate point.

[2] *Parnassus:* The mountain in Greece sacred to Apollo and the Muses, and thus the classical site of poetry.

[3] *Master of Alexander, and the Secretary of the renown'd Zenobia:* The philosopher Aristotle (384–322 B.C.) was the schoolmaster of Alexander the Great of Macedon. Dionysus Cassius Longinus (210?–273), a Greek philosopher and the reputed author of the rhetorical text *Peri Hypsos* (*On the Sublime*), was the secretary of Zenobia, a famous queen of the Roman colony of Palmyra from 267/68 to 272.

Ground, are perpetually throwing down Rubbish, Dirt, and Stones upon us, never suffering us to live in Peace: These Men, while they enjoy the Chrystal Stream of *Helicon*,[4] envy us our common Water, which (thank our Stars) tho it is somewhat muddy, flows in much greater abundance. Nor is this the greatest injustice we have to complain of; for tho' it is evident that we never made the least *Attempt* or *Inrode* into *their* Territories, but lived contented in our Native Fens; they have often, not only committed *Petty Larcenys* upon our Borders, but driven the Country, and carried off at once *whole Cartloads* of our *Manufacture*; to reclaim some of which stolen Goods is part of the Design of this Treatise.

For we shall see in the course of this Work, that our greatest Adversaries have sometimes descended towards us; and doubtless might now and then have arrived at the *Bathos* itself, had it not been for that mistaken Opinion they all entertained, that the *Rules* of the *Antients* were *equally necessary* to the *Moderns*, than which there cannot be a more grievous Error, as will be amply proved in the following Discourse.

And indeed when any of these have gone so far, as by the light of their own Genius to attempt upon *new Models*, it is wonderful to observe, how nearly they have approach'd Us in those particular Pieces; tho' in all their others they differ'd *toto cœlo*[5] from us.

Chap. II.

That the Bathos, *or* Profund, *is the natural Taste of Man, and in particular, of the present Age.*

The Taste of the *Bathos* is implanted by Nature itself in the Soul of Man; 'till perverted by Custom or Example he is taught, or rather compell'd, to relish the *Sublime*. Accordingly, we see the unprejudiced Minds of Children delight only in such Productions, and in such Images, as our true modern Writers set before them. I have observ'd how fast the general Taste is returning to this first Simplicity and Innocence; and if the Intent of all Poetry be to divert and instruct, certainly that Kind which diverts and instructs the greatest Number, is to be preferr'd. Let us look round among the Admirers of Poetry, we shall find those who have a Taste of the *Sublime* to be very few, but the *Profund* strikes universally, and is adapted to every

[4] *Helicon:* In Greek mythology, the mountain where Apollo and the Muses lived.
[5] *toto cœlo:* By the entire extent of the heavens.

Capacity. 'Tis a fruitless Undertaking to write for Men of a nice and foppish *Gusto*,[6] whom, after all, it is almost impossible to please; and 'tis still more Chimerical to write for *Posterity*, of whose Taste we cannot make any Judgment, and whose Applause we can never enjoy. It must be confess'd, our wiser Authors have a present End,

Et prodesse volunt, & delectare Poetæ:[7]

Their true Design is *Profit* or *Gain*; in order to acquire which, 'tis necessary to procure Applause, by administring *Pleasure* to the Reader: From whence it follows demonstrably, that their Productions must be suited to the *present Taste*; and I cannot but congratulate our Age on this peculiar Felicity, that tho' we have made indeed great Progress in all other Branches of Luxury, we are not yet debauch'd with any *high relish* in Poetry, but are in this one Taste, less *nice* than our Ancestors. If an Art is to be estimated by its Success, I appeal to Experience, whether there have not been, in proportion to their Number, as many starving good Poets, as bad ones?

Nevertheless, in making *Gain* the principal End of our Art, far be it from me to exclude any great *Genius's* of *Rank* or *Fortune* from diverting themselves this way. They ought to be praised no less than those Princes, who pass their vacant Hours in some ingenious Mechanical or Manual Art: And to such as these, it would be Ingratitude not to own, that our Art has been often infinitely indebted.

Chap. XIII.

A Project for the Advancement of the Bathos.

Thus have I (my dear Countrymen) with incredible Pains and Diligence, discover'd the hidden Sources of the *Bathos*, or as I may say broke open the Abysses of this *Great Deep*. And having now establish'd the good and wholesome *Laws*, what remains but that all true Moderns with their utmost Might do proceed to put the same in execution? In order whereto, I think I shall in the second place highly deserve of my Country, by proposing such a *Scheme*, as may facilitate this great End.

As our Number is confessedly far superior to that of the Enemy, there seems nothing wanting but Unanimity among our selves. It is

---

[6] *Gusto:* Taste.
[7] *Et . . . delectare Poetæ:* From Horace, *Ars Poetica* 1.333: "Poets want to profit and to please."

therefore humbly offer'd, that all and every Individual of the *Bathos* do enter into a firm *Association*, and incorporate into *one Regular Body*, whereof every Member, even the meanest, will some way contribute to the Support of the whole; in like manner as the weakest Reeds when join'd in one Bundle, become infrangible. To which end our Art ought to be put upon the same foot with other Arts of this Age. The vast Improvement of modern Manufactures ariseth from their being divided into several Branches, and parcel'd out to several *Trades*: For instance, in *Clock-making*, one Artist makes the Balance, another the Spring, another the Crown-Wheels, a fourth the Case, and the principal Workman puts all together; To this OEconomy we owe the Perfection of our modern Watches; and doubtless we also might that of our modern Poetry and Rhetoric, were the several Parts branched out in the like manner.

Nothing is more evident than that divers Persons, no other way remarkable, have each a strong Disposition to the Formation of some particular Trope or Figure. *Aristotle* saith, that the *Hyperbole* is an Ornament of Speech fit for *young Men of Quality*; accordingly we find in those Gentlemen a wonderful Propensity toward it, which is marvellously improv'd by *travelling*. *Soldiers* also and *Seamen* are very happy in the same Figure. The *Periphrasis* or *Circumlocution* is the peculiar Talent of *Country Farmers*, the Proverb and Apologue of *old Men* at their Clubs, the *Ellipsis* or Speech by half-words of *Ministers* and *Politicians*, the *Aposiopesis* of *Courtiers*, the *Littole* or Diminution of *Ladies*, *Whisperers* and *Backbiters*; and the *Anadyplosis*[8] of Common *Cryers* and *Hawkers*, who by redoubling the same Words, persuade People to buy their Oysters, green Hastings, or new Ballads. *Epithets* may be found in great plenty at *Billingsgate*,[9] *Sarcasm* and *Irony* learn'd upon the *Water*, and the *Epiphonema* or *Exclamation* frequently from the *Bear-garden*,[10] and as frequently from the *Hear him* of the House of Commons.

Now each man applying his whole Time and Genius upon his particular Figure, would doubtless attain to Perfection; and when each

---

[8] *Littole . . . Anadyplosis:* Rhetorical figures. Littole is a figure of speech in which an affirmative is expressed by a negative. Anadyplosis involves reduplication, beginning a sentence, line, or clause with the concluding or any prominent word of the one preceding.

[9] *Billingsgate:* Billingsgate Market was situated at the north end of London Bridge. From the sixteenth century, it was principally a fishmarket and became a byword for the low, profane English spoken there.

[10] *Bear-garden:* A place, such as Hockley in the Hole, where bear fights and prize-fights were held and wagered on.

became incorporated and sworn into the Society, (as hath been pro-pos'd;) a Poet or Orator would have no more to do, but to send to the particular Traders in each Kind; to the *Metaphorist* for his *Allegories*, to the *Simile-maker* for his *Comparisons*, to the *Ironist* for his *Sarcasmes*, to the *Apothegmatist* for his *Sentences*, *&c.* whereby a *Dedication* or *Speech* would be compos'd in a Moment, the superior Artist having nothing to do but to put together all the Materials.

I therefore propose that there be contrived with all convenient Dispatch, at the publick Expence, a *Rhetorical Chest of Drawers*, consisting of three Stories, the highest for the *Deliberative*, the middle for the *Demonstrative*, and the lowest for the *Judicial*. These shall be divided into *Loci* or *Places*, being Repositories for Matter and Argument in the several Kinds of Oration or Writing; and every Drawer shall again be sub-divided into Cells, resembling those of Cabinets for Rarities. The Apartment for *Peace* or *War*, and that of the *Liberty* of the *Press*, may in a very few Days be fill'd with several Arguments *perfectly new*; and the *Vituperative Partition* will as easily be replenish'd with a most choice Collection, entirely of the Growth and Manufacture of the present Age. Every Composer will soon be taught the Use of this Cabinet, and how to manage all the Registers of it, which will be drawn out much in the Manner of those of an Organ.

The Keys of it must be kept in honest Hands, by some *Reverend Prelate*, or *Valiant Officer*, of unquestion'd Loyalty and Affection to every present Establishment in *Church* and *State*; which will sufficiently guard against any Mischief which might otherwise be apprehended from it.

And being lodg'd in such Hands, it may be at discretion *let out* by the *Day*, to several great Orators in both Houses; from whence it is to be hop'd much *Profit* or *Gain* will also accrue to our Society.

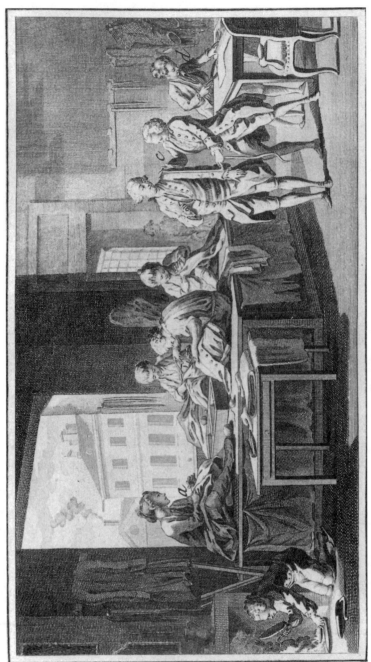

"Tailleur d'Habits" (Tailor Shop), from *Encyclopédie, Recuiel de Planches*

4

Fashioning Gender

This section includes papers and accompanying materials that reflect the role of taste and fashion in the representation of the modern bourgeois character, especially the gendering of that character. In her discussion of what she names "the eighteenth-century myth of passive womanhood," Ellen Pollak explains her use of the term "myth":

> I mean to refer specifically to the representational forms that ideology takes — to the literary and epistemological structures by which certain proportions about the phenomenal world (in this case, women) are made to seem the outgrowths of a strict necessity, consistent with the laws of natural order. (5)

Dress and manners, like literature, serve as structures through which gender can be represented as natural and inevitable. The eighteenth-century myth of passive womanhood was propagated not only through literary rhetoric but also through the rhetorics of style that shaped bodily appearance and social self-presentation. The historical development of the modern notion of innate sexual difference, grounded in biology and so utterly naturalized, is readily apparent in discussions of personal stylization (see Introduction, p. 19). The fascinated anxiety about cross-dressing that abounds in eighteenth-century literature, for example, reveals an urgent effort to erase the gap between innate "natural" sexual identity and external cultural forms of gender representation. The representation of gender difference becomes part of the broader eighteenth-century literary and aesthetic issues of nature vs. artifice. Conversely, literary-aesthetic discussions are often inflected through the metaphors of dress and the figure of the clothed or stripped female body. The eighteenth-century quest for a natural standard of taste and style is inseparable from the modern insistence on a naturalized ground of gender difference. As critics like Thomas Laqueur, Michael McKeon, Ellen Pollak, and Laura Brown have shown, our modern sense that gender difference is inalienably based in inborn biological sexual difference has been largely shaped by the medical, scientific, aesthetic, social, and economic discourses of the eighteenth century.

Textual and pictorial evidence from this period suggests a near obsession with matters of style. Satires on fashion and the fashionable abound, and the discourse of fashion permeates poetry, fiction, and drama. Casual allusions to fashion esoterica in social satire rely on an astounding technical expertise in matters of dress. Discussions of political economy, education, and ethics consider fashion, taste, style, and consumption as matters of urgent concerns in the areas of economy, politics, pedagogy, and morality. As this suggests, fashion talk is about much more than clothing and encompasses all manner of social practices and attitudes. In the early eighteenth century, as in the late twentieth, there are fashionable and unfashionable clothes, hairstyles, foods, houses, furniture, neighborhoods, religions, books, plays, attitudes, beliefs, illnesses, gestures, courtship rituals, modes of combat, people, and pastimes. The lion's share of the attention to fashion is unequivocally negative. Fashion becomes a way to talk about much that is wrong with the world and so a critical category in the rhetoric of reform. Of course, it is because so much of the world revolves around fashion that it can serve as such a fulcrum for cultural criticism.

In the *Tatler* and *Spectator* papers gathered here, fashion itself seems at odds with their ideal human types. Addison's and Steele's contemporaries, so their papers claim, are being lost to fashion. *Spectator* Nos. 275 and 281, which recount the dissection of a beau's brain and a coquette's heart, reveal individuals whose innermost core of rationality and sentiment have been taken over by the fashionable things so avidly consumed in the *beau monde*. This vision speaks of a loss of humanity. At the same time, it reveals exactly where the essentially human is thought to reside: inside, not outside; in the mind and heart, not in mere appearances. The real self, the authentically human, is conceived of as an essentially interior arena of integrity and value. The authentic bourgeois individual exists in a kind of polarized opposition to the blatant cultural codes of fashion. To talk about fashion in this context becomes a way of talking about what is not essentially human, what may in fact impede the development and true representation of human character.

As depicted in Will Honeycomb's account of the Pict-Coquette in *Spectator* No. 41 and more darkly in Swift's "The Progress of Beauty" and "A Beautiful Young Nymph Going to Bed," the drive to discover the natural ground of human identity can take the form of stripping the body, usually the female body, of all artifice. That this discovery is often a disappointment, sometimes even a horror, demonstrates the highly vexed position of women in eighteenth-century life and thought. If women, as Pope asserts in his *Epistle to a Lady,* "have no Characters at all," then under all their artifice there is nothing to find (see p. 568). Swift discovers in his stripped prostitutes only the reek of human despair and the stinking physical decay engendered by lives in thrall to an institution of sexual exploitation. But in *The Tatler* and *The Spectator,* woman's innate fickleness, her apparent lack of character and self-identity, become conditions for her improvement rather than occasions for despair or derision. Precisely because her lack of a self-identity leaves her vulnerable to outside influence and change, woman is malleable; she is open to good influence as well as bad. More optimistic and progressive than Swift and Pope, Addison and Steele want to give women a character, but one that is wholly defined by her domestic and familial roles.

Around the turn of the eighteenth century, the map of social geography was being redrafted to define highly gendered, differentiated spheres of activity: public/masculine/commercial and private/feminine/familial. These realms, like the relationship between the sexes, are conceived of as separate but complementary. Indeed, like the ideal relationship outlined in *Spectator* No. 128, this harmonious complementarity depends on a model of gender in which differences between masculine and feminine are naturalized and essentialized and thus inviolable. In the texts presented here, jurisdiction over fashion, taste, and consumption works to police gender boundaries and sexuality. The history of costume shows that, in line with the increasingly gendered separation of social spheres, gendered distinctions in dress become more marked and more significant. It is not until the eighteenth century that the stylistic rhetoric of male dress starts to develop along a path that is separate from female dress. Earlier modes of male and female dress were certainly not indistinguishable, but they shared many of the same elements and reflected similar principles of ornamentation, structure, and even body type. Thus the softly folding drapery of the legs (in men as pantaloons, in women as skirts), lace, ribbons, and brocade of baroque costume all show up in the clothing of both sexes. In the eighteenth century, however, masculine costume sheds the superfluous ornament and gorgeous fanciness that had been common a century earlier, and just as important, the *cut* of male and female clothes diverges. Thus men's breeches get tighter as women's skirts get fuller. They no longer mirror one another.

The new reserved style of male costume becomes an important mark of masculinity itself, while fancy dress becomes a sign of effeminacy. In *Spectator* No. 156, with its description of the lady's man, effeminacy in dress and attitude is not yet monolithically identified with same-sex desire, with what in the nineteenth century comes to be called homosexuality. Yet this association is beginning to emerge, as we can see in the sodomitical references in *Mundus Foppensis*, in Edward Ward's description of the Mollies' Club, and in the letter from the indignant Pretty Fellow in *Tatler* No. 26 (see p. 467).

Modern gender roles are historical-cultural formations, as are the modern identity categories "heterosexual" and "homosexual." Randolph Trumbach has shown that the shift in gender definitions taking place in the early eighteenth century is rooted in notions of sexual difference that also support the development of the modern, exclusively homosexual effeminate type. There is greater differentiation between the dress of men and women and between that of real men and mollies. Whether it is the overt transvestitism of some of the mollies or the suspicious frippery of the fop, failure to adhere to a sober male uniform begins to look like gender treachery.

But just as there is a drive to get men out of their ribbons, lace, high-heeled red pumps, and makeup and into a more sober, more masculine costume, there is likewise a drive to get women to simplify their dress, to abandon fragrantly artificial styles and overtly affected manners. One might wonder if women are being asked to adopt a masculine mode of dress. Not exactly. As Addison makes clear at the close of *Tatler* No. 116, he by no means wants to deprive women of all their ornaments. But the kinds of ornaments he approves are figured as "natural." In keeping with her own nature as a "beautiful Romantick Animal," Addison's woman "may be adorned with Furs and Feathers, Pearls and Diamonds, Ores and Silks" (see p. 485). The difference between the fashion aesthetic promoted in *The Tatler* and

The Spectator and the one it is meant to displace hinges on this concept of the natural. Women should not hide their true selves beneath their paint or their petticoats. Their dress should represent, not distort or dissimulate, their "natural" identity.

Forces of artifice, irrationalities of style, affectation, and dissimulation are themselves largely identified with a bad sort of femininity. What we can see happening in the *Tatler* and the *Spectator* papers is an effort to purge both male *and* female modes of self-representation of a shared set of "bad feminine" qualities. The ideal male and the ideal female are defined in negative relation to this set of feminine character flaws. As the papers describe their ideal female character, they remove from her the contaminants of the badly feminine: exhibitionist self-display, slavish devotion to irrational and unnatural modes, gadding about in the public world.

The demand for a simpler, more natural style of female dress and manner, then, does not involve a call to masculinize women's costume. Indeed, female dress such as the equestrian costume discussed in *Spectator* No. 435, which transgresses gender limits, hybridizing and confusing sexual differences, is emphatically denounced. Women dressed in the suit jackets and skirts of the eighteenth-century riding costume threaten the ideal of bourgeois femininity not only with a symbolic gender transgression figured by their "Amphibious Dress" but also with more literal and practical transgressions (see p. 539). A woman out riding is a woman gadding abroad, a woman outside the limits of the domestic scene that circumscribes her proper field of experience. Similarly concerned with the scandal of women in masculine attire, Mrs. Crackenthorpe derides an eccentric pair of sisters, Mrs. Margaret and Mrs. Millicent Trott, in No. 8 of *The Female Tatler*, for affecting "every thing that's masculine" (see p. 562). Unlike the lady equestrian in *Spectator* No. 435, these ladies go out in full male drag. But here again, the scandal lies in the access to arenas and experiences outside the domestic sphere that such dress-code violations give women. Got up in their jackets, cloaks, and periwigs, Mrs. Millicent and Mrs. Margaret go out on the town in the confirmed style of the libertine rake: "They'll sit down tightly to a bowl of punch, and then scour the streets, break windows, and have so little regard to their own sex as to abuse every woman they meet" (see pp. 562–63). Unladylike behavior indeed.

Though such hooliganism is also, according to the standards being established in *The Tatler* and *The Spectator*, *ungentlemanly* behavior, and while no one would approve of this rakish dissipation in women, many of Addison's and Steele's contemporaries would, if not applaud, at least wink at it in men. Many people still modeled their notion of the fine, spirited man of style after a type established by the libertine court rakes of the Restoration (1660). Addison and Steele work strenuously to revise this model and admonish the flash, violence, and excesses of the libertine gentleman, though, as in Steele's character sketch of a rake (*Tatler* No. 27), this disapproval may be indulgent and affectionate. One major obstacle to the reform of the rake, the fop, the beau, the pretty fellow, the lady's man, and the coquette is that these social types are fashionable. Embodying attitudes, privileges, and distinctions highly valued in the early eighteenth century, these types were prized for their glamor, social mastery, sex appeal, and worldly prestige. To counter them, Addison and Steele must change the sensibilities of their contemporaries so that the decent, mild-mannered man is the true gentleman, the sensible, unaffected, and modest woman the desirable woman. The success of the reformed characters, manners, and stylistic principles they promote rests not simply on a disavowal of style, fashion, and prestige but also on a reconstitution of the content of these categories. The papers strive to establish a popular taste for the unaffected, modest, simple, natural, and sincere. They want to reform the regime of style that governs polite English life and the genteel English subject.

The Tatler

No. 24
Saturday, June 4, 1709
[Addison (?) on the Pretty Fellow and the Toast of the Town]

White's Chocolate-house, June 2.
    In my Paper of the 28th of the last Month, I mention'd several Characters which want Explanation to the Generality of Readers: Among others, I spoke of a Pretty Fellow. I have since received a kind Admonition in a Letter to take Care that I do not omit to show also what is meant by a *very* Pretty Fellow, which is to be allow'd as a

Character by it self, and a Person exalted above the other by a peculiar Sprightliness; as one who, by a distinguishing Vigour, outstrips
his Companions, and has thereby deserved and obtained a particular
Appellation, or Nick-name of Familiarity. Some have this Distinction
from the Fair Sex, who are so generous as to take into their Protection such as are laugh'd at by the Men, and place 'em for that Reason
in Degrees of Favour.

The chief of this Sort is Colonel *Brunett*, who is a Man of Fashion,
because he will be so; and practises a very janty Way of Behaviour,
because he is too careless to know when he offends, and too sanguine
to be mortified if he did know it. Thus the Colonel has met with a
Town ready to receive him, and can't possibly see why he should not
make use of their Favour, and set himself in the First Degree of Conversation. Therefore he is very successfully loud among the Wits, familiar among the Ladies, and dissolute among the Rakes. Thus he is
admitted in one Place, because he is so in another; and every Man
treats *Brunett* well, not out of his particular Esteem for him, but in
Respect to the Opinion of others. It is to me a solid Pleasure to see
the World thus mistaken on the good-natur'd Side; for 'tis Ten to
One but the Colonel mounts into a General Officer, marries a fine
Lady, and is Master of a good Estate, before they come to explain
upon him. What gives most Delight to me in this Observation, is, that
all this arises from pure Nature, and the Colonel can account for his
Success no more than those by whom he succeeds. For these Causes
and Considerations, I pronounce him a true Woman's Man, and in
the first Degree, *A very Pretty Fellow*.

The next to a Man of this universal Genius, is one who is peculiarly form'd for the Service of the Ladies, and his Merit chiefly is to
be of no Consequence. I am indeed a little in Doubt, Whether he
ought not rather to be call'd a *very Happy*, than a *very Pretty* Fellow?
For he is admitted at all Hours: All he says or does, which would offend in another, are pass'd over in him; and all Actions and Speeches
which please, doubly please if they come from him: No one wonders
or takes Notice when he's wrong; but all admire him when he's in the
Right. — By the Way it is fit to remark, That there are People of better Sense than these, who endeavour at this Character; but they are
out of Nature; and tho', with some Industry, they get the Characters
of Fools, they cannot arrive to be *very*, seldom to be meerly *Pretty
Fellows*. But where Nature has form'd a Person for this Station
amongst Men, he is gifted with a peculiar Genius for Success, and his
very Errors and Absurdities contribute to it; this Felicity attending

him to his Life's End. For it being in a Manner necessary that he should be of no Consequence, he is as well in Old Age as Youth; and I know a Man, whose Son has been some Years a Pretty Fellow, who is himself at this Hour a *very* Pretty Fellow. One must move tenderly in this Place, for we are now in the Ladies Lodgings, and speaking of such as are supported by their Influence and Favour; against which there is not, neither ought there to be, any Dispute or Observation. But when we come into more free Air, one may talk a little more at large.

Give me leave then to mention Three whom I do not doubt but we shall see make considerable Figures; and these are such as, for their *Bacchanalian* Performances,[1] must be admitted into this Order. They are Three Brothers lately landed from *Holland*: As yet, indeed, they have not made their publick Entry, but lodge and converse at *Wapping*. They have merited already on the Water-side particular Titles: The First is called *Hogshead*; the Second, *Culverin*; and the Third, *Musquet*.[2] This Fraternity is preparing for our End of the Town by their Ability in the Exercises of *Bacchus*, and measure their Time and Merit by Liquid Weight, and Power of Drinking. *Hogshead* is a prettier Fellow than *Culverin* by Two Quarts, and *Culverin* than *Musquet* by a full Pint. It is to be fear'd, *Hogshead* is so often too full, and *Culverin* overloaded, that *Musquet* will be the only lasting *very* Pretty Fellow of the Three.

A Third Sort of this Denomination are such as, by very daring Adventures in Love, have purchas'd to themselves Renown and new Names; as *Jo. Carry*, for his excessive Strength and Vigour; *Tom Drybones*, for his generous Loss of Youth and Health; and *Cancrum*,[3] for his meritorious Rottenness.

These Great and Leading Spirits are propos'd to all such of our *British* Youth as would arrive at Perfection in these different Kinds; and if their Parts and Accomplishments were well imitated, it is not doubted, but that our Nation would soon excel all others in Wit and Arts, as they already do in Arms.

N. B. The Gentleman who stole *Betty Pepin*, may own it, for he is allow'd to be a *very* Pretty Fellow.

---

[1] *Bacchanalian Performances:* Drinking and carousing exploits. Bacchus (Dionysus) is the god of wine.

[2] *Hogshead . . . Culverin . . . Musquet:* A hogshead is a large barrel; a culverin is a long, heavy cannon; and a musquet (musket) is a shoulder gun.

[3] *Cancrum:* Canker or cancer.

But we must proceed to the Explanation
of other Terms in our Writings.

To know what a Toast[4] is in the Country, gives as much Perplexity as she her self does in Town: And indeed, the Learned differ very much upon the Original of this Word, and the Acceptation of it among the Moderns. However, it is by all agreed to have a joyous and chearful Import. A Toast in a cold Morning, heighten'd by Nutmeg, and sweeten'd with Sugar, has for many Ages been given to our Rural Dispensers of Justice, before they enter'd upon Causes, and has been of great and politick Use to take off the Severity of their Sentences; but has indeed been remarkable for one ill Effect, that it inclines those who use it immoderately to speak *Latin*, to the Admiration, rather than Information, of the Audience. This Application of a Toast makes it very obvious, that the Word may, without Metaphor, be understood as an apt Name for a Thing which raises us in the most sovereign Degree. But many of the Wits of the last Age will assert, That the Word, in its present Sense, was known among them in their Youth, and had its Rise from an Accident at the Town of *Bath*[5] in the Reign of King *Charles* the Second.[6]

It happen'd, that on a Publick Day a celebrated Beauty of those Times was in the *Cross-Bath*, and one of the Crowd of her Admirers took a Glass of the Water in which the Fair one stood, and drank her Health to the Company. There was in the Place a Gay Fellow, half fuddled, who offer'd to jump in, and swore, Tho' he lik'd not the Liquor, he would have the Toast. He was opposed in his Resolution; yet this Whim gave Foundation to the present Honour which is done to the Lady we mention in our Liquors, who has ever since been call'd a *Toast*.

Tho' this Institution had so trivial a Beginning, it is now elevated into a formal Order; and that happy Virgin who is receiv'd and drank to at their Meetings, has no more to do in this Life, but to judge and accept of the first good Offer. The Manner of her Inauguration is much like that of the Choice of a Doge in *Venice*:[7] It is perform'd by

---

[4] *Toast:* A description of this female type follows. A Toast is a woman celebrated in fashionable society for her beauty, savoir faire, and sex appeal.

[5] *Bath:* A popular resort town in southwest England, Bath is famous for its hot mineral springs.

[6] *Reign of King Charles the Second:* Charles II (1630–1685) reigned from 1660 to 1685.

[7] *Doge in Venice:* The doge was the elected chief magistrate of the former republics of Venice and Genoa.

Balloting; and when she is so chosen, she reigns indisputably for that ensuing Year; but must be elected anew to prolong her Empire a Moment beyond it. When she is regularly chosen, her Name is written with a Diamond on a Drinking-glass. The Hieroglyphick of the Diamond is to show her, that her Value is imaginary; and that of the Glass to acquaint her, that her Condition is frail, and depends on the Hand which holds her. This wise Design admonishes her, neither to over-rate or depreciate her Charms; as well considering and applying, that it is perfectly according to the Humour and Tast of the Company, whether the Toast is eaten or left as an Offal.[8]

The Foremost of the whole Rank of Toasts, and the most undisputed in their present Empire, are Mrs. *Gatty* and Mrs. *Frontlet*: The First, an Agreeable; the Second, an Awful Beauty. These Ladies are perfect Friends; out of a Knowledge, that their Perfections are too different to stand in Competition. He that likes *Gatty*, can have no Relish for so solemn a Creature as *Frontlet*; and an Admirer of *Frontlet*, will call *Gatty* a Maypole Girl.[9] *Gatty* for ever smiles upon you; and *Frontlet* disdains to see you smile. *Gatty*'s Love is a shining quick Flame; *Frontlet*'s a slow wasting Fire. *Gatty* likes the Man that diverts her; *Frontlet* him who adores her. *Gatty* always improves the Soil in which she travels; *Frontlet* lays wast the Country. *Gatty* does not only smile, but laughs at her Lover; *Frontlet* not only looks serious, but frowns at him. All the Men of Wit, and Coxcombs their Followers, are profess'd Servants of *Gatty*: The Politicians and Pretenders give solemn Worship to *Frontlet*. Their Reign will be best judg'd of by its Duration. *Frontlet* will never be chosen more; and *Gatty* is a Toast for Life.

---

[8] *Offal:* Here in the sense of refuse, leftover, remnant.
[9] *Maypole Girl:* A girl dancing around the Maypole on May 1, May Day, a traditional rustic holiday.

No. 26
Thursday, June 9, 1709
[Steele on a Letter from a Pretty Fellow]

From my own Apartment, June 8.

I have read the following Letter with Delight and Approbation, and I hereby order Mr. *Kidney* at St. *James*'s, and Sir *Thomas* at *White*'s,[1] (who are my Clerks for enrolling all Men in their distinct Classes, before they presume to drink Tea or Chocolate in those Places) to take Care, that the Persons within the Descriptions in the Letter be admitted, and excluded according to my Friend's Remonstrance.

SIR,   June 6. 1709

'*Your Paper of* Saturday *has rais'd up in me a noble Emulation, to be recorded in the foremost Rank of Worthies therein mention'd; and if any Regard be had to Merit or Industry, I may hope to succeed in the Promotion, for I have omitted no Toil or Expence to be a Proficient; and if my Friends do not flatter, they assure me, I have not lost my Time since I came to Town. To enumerate but a few Particulars; There's hardly a Coachman I meet with, but desires to be excus'd taking me, because he has had me before. I have compounded Two or Three Rapes; and let out to Hire as many Bastards to Beggars. I never saw above the First Act of a Play: And as to my Courage, it is well known, I have more than once had sufficient Witnesses of my drawing my Sword both in Tavern and Playhouse. Dr.* Wall *is my particular Friend; and if it were any Service to the Publick to compose the Difference between* Martin *and* Sintilaer *the Pearl-driller,[2] I don't know a Judge of more Experience than my self: For in that I may say with the Poet;*

Quae Regio in Villâ nostri non plena Laboris?[3]

'*I omit other lesser Particulars, the necessary Consequences of greater Actions. But my Reason for troubling you at this present is, to*

---

[1] *Mr. Kidney . . . Sir Thomas at White's:* Men who work as drawers, or waiters, at St. James's Coffee-house and White's Chocolate-house.

[2] *Dr. Wall . . . Sintilaer the Pearl-driller:* "Quack doctors," specializing in the cure of venereal disease [Bond].

[3] *Quae. . . plena Laboris?:* Altered from Virgil's *Aeneid* 1.460: *quae regio in terris nostri non plena laboria* ("What country on earth is not full of our works"). Here as altered: "What ward in the city is not full of our works?"

put a Stop, if it may be, to an insinuating, increasing Set of People,[4]
who sticking to the Letter *of your Treatise, and not to the Spirit of
it, do assume the Name of* Pretty Fellows; *nay, and even get new
Names, as you very well hint. Some of them I have heard calling to
one another as I have sat at* White's *and St.* James's, *by the Names of,*
Betty, Nelly, *and so forth. You see them accost each other with effeminate Airs: They have their Signs and Tokens like Free-Masons:
They rail at Womenkind; receive Visits on their Beds in Gowns, and
do a Thousand other unintelligible Prettinesses that I cannot tell
what to make of. I therefore heartily desire you would exclude all this
Sort of Animals.*

   *'There is another Matter I am foreseeing an ill Consequence from,
but may be timely prevented by Prudence; which is, that for the last
Fortnight, prodigious Shoals of Volunteers have gone over to bully
the* French, *upon hearing the Peace*[5] *was just signing; and this is so
true, that I can assure you, all Ingrossing Work about the* Temple[6] *is
risen above* 3 s. *in the Pound for want of Hands. Now as 'tis possible, some little Alteration of Affairs may have broken their Measures, and that they will post back again, I am under the last Apprehension, that these will, at their Return, all set up for* Pretty Fellows,
*and thereby confound all Merit and Service, and impose on us some
new Alteration in our Nightcap-Wigs*[7] *and Pockets, unless you can
provide a particular Class for them. I cannot apply my self better
than to you, and I'm sure I speak the Mind of a very great Number as
deserving as my self.'*

   The Pretensions of this Correspondent are worthy a particular Distinction: He cannot indeed be admitted as a *Pretty,* but is, what we
more justly call, a *Smart Fellow.* Never to pay at the Playhouse in an
Act of Frugality: That lets you into his Character. And his Expedient

---

[4] *Set of People:* As becomes clear from the following description, the correspondent refers to a set of mollies, or effeminate male homosexuals.

[5] *the Peace:* In 1708–09 Louis XIV again sought a peace to end the War of the
Spanish Succession (1701–14), but he finally refused the terms set by the English and
their allies.

[6] *Ingrossing Work about the Temple:* Copying work for the lawyers at the Temple.
The Temple Bar was one of the four Inns of Court housed along Fleet Street in London. Originally owned by the medieval religious and military Order of the Knights
Templar, who built their residence there in the twelfth century, this series of buildings,
known collectively as the Temple, was presented by James I to lawyers for their professional use. It housed both residential and professional legal apartments.

[7] *Nightcap-Wigs:* Short, close-fitting wigs styled like nightcaps.

in sending his Children a begging before they can go, are Characteristical Instances that he belongs to this Class. I never saw the Gentleman; but I know by his Letter, he hangs his Cane on his Button; and by some Lines of it, he should wear red heel'd Shoes; which are essential Parts of the Habit belonging to the Order of *Smart Fellows*.

No. 25
Tuesday, June 7, 1709
[Steele on Dueling]

White's *Chocolate-house, June 6.*

A Letter from a young Lady, written in the most passionate Terms, (wherein she laments the Misfortune of a Gentleman, her Lover, who was lately wounded in a Duel) has turn'd my Thoughts to that Subject, and enclin'd me to examine into the Causes which precipitate Men into so fatal a Folly. And as it has been propos'd to treat of Subjects of Gallantry in the Article from hence, and no one Point in Nature is more proper to be consider'd by the Company who frequent this Place, than that of Duels, it is worth our Consideration to examine into this Chimaerical groundless Humour, and to lay every other Thought aside, till we have strip'd it of all its false Pretences to Credit and Reputation amongst Men.

But I must confess, when I consider what I am going about, and run over in my Imagination all the endless Crowd of Men of Honour who will be offended at such a Discourse; I am undertaking, methinks, a Work worthy an invulnerable Heroe in Romance, rather than a private Gentleman with a single Rapier: But as I am pretty well acquainted by great Opportunities with the Nature of Man, and know of a Truth, that all Men fight *against their Will*, the Danger vanishes, and Resolution rises upon this Subject. For this Reason I shall talk very freely on a Custom which all Men wish exploded, tho' no Man has Courage enough to resist it.

But there is one unintelligible Word which I fear will extremely perplex my Dissertation; and I confess to you I find very hard to explain, which is, the Term *Satisfaction*. An honest Country Gentleman had the Misfortune to fall into Company with Two or Three modern Men of Honour, where he happen'd to be very ill treated; and one of the Company being conscious of his Offence, sends a Note to him in the Morning, and tells him, He was ready to give him Satisfaction.

This is fine Doing (says the plain Fellow): Last Night he sent me away cursedly out of Humour, and this Morning he fancies it would be a Satisfaction to be run through the Body.

As the Matter at present stands, it is not to do handsome Actions denominates a Man of Honour; it is enough if he dares to defend ill ones. Thus you often see a common Sharper in Competition with a Gentleman of the first Rank; tho' all Mankind is convinc'd, that a Fighting Gamester is only a Pick-pocket with the Courage of an Highway-man. One cannot with any Patience reflect on the unaccountable Jumble of Persons and Things in this Town and Nation, which occasions very frequently, that a brave Man falls by a Hand below that of the common Hangman, and yet his Executioner escapes the Clutches of the Hangman for doing it. I shall therefore hereafter consider, how the bravest Men in other Ages and Nations have behav'd themselves upon such Incidents as we decide by Combat; and show, from their Practice, that this Resentment neither has its Foundation from true Reason, or solid Fame; but is an Imposture, made up of Cowardice, Falshood, and Want of Understanding. For this Work, a good History of Quarrels would be very edifying to the Publick, and I apply my self to the Town for Particulars and Circumstances within their Knowledge, which may serve to embellish the Dissertation with proper Cuts. Most of the Quarrels I have ever known, have proceeded from some valiant Coxcomb's persisting in the Wrong, to defend some prevailing Folly, and preserve himself from the Ingenuity of owning a Mistake.

By this Means it is call'd, *Giving a Man Satisfaction*, to urge your Offence against him with your Sword; which puts me in Mind of *Peter*'s Order to the Keeper, in *The Tale of a Tub*: *If you neglect to do all this, damn you and your Generation for ever; and so we bid you heartily farewel.*[1] If the Contradiction in the very Terms of one of our Challenges were as well explain'd, and turn'd into downright *English*, would it not run after this Manner?

Sir,

    '*Your extraordinary Behaviour last Night, and the Liberty you were pleas'd to take with me, makes me this Morning give you this, to tell you, because you are an ill-bred Puppy, I will meet you in*

---

[1] *. . . heartily farewel*: From Jonathan Swift's *A Tale of a Tub* (1704/1710). It is taken from the conclusion of Peter's letter of pardon written to the jailers at Newgate Prison.

Hide-*Park an Hour hence; and because you want both Breeding and Humanity, I desire you would come with a Pistol in your Hand, on Horseback, and endeavour to shoot me through the Head, to teach you more Manners. If you fail of doing me this Pleasure, I shall say, You are a Rascal on every Post in Town: And so, Sir, if you will not injure me more, I shall never forgive what you have done already. Pray Sir, do not fail of getting every Thing ready, and you will infinitely oblige,*

Sir,

Your most Obedient
Humble Servant, &c.'

No. 27
Saturday, June 11, 1709
[Steele on the Rake Defined]

White's Chocolate-house, June 9.

Pacolet being gone a strolling among the Men of the Sword, in order to find out the secret Causes of the frequent Disputes we meet with, and furnish me with Materials for my Treatise on Duelling;[1] I have Room left to go on in my Information to my Country Readers, whereby they may understand the bright People whose Memoirs I have taken upon me to write. But in my Discourse of the 28th of the last Month, I omitted to mention the most agreeable of all bad Characters; and that is, a Rake.

A Rake is a Man always to be pitied; and if he lives is one Day certainly reclaim'd; for his Faults proceed not from Choice or Inclination, but from strong Passions and Appetites, which are in Youth too violent for the Curb of Reason, good Sense, good Manners, and good Nature: All which he must have by Nature and Education, before he can be allow'd to be, or have been, of this Order. He is a poor unweildy Wretch, that commits Faults out of the Redundance of his good Qualities. His Pity and Compassion makes him sometimes a Bubble[2] to all his Fellows, let 'em be never so much below him in

---

[1] *Pacolet . . . Duelling:* Pacolet is an imaginary companion of Bickerstaff's; the treatise on dueling is in *Tatler* No. 25 (p. 469).

[2] *a Bubble:* A dupe.

Understanding. His Desires run away with him through the Strength and Force of a lively Imagination, which hurries him on to unlawful Pleasures, before Reason has Power to come in to his Rescue. Thus, with all the good Intentions in the World to Amendment, this Creature sins on against Heaven, himself, his Friends, and his Country, who all call for a better Use of his Talents. There is not a Being under the Sun so miserable as this: He goes on in a Pursuit he himself disapproves, and has no Enjoyment but what is follow'd by Remorse; no Relief from Remorse, but the Repetition of his Crime. It's possible I may talk of this Person with too much Indulgence; but I must repeat it, that I think this, a Character which is the most the Object of Pity of any in the World. This Man in the Pangs of the Stone, Gout, or any acute Distemper, is not in so deplorable a Condition in the Eye of right Sense, as he that errs and repents, and repents and errs on. The Fellow with broken Limbs justly deserves your Alms for his impotent Condition; but he that can't use his own Reason, is in a much worse State; for you see him in miserable Circumstances, with his Remedy at the same Time in his own Possession, if he would or could use it. This is the Cause, that, of all ill Characters, the Rake has the best Quarter in the World; for when he is himself, and unruffled with Intemperance, you see his natural Faculties exert themselves, and attract an Eye of Favour towards his Infirmities. But if we look round us here, how many dull Rogues are there, that would fain be what this poor Man hates himself for? All the Noise towards Six in the Evening is caused by his Mimicks and Imitators. How ought Men of Sense to be careful of their Actions, if it were meerly from the Indignation of seeing themselves ill drawn by such little Pretenders? Not to say, he that leads, is guilty of all the Actions of his Followers: And a Rake has Imitators whom you would never expect should prove so. Second-hand Vice sure of all is the most nauseous: There is hardly a Folly more absurd, or which seems less to be accounted for, (tho' 'tis what we see every Day) than, that grave and honest Natures give into this Way, and at the same Time have good Sense, if they thought fit to use it: But the Fatality (under which most Men labour) of desiring to be what they are not, makes 'em go out of a Method in which they might be receiv'd with Applause, and would certainly excel, into one, wherein they will all their Life have the Air of Strangers to what they aim at. For this Reason, I have not lamented the Metamorphosis of any one I know so much as of *Nobilis*, who was born with Sweetness of Temper, just Apprehension, and every Thing else that might make him a Man fit for his Order. But instead of the Pursuit of sober Studies, and Applications, in which he would certainly be capable of making a considerable Figure in the noblest Assembly of Men in the World: I say, in Spight of that good Nature, which is his proper Bent, he will say ill-natur'd Things aloud, put such as he was, and still should be, out of Countenance, and drown all the natural Good in him, to receive an artificial ill Character, in which he will never succeed: For *Nobilis* is no Rake. He may guzzle as much Wine as he pleases, talk Bawdy if he thinks fit; but he may as well drink Watergruel, and go twice a Day to Church, for it will never do. I pronounce it again, *Nobilis* is no Rake. To be of that Order, he must be vicious against his Will, and not so by Study or Application. All Pretty Fellows are also excluded to a Man, as well as all Inamaratoes, or Persons of the Epicene Gender,[3] who gaze at one another in the Presence of Ladies. This Class, of which I am giving you an Account, is pretended to also by Men of strong Abilities in Drinking; tho' they are such whom the Liquor, not the Conversation, keeps together. But Blockheads may roar, fight, and stab, and be never the nearer; their Labour is also lost; they want Sense: They are no Rakes.

As a Rake among Men is the Man who lives in the constant Abuse of his Reason, so a Coquet among Women is one who lives in continual Misapplication of her Beauty. The chief of all whom I have the Honour to be acquainted with, is pretty Mrs. *Toss:* She is ever in Practice of something which disfigures her, and takes from her Charms; tho' all she does tends to a contrary Effect. She has naturally a very agreeable Voice and Utterance, which she has chang'd for the prettiest Lisp imaginable. She sees, what she has a Mind to see, at half a Mile Distance; but poring with her Eyes half shut at every one she passes by, she believes much more becoming. The *Cupid* on her Fan and she have their Eyes full on each other, all the Time in which they are not both in Motion. Whenever her Eye is turn'd from that dear Object, you may have a Glance and your Bow, if she is in Humour, return'd as civilly as you make it; but that must not be in the Presence of a Man of greater Quality: For Mr. *Toss* is so thoroughly well bred, that the chief Person present has all her Regards. And she, who giggles at Divine Service, and laughs at her very Mother, can compose her self at the Approach of a Man of a good Estate.

---

[3] *Persons of the Epicene Gender:* People having both masculine and feminine characteristics; effeminate men like those referred to by the correspondent in *Tatler* No. 26 (p. 467).

No. 107
Thursday, December 15, 1709
[Steele on the Coquette]

—— Ah Miser!
Quanta laboras in Charybdi
Digne Puer meliore Flammâ?[1]
— Hor.

Sheer-Lane, December 14.

About Four this Afternoon, which is the Hour I usually put my self
in a Readiness to receive Company, there enter'd a Gentleman who I
believed at first came upon some ordinary Question; but as he approached nearer to me, I saw in his Countenance a deep Sorrow,
mix'd with a certain ingenuous Complacency, that gave me a sudden
Good-will towards him. He star'd, and betray'd an Absence of
Thought as he was going to communicate his Business to me. But at
last, recovering himself, he said, with an Air of great Respect, Sir, It
would be an Injury to your Knowledge in the Occult Sciences to tell
you what is my Distress; I dare say you read it in my Countenance: I
therefore beg your Advice to the most unhappy of all Men.

Much Experience has made me particularly sagacious in the Discovery of Distempers, and I soon saw that his was Love. I then turned
to my Common-place Book, and found his Case under the Word *Coquette*; and reading over the Catalogue which I have collected out of
this great City of all under that Character, I saw at the Name of *Cynthia* his Fit came upon him. I repeated the Name thrice after a musing
Manner, and immediately perceived his Pulse quicken two Thirds;
when his Eyes, instead of the Wildness with which they appeared at
his Entrance, looked with all the Gentleness imaginable upon me, not
without Tears.

Oh! Sir, said he, you know not the unworthy Usage I have met
with from the Woman my Soul doats on. I could gaze at her to the
End of my Being; yet when I have done so, for some Time past I have
found her Eyes fix'd on another. She is now Two and twenty, in the
full Tyranny of her Charms, which she once acknowledg'd she re-
joic'd in, only as they made her Choice of me, out of a Crowd of Admirers, the more obliging. But in the Midst of this Happiness, so it is

---

[1] *Ah Miser! . . . Flammâ?:* From Horace, *Odes,* 1.27.18–20: "Unhappy Youth, / In
what ill State thy Fortune lies, / Thou didst deserve a Dart from kinder Eyes" [Bond].

Mr. *Bickerstaff*, that young *Quicksett*, who is just come to Town, without any other Recommendation then that of being tolerably handsome, and excessively rich, has won her Heart in so shameless a Manner, that she dies for him. In a Word, I would consult you how to cure my self of this Passion for an ungrateful Woman, who triumphs in her Falsehood, and can make no Man happy, because her own Satisfaction consists chiefly in being capable of giving Distress. I know *Quicksett* is at present considerable with her for no other Reason but that he can be without her, and feel no Pain in the Loss. Let me therefore desire you, Sir, to fortify my Reason against the Levity of an Inconstant, who ought only to be treated with Neglect.

All this Time I was looking over my Receipts, and ask'd him if he had any good Winter Boots — Boots Sir! said my Patient — I went on; You may easily reach *Harwich*[2] in a Day, so as to be there when the Packet goes off.

Sir, said the Lover, I find you design me for Travelling; but alas! I have no Language, it will be the same Thing to me as Solitude to be in a strange Country. I have, continued he, sighing, been many Years in Love with this Creature, and have almost lost even my *English*, at least to speak such as any body else does. I asked a Tenant of ours, who came up to Town the other Day with Rent, whether the Flowry Meads near my Father's House in the Country had any Shepherd in it. I have called a Cave a Grotto these Three Years, and must keep ordinary Company, and frequent busie People for some Time, before I can recover my common Words. I smiled at his Raillery upon himself, tho' I well saw it came from an heavy Heart. You are (said I) acquainted to be sure with some of the General Officers; Suppose you made a Campagne? If I did (said he) I should venture more than any Man there, for I should be in Danger of starving; my Father is such an untoward old Gentleman, that he would tell me he found it hard enough to pay his Taxes towards the War[3] without making it more expensive by an Allowance to me. With all this, he is as fond as he is rugged, and I am his only Son.

I looked upon the young Gentleman with much Tenderness, and not like a Physician, but a Friend; for I talked to him so largely, that if I had parcelled my Discourse into distinct Prescriptions, I am confident I gave him Two Hundred Pounds worth of Advice. He heard me with great Attention, bowing, smiling, and showing all other

---

[2] *Harwich*: A borough of southeastern England.
[3] *the War*: The War of the Spanish Succession (1701–14).

Instances of that natural good Breeding which ingenuous Tempers pay to those who are elder and wiser than themselves. I entertained him to the following Purpose: I am sorry, Sir, that your Passion is of so long a Date, for Evils are much more curable in their Beginnings; but at the same Time must allow, that you are not to be blamed, since your Youth and Merit has been abused by one of the most charming, but the most unworthy Sort of Women, the Coquets.

A Coquet is a chast Jilt, and differs only from a common One, as a Soldier who is perfect in Exercise, does from one that is actually in Service. This Grief, like all other, is to be cured only by Time; and altho' you are convinced this Moment, as much as you will be Ten Years hence, that she ought to be scorned and neglected, you see you must not expect your Remedy from the Force of Reason. The Cure then is only in Time, and the hastening of the Cure only in the Manner of employing that Time. You have answered me as to Travel and a Campagne, so that we have only *Great Britain* to avoid her in. Be then your self, and listen to the following Rules, which only can be of Use to you in this unaccountable Distemper, wherein the Patient is often averse even to his Recovery. It has been of Benefit to some to apply themselves to Business; but as that may not lie in your Way, go down to your Estate, mind your Fox-hounds, and venture the Life you are weary of over every Hedge and Ditch in the Country. These are wholesom Remedies; but if you can have Resolution enough, rather stay in Town, and recover your self even in the Town where she inhabits. Take particular Care to avoid all Places where you may possibly meet her, and shun the Sight of every Thing which may bring her to your Remembrance; there is an Infection in all that relates to her: You'll find, her House, her Chariot, her Domesticks, and her very Lap-dog, are so many Instruments of Torment. Tell me seriously, Do you think you could bear the Sight of her Fan? He shook his Head at the Question, and said, Ah! Mr. *Bickerstaff*, you must have been a Patient, or you could not have been so good a Physician. To tell you truly, said I, about the Thirtieth Year of my Age, I received a Wound that has still left a Scar in my Mind, never to be quite worn out by Time or Philosophy.

The Means which I found the most effectual for my Cure, were Reflections upon the ill Usage I had received from the Woman I loved, and the Pleasure I saw her take in my Sufferings.

I considered the Distress she brought upon me, the greatest that could befal an human Creature, at the same Time that she did not in-flict this upon one who was her Enemy, one that had done her an Injury, one that had wish'd her ill; but on the Man who loved her more than any else loved her, and more than it was possible for him to love any other Person.

In the next Place, I took Pains to consider her in all her Imperfections; and that I might be sure to hear of them constantly, kept Company with those her Female Friends who were her dearest and most intimate Acquaintance.

Among her highest Imperfections, I still dwelt upon her Baseness of Mind and Ingratitude, that made her triumph in the Pain and Anguish of the Man who loved her, and of one who in those Days, without Vanity be it spoken, was thought to deserve her Love.

To shorten my Story, she was married to another, which would have distracted me had he proved a good Husband; but to my great Pleasure, he used her at first with Coldness, and afterwards with Contempt. I hear he still treats her very ill; and am informed, that she often says to her Woman, This is a just Revenge for my Falsehood to my first Love: What a Wretch am I, that might have been married to the famous Mr. *Bickerstaff.*

My Patient looked upon me with a kind of melancholy Pleasure, and told me, He did not think it was possible for a Man to live to the Age I now am of, who in his Thirtieth Year had been tortured with that Passion in its Violence: For my Part, (said he) I can neither eat, drink, nor sleep in it; nor keep Company with any body, but Two or Three Friends who are in the same Condition.

There (answered I) you are to blame; for as you ought to avoid nothing more than keeping Company with your self, so you ought to be particularly cautious of keeping Company with Men like your self. As long as you do this, you do but indulge your Distemper.

I must not dismiss you without further Instructions. If possible, transfer your Passion from the Woman you are now in Love with to another; or if you cannot do that, change the Passion it self into some other Passion; that is, to speak more plainly, find out some other agreeable Woman: Or if you can't do this, grow covetous, ambitious, litigious; turn your Love of Woman into that of Profit, Preferment, Reputation; and for a Time, give up your self intirely to the Pursuit.

This is a Method we sometimes take in Physick, when we turn a desparate Disease into one we can more easily cure.

He made little Answer to all this, but crying out, Ah, Sir! For his Passion reduced his Discourse to Interjections.

There is one Thing, added I, which is present Death to a Man in your Condition, and therefore to be avoided with the greatest Care and Caution: That is, in a Word, to think of your Mistress and Rival together, whether walking, discoursing, dallying — The Devil! He cried out, Who can bear it? To compose him, for I pitied him very much, the Time will come, said I, when you shall not only bear it, but laugh at it. As a Preparation to it, ride every Morning an Hour at least with the Wind full in your Face. Upon your Return, recollect the several Precepts which I have now given you, and drink upon them a bottle of *Spaw-Water*.[4] Repeat this every Day for a Month successively, and let me see you at the End of it. He was taking his Leave, with many Thanks, and some Appearance of Consolation in his Countenance, when I called him back to acquaint him, That I had private Information of a Design of the Coquets to buy up all the true *Spaw-Water* in Town: Upon which he took his Leave in haste, with a Resolution to get all Things ready for entring upon his Regimen the next Morning.

No. 110
Thursday, December 22, 1709
[Addison and Steele on Bickerstaff's Court of Honor]

—— *Quae Lucis Miseris tam dira Cupido?*[1]
— Virg.

Sheer-Lane, December 21.

As soon as I had placed my self in my Chair of Judicature, I ordered my Clerk Mr. *Lillie* to read to the Assembly (who were gathered together according to Notice) a certain Declaration, by way of Charge, to open the Purpose of my Session, which tended only to this Explanation, That as other Courts were often called to demand the Execution of Persons dead in Law, so this was held to give the last Orders relating to those who are dead in Reason. The Sollicitor of the new Company of Upholders near the *Hay-Market*[2] appeared in Be-

---

[4] *Spaw-Water:* Spa water, originally from Spa, a resort town in eastern Belgium. Spa water is mineral water taken as a tonic.

[1] *Quae . . . Cupido?:* From Virgil, *Aeneid* 6.721: "What makes the wretches covet light?" [Bond].

[2] *Hay-Market:* Haymarket was an area that ran south from Coventry Street to Pall Mall east. Because it was close to the Royal Mews, in the seventeenth century a market was established here for hay and straw. In 1705 Thomas Betterton brought his company from Lincoln's Inn Fields to a new theater in Haymarket. Within a few years this new Queen's Theatre had become the venue for opera performances.

half of that useful Society, and brought in an Accusation of a young Woman, who her self stood at the Bar before me. Mr. *Lillie* read her Indictment, which was in Substance, That whereas Mrs. *Rebecca Pindust*, of the Parish of St. *Martin in the Fields*, had, by the Use of one Instrument called a Looking-glass, and by the further Use of certain Attire, made either of Cambrick, Muslin, or other Linnen Wares, upon her Head, attained to such an evil Art and magical Force in the Motion of her Eyes and Turn of her Countenance, that she the said *Rebecca* had put to Death several young Men of the said Parish; and that the said young Men had acknowledged in certain Papers, commonly called Love-Letters, (which were produced in Court, gilded on the Edges, and sealed with a particular Wax, with certain amorous and enchanting Words wrought upon the said Seals) that they died for the said *Rebecca*: And whereas the said *Rebecca* persisted in the said evil Practice; This Way of Life the said Society construed to be, according to former Edicts, a State of Death, and demanded an Order for the Interrment of the said *Rebecca*.

I looked upon the Maid with great Humanity, and desired her to make Answer to what was said against her. She said, It was indeed true, that she had practised all the Arts and Means she could to dispose of her self happily in Marriage, but thought she did not come under the Censure express'd in my Writings for the same; and humbly hoped, I would not condemn her for the Ignorance of her Accusers, who, according to their own Words, had rather represented her killing than dead. She further alledged, That the Expressions mentioned in the Papers written to her, were become meer Words, and that she had been always ready to marry any of those who said they died for her; but that they made their Escape as soon as they found themselves pitied or believed. She ended her Discourse, by desiring I would for the future settle the Meaning of the Words, *I Die*, in Letters of Love.

Mrs. *Pindust* behaved her self with such an Air of Innocence, that she easily gained Credit, and was acquitted. Upon which Occasion, I gave it as a standing Rule, That any Persons, who in any Letter, Billet, or Discourse, should tell a Woman he died for her, should, if she pleased, be obliged to live with her, or be immediately interr'd, upon such their own Confession, without Bail or Mainprize.

It happened, that the very next who was brought before me was one of her Admirers, who was indicted upon that very Head. A Letter which he acknowledged to be his own Hand was read; in which were the following Words; *Cruel Creature, I die for you.* It was observable, that he took Snuff all the Time his Accusation was reading. I ask'd him, How he came to use these Words, if he were not a dead Man? He told me, He was in Love with the Lady, and did not know any other Way of telling her so; and that all his Acquaintance took the same Method. Tho' I was moved with Compassion towards him by reason of the Weakness of his Parts, yet for Example's-sake, I was forced to answer, Your Sentence shall be a Warning to all the rest of your Companions not to tell Lies for want of Wit. Upon this, he began to beat his Snuffbox with a very sawcy Air; and opening it again, Faith *Isaac*, said he, thou art a very unaccountable old Fellow — Prithee, who gave thee Power of Life and Death? What-a-Pox hast thou to do with Ladies and Lovers? I suppose thou wouldst have a Man be in Company with his Mistress and say nothing to her. Dost thou call breaking a Jest telling a Lie? Ha! Is that thy Wisdom, old Stiffrump, ha? He was going on with this insipid Common-place Mirth, sometimes opening his Box, sometimes shutting it, then viewing the Picture on the Lid, and then the Workmanship of the Hinge, when, in the midst of his Eloquence, I ordered his Box to be taken from him; upon which he was immediately struck speechless, and carried off stone-dead.

The next who appeared, was a hale old Fellow of Sixty. He was brought in by his Relations, who desired Leave to bury him. Upon requiring a distinct Account of the Prisoner, a credible Witness deposed, That he always rose at Ten of the Clock, played with his Cat till Twelve, smoaked Tobacco till One, was at Dinner till Two, then took another Pipe, played at Backgammon till Six, talked of one Madam *Frances*, an old Mistriss of his, till Eight, repeated the same Account at the Tavern till Ten, then returned Home, took t'other Pipe, and then to Bed. I asked him what he had to say for himself? As to what (said he) they mentioned concerning Madam *Frances* — I did not care for hearing a *Canterbury* Tale,[3] and therefore thought my self seasonably interrupted by a young Gentleman who appeared in the Behalf of the old Man, and prayed an Arrest of Judgment; for that he the said young Man held certain Lands by his the said old Man's Life. Upon this, the Sollicitor of the Upholders took an Occasion to demand him also, and thereupon produced several Evidences that witnessed to his Life and Conversation. It appeared, That each of them divided their Hours in Matters of equal Moment and Importance to themselves and to the Publick. They rose at the same Hour:

---

[3] *Canterbury Tale:* A long, pointless story.

While the old Man was playing with his Cat, the young One was looking out of his Window; while the old Man was smoaking his Pipe, the young Man was rubbing his Teeth; while One was at Dinner, the Other was dressing; while One was at Backgammon, the Other was at Dinner; while the old Fellow was talking of Madam *Frances*, the young One was either at Play, or Toasting Women whom he never conversed with. The only Difference was, that the young Man had never been good for any Thing; the old Man, a Man of Worth before he knew Madam *Frances*. Upon the Whole, I ordered them to be both interred together, with Inscriptions proper to their Characters, signifying, That the old Man died in the year 1689, and was buried in the Year 1709. And over the young One it was said, That he departed this World in the 25th Year of his Death.

The next Class of Criminals, were Authors in Prose and Verse. Those of them who had produced any still-born Work, were immediately dismissed to their Burial, and were followed by others, who, notwithstanding some sprightly Issue in their Life-time, had given Proofs of their Death by some Post-humous Children, that bore no Resemblance to their elder Brethren. As for those who were the Fathers of a mixed Progeny, provided always they could prove the last to be a live Child, they escaped with Life, but not without Loss of Limbs; for in this Case, I was satisfied with Amputation of the Parts which were mortified.

These were followed by a great Crowd of superannuated Benchers[4] of the Inns of Court, Senior Fellows of Colleges, and defunct Statesmen; all of whom I ordered to be decimated indifferently, allowing the rest a Reprieve for one Year, with a Promise of a free Pardon in Case of Resuscitation.

There were still great Multitudes to be examined; but finding it very late, I adjourned the Court; not without the secret Pleasure that I had done my Duty, and furnished out an handsome Execution.

Going out of the Court, I received a Letter, informing me, That in Pursuance of the Edict of Justice in one of my late Visions, all those of the Fair Sex began to appear pregnant who had ran any Hazard of it; as was manifest by a particular Swelling in the Petticoats of several Ladies in and about this great City. I must confess, I do not attribute the Rising of this Part of the Dress to this Occasion, yet must own,

---

[4] *Benchers:* A bencher is a member of the inner or higher bar who acts as a governor of one of the Inns of Court housed in four main buildings on Fleet Street.

that I am very much disposed to be offended with such a new and unaccountable Fashion. I shall however pronounce nothing upon it, till
I have examined all that can be said for and against it. And in the
mean Time, think fit to give this Notice to the fair Ladies who are
now making up their Winter-Suits, that they may abstain from all
Dresses of that Kind, till they shall find what Judgment will be passed
upon them; for it would very much trouble me, that they should put
themselves to an unnecessary Expence; and could not but think my
self to blame, if I should hereafter forbid them the Wearing of such
Garments, when they had laid out Money upon them, without having
given them any previous Admonition.

No. 116
Thursday, January 5, 1710
[Addison on the Hoop-skirt on Trial]

—— *Pars minima est ipsa Puella sui.*[1]
— Ovid.

Sheer-Lane, January 4.

The court being prepared for proceeding on the Cause of the Petticoat, I gave Orders to bring in a Criminal who was taken up as she
went out of the Puppet-Show about Three Nights ago, and was now
standing in the Street with a great Concourse of People about her.
Word was brought me, that she had endeavoured twice or thrice to
come in, but could not do it by reason of her Petticoat, which was
too large for the Entrance of my House, tho' I had ordered both the
Folding-Doors to be thrown open for its Reception. Upon this, I desired the Jury of Matrons, who stood at my Right Hand, to inform
themselves of her Condition, and know whether there were any private Reasons why she might not make her Appearance separate from
her Petticoat. This was managed with great Discretion, and had such
an Effect, that upon the Return of the Verdict from the Bench of Matrons, I issued out an Order forthwith, That the Criminal should be

---

[1] *Pars minima . . . sui:* From Ovid, *Remedia Amoris* 344: "(Her beauty's art, gems,
gold, and rich attire, / Make up the pageant you so much admire; / In all that spacious
figure which you see) / The least, least part of her own self is she." — TATE (in Garth's
Ovid) [Bond].

stripped of her Incumbrances, till she became little enough to enter my House. I had before given Directions for an Engine of several Legs, that could contract or open it self like the Top of an Umbrello, in order to place the Petticoat upon it, by which means I might take a leisurely Survey of it, as it should appear in its proper Dimensions. This was all done accordingly; and forthwith, upon the closing of the Engine, the Petticoat was brought into Court. I then directed the Machine to be set upon the Table, and dilated in such a Manner as to show the Garment in its utmost Circumference; but my great Hall was too narrow for the Experiment; for before it was half unfolded, it described so immoderate a Circle, that the lower Part of it brush'd upon my Face as I sate in my Chair of Judicature. I then enquired for the Person that belonged to the Petticoat; and to my great Surprize, was directed to a very beautiful young Damsel, with so pretty a Face and Shape, that I bid her come out of the Crowd, and seated her upon a little Crock at my Left Hand. My pretty Maid, said I, do you own your self to have been the Inhabitant of the Garment before us? The Girl I found had good Sense, and told me with a Smile, that notwithstanding it was her own Petticoat, she should be very glad to see an Example made of it; and that she wore it for no other Reason, but that she had a Mind to look as big and burly as other Persons of her Quality; That she had kept out of it as long as she could, and till she began to appear little in the Eyes of all her Acquaintance; That if she laid it aside, People would think she was not made like other Women. I always give great Allowances to the Fair Sex upon Account of the Fashion, and therefore was not displeased with the Defence of my pretty Criminal. I then ordered the Vest which stood before us to be drawn up by a Pully to the Top of my great Hall, and afterwards to be spread open by the Engine it was placed upon, in such a Manner, that it formed a very splendid and ample Canopy over our Heads, and covered the whole Court of Judicature with a kind of Silken Rotunda, in its Form not unlike the Cupolo of St. *Paul*'s.[2] I enter'd upon the whole Cause with great Satisfaction as I sate under the Shadow of it.

The Council for the Petticoat was now called in, and ordered to produce what they had to say against the popular Cry which was raised against it. They answered the Objections with great Strength and Solidity of Argument, and expatiated in very florid Harangues,

---

[2] *St. Paul's:* St. Paul's Cathedral was built (1675–1710) by Sir Christopher Wren (1632–1723).

which they did not fail to set off and furbelow[3] (if I may be allowed
the Metaphor) with many Periodical Sentences and Turns of Oratory.
The chief Arguments for their Client were taken, first, from the great
Benefit that might arise to our Woollen Manufactury from this Invention, which was calculated as follows: The common Petticoat has not
above Four Yards in the Circumference; whereas this over our Heads
had more in the Semi-diameter; so that by allowing it Twenty four
Yards in the Circumference, the Five Millions of Woollen Petticoats,
which, (according to Sir *William Petty*)[4] supposing what ought to be
supposed in a well-governed State, that all Petticoats are made of that
Stuff, would amount to Thirty Millions of those of the ancient Mode.
A prodigious Improvement of the Woollen Trade! and what could
not fail to sink the Power of *France*[5] in a few Years.

To introduce the Second Argument, they begged Leave to read a
Petition of the Rope-Makers, wherein it was represented, That the
Demand for Cords, and the Price of 'em, were much risen since this
Fashion came up. At this, all the Company who were present lifted
up their Eyes into the Vault; and I must confess, we did discover
many Traces of Cordage which were interwoven in the Stiffening of
the Drapery.

A Third Argument was founded upon a Petition of the *Greenland*
Trade, which likewise represented the great Consumption of Whale-
bone which would be occasioned by the present Fashion, and the
Benefit which would thereby accrue to that Branch of the *British*
Trade.

To conclude, they gently touched upon the Weight and Unwieldi-
ness of the Garment, which they insinuated might be of great Use to
preserve the Honour of Families.

These Arguments would have wrought very much upon me, (as I
then told the Company in a long and elaborate Discourse) had I not
considered the great and additional Expence which such Fashions
would bring upon Fathers and Husbands; and therefore by no Means
to be thought of till some Years after a Peace. I further urg'd, that it
would be a Prejudice to the Ladies themselves, who could never expect to have any Money in the Pocket, if they laid out so much on the

---

[3] *furbelow:* A furbelow is an ornamental ruffle or flounce; here it is used as a verb,
to decorate as with a ruffle.

[4] *Sir William Petty:* Sir William Petty (1623–1687) was a political economist and
statistician.

[5] *Power of France:* With whom England was at war in the War of the Spanish Succession (1701–14).

Petticoat. To this I added, that great Temptation it might give to Virgins, of acting in Security like married Women, and by that Means give a Check to Matrimony, an Institution always encouraged by wise Societies.

At the same Time, in Answer to the several Petitions produced on that Side, I shewed one subscribed by the Women of several Persons of Quality, humbly setting forth, That since the Introduction of this Mode, their respective Ladies had (instead of bestowing on 'em their Cast-Gowns) cut them into Shreds, and mixed them with the Cordage and Buckram,[6] to compleat the stiffening of their Under-Petticoats. For which, and sundry other Reasons, I pronounced the Petticoat a Forfeiture: But to shew that I did not make that Judgment for the Sake of filthy Lucre, I ordered it to be folded up, and sent it as a Present to a Widow-Gentlewoman, who has five Daughters, desiring she would make each of them a Petticoat out of it, and send me back the Remainder, which I design to cut into Stomachers, Caps, Facings of my Wastcoat-Sleeves, and other Garnitures, suitable to my Age and Quality.

I would not be understood that (while I discard this monstrous Invention) I am an Enemy to the proper Ornaments of the Fair Sex. On the contrary, as the Hand of Nature has poured on them such a Profusion of Charms and Graces, and sent them into the World more amiable and finished than the rest of her Works; so I would have them bestow upon themselves all the additional Beauties that Art can supply them with, provided it does not interfere with, disguise, or pervert, those of Nature.

I consider Woman as a beautiful Romantick Animal, that may be adorned with Furs and Feathers, Pearls and Diamonds, Ores and Silks. The Lynx shall cast its Skin at her Feet to make her a Tippet;[7] the Peacock, Parrot, and Swan, shall pay Contributions to her Muff; the Sea shall be searched for Shells, and the Rocks for Gems; and every Part of Nature furnish out its Share towards the Embellishment of a Creature that is the most consummate Work of it. All this I shall indulge them in; but as for the Petticoat I have been speaking of, I neither can, nor will allow it.

---

[6] *Cordage and Buckram:* Cordage is rope, and buckram is a coarse cotton fabric heavily sized with glue used for stiffening clothes and for bookbinding.
[7] *Tippet:* A kind of stole, often of fur, covering the shoulders and having ends that hang down in front.

No. 151
Tuesday, March 28, 1710
[Addison on Women's Weakness for Dress]

—— Ni Vis Boni
In ipsa inesset Forma, haec Formam extinguerent.[1]
— Ter.

From my own Apartment, March 27.

When Artists would expose their Diamonds to an Advantage, they usually set them to Show in little Cases of black Velvet. By this Means, the Jewels appear in their true and genuine Lustre, while there is no Colour that can infect their Brightness, or give a false Cast to the Water. When I was at the Opera the other Night, the Assembly of Ladies in Mourning made me consider them in the same Kind of View. A Dress wherein there is so little Variety, shows the Face in all its natural Charms, and makes one differ from another, only as it is more or less beautiful. Painters are ever careful of offending against a Rule which is so essential in all just Representations. The chief Figure must have the strongest Point of light, and not be injured by any gay Colourings that may draw away the Attention to any less considerable Part of the Picture. The present Fashion obliges every body to be dressed with Propriety, and makes the Ladies Faces the principal Objects of Sight. Every beautiful Person shines out in all the Excellence with which Nature has adorned her. Gawdy Ribands and glaring Colours being now out of Use, the Sex has no Opportunity given 'em to disfigure themselves, which they seldom fail to do whenever it lies in their Power. When a Woman comes to her Glass, she does not so much employ her Time in making her self look more advantagiously what she really is, but endeavours to be as much another Creature as she possibly can. Whether this happens because they stay so long, and attend their Work so diligently, that they forget the Faces and Persons which they first sat down with, or whatever it is, they seldom rise from the Toilet the same Women they appeared when they began to dress. What Jewel can the charming *Cleora* place in her Ears, that can please her Beholders so much as her Eyes? The Cluster of Diamonds upon the Breast can add no Beauty to the fair Chest of Ivory which supports it. It may indeed tempt a Man to steal a Woman, but never to love her. Let *Thalestris* change her self into a Motly Party-

---

[1] *Ni . . . extinguerent:* From Terence, *Phormio* 107–08: "If she had not such beauty herself, these would have extinguished it" [Bond].

coloured Animal; the Pearl Necklace, the Flowered Stomacher, the Artificial Nosegay, and Shaded Furbelow,[2] may be of Use to attract the Eye of the Beholder, and turn it from the imperfections of her Features and Shape. But if Ladies will take my Word for it, (and as they dress to please Men, they ought to consult our Fancy rather than their own in this Particular) I can assure them, there is nothing touches our Imagination so much as a beautiful Woman in a plain Dress. There might be more agreeable Ornaments found in our own Manufacture, than any that rise out of the Looms of *Persia.*

This I know is a very harsh Doctrine of Womankind, who are carried away with every Thing that is showy, and with what delights the Eye, more than any other Species of Living Creatures whatsoever. Were the Minds of the Sex laid open, we should find the chief Idea in one to be a Tippet,[3] in another a Muff, in a third a Fan, and in a fourth a Fardingal.[4] The Memory of an old Visiting Lady is so filled with Gloves, Silks and Ribands, that I can look upon it as nothing else but a Toy-shop.[5] A Matron of my Acquaintance complaining of her Daughter's Vanity, was observing, that she had all of a sudden held up her Head higher than ordinary, and taken an Air that showed a secret Satisfaction in her self, mixed with a Scorn of others. I did not know, says my Friend, what to make of the Carriage of this fantastical Girl, till I was informed by her elder Sister, that she had a Pair of strip'd Garters on. This odd Turn of Mind often makes the Sex unhappy, and disposes them to be struck with every Thing that makes a Show, however trifling and superficial.

Many a Lady has fetched a Sigh at the Toss of a Wig, and been ruin'd by the Tapping of a Snuff-Box. It is impossible to describe all the Execution that was done by the Shoulder-Knot while that Fashion prevailed, or to reckon up all the Virgins that have fallen a Sacrifice to a Pair of Fringed Gloves. A sincere Heart has not made half so many Conquests as an open Wastcoat; and I should be glad to see an able Head make so good a Figure in a Woman's Company as a Pair of Red Heels. A *Grecian* Hero, when he was asked, Whether he could play upon the Lute? Thought he had made a very good Reply, when he answered, No; But I can make a great City of a little one.

[2] *Furbelow:* An ornamental ruffle or flounce.

[3] *Tippet:* A kind of stole, often of fur, covering the shoulders and having ends that hang down in front.

[4] *Fardingal:* A farthingale, an earlier incarnation of the hoop, a support to hold up a woman's skirt in a horizontal line out from the waist. Farthingales were worn by European women in the sixteenth and seventeenth centuries.

[5] *Toy-shop:* Not a store selling playthings for children, but one furnishing fashionable ladies and gentlemen with ornamental personal accessories and knickknacks.

Notwithstanding his boasted Wisdom, I appeal to the Heart of any Toast[6] in Town, whether she would not think the Lutanist preferable to the Statesman. I do not speak this out of any Aversion that I have to the Sex. On the contrary, I have always had a Tenderness for them; but I must confess, it troubles me very much to see the Generality of them place their Affections on improper Objects, and give up all the Pleasures of Life for Gugaws[7] and Trifles.

Mrs. *Margery Bickerstaff*, my Great Aunt, had a Thousand Pounds to her Portion, which our Family was desirous of keeping among themselves, and therefore used all possible Means to turn off her Thoughts from Marriage. The Method they took was, in any Time of Danger to throw a new Gown or Petticoat in her Way. When she was about Twenty five Years of Age, she fell in Love with a Man of an agreeable Temper and equal Fortune, and would certainly have married him, had not my Grandfather, Sir *Jacob*, dressed her up in a Suit of flowered Sattin; upon which she set so immoderate a Value upon her self, that the Lover was contemned and discarded. In the Fortieth Year of her Age, she was again smitten, but very luckily transferred her Passion to a Tippet, which was presented to her by another Relation who was in the Plot. This, with a white Sarsenet[8] Hood, kept her safe in the Family till Fifty. About Sixty, which generally produces a Kind of latter Spring in amorous Constitutions, my Aunt *Margery* had again a Colt's Tooth[9] in her Head, and would certainly have eloped from the Mansion-House, had not her Brother *Simon*, who was a wise Man and a Scholar, advised to dress her in Cherry-colour'd Ribands, which was the only Expedient that could have been found out by the Wit of Man to preserve the Thousand Pounds in our Family, Part of which I enjoy at this Time.

This Discourse puts me in Mind of an Humorist mentioned by *Horace*, called *Eutrapelus*, who, when he designed to do a Man a Mischief, made him a Present of a gay Suit;[10] and brings to my Memory another Passage of the same Author, when he describes the most ornamental Dress that a Woman can appear in with Two Words, *Simplex Munditiis*,[11] which I have quoted for the Benefit of my Female Readers.

---

[6] *Toast:* See *Tatler* No. 24 (p. 465).

[7] *Gugaws:* Gewgaws.

[8] *Sarsenet:* A kind of silk.

[9] *Colt's Tooth:* A taste for youthful pleasures.

[10] *Horace . . . gay Suit:* A reference to the Roman lyric poet Horace's (65–8 B.C.) *Epistles* 1.18.31 [Bond].

[11] *Simplex Munditiis:* This tag means simple neatness, or elegance (*Odes* 1.5.5). See *Tatler* No. 62 (p. 327).

No. 166
Tuesday, May 2, 1710
[Steele on Tom Modely]

—— *Dicenda, Tacenda, Loquutus.*[1]
— Hor.

White's Chocolate-house, May 1.

The World is so overgrown with Singularities in Behaviour, and Method of Living, that I have no sooner laid before Mankind the Absurdity of one Species of Men, but there starts up to my View some new Sect of Impertinents that had before escaped Notice. This Afternoon, as I was talking with fine Mrs. *Sprightly*'s Porter, and desiring Admittance upon an extraordinary Occasion, it was my Fate to be spy'd by *Tom Modely* riding by in his Chariot. He did me the Honour to stop, and asked, What I did there of a *Monday*? I answered, That I had Business of Importance, which I wanted to communicate to the Lady of the House. *Tom* is one of those Fools who look upon Knowledge of the Fashion to be the only Liberal Science; and was so rough as to tell me, That a well-bred Man would as soon call upon a Lady (who keeps a Day) at Midnight, as on any Day but that on which she professes being at Home.[2] There are Rules and Decorums which are never to be transgressed by those who understand the World; and he who offends in that Kind, ought not to take it ill if he is turned away, even when he sees the Person look out at her Window whom he enquires for. Nay, said he, my Lady *Dimple* is so positive in this Rule, that she takes it for a Piece of good Breeding and Distinction to deny her self with her own Mouth. Mrs. *Comma*, the great Scholar, insists upon it; and I my self have heard her assert, That a Lord's Porter, or a Lady's Woman, cannot be said to lie in that Case, because they act by Instruction; and their Words are no more their own, than those of a Puppet.

He was going on with this Ribaldry, when on a sudden he looked on his Watch, and said, he had Twenty Visits to make, and drove away without further Ceremony. I was then at Leisure to reflect upon the Tastless Manner of Life, which a Set of idle Fellows lead in this

---

[1] *Dicenda, Tacenda, Loquutus:* From Horace, *Epistles* 1.7.72: "Speaking both what is fit, and what is not" [Bond].

[2] *being at Home:* That is, being at home to visitors. Women in society specified certain days when they were "at home," when they would receive visitors dropping by. Much of a woman's social life revolved around giving and receiving such visits in a regular weekly succession.

Town, and spend Youth it self with less Spirit, than other Men do their old Age. These Expletives in Human Society, tho' they are in themselves wholly insignificant, become of some Consideration when they are mixed with others. I am very much at a Loss how to define, or under what Character, Distinction, or Denomination, to place them, except you give me Leave to call them the Order of the *Insipids*. This Order is in its Extent like that of the Jesuits, and you see of them in every Way of Life, and in every Profession. *Tom Modely* has long appeared to me at the Head of this Species. By being habitually in the best Company, he knows perfectly well when a Coat is well cut, or a Periwig well mounted. As soon as you enter the Place where he is, he tells the next Man to him who is your Taylor, and judges of you more from the Choice of your Periwig-maker than of your Friend. His Business in this World is to be well dressed; and the greatest Circumstance that is to be recorded in his Annals is, That he wears Twenty Shirts a Week. Thus, without ever speaking Reason among the Men, or Passion among the Women, he is every where well received; and without any one Man's Esteem, he has every Man's Indulgence.

This Order has produced great Numbers of tolerable Copiers in Painting, good Rhimers in Poetry, and harmless Projectors in Politicks. You may see them at first Sight grow acquainted by Sympathy, insomuch that one who had not studied Nature, and did not know the true Cause of their sudden Familiarities, would think that they had some secret Intimation of each other, like the Free Masons. The other Day at *Will*'s, I heard *Modely*, and a Critick of the same Order, show their equal Talents with great Delight. The Learned Insipid was commending *Racine*'s Turns;[3] the Genteel Insipid, *Duvillier*'s Curls.[4]

These Creatures, when they are not forced into any particular Employment, for want of Idea's in their own Imaginations, are the constant Plaque of all they meet with by Enquiries for News and Scandal, which makes them the Heroes of Visiting Days, where they help the Design of the Meeting, which is to pass away that odious Thing called Time, in Discourses too trivial to raise any Reflections which may put well bred Persons to the Trouble of Thinking.

---

[3] *Racine's Turns:* Jean Racine (1639–1699) was a French neoclassical dramatist.
[4] *Duvillier's Curls:* Duvillier was a famed Parisian wigmaker of the day.

The Spectator

No. 15
Saturday, March 17, 1711
[Addison on Women Taken In
by Shows and Appearances]

Parva leves capiunt animos . . .[1]
— Ovid

When I was in *France*, I used to gaze with great Astonishment at the Splendid Equipages, and Party-coloured Habits, of that Fantastick Nation. I was one Day in particular contemplating a Lady, that sate in a Coach adorned with gilded *Cupids*, and finely painted with the Loves of *Venus* and *Adonis*. The Coach was drawn by six milk-white Horses, and loaden behind with the same Number of powder'd Foot-men. Just before the Lady were a Couple of beautiful Pages, that were stuck among the Harness, and by their gay Dresses, and smiling Features, looked like the elder Brothers of the little Boys that were carved and painted in every Corner of the Coach.

The Lady was the unfortunate *Cleanthe*, who afterwards gave an Occasion to a pretty melancholy Novel. She had, for several Years, received the Addresses of a Gentleman, whom, after a long and intimate Acquaintance she forsook, upon the Account of this shining Equipage, which had been offered to her by one of Great Riches, but a Crazy Constitution. The Circumstances in which I saw her, were, it seems, the Disguises only of a broken Heart, and a kind of Pageantry to cover Distress; for in two Months after she was carried to her Grave with the same Pomp and Magnificence: being sent thither partly by the Loss of one Lover, and partly by the Possession of another.

I have often reflected with my self on this unaccountable Humour in Woman-kind, of being smitten with every thing that is showy and superficial; and on the numberless Evils that befall the Sex, from this light, fantastical Disposition. I my self remember a young Lady, that was very warmly sollicited by a Couple of importunate Rivals, who for several Months together did all they could to recommend themselves, by Complacency of Behaviour, and Agreeableness of Conversation.

---

[1] *Parva leves capiunt animos . . . :* From Ovid, *Ars Amatoria* 1.159: "Light minds are taken with little things" [Bond].

At length, when the Competition was doubtful, and the Lady undetermined in her Choice, one of the young Lovers very luckily bethought himself of adding a supernumerary Lace to his Liveries, which had so good an Effect that he married her the very Week after.

The usual Conversation of ordinary Women very much cherishes this Natural Weakness of being taken with Outside and Appearance. Talk of a new-married Couple, and you immediately hear whether they keep their Coach and six, or eat in Plate;[2] Mention the Name of an absent Lady, and it is ten to one but you learn something of her Gown and Petticoat. A Ball is a great Help to Discourse, and a Birth-Day furnishes Conversation for a Twelve-month after. A Furbelow[3] of precious Stones, an Hat buttoned with a Diamond, a Brocade Waistcoat or Petticoat, are standing Topicks. In short, they consider only the Drapery of the Species, and never cast away a Thought on those Ornaments of the Mind, that make Persons Illustrious in themselves, and Useful to others. When Women are thus perpetually dazling one anothers Imaginations, and filling their Heads with nothing but Colours, it is no Wonder that they are more attentive to the superficial Parts of Life, than the solid and substantial Blessings of it. A Girl, who has been trained up in this kind of Conversation, is in danger of every Embroidered Coat that comes in her Way. A Pair of fringed Gloves may be her Ruin. In a word, Lace and Ribbons, Silver and Gold Galloons,[4] with the like glittering Gew-Gaws, are so many Lures to Women of weak Minds or low Educations, and, when artificially displayed, are able to fetch down the most airy Coquet from the wildest of her Flights and Rambles.

True Happiness is of a retired Nature, and an Enemy to Pomp and Noise; it arises, in the first place, from the Enjoyment of ones self; and, in the next, from the Friendship and Conversation of a few select Companions. It loves Shade and Solitude, and naturally haunts Groves and Fountains, Fields and Meadows: In short, it feels every thing it wants within it self, and receives no Addition from Multitudes of Witnesses and Spectators. On the contrary, false Happiness loves to be in a Crowd, and to draw the Eyes of the World upon her. She does not receive any Satisfaction from the Applauses which she gives her self, but from the Admiration which she raises in others. She

---

[2] *eat in Plate:* To eat from silver-plated dinnerware.

[3] *Furbelow:* An ornamental ruffle or flounce.

[4] *Galloons:* A braid of metallic thread, here gold, used as ornamental trimming on clothes.

flourishes in Courts and Palaces, Theatres and Assemblies, and has no Existence but when she is looked upon.

Aurelia, tho' a Woman of Great Quality, delights in the Privacy of a Country Life, and passes away a great part of her Time in her own Walks and Gardens. Her Husband, who is her Bosom Friend, and Companion in her Solitudes, has been in Love with her ever since he knew her. They both abound with good Sense, consummate Virtue, and a mutual Esteem; and are a perpetual Entertainment to one another. Their Family is under so regular an Oeconomy, in its Hours of Devotion and Repast, Employment and Diversion, that it looks like a little Common-Wealth within it self. They often go into Company, that they may return with the greater Delight to one another; and sometimes live in Town not to enjoy it so properly as to grow weary of it, that they may renew in themselves the Relish of a Country Life. By this means they are Happy in each other, beloved by their Children, adored by their Servants, and are become the Envy, or rather the Delight, of all that know them.

How different to this is the Life of *Fulvia*! she considers her Husband as her Steward, and looks upon Discretion, and good House-Wifery, as little domestick Virtues, unbecoming a Woman of Quality. She thinks Life lost in her own Family, and fancies her self out of the World when she is not in the Ring,[5] the Play-House, or the Drawing-Room: She lives in a perpetual Motion of Body, and Restlesness of Thought, and is never easie in any one Place when she thinks there is more Company in another. The missing of an Opera the first Night, would be more afflicting to her than the Death of a Child. She pities all the valuable Part of her own Sex, and calls every Woman of a prudent modest retired Life, a poor-spirited, unpolished Creature. What a Mortification would it be to *Fulvia*, if she knew that her setting herself to View is but exposing her self, and that she grows Contemptible by being Conspicuous.

I cannot conclude my Paper, without observing that *Virgil* has very finely touched upon this Female Passion for Dress and Show, in the Character of *Camilla*;[6] who, tho' she seems to have shaken off all the other Weaknesses of her Sex, is still described as a Woman in this Particular. This Poet tells us, that after having made a great Slaughter

---

[5] *Ring:* In Hyde Park, a circular road that was a fashionable place to ride and walk.

[6] *Camilla:* The woman warrior who fights against Aeneas in Book 11 of Virgil's (70–19 B.C.) *Aeneid.*

of the Enemy, she unfortunately cast her Eye on a *Trojan* who wore an embroidered Tunick, a beautiful Coat of Mail, with a Mantle of the finest Purple. *A Golden Bow,* says he, *hung upon his Shoulder; his Garment was buckled with a Golden Clasp, and his Head covered with an Helmet of the same shining Mettle.* The *Amazon* immediately singled out this well-dressed Warrior, being seized with a Woman's Longing for the pretty Trappings that he was adorned with:

> ... *Totumque incauta per agmen*
> *Fœmineo prædæ & spoliorum ardebat amore.*[7]

This heedless Persuit after these glittering Trifles, the Poet (by a nice concealed Moral) represents to have been the Destruction of his Female Hero.

No. 16
Monday, March 19, 1711
[Addison on Dress Reform]

Quod verum atque decens curo & rogo, & omnis in hoc sum.[1]
— Hor.

I have receiv'd a Letter, desiring me to be very satyrical upon the little Muff[2] that is now in Fashion; another informs me of a Pair of silver Garters buckled below the Knee, that have been lately seen at the *Rainbow* Coffee-house[3] in *Fleet-street;* a third sends me an heavy Complaint against fringed Gloves. To be brief, there is scarce an Ornament of either Sex which one or other of my Correspondents has not inveighed against with some Bitterness, and recommended to my Observation. I must therefore, once for all inform my Readers, that it is not my Intention to sink the Dignity of this my Paper with Reflec-

---

[7] *... Totumque ... amore:* From Virgil, *Aeneid* 11.781–82: "And she followed him blindly and rashly through the whole army / Burning with the feminine love of plunder and spoils."

[1] *Quod verum ... sum:* From Horace, *Epistles* 1.1.11: "I now design to seek what's good and true, / And that alone" — CREECH [Bond].

[2] *Muff:* At this time both men and women carried muffs.

[3] *Rainbow Coffee-house:* There were at least six coffeehouses of this name; the one in Fleet Street was near Lintot's bookshop [Bond].

tions upon Red-heels or Top-knots,[4] but rather to enter into the Passions of Mankind, and to correct those depraved Sentiments that give Birth to all those little Extravagancies which appear in their outward Dress and Behaviour. Foppish and fantastick Ornaments are only Indications of Vice, not criminal in themselves. Extinguish Vanity in the Mind, and you naturally retrench the little Superfluities of Garniture and Equipage. The Blossoms will fall of themselves, when the Root that nourishes them is destroyed.

I shall therefore, as I have said, apply my Remedies to the first Seeds and Principles of an affected Dress, without descending to the Dress it self; though at the same time I must own, that I have Thoughts of creating an Officer under me to be entituled *The Censor of small Wares*, and of allotting him one Day in a Week for the Execution of such his Office. An Operator of this Nature might act under me with the same Regard as a Surgeon to a Physitian;[5] the one might be employ'd in healing those Blotches and Tumours which break out in the Body, while the other is sweetning the Blood and rectifying the Constitution. To speak truly, the young People of both Sexes are so wonderfully apt to shoot out into long Swords or sweeping Trains, bushy Head-dresses or full-bottom'd Perriwigs, with several other Incumbrances of Dress, that they stand in Need of being pruned very frequently, lest they should be oppressed with Ornaments, and overrun with the Luxuriency of their Habits. I am much in doubt, whether I should give the Preference to a Quaker[6] that is trimmed close and almost cut to the Quick, or to a Beau that is loaden with such a Redundance of Excrescencies. I must therefore desire my Correspondents to let me know now they approve my Project, and whether they think the erecting of such a petty Censorship may not turn to the Emolument of the Publick; for I would not do any thing of this Nature rashly and without Advice.

There is another Set of Correspondents to whom I must address my self in the second Place; I mean such as fill their Letters with pri-

---

[4] *Top-knots:* A ribbon bow worn as part of a woman's headdress.

[5] *Surgeon to a Physitian:* At this time a surgeon was a mere technician without the scientific education and medical training of a physician.

[6] *Quaker:* Member of the Society of Friends, a radical Protestant religious and social sect established by George Fox in England in the mid–seventeenth century. The Friends rejected the ordained ministry and the outward rules and trappings of conventional religious orders. They acquired the name "Quakers" from the way that they reputedly would shake with religious enthusiasm at their meetings. Quakers spurned worldly vanities and cultivated a plain style of dress.

vate Scandal, and black Accounts of particular Persons and Families. The World is so full of Ill-nature, that I have Lampoons sent me by People who cannot spell, and Satyrs compos'd by those who scarce know how to write. By the last Post in particular I receiv'd a Packet of Scandal which is not legible; and have a whole Bundle of Letters in Womens Hands that are full of Blots and Calumnies, insomuch that when I see the Name *Cœlia, Phillis, Pastora*, or the like, at the Bottom of a Scrawl, I conclude on course[7] that it brings me some Account of a fallen Virgin, a faithless Wife, or an amorous Widow. I must therefore inform these my Correspondents, that it is not my Design to be a Publisher of Intreagues and Cuckoldoms, or to bring little infamous Stories out of their present lurking Holes into broad Day light. If I attack the Vicious, I shall only set upon them in a Body; and will not be provoked by the worst Usage I can receive from others, to make an Example of any particular Criminal. In short, I have so much of a *Drawcansir*[8] in me, that I shall pass over a single Foe to charge whole Armies. It is not *Lais* or *Silenus*,[9] but the Harlot and the Drunkard, whom I shall endeavour to expose; and shall consider the Crime as it appears in a Species, not as it is circumstanced in an Individual. I think it was *Caligula*[10] who wished the whole City of *Rome* had but one Neck, that he might behead them at a Blow. I shall do out of Humanity what that Emperour would have done in the Cruelty of his Temper, and aim every Stroak at a collective Body of Offenders. At the same Time I am very sensible, that nothing spreads a Paper like private Calumny and Defamation; but as my Speculations are not under this Necessity, they are not exposed to this Temptation.

In the next Place I must apply my self to my Party-Correspondents, who are continually teazing me to take Notice of one anothers Pro-

---

[7] *on course:* An archaic locution, "of course."

[8] *Drawcansir:* A character in *The Rehearsal*, a play by George Buckingham (1628–1687), which parodies Restoration heroic tragedies. In act 5, scene 1, Drawcansir says: "Others may boast a single man to kill / But I the blood of thousands daily spill."

[9] *Lais or Silenus:* Lais was a famous Athenian hetaera, or female companion, a class of highly educated independent Greek courtesans. Silenus is a mythical Greek creature of the woods, part man and part goat; he is a companion of Dionysus, the god of wine. Both the figures are invoked here as representatives of, respectively, female and male illegitimate sexuality.

[10] *Caligula:* The nickname ("little boots") of Gaius Caesar Germanicus (A.D. 12–41), the wildly despotic Roman emperor who ruled from 37–41. The statement referred to here is recorded by the Roman biographer Gaius Suetonius Tranquillus (A.D. 69–after 122), in his *Caligula* 30 [Bond].

ceedings. How often am I asked by both Sides, if it is possible for me to be an unconcerned Spectator of the Rogueries that are committed by the Party which is opposite to him that writes the Letter. About two Days since I was reproached with an old *Grecian* Law,[11] that forbids any Man to stand as a Neuter or a Looker-on in the Divisions of his Country. However, as I am very sensible my Paper would lose its whole Effect, should it run into the Outrages of a Party, I shall take Care to keep clear of every thing which looks that Way. If I can any way asswage private Inflamations, or allay publick Ferments, I shall apply my self to it with my utmost Endeavours; but will never let my Heart reproach me with having done any thing towards encreasing those Feuds and Animosities that extinguish Religion, deface Government, and make a Nation miserable.

What I have said under the three foregoing Heads, will, I am afraid, very much retrench the Number of my Correspondents: I shall therefore acquaint my Reader, that if he has started any Hint which he is not able to pursue, if he has met with any surprizing Story which he does not know how to tell, if he has discovered any epidemical Vice which has escaped my Observation, or has heard of any uncommon Vertue which he would desire to publish; in short, if he has any Materials that can furnish out an innocent Diversion, I shall promise him my best Assistance in the working of them up for a publick Entertainment.

This Paper my Reader will find was intended for an Answer to a Multitude of Correspondents; but I hope he will pardon me if I single out one of them in particular, who has made me so very humble a Request, that I cannot forbear complying with it.

[11] *old Grecian Law:* A reference to the reformed Athenian law code of the statesman and poet Solon (630–560 B.C.). According to the Greek historian and biographer Plutarch (A.D. 46–119), Solon made a "peculiar and surprising" law, which ordained that a man who in time of faction takes neither side shall be disenfranchised (*Solon* 20.1) [Bond].

No. 41
Tuesday, April 17, 1711
[Steele on the Modern "Pict" Exposed]

. . . Tu non inventa reperta es.[1]
— Ovid.

Compassion for the Gentleman who writes the following Letter, should not prevail upon me to fall upon the Fair Sex, if it were not that I find they are frequently Fairer than they ought to be. Such Impostures are not to be tolerated in Civil Society; and I think his Misfortune ought to be made publick, as a Warning for other Men always to Examine into what they Admire.

SIR,

'Supposing you to be a Person of General Knowledge, I make my Application to you on a very particular Occasion. I have a great Mind to be rid of my Wife, and hope, when you consider my Case, you will be of Opinion I have very just Pretentions to a Divorce. I am a mere Man of the Town, and have very little Improvement, but what I have got from Plays. I remember in *The Silent Woman*[2] the Learned Dr. *Cutberd*, or Dr. *Otter* (I forget which) makes one of the Causes of Separation to be *Error Personæ*,[3] when a Man marries a Woman, and finds her not to be the same Woman whom he intended to marry, but another. If that be Law, it is, I presume, exactly my Case. For you are to know, Mr. *Spectator*, that there are Women who do not let their Husbands see their Faces 'till they are married.

'Not to keep you in suspense, I mean plainly, that part of the Sex who paint. They are some of them so Exquisitely skilful this Way, that give them but a Tolerable Pair of Eyes to set up with, and they will make Bosom, Lips, Cheeks, and Eyebrows, by their own Industry. As for my Dear, never Man was so inamour'd as I was of her fair Forehead, Neck and Arms, as well as the bright Jett of her Hair; but to my great Astonishment, I find they were all the Effect of Art: Her Skin is so Tarnished with this Practice, that when she first wakes in a

---

[1] *Tu non inventa reperta es:* Adapted from Ovid, *Metamorphoses* 1.654–55: "Undiscovered thou art discovered" [Bond].

[2] *The Silent Woman:* Ben Jonson's (1572/73–1637) play *Epicoene, or the Silent Woman,* 5.1 [Bond].

[3] *Error Personæ:* Mistaken identity.

Morning, she scarce seems young enough to be the Mother of her whom I carried to Bed the Night before. I shall take the Liberty to part with her by the first Opportunity, unless her Father will make her Portion suitable to her real, not her assumed, Countenance. This I thought fit to let him and her know by your means.

I am, SIR,

Your most Obedient,

Humble Servant.'

I cannot tell what the Law, or the Parents of the Lady, will do for this Injured Gentleman, but must allow he has very much Justice on his side. I have indeed very long observed this Evil, and distinguished those of our Women who wear their own, from those in borrowed Complexions, by the *Picts*[4] and the *British*. There does not need any great Discernment to judge which are which. The *British* have a lively, animated Aspect; the *Picts*, tho' never so Beautiful, have dead, uninformed Countenances. The Muscles of a real Face sometimes swell with soft Passion, sudden Surprize, and are flushed with agreeable Confusions, according as the Objects before them, or the Ideas presented to them, affect their Imagination. But the *Picts* behold all things with the same Air, whether they are Joyful or Sad; The same fix'd Insensibility appears upon all Occasions. A *Pict*, tho' she takes all that Pains to invite the Approach of Lovers, is obliged to keep them at a certain Distance; a Sigh in a Languishing Lover, if fetched too near her, would dissolve a Feature; and a Kiss snatched by a Forward one, might transfer the Complexion of the Mistress to the Admirer. It is hard to speak of these false Fair Ones, without saying something uncomplaisant, but I would only recommend to them to consider how they like coming into a Room new Painted; they may assure themselves, the near Approach of a Lady who uses this Practice is much more offensive.

WILL. HONEYCOMB[5] told us, one Day, an Adventure he once had with a *Pict*. This Lady had Wit, as well as Beauty, at Will, and made it her Business to gain Hearts, for no other Reason, but to rally the Torments of her Lovers. She would make great Advances to insnare

---

[4] *Picts:* Ancient inhabitants of northern Britain who used woad, a blue vegetable dye, as war paint.

[5] *WILL. HONEYCOMB:* An aging relic of the Restoration, the rakish man-about-town Will Honeycomb is a member of the Spectator club introduced in *Spectator* No. 2 (see p. 83).

Men, but without any manner of Scruple break off when there was no Provocation. Her Ill-Nature and Vanity made my Friend very easily Proof against the Charms of her Wit and Conversation; but her beauteous Form, instead of being blemished by her Falshood and Inconstancy, every Day increased upon him, and she had new Attractions every time he saw her. When she observed WILL. irrevocably her Slave, she began to use him as such, and after many steps toward such a Cruelty, she at last utterly banished him. The unhappy Lover strove in vain, by servile Epistles, to revoke his Doom, till at length he was forced to the last Refuge, a round Sum of Mony to her Maid. This corrupt Attendant placed him early in the Morning behind the Hangings in her Mistress's Dressing-Room. He stood very conveniently to observe, without being seen. The *Pict* begins the Face she designed to wear that Day, and I have heard him protest she had worked a full half Hour before he knew her to be the same Woman. As soon as he saw the Dawn of that Complexion, for which he had so long languished, he thought fit to break from his Concealment, repeating that of *Cowley*:[6]

> Th' adorning Thee, with so much Art,
>   Is but a barbarous Skill;
> 'Tis like the Pois'ning of a Dart,
>   Too apt before to kill.

The *Pict* stood before him in the utmost Confusion, with the prettiest Smirk imaginable on the finish'd side of her Face, pale as Ashes on the other. HONEYCOMB seized all her Gally-Pots[7] and Washes, and carried off his Handkerchief full of Brushes, Scraps of *Spanish* Wool,[8] and Phials of Unguents. The Lady went into the Country, the Lover was cured.

It is certain no Faith ought to be kept with Cheats, and an Oath made to a *Pict* is of it self void. I would therefore exhort all the *British* Ladies to single them out, nor do I know any but *Lindamira*, who should be Exempt from Discovery; for her own Complexion is

---

[6] *Cowley:* Abraham Cowley (1618–1667) was a seventeenth-century English metaphysical poet. This passage is from his poem, "The Waiting Maid," in *The Mistress*, stanza 4 (*Poems*, ed. Waller, p. 138) [Bond].

[7] *Gally-Pots:* Small earthenware pots used by apothecaries for medicinal ointments and washes.

[8] *Spanish Wool:* Wool treated with red dye and used as a cosmetic, like blush for the cheeks.

so delicate, that she ought to be allowed the Covering it with Paint, as a Punishment for chusing to be the worst Piece of Art extant, instead of the Masterpiece of Nature. As for my part, who have no Expectations from Women, and Consider them only as they are part of the Species, I do not half so much fear offending a Beauty, as a Woman of Sense; I shall therefore produce several Faces which have been in Publick this many Years, and never appeared; it will be a very pretty Entertainment in the Play-House (when I have abolished this Custom) to see so many Ladies, when they first lay it down, *incog*,[9] in their own Faces.

In the mean time, as a Pattern for improving their Charms, let the Sex study the agreeable *Statira*. Her Features are enlivened with the Chearfulness of her Mind, and good Humour gives an Alacrity to her Eyes. She is Graceful without Affecting an Air, and Unconcerned without appearing Careless. Her having no manner of Art in her Mind, makes her want none in her Person.

How like is this Lady, and how unlike is a *Pict*, to that Description Dr. *Donne*[10] gives of his Mistress?

> . . . *Her Pure and Eloquent Blood*
> *Spoke in her Cheeks, and so distinctly Wrought,*
> *That one would almost say her Body Thought.*

---

[9] *incog:* Incognito.

[10] *Dr. Donne:* John Donne (1572–1631), leading English metaphysical poet and dean of St. Paul's Cathedral. Donne is famous for his love poetry, his devotional verse, and his sermons. The passage here is from "Of the Progress of the Soul (the Second Anniversary)," 244–46.

No. 66
Wednesday, May 16, 1711
[Steele on Female Education]

Motus Doceri gaudet Jonicos
Matura Virgo, & fingitur Artibus
Jam nunc, & incestos amores
De Tenero meditatur Ungui.[1]
— Hor.

The two following Letters are upon a Subject of very great Importance, tho' expressed without any Air of Gravity.

To the SPECTATOR.

SIR,

'I take the Freedom of asking your Advice in Behalf of a young Country Kinswoman of mine who is lately come to Town, and under my Care for her Education. She is very pretty, but you can't imagine how unform'd a Creature it is. She comes to my Hands just as Nature left her, half finish'd, and without any acquir'd Improvements. When I look on her I often think of the *Belle Sauvage*[2] mention'd in one of your Papers. Dear Mr. SPECTATOR, help me to make her comprehend the visible Graces of Speech, and the dumb Eloquence of Motion; for she is at present a perfect Stranger to both. She knows no Way to express her self but by her Tongue, and that always to signify her Meaning. Her Eyes serve her yet only to see with, and she is utterly a Forreigner to the Language of Looks and Glances. In this I fancy you could help her better than any Body. I have bestow'd two Months in teaching her to sigh when she is not concern'd, and to smile when she is not pleas'd; and am asham'd to own she makes little or no improvement. Then she is no more able now to walk, than she was to go at a Year old. By Walking you will easily know I mean that regular but easy Motion, which gives our Persons so irresistible a Grace

---

[1] *Motus . . . Ungui:* From Horace, *Odes* 3.6.21–24: "The maiden early takes delight in learning Grecian dances, and trains herself in coquetry e'en now, and plans unholy amours, from childhood" [Bond].

[2] *Belle Sauvage:* French, the beautiful wildwoman. The reference is to *Spectator* 28 on London shop signs: "As for the Bell-Savage, which is the Sign of a savage Man standing by a Bell, I was formerly very much puzzled upon the Conceit of it, till I accidently fell into the reading of an old Romance translated out of the *French*; which gives an Account of a very beautiful Woman who was found in a Wilderness, and is called in *French la belle Sauvage.*"

as if we mov'd to Musick, and is a Kind of disengag'd Figure, or, if I may so speak, recitative Dancing. But the Want of this I cannot blame in her, for I find she has no Ear, and means nothing by Walking but to change her Place. I cou'd pardon too her Blushing if she knew how to carry her self in it, and if it did not manifestly injure her Complexion.

'They tell me you are a Person who have seen the World, and are a Judge of fine Breeding; which makes me ambitious of some Instructions from you for her Improvement: Which when you have favour'd me with, I shall further advise with you about the Disposal of this fair Forrester in Marriage; for I will make it no Secret to you, that her Person and Education are to be her Fortune.

I am,

Sir,

Your very humble Servant,

Celimene.'

SIR,

'Being employed by *Celimene* to make up and send to you her Letter, I make bold to recommend the Case therein mentioned to your Consideration, because she and I happen to differ a little in our Notions. I, who am a rough Man, am afraid the young Girl is in a fair Way to be spoiled: Therefore pray Mr. SPECTATOR let us have your Opinion of this fine thing called *Fine Breeding*; for I am afraid it differs too much from that plain thing called *Good Breeding*.

Your most humble Servant.'

The general Mistake among use in the educating our Children, is, That in our Daughters we take Care of their Persons and neglect their Minds; in our Sons, we are so intent upon adorning their Minds, that we wholly neglect their Bodies. It is from this that you shall see a young Lady celebrated and admired in all the Assemblies about Town; when her elder Brother is afraid to come into a Room. From this ill Management it arises, That we frequently observe a Man's Life is half spent before he is taken Notice of; and a Woman in the Prime of her Years is out of Fashion and neglected. The Boy I shall consider upon some other Occasion, and at present stick to the Girl: And I am the more inclined to this, because I have several Letters which complain to me that my female Readers have not understood me for some Days last past, and take themselves to be unconcerned in the present Turn of my Writings. When a Girl is safely brought from her Nurse, before she is capable of forming one simple Notion of any thing in Life, she is delivered to the Hands of her Dancing-Master; and with a Collar round her Neck,[3] the pretty wild thing is taught a fantastical Gravity of Behaviour, and forced to a particular Way of holding her Head, heaving her Breast, and moving with her whole Body; and all this under Pain of never having an Husband, if she steps, looks, or moves awry. This gives the young Lady wonderful Workings of Imagination, what is to pass between her and this Husband that she is every Moment told of, and for whom she seems to be educated. Thus her Fancy is engaged to turn all her Endeavours to the Ornament of her Person, as what must determine her Good and Ill in this Life; and she naturally thinks, if she is tall enough she is wise enough for any thing for which her Education makes her think she is designed. To make her an agreable Person is the main Purpose of Her Parents; to that is all their Cost, to that all their Care directed; and from this general Folly of Parents we owe our present numerous Race of Coquets. These Reflections puzzle me, when I think of giving my Advice on the Subject of managing the wild thing mentioned in the Letter of my Correspondent. But sure there is a middle Way to be followed; the Management of a young Lady's Person is not to be overlooked, but the Erudition of her Mind is much more to be regarded. According as this is managed, you will see the Mind follow the Appetites of the Body, or the Body express the Virtues of the Mind.

Cleomira dances with all the Elegance of Motion imaginable; but her eyes are so chastised with the Simplicity and Innocence of her Thoughts, that she raises in her Beholders Admiration and good Will, but no loose Hope or wild Imagination. The true Art in this Case is, To make the Mind and Body improve together; and if possible, to make Gesture follow Thought, and not let Thought be employed upon Gesture.

---

[3] *Collar round her Neck:* It was a common practice to put young girls in back braces to train their spines to grow straight.

No. 73
Thursday, May 24, 1711
[Addison on Female "Idols"]

... *O Dea certè!*[1]
— Virg.

It is very strange to consider, that a Creature like Man, who is sensible of so many Weaknesses and Imperfections, should be actuated by a Love of Fame: That Vice and Ignorance, Imperfection and Misery should contend for Praise, and endeavour as much as possible to make themselves Objects of Admiration.

But notwithstanding Man's Essential Perfection is but very little, his Comparative Perfection may be very considerable. If he looks upon himself in an abstracted Light, he has not much to boast of; but if he considers himself with regard to others, he may find Occasion of glorying, if not in his own Virtues, at least in the Absence of another's Imperfections. This gives a different Turn to the Reflections of the Wise Man and the Fool. The first endeavours to shine in himself, and the last to outshine others. The first is humbled by the Sense of his own Infirmities, the last is lifted up by the Discovery of those which he observes in other Men. The Wise Man considers what he wants, and the Fool what he abounds in. The Wise Man is happy when he gains his own Approbation, and the Fool when he Recommends himself to the Applause of those about him.

But however unreasonable and absurd this Passion for Admiration may appear in such a Creature as Man, it is not wholly to be discouraged; since it often produces very good Effects, not only as it restrains him from doing any thing which is mean and contemptible, but as it pushes him to Actions which are great and glorious. The Principle may be defective or faulty, but the Consequences it produces are so good, that, for the benefit of Mankind, it ought not to be extinguished.

It is observed by *Cicero*,[2] that Men of the greatest and the most shining Parts are the most actuated by Ambition; and if we look into the two Sexes, I believe we shall find this Principle of Action stronger in Women than in Men.

---

[1] *O Dea certè!*: From Virgil, *Aeneid* 1.328: "O goddess surely!" [Bond].

[2] *Cicero*: Marcus Tullius Cicero (106–43 B.C.), the famous Roman orator, philosopher, and statesman. He makes this observation in *De Officiis* (*On Duty*) 1.8.26 and *Tusculan Disputations* 5.24.68 [Bond].

The Passion for Praise, which is so very vehement in the fair Sex, produces excellent Effects in Women of Sense, who desire to be admired for that only which deserves Admiration: and I think we may observe, without a Compliment to them, that many of them do not only live in a more uniform Course of Virtue, but with an infinitely greater Regard to their Honour, than what we find in the Generality of our own Sex. How many Instances have we of Chastity, Fidelity, Devotion? How many Ladies distinguish themselves by the Education of their Children, Care of their Families, and Love of their Husbands, which are the great Qualities and Atchievements of Womankind: As the making of War, the carrying on of Traffick, the Administration of Justice, are those by which Men grow famous, and get themselves a Name.

But as this Passion for Admiration, when it works according to Reason, improves the beautiful Part of our Species in every thing that is Laudable; so nothing is more Destructive to them when it is governed by Vanity and Folly. What I have therefore here to say, only regards the vain Part of the Sex, whom for certain Reasons, which the Reader will hereafter see at large, I shall distinguish by the Name of *Idols*. An *Idol* is wholly taken up in the Adorning of her Person. You see in every Posture of her Body, Air of her Face, and Motion of her Head, that it is her Business and Employment to gain Adorers. For this Reason your *Idols* appear in all publick Places and Assemblies, in order to seduce Men to their Worship. The Playhouse is very frequently filled with *Idols*; several of them are carried in Procession every Evening about the Ring,[3] and several of them set up their Worship even in Churches. They are to be accosted in the Language proper to the Deity. Life and Death are in their Power: Joys of Heaven and Pains of Hell are at their disposal: Paradise is in their Arms, and Eternity in every Moment that you are present with them. Raptures, Transports and Extasies are the Rewards which they confer: Sighs and Tears, Prayers and broken Hearts are the Offerings which are paid to them. Their Smiles make Men happy; their Frowns drive them to Despair. I shall only add under this Head, that *Ovid*'s Book of the Art of Love[4] is a kind of Heathen Ritual, which contains all the Forms of Worship which are made use of to an *Idol*.

---

[3] *the Ring:* In Hyde Park, a circular road that was a fashionable place to ride and walk.

[4] *Art of Love:* A translation of the Roman lyric poet Ovid's (43 B.C.–A.D. 17/18) *Art of Love, together with his Remedy of Love,* "by several eminent hands" (Dryden, Congreve, and Nahum Tate) had been published in 1709 [Bond].

It would be as difficult a Task to reckon up these different kinds of *Idols*, as *Milton*'s[5] was to number those that were known in *Canaan*, and the Lands adjoining. Most of them are Worshipped, like *Moloch*, in Fires and Flames. Some of them, like *Baal*, love to see their Votaries cut and slashed, and shedding their Blood for them. Some of them, like the *Idol* in the *Apocrypha*,[6] must have Treats and Collations prepared for them every Night. It has indeed been known, that some of them have been used by their incensed Worshippers like the *Chinese Idols*, who are Whipped and Scourged when they refuse to comply with the Prayers that are offered to them.

I must here observe, that those Idolaters who devote themselves to the *Idols* I am here speaking of, differ very much from all other kinds of Idolaters. For as others fall out because they Worship different *Idols*, these Idolaters quarrel because they Worship the same.

The Intention therefore of the *Idol* is quite contrary to the Wishes of the Idolater; as the one desires to confine the *Idol* to himself, the whole Business and Ambition of the other is to multiply Adorers. This Humour of an *Idol* is prettily described in a Tale of *Chaucer*;[7] He represents one of them sitting at a Table with three of her Votaries about her, who are all of them courting her Favour, and paying their Adorations: She smiled upon one, drank to another, and trod upon the other's Foot which was under the Table. Now which of these three, says the old Bard, do you think was the Favourite? In troth, says he, not one of all the three.

The Behaviour of this old *Idol* in *Chaucer*, puts me in mind of the Beautiful *Clarinda*, one of the greatest *Idols* among the Moderns. She is Worshipped once a Week by Candle-light in the midst of a large Congregation generally called an Assembly. Some of the gayest Youths in the Nation endeavour to plant themselves in her Eye, while she sits in form with multitudes of Tapers burning about her. To encourage the Zeal of her Idolaters, she bestows a Mark of her Favour upon every one of them before they go out of her Presence. She asks a

---

[5] *Milton's:* John Milton (1608–1674) was an English poet, radical Protestant thinker, and scholar. Here, Milton describes these demons in book 1 of his *Paradise Lost*.

[6] *Apocrypha:* The Apocrypha are the fourteen books of the Septuagint included in the Catholic Latin Vulgate Bible but considered noncanonical by Protestants because they are not part of Hebrew Scripture. This is a reference to the *History of the Destruction of Bel and the Dragon*, 5.3 [Bond].

[7] *Chaucer:* An allusion to a pseudo-Chaucerian poem, "The Remedie of Love," stanzas 8 and 9 [Bond]. Geoffrey Chaucer (1340?–1400) is the author of the collection of narrative poems the *Canterbury Tales* (1382–1400).

Question of one, tells a Story to another, glances an Ogle upon a third, takes a Pinch of Snuff from the fourth, lets her Fan drop by accident to give the fifth an occasion of taking it up. In short, every one goes away satisfied with his Success, and encouraged to renew his Devotions on the same Canonical Hour that Day Seven-night.

An *Idol* may be Undeified by many accidental Causes. Marriage in particular is a kind of Counter-*Apotheosis*, or a Deification inverted. When a Man becomes familiar with his Goddess, she quickly sinks into a Woman.

Old Age is likewise a great Decayer of your *Idol*: The truth of it is, there is not a more unhappy Being than a Superannuated *Idol*, especially when she has contracted such Airs and Behaviour as are only Graceful when her Worshippers are about her.

Considering therefore that in these and many other Cases the *Woman* generally outlives the *Idol*, I must return to the Moral of this Paper, and desire my fair Readers to give a proper Direction to their Passion for being admired: In order to which, they must endeavour to make themselves the Objects of a reasonable and lasting Admiration. This is not to be hoped for from Beauty, or Dress, or Fashion, but from those inward Ornaments which are not to be defaced by Time or Sickness, and which appear most amiable to those who are most acquainted with them.

No. 81
Saturday, June 2, 1711
[Addison on Party Patches]

Qualis ubi audito venantum murmure Tigris
Horruit in maculas . . .[1]
— Statius.

About the middle of last Winter I went to see an *Opera* at the Theatre in the *Hay-Market*,[2] where I could not but take notice of two Parties of very Fine Women, that had placed themselves in the opposite Side-Boxes,[3] and seemed drawn up in a kind of Battel Array one against another. After a short Survey of them, I found they were *Patched*[4] differently; the Faces, on one Hand, being Spotted on the Right Side of the Forehead, and those upon the other on the Left. I quickly perceived that they cast Hostile Glances upon one another; and that their Patches were placed in those different Situations, as Party Signals to distinguish Friends from Foes. In the Middle-Boxes, between these two opposite Bodies, were several Ladies who Patched indifferently on both sides of their Faces, and seemed to sit there with no other Intention but to see the *Opera*. Upon Enquiry I found that the Body of *Amazons*[5] on my Right Hand were Whigs, and those on my Left, Tories; and that those who had placed themselves in the Middle-Boxes were a Neutral Party, whose Faces had not yet declared themselves. These last however, as I afterwards found, diminished daily, and took their Party with one Side or the other, insomuch that I observed in several of them, the Patches which were before dispersed equally, are now all gone over to the Whig or Tory[6] Side of

---

[1] *Qualis . . . in maculas:* From Statius, *Thebaid* 2.128–29: "As when the tigress hears the hunters' din, / Dark angry spots distain her glossy skin" [Bond].

[2] *Hay-Market:* Haymarket was an area that ran south from Coventry Street to Pall Mall east. Because it was close to the Royal Mews, in the seventeenth century a market was established here for hay and straw. In 1705 Thomas Betterton brought his company from Lincoln's Inns Fields to a new theater in Haymarket. Within a few years this new Queen's Theatre had become the venue for opera performances.

[3] *Side-Boxes:* In general at this time the custom seems to have been for the men to occupy the side boxes and the women the front of middle boxes [Bond].

[4] *Patched:* Patches are small rounds of silk used cosmetically as artificial beauty marks on the face, neck, and shoulders.

[5] *Amazons:* The mythical nation of women warriors who reputedly lived in ancient Scythia.

[6] *Whig or Tory:* The two political parties of the day. The Whigs had lost power in 1710, and so at this time the Tories were in ascendancy. See Introduction (p. 22).

the Face. The Censorious say, That the Men whose Hearts are aimed at are very often the Occasions that one part of the Face is thus Dishonoured, and lyes under a kind of Disgrace, while the other is so much Set off and Adorned by the Owner; and that the Patches turn to the Right or to the Left, according to the Principles of the Man who is most in Favour. But whatever may be the Motives of a few Fantastical Coquets, who do not Patch for the Publick Good, so much as for their own Private Advantage, it is certain that there are several Women of Honour who Patch out of Principle, and with an Eye to the Interest of their Country. Nay, I am informed, that some of them adhere so stedfastly to their Party, and are so far from Sacrificing their Zeal for the Publick to their Passion for any particular Person, that in a late Draught of Marriage Articles a Lady has stipulated with her Husband, That, whatever his Opinions are, she shall be at Liberty to Patch on which side she pleases.

I must here take notice, that *Rosalinda*, a Famous Whig Partizan, has most unfortunately a very beautiful Mole on the Tory part of her Forehead, which, being very conspicuous, has occasioned many Mistakes, and given an Handle to her Enemies to misrepresent her Face, as though it has Revolted from the Whig Interest. But whatever this natural Patch may seem to intimate, it is well known that her Notions of Government are still the same. This unlucky Mole however has mis-led several Coxcombs, and, like the hanging out of false Colours, made some of them Converse with *Rosalinda* in what they thought the Spirit of her Party, when on a sudden she has given them an unexpected Fire, that has sunk them all at once. If *Rosalinda* is unfortunate in her Mole, *Nigranilla* is as unhappy in a Pimple which forces her, against her Inclinations, to Patch on the Whig side.

I am told that many Virtuous Matrons, who formerly have been taught to believe that this Artificial Spotting of the Face was unlawful, are now reconciled by a Zeal for their Cause, to what they could not be prompted by a Concern for their Beauty. This way of declaring War upon one another, puts me in mind of what is reported of the Tigress, that several Spots rise in her Skin when she is angry; or as Mr. *Cowley*[7] has imitated the Verses that stand as the Motto of this Paper,

> — *She Swells with angry Pride,*
> *And calls forth all her Spots of every side.*

[7] *Cowley:* From Abraham Cowley's (1618–1667) unfinished epic the *Davideis* 3.403–04 [Bond].

When I was in the Theatre the time above-mentioned, I had the Curiosity to count the Patches on both Sides, and found the Tory Patches to be about twenty Stronger than the Whig; but to make amends for this small Inequality, I the next Morning found the whole Puppet-show filled with Faces spotted after the Whiggish manner. Whether or no the Ladies had retreated hither in order to rally their Forces I cannot tell, but the next Night they came in so great a Body to the Opera, that they out-numbered the Enemy.

This Account of Party-Patches will, I am afraid, appear improbable to those who live at a distance from the fashionable World, but as it is a Distinction of a very singular Nature, and what perhaps may never meet with a Parallel, I think I should not have discharged the Office of a faithful Spectator had I not recorded it.

I have, in former Papers,[8] endeavoured to expose this Party Rage in Women, as it only serves to aggravate the Hatreds and Animosities that reign among Men, and in a great measure deprive the Fair Sex of those peculiar Charms with which Nature has endowed them.

When the *Romans* and *Sabines*[9] were at War, and just upon the point of giving Battel, the Women, who were allied to both of them, interposed with so many Tears and Intreaties that they prevented the mutual Slaughter which threatned both Parties, and united them together in a firm and lasting Peace.

I would recommend this noble Example to our *British* Ladies, at a time when their Country is torn with so many unnatural Divisions, that if they continue, it will be a Misfortune to be born in it. The *Greeks* thought it so improper for Women to interest themselves in Competitions and Contentions, that for this Reason, among others, they forbad them, under Pain of Death, to be present at the *Olympick* Games, notwithstanding these were the Publick Diversions of all *Greece.*

As our *English* Women excell those of all Nations in Beauty, they should endeavour to outshine them in all other Accomplishments proper to the Sex, and to distinguish themselves as tender Mothers and faithful Wives, rather than as furious Partizans. Female Virtues

---

[8] *former Papers:* In *Spectator* No. 57.

[9] *Romans and Sabines:* The Sabines were an ancient Italic tribe. The Romans and Sabines fought a series of skirmishes until the Romans gained a victory in 449 B.C. Later in 290 B.C., the Romans decisively conquered the Sabines, absorbing them into Roman Italy; the Sabines became full Roman citizens in 268 B.C. The story referred to here appears in the Roman historian Livy's (59 B.C.–A.D. 17) *History of Rome,* 1.13 [Bond].

are of a Domestick turn. The Family is the proper Province for Private Women to Shine in. If they must be showing their Zeal for the Publick, let it not be against those who are perhaps of the same Family, or at least of the same Religion or Nation, but against those who are the open, professed, undoubted Enemies of their Faith, Liberty, and Country. When the *Romans* were pressed with a Foreign Enemy, the Ladies voluntarily contributed all their Rings and Jewels to assist the Government under a publick Exigence, which appeared so laudable an Action in the Eyes of their Countrymen, that from thenceforth it was permitted by a Law to pronounce publick Orations at the Funeral of a Woman in Praise of the deceased Person, which till that time was peculiar to Men. Would our *English* Ladies instead of sticking on a Patch against those of their own Country, show themselves so truly Publick-spirited as to Sacrifice every one her Necklace against the Common Enemy, what Decrees ought not to be made in favour of them?

Since I am recollecting upon this Subject such Passages as occur to my Memory out of ancient Authors, I cannot omit a Sentence in the Celebrated Funeral Oration of *Pericles*,[10] which he made in Honour of those brave *Athenians*, that were Slain in a Fight with the *Lacedemonians*.[11] After having addressed himself to the several Ranks and Orders of his Countrymen, and shewn them how they should behave themselves in the Publick Cause, he turns to the Female part of his Audience; 'And as for you (says he) I shall advise you in very few Words; Aspire only to those Virtues that are peculiar to your Sex; follow your natural Modesty, and think it your greatest Commendation not to be talked of one way or other.'

---

[10] *Pericles:* The Athenian statesman (d. 429 B.C.) famous for promoting Athenian democracy, extending the Athenian empire, and building the Parthenon, the Temple of Athena on the Athenian Acropolis. The Funeral Oration is given in the Athenian historian Thucydides' (460?–400? B.C.) *History of the Peloponnesian War*, 2.45.

[11] *Lacedemonians:* The Spartans. Athens and Sparta were the two most powerful Greek city-states and were at war from 431–404 B.C. (the Peloponnesian War).

No. 119
Tuesday, July 17, 1711
[Addison on Different Manners in Country and City]

Urbem quam dicunt Romam, Meliboee, putavi
Stultus ego huic nostræ similem . . .[1]
— Virg.

The first and most obvious Reflections which arise in a Man who changes the City for the Country, are upon the different Manners of the People whom he meets with in those two different Scenes of Life. By Manners I do not mean Morals, but Behaviour and Good Breeding, as they show themselves in the Town and in the Country.

And here, in the first place, I must observe a very great Revolution that has happened in the Article of Good Breeding. Several obliging Deferencies, Condescensions and Submissions, with many outward Forms and Ceremonies that accompany them, were first of all brought up among the politer Part of Mankind who lived in Courts and Cities, and distinguished themselves from the Rustick part of the Species (who on all Occasions acted bluntly and naturally) by such a mutual Complaisance and Intercourse of Civilities. These Forms of Conversation by degrees multiplied and grew troublesome; the Modish World found too great a Constraint in them, and have therefore thrown most of them aside. Conversation, like the *Romish* Religion,[2] was so encumbered with Show and Ceremony, that it stood in need of a Reformation to retrench its Superfluities, and restore it to its natural good Sense and Beauty. At present therefore an unconstrained Carriage, and a certain Openness of Behaviour are the height of Good Breeding. The Fashionable World is grown free and easie; our Manners, sit more loose upon us: Nothing is so modish as an agreeable Negligence. In a word, Good Breeding shows it self most, where to an ordinary Eye it appears the least.

If after this we look on the People of Mode in the Country, we find in them the Manners of the last Age. They have no sooner fetched themselves up to the fashion of the Polite World, but the Town has dropped them, and are nearer to the first State of Nature than to those Refinements which formerly reigned in the Court, and still prevail in

---

[1] *Urbem . . . similem . . .*: From Virgil, *Eclogues* 1.19–20: "Fool that I was, I thought Imperial *Rome* / Like *Mantua*" — DRYDEN [Bond].
[2] *Romish Religion*: Roman Catholicism.

the Country. One may now know a Man that never conversed in the World by his Excess of Good Breeding. A Polite Country Squire shall make you as many Bows in half an Hour, as would serve a Courtier for a Week. There is infinitely more to do about Place and Precedence in a Meeting of Justices Wives, than in an Assembly of Dutchesses.

This Rural Politeness is very troublesome to a Man of my Temper, who generally take the Chair that is next me, and walk first or last, in the Front or in the Rear, as Chance directs. I have known my Friend Sir ROGER's[3] Dinner almost cold before the Company could adjust the Ceremonial, and be prevailed upon to sit down; and have heartily pitied my old Friend, when I have seen him forced to pick and cull his Guests, as they sat at the several Parts of his Table, that he might drink their Healths according to their respective Ranks and Qualities. Honest *Will. Wimble*, who I should have thought had been altogether uninfected with Ceremony, gives me abundance of Trouble in this Particular; though he has been fishing all the Morning, he will not help himself at Dinner 'till I am served. When we are going out of the Hall he runs behind me, and last Night, as we were walking in the Fields, stopped short at a Stile till I came up to it, and upon my making Signs to him to get over, told me, with a serious Smile, that sure I believed they had no Manners in the Country.

There has happened another Revolution in the Point of Good Breeding, which relates to the Conversation among Men of Mode, and which I cannot but look upon as very extraordinary. It was certainly one of the first Distinctions of a well-bred Man to express every thing that had the most remote Appearance of being obscene in modest Terms and distant Phrases; whilst the Clown, who had no such Delicacy of Conception and Expression, cloathed his *Ideas* in those plain homely Terms that are the most obvious and natural. This kind of Good Manners was perhaps carried to an Excess, so as to make Conversation too stiff, formal and precise; for which Reason (as Hypocrisy in one Age is generally succeeded by Atheism in another) Conversation is in a great measure relapsed into the first Extream; So that at present several of our Men of the Town, and particularly those who have been polished in *France*, make use of the most coarse uncivilized Words in our Language, and utter themselves often in such a manner as a Clown would blush to hear.

---

[3] *Sir ROGER's:* Sir Roger de Coverley, the Tory country gentleman who is one of the most recurrent and prominent characters of the Spectator Club introduced in *Spectator* No. 2 (see p. 83).

This infamous Piece of Good Breeding, which reigns among the Coxcombs of the Town, has not yet made its way into the Country; and as it is impossible for such an irrational way of Conversation to last long among a People that make any Profession of Religion, or Show of Modesty, if the Country Gentlemen get into it they will certainly be left in the Lurch; their Good Breeding will come too late to them, and they will be thought a parcel of lewd Clowns, while they fancy themselves talking together like Men of Wit and Pleasure.

As the two Points of Good Breeding, which I have hitherto insisted upon, regard Behaviour and Conversation, there is a third which turns upon Dress. In this too the Country are very much behind hand. The Rural Beaus are not yet got out of the Fashion that took place at the time of the Revolution, but ride about the Country in red Coats and laced Hats, while the Women in many Parts are still trying to outvie one another in the Height of their Head-Dresses.

But a Friend[4] of mine, who is now upon the Western Circuit, having promised to give me an Account of the several Modes and Fashions that prevail in the different Parts of the Nation through which he passes, I shall defer the enlarging upon this last Topick till I have received a Letter from him, which I expect every Post.

No. 128
Friday, July 27, 1711
[Addison on Successful Marriage]

. . . *Concordia discors.*[1]
— Luc.

Women in their Nature are much more gay and joyous than Men; whether it be that their Blood is more refined, their Fibres more delicate, and their animal Spirits more light and volatile; or whether, as some have imagined, there may not be a kind of Sex in the very Soul, I shall not pretend to determine. As Vivacity is the Gift of Women, Gravity is that of Men. They should each of them therefore keep a Watch upon the particular Biass which Nature has fixed in their Minds, that it may not *draw* too much, and lead them out of the

---

[4] *a Friend:* His letter is printed in *Spectator* No. 129.
[1] *Concordia discors:* From Lucan, *Pharsalia* 1.98: "Jarring harmony" [Bond].

Paths of Reason. This will certainly happen, if the one in every Word and Action affects the Character of being rigid and severe, and the other of being brisk and airy. Men should beware of being captivated by a kind of savage Philosophy, Women by a thoughtless Gallantry. Where these Precautions are not observed, the Man often degenerates into a Cynick, the Woman into a Coquet; the Man grows sullen and morose, the Woman impertinent and fantastical.

By what I have said we may conclude, Men and Women were made as Counterparts to one another, that the Pains and Anxieties of the Husband might be relieved by the Sprightliness and good Humour of the Wife. When these are rightly tempered, Care and Chearfulness go Hand in Hand; and the Family, like a Ship that is duly trimmed, wants neither Sail nor Ballast.

Natural Historians observe, (for whilst I am in the Country I must fetch my Allusions from thence) That only the Male Birds have Voices; That their Songs begin a little before Breeding-time, and end a little after: That whilst the Hen is covering her Eggs, the Male generally takes his Stand upon a neighbouring Bough within her Hearing; and by that Means amuses and diverts her with his Songs during the whole Time of her Sitting.

This Contract among Birds lasts no longer than till a Brood of young ones arises from it; so that in the feather'd Kind, the Cares and Fatigues of the married State, if I may so call it, lie principally upon the Female. On the contrary, as in our Species the Man and Woman are joined together for Life, and the main Burden rests upon the former, Nature has given all the little Arts of soothing and Blandishment to the Female, that she may chear and animate her Companion in a constant and assiduous Application to the making a Provision for his Family, and the educating of their common Children. This however is not to be taken so strictly, as if the same Duties were not often reciprocal, and incumbent on both Parties; but only to set forth what seems to have been the general Intention of Nature, in the different Inclinations and Endowments which are bestowed on the different Sexes.

But whatever was the Reason that Man and Woman were made with this Variety of Temper, if we observe the Conduct of the fair Sex, we find that they choose rather to associate themselves with a Person who resembles them in that light and volatile Humour which is natural to them, than to such as are qualified to moderate and counter-ballance it. It has been an old Complaint, That the Coxcomb carries it with them before the Man of Sense. When we see a Fellow loud and talkative, full of insipid Life and Laughter, we may venture to pronounce him a female Favourite: Noise and Flutter are such Accomplishments as they cannot withstand. To be short, the Passion of an ordinary Woman for a Man, is nothing else but Self-love diverted upon another Object: She would have the Lover a Woman in every thing but the Sex. I do not know a finer Piece of Satyr on this Part of Womankind than those Lines of Mr. *Dryden*,

> *Our thoughtless Sex is caught by outward Form*
> *And empty Noise, and loves it self in Man.*[2]

This is a Source of infinite Calamities to the Sex, as it frequently joins them to Men who in their own Thoughts are as fine Creatures as themselves; or if they chance to be good-humoured, serve only to dissipate their Fortunes, inflame their Follies, and aggravate their Indiscretions.

The same female Levity is no less fatal to them after Marriage than before; it represents to their Imaginations the faithful prudent Husband as an honest tractable and domestick Animal; and turns their Thoughts upon the fine gay Gentleman that laughs, sings, and dresses so much more agreeably.

As this irregular Vivacity of Temper leads astray the Hearts of ordinary Women in the Choice of their Lovers and the Treatment of their Husbands, it operates with the same pernicious Influence towards their Children, who are taught to accomplish themselves in all those sublime Perfections that appear captivating in the Eye of their Mother. She admires in her Son what she loved in her Gallant; and by that Means contributes all she can to perpetuate herself in a worthless Progeny.

The younger *Faustina*[3] was a lively Instance of this Sort of Women. Notwithstanding she was married to *Marcus Aurelius*, one of the greatest, wisest, and best of the *Roman* Emperors, she thought a common Gladiator much the prettier Gentleman; and had taken such Care to accomplish her Son *Commodus* according to her own Notions of a fine Man, that when he ascended the Throne of his Father, he became the most foolish and abandoned Tyrant that was ever placed at the Head of the *Roman* Empire, signalizing himself in

---

[2] ... *in Man:* From John Dryden's (1631–1700) *Oedipus* 1.1: "That thoughtless Sex" [Bond].

[3] *Faustina:* Annia Galeria Faustina (125–176), the daughter of the Roman emperor Antoninus Pius and wife of the philosopher-emperor Marcus Aurelius (121–180, ruled 161–180). Commodus (161–192), their son, ruled from 180 to 192.

nothing but the fighting of Prizes, and knocking out Mens Brains. As he had no Taste of true Glory, we see him in several Medals and Statues which are still extant of him, equipped like an *Hercules* with a Club and a Lion's Skin.

I have been led into this Speculation by the Characters I have heard of a Country-Gentleman and his Lady, who do not live many Miles from Sir ROGER. The Wife is an old Coquet, that is always hankering after the Diversions of the Town; the Husband a morose Rustick, that frowns and frets at the Name of it: The Wife is overrun with Affection, the Husband sunk into Brutality: The Lady cannot bear the Noise of the Larks and Nightingales, hates your tedious Summer-Days, and is sick at the Sight of shady Woods and purling Streams; the Husband wonders how any one can be pleased with the Fooleries of Plays and Operas, and rails from Morning to Night at essenced Fops and tawdry Courtiers. The Children are educated in these different Notions of their Parents. The Sons follow the Father about his Grounds, while the Daughters read Volumes of Love-Letters and Romances to their Mother. By this Means it comes to pass, that the Girls look upon their Father as a Clown, and the Boys think their Mother no better than she should be.

How different are the Lives of *Aristus* and *Aspatia*? The innocent Vivacity of the one is tempered and composed by the chearful Gravity of the other. The Wife grows Wise by the Discourses of the Husband, and the Husband good-humour'd by the Conversations of the Wife. *Aristus* would not be so amiable were it not for his *Aspatia*, nor *Aspatia* so much to be esteemed were it not for her *Aristus*. Their Virtues are blended in their Children, and diffuse through the whole Family a perpetual Spirit of Benevolence, Complacency, and Satisfaction.

No. 154
Monday, August 27, 1711
[Steele on the Reformed Rake-Manque]

Nemo repente fuit Turpissimus . . .[1]
— Juv.

Mr. SPECTATOR,

'You are frequent in the Mention of Matters which concern the feminine World, and take upon you to be very severe against Men upon all those Occasions: But all this while I am afraid you have been very little conversant with Women, or you would know the Generality of them are not so angry as you imagine at the general Vices amongst us. I am apt to believe (begging your Pardon) that you are still what I my self was once, a queer modest Fellow; and therefore, for your Information, shall give you a short Account of my self, and the Reasons why I was forced to wench, drink, play, and do every thing which are necessary to the Character of a Man of Wit and Pleasure, to be well with the Ladies.

'You are to know then that I was bred a Gentleman, and had the finishing Part of my Education under a Man of great Probity, Wit, and Learning in one of our Universities. I will not deny but this made my Behaviour and Mein bear in it a Figure of Thought rather than Action; and a Man of a quite contrary Character, who never thought in his Life, rallied me one Day upon it, and said He believ'd I was still a Virgin. There was a young Lady of Virtue present; and I was not displeased to favour the Insinuation: But it had a quite contrary Effect from what I expected, I was ever after treated with great Coldness both by that Lady and all the rest of my Acquaintance. In a very little Time I never came into a Room but I could hear a Whisper, Here comes the Maid: A Girl of Humour would on some Occasions say, Why how do you know more than any of us? An Expression of that kind was generally followed by a loud Laugh: In a Word, for no other Fault in the World than that they really thought me as innocent as themselves, I became of no Consequence among them, and was receiv'd always upon the Foot of a Jest. This made so strong an Impression upon me, that I resolv'd to be as agreeable as the best of the Men who laughed at me; but I observed it was Nonsense for me to be im-

---

[1] *Nemo . . . Turpissimus . . . :* From Juvenal, *Satires* 2.83: "No man e're reach'd the heights of Vice at first" — TATE [Bond].

pudent at first among those who knew me: My Character for Modesty was so notorious wherever I had hitherto appeared, that I resolved to shew my new Face in new Quarters of the World. My first Step I chose with Judgment, for I went to *Astrop*; and came down among a Crowd of Academicks, at one Dash, the impudentest Fellow they had ever seen in their Lives. Flushed with this Success, I made Love and was happy. Upon this Conquest I thought it would be unlike a Gentleman to stay long with my Mistress, and crossed the Country to *Bury*: I could give you a very good Account of my self at that Place also. At these two ended my first Summer of Gallantry. The Winter following, you would wonder at it, but I relapsed into Modesty upon coming among People of Figure in *London*, yet not so much but that the Ladies who had formerly laughed at me said, Bless us! how wonderfully that Gentleman is improved? Some Familiarities about the Play-houses towards the End of the ensuing Winter, made me conceive new Hopes of Adventures; and instead of returning the next Summer to *Astrop* or *Bury*, I thought my self qualified to go to *Epsom*, and followed a young Woman, whose Relations were jealous of my Place in her Favour, to *Scarborough*. I carried my Point, and in my third Year aspired to go to *Tunbridge*, and in the Autumn of the same Year made my Appearance at *Bath*.[2] I was now got into the Way of Talk proper for Ladies, and was run into a vast Acquaintance among them, which I always improved to the *best Advantage*. In all this Course of Time, and some Years following, I found a sober modest Man was always looked upon by both Sexes as a precise unfashioned Fellow of no Life or Spirit. It was ordinary for a Man who had been drunk in good Company, or passed a Night with a Wench, to speak of it next Day before Women for whom he had the greatest Respect. He was reproved, perhaps, with a Blow of the Fan or an oh Fie, but the angry Lady still preserved an apparent Approbation in her Countenance: He was called a strange wicked Fellow, a sad Wretch; he shrugs his Shoulders, swears, receives another Blow, swears again he did not know he swore, and all was well. You might often see Men game in the Presence of Women, and throw at once for more than they were worth, to recommend themselves as Men of Spirit. I found by long Experience, that the loosest Principles and most abandoned Behaviour, carried all before them in Pretensions to Women of Fortune. The Encouragement given to People of this

---

[2] *Astrop . . . Bath:* All the place names here are spas and the correspondent, Simon Honeycomb, travels to them in an order of ascending fashionability, Astrop being the least and Bath the most modish [Bond].

Stamp, made me soon throw off the remaining Impressions of a sober Education. In the above-mentioned Places, as well as in Town, I always kept Company with those who lived most at large; and in due Process of Time I was a very pretty Rake among the Men, and a very pretty Fellow among the Women. I must confess I had some melancholy Hours upon the Account of the Narrowness of my Fortune, but my Conscience at the same Time gave me the Comfort that I had qualified my self for marrying a Fortune.

'When I had lived in this Manner for some Time, and became thus accomplished, I was now in the Twenty seventh Year of my Age, and about the Forty seventh of my Constitution, my Health and Estate wasting very fast; when I happened to fall into the Company of a very pretty young Lady in her own Disposal. I entertained the Company, as we Men of Gallantry generally do, with the many Haps and Disasters, Watchings under Windows, Escapes from jealous Husbands, and several other Perils. The young thing was wonderfully charmed with one that knew the World so well and talked so fine; with *Desdemona*, all her Lover said affected her; *it was strange, 'twas wond'rous strange.*[3] In a Word, I saw the Impression I had made upon her, and with a very little Application the pretty thing has married me. There is so much Charm in her Innocence and Beauty, that I do now as much detest the Course I have been in for many Years, as ever I did before I entred into it.

'What I intend, Mr. SPECTATOR, by writing all this to you, is, that you would, before you go any further with your Panegyricks on the fair Sex, give them some Lectures upon their silly Approbations. It is that I am weary of Vice, and that it was not in my natural Way, that I am now so far recovered as not to bring this believing dear Creature to Contempt and Poverty for her Generosity to me. At the same Time tell the Youth of good Education of our Sex, that they take too little Care of improving themselves in little things: A good Air at entring into a Room, a proper Audacity in expressing himself with Gayety and Gracefulness, would make a young Gentleman of Virtue and Sense capable of discountenancing the shallow impudent Rogues that shine among the Women.

'Mr. SPECTATOR, I don't doubt but you are a very sagacious Person, but you are so great with *Tully*[4] of late, that I fear you will

---

[3] *it was . . . strange:* From William Shakespeare's (1564–1616) tragedy *Othello* 1.3.160–61.

[4] *Tully:* Marcus Tullius Cicero (106–43 B.C.), the famous Roman orator, philosopher, and statesman.

contemn these things as Matters of no Consequence: But believe me, Sir, they are of the highest Importance to humane Life; and if you can do any thing towards opening fair Eyes, you will lay an Obligation upon all your Contemporaries who are Fathers, Husbands, or Brothers to Females.

> *Your most affectionate humble Servant,*
> Simon Honeycomb.'

No. 156
Wednesday, August 29, 1711
[Steele on the Woman's Man]

> . . . *Sed tu simul obligasti*
> *Perfidum votis caput, enitescis*
> *Pulchrior multo . . .* [1]
> — Hor.

I do not think any thing could make a pleasanter Entertainment, than the History of the reigning Favourites among the Women from Time to Time about this Town. In such an Account we ought to have a faithful Confession of each Lady for what she liked such and such a Man, and he ought to tell us by what particular Action or Dress he believed he should be most successful. As for my Part, I have always made as easy a Judgment when a Man dresses for the Ladies, as when he is equipped for Hunting or Coursing. The Woman's Man is a Person in his Air and Behaviour quite different from the rest of our Species: His Garb is more loose and negligent, his Manner more soft and indolent; that is to say, in both these Cases there is an apparent Endeavour to appear unconcerned and careless. In catching Birds the Fowlers have a Method of imitating their Voices to bring them to the Snare; and your Women's Men have always a Similitude of the Creature they hope to betray, in their own Conversation. A Woman's Man is very knowing in all that passes from one Family to another, has little pretty Officiousnesses, is not at a Loss what is good for a Cold, and it is not amiss if he has a Bottle of Spirits in his Pocket in case of any sudden Indisposition.

---

[1] *Sed . . . Pulchrior multo:* From Horace, *Odes* 2.8.5–7: "But you, though perjured and forsworn, / Yet still shine out more bright and fair" [Bond].

Curiosity having been my prevailing Passion, and indeed the sole Entertainment of my Life, I have sometimes made it my Business to examine the Course of Intreagues, as well as the Manners and Accomplishments of such as have been most successful that Way. In all my Observation, I never knew a Man of good Understanding a general Favourite; some Singularity in his Behaviour, some Whim in his Way of Life, and what would have made him ridiculous among the Men, has recommended him to the other Sex. I should be very sorry to offend a People so fortunate as these of whom I am speaking; but let any one look over the old Beaux, and he will find the Man of Success was remarkable for quarrelling impertinently for their Sakes, for dressing unlike the rest of the World, or passing his Days in an insipid Assiduity about the fair Sex, to gain the Figure he made amongst them. Add to this that he must have the Reputation of being well with other Women, to please any one Woman of Gallantry; for you are to know, that there is a mighty Ambition among the light Part of the Sex to gain Slaves from the Dominion of others. My Friend WILL. HONEYCOMB says it was a common Bite[2] with him to lay Suspicions that he was favoured by a Lady's Enemy, that is some rival Beauty, to be well with her herself. A little Spite is natural to a great Beauty; and it is ordinary to snap up a disagreeable Fellow least another should have him. That impudent Toad *Bareface* fares well among all the Ladies he converses with, for no other Reason in the World but that he has the Skill to keep them from Explanation with one another. Did they know there is not one who likes him in her Heart, each would declare her Scorn of him the next Moment; but he is well received by them because it is the Fashion, and Opposition to each other brings them insensibly into an Imitation of each other. What adds to him the greatest Grace is, that the pleasant Thief, as they call him, is the most inconstant Creature living, has a wonderful deal of Wit and Humour, and never wants something to say; besides all which he has a most spiteful dangerous Tongue if you should provoke him.

To make a Woman's Man, he must not be a Man of Sense or a Fool; the Business is to entertain, and it is much better to have a Faculty of arguing than a Capacity of judging right. But the pleasantest of all the Women's Equipage are your regular Visitants; these are Volunteers in their Service without Hopes of Pay or Preferment: It is

---

[2] *WILL. HONEYCOMB* . . . *Bite:* A member of the Spectator Club introduced in *Spectator* No. 2 (see p. 83). A "Bite" is a verbal deception.

enough that they can lead out from a publick Place, that they are admitted on a publick Day, and can be allowed to pass away Part of
that heavy Load, their Time, in the Company of the Fair. But commend me above all others to those who are known for your Ruiners
of Ladies; these are the choicest Spirits which our Age produces. We
have several of these irresistible Gentlemen among us when the Company is in Town. These Fellows are accomplished with the Knowledge of the ordinary Occurrences about Court and Town, have that
sort of good Breeding which is exclusive of all Morality, and consists
only in being publickly decent, privately dissolute.

It is wonderful how far a fond Opinion of herself can carry a
Woman to make her have the least Regard to a professed known
Woman's Man: But as scarce one of all the Women who are in the
Tour of Gallantries ever hears any thing of what is the common Sense
of sober Minds, but are entertained with a continual Round of Flatteries, they cannot be Mistresses of themselves enough to make Arguments for their own Conduct from the Behaviour of these Men to
others. It is so far otherwise, that a general Fame for Falshood in this
kind is a Recommendation; and the Coxcomb, loaded with the
Favours of many others, is received like a Victor that disdains his
Trophies to be a Victim to the present Charmer.

If you see a Man more full of Gesture than ordinary in a publick
Assembly, if loud upon no Occasion, if negligent of the Company
round him, and yet laying wait for destroying by that Negligence,
you may take it for granted that he has ruined many a fair One. The
Woman's Man expresses himself wholly in that Motion which we
call Strutting: An elevated Chest, a pinched[3] Hat, a measurable Step,
and a sly surveying Eye, are the Marks of him. Now and then you see
a Gentleman with all these Accomplishments; but alass any one of
them is enough to undo thousands: When a Gentleman with such
Perfections adds to it suitable Learning, there should be publick
Warning of his Residence in Town, that we may remove our Wives
and Daughters. It happens sometimes that such a fine Man has read
all the Miscellany Poems, a few of our Comedies, and has the Translation of *Ovid*'s Epistles[4] by Heart. Oh if it were possible that such a
one could be as true as he is charming! but that is too much, the
Women will share such a dear false Man: 'A little Gallantry to hear

---

[3] *pinched:* Pleated, gathered.
[4] *Ovid's Epistles:* A translation of the Roman lyric poet Ovid's (43 B.C.–A.D.
17/18) *Epistles* by Dryden and others was published in 1680 [Bond].

him Talk one would indulge one's self in, let him reckon the Sticks of one's Fan, say something of the Cupids in it, and then call one so many soft Names which a Man of his Learning has at his Fingers Ends. There sure is some Excuse for Frailty when attack'd by such Force against a weak Woman.' Such is the Soliloquy of many a Lady one might name, at the Sight of one of these who makes it no Iniquity to go on from Day to Day in the Sin of Woman-slaughter.

It is certain that People are got into a way of Affection with a manner of overlooking the most solid Virtues, and admiring the most trivial Excellencies. The Woman is so far from expecting to be contemned for being a very injudicious silly Animal, that while she can preserve her Features and her Mein she knows she is still the Object of Desire; and there is a sort of secret Ambition, from reading frivolous Books, and keeping as frivolous Company, each-side to be amiable in Imperfection, and arrive at the Characters of the dear Deceiver and the perjured Fair.

No. 187
Thursday, October 4, 1711
[Steele on Female Jilts]

> . . . *Miseri quibus*
> *Intentata nites . . .* [1]
> — Hor.

The Intelligence given by this Correspondent is so important and useful, in order to avoid the Persons he speaks of, that I shall insert his Letter at length.

Mr. SPECTATOR,

'I do not know that you have ever touched upon a certain Species of Women, whom we ordinarily call Jilts. You cannot possibly go upon a more useful Work, than the Consideration of these dangerous Animals. The Coquet is indeed one degree towards the Jilt; but the Heart of the former is bent upon admiring her self, and giving false Hopes to her Lovers, but the latter is not contented to be extreamly

---

[1] *Miseri . . . nites:* From Horace, *Odes* 1.5.12–13: "Unhappy they by whom thy charms are seen, but not thy wiles" [Bond].

Amiable, but she must add to that Advantage a certain Delight in being a Torment to others. Thus when her Lover is in the full Expectation of Success, the Jilt shall meet him with a sudden Indifference, an Admiration in her Face at his being surprised that he is received like a Stranger, and a Cast of her Head another way with a pleasant Scorn of the Fellow's Insolence. It is very probable the Lover goes home utterly astonished and dejected, sits down to his Scrutore,[2] sends her Word, in the most abject Terms, That he knows not what he has done, that all which was desirable in this Life is so suddenly vanished from him, that the Charmer of his Soul should withdraw the vital Heat from the Heart which pants for her. He continues a Mournful Absence for some time pining in secret, and out of Humour with all things which he meets with. At length he takes a Resolution to try his Fate, and explain with her resolutely upon her unaccountable Carriage. He walks up to her Apartment, with a thousand Inquietudes and Doubts in what manner he shall meet the first Cast of her Eye; when upon his first Appearance she flies towards him, wonders where he has been, accuses him of his Absence, and treats him with a Familiarity as surprising as her former Coldness. This good Correspondence continues till the Lady observes the Lover grows happy in it, and then she interrupts it with some new Inconsistency of Behaviour. For (as I just now said) the Happiness of a Jilt consists only in the Power of making others Uneasie. But such is the Folly of this Sect of Women, that they carry on this pretty skittish Behaviour, 'till they have no Charms left to render it supportable. *Corinna*, that used to torment all who conversed with her with false Glances, and little heedless unguarded Motions, that were to betray some Inclination towards the Man she would ensnare, finds at present all she attempts that way unregarded; and is obliged to indulge the Jilt in her Constitution, by laying Artificial Plots, writing perplexing Letters from unknown Hands, and making all the young Fellows in Love with her, 'till they find out who she is. Thus as before she gave Torment by disguising her Inclination, she now is obliged to do it by hiding her Person.

'As for my own part, *Mr.* SPECTATOR, it has been my Unhappy Fate to be Jilted from my Youth upward, and as my Taste has been very much towards Intreague, and having Intelligence with Women of Wit, my whole Life has passed away in a Series of Impositions. I shall, for the benefit of the present Race of young Men, give some account of my Loves. I know not whether you have ever heard of the

---

[2] *Scrutore:* An archaic form of escritoire, a writing table, desk.

famous Girl about Town called *Kitty*, this Creature (for I must take Shame upon my self) was my Mistress in the Days when Keeping was in Fashion. *Kitty*, under the Appearance of being Wild, Thoughtless and Irregular in all her Words and Actions, concealed the most accomplish'd Jilt of her time. Her Negligence had to me a Charm in it like that of Chastity, and want of Desires seemed as great a Merit as the Conquest of them. The Air she gave her self was that of a Romping Girl, and whenever I talked to her with any turn of Fondness, she would immediately snatch off my Perriwig, try it upon her self in the Glass, clap her Arms a Kimbow, draw my Sword, and make Passes on the Wall, take off my Cravat, and seize it to make some other use of the Lace, or run into some other unaccountable Rompishness, 'till the time I has appointed to pass away with her was over: I went from her full of Pleasure at the Reflection that I had the keeping of so much Beauty in a Woman, who as she was too heedless to please me, was also too unattentive to form a design to wrong me. Long did I divert every Hour that hung heavy upon me in the Company of this Creature, whom I looked upon as neither Guilty or Innocent, but could laugh at my self for my unaccountable Pleasure in an Expence upon her, 'till in the end it appeared my pretty Insensible was with Child by my Footman.

'This Accident roused me into a Disdain against all Libertine Women, under what Appearance soever they hid their Insincerity, and I resolved after that time to converse with none but those who lived within the Rules of Decency and Honour. To this End, I formed my self into a more regular Turn of Behaviour, and began to make Visits, frequent Assemblies, and lead out Ladies from the Theatres, with all the other insignificant Duties which the professed Servants of the Fair place themselves in constant readiness to perform. In a very little time, (having a plentiful Fortune) Fathers and Mothers began to regard me as a good Match, and I found easie Admittance into the best Families in Town to observe their Daughters; but I, who was born to follow the Fair to no purpose, have by the force of my ill Stars made my Application to Three Jilts successively.

'*Hyæna* is one of those who form themselves into a melancholy and indolent Air, and endeavour to gain Admirers from their Inattention to all around them. *Hyæna* can loll in her Coach, with something so fixed in her Countenance, that it is impossible to conceive her Meditation is employed only on her Dress and her Charms in that Posture. If it were not too coarse a Simile, I should say *Hyæna*, in the Figure she affects to appear in, is a Spider in the midst of a Cobweb, that is sure to destroy every Fly that approaches it. The Nett *Hyæna*

throws is so fine, that you are taken in it before you can observe any
Part of her Work. I attempted her for a long and weary Season; but I
found her Passion went no further than to be admired, and she is of
that unreasonable Temper as not to value the Inconstancy of her
Lovers, provided she can boast she once had their Addresses.

'*Biblis* was the second I aimed at, and her Vanity lay in purchasing
the Adorers of others, and not in rejoicing in their Love it self. *Biblis*
is no Man's Mistress, but every Woman's Rival. As soon as I found
this, I fell in Love with *Chloe*, who is my present Pleasure and Torment. I have writ to her, danced with her, and fought for her, and
have been her Man in the sight and expectation of the whole Town
this three Years, and thought my self near the end of my Wishes,
when the other Day she called me into her Closet, and told me, with
a very grave Face, that she was a Woman of Honour, and scorned to
deceive a Man who loved her with so much Sincerity as she saw I did,
and therefore she must inform me that she was by Nature the most
inconstant Creature breathing, and begged of me not to Marry her: If
I insisted upon it, I should; but that she was lately fallen in Love with
another. What to do or say I know not, but desire you to inform me,
and you will infinitely Oblige,

SIR,

Your Most Humble Servant,

Charles Yellow.'

No. 275
Tuesday, January 15, 1712
[Addison on the Dissection of a Beau's Brain]

. . . *tribus Anticyris caput insanabile* . . . [1]

— Juv.

I was Yesterday engaged in an Assembly of Virtuoso's,[2] where one
of them produced many curious Observations, which he had lately
made in the Anatomy of an Human Body. Another of the Company
communicated to us several wonderful Discoveries, which he had

---

[1] *tribus . . . insanabile:* From Horace, *Ars Poetica* 300: "A head which three doses
of hellebore cannot cure"[Bond].

[2] *Assembly of Virtuoso's:* Here, a set of amateur scientific enthusiasts.

also made on the same Subject, by the help of very fine Glasses. This gave Birth to a great Variety of uncommon Remarks, and furnished Discourse for the remaining Part of the Day.

The different Opinions which were started on this Occasion presented to my Imagination so many new Ideas, that by mixing with those which were already there, they employed my Fancy all the last Night, and composed a very wild Extravagant Dream.

I was invited, methought, to the Dissection of a *Beau's Head* and of a *Coquet's Heart*, which were both of them laid on a Table before us. An imaginary Operator opened the first with a great deal of Nicety, which, upon a cursory and superficial View, appeared like the Head of another Man; but, upon applying our Glasses to it, we made a very odd Discovery, namely, that what we looked upon as Brains, were not such in reality, but an Heap of strange Materials wound up in that Shape and Texture, and packed together with wonderful Art in the several Cavities of the Skull. For, as *Homer* tells us,[3] that the Blood of the Gods is not real Blood, but only something like it; so we found that the Brain of a Beau is not real Brain, but only something like it.

The *Pineal Gland*,[4] which many of our Modern Philosophers suppose to be the Seat of the Soul, smelt very strong of Essence and Orange-Flower Water, and was encompassed with a kind of Horny Substance, cut into a thousand little Faces or Mirrours, which were imperceptible to the naked Eye, insomuch that the Soul, if there had been any here, must have been always taken up in contemplating her own Beauties.

We observed a large *Antrum* or Cavity in the *Sinciput*,[5] that was filled with Ribbons, Lace and Embroidery, wrought together in a most curious Piece of Network, the Parts of which were likewise imperceptible to the naked Eye. Another of these *Antrums* or Cavities, was stuffed with invisible Billet-doux,[6] Love-Letters, pricked Dances,[7] and other Trumpery of the same nature. In another we found a kind of Powder, which set the whole Company a Sneezing, and by the Scent discovered it self to be right *Spanish*.[8] The several

---

[3] *as Homer tells us:* In his Greek epic the *Iliad* 5.339–43 [Bond].

[4] *Pineal Gland:* A small organ in the back of the head that secretes the hormone melatonin.

[5] *Sinciput:* The front part of the head.

[6] *Billet-doux:* Love letters.

[7] *pricked Dances:* To prick is to set down music by means of pricks or notes; here it would be the music for such dances [Bond].

[8] *right Spanish:* Authentic Spanish snuff, a kind of powdered tobacco inhaled through the nose.

other Cells were stored with Commodities of the same kind, of which it would be tedious to give the Reader an exact Inventory.

There was a large Cavity on each side of the Head, which I must not omit. That on the right side was filled with Fictions, Flatteries and Falsehoods, Vows, Promises and Protestations; that on the left with Oaths and Imprecations. There issued out a *Duct* from each of these Cells, which ran into the Root of the Tongue, where both joined together, and passed forward in one common *Duct* to the Tip of it. We discovered several little Roads or Canals running from the Ear into the Brain, and took particular Care to trace them out through their several Passages. One of them extended it self to a bundle of Sonnets and little Musical Instruments. Others ended in several Bladders which were filled either with Wind or Froth. But the large Canal entered into a great Cavity of the Skull, from whence there went another Canal into the Tongue. This great Cavity was filled with a kind of Spongy Substance, which the *French* Anatomists call *Galimatias*, and the *English*, Nonsense.

The Skins of the Forehead were extreamly tough and thick, and what very much surprized us, had not in them any single Blood-Vessel that we were able to discover, either with or without our Glasses; from whence we concluded, that the Party when alive must have been entirely deprived of the Faculty of Blushing.

The *Os Cribriforme*[9] was exceedingly stuffed, and in some places damaged with Snuff. We could not but take Notice in particular of that small Muscle, which is not often discovered in Dissections, and draws the Nose upwards, when it expresses the Contempt which the Owner of it has, upon seeing any thing he does not like, or hearing any thing he does not understand. I need not tell my learned Reader, this is that Muscle which performs the Motion so often mentioned by the *Latin* Poets,[10] when they talk of a Man's cocking his Nose, or playing the Rhinoceros.

We did not find any thing very remarkable in the Eye, saving only, that the *Musculi Amatorii*, or as we may translate it into *English*, the *Ogling Muscles*, were very much worn and decayed with use; whereas on the contrary, the *Elevator* or the Muscle which turns the Eye towards Heaven, did not appear to have been used at all.

[9] *Os Cribriforme*: A sievelike opening.
[10] *Latin Poets*: For example, the Roman epigrammatist Martial (c. A.D. 40–c. 140), *Epigrams* 1.3.5–6 [Bond].

I have only mentioned in this Dissection such new Discoveries as we were able to make, and have not taken any Notice of those Parts which are to be met with in common Heads. As for the Skull, the Face, and indeed the whole outward shape and figure of the Head, we could not discover any difference from what we observe in the Heads of other Men. We were informed, that the Person to whom this Head belonged, had passed for *a Man* above five and thirty Years; during which time he Eat and Drank like other People, dressed well, talked loud, laught frequently, and on particular Occasions had acquitted himself tolerably at a Ball or an Assembly; to which one of the Company added, that a certain knot of Ladies took him for a Wit. He was cut off in the flower of his Age by the blow of a Paring-Shovel, having been surprized by an eminent Citizen, as he was tendring some Civilities to his Wife.

When we had thoroughly examin'd this Head with all its Apartments, and its several kinds of Furniture, we put up the Brain, such as it was, into its proper place, and laid it aside under a broad piece of Scarlet Cloth, in order to be *prepared*, and kept in a great Repository of Dissections; our Operator telling us that the Preparation would not be so difficult as that of another Brain, for that he had observed several of the little Pipes and Tubes which ran through the Brain were already filled with a kind of Mercurial Substance, which he looked upon to be true Quick-Silver.

He applied himself in the next place to the *Coquet's Heart*, which he likewise laid open with great Dexterity. There occurred to us many Particularities in this Dissection; but being unwilling to burden my Reader's Memory too much, I shall reserve this Subject for the Speculation of another Day.

No. 281
Tuesday, January 22, 1712
[Addison on the Dissection of a Coquette's Heart]

Pectoribus inhians spirantia consulit exta. [1]
— Virg.

Having already given an Account of the Dissection of a *Beau's Head*,[2] with the several Discoveries made on that Occasion; I shall here, according to my Promise, enter upon the Dissection of a *Coquet's Heart*, and communicate to the Publick such Particularities as we observed in that curious Piece of Anatomy.

I should perhaps have waved this Undertaking, had not I been put in mind of my Promise by several of my unknown Correspondents, who are very importunate with me to make an Example of the Coquet, as I have already done of the Beau. It is therefore in Compliance with the Request of Friends, that I have looked over the Minutes of my former Dream, in order to give the Publick an exact Relation of it, which I shall enter upon without further Preface.

Our Operator, before he engaged in this Visionary Dissection, told us, that there was nothing in his Art more difficult, than to lay open the Heart of a Coquet, by reason of the many Labyrinths and Recesses which are to be found in it, and which do not appear in the Heart of any other Animal.

He desired us first of all to observe the *Pericardium*, or outward Case of the Heart, which we did very attentively; and by the help of our Glasses discerned in it Millions of little Scars, which seem'd to have been occasioned by the Points of innumerable Darts and Arrows, that from time to time had glanced upon the outward Coat; though we could not discover the smallest Orifice, by which any of them had entered and pierced the inward Substance.

Every Smatterer in Anatomy knows, that this *Pericardium*, or Case of the Heart, contains in it a thin reddish Liquor, supposed to be bred from the Vapours which exhale out of the Heart, and being stopt here, are condensed into this watry Substance. Upon examining this Liquor, we found that it had in it all the Qualities of that Spirit which is made use of in the Thermometer, to shew the Change of Weather.

---

[1] *Pectoribus . . . exta:* From Virgil, *Aeneid* 4.64: "And anxiously the panting Entrails views" — DRYDEN [Bond].

[2] *Beau's Head:* In *Spectator* No. 275 (p. 528).

Nor must I here omit an Experiment one of the Company assured us he himself had made with this Liquor, which he found in great quantity about the Heart of a Coquet whom he had formerly dissected. He affirmed to us, that he had actually enclosed it in a small Tube made after the manner of a Weather-Glass;[3] but that instead of acquainting him with the Variations of the Atmosphere, it showed him the Qualities of those Persons who entered the Room where it stood. He affirmed also, that it rose at the Approach of a Plume of Feathers, an embroidered Coat, or a Pair of fringed Gloves; and that it fell as soon as an ill-shaped Perriwig, a clumsy pair of Shoes, or an unfashionable Coat came into his House: Nay, he proceeded so far as to assure us, that upon his Laughing aloud when he stood by it, the Liquor mounted very sensibly, and immediately sunk again upon his looking serious. In short, he told us, that he knew very well by this Invention whenever he had a Man of Sense or a Coxcomb in his Room.

Having cleared away the *Pericardium*, or the Case and Liquor above-mentioned, we came to the Heart itself. The outward Surface of it was extremely slippery, and the *Mucro*, or Point, so very cold withal, that upon endeavouring to take hold of it, it glided through the Fingers like a smooth piece of Ice.

The Fibres were turned and twisted in a more intricate and perplexed manner than they are usually found in other Hearts; insomuch, that the whole Heart was wound up together like a Gordian Knot,[4] and must have had very irregular and unequal Motions, whilst it was employed in its Vital Function.

One thing we thought very observable, namely, that upon examining all the Vessels which came into it or issued out of it, we could not discover any Communication that it had with the Tongue.

We could not but take Notice likewise, that several of those little Nerves in the Heart which are affected by the Sentiments of Love, Hatred, and other Passions, did not descend to this before us from the Brain, but from the Muscles which lie about the Eye.

Upon weighing the Heart in my Hand, I found it to be extreamly light, and consequently very hollow, which I did not wonder at when upon looking into the Inside of it, I saw Multitudes of Cells and Cavities running one within another, as our Historians describe the

---

[3] *Weather-Glass:* A barometer or thermometer.

[4] *Gordian Knot:* An intricate knot tied by King Gordius of Phrygia and cut by Alexander the Great after he heard that whoever undid the knot would rule Asia.

Appartments of *Rosamond*'s Bower. Several of these little Hollows were stuffed with innumerable sorts of Trifles, which I shall forbear giving any particular Account of, and shall therefore only take Notice of what lay first and uppermost, which upon our unfolding it and applying our Microscope to it appeared to be a Flame-coloured Hood.

We were informed that the Lady of this Heart, when living, received the Addresses of several who made Love to her, and did not only give each of them Encouragement, but made every one she conversed with believe that she regarded him with an Eye of Kindness; for which Reason we expected to have seen the Impression of Multitudes of Faces among the several Plaites and Foldings of the Heart, but to our great Surprize not a single Print of this nature discovered it self till we came into the very Core and Center of it. We there observed a little Figure, which, upon applying our Glasses to it, appeared dressed in a very Fantastick manner. The more I looked upon it, the more I thought I had seen the Face before, but could not possibly recollect either the Place or Time; when at length one of the Company, who had examined this Figure more nicely than the rest, shew'd us plainly by the make of its Face, and the several turns of its Features, that the little Idol which was thus lodged in the very Middle of the Heart was the Deceased Beau, whose Head I gave some Account of in my last *Tuesday*'s Paper.

As soon as we had finished our Dissection, we resolved to make an Experiment of the Heart, not being able to determine among our selves the Nature of its Substance, which differed in so many Particulars from that of the Heart in other Females. Accordingly we laid it into a Pan of burning Coals, when we observed in it a certain Salamandrine Quality, that made it capable of living in the midst of Fire and Flame, without being consum'd, or so much as sindged.

As we were admiring this strange *Phænomenon*, and standing round the Heart in a Circle, it gave a most prodigious Sigh or rather Crack, and dispersed all at once in Smoke and Vapour. This imaginary Noise, which methoughts was louder than the burst of a Cannon, produced such a violent Shake in my Brain, that it dissipated the Fumes of Sleep, and left me in an instant broad awake.

No. 302
Friday, February 15, 1712
[Hughes on Emilia, the Picture of the Good Woman]

... Lachrymæque decoræ,
Gratior & pulchro veniens in corpore Virtus.[1]
— Vir. Æn. 5.

I read what I give for the Entertainment of this Day with a great deal of Pleasure, and publish it just as it came to my Hands. I shall be very glad to find there are many guessed at for *Emilia*.

Mr. SPECTATOR,

'If this Paper has the good Fortune to be honoured with a Place in your Writings, I shall be the more pleased, because the Character of *Emilia* is not an imaginary but a real one. I have industriously obscured the whole by the Addition of one or two Circumstances of no Consequence, that the Person it is drawn from might still be concealed; and that the Writer of it might not be in the least suspected, and for some other Reasons, I chuse not to give it the Form of a Letter: But if, besides the Faults of the Composition, there be any thing in it more proper for a Correspondent than the SPECTATOR himself to write, I submit it to your better Judgment, to receive any other Model you think fit.

I am,
SIR,
Your very humble Servant.

There is nothing which gives one so pleasing a Prospect of humane Nature, as the Contemplation of Wisdom and Beauty: The latter is the peculiar Portion of that Sex which is therefore called Fair; but the happy Concurrence of both these Excellencies in the same Person, is a Character too celestial to be frequently met with. Beauty is an overweaning self-sufficient thing, careless of providing it self any more substantial Ornaments; nay so little does it consult its own Interests, that it too often defeats it self, by betraying that Innocence which renders it lovely and desirable. As therefore Virtue makes a beautiful Woman appear more beautiful, so Beauty makes a virtuous Woman really more virtuous. Whilst I am considering these two Perfections

---

[1] *Lachrymæque ... Virtus:* From Virgil, *Aeneid* 5.343–44: "The lovely Grief to Pity won, / And Virtue, grace'd with Beauty, brighter shone" [Bond].

gloriously united in one Person, I cannot help representing to my Mind the Image of *Emilia*.

Who ever beheld the charming *Emilia*, without feeling in his Breast at once the Glow of Love and the Tenderness of virtuous Friendship? The unstudied Graces of her Behaviour, and the pleasant Accents of her Tongue, insensibly draw you on to wish for a nearer Enjoyment of them; but even her Smiles carry in them a silent Reproof to the Impulses of licentious Love. Thus, tho' the Attractives of her Beauty play almost irresistibly upon you and create Desire, you immediately stand corrected not by the Severity but the Decency of her Virtue. That Sweetness and Good-humour which is so visible in her Face, naturally diffuses it self into every Word and Action: A Man must be a Savage, who, at the Sight of *Emilia*, is not more inclined to do her Good than gratify himself: Her Person as it is thus studiously embellished by Nature, thus adorned with unpremeditated Graces, is a fit Lodging for a Mind so fair and lovely; there dwell rational Piety, modest Hope, and chearful Resignation.

Many of the prevailing Passions of Mankind do undeservedly pass under the Name of Religion; which is thus made to express it self in Action, according to the Nature of the Constitution in which it resides: So that were we to make a Judgment from Appearances, one would imagine Religion in some is little better than Sullenness and Reserve, in many Fear, in others the Despondings of a melancholly Complexion, in others the Formality of insignificant unaffecting Observances, in others Severity, in others Ostentation. In *Emilia* it is a Principle founded in Reason and enlivened with Hope; it does not break forth into irregular Fits and Sallies of Devotion, but is an uniform and consistent Tenour of Action: It is strict without Severity, compassionate without Weakness; it is the Perfection of that good Humour which proceeds from the Understanding, not the Effect of an easy Constitution.

By a generous Sympathy in Nature, we feel our selves disposed to mourn when any of our Fellow Creatures are afflicted; but injured Innocence and Beauty in Distress, is an Object that carries in it something inexpressibly moving: It softens the most manly Heart with the tenderest Sensations of Love and Compassion, till at length it confesses its Humanity and flows out into Tears.

Were I to relate that Part of *Emilia*'s Life which has given her an Opportunity of exerting the Heroism of Christianity, it would make too sad, too tender a Story: But when I consider her alone in the Midst of her Distresses, looking beyond this gloomy Vale of Affliction and Sorrow in the Joys of Heaven and Immortality, and when I see her in Conversation thoughtless and easy as if she were the most happy Creature in the World, I am transported with Admiration. Surely never did such a Philosophic Soul inhabit such a beauteous Form! For Beauty is often made a Privilege against Thought and Reflexion; it laughs at Wisdom, and will not abide the Gravity of its Instructions.

Were I able to represent *Emilia*'s Virtues in their proper Colours and their due to Proportions, Love or Flattery might perhaps be thought to have drawn the Picture larger than Life; but as this is but an imperfect Draught of so excellent a Character, and as I cannot, will not hope to have any Interest in her Person, all that I can say of her is but impartial Praise extorted from me by the prevailing Brightness of her Virtues. So rare a Pattern of Female Excellence ought not to be concealed, but should be set out to the View and Imitation of the World; for how amiable does Virtue appear thus as it were made visible to us in so fair an Example!

Honoria's Disposition is of a very different Turn: Her Thoughts are wholly bent upon Conquest and arbitrary Power. That she has some Wit and Beauty no Body denies, and therefore has the Esteem of all her Acquaintance as a Woman of an agreeable Person and Conversation; but (whatever her Husband may think of it) that is not sufficient for *Honoria*: She waves that Title to Respect as a mean Acquisition, and demands Veneration in the Right of an Idol; for this Reason her natural Desire of Life is continually checked with an inconsistent Fear of Wrinkles and old Age.

Emilia cannot be supposed ignorant of her personal Charms, tho' she seems to be so; but she will not hold her Happiness upon so precarious a Tenure, whilst her Mind is adorned with Beauties of a more exalted and lasting Nature. When in the full Bloom of Youth and Beauty we saw her surrounded with a Croud of Adorers, she took no Pleasure in Slaughter and Destruction, gave no false deluding Hopes which might encrease the Torments of her disappointed Lovers; but having for some Time given to the Decency of a Virgin Coyness, examined the Merit of their several Pretensions, she at length gratified her own, by resigning herself to the ardent Passion of *Bromius*. *Bromius* was then Master of many good Qualities and a moderate Fortune, which was soon after unexpectedly encreased to a plentiful Estate. This for a good while prov'd his Misfortune, as it furnish'd his unexperienc'd Age with the Opportunities of evil Company and a sensual Life. He might have longer wander'd in the Labyrinths of

Vice and Folly, had not *Emilia's* prudent Conduct won him over to the Government of his Reason. Her Ingenuity has been constantly employed in humanizing his Passions and refining his Pleasures. She has shew'd him by her own Example, that Virtue is consistent with decent Freedoms and good Humour, or rather, that it cannot subsist without 'em. Her good Sense readily instructed her, that a silent Example and an easy unrepining Behaviour, will always be more perswasive than the Severity of Lectures and Admonitions; and that there is so much Pride interwoven into the Make of Humane Nature, that an obstinate Man must only take the Hint from another, and then be left to advise and correct himself. Thus by an artful Train of Management and unseen Perswasions, having at first brought him not to dislike, and at length to be pleased with that which otherwise he would not have bore to hear of, she then knew how to press and secure this Advantage, by approving it as his Thought, and seconding it as his Proposal. By this Means she has gain'd an Interest in some of his leading Passions, and made them accessary to his Reformation.

There is another Particular of *Emilia's* Conduct which I can't forbear mentioning: To some perhaps it may at first Sight appear but a trifling inconsiderable Circumstance; but for my Part, I think it highly worthy of Observation, and to be recommended to the Consideration of the fair Sex. I have often thought wrapping Gowns and dirty Linnen, with all that huddled Oeconomy of Dress which passes under the general Name of a Mob, the Bane of conjugal Love, and one of the readiest Means imaginable to alienate the Affection of an Husband, especially a fond one. I have heard some Ladies who have been surprized by Company in such a Deshabille, apologize for it after this Manner; *Truly I am ashamed to be caught in this Pickle; but my Husband and I were sitting all alone by our selves, and I did not expect to see such good Company* — This by the Way is a fine Compliment to the good Man, which 'tis ten to one but he returns in dogged Answers and a churlish Behaviour, without knowing what it is that puts him out of Humour.

Emilia's Observation teaches her, that as little Inadvertencies and Neglects cast a Blemish upon a great Character; so the Neglect of Apparel, even among the most intimate Friends, does insensibly lessen their Regards to each other, by creating a Familiarity too low and contemptible. She understands the Importance of those things which the Generality account Trifles; and considers every thing as a Matter of Consequence, that has the least Tendency towards keeping up or abating the Affection of her Husband; him she esteems a fit Object to employ her Ingenuity in pleasing, because he is to be pleased for Life.

By the Help of these, and a thousand other nameless Arts, which 'tis easier for her to practise than for another to express, by the Obstinacy of her Goodness and unprovoked Submission, in spight of all her Afflictions and ill Usage, *Bromius* is become a Man of Sense and a kind Husband, and *Emilia* a happy Wife.

Ye guardian Angels to whose Care Heaven has entrusted its dear *Emilia*, guide her still forward in the Paths of Virtue, defend her from the Insolence and Wrongs of this undiscerning World; at length when we must no more converse with such Purity on Earth, lead her gently hence innocent and unreprovable to a better Place, where by an easy Transition from what she now is, she may shine forth an Angel of Light.

No. 435
Saturday, July 19, 1712
[Addison against Female Equestrian Costume]

Among the several Female Extravagancies I have already taken Notice of, there is one which still keeps its Ground. I mean that of the Ladies who dress themselves in a Hat and Feather, a Riding-coat and a Perriwig; or at least tie up their Hair in a Bag or Ribbond, in imitation of the smart Part of the opposite Sex. As in my Yesterday's Paper I gave an Account of the Mixture of two Sexes in one Commonwealth, I shall here take notice of this Mixture of two Sexes in one Person. I have already shewn my Dislike of this Immodest Custom more than once;[1] but in Contempt of every thing I have hitherto said, I am informed that the Highways about this great City are still very much infested with these Female Cavaliers.

I remember when I was at my Friend Sir ROGER DE COVERLY's[2] about this time Twelve-month, an Equestrian Lady of this Order appeared upon the Plains which lay at a distance from his House. I was at that time walking in the Fields with my old Friend; and as his Tenants ran out on every side to see so strange a Sight, Sir ROGER asked one of them who came by us what it was? To which the Country Fellow reply'd, 'Tis a Gentlewoman, saving your Worship's Presence, in

---

[1] . . . *more than once:* In *Spectator* Nos. 104 and 331.
[2] Sir ROGER DE COVERLY's: See *Spectator* No. 119, note 3 (p. 514).

a Coat and Hat. This produced a great deal of Mirth at the Knight's House, where we had a Story at the same time of another of his Tenants, who meeting this Gentleman-like Lady on the High-way, was asked by her *whether that was* Coverly-Hall, the Honest Man seeing only the Male part of the Querist, replied, *Yes, Sir*; but upon the second Question, *whether Sir* ROGER DE COVERLY *was a Married Man*, having dropped his Eye upon the Petticoat, he chang'd his Note into *No Madam.*

Had one of these Hermaphrodites appeared in *Juvenal*'s Days,[3] with what an Indignation should we have seen her described by that excellent Satyrist. He would have represented her in her Riding Habit, as a greater Monster than the Centaur. He would have called for Sacrifices, or Purifying Waters, to expiate the Appearance of such a Prodigy. He would have Invoked the Shades of *Portia* or *Lucretia*, to see into what the *Roman* Ladies had transformed themselves.

For my own part, I am for treating the Sex with greater Tenderness, and have all along made use of the most gentle Methods to bring them off from any little Extravagance, into which they are sometimes unwarily fallen: I think it however absolutely necessary to keep up the Partition between the two Sexes, and to take Notice of the smallest Encroachments which the one makes upon the other. I hope therefore that I shall not hear any more Complaints on this Subject. I am sure my She-Disciples who peruse these my daily Lectures, have profited but little by them, if they are capable of giving into such an Amphibious Dress. This I should not have mentioned, had not I lately met one of these my Female Readers in *Hide-Park*,[4] who looked upon me with a masculine Assurance, and cocked her Hat full in my Face.

For my part, I have one general Key to the Behaviour of the Fair Sex. When I see them singular in any Part of their Dress, I conclude it is not without some Evil Intention; and therefore question not but the Design of this strange Fashion is to smite more effectually their Male Beholders. Now to set them right in this Particular, I would fain have them consider with themselves whether we are not more likely to be struck by a Figure entirely Female, than with such an one as we may see every Day in our Glasses: Or, if they please, let them reflect upon their own Hearts, and think how they would be affected should they

[3] *Juvenal's Days:* In the time of the Roman satirist Juvenal (60?–140?).
[4] *Hide-Park:* Hyde Park, the largest of the London parks, where it was fashionable to walk and ride along the circular road called the Ring.

meet a Man on Horseback, in his Breeches and Jack-boots, and at the same time dressed up in a Commode and a Night-raile.[5]

I must observe that this Fashion was first of all brought to us from *France*, a Country which has Infected all the Nations of *Europe* with its Levity. I speak not this in derogation of a whole People, having more than once found fault with those general Reflections which strike at Kingdoms or Common-wealths in the Gross: a piece of Cruelty, which an ingenious Writer of our own compares to that of *Caligula*, who wished the *Roman* People had all but one Neck, that he might behead them at a Blow,[6] I shall therefore only Remark, that as Liveliness and Assurance are in a peculiar manner the Qualifications of the *French* Nation, the same Habits and Customs will not give the same Offence to that People, which they produce among those of our own Country. Modesty is our distinguishing Character, as Vivacity is theirs: And when this our National Virtue appears in that Female Beauty, for which our *British* Ladies are celebrated above all others in the Universe, it makes up the most amiable Object that the Eye of Man can possibly behold.

No. 467
Tuesday, August 26, 1712
[On Manilius, the Character of a Good Man]

> *... Quodcunque meæ poterunt Audere Camœnæ*
> *Seu Tibi par poterunt, seu, quod spes abnuit ultra;*
> *Sive minus; certeque canent minus; omne vovemus*
> *Hoc tibi; nec tanto careat mihi nomine Charta.*[1]
> — Tibull. ad Messalam.

The Love of Praise is a Passion deeply fix'd in the Mind of every extraordinary Person, and those who are most affected with it, seem most to partake of that Particle of the Divinity which distinguishes Mankind from the inferior Creation. The supreme Being it self is

[5] *Night-raile:* Nightdress.
[6] *Caligula ... at a Blow:* See *Spectator* No. 16, note 10 (p. 496).
[1] *... Quodcunque ... Charta:* From Tibullus, *Elegies* 4.1.24–27:

> Whate'er my Genius dares attempt to write,
> Or whether worthy your judicious Sight;
> Or whether Joys beneath your Taste I sing,
> (Beyond that noble Taste no Muse can wing)

542   Fashioning Gender: *The Spectator*

most pleased with Praise and Thanksgiving; the other Part of our
Duty is but an Acknowledgment of our Faults, whilst this is the immediate Adoration of his Perfections. 'Twas an excellent Observation, That we then only despise Commendation when we cease to deserve it; and we have still extant two Orations of *Tully* and *Pliny*,[2]
spoken to the greatest and best Princes of all the *Roman* Emperors,
who, no Doubt, heard with the greatest Satisfaction, what even the
most disinterested Persons, and at so large a Distance of Time, cannot read without Admiration. *Cæsar* thought his Life consisted in the
Breath of Praise, when he profess'd he had liv'd long enough for himself when he had for his Glory; others have sacrific'd themselves for a
Name which was not to begin till they were dead, giving away themselves to purchase a Sound which was not to commence till they were
out of hearing: But by Merit and superior Excellencies not only to
gain, but, whilst living, to enjoy a great and universal Reputation, is
the last Degree of Happiness which we can hope for here. Bad Characters are dispers'd abroad with Profusion, I hope for Example Sake,
and (as Punishments are design'd by the Civil Power) more for the de-
terring the Innocent, than the chastising the Guilty. The Good are less
frequent, whether it be that there are indeed fewer Originals of this
Kind to copy after, or that, thro' the Malignity of our Nature, we
rather delight in the Ridicule than the Virtues we find in others. However, it is but just, as well as pleasing, even for Variety, sometimes to
give the World a Representation of the bright Side of humane Nature, as well as the dark and gloomy! The Desire of Imitation may,
perhaps, be a greater Incentive to the Practice of what is good, than
the Aversion we may conceive at what is blameable; the one immediately directs you what you shou'd do, whilst the other only shews
you what you shou'd avoid: And I cannot at present do this with
more Satisfaction, than by endeavouring to do some Justice to the
Character of *Manilius*.[3]

All I devote or to your Praise or Scorn,
That such a Patron may my Page adorn. [Bond]
    [2] *two Orations of Tully and Pliny:* For Cicero's [106–43 B.C.] praise of Caesar see
the oration *Pro Marcello,* delivered 46 B.C. The only surviving speech of the Roman
consul and writer Pliny the younger [A.D. 62?–113?] is the panegyric which he delivered in A.D. 100 in praise of the reforms of the Emperor Trajan [53–117] [Bond].
    [3] *Manilius:* Probably the Whig politician, lawyer, and first lord high chancellor of
England, Lord Cowper, William Cowper (1665–1723), created Baron Cowper in
1706.

It wou'd far exceed my present Design, to give a particular Description of *Manilius* thro' all the Parts of his excellent Life: I shall now only draw him in his Retirement, and pass over in Silence the various Arts, the courtly Manners, and the undesigning Honesty by which he attained the Honours he has enjoy'd, and which now give a Dignity and Veneration to the Ease he does enjoy. 'Tis here that he looks back with Pleasure on the Waves and Billows thro' which he has steered to so fair an Haven; he is now intent upon the Practice of every Virtue, which a great Knowledge and Use of Mankind has discovered to be the most useful to them. Thus in his private domestick Employments he is no less glorious than in his publick; for 'tis in Reality a more difficult Task to be conspicuous in a sedentary inactive Life, than in one that is spent in Hurry and Business; Persons engag'd in the latter, like Bodies violently agitated, from the Swiftness of their Motion have a Brightness added to them, which often vanishes when they are at Rest; but if it then still remain, it must be the Seeds of intrinsick Worth that thus shine out without any foreign Aid or Assistance.

His Liberality in another might almost bear the Name of Profusion; he seems to think it laudable even in the Excess, like that River which most enriches when it overflows: But *Manilius* has too perfect a Taste of the Pleasure of doing good, ever to let it be out of his Power; and for that Reason he will have a just Oeconomy, and a splendid Frugality at home, the Fountain from whence those Streams should flow which he disperses abroad. He looks with Disdain on those who propose their Death as the Time when they are to begin their Munificence; he will both see and enjoy (which he then does in the highest Degree) what he bestows himself; he will be the living Executor of his own Bounty, whilst they who have the Happiness to be within his Care and Patronage at once, pray for the continuation of his Life, and their own good Fortune. No one is out of the reach of his Obligations; he knows how, by proper and becoming Methods, to raise himself to a Level with those of the highest Rank; and his good Nature is a sufficient Warrant against the want of those who are so unhappy as to be in the very lowest. One may say of him, as *Pindar* bids his Muse say of *Theron*.

> *Swear, that* Theron *sure has sworn,*
> *No one near him shou'd be Poor.*
> *Swear that none e'er had such a graceful Art,*
> *Fortune's Free-Gifts as freely to impart,*
> *With an unenvious Hand, and an unbounded Heart.*

Never did *Atticus* succeed better in gaining the universal Love and Esteem of all Men, nor steer with more Success betwixt the Extreams of two contending Parties. 'Tis his peculiar Happiness, that while he espouses neither with an intemperate Zeal, he is not only admir'd, but, what is a more rare and unusual Felicity, he is belov'd and carress'd by both; and I never yet saw any Person, of whatsoever Age or Sex, but was immediately struck with the Merit of *Manilius*. There are many who are acceptable to some particular Persons, whilst the rest of Mankind look upon them with Coldness and Indifference; but he is the first whose entire good Fortune it is ever to please and to be pleased, where-ever he comes to be admir'd, and where-ever he is absent to be lamented. His Merit fares like the Pictures of *Raphael*, which are either seen with Admiration by all, or at least no one dare own he has no Taste for a Composition which has received so universal an Applause. Envy and Malice find it against their Interest to indulge Slander and Obloquy. 'Tis as hard for an Enemy to detract from, as for a Friend to add to his Praise. An Attempt upon his Reputation is a sure lessening of one's own; and there is but one Way to injure him, which is to refuse him his just Commendations, and be obstinately silent.

It is below him to catch the Sight with any Care of Dress; his outward Garb is but the Emblem of his Mind, it is genteel, plain, and unaffected; he knows that Gold and Embroidery can add nothing to the Opinion which all have of his Merit, and that he gives a Lustre to the plainest Dress, whilst 'tis impossible the richest should communicate any to him. He is still the principal Figure in the Room: He first engages your Eye, as if there were some Point of Light which shone stronger upon him than on any other Person.

He puts me in mind of a Story of the famous *Bussy d'Amboise*, who at an Assembly at Court, where every one appear'd with the utmost Magnificence, relying upon his own superior Behaviour, instead of adorning himself like the rest, put on that Day a plain Suit of Cloaths, and dress'd all his Servants in the most costly gay Habits he could procure: The Event was, that the Eyes of the whole Court were fix'd upon him, all the rest look'd like his Attendants, whilst he alone had the Air of a Person of Quality and Distinction.

Like *Aristippus*, whatever Shape or Condition he appears in, it still sits free and easy upon him; but in some Part of his Character, 'tis true, he differs from him; for as he is altogether equal to the Largeness of his present Circumstances, the Rectitude of his Judgment has so far corrected the Inclinations of his Ambition, that he will not trouble himself with either the Desires or Pursuits of any thing beyond his present Enjoyments.

A thousand obliging Things flow from him upon every Occasion, and they are always so just and natural, that it is impossible to think he was at the least Pains to look for them. One would think it were the Dæmon of good Thoughts that discovered to him those Treasures, which he must have blinded others from seeing, they lay so directly in their Way. Nothing can equal the Pleasure is taken in hearing him speak, but the Satisfaction one receives in the Civility and Attention he pays to the Discourse of others. His Looks are a silent Commendation of what is good and praise-worthy, and a secret Reproof to what is licentious and extravagant. He knows how to appear free and open without Danger of Intrusion, and to be cautious without seeming reserved. The Gravity of his Conversation is always enlivened with his Wit and Humour, and the Gayety of it is temper'd with something that is instructive, as well as barely agreeable. Thus with him you are sure not to be merry at the Expence of your Reason, nor serious with the Loss of your good Humour; but, by a happy Mixture in his Temper, they either go together, or perpetually succeed each other. In fine, his whole Behaviour is equally distant from Constraint and Negligence, and he commands your Respect, whilst he gains your Heart.

There is in his whole Carriage such an engaging Softness, that one cannot perswade one's self he is ever actuated by those rougher Passions, which, wherever they find Place, seldom fail of shewing themselves in the outward Demeanour of the Persons they belong to: But his Constitution is a just Temperature between Indolence on one Hand and Violence on the other. He is mild and gentle, wherever his Affairs will give him Leave to follow his own Inclinations; but yet never failing to exert himself with Vigour and Resolution in the Service of his Prince, his Country, or his Friend.

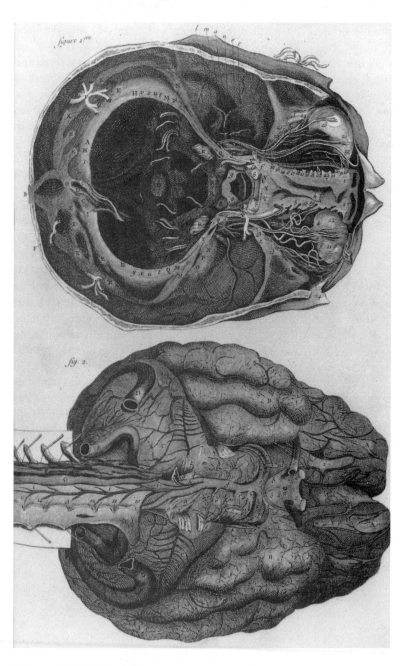

"Anatomie" (of a brain).

Cultural Contexts

EDWARD WARD

"The Beau's Club" and "The Mollies' Club"
(From The Secret History of the London Clubs*)*

As we see in his character sketches of a modern critic and of a beau (see pp. 436 and 550), the satirist Edward Ward (1667–1731) sprinkled the narrative of his *London Spy* with "characters" of the contemporary types he observed during his rambles through London. In his *Secret History of the London Clubs* (1710), Ward also writes "characters," here of "The Beau's Club" and "The Mollies' Club." In these two sketches Ward observes two sets of dubious masculine types: the molly, or effeminate male homosexual, and the beau, the ludicrously affected, fashionable man of the town. While considerable attention was paid to proper female types during this period, there was equal, if not greater, concern about the masculine character. Anxiety over the nature and representation of masculinity surfaces as well in the selection from *Mundus Foppensis* (p. 602). (For more information on Edward Ward and *The London Spy*, see Chapter 1's Cultural Contexts, p. 144.)

The Beau's Club.

This Finikin Society or Lady's Lap-dog Club is now kept at a certain Tavern near *Covent Garden*[1] where, every afternoon the Fantastical Idols, assemble themselves in a Body, to compare Dresses, invent new Fashions, talk Bawdy, and drink Healths to their Mistresses. At the upper end of their Club Room stands a Side-Board Table, which is constantly furnished with a Dozen of Flannel Muckinders,[2] folded up for rubbing the dust off of their Upper-Leathers, or an unfortunate speck off their Scabbards of their Swords. Next to these cleanly necessaries, stands an Olive-Box,[3] full of the best perfum'd Powder,

---

[1] *Covent Garden:* Established in 1670, Covent Garden was the chief flower, fruit, and vegetable market in London. Because it was located in the midst of the theater district, Covent Garden acquired a reputation as a center of dissipated pleasures.

[2] *Muckinders:* Pocket handkerchiefs.

[3] *Olive-Box:* Box made of olive wood.

crown'd with three or four mighty Combs, that their Wigs may be continually new scented, and every stragling Hair that has been rufled by a Storm of their Mistresses Breath, may be carefully put into Orders. Round the edges of the Table lies strew'd by way of Garnish Scissors, Tooth-pickers, & Tweezers, Patches,[4] Essences, Pomatums, Pastes, & Washes, with all the artful implements Woman can invent to turn Men into Monkeys: so that the Sir Foplings are no sooner met, but they are as busie as so many Stage-Players before a Comedy, dizening their ill shap'd Carcesses and Apes Faces. Then down they sit to their *Champaigne, Burgundy, & Hermitage,*[5] pull out their gilt Snush-Boxes, with *Orangeree, Brazil,* and plain *Spanish*[6] that each may fill his Elephant Trunk with Odoriferous Dust, & make his Breath as sweet as an *Arabian* breeze to the Nostrils of a Seaman; & when they are thus scented, down goes a delicious Health to some celebrated Harlot, Play-House Punk,[7] or Court Courtezan. When the Modish Fops, *Amorettas,* have drank so many select Healths to their Mistresses, without the danger of raising Pimples on their Faces, then they pay their Reckonings, tipp up the Fore-tops of their Wiggs, with their Alabaster figures, and walk bare-headed to the Play-house, where they commonly arrive about the Third Act, by which time the Ladies, who care not much to appear by Day-Light, are bolted from their Stews, and *Drury Lane*[8] Alleys, to sneak into the Pit and Eighteen-penny Gallery without Tickets at the Courtisie of the Door-Keepers, when these gaudy, cringing Coxcombs, have thus met with their Matches, they tattle away Play-time among their Half-Crown Punks, till one of the Fraternity of sham Heroes makes an humble Bow to the Box-Ladies, and the rest follow him according to their custom to Drinking, W——g, and Gaming till next Morning.

> To be a Modish Fop, a Beau compleat,
> Is to pretend to, but be void of, wit,
> 'Tis to be Squeamish, Critical, and nice
> In all things, & Fantastic to a Vice.
> 'Tis to seem knowing, tho' he nothing nowse

---

[4] *Patches:* Patches are small rounds of silk used cosmetically as artificial beauty marks on the face, neck, and shoulders.

[5] *Champaigne . . . Hermitage:* Types of wine.

[6] *Orangeree . . . plain Spanish:* Types of snuff, a form of powdered tobacco inhaled through the nose.

[7] *Punk:* Whore.

[8] *Stews . . . Drury Lane:* Stews are brothels; Drury Lane was a notorious haunt of prostitutes.

& vainly lewd to please his Brother Beaus,
'Tis in his dress to be profusely gay,
& to affect gay-like a wanton way.
'Tis to be charmed with each new fashion'd whim
& to be Modish to a vain extream.
That each gay Punk, a lustful eye may rowl,
& for his Shapes admire the pretty fool:
'Tis to attack the Ladies with a grace,
& still transfer his love to each new Face,
Flutter about his charms, till like a Fly,
Burnt by the Flame, he's scorch'd amidst his Joy.

The Mollies' Club.

There are a particular Gang of Wretches in Town, who call themselves *Mollies*,[1] & are so far degenerated from all Masculine Deportment or Manly exercises that they rather fancy themselves Women,
imitating all the little Vanities that Custom has reconcil'd to the Female sex, affecting to speak, walk, tattle, curtsy, cry, scold, & mimick all manner of Effeminacy. At a certain Tavern in the City, whose
sign I shall not mention, because I am unwilling to fix an Odium on
the House, they have a settled & constant Meeting. When they are
met, together, their usual Practice is to mimick a female Gossiping &
fall into all the impertinent Tittle Tattle that a merry Society of good
Wives can be subject to. Not long since they had cushioned up one of
their Brethren, or rather Sisters, according to Female Dialect, disguising him in a Woman's Night-Gown, Sarsanet,[2] Hood, & Night-rail[3]
who when the Company were men, was to mimick a woman, produce a jointed Baby[4] they had provided, which wooden Offspring
was to be afterwards Christened, whilst one in a High Crown'd Hat,
I am old Beldam's Pinner,[5] representing a Country Midwife, & another dizen'd up in a Huswife's Coif[6] for a Nurse & all the rest of an
impertinent *Decorum* of a Christening.

And for the further promotion of their unbecoming mirth, every
one was to talk of their Husbands & Children, one estolling the
Virtues of her Husband, another the genius & wit of their Children;

---

[1] *Mollies:* Effeminate male homosexuals. See *Tatler* No. 26 (p. 467).
[2] *Sarsanet:* A kind of silk.
[3] *Night-rail:* A nightgown or dressing gown.
[4] *Baby:* A doll.
[5] *Pinner:* A kind of headdress.
[6] *Coif:* A cap.

whilst a Third would express himself sorrowfully under the character of a Widow.

Thus every one in his turn makes scoff of the little Effeminacy & Weaknesses, which Women are subject to, when gossiping o'er their cups on purpose to extinguish that Natural Affection which is due to the Fair Sex & to turn their Juvenile desires towards preternatural polotions. They continued their practices till they were happily routed by the conduct of some of the under Agents to the Reforming Society, so that several of them were brought to open Punishment, which happily put a Period to their *Scandalous Revels.*

EDWARD WARD

Character of a Beau
(From The London Spy*)*

The self-absorption, devotion to appearances, and affectation that mark Addison and Steele's faulty character types, both male and female, emerge in full force in Ward's description of the beau. Although in many aspects an effeminate type, the beau is distinguished from the effeminate molly by his sexual love for women. As Ward crudely puts it, there are two things the largely worthless beau is good for: "to give a poor fellow dinner . . . and to help to serve the turn of an insatiate woman, instead of a dildo." The beau's heterosexuality, however, is compromised even as it is invoked: he is the passive sex toy of the aggressive, "insatiate" woman. Mrs. Crackenthorpe presents her satire on this type in her character of Beau Maskwell in *The Female Tatler* No. 34 (p. 561). For more information on Edward Ward, see other Ward documents (pp. 144, 246, and 436).

The text reprinted here is taken from *The London Spy*, ed. Paul Hyland (East Lansing: Colleagues Press, 1993), Part 16, 295–96.

He is a Narcissus[1] that is fallen in love with himself and his own shadow. Within doors he's a great friend to a great glass, before which he admires the works of his tailor more than the whole cre-

---

[1] *Narcissus:* In Greek mythology, a beautiful young man who fell in love with his own reflection in a pool of water.

ation. Without doors he adores the sun like a Persian and walks always in his rays, though at midsummer, to please himself with a moving copy of his own proportion. His body's but a poor stuffing of a rich case, like bran in a lady's pincushion, that when the outside is stripped off, there remains nothing that's valuable. His head is a fool's egg which lies hid in a nest of hair. His brains are the yolk, which conceit has addled. He's a strolling assistant to drapers and tailors, showing every other day a new pattern and a new fashion. He's a walking argument against immortality, for no man, by his actions or his talk, can find he has more soul than a goose.

He's a very troublesome guest in a tavern, and must have good wine changed three or four times, till they bring him the worst in the cellar, before he'll like it. His conversation is as intolerable as a young counsel in term-time, talking as much of his mistresses as the other does of his motions, and will have the most words, though all that he says is nothing. He's a bubble[2] to all he deals with, from his whore to his periwig-maker, and hates the sordid rascal that won't flatter him. He scorns to condescend so low as to speak to any person beneath the dignity of a nobleman. The Duke of Such-a-place, and my Lord Such-a-one, are his common cronies, from whom he knows all the secrets of the Court, but dares not impart 'em to his best friends, because the Duke enjoined him to secrecy.

He is always furnished with new jests from the last new play, which he most commonly spoils in repeating. His watch he compares with every sundial, swears it corrects the sun, and plucks it out so frequently in company that his fingers go oftener in a day to his fob[3] than they do to his mouth; spending more time every week in showing the rarity of the work than the man did in making on't, and being as fond to tell the price of it, without desiring, as he is to tell the hour, without asking. He is as constant a visitor of a coffee-house as a Drury Lane whore is of Covent Garden Church, where he cons over the newspapers with as much indifference as the other prays, reading only for fashion's sake, and not for information.

He's commonly of a small standing at one of the universities, though all he has learned there is to know how many taverns there are in the town and what vintner has the handsomest wife. Though his parents have given him an expensive education, he's as dumb to rhetoric as a fool to reason; as blind to philosophy as an owl in the

[2] *bubble:* Dupe.
[3] *fob:* A small pocket for a watch in a man's coat.

sunshine; and as deaf to understanding as a priest to charity. He often hopes to pass for a wit by calling other people fools, and his fine apparel is his only armour that defends him from contempt. He's a coward amongst brave men, and a brave fellow among cowards; a fool amongst wise men, and a wit in fools' company. All that I know he's good for is to give a poor fellow a dinner, so that he will do him homage, and to help to serve the turn of an insatiate woman, instead of a dildo.

BERNARD MANDEVILLE

The Vanity of Men and Women
(From The Fable of the Bees)

In these selections from his *Fable of the Bees*, Bernard Mandeville (1670–1733) presents a picture of human nature driven by pride and vanity. In "Remark R" Mandeville reflects on masculine pride and cites male vanity as the great motive behind martial honor. The military man is seduced into the pursuit of glory not, as is conventionally and romantically believed, by the desire to impress a beautiful woman, but by the desire to make a fine personal showing in a fancy uniform. This discussion of vainglory leads straight into a critique of honor and of the practice of dueling through which honor was defended. Like Steele, Mandeville is no advocate of the duel (see *Tatler* No. 25, p. 469), but his objection is not simply that this is a misguided way of preserving honor but that the whole concept of honor is "without virtue," based as it is on sheer pride.

In the selections from "Remark T" and from "A Search into the Nature of Society," Mandeville looks at female vanity and the consumption of luxury goods that feeds it. Far from being a detriment to society, these vices of female vanity, pride, and luxury are a boon to industry and so promote employment, production, and the overall wealth of the nation. For more information on Bernard Mandeville, see Chapter 2's Cultural Contexts (p. 298).

The text excerpted here is taken from Bernard Mandeville's *Fable of the Bees*, with commentary by F. B. Kaye (Oxford: Clarendon Press, 1925), 216–20, 356–58, and 225–28.

Remark R

I have made this Digression chiefly to shew the Strength of human Nature, and what meer Man may perform by Pride and Constitution alone. Man may certainly be as violently rous'd by his Vanity, as a Lion is by his Anger; and not only this, Avarice, Revenge, Ambition, and almost every Passion, Pity not excepted, when they are extraordinary, may by overcoming Fear, serve him instead of Valour, and be mistaken for it even by himself; as daily Experience must teach every Body that will examine and look into the Motives from which some Men act. But that we may more clearly perceive what this pretended Principle is really built upon, let us look into the Management of Military Affairs, and we shall find that Pride is no where so openly encouraged as there. As for Clothes, the very lowest of the Commission Officers have them richer, or at least more gay and splendid, than are generally wore by other People of four or five times their Income. Most of them, and especially those that have Families, and can hardly subsist, would be very glad, all *Europe* over, to be less Expensive that way; but it is a Force put upon them to uphold their Pride, which they don't think on.

But the ways and means to rouse Man's Pride, and catch him by it, are no where most grosly conspicuous than in the Treatment which the Common Soldiers receive, whose Vanity is to be work'd upon (because there must be so many) at the cheapest rate imaginable. Things we are accustom'd to we don't mind, or else what Mortal that never had seen a Soldier could look without laughing upon a Man accoutred with so much paltry Gaudiness and affected Finery? The coarsest Manufacture that can be made of Wool, dy'd of a Brick-dust Colour, goes down with him, because it is in Imitation of Scarlet or Crimson Cloth; and to make him think himself as like his Officer as 'tis possible with little or no Cost, instead of Silver or Gold Lace, his Hat is trim'd with white or yellow Worsted, which in others would deserve Bedlam[1]; yet these fine Allurements, and the Noise made upon a Calf's Skin, have drawn in and been the Destruction of more Men in reality, than all the killing Eyes and bewitching Voices of Women ever slew in Jest. To Day the Swineherd puts on his Red Coat, and believes every body in earnest that calls him Gentleman,

---

[1] *Bedlam:* "Bedlam" is a colloquial corruption of "Bethlehem" and refers to the hospital of St. Mary of Bethlehem for the insane.

and two Days after Serjeant *Kite*[2] gives him a swinging wrap with his Cane, for holding his Musket an Inch higher than he should do. As to the real Dignity of the Employment, in the two last Wars, Officers, when Recruits were wanted, were allow'd to list Fellows convicted of Burglary and other Capital Crimes, which shews that to be made a Soldier is deem'd to be a Preferment next to hanging. A Trooper is yet worse than a Foot-Soldier; for when he is most at ease, he has the Mortification of being Groom to a Horse that spends more Money than himself. When a Man reflects on all this, the Usage they generally receive from their Officers, their Pay, and the Care that is taken of them, when they are not wanted, must he not wonder how Wretches can be so silly as to be proud of being call'd *Gentlemen Soldiers?* Yet if they were not, no Art, Discipline or Money would be capable of making them so Brave as Thousands of them are.

If we will mind what Effects Man's Bravery, without any other Qualifications to sweeten him, would have out of an Army, we shall find that it would be very pernicious to the Civil Society; for if Man could conquer all his Fears, you would hear of nothing but Rapes, Murthers and Violence of all sorts, and Valiant Men would be like Giants in Romances: Politicks therefore discovered in Men a mixt-mettle Principle, which was a Compound of Justice, Honesty and all the Moral Virtues join'd to Courage, and all that were possess'd of it turned Knights-Errant of course. They did abundance of Good throughout the World, by taming Monsters, delivering the Distress'd, and killing the Oppressors: But the Wings of all the Dragons being clipt, the Giants destroyed, and the Damsels every where set at liberty, except some few in *Spain* and *Italy*, who remain'd still captivated by their Monsters, the Order of Chivalry, to whom the Standard of Ancient Honour belonged, has been laid aside some time. It was like their Armours very massy and heavy; the many Virtues about it made it very troublesome, and as Ages grew wiser and wiser, the Principle of Honour in the beginning of the last Century was melted over again, and brought to a new Standard; they put in the same Weight of Courage, half the Quantity of Honesty, and a very little Justice, but not a Scrap of any other Virtue, which has made it very easy and portable to what it was. However, such as it is, there would be no living without it in a large Nation; it is the tye of Society, and though we are beholden to our Frailties for the chief Ingredi-

---

[2] *Serjeant Kite:* The recruiting sergeant in the Irish playwright George Farquhar's (1678–1707) comedy *The Recruiting Officer* (1706).

ent of it, there is no Virtue, at least that I am acquainted with, that has been half so instrumental to the civilizing of Mankind, who in great Societies would soon degenerate into cruel Villains and treacherous Slaves, were Honour to be removed from among them.

As to the Duelling Part which belongs to it, I pity the Unfortunate whose Lot it is; but to say, that those who are guilty of it go by false Rules, or mistake the Notions of Honour, is ridiculous; for either there is no Honour at all, or it teaches Men to resent Injuries, and accept of Challenges. You may as well deny that it is the Fashion what you see every body wear, as to say that demanding and giving Satisfaction is against the Laws of true Honour. Those that rail at Duelling don't consider the Benefit the Society receives from that Fashion: If every ill-bred Fellow might use what Language he pleas'd, without being called to an Account for it, all Conversation would be spoil'd. Some grave People tell us, that the *Greeks* and *Romans* were such valiant Men, and yet knew nothing of Duelling but in their Country's Quarrel: This is very true, but for that Reason the Kings and Princes in *Homer*[3] gave one another worse Language than our Porters and Hackney Coachmen would be able to bear without Resentment.

Would you hinder Duelling, pardon no body that offends that way, and make the Laws against it as severe as you can, but don't take away the thing it self, the Custom of it. This will not only prevent the Frequency of it, but likewise by rendring the most resolute and most powerful cautious and circumspect in their Behaviour, polish and brighten Society in general. Nothing civilizes a Man equally as his Fear, and if not all, (as my Lord *Rochester*[4] said) at least most Men would be Cowards if they durst: The dread of being called to an Account keeps abundance in awe, and there are thousands of mannerly and well-accomplish'd Gentlemen in *Europe*, who would have been insolent and insupportable Coxcombs without it; besides if it was out of Fashion to ask Satisfaction for Injuries which the Law cannot take hold of, there would be twenty times the Mischief done there is now, or else you must have twenty times the Constables and other Officers to keep the Peace. I confess that though it happens but seldom, it is a Calamity to the People, and generally the Families it

[3] *Homer:* The ninth-century B.C. Greek epic poet, author of the *Iliad* and the *Odyssey.*
[4] *Lord Rochester:* John Wilmot, second Earl of Rochester (1647–1680), an English satiric poet and renowned Restoration wit and libertine. This line is from his *Satyr Against Mankind.*

falls upon; but there can be no perfect Happiness in this World, and all Felicity has an Allay. The Act it self is uncharitable, but when above thirty in a Nation destroy themselves in one Year, and not half that Number are killed by others, I don't think the People can be said to love their Neighbours worse than themselves. It is strange that a Nation should grudge to see perhaps half a dozen Men sacrific'd in a Twelvemonth to obtain so valuable a Blessing, as the Politeness of Manners, the Pleasure of Conversation, and the Happiness of Company in general, that is often so willing to expose, and sometimes loses as many thousands in a few Hours, without knowing whether it will do any good or not.

Remark T

What our common Rogues when they are going to be hanged chiefly complain of, as the Cause of their untimely End, is, next to the neglect of the Sabbath, their having kept Company with ill Women, meaning Whores; and I don't question, but that among the lesser Villains many venture their Necks to indulge and satisfy their low Amours. But the Words that have given Occasion to this Remark, may serve to hint to us, that among the great ones Men are often put upon such dangerous Projects, and forced into such pernicious Measures by their Wives, as the most subtle Mistress never could have persuaded them to. I have shewn already that the worst of Women and most profligate of the Sex did contribute to the Consumption of Superfluities, as well as the Necessaries of Life, and consequently were Beneficial to many peaceable Drudges, that work hard to maintain their Families, and have no worse design than an honest Livelihood. — Let them be banished notwithstanding, says a good Man: When every Strumpet is gone, and the Land wholly freed from Lewdness, God Almighty will pour such Blessings upon it as will vastly exceed the Profits that are now got by Harlots. — This perhaps would be true; but I can make it evident, that with or without Prostitutes, nothing could make amends for the Detriment Trade would sustain, if all those of that Sex, who enjoy the happy State of Matrimony, should act and behave themselves as a sober wise Man could wish them.

The variety of Work that is perform'd, and the number of Hands employ'd to gratify the Fickleness and Luxury of Women is prodigious, and if only the married ones should hearken to Reason and just Remonstrances, think themselves sufficiently answer'd with the first refusal, and never ask a second time what had been once denied them: If, I say, Married Women would do this, and then lay out no Money but what their Husbands knew and freely allowed of, the Consumption of a thousand things, they now make use of, would be lessened by at least a fourth Part. Let us go from House to House and observe the way of the World only among the middling People, creditable Shop-keepers, that spend Two or Three Hundred a Year, and we shall find the Women when they have half a Score Suits of Clothes, Two or Three of them not the worse for wearing, will think it a sufficient Plea for new Ones, if they can say that they have never a Gown or Petticoat, but what they have been often seen in, and are known by, especially at Church; I don't speak now of profuse extravagant Women, but such as are counted Prudent and Moderate in their Desires.

If by this Pattern we should in Proportion judge of the highest Ranks, where the richest Clothes are but a trifle to their other Expences, and not forget the Furniture of all sorts, Equipages, Jewels, and Buildings of Persons of Quality, we should find the fourth Part I speak of a vast Article in Trade, and that the Loss of it would be a greater Calamity to such a Nation as ours, than it is possible to conceive any other, a raging Pestilence not excepted: for the Death of half a Million People could not cause a tenth Part of the Disturbance to the Kingdom, that the same Number of Poor unemploy'd would certainly create, if at once they were to be added to those, that already one way or other are a Burthen to the Society.

Some few Men have a real Passion for their Wives, and are fond of them without reserve; others that don't care, and have little Occasion for Women, are yet seemingly uxorious, and love out of Vanity; they take Delight in a handsome Wife, as a Coxcomb does in a fine Horse, not for the use he makes of it, but because it is His: The Pleasure lies in the consciousness of an uncontrolable Possession, and what follows from it, the Reflexion on the mighty Thoughts he imagines others to have of his Happiness. The Men of either sort may be very lavish to their Wives, and often preventing their Wishes croud New Clothes and other Finery upon them faster than they can ask it, but the greatest part are wiser than to indulge the Extravagances of their Wives so far, as to give them immediately every thing they are pleas'd to fancy.

It is incredible what vast quantity of Trinkets as well as Apparel are purchas'd and used by Women, which they could never have come at by any other means, than pinching their Families, Marketting, and other ways of cheating and pilfering from their Husbands: Others by ever teazing their Spouses, tire them into Compliance, and conquer even obstinate Churls by perseverance and their assiduity of asking; A Third sort are outrageous at a denial, and by downright Noise and Scolding bully their tame Fools out of any thing they have a mind to; while thousands by the force of Wheedling know how to overcome the best weigh'd Reasons and the most positive reiterated Refusals; the Young and Beautiful especially laugh at all Remonstrances and Denials, and few of them scruple to employ the most tender Minutes of Wedlock to promote a sordid Interest. Here had I time I could inveigh with warmth against those Base, those wicked Women, who calmly play their Arts and false deluding Charms against our Strength and Prudence, and act the Harlots with their Husbands! Nay, she is worse than Whore, who impiously prophanes and prostitutes the Sacred Rites of Love to Vile Ignoble Ends; that first excites to Passion and invites to Joys with seeming Ardour, then racks our Fondness for no other purpose than to extort a Gift, while full of Guile in Counterfeited Transports she watches for the Moment when Men can least deny.

A Search into the Nature of Society

I protest against Popery as much as ever *Luther* and *Calvin* did, or Queen *Elizabeth*[1] herself, but I believe from my Heart, that the Reformation has scarce been more Instrumental in rend'ring the Kingdoms and States that have embraced it, flourishing beyond other Nations, than the silly and capricious Invention of Hoop'd and Quilted Petticoats. But if this should be denied me by the Enemies of Priestly Power, at least I am sure that, bar the great Men who have fought for and against that Lay-Man's Blessing, it has from its first beginning to this Day not employ'd so many Hands, honest industrious labouring Hands, as the abominable improvement on Female Luxury I named has done in few Years. Religion is one thing and Trade is another. He

---

[1] *Luther . . . Calvin . . . Queen Elizabeth:* All three figures were instrumental in the Protestant Reformation of the Roman Catholic Church ("Popery"). A sixteenth-century religious movement, the Reformation resulted in the establishment of Protestant religions. Its three great leaders were Martin Luther (1483–1546) in Germany, John Calvin (1509–1564) in Geneva, and John Knox (c. 1514–1572) in Scotland. Queen Elizabeth (1558–1603) consolidated the form of English Protestantism known as Anglicism. Protestants stressed the authority of Scripture over that of priests, and justification by faith rather than by works; they rejected the doctrine of transubstantiation, the cult of the Virgin Mary, and the authority of the Pope.

that gives most Trouble to thousands of his Neighbours, and invents the most operose Manufactures is, right or wrong, the greatest Friend to the Society.

What a Bustle is there to be made in several Parts of the World, before a fine Scarlet or crimson Cloth can be produced, what Multiplicity of Trades and Artificers must be employ'd! Not only such as are obvious, as Wool-combers, Spinners, the Weaver, the Cloth-worker, the Scourer, the Dyer, the Setter, the Drawer and the Packer; but others that are more remote and might seem foreign to it; as the Millwright, the Pewterer and the Chymist,[2] which yet are all necessary as well as a great Number of other Handicrafts to have the Tools, Utensils and other Implements belonging to the Trades already named: But all these things are done at home, and may be perform'd without extraordinary Fatigue or Danger; the most frightful Prospect is left behind, when we reflect on the Toil and Hazard that are to be undergone abroad, the vast Seas we are to go over, the different Climates we are to endure, and the several Nations we must be obliged to for their Assistance. *Spain* alone it is true might furnish us with Wool to make the finest Cloth; but what Skill and Pains, what Experience and Ingenuity are required to Dye it of those Beautiful Colours! How widely are the Drugs and other Ingredients dispers'd thro' the Universe that are to meet in one Kettle! Allum indeed we have of our own; Argol we might have from the *Rhine*, and Vitriol from *Hungary*; all this is in *Europe*; but then for Saltpetre in quantity we are forc'd to go as far as the *East-Indies*. Cochenille,[3] unknown to the Ancients, is not much nearer to us, tho' in a quite different part of the Earth: we buy it 'tis true from the *Spaniards*; but not being their Product they are forc'd to fetch it for us from the remotest Corner of the New World in the *West-Indies*. While so many Sailors are broiling in the Sun and sweltered with Heat in the *East* and *West* of us, another set of them are freezing in the *North* to fetch Potashes[4] from *Russia*.

When we are thoroughly acquainted with all the Variety of Toil and Labour, the Hardships and Calamities that must be undergone to

---

[2] *Chymist:* Chemist.

[3] *Argol . . . Cochenille:* Argol is the tartar from fermented wines deposited on the sides of wine casks; it is a form of bitartite of potassium, which is refined into cream of tartar. Saltpeter, or potassium nitrate, is the chief constituent of gunpowder. Cochineal is made from the dried bodies of the insect *Coccus cacti* and is used for making carmine, a brilliant scarlet dye.

[4] *Potashes:* Compounds containing potassium that are used as fertilizers.

compass the End I speak of, and we consider the vast Risques and Perils that are run in those Voyages, and that few of them are ever made but at the Expence, not only of the Health and Welfare, but even the Lives of many: When we are acquainted with, I say, and duly consider the things I named, it is scarce possible to conceive a Tyrant so inhuman and void of Shame, that beholding things in the same View, he should exact such terrible Services from his Innocent Slaves; and at the same time dare to own, that he did it for no other Reason, than the Satisfaction a Man receives from having a Garment made of Scarlet or Crimson Cloth. But to what Height of Luxury must a Nation be arrived, where not only the King's Officers, but likewise his Guards, even the private Soldiers should have such impudent Desires!

But if we turn the Prospect, and look on all those Labours as so many voluntary Actions, belonging to different Callings and Occupations that Men are brought up to for a Livelihood, and in which every one Works for himself, how much soever he may seem to Labour for others: If we consider, that even the Sailors who undergo the greatest Hardships, as soon as one Voyage is ended, even after Ship-wrack,[5] are looking out and solliciting for Employment in another: If we consider, I say, and look on these things in another View, we shall find that the Labour of the Poor is so far from being a Burthen and an Imposition upon them; that to have Employment is a Blessing, which in their Addresses to Heaven they pray for, and to procure it for the generality of them is the greatest Care of every Legislature.

As Children and even Infants are the Apes of others, so all Youth have an ardent desire of being Men and Women, and become often ridiculous by their impatient Endeavours to appear what every body sees they are not; all large Societies are not a little indebted to this Folly for the Perpetuity or at least long Continuance of Trades once Established. What Pains will young People take, and what Violence will they not commit upon themselves, to attain to insignificant and often blameable Qualifications, which for want of Judgment and Experience they admire in others, that are Superior to them in Age! This fondness of Imitation makes them accustom themselves by degrees to the Use of things that were Irksome, if not intolerable to them at first, till they know not how to leave them, and are often very Sorry for having inconsiderately increas'd the Necessaries of Life without any

---

[5] *Ship-wrack:* Shipwreck.

Necessity. What Estates have been got by Tea and Coffee! What a vast Traffick is drove, what a variety of Labour is performed in the World to the Maintenance of Thousands of Families that altogether depend on two silly if not odious Customs; the taking of Snuff and smoking of Tobacco; both which it is certain do infinitely more hurt than good to those that are addicted to them! I shall go further, and demonstrate the Usefulness of private Losses and Misfortunes to the Publick, and the folly of our Wishes, when we pretend to be most Wise and Serious. The Fire of *London*,[6] was a great Calamity, but if the Carpenters, Bricklayers, Smiths, and all, not only that are employed in Building but likewise those that made and dealt in the same Manufactures and other Merchandizes that were Burnt, and other Trades again that got by them when they were in full Employ, were to Vote against those who lost by the Fire; the Rejoicings would equal if not exceed the Complaints. In recruiting what is lost and destroy'd by Fire, Storms, Sea-fights, Sieges, Battles, a considerable part of Trade consists; the truth of which and whatever I have said of the Nature of Society will plainly appear from what follows.

Masculine Women, Beaux, and Prudes (From The Female Tatler *Nos. 8, 34, and 71)*

In her censure of the cross-dressing sisters Mrs. Margaret and Mrs. Millicent Trott (*The Female Tatler* No. 8), Mrs. Crackenthorpe expresses anxiety about the clear demarcation of gender roles. While gender is being more completely understood as a natural, inalterable biological condition, its dependence for its representation on external, artificial, transferable signs, especially clothes, becomes newly problematic. That these signs may mislead, that both men and women may successfully cross-dress, becomes a matter of considerable concern. We see this concern as well in *Spectator* No. 435, in which a gentleman correspondent is outraged at the "amphibious" equestrian costume, and in Ward's description of the Mollies' Club, where men indulge in transvestism (see pp. 539 and 549).

In the two other papers included here, Mrs. Crackenthorpe provides characters of the beau (No. 34) and of the prude (No. 71) that complement the pictures sketched by Ward (p. 550) and by Addison and Steele

---

[6] *Fire of London:* In 1666.

(see *Tatler* No. 107 and *Spectator* No. 275, pp. 474 and 528). For more information on *The Female Tatler,* see Chapter 1's Cultural Contexts (p. 129).

The text reprinted here is from *The Female Tatler,* ed. Fidelis Morgan (Rutland, VT: Charles Tuttle/Everyman's, 1992).

No. 8
Friday, July 22, to Monday, July 25

I'm obliged to the gentleman, who wrote the following letter, for the compliments he makes me. But if he saw my face he'd think no more of adoration. Beauty was ever the least of my aim, I would rather chose to recommend myself by a tolerable understanding. 'Tis true, it heightens a lady's character, and when a fine woman shall deliver herself in an elegant manner, her beauty, like sweetening a note in music, is a grace to her expression, and the men are ravish'd with her, when they'd be but barely pleas'd with one less agreeable. But, if gentlemen would not value a woman chiefly for her person, and think the silliest things wit, that come from youth and beauty, our sex would employ some time in cultivating their minds, and take more pains to place their words, than their patches . . .

An express from Peckham gives an account that Mrs Margaret and Mrs Millicent Trott are grown so very ridiculous not a neighbour will receive a visit from them. They affect every thing that's masculine, their shifts are called shirts, their headclothes are their perriwigs, their wrapper is their double-button'd coat, and their furbelow-scarves their roquelaures.[1] They are very intimate with Obadiah Subpoena, an impudent attorney, and Frank Fore-castle, a ranting sea-captain, are frequently dress'd in man's clothes, and gallop with 'em to the Palatines, where, tho' they have not taught 'em English, 'tis suspected they have given some of 'em to understand that conversation may be held between people of different nationals without knowing one another's language. But the worth of the matter is, they have seduc'd Miss Lack-it from the boarding-school, who steals out when her mistress is a-bed, to ramble with 'em. They'll sit down tightly to a bowl of punch, and then scour the streets, break windows, and have so little regard to their own sex as to abuse every

---

[1] *their furbelow-scarves their roquelaures:* They wear their flounced scarves as their knee-length cloaks.

woman they meet. They are women of condition as well as fortune, and their relations, having in vain us'd all arguments to reclaim 'em, were forc'd to entreat a public reprimand.

The two ladies I have little to say to. A wound taken early may be easily cur'd, and one foolish frolic the town may have good nature enough to forget; but a reputation once lost, like a mortification, is almost irrecoverable. As to the girl, her mistress is more to blame for not keeping a stricter eye over her. Her actions confirm me in the dislike I ever had to boarding-schools. People of fashion nowadays educate their children at home, and whereas, formerly, Miss was a romp at twenty, she is now, by the management of her parents, a discreet young lady at fifteen.

A ship laden with monkeys is lately come into the river; the young ones are fit for ladies' pages, the middle ag'd ones, ladies' impertinents, and the old ones will make admirable C——n C——l men.[2] They are to be seen any hour of the day, at the St George[3] near the Tower.

No. 34
Wednesday, September 21, to Friday, September 23

The gay part of mankind, who frequent park, plays, chocolate-houses, and every little fashionable assembly, that rid away many a tedious hour in reading *Tatlers*, eating jellies, disputing on twenty different sorts of snuff, and making pretty satirical observations upon one another, must have observed Beau Maskwell, one of the walking gentlemen of the age; a person Sans Consequence,[1] who every day makes his tour of public places with a kind of thoughtless serenity, and with no other seeming design, than the many saunterers of estate. He is what we call a clean dressed fellow, who instead of alarming people with a scarlet lace suit, tissue facings or embroidery, or elbowing thro' a coffee-house with a monstrous full-blown wig, affects pretty fancied druggets,[2] with a gold button, or a black and silver binding, a modest French nightcap, a nice white glove, with a diamond ring over the little finger, and a colberteen[3] neckcloth. You

---

[2] *C——n C——l men:* Common Council men.
[3] *the St George:* A tavern.
[1] *Sans Consequence:* Of no importance.
[2] *druggets:* A partially woolen fabric.
[3] *colberteen:* A netlike lace.

meet him everywhere dangling after a particular set of Baronets, who are observed in public places to be very much upon the whisper, and to have a secret value for one another. He is intimate in their families, and their ladies think him a modest, sober, discreet person, that lives prettily on a younger brother's fortune, and they have a mighty value in this age for everybody that keeps within compass.

But as there are a sort of tricking people, that pass through the world without noise, and had rather pick up a moderate subsistence with security and reputation, than publicly to expose their way of living, by publishing at great matters, Beau Maskwell is not the least politic of these. He is extremely indifferent whether you call for cards or no, had as live play for sixpences as half-crowns, and if he comes off ten shillings winner, the ladies think that his company repays it, and cannot suppose such trifling play should be a gentleman's support, but, as incredible estates have by assiduity and cunning been raised from the most abject callings, Maskwell, who has studied Piquet more than Aesculapius[4] ever did Physics, can slightly place the cards to his own advantage, and commit solecisms without being the least out of countenance, has for several years past genteely shuffled himself thro' all the difficulties of life. His associating with some of the better sort, makes people regard him with a kind of deference, 'tis not material nowadays, whether a man has birth, fortune, wit, sense, religion or morality; if the world stamps him a pretty gentleman, he passes current in all company. As such, Beau Maskwell has been looked upon and there's scarce a dancing-bout, basset night or collation,[5] but he's one of the Cabal.

Sometime past he had an invitation to supper where he found a select, genteel society; amongst the rest, Hillaria, an easy, unaffected young lady of about six thousand pounds fortune, was the life of the company. Her youth and good humour made her a little folicsome. She was equally pleasant, witty and familiar with strangers, as well as acquaintance, and the ladies were as much charmed with her gaiety, as the men were ravished with her beauty. They laughed, they danced, played at questions and commands, Hillaria romped a little. Everybody seemed wonderfully pleased with each other, and they only lamented the misfortune of being obliged to part at the break of day. Two days after, the same company assembled on another invitation. Maskwell was there, and asked leave to introduce a particular

---

[4] *Aesculapius:* In Greek mythology, the god of healing.
[5] *collation:* A meal.

friend after supper. The vote was unanimous for cards, except Maskwell, who so strongly opposed to his darling pleasure and profession, and was so strangely eager for questions and commands, that some people began to suspect his good manners. However, the reconciling Hillaria, to make everybody easy, that she might be so herself, proposed both diversions. The company were to be first questioned and then commanded to cards. Maskwell discovered no small satisfaction at being obliged in so seeming a trifle, and when he assumed the title of King, and the bright Hillaria condescended to be his subject, he commanded her to marry him, and that the person he had introduced, should perform the priestly office. The giddy nymph, who was for Clapperdepouch,[6] or anything, readily consents, banters him with having gnawed the sheets[7] a great while; that the war has made such havoc among the men she was afraid she should have died of the pip,[8] but that, (thanks to her better stars) she had now got a husband before her elder sister. And the stranger, praising himself for an admirable memory, repeated the service between 'em. Maskwell sends immediately for gloves and favours, Hillaria is ready to die with laughing, the company thinks them comical creatures, and the romantic airs of this new married couple afforded so much of what they call pastime, that several wish it had been a match in earnest, and thought it unnatural to part without throwing the stocking.

Maskwell the next morning attends his bride, was careless enough as to her person, but demanded her fortune. Hillaria laughs still, he commends her good humour and hopes his claim won't in the least divert it, but says they were actually married the night before, and that the person who performed the ceremony was a clergyman in the Fleet, whom he had introduced in lay-habit for that purpose. Hillaria then began to change, her relations were summoned upon the matter, but Maskwell impudently asserting the marriage, and being a fellow of too much craft to be bantered, bullied or baffled, the trembling Hillaria, to prevent town-talk, and the cognisance of Doctor's Commons[9] for making a jest of sacred things, gave him a thousand pounds to waive his pretensions to her. Maskwell now flourished like

[6] *Clapperdepouch:* A game.

[7] *gnawed the sheets:* Become anxious and impatient.

[8] *the pip:* Ill humor or poor health. To get or have the pip is to be depressed and despondent.

[9] *Doctor's Commons:* The common table and dining hall of the Association or College of Doctors of Civil Law in London. The buildings were located in the City, south of St. Paul's Cathedral.

his Baronets, they published him a man of estate, recommended him to fortunes, and about a month past he was marry to a lady of three thousand pounds, and made her a jointure in Utopia.[10]

Mrs Penelope Penny-royal, a middle-aged maid, that has three thousand pounds and plays finely on the organ, having many years, to no purpose, pretended to a coach, is now willing to dispose herself at reasonable rates. She may be seen most hours in the day standing at the door, near Catherine Street in the Strand. She's a fresh-coloured lady in a yellow damask gown, her pinners[11] not above a quarter of a yard higher than other people's, the furbelow of her nightrail[12] don't quite touch the ground, nor does her watch hang much below her knee. Whoever thinks fit to engage in her service, will have a very cordial reception.

No. 71
Friday, December 16, to Monday, December 19
Arabella's Day

Since Emilia took upon her last time, to vindicate Altamira's character and conduct, especially since her wise choice in one of the first mice of quality, the Court prudes are all in an uproar, and have resolved to load that deserving beauty with all the secret scandal, wit or envy can invent. To anticipate which design, I shall endeavour to draw their pictures in miniature, and find them in full employ to blot out the gaieties I have designed for them, if they like not their own faces when they see them in proper colouring or else to daub them over with varnish that may disguise the painting.

A prude is a woman who places her virtue in having wit enough to keep a man from prying in to her faults, and modest enough to hinder him from climbing into her bed-chamber. She simpers before company, as if butter would not melt in her mouth, but in private is an errant Miss Romps, and shows her teeth to her chamber-maid, as certain as she bites her lip in public conversation. Where she is so circumspect that she divides her eyes among the company, reserving always one half to herself, except by chance, she gives a glance now and then upon some gold watch, diamond ring, or other piece of fin-

---

[10] *jointure in Utopia:* A jointure in a marriage contract specified the amount of his property a man would share with his wife. Utopia (literally "noplace") is thus an ideal realm.

[11] *pinners:* Headdress.

[12] *nightrail:* Dressing gown or nightgown.

ery that is before her. When she sits at her tea-table, she moulds her face into a regular figure, which vanishes away at the introduction of a dram of right Nantz.[1] And that art before which persuaded her to keep a secret, now yields with pleasure to the power of nature, which triumphs in revealing it. She consults her face every morning so long, till she goes away convinced that she is fair, and then commends her glass because it does not flatter her. She is of that reserved prim that, though her ears are guilty of hearing many things, she scorns her tongue should tell of any of them, so she cannot be censured by the world for sinning with her understanding. She seems to be bred in the stoic philosophy, for she neglects her equals and despises her betters, so that her vanity seldom can be said to exceed condescension.

She plumes herself and puts a value upon her wit if she can gain a gay lover that is remarkable for a fool that she may have the pleasure and, as she thinks, the applause of the world for laughing at his simplicity. Then the men will call her a hard-hearted and cruel creature, and the women perhaps say she is a shy lady, and too nice for a wife. If she loves at all, as it is ten to one she does, she loves not the man, but his equipage, the laced liveries and the saucy fellows that wear them. Her lightness makes her swim on the top of her acquaintance, because they visit her not in such clean linen as she dresses in. Her devotion is in a new suit of clothes that carries her to church in the top of the fashion, where she lifts up her eyes instead of her heart, to know who looks upon her, not who she is praying to. The most necessary attendants about her are her woman and her lap-dog, and the greatest curiosities she is guilty of is a better jewel, or a finer gown.

ALEXANDER POPE

Epistle to a Lady

Alexander Pope (1688–1743) published his *Epistle to a Lady* early in 1735 and then included it in *Epistles to Several Persons,* the 1735 collection of his *Works.* This collection is sometimes called Pope's *Moral Essays;* the poems, which are modeled on Horace's satiric epistles, are concerned with ethical standards and the content of human character.

This poem proceeds as a tour through a gallery of portraits of contemporary female types, each of which the narrator describes in succes-

---

[1] *right Nantz:* Authentic Nantz brandy.

sion. The lady addressed is Martha Blount (1690–1763), a close and longtime friend of Pope's. And while Blount may seem to escape Pope's satiric censure of female fickleness and contrariness, her virtue is itself built on a contradiction: the only way a woman can acquire ethical validity is to acquire virtues that are essentially masculine and so at odds with her female nature. As Pope says, "Woman's at best a Contradiction still. / Heav'n, when it strives to polish all it can / Its last best work, but forms a softer Man" (ll. 279–81).

Of the Characters of Women
Argument

Of the Characters of *Women* (consider'd only as contradistinguished from the other Sex.) That these are yet more inconsistent and incomprehensible than those of Men, of which Instances are given even from such Characters as are plainest, and most strongly mark'd; as in the *Affected*, Ver. 7, &c. The *Soft-natur'd*. 29. the *Cunning*, 45. the *Whimsical*, 53. the *Wits and Refiners*, 87. the *Stupid* and *Silly*, 101. How Contrarieties run thro' them all.

But tho' the *Particular Characters* of this Sex are more various than those of Men, the *General Characteristick*, as to the *Ruling Passion*, is more uniform and confin'd. In what That lies, and whence it *proceeds*, 207, &c. Men are best known in publick Life, Women in private, 199. What are the *Aims*, and the *Fate* of the Sex, both as to *Power* and *Pleasure*? 219, 231, &c. Advice for their true Interest, 249. The Picture of an esteemable Woman, made up of the best kind of Contrarieties, 269, &c.

Nothing so true as what you once let fall,
'Most Women have no Characters at all'.
Matter too soft a lasting mark to bear,
And best distinguish'd by black, brown, or fair.

   How many pictures of one Nymph we view,   5
All how unlike each other, all how true!
Arcadia's Countess° here, in ermin'd pride,

7. *Arcadia's Countess:* A reference to *The Countess of Pembroke's Arcadia*, the heroic and pastoral romance written by the English poet Sir Philip Sidney (1554–1586) for the amusement of his sister, Mary Herbert, Countess of Pembroke (1561–1621).

Is there, Pastora by a fountain side:
Here Fannia, leering on her own good man,
Is there, a naked Leda with a Swan.°　　　　　　　　　10
Let then the Fair one beautifully cry,
In Magdalen's° loose hair and lifted eye,
Or drest in smiles of sweet Cecilia shine,
With simp'ring Angels, Palms, and Harps divine;
Whether the Charmer sinner it, or saint it,　　　　　15
If Folly grows romantic, I must paint it.
　　Come then, the colours and the ground prepare!
Dip in the Rainbow, trick her off in Air,
Chuse a firm Cloud, before it fall, and in it
Catch, ere she change, the Cynthia of this minute.　　20
　　Rufa, whose eye quick-glancing o'er the Park,°
Attracts each light gay meteor of a Spark,°
Agrees as ill with Rufa studying Locke,°
As Sappho's° diamonds with her dirty smock,
Or Sappho at her toilet's greasy task,　　　　　　25
With Sappho fragrant at an ev'ning Mask:
So morning Insects that in muck begun,
Shine, buzz, and fly-blow in the setting-sun.
　　How soft is Silia! fearful to offend,
The Frail one's advocate, the Weak one's friend:　　30

The *Arcadia* was first published in 1590 and reprinted throughout the seventeenth century.

10. *Leda with a Swan:* In Greek mythology, Leda was raped by the god Zeus, who attacked her in the form of a swan; she gave birth to the Heavenly Twins, Castor and Pollux.

12. *Magdalen's:* A former prostitute, Mary Magdalene (first century A.D.) was one of Jesus' most celebrated disciples and the first person to see the resurrected Christ (Mark 16:9–10; John 20:14–17).

21. *the Park:* St. James's Park, the oldest of London's royal parks and a resort of the sovereign and the court through the Restoration.

22. *a Spark:* A fancy, frivolous, fashionable man.

23. *Locke:* John Locke (1632–1704), the English philosopher whose *Essay Concerning Human Understanding* (1690) explores the nature of the human mind and its cognitive abilities.

24. *Sappho's:* A reference to Lady Mary Wortley Montagu, a sometime friend of Pope who was renowned as a letter writer (especially for her letters from the British Embassy in Turkey), poet, and essayist. Sappho was a Greek poet born in the late seventh century B.C. on the island of Lesbos. This is a derogatory characterization of Lady Mary Wortley Montagu, suggesting that she is an unchaste woman with ludicrous pretensions to literary skill.

To her, Calista° prov'd her conduct nice,
And good Simplicius° asks of her advice.
Sudden, she storms! she raves! You tip the wink,
But spare your censure; Silia does not drink.
All eyes may see from what the change arose,   35
All eyes may see — a Pimple on her nose.
    Papillia,° wedded to her doating spark,
Sighs for the shades — 'How charming is a Park!'
A Park is purchas'd, but the Fair he sees
All bath'd in tears — 'Oh odious, odious Trees!'   40
    Ladies, like variegated Tulips, show,
'Tis to their Changes that their charms we owe;
Their happy Spots the nice admirer take,
Fine by defect, and delicately weak.
'Twas thus Calypso° once each heart alarm'd,   45
Aw'd without Virtue, without Beauty charm'd;
Her Tongue bewitch'd as odly as her Eyes,
Less Wit than Mimic, more a Wit than wise:
Strange graces still, and stranger flights she had,
Was just not ugly, and was just not mad;   50
Yet ne'er so sure our passion to create,
As when she touch'd the brink of all we hate.
    Narcissa's° nature, tolerably mild,
To make a wash,° would hardly stew a child,
Has ev'n been prov'd to grant a Lover's pray'r,   55
And paid a Tradesman once to make him stare,
Gave alms at Easter, in a Christian trim,
And made a Widow happy, for a whim.
Why then declare Good-nature is her scorn,
When 'tis by that alone she can be born?   60
Why pique all mortals, yet affect a name?
A fool to Pleasure, and a slave to Fame:

---

31. *Calista:* Calista is a character in Nicholas Rowe's (1674–1718) play *The Fair Penitent* (1703).
    32. *Simplicius:* A sixth-century A.D. neoplatonic philosopher.
    37. *Papillia:* In Latin, *papilio* means butterfly (French, *papillon*).
    45. *Calypso:* In Greek legend, a sea nymph who kept the hero Odysseus, returning home to Greece from the Trojan war, for seven years on the island of Ogygia. She appears in Book 5 of Homer's epic poem, the *Odyssey.*
    53. *Narcissa's:* A vain, self-infatuated woman. In Greek mythology, Narcissus was a beautiful young man who fell in love with his own reflection in a pool.
    54. *wash:* A cosmetic facial wash.

Now deep in Taylor and the Book of Martyrs,°
Now drinking citron with his Grace and Chartres.°
Now Conscience chills her, and now Passion burns;   65
And Atheism and Religion take their turns;
A very Heathen in the carnal part,
Yet still a sad, good Christian at her heart.
  See Sin in State, majestically drunk,
Proud as a Peeress, prouder as a Punk;   70
Chaste to her Husband, frank to all beside,
A teeming Mistress, but a barren Bride.
What then? let Blood and Body bear the fault,
Her Head's untouch'd, that noble Seat of Thought:
Such this day's doctrine — in another fit   75
She sins with Poets thro' pure Love of Wit.
What has not fir'd her bosom or her brain?
Caesar and Tall-boy, Charles and Charlema'ne.°
As Helluo,° late Dictator of the Feast,
The Nose of Hautgout,° and the Tip of Taste,   80
Critick'd your wine, and analyz'd your meat,
Yet on plain Pudding deign'd at-home to eat;
So Philomedé, lect'ring all mankind
On the soft Passion, and the Taste refin'd,
Th' Address, the Delicacy — stoops at once,   85
And makes her hearty meal upon a Dunce.
  Flavia's a Wit, has too much sense to Pray,
To Toast our wants and wishes, is her way;
Nor asks of God, but of her Stars to give
The mighty blessing, 'while we live, to live.'   90
Then all for Death, that Opiate of the soul!

  63. *Taylor and the Book of Martyrs:* Jeremy Taylor's (1613–1667) *The Rule and Exercises of Holy Living* (1650) and *The Rule and Exercises of Holy Dying* (1651); John Foxe's (1516–1587) Protestant martyrology, *Actes and Monuments* (1563).
  64. *drinking citron with his Grace and Chartres:* Drinking citron water, a kind of brandy flavored with citron or lemon peel, with a duke and Francis Chartres (1675–1732), an infamously vicious gambler, moneylender, and rapist.
  78. *Caesar and Tall-boy, Charles and Charlema'ne:* Julius Caesar (100–44 B.C.) was a Roman general, statesman, and historian; he was appointed dictator by the people of Rome. Tall-boy is a booby character in Richard Brome's comedy *The Jovial Crew* (1641). Charles is a generic name for a footman. Charlemagne (742?–814) was king of the Franks and founder of the first empire in Western Europe after the fall of Rome.
  79. *Helluo:* In Latin, a glutton.
  80. *Hautgout:* Something with a strong taste or smell.

Lucretia's dagger, Rosamonda's bowl.°
Say, what can cause such impotence of mind?
A Spark too fickle, or a Spouse too kind.
Wise Wretch! with Pleasures too refin'd to please,   95
With too much Spirit to be e'er at ease,
With too much Quickness ever to be taught,
With too much Thinking to have common Thought:
Who purchase Pain with all that Joy can give,
And die of nothing but a Rage to live.°   100
    Turn then from Wits; and look on Simo's Mate,
No Ass so meek, no Ass so obstinate:
Or her, that owns her Faults, but never mends,
Because she's honest, and the best of Friends:
Or her, whose life the Church and Scandal share,   105
For ever in a Passion, or a Pray'r:
Or her, who laughs at Hell, but (like her Grace)
Cries, 'Ah! how charming if there's no such place!'
Or who in sweet vicissitude appears
Of Mirth and Opium, Ratafie and Tears,   110
The daily Anodyne, and nightly Draught,
To kill those foes to Fair ones, Time and Thought.
Woman and Fool are two hard things to hit,
For true No-meaning puzzles more than Wit.
    But what are these to great Atossa's° mind?   115
Scarce once herself, by turns all Womankind!
Who, with herself, or others, from her birth
Finds all her life one warfare upon earth:
Shines, in exposing Knaves, and painting Fools,
Yet is, whate'er she hates and ridicules.   120
No Thought advances, but her Eddy Brain
Whisks it about, and down it goes again.
Full sixty years the World has been her Trade,
The wisest Fool much Time has ever made.
From loveless youth to unrespected age,   125

92. *Lucretia's dagger, Rosamonda's bowl:* Lucrezia Borgia (1450–1519) was a noblewoman of the powerful and corrupt Borgia family of Renaissance Italy. She is suspected of committing incest with her father and of having a hand in the political intrigues and assassinations pursued by her family. Rosamonde Clifford (d. 1177) was the mistress of Henry II (1133–1189) and was poisoned by his queen.

115. *Atossa's:* Atossa was the daughter of Cyrus the Great (sixth century B.C.), the founder of the Persian empire, and the sister of Cambyses. She became the wife of three Persian kings and the mother of Xerxes.

No Passion gratify'd except her Rage.
So much the Fury still out-ran the Wit,
The Pleasure miss'd her, and the Scandal hit.
Who breaks with her, provokes Revenge from Hell,
But he's a bolder man who dares be well: 130
Her ev'ry turn with Violence pursu'd,
Nor more a storm her Hate than Gratitude.
To that each Passion turns, or soon or late;
Love, if it makes her yield, must make her hate:
Superiors? death! and Equals? what a curse!   135
But an Inferior not dependant? worse.
Offend her, and she knows not to forgive;
Oblige her, and she'll hate you while you live:
But die, and she'll adore you — Then the Bust
And Temple rise — then fall again to dust.   140
Last night, her Lord was all that's good and great,
A Knave this morning, and his Will a Cheat.
Strange! by the Means defeated of the Ends,
By Spirit robb'd of Pow'r, by Warmth of Friends,
By Wealth of Follow'rs! without one distress   145
Sick of herself thro' very selfishness!
Atossa, curs'd with ev'ry granted pray'r,
Childless with all her Children, wants an Heir.
To Heirs unknown descends th' unguarded store
Or wanders, Heav'n-directed, to the Poor.   150
   Pictures like these, dear Madam, to design,
Asks no firm hand, and no unerring line;
Some wand'ring touch, or some reflected light,
Some flying stroke alone can hit 'em right:
For how should equal Colours do the knack?   155
Chameleons who can paint in white and black?
   'Yet Cloe sure was form'd without a spot — '
Nature in her then err'd not, but forgot.
'With ev'ry pleasing, ev'ry prudent part,
Say, what can Cloe want?' — she wants a Heart.   160
She speaks, behaves, and acts just as she ought;
But never, never, reach'd one gen'rous Thought.
Virtue she finds too painful an endeavour,
Content to dwell in Decencies for ever.
So very reasonable, so unmov'd,   165
As never yet to love, or to be lov'd.

She, while her Lover pants upon her breast,
Can mark the figures on an Indian chest;
And when she sees her Friend in deep despair,
Observes how much a Chintz exceeds Mohair.   170
Forbid it Heav'n, a Favour or a Debt
She e'er should cancel — but she may forget.
Safe is your Secret still in Cloe's ear;
But none of Cloe's shall you ever hear.
Of all her Dears she never slander'd one,   175
But cares not if a thousand are undone.
Would Cloe know if you're alive or dead?
She bids her Footman put it in her head.
Cloe is prudent — would you too be wise?
Then never break your heart when Cloe dies.   180
    One certain Portrait may (I grant) be seen,
Which Heav'n has varnish'd out, and made a *Queen*:°
The same for ever! and describ'd by all
With Truth and Goodness, as with Crown and Ball:
Poets heap Virtues, Painters Gems at will,   185
And show their zeal, and hide their want of skill.
'Tis well — but, Artists! who can paint or write,
To draw the Naked is your true delight:
That Robe of Quality so struts and swells,
None see what Parts of Nature it conceals.   190
Th' exactest traits of Body or of Mind,
We owe to models of an humble kind.
If QUEENSBERRY° to strip there's no compelling,
'Tis from a Handmaid we must take a Helen.
From Peer or Bishop 'tis no easy thing   195
To draw the man who loves his God, or King:
Alas! I copy (or my draught would fail)
From honest Mah'met,° or plain Parson Hale.°
    But grant, in Public Men sometimes are shown,
A Woman's seen in Private life alone: 200
Our bolder Talents in full light display'd,

---

182. *Queen:* Queen Caroline (1683–1737), wife of George II.
193. *QUEENSBERRY:* Catherine Hyde, Duchess of Queensbury (1700–1777) was famous for her personal beauty.
198. *Mah'met:* The Turkish servant to the late king, George I.   *Parson Hale:* Dr.
Stephen Hales (1637–1761), a famous physiologist who witnessed Pope's will [Bond].

Your Virtues open fairest in the shade.
Bred to disguise, in Public 'tis you hide;
There, none distinguish 'twixt your Shame or Pride,
Weakness or Delicacy; all so nice,   205
That each may seem a Virtue, or a Vice.
    In Men, we various Ruling Passions find,
In Women, two almost divide the kind;
Those, only fix'd, they first or last obey,
The Love of Pleasure, and the Love of Sway.   210
    That, Nature gives; and where the lesson taught
Is but to please, can Pleasure seem a fault?
Experience, this; by Man's oppression curst,
They seek the second not to lose the first.
    Men, some to Bus'ness, some to Pleasure take;   215
But ev'ry Woman is at heart a Rake:
Men, some to Quiet, some to public Strife;
But ev'ry Lady would be Queen for life.
    Yet mark the fate of a whole Sex of Queens!
Pow'r all their end, but Beauty all the means.   220
In Youth they conquer, with so wild a rage,
As leaves them scarce a Subject in their Age:
For foreign glory, foreign joy, they roam;
No thought of Peace or Happiness at home.
But Wisdom's Triumph is well-tim'd Retreat,   225
As hard a science to the Fair as Great!
Beauties, like Tyrants, old and friendless grown,
Yet hate to rest, and dread to be alone,
Worn out in public, weary ev'ry eye,
Nor leave one sight behind them when they die.   230
    Pleasures the sex, as children Birds, pursue,
Still out of reach, yet never out of view,
Sure, if they catch, to spoil the Toy at most,
To covet flying, and regret when lost:
At last, to follies Youth could scarce defend,   235
'Tis half their Age's prudence to pretend;
Asham'd to own they gave delight before,
Reduc'd to feign it, when they give no more:
As Hags hold Sabbaths, less for joy than spight,
So these their merry, miserable Night;   240
Still round and round the Ghosts of Beauty glide,
And haunt the places where their Honour dy'd.

See how the World its Veterans rewards!
A Youth of frolicks, an old Age of Cards,
Fair to no purpose, artful to no end,   245
Young without Lovers, old without a Friend,
A Fop their Passion, but their Prize a Sot,
Alive, ridiculous, and dead, forgot!
   Ah Friend! to dazzle let the Vain design,
To raise the Thought and touch the Heart, be thine!   250
That Charm shall grow, while what fatigues the Ring
Flaunts and goes down, an unregarded thing.
So when the Sun's broad beam has tir'd the sight,
All mild ascends the Moon's more sober light,
Serene in Virgin Modesty she shines,   255
And unobserv'd the glaring Orb declines.
   Oh! blest with Temper, whose unclouded ray
Can make to morrow chearful as to day;
She, who can love a Sister's charms, or hear
Sighs for a Daughter with unwounded ear;   260
She, who ne'er answers till a Husband cools,
Or, if she rules him, never show she rules;
Charms by accepting, by submitting sways,
Yet has her humour most, when she obeys;
Lets Fops or Fortune fly which way they will;   265
Disdains all loss of Tickets, or Codille;°
Spleen, Vapours, or Small-pox, above them all,
And Mistress of herself, tho' China fall.
   And yet, believe me, good as well as ill,
Woman's at best a Contradiction still.   270
Heav'n, when it strives to polish all it can
Its last best work, but forms a softer Man;
Picks from each sex, to make its Fav'rite blest,
Your love of Pleasure, our desire of Rest,
Blends, in exception to all gen'ral rules,   275
Your Taste of Follies, with our Scorn or Fools,
Reserve with Frankness, Art with Truth ally'd,
Courage with Softness, Modesty with Pride;
Fix'd Principles, with Fancy ever new;
Shakes all together, and produces — You.   280

---

266. *Tickets, or Codille:* Lottery tickets; codille is a term used in the fashionable
card game ombre.

Be this a Woman's Fame: with this unblest,
Toasts live a scorn, and Queens may die a jest.
This Phoebus promis'd (I forget the year)
When those blue eyes first open'd on the sphere;
Ascendant Phoebus watch'd that hour with care,   285
Averted half your Parents simple Pray'r,
And gave you Beauty, but deny'd the Pelf
Which buys your sex a Tyrant o'er itself.
The gen'rous God, who Wit and Gold refines,
And ripens Spirits as he ripens Mines,   290
Kept Dross for Duchesses, the world shall know it,
To you gave Sense, Good-humour, and a Poet.

JONATHAN SWIFT

"The Progress of Beauty" and "A Beautiful Young Nymph Going to Bed"

Jonathan Swift (1667–1745) was a prolific poet, and some of his best-known poems are scathingly bleak descriptions of the dynamics of sexual desire and, as in the two works included here, the effects of that desire on the bodies of women. The women in these poems are both prostitutes, or as Swift with ironic euphemism dubs them, "nymphs of Drury Lane." But in other poems, such as "A Lady's Dressing Room" and "Phyllis, or, The Progress of Love," Swift deals with similar themes as they affect bourgeois women. He sharply exposes the discrepancy, as well as the connection, between the idealized conventions of feminine beauty and sexual love, and the ugly, deathly realities of these women's lives. Eaten away by venereal disease and poverty, these "nymphs" must still try to put themselves together in a fashion that conforms to the highly idealized, disembodied, masculine ideal of female beauty. Swift strips these women of the artifice that society demands of them and reveals the corruption imposed on their bodies.

"The Progress of Beauty" was written in 1719 or 1720 and first published in the Pope-Swift *Miscellanies* of 1727. "A Beautiful Young Nymph Going to Bed" was published in 1734 in a pamphlet that also included Swift's "Strephon and Chloe" and "Cassinus and Peter." (See also headnote to Jonathan Swift, *A Proposal for Correcting the English Tongue*, Chapter 3's Cultural Contexts, p. 403.)

The poems have been taken from *Jonathan Swift: The Complete Poems*, ed. Pat Rogers (New York: Penguin Books, 1983).

The Progress of Beauty

When first Diana° leaves her Bed
Vapors and Steams her Looks disgrace,
A frouzy dirty colour'd red
Sits on her cloudy wrinkled Face.

But by degrees when mounted high
Her artificiall Face appears
Down from her Window in the Sky,
Her Spots are gone, her Visage clears.

'Twixt earthly Femals and the Moon
All Parallells exactly run;   10
If Celia should appear too soon
Alas, the Nymph would be undone.

To see her from her Pillow rise
All reeking in a cloudy Steam,
Crackt Lips, foul Teeth, and gummy Eyes,
Poor Strephon, how would he blaspheme!

The Soot or Powder which was wont
To make her Hair look black as Jet,
Falls from her Tresses on her Front
A mingled Mass of Dirt and Sweat.   20

Three Colours, Black, and Red, and White,
So gracefull in their proper Place,
Remove them to a diff'rent Light
They form a frightfull hideous Face,

For instance; when the Lilly slipps
Into the Precincts of the Rose,
And takes Possession of the Lips,
Leaving the Purple to the Nose.

So Celia went entire to bed,
All her Complexions safe and sound,   30

---

1. *Diana:* In Roman mythology, Diana is the virgin goddess of childbirth and the hunt; she is associated with the moon.

But when she rose, the black and red
Though still in Sight, had chang'd their Ground.

    The Black, which would not be confin'd
A more inferior Station seeks
Leaving the fiery red behind,
And mingles in her muddy Cheeks.

    The Paint by Perspiration cracks,
And falls in Rivulets of Sweat,
On either Side you see the Tracks,
While at her Chin the Conflu'ents met.   40

    A Skillfull Housewife thus her Thumb
With Spittle while she spins, anoints,
And thus the brown Meanders come
In trickling Streams betwixt her Joynts.

    But Celia can with ease reduce
By help of Pencil, Paint and Brush
Each Colour to it's Place and Use,
And teach her Cheeks again to blush.

    She knows her Early self no more,
But fill'd with Admiration, stands,   50
As Other Painters oft adore
The Workmanship of their own Hands.

    Thus after four important Hours
Celia's the Wonder of her Sex;
Say, which among the Heav'nly Pow'rs
Could cause such wonderfull Effects.

    Venus, indulgent to her Kind
Gave Women all their Hearts could wish
When first she taught them where to find
White Lead, and Lusitanian° Dish.   60

    Love with White lead° cements his Wings,
White lead was sent us to repair
Two brightest, brittlest earthly Things
A Lady's Face, and China ware.

    She ventures now to lift the Sash,
The Window is her proper Sphear;

---

60. *Lusitanian:* From Lusitania, an ancient Roman province in the Iberian Peninsula.
61. *White lead:* Facial foundation was made from powdered white lead.

Ah Lovely Nymph be not too rash,
Nor let the Beaux approach too near.

Take Pattern by your Sister Star,
Delude at once and Bless our Sight,   70
When you are seen, be seen from far,
And chiefly chuse to shine by Night.

In the Pell-mell° when passing by,
Keep up the Glasses of your Chair,°
Then each transported Fop will cry,
G—d d—m me Jack, she's wondrous fair.

But, Art no longer can prevayl
When the Materialls all are gone,
The best Mechanick Hand must fayl
Where Nothing's left to work upon.   80

Matter, as wise Logicians say,
Cannot without a Form subsist,
And Form, say I, as well as They,
Must fayl if Matter brings no Grist.

And this is fair Diana's Case
For, all Astrologers maintain
Each Night a Bit drops off her Face
When Mortals say she's in her Wain.

While Partridge° wisely shews the Cause
Efficient of the Moon's Decay,   90
That Cancer with his pois'nous Claws
Attacks her in the milky Way:

But Gadbury° in Art profound
From her pale Cheeks pretends to show
That Swain Endymion° is not sound,
Or else, that Mercury's° her Foe.

---

73. *Pell-mell:* Pall Mall, a fashionable street in St. James's so called because it had
been an alley where Pall-Mall, a croquetlike game, was played.
74. *Chair:* Sedan chair in which people were carried.
89. *Partridge:* John Partridge (1644–1715), a quack astrologer against whom
Swift, as Isaac Bickerstaff, launched a satirical attack in his Bickerstaff papers,
1708–09 (see Introduction, p. 28).
93. *Gadbury:* John Gadbury (1627–1704), an astrologer.
95. *Endymion:* In Greek mythology, the young man beloved by the goddess
Diana.
96. *Mercury:* The metal mercury was used to treat syphilis.

But, let the Cause be what it will,
In half a Month she looks so thin
That Flamstead° can with all his Skill
See but her Forehead and her Chin.   100

Yet as she wasts, she grows discreet,
Till Midnight never shows her Head;
So rotting Celia stroles the Street
When sober Folks are all a-bed.

For sure if this be Luna's Fate,
Poor Celia, but of mortall Race
In vain expects a longer Date
To the Materialls of Her Face.

When Mercury her Tresses mows
To think of Oyl and Soot, is vain,   110
No Painting can restore a Nose,
Nor will her Teeth return again.

Two Balls of Glass may serve for Eyes,
White Lead can plaister up a Cleft,
But these alas, are poor Supplyes
If neither Cheeks, nor Lips be left.

Ye Pow'rs who over Love preside,
Since mortal Beautyes drop so soon,
If you would have us well supply'd,
Send us new Nymphs with each new Moon.   120

A Beautiful Young Nymph Going to Bed

Corinna, Pride of *Drury-Lane*,°
For whom no Shepherd sighs in vain;
Never did *Covent Garden*° boast
So bright a batter'd, strolling Toast;
No drunken Rake to pick her up,
No Cellar where on Tick to sup;°
Returning at the Midnight Hour;

---

99. *Flamstead:* John Flamsteed (1646–1719), the first royal astronomer (1675).

1. *Drury-Lane:* In the theater district around Covent Garden, Drury Lane was a notorious haunt of prostitutes.

3. *Covent Garden:* Covent Garden, in the midst of the theater district, acquired a reputation as a center of dissipated pleasures.

6. *on Tick to sup:* To run up a bill at a restaurant.

Four Stories climbing to her Bow'r;
Then, seated on a three-legg'd Chair,
Takes off her artificial Hair: 10
Now, picking out a Crystal Eye,
She wipes it clean, and lays it by.
Her Eye-Brows from a Mouse's Hyde,
Stuck on with Art on either Side,
Pulls off with Care, and first displays 'em,
Then in a Play-Book smoothly lays 'em.
Now dextrously her Plumpers draws,
That serve to fill her hollow Jaws.
Untwists a Wire; and from her Gums
A Set of Teeth completely comes.   20
Pulls out the Rags contriv'd to prop
Her flabby Dugs and down they drop.
Proceeding on, the lovely Goddess
Unlaces next her Steel-Rib'd Bodice;
Which by the Operator's Skill,
Press down the Lumps, the Hollows fill,
Up goes her Hand, and off she slips
The Bolsters that supply her Hips.
With gentlest Touch, she next explores
Her Shankers, Issues, running Sores,   30
Effects of many a sad Disaster;
And then to each applies a Plaister.
But must, before she goes to Bed,
Rub off the Dawbs of White and Red;
And smooth the Furrows in her Front,
With greasy Paper stuck upon't.
She takes a *Bolus*° e'er she sleeps;
And then between two Blankets creeps.
With Pains of Love tormented lies;
Or if she chance to close her Eyes,   40
Of *Bridewell* and the *Compter*° dreams,

---

37. *Bolus:* A pill.
41. *Bridewell and the Compter:* Originally a royal palace built 1515–20 for Henry
VIII, Bridewell was named after a holy well dedicated to St. Bride. In 1553, Edward VI
gave the palace to the city of London to house vagrants and homeless children and to
use as a correctional institution for petty offenders and wayward women. In 1556 the
city took possession and, with the confirmation of Queen Mary, turned the palace into
a prison, hospital, and workhouse. A compter was a city prison.

And feels the Lash, and faintly screams;
Or, by a faithless Bully drawn,
At some Hedge-Tavern lies in Pawn;
Or to *Jamaica* seems transported,°
Alone, and by no Planter courted;
Or, near *Fleet-Ditch*'s° oozy Brinks,
Surrounded with a Hundred Stinks,
Belated, seems on watch to lye,
And snap some Cully passing by;   50
Or, struck with Fear, her Fancy runs
On Watchmen, Constables and Duns,
From whom she meets with frequent Rubs;
But, never from Religious Clubs;
Whose Favour she is sure to find,
Because she pays 'em all in Kind.
    Corinna wakes. A dreadful Sight!
Behold the Ruins of the Night!
A wicked Rat her Plaister stole,
Half eat, and dragg'd it to his Hole.   60
The Crystal Eye, alas, was miss't;
And *Puss* had on her Plumpers p——st.°
A Pigeon pick'd her Issue-Peas;°
And *Shock* her Tresses fill'd with Fleas.
    The Nymph, tho' in this mangled Plight,
Must ev'ry Morn her Limbs unite.
But how shall I describe her Arts
To recollect the scatter'd Parts?
Or shew the Anguish, Toil, and Pain,
Of gath'ring up herself again?   70
The bashful Muse will never bear
In such a Scene to interfere.
Corinna in the Morning dizen'd,
Who sees, will spew; who smells, be poison'd.

45. *transported:* Transportation to the Americas was a common penal sentence.
47. *Fleet-Ditch:* An open sewer running between Ludgate Hill and Fleet Street
into the Thames.
62. *p——st:* Pissed.
63. *Issue-Peas:* A small, round piece of material placed in surgical incisions to
drain infection.

MARY EVELYN

From *Mundus Muliebris: or, The Ladies Dressing-Room Unlock'd* and *The Fop-Dictionary*

Mary Evelyn (1665–1685) was the daughter of John Evelyn (1620–1706), a prominent figure in Restoration government and a leading member of the Royal Society. John Evelyn published *Mundus Muliebris* (*The Woman's World*) in 1690, five years after the death of his daughter. The Preface is probably his.

Built around the conceit of offering advice to a young man who would outfit a modern young lady in order to sail with her into marriage ("Maryland"), this satire on female extravagance offers a heavily detailed and topical picture of what went into the composition of the late-seventeenth-century woman of fashion. The poem gives a clear sense of the Frenchness, the foreignness of high fashion. The accompanying *Fop-Dictionary* provides a useful glossary to many French words for specific modes of dress and hairstyle: fashion is French, and in order to master fashion one must master at least a good handful of French words and phrases. Style, as this poem makes clear, is full of arcane and technical distinctions, the mastery of which must have demanded considerable time and attention.

A rebuttal to Evelyn's satire on female vanity is given in *Mundus Foppensis*, a satire on male vanity (p. 602).

Preface.

This Paper was not to come abroad without a Preface as well as Comment, for Instruction of our young Master, who newly launch'd from the University (where he has left a year or two) is not yet Travell'd, or if haply he has made le petit Tour *(with the formal thing his Governour)*[1] *having never yet Read* Tully's Offices[2] *through, since he came from School sets up for a* Beau, *and Equipp'd for the Town at his Return, comes to seek Adventures in an Ocean full of Rocks, and*

---

[1] *le petit Tour . . . his Governour:* Made the small tour of Europe with an older gentleman, the governor appointed to look after him.

[2] *Tully's Offices:* Tully is Marcus Tullius Cicero (106–43 B.C.), the Roman orator, philosopher, and statesman. The *Offices* is his *De Officiis (On Duties)* in which Cicero lays out a moral code of conduct.

Shelves, and wants a skilful Pilot to Steer him, as much as any Vessel that goes to the Indies[3]; *and oftentimes returns home Leaky, and as poorly freighted, as those who have been near Shipwrack'd,*[4] *or left their Voyage.*

It is for direction of such as are setting out towards this great and famous Emporium[5] *(whether the design be Miss or Marriage) what Cargo he must provide; not as Merchants do for* America, Glass Beads, *and Baubles in exchange for Gold and Pearl; but Gold and Pearl, and all that's precious, for that which is of less value than Knives and Childrens Rattles.*

You see, Squires, what you are to prepare for as Adventurers, or by way of Barter, if you think to Traffick here, and to carry the Fair One, especially if she be at her own disposal (or being come some considerable time out of the Country) has been initiated into the Conversation of the Town: The Refined Lady expects her Servants and humble Admirers should Court her in the Forms and Decencies of making Love in Fashion: In order to this, you must often Treat her at the Play, *the* Park,[6] *and the* Musick; *present her at the* Raffle,[7] *follow her to* Tunbridge[8] *at the season of drinking of Waters, though you have no need of them your self: You must improve all occasions of celebrating her Shape, and how well the Mode becomes her, though it be ne'er so Fantastical and Ridiculous; that she Sings like an Angel, Dances like a Goddess; and that you are Charm'd with her Wit and Beauty: Above all, you must be sure to find some Fault or Imperfection in all other Ladies of the Town, and to laugh at the Fopps like your self: With this, a little Practice will qualifie you for the Conversation and Mistery of the* Ruelle[9]; *and if the whole Morning be spent between the Glass and the Comb, that your Perruque*[10] *fit well, and Cravat-Strings be adjusted as things of importance; with these and*

---

[3] *the Indies:* The East Indies comprised India and East Asia; the chief English possessions in the West Indies were Barbados and Jamaica.

[4] *Shipwrack'd:* Shipwrecked.

[5] *Emporium:* Here Evelyn is figuring the social world of courtship as an emporium or fashionable marketplace of women and offering advice on how a modern suitor can best obtain his goods, "Miss or Marriage."

[6] *the Park:* St. James's Park, the oldest of London's royal parks and a resort of the sovereign and the court through the Restoration.

[7] *the Raffle:* Lotteries were extremely popular at this time; see Chapter 2, *Tatler* Nos. 124 and 203 (pp. 177 and 181).

[8] *Tunbridge:* Tunbridge Wells, a fashionable resort spa.

[9] *Ruelle:* Alley.

[10] *Perruque:* A kind of wig worn by men.

the like accomplishments you'l emerge a consummate Beau, Anglice,[11] *a* Coxcomb. *But the Dancing-Master will still be necessary to preserve your good Meen,*[12] *and fit you for the Winter-Ball.*

Thus you see, young Sparks, how the Stile and Method of Wooing is quite changed as well as the Language, since the days of our Fore-Fathers (of unhappy Memory, simple and plain Men as they were) who Courted and chose their Wives for their Modesty, Frugality, keeping at Home, Good-Housewifery, and other Oeconomical Virtues then in Reputation: And when the young Damsels were taught all these in the Country, and their Parents Houses, the Portion they brought was more in Virtue than Money, and she was a richer Match than one who could have brought a Million, and nothing else to commend her. The Presents which were made when all was concluded, were a Ring, a Necklace of Pearl, and perhaps another fair Jewel, the Bona paraphernalia[13] *of her prudent Mother, whose Nuptial Kirtle,*[14] *Gown and Petticoat lasted as many Anniversaries as the happy Couple liv'd together, and were at last bequeathed with a Purse of old Gold, Rose-Nobles, Spur-Royals, and Spankers,*[15] *as an House-Loom to her Grand Daughter.*

They had Cupboards of Ancient, Useful Plate, whole Chests of Damask for the Table, and store of fine Holland Sheets (white as the driven Snow) and fragrant of Rose and Lavender for the Bed; and the sturdy Oaken Bedstead, and Furniture of the House, lasted one whole Century; the Shovel-Board[16] *and other long Tables both in Hall and Parlour were as fixed as the Freehold; nothing was moveable save Joynt-Stools, the Black-Jacks,*[17] *Silver Tankards, and Bowls: And though many things fell out between the Cup and the Lip, when Nappy Ale,* March Beer, Metheglin, Malmesey,[18] *and Old Sherry, got the Ascendant amongst the Blew-Coats, and Badges,*[19] *they sung Old*

[11] *Anglice:* In English.

[12] *good Meen:* Good mien, a good manner or countenance.

[13] *Bona paraphernalia:* The fine personal effects. In Medieval Latin, *paraphernalia* refers to a married woman's personal property, exclusive of her dowry.

[14] *Nuptial Kirtle:* A skirt worn as part of the wedding dress.

[15] *Rose-Nobles, Spur-Royals, and Spankers:* Outdated forms of currency.

[16] *Shovel-Board:* The table upon which the game of shovel-board, in which a coin was tossed along a board marked with transverse lines, was played.

[17] *Black-Jacks:* A large, tar-coated leather jug used for wine.

[18] *Metheglin, Malmesey:* Metheglin is a spiced or medicated form of mead, a liquor made of fermented honey. Malmsey is a strong, sweet wine.

[19] *Blew-Coats, and Badges:* Servants and other members of the lower orders traditionally wore blue coats. "Badges" here probably also refers metonymically to household retainers, whose affiliation was marked by badges on their clothes.

Symon, *and* Cheviot-Chase, *and danc'd brave* Arthur,[20] *and were able to draw a Bow, that made the Proud Monsieur Tremble at the Whizze of the Grey Goose-Feather: 'Twas then Ancient Hospitality was kept up in Town, and Country, by which the Tenants were enabled to pay their Landlords at punctual day: The Poor were Relieved bountifully, and Charity was as warm as the Kitchin, where the Fire was perpetual.*

In those happy days, Sure-Foot, the grave and steady Mare, carried the Good Knight, and his Courteous Lady behind him to Church, and to Visit the Neighbourhood; without so many Hell Carts, Ratling Coaches, and a crue of Damme-Lacqueys, *which a Grave Livery Servant or two supply'd, who Rid before and made way for his Worship.*

Things of Use were Natural, Plain, and Wholesome nothing was superfluous, nothing necessary wanting; and Men of Estate studied the Publick Good, and gave Example of true Piety, Loyalty, Justice, Sobriety, Charity, and the good Neighbourhood compos'd most differences: Perjury, Suborning Witnesses, Alimony, Avowed Adulteries, and Misses (publickly own'd) were Prodigies in those days, and Laws were Reason, not Craft, when Mens Titles were secure, and they served their Generation with Honour; left their Patrimonial Estates improv'd, to an Hopeful Heir, who passing from the Free-School to the Colledge, and thence to the Inns of Court,[21] acquainting himself with a competent Tincture of the Laws of his Country, followed the Example of his Worthy Ancestors; and if he Travell'd abroad, it was not to count Steeples, and bring home Feather, and Ribbon, and the Sins of other Nations; but to gain such Experience, as rendered him useful to his Prince and Country upon occasion, and confirm'd him in the Love of both of 'em above any other.

The Virgins and Young Ladies of that Golden Age quæsierunt lanam & linum;[22] *put their hands to the Spindle, nor disdain'd they the Needle; were obsequious, and helpful to their Parents; instructed*

---

[20] *sung Old Symon, and Cheviot-Chase, and danc'd brave Arthur:* "Old Symon" and "Cheviot-Chase" (or "Chevy Chase") are traditional ballads; "brave Arthur" is probably also a traditional song and the dance that accompanied it.

[21] *Inns of Court:* The four Inns of Court were housed along Fleet Street in London. Originally owned by the medieval religious and military order the Knights Templar, who built their residence there in the twelfth century, this series of buildings, known collectively as the Temple, was presented by James I to lawyers for their professional use. It housed both residential and professional legal apartments.

[22] *quæsierunt lanam & linum:* They seek out wool and flax.

*in the Managery of the Family, and gave Presages of making excellent Wives; nor then did they Read so many Romances, see so many Plays, and smutty Farces; set up for Visits, and have their days of Au*dience, *and Idle pass-time. Honest* Gleek, Ruff *and* Honours,[23] *diverted the Ladies at* Christmas, *and they knew not so much as the Names of* Ombre, Comet, *and* Basset.[24] *Their Retirements were Devout and Religious Books, and their Recreations in the Distillatory, the knowledge of Plants and their Virtues, for the comfort of their poor Neighbours, and use of the Family, which wholsome plain Dyet, and Kitching Physick, preserved in perfect Health: In those days, the Scurvy, Spleen,*[25] &c. *were scarce heard of, till Foreign Drinks and Mixtures were wantonly introduc'd. Nor were the young Gentlewomen so universally afflicted with Hysterical Fits*[26]; *nor, though extreamly modest, at all Melancholy, or less Gay, and in good Humour; they could touch the Lute, and Virginal,*[27] *sing like to the Damask Rose—and their Breath was as sweet as their Voices: They danc'd the* Canarys, Spanish Pavan, *and* Selengers Round *upon Sippets*[28] *with as much Grace and Loveliness, as any* Isaac, Monsieur, *or* Italian *of them all, can Teach with his Fop-call, and Apish Postures.*

To shew you then, how the World is alter'd among us, since Foreign Manners, the Luxury (more than Asiatick, *which was the final Ruine of the Greatest, Wisest, and most Noble Monarchy*[29] *upon Earth) has universally obtain'd among us, corrupting ancient simplicity; and in what extravagant Form the young Gallant we describ'd, is to Court the Sex, and make his Addresses (whether his Expedition be for Marriage or Mistress) it has been thought good by some Chari-*

---

[23] *Honest Gleek, Ruff and Honours:* Formerly fashionable card games. Ruff and Honours is also called Trump.

[24] *Ombre, Comet, and Basset:* Currently fashionable card games.

[25] *Scurvy, Spleen:* Scurvy is a disease of the gums and skin caused by vitamin C deficiency. The spleen (also the vapors, hypochondria) was a modish psychosomatic nervous disorder characterized by bad temper, ennui, and depression.

[26] *Hysterical Fits:* Fainting and crying fits, among the set of symptoms that characterize the vapors.

[27] *Lute, and Virginal:* By this time archaic, the lute and virginal were popular in the Renaissance. The lute is a stringed instrument, and the virginal, an early form of the harpsichord, is a small, legless rectangular keyboard instrument.

[28] *Canarys . . . Sippets:* The Canarys was a lively Spanish dance said to have been derived from the aborigines of the Canary Islands. The Pavan was a grave and stately dance introduced into England in the sixteenth century. The Sellengers Round was a country dance popular in England during the sixteenth and seventeenth centuries.

[29] *Noble Monarchy:* A reference to the rule of Alexander the Great (356–323 B.C.), which was corrupted, as his detractors claimed, by the influx of Persian manners and luxury into his court.

*table hands, that have contributed to this Catalogue, to present him
with an Enumeration of particulars, and Computation of the Charges
of the Adventurer, as follows.*

A Voyage to Maryland; or, the Ladies Dressing-Room.

> *Negotii sibi volet qui vim parare,*
> *Navim, & Mulierem, hæc duo comparato.*
> *Nam nullæ magis Res duæ plus Negotii*
> *Habent, forte si occeperis exornare.*
> *Neque unquam satis hæ duæ Res ornantur.*
> *Neque eis ulla ornandi satis satietas est.*
> > Plaut. Poenulus. Act. I. Scen. 2.[1]

Whoever has a mind to abundance of trouble,
Let him furnish himself with a Ship and a Woman,
For no two things will find you more Employment,
If once you begin to rig them out with all their Streamers,
Nor are they ever sufficiently adorned,
Or satisfy'd, that you have done enough to set them forth.

He that will needs to *Marry-Land*
Adventure, first must understand
For's [for his] Bark, what Tackle to prepare,
Gainst Wind and Weather, wear and tare:
Of Point *d'Espagne* a rich *Cornet*°   5
Two *Night-Rails*, and a *Scarf* beset
With a great Lace, a *Colleret.*°
One black Gown of Rich Silk, which odd is
Without one Colour'd, Embroider'd *Bodice:*
Four Petticoats for Page to hold up,   10
Four short ones nearer to the Crup:°
Three *Manteaus,*° nor can Madam less

---

[1] *Negotii . . . Scen. 2.:* A passage from *Poenulus* (*The Little Carthaginian*, 191 B.C.) by the Roman comic playwright Plautus: "A man who wants to make a lot of trouble for himself should get himself a ship and a woman, just these two things. For nothing is more trouble than these two things, if you happen to take on fitting them out. And there is no fitting them out satisfactorily enough to suffice" (ll. 210–14).
    5. *Of Point d'Espagne a rich Cornet:* A rich collar of Spanish lace.
    7. *Colleret:* See the *Fop-Dictionary.*
    11. *Crup:* The hindquarters, the rear.
    12. *Manteaus:* A style of woman's outer gown.

Provision have for due undress;
Nor *demy Sultane, Spagnolet,*°
Nor Fringe to sweep the Mall forget: 15
Of under Bodice three neat pair
Embroider'd, and of Shoos as fair:
Short under Petticoats pure fine,
Some of *Japan* Stuff, some of *Chine,*
With Knee-high Galoon° bottomed,   20
Another quilted White and Red;
With a broad *Flanders* Lace below:
Four pair of *Bas de soy*° shot through
With Silver, Diamond Buckles too,
For Garters, and as Rich for Shoo.   25
Twice twelve day Smocks of *Holland* fine,
With *Cambric* Sleeves, rich Point° to joyn,
(For she despises *Colbertine*°)
Twelve more for night, all *Flanders* lac'd,
Or else she'll think her self disgrac'd: 30
The same her Night-Gown must adorn,
With Two Point Wastcoats° for the Morn:
Of Pocket *Mouchoirs*° Nose to drain,
A dozen lac'd, a dozen plain:
Three Night-Gowns of rich *Indian* Stuff,°   35
Four Cushion-Cloths are scarce enough,
Of Point, and *Flanders,* not forget
Slippers embroidered on Velvet:
A *Manteau* Girdle, Ruby Buckle,
And *Brillant* Diamond Rings for Knuckle: 40
Fans painted, and perfumed three;
Three Muffs of *Sable, Ermine, Grey*°;
Nor reckon it among the Baubles,

---

14. *demy Sultane, Spagnolet:* See the *Fop-Dictionary.*
20. *Galoon:* A braid of metallic thread, here gold, used as an ornamental trimming on clothes.
23. *Bas de soy:* See the *Fop-Dictionary.*
26–27. *Holland . . . Point:* Smocks made of glazed linen with gauzy cambric sleeves, which are joined to the body of the gown by a fine lacing.
28. *Colbertine:* See the *Fop-Dictionary.*
32. *Two Point Wastcoats:* Vests joined by two points of laces.
33. *Mouchoirs:* Pocket handkerchieves.
35. *Indian Stuff:* Fabric from India, muslin.
42. *Sable, Ermine, Grey:* Furs; grey refers to the grey fox.

A *Palatine*° also of *Sables*.
A Saphire Bodkin for the Hair,   45
Or sparkling Facet Diamond there:
Then *Turquois*, *Ruby*, *Emrauld* Rings
For Fingers, and such petty things;
As Diamond Pendants for the Ears,
Must needs be had, or two Pearl Pears,   50
Pearl Neck-lace, large and Oriental,
And Diamond, and of Amber pale;
For Oranges bears every Bush,
Nor values she cheap things a rush.
Then Bracelets for her Wrists bespeak,   55
(Unless her Heart-strings you will break)
With Diamond *Croche*° for Breast and Bum,
Till to hang more on there's no room.
Besides these Jewels you must get
Cuff Buckles, and an handsom Set   60
Of Tags for Palatine, a curious Hasp
The Manteau 'bout her Neck to clasp:
Nor may she want a Ruby Locket,
Nor the fine sweet quilted Pocket;
To play at *Ombre*, or *Basset*,°   65
She a rich *Pulvil* Purse° must get,
With Guineas fill'd, on Cards to lay,
With which she fancies most to play:
Nor is she troubled at ill fortune,
For should the bank be so importune,   70
To rob her of her glittering Store,
The amorous Fop will furnish more.
Pensive and mute, behind her shoulder
He stands, till by her loss grown bolder,
Into her lap *Rouleau*° conveys,   75
The softest thing a Lover says:

44. *Palatine:* A tippet, or small stole, of sable, so called after the Princess Palatine, wife of the Duke of Orleans, who brought it into fashion in the later seventeenth century.
57. *Croche:* A hook.
65. *Ombre . . . Basset:* Fashionable card games.
66. *Pulvil Purse:* See the *Fop-Dictionary*. This powder was used on the body and on wigs.
75. *Rouleau:* A number of gold coins made up into a cylindrical packet.

She grasps it in her greedy hands,
Then best his Passion understands;
When tedious anguishing has fail'd,
Rouleau has constantly prevail'd.   80
But to go on where we left off,
Though you may think what's said enough;
This is not half that does belong
To the fantastick Female Throng:
In Pin-up Ruffles now she flaunts,   85
About her Sleeves are *Engageants*:°
Of Ribbon, various *Echelles*,°
Gloves trimm'd, and lac'd as fine as *Nell*'s,°
Twelve dozen *Martial*,° whole, and half,
Of *Jonquil, Tuberose*, (don't laugh)   90
Frangipan, Orange, Violett,
Narcissus, Jassemin, Ambrett:
And some of *Chicken* skin° for night,
To keep her Hands plump, soft, and white:
Mouches for pushes,° to be sure,   95
From *Paris* the *tré-fine* procure,
And *Spanish* Paper,° Lip, and Cheek,
With Spittle sweetly to belick:
Nor therefore spare the next place,
The Pocket *Sprunking* Looking-Glass;°   100
Calembuc Combs° in *Pulvil* case,
To set, and trim the Hair and Face:
And that the Cheeks may both agree,
Plumpers° to fill the Cavity.
The *Settée, Cuple* place aright,   105
Frelange, Fontange, Favorite;
Monté la haut, and *Palisade*,

86. *Engageants:* See the *Fop-Dictionary*.
87. *Echelles:* See the *Fop-Dictionary*.
88. *Nell's:* Eleanor (Nell) Gwyn (1650–1687), an actress and mistress of Charles II.
89. *Martial:* See the *Fop-Dictionary*. This passage describes various kinds of perfumed gloves.
93. *Chicken skin:* For softening the hands.
95. *Mouches for pushes:* Patches to cover up pimples. See the *Fop-Dictionary* for *Mouches*.
97. *Spanish Paper:* See the *Fop-Dictionary*.
100. *Pocket Sprunking Looking-Glass:* See the *Fop-Dictionary*.
101. *Calembuc Combs:* See the *Fop-Dictionary*.
104. *Plumpers:* See the *Fop-Dictionary*.

Sorti, Flandan, (great helps to Trade)
Burgoigne, Jardiné, Cornett,
Frilal° next upper Pinner set,   110
Round which it does our Ladies please
To spread the Hood call'd *Rayonnés*:
Behind the Noddle every Baggage
Wears bundle *Choux,* in *English* Cabbage.
Nor *Cruches* she, nor *Confidents,*   115
Nor *Passagers* nor *Bergers*° wants;
And when this Grace Nature denies,
An Artificial *Tour* supplies;
All which with *Meurtriers*° unite,
And *Creve-Cœurs*° silly Fops to smite,   120
Or take in Toil at *Park*° or *Play,*
Nor Holy *Church* is safe, they say,
Where decent Veil was wont to hide
The modest Sex Religious Pride:
Lest these yet prove too great a Load,   125
'Tis all compris'd in the *Commode*;°
Pins tipt with Diamond Point, and head,
By which the Curls are fastened,
In radiant *Firmament* set out,
And over all the Hood *sur-tout*:°   130
Thus Face that *Erst* near head was plac'd
Imagine now about the Wast,
for *Tour* on *Tour,* and *Tire* on *Tire,*
Like Steeple *Bow,* or *Grantham* Spire,
Or *Septizonium* once at *Rome,*°   135
(But does not half so well become
Fair Ladies Head) you here behold
Beauty by Tyrant Mode controll'd.
The graceful *Oval,* and the *Round,*

105–10. *Settée . . . Frilal:* All various modes of dressing the head. See the *Fop-Dictionary.*
116. *Passagers nor Bergers:* Ways of curling the hair. See the *Fop-Dictionary.*
181–19. *Tour . . . Meurtriers:* Hairstyles. See the *Fop-Dictionary.*
120. *Creve-Cœurs:* See the *Fop-Dictionary.*
121. *Park:* St. James's Park, the oldest of London's royal parks and a resort of the sovereign and the court through the Restoration.
126. *Commode:* See the *Fop-Dictionary.*
130. *sur-tout:* See the *Fop-Dictionary.*
135. *Septizonium once at Rome:* See the *Fop-Dictionary.*

This *House* Tire does quite confound;   140
And Ears like *Satyr*, Large and Raw,
And bony Face, and hollow Jaw;
This monstrous Dress does now reveal
Which well plac'd Curles did once conceal.
Besides all these, 'tis always meant   145
You furnish her Appartment,
With *Moreclack* Tapistry,° Damask Bed,
Or Velvet richly embroidered:
Branches, *Brasero*, *Cassolets*,
A *Cofre fort*,° and Cabinets,   150
Vases of Silver, *Procelan*, store
To set, and range about the Floor:
The Chimney Furniture of Plate,
(For Iron's now quite out of date:)
Tea-Table, *Skreens*, Trunks, and Stand,   155
Large Looking-Glass richly *Japan'd*,°
An hanging Shelf, to which belongs
Romances, Plays, and Amorous Songs;
Repeating Clocks, the hour to show,
When to the Play 'tis time to go,   160
In Pompous Coach, or else Sedan'd ⎫
With Equipage along the *Strand*,   ⎬
And with her new *Beau* Foppling mann'd. ⎭
A new Scene to us next presents,
The Dressing-Room, and Implements,   165
Of Toilet Plate Gilt, and Emboss'd,
And several other things of Cost:
The Table *Mirror*, one Glue Pot,
One for *Pomatum*, and what not?
Of *Washes*, *Unguents*, and *Cosmeticks*,   170
A pair of Silver Candlesticks;
Snuffers, and Snuff-dish, Boxes more,
For Powders, Patches, Waters store,
In silver Flasks, or Bottles, Cups
Cover'd, or open, to wash Chaps;   175

---

147. *Moreclack Tapistry:* Morteclacke or Mortlake; a kind of tapestry woven in
the town of Mortlake in Surrey, England, in the early seventeenth century.
    149–50. *Brasero, Cassolets,* / *A Cofre fort:* See the *Fop-Dictionary.*
    156. *Japan'd:* Decorated with lacquer work.

Nor may *Hungarian* Queen's be wanting,
Nor store of Spirits against fainting:°
Of other waters rich, and sweet,
To sprinkle Handkerchief is meet;
D'Ange, Orange, Mill-Fleur, Myrtle,°   180
Whole Quarts the Chamber to bequirtle:
Of essence *rare, & le meilleure*°
From *Rome*, from *Florence, Montpellier,*
In *Filgran Casset*° to repel,
When Scent of *Gousset*° does rebel,   185
Though powder'd *Allom*° be as good
Well strew'd on, and well understood;
For Vapours that offend the Lass,
Of *Sal-armoniack*° a Glass:
Nor Brush for Gown, nor Oval Salver,   190
Nor Pincushion, nor Box of Silver,
Baskets of *Fil gran,*° long and round,
Or if *Japonian* to be found,
And the whole Town so many yield,
Calembuc Combs by dozens fill'd   195
You must present, and a world more,
She's a poor Miss can count her store.
The Working Apron too from *France*,
Will all its trim Apurtenance;
Loo Masks, and whole, as Wind do blow,   200
And Miss abroad's dispos'd to go:
Hoods by whole dozens, White and Black, ⎫
And store of Coiffs° she must not lack, ⎬
Nor Velvet Scarfs about her Back,   ⎭
To keep her warm; all these at least   205
In *Amber'd* Skins, or quilted Chest
Richly perfum'd, she Lays, and rare

176–77. *Hungarian Queen's . . . Spirits against fainting:* A reference to Hungary water, a distilled infusion of herbs taken as a tonic and used as a cosmetic wash.
180. *D'Ange . . . Myrtle:* Types of toilet water.
182. *rare, & le meilleure:* See the *Fop-Dictionary.*
184. *Filgran Casset:* See the *Fop-Dictionary.*
185. *Scent of Gousset:* Probably a scent created by a perfumer named Gousset.
186. *Allom:* Alum.
189. *Sal-armoniack:* Sal ammoniac, ammonium chloride.
192. *Baskets of Fil gran:* See the *Fop-Dictionary.*
203. *Coiffs:* Caps.

Powders for Garments, some for Hair
Of *Cyprus*, and of *Corduba*,
And the Rich *Polvil* of *Goa*:   210
Nor here omit the Bob of Gold
Which a *Pomander* Ball does hold,
This to her side she does attach
With Gold *Crochet*, or *French Pennache*,°
More useful far then *Ferula*,°   215
For any saucy Coxcomb's Jaw:
A graceful Swing to this belongs,
Which he returns in Cringe, and Songs,
And languishings to kiss the hand,
That can Perfumed blows command.   220
All these, and more in order set,
A large rich Cloth of Gold *Toilet*
Does cover, and to put up Rags,
Two high Embroider'd Sweet Bags,
Or a large Perfum'd *Spanish* Skin,°   225
To wrap up all these Trinkets in.
But I had almost quite forgot,
A *Tea* and *Chocolate* Pot,
With *Molionet*,° and Caudle Cup,
Restoring Breakfast to sup up: 230
Porcelan Saucers, Spoons of Gold,
Dishes that refin'd Sugars hold;
Pastillios de Bocca° we
In Box of beaten Gold do see,
Inchas'd with Diamonds, and *Tweeze*   235
As Rich and Costly as all these,
To which a bunch of *Onyxes*,
And many a Golden Seal there dangles,
Mysterious Cyphers, and new fangles.
Gold is her Toothpick, Gold her Watch is,   240
And Gold is every thing she touches
But tir'd with numbers I give o're,

214. *Gold Crochet . . . French Pennache:* See the *Fop-Dictionary.*
215. *Ferula:* See the *Fop-Dictionary.*
225. *Spanish Skin:* Cordovan leather made of goatskin.
229. *Molionet:* See the *Fop-Dictionary.*
233. *Pastillios de Bocca:* Candies, bonbons.

Arithmetick can add no more,
Thus Rigg'd the Vessel, and Equipp'd,
She is for all Adventures Shipp'd,   245
And Portion e're the year goes round,
Does with her Vanity confound.

The Fop-Dictionary.
Or,
An Alphabetical Catalogue of the hard and foreign Names, and Terms of the Art *COSMETICK*, &c. together with their Interpretations, for Instruction of the Unlearned.

Attache.
Any thing which fastens to another, &c.

Bas de soye shot through.
Silk Stockings with Gold, or Silver thread wove into the Clock.

Berger.
A plain small Lock (*a la Shepherdesse*) turn'd up with a Puff.

Bourgoigne.
The first part of the Dress for the Head next the Hair.

Branches.
Hanging Candlesticks, like those used in Churches.

Brasiere.
A large Vessel, or moving-Hearth of Silver for Coals, transportable into any Room, much used in *Spain*.

Calumbuc.
A certain precious Wood, of an agreeable Scent, brought from the *Indies*.

Campaine.
A kind of narrow picked Lace.

Casset.
A Dressing Box.

Cassolet.
Perfuming Pot or Censer.

Choux.
The great round Boss or Bundle, resembling a Cabbage from whence the *French* give it that name.

Cifre-fort.

A strong Box of some precious or hard wood, &c. bound with gilded Ribs.

Colbertine.

A Lace resembling Net-work, of the Fabrick of Monsieur *Colbert*, Superintendent of the *French* Kings Manufactures.

Collaret.

A sort of Gorget.

Commode.

A Frame of Wire, cover'd with Silk, on which the whole Head-Attire is adjusted at once upon a *Bust*, or property of Wood carved to the Breasts, like that which Perruque-makers set upon their Stalls.

Confidants.

Smaller *Curles* near the Ears.

Cornet.

The upper *Pinner*, dangling about the Cheeks, like *Hounds Ears*.

Cosmeticks.

Here used for any Effeminate Ornament, also artificial Complections and Perfumes.

Creve-cœur.

Heart-breakers, the two small curl'd Locks at the Nape of the Neck.

Crochet.

The Hook to which are chain'd the Ladies Watch, Seals, and other *Intaglias*, &c.

Cruches.

Certain smaller Curles, placed on the Forehead.

Cuppée.

A kind of Pinner.

Echelles.

A Pectoral, or Stomacher lac'd with Ribbon, like the rounds of a Ladder.

Engageants.

Deep double Ruffles, handing down to the Wrists.

Favorites.

Locks dangling on the Temples.

Ferula.
An Instrument of Wood us'd for Correction of lighter faults, more sensibly known to School-Boys than to Ladies.

Fil-grain'd.
Dressing-Boxes, Baskets, or whatever else is made of Silver Wire-work.

Flandan.
A kind of Pinner joyning with the *Bonnet*.

Firmament.
Diamonds, or other precious Stones heading the *Pins* which they stick in the *Tour*, and Hair, like Stars.

Frelan.
Bonnet and Pinner together.

Font-Ange.
The Top-knot, so call'd from *Mademoiselle de Fontange*, one of the *French* King's Mistresses, who first wore it.

Gris.
The Grey Furr of Squirrels bellies.

Japonian.
Any thing Varnish'd with *Laccar*, or *China* Polishing, or that is old or fantastical.

Jardinée.
That single *Pinner* next the *Bourgogne*.

Loo Maske.
An half Mask.

Martial.
The Name of a famous *French* Perfumer, emulateing the *Frangipani* of *Rome*.

Miroir.
In general, any Looking-Glass; but here, for the Table, Toilet, or Pocket *Sprunking*-Glass.

Molionet.
The Instrument us'd to mingle *Chocolate* with the Water.

Monte la haut.
Certain degrees of Wire to raise the Dress.

Mouchoire.

It were Rude, Vulgar, and Uncourtly to call it Handkerchief.

Mouches.

Flies, or, Black Patches, by the Vulgar.

Meurtrieres.

Murderers; a certain Knot in the Hair, which ties and unites the Curls.

Palatine.

Formerly call'd *Sables*, or *Tippet*, because made of the Tails of that Animal.

Palisade.

A Wire sustaining the Hair next to the *Dutchess*, or first Knot.

Passagere.

A Curl'd Lock next the Temples.

Pastillo di Bocca.

Perfum'd Lozenges to improve the Breath.

Pennache.

Any Bunch or Tassel of small Ribbon.

Plumpers.

Certain very thin, round, and light Balls, to plump out, and fill up the Cavities of the Cheeks, much us'd by old Court-Countesses.

Polvil.

The *Portugal* term for the most exquisite Powders and Perfumes.

Raggs.

A Compendious Name generally us'd for all sorts of Point, Lace, &c. whence the Women who bring them to Ladies Chambers are call'd *Ragg*-Women; but whilst in their Shops, Exchange-Women.

Rare, le meilleures.

Best, and most Excellent; but in *Language de beau, rare & le meilleure*, happily rhyming with *Montpellier*.

Rayonné.

Upper Hood, pinn'd in Circle, like the *Sun-Beams*.

Rouleau.

Is Forty Nine Guineas, made up in a Paper Roll, which *Monsier F——— Sir J———* and Father *B———* lend to losing Gamesters, that are good Men, and have Fifty in Return.

Ruffles.

By our Fore-fathers call'd Cuffs.

Settée.

The double Pinner.

Sorti.

A little Knot of small Ribbon, peeping out between the Pinner and Bonnet.

Septizonium.

A very high Tower in *Rome*, built by the Emperour *Severus*,[1] of Seven Ranks of Pillars, set one upon the other, and diminishing to the Top, like the Ladies new Dress for their Heads, which was the mode among the *Roman* Dames, and is exactly describ'd by *Juvenal*[2] in his *6th* Satyr.

> Such Rows of Curles press'd on each other lye,
> She builds her Head so many Stories high,
> That look on her before, and you would swear
> *Hector*'s tall Wife *Andromache* she were,
> Behind a Pigmy ———.

Spanish Paper.

A beautiful red Colour, which the Ladies, *&c.* in *Spain* paint their Faces withal.

Spagnolet.

A kind of narrow-sleev'd Gown, *a la Spagnole.*[3]

Sprunking.

A *Dutch* term for Pruning, Tiffing, Trimming, and setting out, by the Glass or Pocket *Miroir.*

Sultane.

A Gown trimm'd with Buttons, and Loops.

Surtout.

A Night-Hood covering the entire Dress.

Toilet.

Corruptly call'd the *Twilight*, but originally signifying a little Cloth.

Tour.

An artificial Dress of Hair on the Forehead, *&c.*

Tré fine.

Langage de beau. Extreamly fine, and delicate, *cum multis, aliis.*

---

[1] *Severus:* Lucius Septimus Severus (146–211) was emperor of Rome from 193 to 211.
[2] *Juvenal:* Juvenal (60?–140?) was a satirist who wrote against the corruption and luxury of the Roman elite.
[3] *a la Spagnole:* In the Spanish style.

For besides these, there are a world more, as *Assasin*, or *Venez a moy*, A certain Breast-knot, as much as to say, Come to me, Sir, *&c.*

Dutchesse. A Knot next the Hair, immediately above the *Tour*, *&c.* with innumerable others now obsolete, and for the present out of use; but we confine our selves to those in *Vogue.*

To conclude, Those who have the curiosity, by comparing these Terms with the Ancients, thereby to inform themselves, how this elegant Science is improv'd, especially since we have submitted to, and still continue under the Empire of the *French*, (for want of some *Royal* or Illustrious Ladies Invention and Courage, to give the Law of the *Mode* to her own Country, and to Vindicate it from Foreign Tyranny) may for Divine History consult *Isaiah 6th ch. ver.* 16, *&c.* and for Prophane, read *Plautus* his *Poenulus, Act.* 1. *Scen.* 2. and his *Aulularia, Act.* 3. *Scen.* 5.

Mundus Foppensis (*The World of Foppery*)

A rebuttal to Mary Evelyn's satire on female vanity in her *Mundus Muliebris* (1690; see p. 584), the anonymous, probably female, author of *Mundus Foppensis* launches an attack on male vanity that takes up the themes of masculinity, effeminacy, and modishness so apparent in *Tatler* Nos. 26 and 166 and *Spectator* No. 275, in Ward's "Beau's Club" and "Mollies' Club," and in the characters of the beau sketched by Ward and Mrs. Crackenthorpe. The argument here is that men have abandoned women, that they have indeed taken on many of the roles and attitudes of women and so sacrificed their masculinity to an effeminacy bred by French fashion and corrupt urban high life.

... Now let us then the *Beau* survey,   5
Has he no Baubles to display:
There's first the *Dango*, and the *Snake*,°
Those *Dildoes* in the Nape of Neck;
That dangle down behind, to shew
Dimensions of the *Snake* below: 10
'Tis thick, and long; but pizzl'd at th' end,

7. *Dango . . . Snake:* Styles of curls men wore down their necks.

And would be thought the Woman's Friend:
Yet they who many times have try'd,
By *Dango* swear the *Snake* bely'd.
Then th' insignificant *Knee-Rowl*,° 15
A mere *Whim-wham*, upon my Soul;
For that 'twas never made, I fear,
To save the Master's Knees at Prayer:
Which being worn o'th' largest size,
That Man *Rolls* full, the Bully cries. 20
A Term of Art for Knees Concinnity,°
Beyond the Sense of School-Divinity.
　　What *Beau* himself would so unman,
To ride in scandalous Sedan?°
A Carriage only fit for Midwives, 25
That of their Burthens go to rid Wives;
Unless to hide, from Revelation,
Th' Adulterer's haste to Assignation.
　　What Dunces are our Tonsors° grown,
Where's their Gold Filings in an Amber Box, 30
To strew upon their Masters Locks,
And make 'em glitter in the Sun?
Sure English *Beaus* may out-vie *Venus*,
As well as *Commodus*, or *Gallienus*.°
'Twas Goldilocks, my lovely Boy, 35
Made *Agamemnon* ruine *Troy*.°
　　I could produce ye Emperours
That sate in Womens Dress whole hours,
Expos'd upon the publick Stage
Their Catamites, Wives by Marr'age. 40

---

15. *Knee-Rowl:* A style calling for rolled fabric at the knees of a man's britches.
21. *Concinnity:* Elegance.
24. *Sedan:* Chair in which individuals were carried through the city streets.
29. *Tonsors:* Barbers.
34. *Commodus . . . Gallienus:* Two Roman emperors. Commodus (161–192), the son of Marcus Aurelius, was despotic, cruel, and ultimately mad. When insane, he dressed up as the god Hercules, whom he believed himself to be. Gallienus (218–268) had a less infamous career, though he ruled at a time when the empire was disintegrating under the pressure of foreign invasion.
36. *Agamemnon ruine Troy:* In Greek legend, Agamemnon was the King of Macedon and leader of the Greek forces against Troy. "Goldilocks" is Helen of Troy, the wife of Agamemnon's brother Menelaus. Helen's abduction by the Trojan prince, Paris, started the Trojan War.

Your old Trunk-hose are laid aside,
For what-d'-ye-call-em's Tail to hide;
So strait and close upon the Skin,
As onely made for Lady's Eyne;
To see the shape of Thighs and Groin: 45
Hard case *Priapus°* should be so restrain'd,
That had whole Orchards at command.
Yet these are Toys, in Men, more wise,
To Womens innocent Vanities.
While soft Sir *Courtly Nice°* looks great,   50
With the unmortgag'd Rents of his Estate:
What is the Learning he adores,
But the Discourse of Pimps and Whores?
She who can tye, with quaintest Art,
The spruce Cravat-string,° wins his Heart;   55
Where that same Toy does not exactly sit,
He's not for common Conversation fit,
How is the Barber held Divine,
That can a Perriwig *Carine!°*
Or else *Correct* it; which you please;   60
For these are *Terms* too, now-a-days,
Of modern Gallants to entice
The Barber to advance his Price:
For if a Barber be not dear,
He must not cover Coxcomb's Ear.   65
    Bless us! what's there? 'tis something walks,
A piece of Painting, and yet speaks:
Hard Case to blame the Ladies Washes,
When Men are come to mend their Faces.
Yet some there are such Women grown,   70
They cann't be by their Faces known:
Some wou'd be like the fair *Adonis*;°
Some would be *Hyacinthus°* Cronies;

---

46. *Priapus:* In Greek and Roman mythology, Priapus is the personification of the erect phallus, the god of procreation, the guardian of gardens and vineyards.

50. *Sir Courtly Nice:* Any foppish courtier.

55. *Cravat-string:* Necktie.

59. *a Perriwig Carine:* Order a perriwig from a wigmaker.

72. *Adonis:* In Greek mythology, Adonis was a beautiful young man whom Aphrodite loved.

73. *Hyacinthus:* In Greek mythology, a beautiful young man loved by Apollo but killed by accident. The hyacinth flower sprang up from his blood.

And then they study wanton use
Of Spanish Red, and white Ceruse;°   75
The only Painters to the Life,
That seem with Natures self at strife;
As if she only the dead Colours laid,
But they the Picture perfect made.
What *Zeuxis*° dare provoke these Elves,   80
That to out-doe him paint themselves?
For tho' the Birds his painted Grapes did crave,
These paint and all Mankind deceive.
This sure must spend a World of Morning,
More than the Ladies quick adorning;   85
They have found out a shorter way,
Not as before, to wast the day;
They only comb, wash hands and face,
And streightway, with a comely Grace,
On the admired *Helmet* goes,   90
As ready rigg'd as their lac'd Shoes.
Far much more time Men trifling wast,
E'er their soft Bodies can be drest;
The Looking-Glass hangs just before,
And each o'th' Legs requires an hour: 95
Now thereby, Ladies, hangs a Tale,
A Story for your Cakes and Ale.
A certain *Beau* was lately dressing,
But sure, e'er he had crav'd Heavens Blessing;
When in comes Friend, and finds him laid   100
In mournfull plight, upon his Bed.
Dear *Tom*, quoth he, such a Mischance
As ne'er befell the Foes of *France*;
Nay, I must tell thee, *Fleury* Battel°
Was ne'er to *Europe* half so fatal;   105
For by I know not what ill luck,

75. *Spanish Red, and white Ceruse:* Types of cosmetic coloring. Spanish Red is also called "Spanish Paper" and was used as a rouge or blusher. Ceruse is a white lead pigment used as a foundation on the face.

80. *Zeuxis:* A fifth-century B.C. Athenian painter, reputedly the first to use shading. His pictures were said to be so realistic that birds tried to eat the grapes from one of them.

104. *Fleury Battel:* The Battle of Fleurus occurred in 1690 during the Nine Years War. The English and their allies were defeated by French forces.

My Glass this Morn fell down and broke
Upon my Shin, just in my Rolling;°
Now is not this worth thy condoling?
See Stocking cut, and bloody Shin,   110
Besides the Charge of healing Skin.
'Twas the only Kindness of my Fate,
It mist the solid Piece, my Pate.
    Ladies, this was ill luck, but you
Have much the worser of the two;   115
The World is chang'd I know not how,
For Men kiss Men, not Women now;
And your neglected Lips in vain,
Of smugling *Jack*, and *Tom* complain:
A most unmanly nasty Trick;   120
One Man to lick the other's Cheek;
And only what renews the shame
Of *J.* the first, and *Buckingham*:
He, true it is, his Wives Embraces fled
To slabber his lov'd *Ganimede*;°   125
But to employ, those Lips were made
For Women in *Gomorrha*'s° Trade;
Bespeaks the Reason ill design'd,
Of railing thus 'gainst Woman-kind:
For who that loves as Nature teaches,   130
That had not rather kiss the Breeches
Of Twenty Women, than to lick
The Bristles of one Male dear *Dick*?
    Now wait on *Beau* to his *Alsatia*,
A Place that loves no *Dei Gratia*;°   135
Where the Undoers live, and Undone,
In *London*, separate from *London*;
Where go but Three Yards from the street,

---

108. *Rolling:* Of his britches at the knees; see note for line 15.
123–25. *J. the first, and Buckingham . . . Ganimede:* George Villiers, First Duke of
Buckingham (1592–1628), was a royal favorite, and indeed the lover of King James I,
who more or less ruled England during the last years of James's reign and the first of
Charles I's. In Greek mythology, the beautiful young man Ganymede was Zeus's cup
bearer and his favorite.
127. *Gomorrha:* In the Old Testament, Gomorrah was one of the five notoriously
sinful "cities of the plain" destroyed by "brimstone and fire" (Genesis 19:24).
135. *Dei Gratia:* By the grace of God.

And you with a new Language° meet:
Prig, Prigster, Bubble, Caravan,   140
Pure Tackle, Buttock, Purest pure.
Sealers, Putts, Equipp, and *Bolter;*
Lug out, Scamper, rub and *scowre.*
Ready, Rhino, Coal, and *Darby,*
Meggs, and *Smelts,* and *Hoggs,* and *Decus;*   145
Tathers, Fambles, Tatts and *Doctors,*
Bowsy, Smoaky, Progg, and *Cleare,*
Bolter, Banter, Cut a shamm;
With more a great deal of the same.
Should *Saffold°* make but half this Rattle,   150
When Maidens visit his O-racle,
They'd take him for some Son of *Cham,°*
Calling up Legion by his Name.
  Add but to this the Flanty-Tant°
Of Fopling Al-a-mode Gallant;   155
Why should not *Gris,* or *Jardine,*
Be as well allow'd as *Bien gaunte;°*
Cloaths is a paltry Word *Ma foy;*
But Grandeur in the French *Arroy.*
Trimming's damn'd English, but *le Grass*   160
Is that which must for Modish pass.
To call a Shoe a Shoe, is base;
Let the genteel *Picards* take Place.
Hang *Perriwig,* 'tis only fit
For Barbers Tongues that ne'er spoke Wit;   165
But if you'd be i'th' Fashion, choose
The far politer Term, *Chedreux*
What Clown is he that proudly moves,

---

139. *new Language:* The italicized words that follow are examples of contemporary seventeenth-century street slang, or, as it was then called, "cant."
  150. *Saffold:* Thomas Saffold (d. 1691) was a quack doctor.
  152. *Son of Cham:* A descendant of Ham (Cham), one of Noah's three sons. Genesis 9:20–27 tells how Noah cursed Ham and his descendants after Ham dishonored Noah by looking on his nakedness. Noah's sons, Shem, Japheth, and Ham, are often seen as the progenitors of three races of mankind; Ham's is then the accursed race.
  154. *Flanty-Tant:* Nonsense.
  156–57. *Gris ... Jardine ... Bien gaunte:* Why shouldn't one be able to use the French words for gray (*gris*) or garden (*jardine*), as well as for the expression, "fashionable in his gloves" (*bien gaunte*). What follows is a series of English words and their French equivalents.

With on his hands what we call Gloves?
No Friend, for more refin'd converse   170
Will tell ye they are *Orangers*.
So strangely does *Parisian* Air
Change English Youth, that half a year
Makes 'em forget all Native Custome,
To bring French Modes, and *Gallic*° Lust home;   175
Nothing will these Apostates please,
But *Gallic* Health, and French Disease.
In French their Quarrels, and their Fears,
Their Joys they publish, and their Cares;
In French they quarrel, and in French   180
Mon coeur,° they cry, to paltry Wench.
    Why then should these Extravagants
Make such Rhime-doggeril Complaints
Against the Ladies Dressing-Rooms,
And closets stor'd with rich Perfumes?   185
There's nothing there but what becomes
The Plenty of a fair Estate:
Tho' Chimney Furniture of Plate,
Tho' Mortlake Tapestry,° Damask-Bed;
Or Velvet all Embroidered;   190
Tho' they affect a handsome store,
Of part for State, of usefull more;
They're Glories not to be deny'd
To Women, stopping there their Pride;
For such a Pride has nothing ill,   195
But only makes them more genteel.
Should Nature these fine Toys produce,
And Women be debarr'd the use?
These are no Masculine Delights;
Studies of Books for Men are sights;   200
A Stable with good Horses stor'd,
And Payment punctual to their Word:
Proportion these things to my Wishes,
Let Women take the Porcelan Dishes;

175. *Gallic:* French.
181. *Mon coeur:* "My heart," a term of romantic endearment.
189. *Mortlake Tapestry:* A kind of tapestry woven in the town of Mortlake in Surrey, England, in the early seventeenth century.

The Toylet Plates gilt and embost, 205
With all the rest of little cost:
Such small Diffusion feeds the Poor,
While Misers hoard up all their store.
  Our Satyr then was one of those
Who ne'er had Wealth at his dispose; 210
Or being sped to live in Plenty,
Posted to find his Coffers empty;
Addicted all to sport and Gaming,
And that same Vice not worth the naming;
Till deeply dipp'd in Us'rers° Books, 215
And over-rid by Cheats and Rooks,°
The *Mint*° becomes his Sanctuary,
Where not of his past Errors weary,
But aged grown, and impotent,
Alike in Purse and Codpiece spent, 220
He *Cynic* turns, in *King's-Bench* Tub,°
And vents the Froth of Brewers Bub:
Where we will leave him melancholly,
Bewailing Poverty, and Folly.

A Short *Supplement* to the *Fop-Dictionary*, so far as concerns the present Matter.

Adieu donce me Cheres.
Farewell my dear Friends.

Arroy.
A Suit of Cloaths.

To adjust a Man's self.
That is, to dress himself.

Beau.
A Masculine French Adjective, signifying fine; but now naturaliz'd into *English* to denote a sparkish dressing Fop.

---

215. *Us'rers:* Usurers were moneylenders who charged exorbitant interest.
216. *Rooks:* A con artist, a cheat.
217. *The Mint:* The site of a mint established at Suffolk Place in London around 1543 by Henry VIII. The mint itself was demolished in 1557. The area was a recognized sanctuary for debtors and thieves up through the early eighteenth century.
221. *King's-Bench Tub:* King's Bench Prison in Southwark, mostly populated by debtors.

Beaux Esprits.
A Club of Wits, who call'd themselves so.

Bachique.
A Drinking Song or Catch.

The Brilliant of Language.
Sharpness and wittiness of Expression.

A Brandenburgh.
A Morning Gown.

To Carine a Perriwig.
That is, to order it.

Chedreux.
A Perriwig.

Correct.
The same as *Carine.*

Deshabille.
Undrest, or rather in a careless Dress.

En Cavalier.
Like a Gentleman.

Esclat.
Of Beauty, or the Lustre of Beauty.

Eveille.
I observ'd her more *Eveille* than other Women; that is, more sprightly and airey.

Equipt.
That is, well furnish'd with Money and Cloaths.

Gaunte Bien Gaunte.
Modish in his Gloves.

Grossier.
The World is very *Grossier*; that is, very dull, and ill bred.

Levee and *Couchee.*
Is to attend a Gentleman at his rising or going to Bed.

Le Grass.
The Furniture of a Suit.

Orangers.
The Term for Gloves scented with Oranges.

Picards.
Shoes in downright English.

Pulvillio.

Sweet Powder for the Hair.

Rolls.

A sort of Dress for the Knees, invented as some say by the Roman Catholicks, for the conveniency of Kneeling, but others ascribe the lucky Fancy to Coll. *S——*.

A Revoir.

Till I see you again.

Surtout.

The great Coat which covers all.

For the rest you are referr'd to the Dilucidations of the *Alsatian* Squire.

Selected Bibliography

This bibliography is divided into two parts, "Works Cited" and "Suggestions for Further Reading." The first part contains all primary and secondary works quoted or discussed in the general or chapter introductions. The second part is a selective list of materials that will be useful to students who want to know more. With one or two exceptions, a book or article that appears in "Works Cited" is not recorded again under "Suggestions for Further Reading." Thus, both lists should be consulted.

Works Cited

Brown, Laura. *Alexander Pope*. Rereading Literature Series. Ed. Terry Eagleton. Oxford: Blackwell, 1985.

———. *Ends of Empire: Women and Ideology in Early Eighteenth-Century English Literature*. Ithaca: Cornell UP, 1993.

Defoe, Daniel. *The Complete English Tradesman*. 2 vols. 1726. Reprints of Economic Classics. New York: Augustus M. Kelley, 1969.

———. *The Life and Strange Surprizing Adventures of Robinson Crusoe*. 1719. Ed. J. Donald Crowley. The World's Classics. Oxford: Oxford UP, 1972.

Dickson, P. G. M. *The Financial Revolution in England: A Study in the Development of Public Credit*. London: Macmillan; New York: St. Martin's, 1967.

Eagleton, Terry. *The Function of Criticism: From* The Spectator *to Post-Structuralism.* London: Verso, 1984.

Etherege, George. *The Man of Mode.* Ed. W. B. Carnochan. Regents Restoration Drama Series. Lincoln: U of Nebraska P, 1966.

Habermas, Jürgen. *The Structural Transformation of the Public Sphere: An Inquiry into a Category of Bourgeois Society.* Trans. Thomas Burger with Frederick Lawrence. Studies in Contemporary German Social Thought. Cambridge: MIT P, 1989.

Hill, Christopher. *The Century of Revolution: 1603–1714.* London: Nelson, 1961.

Johnson, Samuel. *Life of Addison.* In *Lives of the English Poets.* With an Introduction by Arthur Waugh. London: Oxford UP, 1959. 399–449.

Laqueur, Thomas. *Making Sex: Body and Gender from the Greeks to Freud.* Cambridge: Harvard UP, 1990.

Lewis, C. S. "Addison." *Essays on the Eighteenth Century Presented to David Nichol Smith.* Oxford: Clarendon/Oxford UP, 1945. 1–14.

McKendrick, Neil. "Introduction: The Birth of a Consumer Society."Neil McKendrick, John Brewer, and J. H. Plumb. *The Birth of a Consumer Society: The Commercialization of Eighteenth-Century England.* Bloomington: Indiana UP, 1982. 1–33.

McKeon, Michael. "Historicizing Patriarchy: The Emergence of Gender Difference in England, 1660–1760." *Eighteenth-Century Studies* 28 (1995): 295–322.

———. *The Origins of the English Novel 1600–1740.* Baltimore: Johns Hopkins UP, 1987.

Pollak, Ellen. *The Poetics of Sexual Myth: Gender and Ideology in the Verse of Swift and Pope.* Chicago: U of Chicago P, 1985.

Pope, Alexander. *Poetry and Prose of Alexander Pope.* Ed. Aubrey Williams. Riverside Editions. Boston: Houghton, 1969.

Shevelow, Kathryn. *Women and Print Culture: The Constitution of Femininity in the Early Periodical.* New York and London: Routledge, 1989.

The Spectator. Ed. Donald F. Bond. 5 vols. Oxford: Clarendon/Oxford UP, 1965.

Spencer, Jane. *The Rise of the Woman Novelist, From Aphra Behn to Jane Austen.* Oxford: Blackwell, 1986.

Stallybrass, Peter, and Allon White. "The Grotesque Body and the Smithfield Muse: Authorship in the Eighteenth Century." *The Politics and Poetics of Transgression.* Ithaca: Cornell UP, 1986. 80–124.

Stephen, Leslie. *English Literature and Society in the Eighteenth Century.* New York: Putnam, 1904.

Swift, Jonathan. *Bickerstaff Papers and Pamphlets on the Church.*
Ed. Herbert Davis. Oxford: Blackwell, 1940.
———. *A Tale of a Tub, with Other Early Works, 1696–1707.* Ed.
Herbert Davis. Oxford: Blackwell, 1957.
The Tatler. Ed. Donald F. Bond. 3 vols. Oxford: Clarendon/Oxford
UP, 1987.
Trumbach, Randolph. "The Birth of the Queen: Sodomy and the
Mergence of Gender Equality in Modern Culture, 1660–1750."
Hidden from History: Reclaiming the Gay and Lesbian Past. Ed.
Martin Duberman, Martha Vicinus, and George Chauncey.
Markham, ON: New American Library/Penguin, 1989. 129–40.
———. "London's Sodomites: Homosexual Behavior and Western
Culture in the Eighteenth Century." *Journal of Social History* 11
(1977): 1–33.
Ward, Edward. *The London Spy.* 1709. Ed. Paul Hyland. East Lansing: Colleagues, 1993.

Suggestions for Further Reading

Altick, Robert. *The Shows of London.* Cambridge: Harvard UP,
1978.
Bloom, Edward A., and Lillian D. Bloom, eds. *Addison and Steele:
The Critical Heritage.* Boston: Routledge, 1980.
Bloom, Edward A., Lillian D. Bloom, and Edmund Leites. *Educating
the Audience: Addison, Steele, & Eighteenth-Century Culture:
Papers Presented at a Clark Library Seminar 15 November
1980.* Los Angeles: William Andrews Clark Memorial Library,
U of California P, 1984.
Bond, Richmond P. The Tatler: *The Making of a Literary Journal.*
Cambridge: Harvard UP, 1971.
Bourdieu, Pierre. *Distinction: A Social Critique of the Judgement of
Taste.* 1979. Trans. Richard Nice. Cambridge: Harvard UP,
1984.
Braudel, Fernand. *Capitalism and Material Life 1400–1800.* Trans.
Miriam Kochan. London: Weidenfeld, 1967.
———. *Civilization and Capitalism 15th–18th Century.* Vol. 1. *The
Structures of Everyday Life: The Limits of the Possible.* Vol. 2.
The Wheels of Commerce. Trans. Sian Reynolds. New York:
Harper, 1981–82.
Brewer, John, and Roy Porter, ed. *Consumption and the World of
Goods.* London and New York: Routledge, 1993.
Buck, Anne. *Dress in Eighteenth-Century England.* London: Batsford, 1979.
Calhoun, Craig, ed. *Habermas and the Public Sphere.* Cambridge:
MIT P, 1992.

Castle, Terry. *Masquerade and Civilization: The Carnivalesque in Eighteenth-Century English Culture and Fiction*. Stanford: Stanford UP, 1986.

Consumption and Culture in the Seventeenth and Eighteenth Centuries: A Bibliography. Comp. Dorothy K. Auyong, Dorothy Porter, and Roy Porter. Ed. John Brewer. Los Angeles: The UCLA Center for 17th & 18th Century Studies and The William Andrews Clark Memorial Library, 1991.

Cunnington, C. Willet, and Phillis Cunnington. *Handbook of English Costume in the Eighteenth Century*. Boston: Plays, 1972.

Davis, Dorothy. *Fairs, Shops, and Supermarkets: A History of English Shopping*. Toronto: U of Toronto P, 1966.

Douglas, Mary, and Baron Isherwood. *The World of Goods: Towards an Anthropology of Consumption*. New York: Basic, 1979.

Eagleton, Terry. *Ideology of the Aesthetic*. Oxford: Blackwell, 1990.

Ellis, Aytoun. *The Penny Universities: A History of the Coffee-Houses*. London: Secker, 1956.

George, M. Dorothy. *London Life in the Eighteenth Century*. London: Penguin, 1965.

Graham, Walter. *The Beginnings of English Literary Periodicals*. New York, London: Oxford UP, 1926.

Hagstrum, Jean H. *Sex and Sensibility: Ideal and Erotic Love from Milton to Mozart*. Chicago: U of Chicago P, 1980.

Hill, Christopher. *Reformation to Industrial Revolution: A Social and Economic History of Britain*. London: Weidenfeld, 1967.

Hirschman, Albert O. *The Passions and the Interests: Political Arguments for Capitalism Before Its Triumph*. Princeton: Princeton UP, 1977.

Hohendahl, Peter Uwe. *The Institution of Criticism*. Ithaca: Cornell UP, 1982.

Holub, Robert C. "The Rise of Aesthetics in the Eighteenth Century." *Comparative Literature Studies* 15, no. 3 (September 1978): 271–283.

Ketcham, Michael G. *Transparent Designs: Reading, Performance, and Form in the* Spectator *Papers*. Athens: U Georgia P, 1985.

Knight, Charles A. *Joseph Addison and Richard Steele: A Reference Guide, 1730–1991*. New York: G. K. Hall/Simon & Schuster Macmillan, 1994.

McCracken, Grant. *Culture and Consumption: New Approaches to the Symbolic Character of Consumer Goods and Activities*. Bloomington: Indiana UP, 1988.

McCrea, Brian. *Addison and Steele are Dead: The English Department, Its Canon, and the Professionalization of Literary Criticism*. Newark: U of Delaware P, 1990.

McKendrick, Neil, John Brewer, and J. H. Plumb. *The Birth of a Consumer Society: The Commercialization of Eighteenth-Century England.* Bloomington: Indiana UP, 1982.

Macpherson, C. P. *The Political Theory of Possessive Individualism: Hobbes to Locke.* Oxford: Oxford UP, 1962.

Marx, Karl. *Capital.* Trans. Ben Fowkes. London and New York: Penguin/New Left Review, 1976.

Mukerji, Chandra. *From Graven Images: Patterns of Modern Materialism.* New York: Columbia UP, 1983.

Pocock, J. G. A. *Virtue, Commerce, and History: Essays on Political Thought and History, Chiefly in the Eighteenth Century.* Cambridge: Cambridge UP, 1985.

Porter, Roy. *English Society in the Eighteenth Century.* The Pelican Social History of Britain. Ed. J. H. Plumb. New York: Penguin, 1982.

Robbins, Bruce, ed. *The Phantom Public Sphere.* Cultural Politics Series. Vol. 5. The Social Text Collective. Minneapolis: U of Minnesota P, 1993.

Rogers, Pat. *Literature and Popular Culture in Eighteenth-Century England.* Sussex: Harvester Press; Totowa: Barnes & Noble, 1985.

Sennett, Richard. *The Fall of Public Man: On the Social Psychology of Capitalism.* New York: Vintage/Random House, 1978.

Shevelow, Kathryn. "Fathers and Daughters: Women as Readers of the *Tatler.*" *Gender and Reading: Essays on Readers, Texts, and Contexts.* Ed. Elizabeth A. Flynn and Patrocino P. Schweickart. Baltimore: Johns Hopkins UP, 1986. 107–23.

Smithers, Peter. *The Life of Joseph Addison.* 2nd ed. Oxford: Clarendon/Oxford UP, 1968.

Stallybrass, Peter, and Allon White. *The Poetics and Politics of Transgression.* Ithaca: Cornell UP, 1986.

Stone, Lawrence. *The Family, Sex, and Marriage in England 1500–1800.* New York: Harper, 1979.

Thompson, E. P. *Customs in Common.* New York: New Press, 1991.

Todd, Janet. *Sensibility: An Introduction.* London: Methuen, 1986.

Warner, Michael. *The Letters of the Republic: Publication and the Public Sphere in Eighteenth-Century America.* Cambridge: Harvard UP, 1990.

Winton, Calhoun. *Captain Steele: The Early Career of Richard Steele.* Baltimore: Johns Hopkins UP, 1964.

Text Acknowledgments

The texts of *The Tatler* and *The Spectator* are reprinted from *The Tatler,* edited by Donald F. Bond (1987), and *The Spectator,* edited by Donald F. Bond (1965). Reprinted by permission of Oxford University Press.

Excerpts from *The Female Tatler,* edited by Fidelis Morgan (1992), reprinted by permission of J. M. Dent.

Excerpts from *The Guardian,* edited by John Calhoun Stephens (1982), reprinted by permission of the University Press of Kentucky.

Sir John Denham, excerpts from *Coopers Hill,* from *Expans'd Hieroglyphicks: A Critical Edition of Sir John Denham's COOPERS HILL,* edited by Brendan Hehir (1969), reprinted by permission of the University of California Press.

John Gay, excerpts from *John Gay: Poetry and Prose,* edited by Vinton A. Dearing (1974), reprinted by permission of Oxford University Press.

Bernard Mandeville, excerpts from *The Fable of the Bees,* edited by F. B. Kaye (1925), reprinted by permission of Oxford University Press.

Alexander Pope, excerpts from *The Poems of Alexander Pope,* edited by John Butt (1963), reprinted by permission of Routledge Press.

Edward Ward, excerpts from *The London Spy,* edited by Paul Hyland (1993), reprinted by permission of Colleagues Press.

Illustration Credit

Woman's silk brocade shoe, England, circa 1720, Alice Schott Bequest, Los Angeles County Museum of Art, copyright © 1996 Museum Associates. Reprinted by permission of the Los Angeles County Museum of Art.